J. Alberto Soggin

INTRODUCTION TO THE OLD TESTAMENT

THE OLD TESTAMENT LIBRARY

General Editors

PETER ACKROYD, University of London
JAMES BARR, Oxford University
BERNHARD W. ANDERSON, Princeton Theological Seminary
JAMES L. MAYS, Union Theological Seminary, Richmond, Virginia

Advisory Editor

JOHN BRIGHT, Union Theological Seminary, Richmond, Virginia

J. ALBERTO SOGGIN

INTRODUCTION TO THE OLD TESTAMENT

FROM ITS ORIGINS TO THE CLOSING
OF THE ALEXANDRIAN CANON

Third Edition

WESTMINSTER/JOHN KNOX PRESS
LOUISVILLE, KENTUCKY

Translated by John Bowden from the Italian
Introduzione all'Antico Testamento,
Fourth edition, published by Paideia Editrice, Brescia 1987
© Paideia Editrice, Brescia 1987
Translation © John Bowden 1989

Published by Westminster/John Knox Press
Louisville, Kentucky

PRINTED IN THE UNITED STATES OF AMERICA
2 4 6 8 9 7 5 3 1

Library of Congress Cataloging-in-Publication Data

Soggin, J. Alberto.
  Introduction to the Old Testament.

  (The Old Testament library)
  Translation of the 4th ed. of: Introduzione all'Antico
Testamento.
  Bibliography: p.
  Includes index.
  1. Bible. O.T.—Introductions.   I. Title.   II. Series.
BS1140.2.S6713 1989   221.6'1   88-33951
ISBN 0-664-21331-6

TO MY WIFE

'As a man trained from early days to read the Bible in Hebrew, Livy in Latin and Herodotus in Greek, I have never found the task of interpreting the Bible any more complex than that of interpreting Livy or Herodotus' (Arnaldo Momigliano, 1981).

PREFACE TO THE FOURTH ITALIAN
EDITION AND THE
THIRD ENGLISH EDITION

This *Introduction* first appeared in Italian about twenty years ago. That is a long time for a textbook which seeks to train the new generations of students in the subject and bring others up to date. The problems now are different, the approach to them is different and the methods used to solve them are different also.

This fourth Italian edition, which is appearing here as the third English edition, is therefore a new work. In the second and third Italian editions I limited myself to updating the bibliographies and inserting additional material here and there in the text, and these changes were also made in the English edition, but the basic approach of the work remained the same. However, in this fourth edition many parts have been rewritten. The most thorough rewriting has been done in the first, second and third parts, but elsewhere, too, no page has in fact remained entirely unchanged. It is for the reader to judge whether the result can be considered a step forward from the other editions; I personally think that it is, though there will be certainly some for whom the new approach to the problems and the solutions put forward will seem too radical, while for others they will not be radical enough. Thus, to take an example, the basic structure of the work has remained the same as that of the first three editions: the text continues to follow a compromise between the canonical order and the chronological order of the books of the Bible and ends with a section devoted to the Alexandrian collection and two appendices on epigraphic texts. However, I am no longer completely sure that this is the right structure: I have become increasingly convinced, and now that the typescript is finished am almost completely convinced, that I should have begun with Deuteronomy and the so-called 'Deuteronomistic' history to which we also owe the first edition of the Pentateuch and the Latter Prophets, and also the last edition of the Former Prophets. Or, in speaking of Proto-, Deutero- and Trito-Isaiah I should have taken over the results of the most

recent studies (cf. below, 20.1,3) of R.E.Clements, O.Kaiser and
R.Rendtorff, and regarded these three works, the division of which
is now one of the axioms of historical criticism, as a single redactional
complex. In other words, I should have begun with the Babylonian
exile, which is truly the bridge between early Israel and what appears
in the Bible. That must be left for a further edition; at all events I offer
the reader the necessary ingredients, which, suitably rearranged, can
provide an *Introduction* more in keeping with contemporary methods.

In the past some reviews have criticized two apparent gaps in the
work.

(*a*) Leonhard Rost (*TLZ* 101, 1976, 179f.) has criticized the fact
that the book does not devote enough attention to the problems of
Hebrew metre (cf. below, 6.4). That is certainly true. However, I
have to admit that I have never succeeded in understanding, far less
in applying, the various methods proposed, foremost among which
is that formulated at the beginning of this century by E.Sievers. The
reasons are simple; what is involved here is studying the metre of a
language which has been transmitted in a vocalization which is
certainly not original, and derives from some centuries after the
original writings, even if it is based on an authoritative tradition.
Nor do we possess the original texts, but texts which have gone
through many hands, manipulated and commented on to meet the
needs of the believing community, and the product of many re-
readings. And in addition to the vocalization, we know nothing about
the original accentuation or about the division of words into syllables.
Moreover even those responsible for the vocalization in the second
half of the first millennium CE do not seem to have had any
recollection of a metrical reading. And above all, it should be noted
that we cannot even know whether there ever was such a reading,
and the suspicion arises that the presupposition is based solely on
the analogy of ancient Greek and Latin poetry; but here too, as is
well known, we are in a phase of substantial revision.

It has therefore seemed to me not only unwise but also unproduc-
tive to discuss a problem which is so complex and which has so little
prospect of being solved unless there are new developments in this
field. One of these seems to be the suggestion of a method which the
author calls stichometric, developed by O.Loretz at the University
of Münster and presented several times in the journal *UF* and the
writings which arise out of it; however, even this method has not yet
produced incontestable results, nor has it developed a methodology
which allows it to be used by anyone who has not worked with Loretz.
Therefore it needs to be made rather more precise before it can be
applied on a large scale.

For all these reasons I reject conjectures and emendations for the sake of metre, which often appear in critical editions and commentaries.

(*b*) Gianfranco Ravasi (*La scuola cattolica* 102, 1975, 664f.) would have liked the *Introduction* also to consider problems in the light of 'the new perspectives of stylistic, linguistic and hermeneutical analysis, the examples of an exegesis more as literary criticism', and Maas Boertien of the Free University of Amsterdam made the same point in a letter of 12 July 1977. I must, however, confess that I do not have that capacity for aesthetic criticism which is necessary to carry through work of this kind, so I am forced to leave it to others. Certainly the Hebrew Bible is also, and primarily, a literary work. So it is always legitimate, and in some cases necessary, to treat it from this point of view. But unlike so many literary works it is not just a literary work; it is a work of sacred history, the normative sacred scripture of two faiths, Jewish and Christian; and in addition it is a collection of texts from the ancient Near East, texts which reflect particular historical, political and social situations. While appreciating the literary and aesthetic value of the various components the student must therefore avoid being blind to this point; the other elements I have mentioned also form an integral part of the texts that we are to study. So the demand of the practitioners of literary criticism that they should be allowed to make their analysis is legitimate, and they are right in asking that it should be done by others before proceeding further; but it would be to do an injustice to the texts if we left them at this point, without investigating the other information that they can offer.

For examples of literary analysis see *inter alia*: R.Alter, *The Art of Biblical Narrative*, New York 1981; J.Fokkelman, *Narrative Art in Genesis*, Assen 1975; id., *Narrative Art and Poetry in the Books of Samuel*, Assen I, 1981; II, 1986 (two further volumes are announced); M.Weiss, *The Bible from Within*, Jerusalem 1986; R.Alter and F.Kermode, *The Literary Guide to the Bible*, New York and London 1987. For the problem see my 'Critica letteraria e critica storica', *Hen* 5, 1983, 268-72, and D.Vetter, 'Was leistet die biblische Erzählung?', *BerTh* 3, 1986, 190-206.

For the history of Israel see my *A History of Israel. From the Beginnings to the Bar Kochba Revolt, AD 135*, London and Philadelphia 1984.

In this book I have preferred to use when possible the expression 'Hebrew Bible' rather than Old Testament: in this way I am trying to avoid a canonical approach to problems. One can in fact speak of the Old Testament only with the entrance of the New Testament into the Christian canon. I also prefer to transcribe the divine name as YHWH rather than using Yahweh; there is no certainty over the transcription of the name but it is certain that it was never pronounced in the historical period. The terms BCE and CE replace BC and AD throughout.

I end by thanking the University of Rome – La Sapienza and the Waldensian Faculty of Theology which have allowed me the time I needed; and the University Library of Basle, which during the months of September, October and November 1986 kindly provided me with a desk in the room reserved for professors, and allowed me to have access to the stacks. That was essential for me to to complete this work.

For this third English edition the bibliographies have been further updated and a few additions have been made to the text here and there. I am most grateful to Richard Coggins for all his help.

University of Rome – La Sapienza
July 1988

CONTENTS

PART FOUR

THE EXILIC AND POST-EXILIC PROPHETS

PART FIVE

THE WRITINGS

ABBREVIATIONS

A	Greek translation of the Hebrew Bible by Aquila
AASOR	*Annual of the American Schools of Oriental Research*
AB	Anchor Bible, New York
AbrNah	*Abr Naharain*
ADPV	Abhandlungen des Deutschen Palästinavereins
ABLAK	M.Noth, *Abhandlungen zur biblischen Landes- und Altertumskunde*, Neukirchen 1971 (= *ZDPV*)
AfO	Archiv für Orientforschung
AfR	Archiv für Religionswissenschaft
AHw	W.von Soden, *Akkadisches Handwörterbuch*, Wiesbaden 1965-1981
AION	*Annali dell'Istituto orientale di Napoli*
AJBI	*Annual of the Japanese Biblical Institute*
AnBibl	Analecta Biblica
ANET	J.B.Pritchard (ed.), *Ancient Near Eastern Texts Relating to the Old Testament*, Princeton ³1969
ANEP	J.B.Pritchard (ed.), *The Ancient Near East in Pictures*, Princeton 1969
Ang	*Angelicum*
ANL-MR	*Atti dell Accademia nazionale dei Lincei – Memorie/ Rendiconti*
Ant	*Antonianum*
AOAT	Alter Orient und Altes Testament
AOF	*Altorientalische Forschungen*
ArchOr	*Archiv Orientální*
ARM	Archives royales de Mari
ASNSP	*Annali della Scuola Normale Superiore di Pisa*
ASOR	The American Schools of Oriental Research
ASTI	*Annual of the Swedish Theological Institute*
Aug	*Augustinianum*
AustBR	*Australian Biblical Review*

BA	*The Biblical Archaeologist*
Bab	*The Babylonian Talmud*
BASOR	*Bulletin of the ASOR*
BCE	Before the Common Era
BeO	*Bibbia e Oriente*
BerThZ	*Berliner theologische Zeitschrift*
BHH	*Biblisch-historisches Handwörterbuch*, 4 vols, Göttingen 1962-1979
BHK	*Biblia Hebraica*, ed. R.Kittel
BHS	*Biblia Hebraica Stuttgartensia* (= *BHK*4)
Bibl	*Biblica*
BiblRes	*Biblical Research*
BJ	La Bible... de Jérusalem
BJRL	*Bulletin of the John Rylands Library*
BN	*Biblische Notizen*
BO	*Bibliotheca Orientalis*
BTB	*Biblical Theology Bulletin*
BZ	*Biblische Zeitschrift*
CAH	The Cambridge Ancient History
CAT	Commentaire de l'Ancien Testament
CBQ	*The Catholic Biblical Quarterly*
CE	Common Era
CRAIBL	*Comptes rendus de l'Académie des inscriptions et belles lettres*
CTA	A.Herdner, *Corpus des tablettes alphabétiques découvertes à Ras Shamra-Ugarit 1929-1939*, Paris 1963
DBAT	*Dielheimer Blätter zum Alten Testament*
EA	J.A.Knudtzon, *Die El Amarna Tafeln*, Leipzig I, 1908; II, 1915; and A.F.Rainey, *The El Amarna Tablets*, AOAT 8, Kevelaer 1973
EI	*Ereṣ Iśra'el*
EncBibl	*Encyclopaedia Biblica* (in Hebrew)
EncJud	*Encyclopaedia Judaica*
EstBibl	*Estudios Bíblicos*
ET	English translation
ETL	*Ephemerides Theologicae Lovanienses*
ETR	*Études théologiques et religieuses*
EvTh	*Evangelische Théologie*
ExpT	*Expository Times*
FS	Festschrift
GA	Gesammelte Aufsätze
GesK	*Gesenius' Hebrew Grammar* (ed. E.Kautzsch, second

	English edition by A.E.Cowley, Oxford)
Greg	*Gregorianum*
Hen	*Henoch*
HorBTh	*Horizons in Biblical Theology*
HTR	*Harvard Theological Review*
HUCA	*Hebrew Union College Annual*
IDB	*The Interpreters' Dictionary of the Bible*
IDB-SV	*The Interpreters' Dictionary of the Bible-Supplementary Volume*
IEJ	*The Israel Exploration Journal*
Int	*Interpretation*
JAAR	*Journal of the American Academy of Religion*
JANESCU	*Journal of the Ancient Near Eastern Society, Columbia University*
JAOS	*Journal of the American Oriental Society*
JBL	*Journal of Biblical Literature*
JCS	*Journal of Cuneiform Studies*
JEA	*Journal of Egyptian Archaeology*
Jerus	Jerusalem Talmud
JESHO	*Journal of the Economic and Social History of the Orient*
JJS	*Journal of Jewish Studies*
JNES	*Journal of Near Eastern Studies*
JNWSL	*Journal of North West Semitic Languages*
JPOS	*Journal of the Palestine Oriental Society*
JQR	*Jewish Quarterly Review*
JSJ	*Journal for the Study of Judaism*
JSOT-SS	*Journal for the Study of the Old Testament* – Supplement Studies
JSS	*Journal of Semitic Studies*
JTS	*Journal of Theological Studies*
KAI	H.Donner and W.Röllig, *Kanaanäische und Aramäische Inschriften*, Wiesbaden ²1966-70
KB	L.Kohler and W.Baumgartner, *Lexicon in Veteris Testamenti Libros*, Leiden ³1967-83 (three fascicles published)
KS	Kleine Schriften
KuD	*Kerygma und Dogma*
LA-SBF	*Liber Annuus – Studii Biblici Franciscani*
Lat	*Lateranum*
LXX	The Septuagint, Greek translation of the Hebrew Bible
MIO	*Mitteilungen des Instituts für Orientforschung*

ND	Name of deity
NICOT	New International Commentaries on the Old Testament
NKZ	*Neue kirchliche Zeitschrift*
NP	Name of person
NTT	*Nederlands theologisch tijdschrift*
OA	*Oriens Antiquus*
OBO	Orbis Biblicus et Orientalis
OLZ	*Orientalische Literaturzeitung*
Or	*Orientalia*
OTOS	J.A.Soggin, *Old Testament and Oriental Studies*, BiblOr 29, Rome 1975
OTS	*Oudtestamentische Studiën*
OTW	M.Noth, *The Old Testament World*, ET Philadelphia and London 1966
PEQ	*Palestine Exploration Quarterly*
PG	Patrologia Graeca, ed. J.P.Migne
PJB	*Palästina Jahrbuch*
PL	Patrologia Latina, ed. J.P.Migne
PP	*La parola del passato*
Prot	*Protestantesimo*
RA	*Revue d'Assyrologie*
RB	*Revue biblique*
RGG	*Die Religion in Geschichte und Gegenwart*
RHPR	*Revue d'histoire et de philosophie religieuses*
RHR	*Revue d'histoire des religions*
RiBib	*Rivista biblica*
RIDA	*Revue internationale des droits de l'antiquité*
RSF	*Rivista di studi fenici*
RSLR	*Rivista di storia e di letteratura religiosa*
RSO	*Rivista di studi orientali*
RSR	*Religious Studies Review*
RTL	*Revue théologique de Louvain*
RTP	*Revue de théologie et de philosophie*
SBFLA	*Studii biblici Franciscani liber annuus*
SBS	Stuttgarter Bibelstudien
SBT	Studies in Biblical Theology
ScrHier	*Scripta Hierosolymitana*
SDB	Supplément au *Dictionnaire de la Bible*
SEÅ	*Svensk Exegetisk Årsbok*
SJT	*Scottish Journal of Theology*
SMSR	*Studi e Materiali di Storia delle Religioni*

SSI	J.C.L.Gibson, *Textboook of Syrian Semitic Inscriptions*, Oxford I, 1971; II, 1975; III, 1982
SSR	*Studi di Storia delle Religioni*
SVT	Supplements to *Vetus Testamentum*
TDNT	*Theological Dictionary of the New Testament*
TDOT	*Theological Dictionary of the Old Testament*
Tg	Targum, Aramaic translation of the Hebrew Bible
TGUOS	*Transactions of the Glasgow University Oriental Society*
TLZ	*Theologische Literaturzeitung*
TR	*Theologische Rundschau*
TRE	*Theologische Realenzyklopädie*, Berlin 1976ff.
TS	*Theological Studies*
TV	Theologische Versuche
TZ	*Theologische Zeitschrift*
UF	*Ugarit-Forschungen*
Vg	Vulgate – Jerome's Latin translation
VuF	*Verkündigung und Forschung*
VT	*Vetus Testamentum*
WHJP	B.Mazar (ed.), *The World History of the Jewish People*, Jerusalem 1964ff.
WissZ	*Wissenschaftliche Zeitschrift*
WuD	*Wort und Dienst*
WUS	J.Aistleitner, *Wörterbuch der ugaritischen Sprache*, Berlin 1963
ZAW	*Zeitschrift für die Alttestamentliche Wissenschaft*
ZNW	*Zeitschrift für die Neutestamentliche Wissenschaft*
ZDMG	*Zeitschrift der Deutschen morgenländischen Gesellschaft*
ZDPV	*Zeitschrift der Deutschen Palästinavereins*
ZTK	*Zeitschrift für Theologie und Kirche*
Θ	Theodotion's Greek translation of the Hebrew Bible
Σ	Symmachus's Greek translation of the Hebrew Bible
co-ord	Coordinates on the 1:250,000 and 1:100,000 maps of the Survey of Israel

GENERAL BIBLIOGRAPHY

I. Introductions to the Old Testament (cited in the text with *)

1. G.W.Anderson, *A Critical Introduction to the Old Testament*, London 1959 (Protestant, popular)
2. T.Ballarini (ed.), *Introduzione alla bibbia*, Turin then Bologna, I, 1965; II, 1969; II.2, 1971; III, 1978 (Catholic, the other volumes deal with the New Testament)
3. A.Bentzen, *Introduction to the Old Testament*, Copenhagen ³1957 (valuable introduction to the methods of the Scandinavian school)
4. J.A.Bewer, *The Literature of the Old Testament*, New York ³1962, ed. E.G.Kraeling (Protestant, technical)
5. L.Boadt, *Reading the Old Testament. An Introduction*, New York 1984 (Catholic, solidly popular)
6. U.Cassuto, 'La letteratura ebraica antica', in *Le civiltà dell'Oriente* II, Rome 1957, 151-89, reprinted in *La rassegna mensile di Israel* 27, 1961, 310-20, 391-401, 437-47, collected in one fascicle, Rome 1961 (in Hebrew)
7. H.Cazelles, *Introduction critique à l'Ancien Testament*, Paris 1973 (the third edition of A.Robert-A.Feuillet, *Introduction à la Bible* I, Paris ²1959, which was controversial in its time: Catholic, technical)
8. B.S.Childs, *Introduction to the Old Testament as Scripture*, London and Philadelphia 1979 (Protestant)
9. O.Eissfeldt, *The Old Testament: An Introduction*, ET Oxford 1965 (Protestant, technical)
10. G.Fohrer, *Das Alte Testament*, Gütersloh I, 1969, II-III 1970 (Protestant)
11. N.K.Gottwald, *The Hebrew Bible. A Socio-Literary Introduction*, Philadelphia 1985 (Protestant, technical)
12. J.H.Hayes, *An Introduction to Old Testament Study*, Nashville and London 1979 (Protestant, technical)
13. O.Kaiser, *Introduction to the Old Testament*, ET Oxford 1975 (Protestant, technical)
14. A.Lods, *Histoire de la littérature hébraïque et juive*, Paris 1950 (Protestant, technical)
15. R.Mayer, *Einleitung in das Alte Testament*, Munich I, 1965; II, 1967 (Catholic)
16. F.Michelini Tocci, *La letteratura ebraica*, Florence 1970 (secular)

17. R.H.Pfeiffer, *Introduction to the Old Testament*, New York [2]1948 (Protestant, technical)

18. G.Rinaldi, *La letteratura ebraica biblica*, Turin 1954 (Catholic)

19. R.Rendtorff, *Das Werden des Alten Testaments*, Neukirchen [2]1965 (popular, Protestant)

20. Id., *The Old Testament. An Introduction*, ET London and Philadelphia 1985

21. H.H.Rowley, *The Growth of the Old Testament*, London 1954 (Protestant, popular)

22. W.H.Schmidt, *Introduction to the Old Testament*, ET New York and London 1984

23. (E.Sellin-)L.Rost, *Einleitung in das alte Testament*, Heidelberg [9]1959 (Protestant, technical)

24. (E.Sellin-)G.Fohrer, *Introduction to the Old Testament*, ET Nashville 1968 and London 1970 (Protestant, technical)

25. R.Smend, *Die Entstehung des Alten Testaments*, Stuttgart 1978, [3]1984 (Protestant, technical)

26. G.Stemberger, *Geschichte der jüdischen Literatur*, Munich 1977 (Jewish, technical)

27. T.C.Vriezen and A.S.van der Woude, *De literatuur van Oud-Israël*, Wassenaar 1961, [4]1973 (Protestant, technical)

28. A.Weiser, *Introduction to the Old Testament*, ET London 1961 (Protestant)

Because the Hebrew Bible is sacred scripture, its main scholars and commentators have been members of the synagogue or the Christian church. Therefore works with an essentially secular approach are rare. Nos. 14 and 17 above are very critical and often start from presuppositions which are disputable today; nos. 7, 8, 28 also take into account the theological value of the material they examine; nos. 4, 7, 9, 11, 23, 24 are technical and critical in character despite their confessional approach, while no.3 is an excellent introduction to the questions and methods of the Scandinavian school. Nos. 2, 7 and 18, albeit in a scholarly way, reflect the directives of the Catholic magisterium, though with differing accents; 6, 16 and 18 are very good indeed despite their brevity; no.6 is an excellent introduction to the study of the material as it is perceived in advanced Jewish circles and to the theories of the authors; nos. 16 and 26 deal with all Jewish literature from its origins to contemporary writings in the state of Israel. No.5 is a popular work of a high standard, with a conservative approach to the texts; no.11 interprets the Bible in a Marxist-revolutionary perspective, but with a conservative approach to the texts.

Three works which I have had no access to, which belong to the conservative trend within Protestantism, are:

R.K.Harrison, *Introduction to the Old Testament*, London and Grand Rapids, Mich. 1969

W.S.LaSor, D.A.Hubbard and F.W.Bush, *Old Testament Survey: the Message, Form and Background of the Old Testament*, Grand Rapids, Mich. 1982

P.C.Craigie, *The Old Testament, its Background, Growth and Content*, Nashville 1986

2. Commentaries on the whole Hebrew Bible

La Sainte Bible, ed. L.Pirot and A.Clamer, Paris (Catholic)
La Sainte Bible (de Jérusalem), Paris (Catholic)
La Bible de la Pléiade, Paris (Protestant in inspiration)
The Interpreter's Bible, New York and Nashville (Protestant, theological, uneven in quality – depending on the author)
Das Alte Testament Deutsch, Göttingen (Protestant, learned popularization); many of the volumes have been included in
The Old Testament Library, London and Philadelphia, which has much the same character
Handbuch zum Alten Testament, Tübingen (technical)
Commentaire de l'Ancien Testament, Geneva (Protestant)
Kommentar zum Alten Testament, Gütersloh (technical)
Biblischer Kommentar, Neukirchen (Protestant)
The International Critical Commentary, Edinburgh (technical)

Detailed references will be made to all these commentaries in the course of the examination of individual books. The last six appear at irregular intervals and are not yet complete.

3. Encyclopaedias and biblical dictionaries

Supplément au *Dictionnaire de la Bible*, Paris 1927ff. (complete up to Vol.XI, 1988)
Die Religion in Geschichte und Gegenwart, 7 vols, Tübingen ³1957-1964
Bibel-Lexikon, Einsiedeln ²1958, third edition in preparation
The Interpreter's Dictionary of the Bible, 4 vols, New York and Nashville 1962; supplementary volume 1976
Biblisch-historisches Handwörterbuch, 4 vols, Göttingen 1962-1979
Enciclopedia della Bibbia, 6 vols, Turin 1969-71
Biblisches Reallexikon, ed.K.Galling, Tübingen ²1977
Theologische Realenzyklopädie, Berlin 1977ff. (complete to Vol.XVI, 1987)

4. Histories of Israel

W.F.Albright, *From the Stone Age to Christianity*, Baltimore 1940, ²1957
J.Bright, *A History of Israel*, Philadelphia and London 1959, ³1981
G.Fohrer, *Geschichte Israels*, Heidelberg ³1982
A.H.Gunneweg, *Geschichte Israels bis Bar Kochba*, Stuttgart ⁴1982
J.H.Hayes and J.M.Miller (eds.), *Israelite and Judaean History*, London and Philadelphia 1977
S.Herrmann, *A History of Israel in Old Testament Times*, ET London and Philadelphia ²1981
H.Jagersma, *A History of Israel in the Old Testament Period*, ET London and Philadelphia 1982

Id., *A History of Israel from Alexander the Great to Bar Kochba*, ET London and Philadelphia 1986

B.Mazar (ed.), *The World History of the Jewish People* (8 vols), Jerusalem and London 1964-86

J.M.Miller and J.H.Hayes, *The History of Israel and Judah*, Philadelphia and London 1986

M.Noth, *History of Israel*, ET London ²1959

P.Sacchi, *Storia del mondo giudaico*, Turin 1976 (basic for the study of Judaism from the exile to the New Testament period)

J.A.Soggin, *A History of Israel from the Beginnings to the Bar Kochba Revolt*, ET London and Philadelphia 1984

R.de Vaux, *History of Ancient Israel*, 2 vols, ET London and New York 1978 (only up to the period of the Judges)

5. History and thought of the ancient Near East

H. and H.A.Frankfort (eds.), *The Intellectual Adventure of Ancient Man*, Chicago 1946

T.Delaporte, *Le Proche-Orient asiatique*, Paris 1948

A.Scharff and A.Moortgat, *Ägypten und Vorderasien im Altertum*, Munich 1950

S.Moscati, *I predecessori d'Israele*, Rome 1956

Id., *Le antiche civiltà semitiche*, Bari ²1958

H.Schmökel, *Kulturgeschichte des alten Orients*, Stuttgart 1961

M.Liverani, *Antico Oriente: storia, società, economia*, Bari 1988

P.Garelli, *Le Proche-Orient asiatique*, Paris 1969

The Cambridge Ancient History, Cambridge I.1, ³1970; I.2, ³1971; II.1, ³1973; II.2, ³1975; III.1, ²1982; III.3, ²1982

L'alba della civiltà, ed.S.Moscati and others, 3 vols., Turin 1976

6. Histories of technical criticism

L.Diestel, *Geschichte des Alten Testaments in der christlichen Kirche*, Halle 1869 (a reprint has been announced for years)

E.G. Kraeling, *The Old Testament since the Reformation*, London 1955

H.-J.Kraus, *Geschichte der historisch-kritischen Erforschung des Alten Testaments*, Neukirchen 1956, ³1982

R.E.Clements, *A Century of Old Testament Interpretation*, London and Philadelphia 1975

A.H.J.Gunneweg, *Understanding the Old Testament*, ET London and Philadelphia 1978

7. The religion of Israel

A.Penna, *La religione d'Israele*, Brescia 1958

H.Ringgren, *Israelite Religion*, ET London 1966

T.C.Vriezen, *The Religion of Israel*, ET London 1967

W.Eichrodt, *Religionsgeschichte Israels*, Bern 1969
G.Fohrer, *History of Israelite Religion*, ET Nashville 1972 and London 1973
E.Jenni-C.Westermann (eds.), *Theologisches Handwörterbuch zum Alten Testament*, Munich I, 1971; II, 1976
W.H.Schmidt, *The Faith of the Old Testament*, ET Oxford 1983
G.J.Botterweck-H.Ringgren (eds.), *Theological Dictionary of the Old Testament*, London and Grand Rapids (the last complete volume is V, 1986)

8. Collections of Ancient Near Eastern texts

J.B.Pritchard (ed.), *The Ancient Near East in Texts and Pictures*, Princeton ³1969
D.W.Thomas (ed.), *Documents from Old Testament Times*, London 1958
F.Michaeli, *Textes de la Bible et de l'ancien Orient*, Neuchâtel 1961
K.Galling, *Textbuch zur Geschichte Israels*, Tübingen ²1968
H.Donner and W.Röllig, *Kanaanäische und aramäische Inschriften*, 3 vols, Wiesbaden ³1971-6
J.C.L.Gibson, *Syrian Semitic Inscriptions*, 3 vols., Oxford 1971-81

9. Bibliographical information

Elenchus bibliographicus biblicus (supplement to *Biblica*)
Internationale Zeitschriftenschau für Bibelwissenschaft und Grenzgebiete
Annual *Book List* of the *Society for Old Testament Study*
Old Testament Abstracts
Zeitschrift für die alttestamentliche Wissenschaft: the review of reviews and books (Zeitschriftenschau and Bücherschau)
There are bibliographies in *TR*, *ETL*, *VuF* and *BTB*

10. The Qumran sect

L.Moraldi (ed.), *I manoscritti di Qumran*, Turin ²1986
G.Vermes., *The Dead Sea Scrolls in English*, Harmondsworth ³1987
Id., *The Dead Sea Scrolls*, Philadelphia and London ²1982

PART ONE

THE HEBREW BIBLE:
HISTORY AND GENERAL PROBLEMS

I

INTRODUCTION TO THE HEBREW BIBLE

1. Description and definition of the material

(*a*) The term 'Introduction', Greek *eisagōgē*, Latin *introductio*, was used for the first time, as far as we know, by the Antiochene monk Hadrian, who died around 440. Nowadays it is used to denote that science which studies the biblical literature from a historical-critical and literary perspective; in this sense it appears at the end of the seventeenth century, from the works of the German scholar J.D. Michaelis on. It is now part of the current terminology of the faculties of theology and the arts.

In fact the concept is already present in a very early period and sometimes begins with the first drafting of the biblical text. The redactors, and more rarely the authors, of the texts already felt the need to prefix to the material in their collections certain observations which were meant to make it easier to understand, putting it in a proper historical and ideological context. So we have the superscriptions of the Psalms (which in modern translations are not always counted in the numbering of the verses, because of their redactional character): they try to relate the compositions in question to events and persons in the history of Israel or to particular liturgical situations. There are also superscriptions to some passages of the prophetic and wisdom books, superscriptions which usually seek to identify an author and sometimes a historical situation. Some of them may go back to the prophets themselves or their disciples, who will have collected them from the words of the master. A very well-known example of this is the beginning of Isa.6.1: 'In the year in which king Uzziah died I saw the Lord...', i.e. around 742 or 736 BCE (the date is uncertain), even if in cases like this we have to take the possibility of pseudepigraphy (below, p.8) seriously into consideration. Other superscriptions in the prophetic and wisdom books, however, are clearly the work of redactors and therefore later;

they can be recognized because they are independent of the context: for example the words with which the book of Jeremiah begins (1.1ff.).

These examples, though differing in quality, have in common the awareness that it is impossible to understand the attitude of persons and schools of thought, and therefore of the writings which derive from them, without knowing the events or the situations which shaped them wholly or in part. For example, ignorance of Canaanite religion would notably limit our understanding of the prophetic message, in continual struggle against religious syncretism; nor could we understand adequately the political or social message of biblical prophecy were we ignorant of the situation which moulded it.

So we find in the Hebrew Bible itself a number of what have rightly been called 'introductory notes', some (and which these are is always controversial) perhaps going back directly or indirectly to the authors of the works, and others (the majority) introduced by the redactors to whom we also owe the final edition of the text. The latter in particular are fairly easy to recognize because they do not fit into the context.

Rabbinic literature continued along these lines, and sometimes we can derive introductory information from it which is important because it is based on trustworthy traditions; however, for the most part we have traditions which cannot be verified and sometimes are even improbable, governed by the demands of edification or catechesis and therefore irrelevant for the historical understanding of the passages to which they refer.

But the need for an introduction is not felt in the same way on all sides. There are those who, like the Israeli M.Weiss, think that the difficulties of identifying the original situation in which certain passages were composed are so great (and the controversial character of the results bears witness to this) that it *a priori* discourages the majority of research in this direction. He considers it more useful, and also more in keeping with the nature of the texts, to concentrate on the aesthetic and dramatic characteristics of the texts and their content. I hope that I shall succeed in demonstrating in the next paragraph why I do not feel able to share this position (moreover I have already alluded to the problem in the Preface, above, p.xi).

The need to interpret a literature in its particular historical, ideological and social context is not, moreover, peculiar to the biblical literature. It appears every time the readers (in this case our contemporaries) have no immediate and direct contact with the circumstances in which a certain type of literature came into being.

That can happen for various reasons: geographical distance (for example, in the case of literature near to us in time but geographically remote and therefore remote in customs, institutions and language); it can also be caused by there being a considerable distance in time between the readers and the events narrated, though these events may have taken place in their geographical vicinity (for example in the West classical Latin and Greek literature, mediaeval literature and Renaissance literature). In the case of the Hebrew Bible and of all the literature of the ancient Near East we face a considerable distance on both the geographical and the chronological levels; modern readers, especially modern Western readers, come up against people (and therefore literatures, practices, institutions, mentalities) with which they have little or nothing in common. So it goes without saying that unless a reader has a remarkable and specialized education, he or she will be ignorant for the most part of the historical, political, economic, social, historical and religious facts to which the text refers. To this must be added the problem of the language, which most of the time is an insuperable obstacle to a direct knowledge of the sources. Finally, the biblical texts present a particular problem, since in the Hebrew Bible we have a work which for millennia has been, as it still is, the sacred scripture of Judaism and Christianity, and therefore Western readers who have grown up in the sphere of the Jewish-Christian tradition have unconsciously assimilated a whole theological and ecclesiastical tradition which will not fail to make its own weight felt on the explanation of the texts. Centuries of exegesis which are far from lacking in preconceptions can impel readers, without their being aware of it, either towards the uncritical acceptance of certain non-proven statements, or paradoxically towards the equally uncritical rejection of certain positions simply because these positions have been traditionally held within the sphere of certain religious communities. The need for an introductory science which offers a critical view of the biblical literature should therefore be evident to anyone.

(b) I propose the following definition of the subject: We may term that discipline Introduction to the Hebrew Bible (or New Testament) which sets out to present, where possible, the information needed to identify the authors of a text, its literary genre, the milieu from which it derives, and so on, thus making it comprehensible against the background of the events and the problems which shaped it. As can be seen, this definition is more descriptive than systematic, but it should cover the substance of the problem. The task is much more complicated than it might appear at first glance, especially in the sphere of Semitic literature, as we shall see in the course of the discussion.

(c) So if there is not and never has been a period in which the reader of the Bible has not felt the need to gain information about the circumstances which accompanied and often conditioned the genesis of a particular text, whether it is read as sacred scripture or as literature, there is also a need to recognize that first the synagogue and then the Christian church down to the Renaissance were not very concerned to establish in an independent and original form the circumstances in which the sacred books originated (here we should leave on one side the Antiochene school and the figures of St Jerome and Nicolas of Lyra). The church usually contented itself with taking over the traditional opinions of the synagogue. Allegorical exegesis, soon practised on a large scale in the mediaeval church, avoided the problems by means of that very special form of ahistorical sublimation which is the nature of allegory; therefore the problem of the divergence between the present reality of the texts and their traditional interpretation did not arise until the beginning of the sixteenth century, with humanistic exegesis. That also happened because with the exceptions of St Jerome and later Nicolas of Lyra, mentioned above, Hebrew was virtually unknown in the West and the Bible was read in the Latin version. It was humanism, with its principle of a return to the sources, that was to be the foundation of scientific-critical Introduction, and the acceptance of this principle by the Protestant Reformation in the sixteenth century may be said to have constituted the decisive step in this direction in church circles also. Despite that, the first attempt at historical-critical Introduction did not take place, paradoxically, within Protestantism, if we leave aside the theses put forward at Wittenberg by Karlstadt in 1520 and rejected by Luther. Rather, it took place in Judaism in the person of the dissident Baruch de Spinoza (in his *Tractatus theologico-politicus*, Amsterdam 1670) and in the Catholicism of the Counter-Reformation with the work of the Oratorian Richard Simon (in his *Histoire critique du Vieux Testament*, Paris 1678). The first modern Introductions came to birth with these works. But neither Judaism nor the Catholic Church of the time accepted their potentialities. Spinoza was anathematized, and Simon had to leave his order. It was only during the second half of the eighteenth century, i.e. in the developed Enlightenment, that Introduction succeeded in freeing itself from its dogmatic and ecclesiastical presuppositions and becoming an independent critical science.

(d) This connection with the Enlightenment and therefore with its rational approach to problems was then to prove, for more than a century, a burden on Introduction, both in respect of its freedom from presuppositions (the dogma of the synagogue or the church was in fact replaced very soon by the dominant philosophy of each era: idealism in its Kantian and Hegelian forms, evolutionism, historicism and so on) and in respect of its own relations to the synagogue and the Christian churches, for which it did the majority of its work in the sphere of the rabbinic seminaries and faculties of theology, which were in fact concerned with preparing ministers for the church and its worship. But in no way can it be said that Introduction suffered from the change, despite certain contingent difficulties; in the face of philosophical doctrines it was possible to engage in debate and even in polemic, but this was not so easy in the face of the doctrines of the church and the synagogue (as the two cases cited indicate). Moreover these philosophical theories did not necessarily have preconceived opinions on the origin and development of the biblical books. So it was possible to embark, at least in countries with a 'Protestant' tradition, on a collaboration between the faculties of theology (almost always in universities) and those of literature; this collaboration was not always an easy one, but in the long run it was fruitful. Those divisions did not occur which we tend to find in Roman Catholic or Eastern Orthodox countries or even in wide areas of Judaism. At the same time, however, this collaboration led to a more or less open conflict between the faculties of theology and the churches who drew their ministers from them, a conflict which has still not completely been overcome.

(e) The new situation of freedom of research in which Introduction found itself coincided with the progressive rediscovery of the world of the ancient Near East. From Napoleon's expedition to Egypt and the discovery (1798) and decipherment of the Rosetta Stone, throughout the nineteenth century and the first half of the twentieth, discoveries were made of the world in which Israel had lived and in which its main figures had been active. Practices and customs; religious, political, legal and social institutions; peoples, places and indeed nations unknown or inadequately known beforehand and, even more important, the various languages and the texts composed in them began to take shape. The biblical narratives and poems, first read almost exclusively in the sphere of the synagogue and of the Christian churches, thus came to be restored to their natural environment, to their own basis, to their proper place in universal history, by the elimination of often fictitious and outdated content, interpretations and explanations created by the tradition of the synagogue and the church. Finally it was possible to study the biblical text on its own merits, without other interference.

(*f*) Those nowadays who want to devote themselves to the study of Introduction to the Hebrew Bible will soon find themselves confronted with a problem which much of the biblical literature has in common with the other literature of the Ancient Near East: the anonymity of the majority of the texts. It should be noted that in the ancient Near East we know only the signatories of letters and treaties, two literary genres which are rare in the Hebrew Bible. Another difficulty is presented by pseudepigraphy, i.e. the tendency to attribute a writing to a person with an acknowleged reputation. Moreover, there are often no objective elements for anything other than conjectural dating; chronology can therefore be arrived at only by subjective criteria, which, apart from being open to question, inevitably change over the generations, as various techniques are improved. There are cases in which particular interpretations of the biblical text are simply the product of exegetical fashions: at the beginning of the century we find the *Babel-Bibel* (Babylonia and the Bible) polemic between authors who wanted to derive the whole of Hebrew thought from Mesopotamia and more moderate authors. Later there was a tendency to give very late dates to the Psalms and the poetical compositions of the Hebrew Bible generally, dates not prior to the Maccabaean period (cf. below, 34.4), and also to those compositions which clearly presuppose the existence of the monarchy and which were then attributed to the Hasmonaean rulers. But there is another example in the opposite direction: the attempts made particularly between the 1930s and the 1960s by a group of American philologists and archaeologists to back-date particular compositions, especially poetry (sometimes to the pre-monarchical or even pre-Israelite period) on the basis of the presence, whether real or presumed, of Canaanite or generally archaic elements. This was done without reflecting that Israelites and Canaanites spoke basically the same language and lived side by side for more than a millennium, down to the Hellenistic and Roman period, so that the presence of Canaanite elements in a composition (even given that it can be demonstrated that these are what they are) proves nothing on the chronological level, at least not to anyone who is not content merely to paraphrase what Israel said about its own prehistory but tries to arrive at a critical opinion. Moreover poetry tends always to use a conservative language, more archaic than current written language, and there is no reason to suppose that things will have been otherwise in Israel. So much is that the case that archaic terms and expressions have been found in the work of Ben Sirach, at the beginning of the second century BCE (cf. below, 48.2).

These fashions may not lead anywhere, but they are often not superseded without having first done some damage. However, their frequency is not due just to the inadequacies of scholars; the lack of objective elements for dating, especially for texts which are considered archaic and for poetry in general, makes some contribution to the creation of a situation which is confused in any case. That explains the perplexity of some scholars (above, p.4) when faced with attempts to obtain any information which does not immediately pose problems.

(g) It is for this reason that, despite the attempt by A.Lods* (1950) to write a history of Hebrew and Jewish literature while aware of the problems that such an attempt involves, the writing of any such history on the model of histories of the classical and modern worlds proves impossible. That is also why I too prefer to go on using the now time-honoured term 'Introduction'. In fact the only Hebrew 'literature' that we have is that selection of texts which has been handed down in the form of the 'canon', with the sole exception of late pseudepigraphical material handed down in other languages, and the very sparse epigraphical material that has come down to us (cf. Appendices 1 and 2). Of course if by 'history of literature' we mean that of the various traditions, only partly oral and for the most part written, and the literary genres represented in them (cf. below, 6.3), then we are applying to the texts a method which is not alien to them but also valid for the other literature of the ancient Near East, instead of trying to force it into whole schemes and criteria drawn from classical and Western literature which are not applicable to the situation in the ancient Near East.

2. The scope and limits of Introduction

(a) The anonymity of large parts of the texts, the pseudepigraphy of so many others and the difficulty of dating the major part of the Hebrew Bible by objective criteria therefore means that the problems of Introduction are quite special and the analogies with Western literature few. So the scholar must seek comparative material in the ancient Near East; the classical schemes which are still dominant in the West will be of little use. But the situation of the biblical writings is also quite different from that of the ancient Near East. In this latter case we have epigraphical texts which have rarely been tampered with, discovered in archaeological excavations, the *terminus ante quem* of which is almost always clear; in the Bible, on the other hand, updatings and continual re-readings have distorted the original text beyond any reasonable possibility of restoration right down to the beginning of the common era.

(b) I shall begin by defining chronologically the material with which we shall be concerned. By almost general consent Old Testament literature begins with the Song of Deborah in Judg.5 (cf. below, 14.3). This song, until recently dated about the twelfth or eleventh century BCE, has meanwhile proved to be much more recent, the earliest parts of it not being earlier than the ninth century BCE, even if the episode narrated is probably to be dated to the twelfth or eleventh century BCE. It is now inserted into a different context, which no longer hymns the ancient Israelite epic but the glories of YHWH, the God of Israel. Thus it can hardly reflect the religious situation of the pre-monarchical period or of the first years of the monarchy. If we go to the other extreme and consider the pseudepigraphical books of late Judaism and the Qumran writings, we come up to the period when there was a fundamental split within Judaism: the birth of the Christian church during the second half of the first century CE. This is why we also have Introduction to the New Testament, though to be strictly logical, much of the New Testament, too, by no means lies outside the literature of Israel. This means that Introduction to the Hebrew Bible must take account not only of the canonical text but also of the deutero-canonical writings, the pseudepigraphical and apocalyptic writings, and those of the Qumran sect. The present work will be limited to the biblical texts and will discuss only the writings of the Hebrew canon and those of Alexandrian Judaism (for a definition see the next chapter).

(c) In the course of our study we shall try to identify, where possible, the authors of individual books or of smaller literary units, isolating passages which are certainly inauthentic and those of doubtful authenticity; we shall also try to see how they came to appear in their present context. We shall consider the literary genres of each unit, study those which preceded them in the tradition and attempt to discover the setting in everyday life: the cult, religious polemic, politics, invective against social situations which were considered unacceptable. We shall see the message that the author, whether or not we know his name, sought to hand on to his own contemporaries and to posterity and how later generations re-read it and applied it to their own situation, even misunderstanding the original intention. These are ambitious aims, and I have no illusions about achieving them completely. In our work we shall be making use of a series of sister disciplines: linguistics and comparative philology (especially Hebrew and biblical Aramaic, but also the Western Semitic languages: Ugaritic, Phoenician, Moabite, Aramaic; sometimes also Akkadian). For the ancient translations we shall use Greek, Latin and Syriac, the history of religions, especially that of the ancient religions of Western Asia and the general history of the ancient Near East.

(d) One last observation. As I indicated at the beginning of this chapter, the course taken by Introduction to the Hebrew Bible for about two centuries has never been the monopoly of a single faculty, that of theology; through history, linguistics and comparative philology the material has come to be an integral part of the subject-matter of the faculties of the arts and philosophy. Moreover the legal material in the Bible, along with the legal codes of the ancient Near East, has a place in the teaching of the faculty of law. The difference between the faculty of theology and the other faculties cannot in any way be over material and methods: a theology which does not use the recognized methods of textual and historical criticism will only produce bad theology. Rather, the difference lies in the final decision between faith and unbelief. In other words, the theologian reads the texts as something more than a philologist and historian. The fact that for the Jewish and Christian believer the Hebrew Bible is also sacred scripture and therefore has a normative value which it evidently does not have for the unbeliever should not prevent believers from achieving a proper objectivity. On the contrary, it should compel them to listen humbly to what the texts say. This is not a paradox. They should therefore make as calm and detached an examination of the text as possible, taking care not to read into it what is not there. Thus the criterion of scientific objectivity, as well as being an ethical postulate for all scholars, applies first of all to believers, if they want to hear the word of the Lord instead of their own, and if they want to have a dialogue with the Lord instead of a monologue with themselves and their own opinions. So we are right to ask of all scholars, whether or not they are believers, to examine the biblical text with the objectivity that they would bring to any other ancient text, whether Near Eastern or classical.

As I have indicated, this attitude of historical and critical objectivity has come to be endorsed for the most part in theological faculties, particularly in universities, in the course of the last two centuries. It should not therefore surprise believers, much less scandalize them, as often happens: its aim is a better understanding of the texts, while at the same time it opens the door to collaboration, encounter and constructive debate with the other faculties, especially those of literature, philosophy and law.

BIBLIOGRAPHY

1. For the figure of R.Simon cf. J.Steinmann, *Richard Simon et les origines de l'exégèse biblique*, Paris 1969. For Spinoza, see in addition to the bibliographies listed in the various encyclopaedias L.Strauss, *Die Religionsphilosophie Spinozas als Grund seiner Bibelwissenschaft*, Berlin 1930, and G.Semerari, *I problemi dello Spinozismo*, Trani 1952.

For the widespread and disconcerting ignorance of Hebrew in Western mediaeval Christendom and therefore ignorance of the text of the Bible, a phenomenon which lasted until the beginning of the sixteenth century, cf. M.Thiels, 'Grundlagen und Gestalt der Hebräischkenntnisse des frühen Mittelalters', *Studi medievali* 10.3, 1969, 9-212.

For pseudepigraphy see now D.G.Meade, *Pseudonymity and Canon – an Investigation into the Relation of Authorship and Authority in Jewish and Christian Tradition*, Tübingen 1988.

2. Whether or not it is possible to write a history of Hebrew literature in the biblical period has been discussed by M.Noth, *Tradition History of the Pentateuch*, ET Englewood Cliffs NY, 1972, with a new and noteworthy introduction.

For present problems see K.-H.Bernhardt, 'Problematik und Probleme der alttestamentliche Einleitungswissenschaft', *TLZ* 98, 1973, 481-96, and R.Smend, 'Ein halbes Jahrhundert alttestamentlicher Einleitungswissenschaft', *TR* 49, 1984, 3-30. See also M.Weiss, *The Bible from Within*, Jerusalem 1986, 38ff., 144ff.

2

THE CANON

1. Traditions about the Palestinian canon

The term 'canon' is almost certainly of Semitic origin: it probably derives from the Akkadian *qanū*, Hebrew *qāneh*, which means 'measuring rod': in Greek we have the term *kanōn*, which generally means 'measure' and in philosophy 'norm'. Philo of Alexandria seems to have been the first to use the term to indicate the collection of books normative for faith, in contrast to other works which may be useful for edification but are not considered normative in the above sense.

We have two traditions about the formation of the Palestinian canon and the criteria according to which books were included in it; they come from the end of the first century CE and are a report by Flavius Josephus and a passage preserved in the pseudepigraphical IV Ezra. They do not therefore derive from orthodox Judaism.

(*a*) Flavius Josephus, *Contra Apionem* 1.8, lists the following qualifications needed by a book for it to become part of the canon as conceived by the Pharisaic movement.

1. It had to have been composed during the period between Moses and Ezra; in other words, a *terminus ad quem* was set for the composition of books which were divinely inspired and therefore eligible to enter the canon with the reign of Artaxerxes I of Persia in the fifth century BCE.

2. It had to have a certain objective sacred quality which differentiated it from all other non-sacred books. In consequence of this principle, anyone who approached the sacred book had to undergo certain rites, in the same way as with particular priestly functions.

3. It had to be included in the number of the twenty-two books listed by Josephus. According to present-day reckoning, these books amount to thirty-eight; the reason is that Josephus' figure is arrived at by a different calculation and excludes the Song of Songs (cf. below, 39.2).

The untouchability and hence the immutability of a text derived from these qualifications.

(b) The tradition preserved in the pseudepigraphical book IV Ezra 14.18ff. tells how Ezra caused to be written, by dictating them to assistants, all the writings which had been lost during the siege and destruction of Jerusalem in 587 BCE. He did this about thirty years afterwards, i.e. about 557, following a divine vision which commanded him to act in this way. It should be noted how this chronology antedates the real chronology by about a century (cf. below, 43.3). In this way Ezra is made to have written the twenty-four canonical books (this figure does not differ much from the one given by Flavius Josephus and is probably arrived at by an analogous procedure) and in addition seventy secret books intended for the wise. If this last note has any historical basis, it may refer to the composition of the apocalyptic and pseudepigraphical books, only some of which have come down to us and even then only in a variety of translations.

We are not in a position to pronounce on the normative value of these two traditions in orthodox Judaism at the end of the first century CE, and in any case they do not seem to have any historical foundation. They do, however, agree in one detail about which we might be more positive and which therefore seems to be of some importance: the time of Ezra was the lower chronological limit for a canonical book. Anything written later (and Josephus recognizes the existence of important Hebrew literature after this era, though it had no sacred character because the gift of prophecy had ceased) was *ipso facto* excluded from the canon, even if the work was of such a notable spiritual character as I Maccabees or Ecclesiasticus (cf. Part Six below), because it could not have been composed within the dates fixed.

The theory that the canon will have been closed at the time of Ezra was accepted uncritically down to the eighteenth century, but its only historical foundation is that it expresses the intention of those who decided (and we do not know who they were) whether a book was canonical or not. In the first place it in fact conflicts with the dates of certain books or individual literary units which are certainly later than the period of Ezra but have nevertheless become part of the canon; it does not explain why the only part of the canon accepted by the Samaritans was the Pentateuch, since the whole of the Hebrew Bible would have been completed and made a canon by the time of the schism; furthermore, it leaves unexplained the origins of the Alexandrian canon (some would have it that this was just a collection), which contains a much larger number of books than the Palestinian canon and additions to the canonical books. In reality the process which led to the creation of the canon was remarkably complex and extended over a lengthy period; in any case it was not the product of formal decision, far less of spontaneous dictation.

I have said that the criterion adopted, namely that books must not have been written after the time of Ezra, conflicts with the fact that later sections found their way into the canon, and we have seen that this criterion was really more an intention of the compilers than an actual fact. The same is true of the New Testament canon; here too the books were chosen according to a criterion, that of apostolicity; books after the apostolic age should not therefore have been chosen. But here too works which were certainly later found their way into the canon. The intention is thus combined with a remarkable lack of information; in other words, if scholars of the Hebrew Bible then had all the information available today, the canon would have been different or other criteria for inclusion would have been used.

2. Information about the origin of the Palestinian canon known to us

The traditional divisions of the Hebrew Bible still give useful, albeit few, indications for following the origins and development of the Palestinian canon. The Hebrew Bible is divided into three parts: the Pentateuch (Hebrew *tōrāh* = instruction, then synonymous with law and therefore translated *nomos* by the LXX and the New Testament); the Prophets (Hebrew *n⁰bī'īm*, which are further divided into Former, Hebrew *rīš'ōnīm*, i.e. the historical books of Joshua, Judges, Samuel and Kings, and Latter, Hebrew *'ahᵃrōnīm*, including all the prophets except Daniel, which Israel rightly did not consider to be a prophetic book); finally the Writings (Hebrew *k⁰tūbīm*, making up the rest). The term 'sacred scripture' for this collection appears only in II Macc.8.23, in the second half of the second century BCE; however, as often happens in cases like this, the idea is much older: whatever has been communicated by God to man through Moses, the prophets and other inspired authors, has authority independently of the expressions used.

In any case – and here we note a difference between earlier and more recent times – all this material, whether oral or written (for the problem of oral tradition see below, 6.2) seems to have circulated in the Jewish community with remarkable freedom. The community used it for liturgical purposes and for instruction, and did not hesitate to adapt it continually to its own changing needs. That seems to have been the situation before the recognition and closing of the canon, and here we have the explanation of the material added to the ancient texts at a later date. But we do not have any indication that this fixing of the tradition and closing of the canon took place before the end of the first century CE; before this period material, even material considered 'holy scripture', had a somewhat fluid character, and it was only after the catastrophes which befell Judaism in 70 and 134 CE that it became necessary to give scripture a fixed form because of the dispersion of the community and hence the danger that the tradition might become corrupt or be lost.

We shall now examine in detail the three or four parts into which the Hebrew Bible is traditionally divided.

(a) The Pentateuch. This is the collection which enjoys the greatest canonical authority in Israel and has always been the standard by which the canonicity of the other writings has been assessed. It has also been accepted from time immemorial with the same status by the Samaritans; they have their own version of it which has a number of variants from the Jewish Pentateuch (cf. below, § 7). This may be taken to indicate that at the time when the schism between Jews and Samaritans took place, an event the date of which cannot be determined with any certainty but which cannot have been after the end of the fourth century BCE, the Pentateuch must have been virtually complete in its present form and must have had undisputed canonical authority. On the other hand passages like Ezek.40-48 and the fact that the final redaction of the Pentateuch was made on the basis of the source P (cf. below, 10.5) demonstrate that the final redaction took place in the post-exilic period, regardless - as is obvious - of the dating of the individual traditions contained in it. This period is near to the time of Ezra and Nehemiah (middle of the fifth century BCE, cf. below, 43, though the date is only an approximate one) and their reforms, which probably laid the foundation for the final split between Jews and Samaritans (for this problem, cf my *History*, XIII.4). As can be seen, here too the difficulties presented by the texts and the impossibility of establishing absolute dates only allow us to put forward hypothetical solutions.

(b) The earliest parts of the Former Prophets are made up of material contemporary with, or a little later than, the earliest sources of the Pentateuch with which up to a few years ago they were wrongly connected (cf. below, 8), but the latest authentic passages cannot be earlier than the events described in II Kings 25.27-30 (c.561 BCE). This material, which therefore does not go back beyond the first twenty-five years of the second exile in Babylon, has been reworked by a school known, as we shall see (below, 12.1) as the Deuteronomistic school because it makes use of the directives given in the fifth and last book of the Pentateuch as criteria for the revision of the ancient traditions. The work of this school took place during and immediately after the exile, perhaps in three stages, and certainly not earlier nor much later than the sixth century BCE. The differences betwen this work and that of the Chronicler (beginning of the fourth century BCE, cf. below, 42), which largely draws on the same sources, may be a sign that the Deuteronomistic work was also finished at this time and enjoyed canonical authority. It was not accepted by the Samaritans, which might indicate that it was brought to a conclusion after the schism, but the reason for this may also be that the whole work is orientated on the centralization of the cult in Jerusalem effected under King Josiah in 622-21, a position which the Samaritans rejected and still reject today. The two explanations are not mutually exclusive.

(c) The Latter Prophets (below, 17) sometimes wrongly called the writing prophets (because in contrast to the Former Prophets we possess books to which they have given their names) derive their canonical authority from the fact that their words are presented as messages which the God of Israel reveals to his people by means of them. We may recall that Josephus set the time of the closing of the canon in the period of Ezra because from then on there were no more prophets (above, 1). It is possible that originally there was a larger collection: prophets like Elijah and Elisha (I Kings 17 – II Kings 10, ninth century BCE) were well known, and the former came to be celebrated, especially in late Judaism, as the precursor of the Messiah (on the basis of Mal.3.23, EVV 4.5), a function which believing and practising Jews still believe him to have. However, very few of the sayings of these two prophets have been preserved. A prophet like Micaiah ben Imlah (I Kings 22.10ff., from the same period) may also have spoken more words than the few of his which have been transmitted. But here too we can do no more than guess: the fact is that the texts restrict themselves to reporting a few words and a number of episodes form the lives of these figures.

The prophets were essentially preachers and not writers. Their sayings were rarely fixed in writing on their own initiative; their books are generally the work of disciples and schools which formed around them. Isaiah 8.16ff. makes explicit mention of the master's disciples, while in Jer.36 and elsewhere in the book we are given the name of the prophet's 'secretary'; this last chapter is also the first to state explicitly that a sizeable collection of prophetic sayings had been put in writing. We do not, however, have the slightest indication when any single prophetic book was finished; we know, rather, that often oracles which were centuries later, or even from the same period but written by different authors, were interpolated in or added to the authentic words of particular prophets. The problem sometimes becomes so complex that there are scholars who would prefer to give up attempting to identify the authentic sayings of the various prophets. In certain cases it is possible to explain the phenomenon by the hypothesis that the school founded by a prophet continued his work for a long time afterwards and that the writings stemming from it circulated under the name of the prophet in question, which was then the name of the school (for example in the case of Isaiah); in other cases, however, the phenomenon is inexplicable.

Even here, however, we have a fixed date, though it is relatively late: the deutero-canonical book of Ecclesiasticus (beginning of the second century BCE, cf. below, 48) 48.22-49.10 knows the three major prophets (it will be remembered that the Hebrew Bible does not consider Daniel to be a prophet) and the twelve minor prophets with whom, a little later, towards the end of the third century BCE, the collection was thought to be closed. It was then probably considered canonical.

(d) The Writings have always been the part of the Hebrew Bible which, apart from the Psalms, has enjoyed the least authority in Israel. Some of the books which belong here have now been recognized to be certainly late (e.g. Daniel); others were certainly introduced only after laborious discussions (e.g. Song of Songs and Esther). However, among the Psalms and in Proverbs there are texts which belong to the earliest traditions of Israel (e.g. Psalms 29 and 68); these passed over to Israel from Canaan after some alterations in a monotheistic direction which can sometimes be clearly recognized by the attentive reader.

3. The Alexandrian collection

Alexandrian Judaism does not seem to have accepted the chronological limitations imposed by Palestinian Judaism on the canon, and admitted among its writings works which can be dated up to the end of the first millennium BCE. It is not easy to determine the canonical character of this collection: it is possible, for example, to suppose that the Jews of Alexandria simply wanted to collect together all the books used in worship without raising the problem of their normative character for faith. It is no coincidence, however, that the

Greek translation, the LXX (cf. below, § 6), which contains a number of books that are not in the Hebrew Bible (below, Part Six), was acquiring increasing authority to the point of being considered inspired and being adopted by the Christian church. In any case its influence was limited to Hellenistic Judaism, from which it then passed to the church, the community of which was initially founded in the milieu of the Hellenistic synagogue outside Palestine and often had a very scanty knowledge of Hebrew and Aramaic. Then as the church gradually spread first into the Hellenistic and then into the Roman world, it is not surprising that the LXX translation found increasing acceptance (though Israel had meanwhile shown some reservations about it) and with it also those works and additions which had not been included in the Palestinian canon. Even today, moreover, the status of the books in the Alexandrian canon is a matter of controversy among the various Christian churches: while the Roman Catholic church after the Council of Trent accepted the canonicity of the greater part of the Alexandrian canon (but not all; it excluded III Ezra and III-IV Maccabees), some Eastern Orthodox churches maintain an equivocal attitude, while others have included different books in their canon; the Protestant and Anglican churches have generally rejected their canonicity, for the most part merely according them the status of devotional books; thus up to the first decades of the nineteenth century they could often be found printed in an appendix in Protestant editions of the Bible also. For the church, the problem is rather like that of ecclesiastical Byzantinism, since while the books in question fill a chronological gap of some centuries (for the Christian church, there would otherwise be no valid traces of Israelite faith between the fourth century BCE and the first century CE) they do not add to or detract from any doctrine of scripture (except through abuses in exegesis) and should not therefore be a matter of controversy. The position of Judaism is of course different: the synagogue has never accepted these books, just as it has always, as we shall see, rejected the LXX translation, accepting only the Hebrew Bible. Finally, all the Christian traditions have kept the order of the Greek Bible.

We shall deal with the Alexandrian canon in Part Six of this book. In view of its problematical character, I have chosen to use the term 'deutero-canonical books', which is historically more neutral and correct, instead of apocrypha, often used in Protestantism, which is polemical and historically incorrect.

4. The closing of the Palestinian canon

The closing of the Palestinian canon is, then, to be sought in the last years of the first century and the first years of the second century CE. Jewish traditions mention assemblies (in the West sometimes wrongly called synods), one of which met in Jerusalem around 65 CE, i.e. before the first destruction of the capital in 70 CE, and another at Jabneh (Greek Jamnia) around 90, i.e. before the last rebellion, that of Bar Kochba, in 132-135. Among the other important matters discussed it seems that these assemblies decided on the inclusion or rejection of a number of controversial books: Song of Songs, Esther and Ecclesiastes; their inclusion thus took place at a late date and was not without opposition. Among the books discussed was also the book of Ezekiel, the last part of which, chapters 40-48, differs in some of its contents from the Pentateuch which, as we have seen, was considered the touchstone for judging the canonicity of a book. Whole books like that of Daniel, and sections like Isa.24-27: Zech.12-14, though later than the time of Ezra, were retained because they were attributed to authors living before the terminus in question.

However, recently good reasons have been presented for questioning whether such assemblies ever took place, since the evidence we have is purely circumstantial. At all events, the fact remains that the Hebrew Bible was complete by the end of the first century CE, at least in its consonantal text (the western and southern Semitic languages were originally written without vowels, which were added to the consonantal text at a later stage). However, many recensions remained in circulation and we can distinguish between a Babylonian text, some fragments of which we possess, a Palestinian text, deriving from the temple of Jerusalem and on the basis of which, as we shall see shortly, the text of the LXX seems to have been translated, and the Pharisaic text, which increasingly established itself after the catastrophes of 70 and 135 CE, the father of the present *textus receptus* or Massoretic text. The Isaiah text of Qumran largely corresponds to this last (11 real variants in 66 chapters); but the Qumran texts, as again we shall see, also bear witness to other textual traditions, epecially in the 4QSam[abc] fragments.

5. The Hebrew Bible: the text

(a) So far we have been occupied with the divisions of the Hebrew Bible and with the canon (above, § 2); we shall now turn our attention to the text (or, better, texts). In addition to this we shall also consider the two most celebrated translations, the Greek translation known as the LXX and the Latin translation by Jerome.

The Hebrew text now in our possession has one peculiarity: despite its supposed antiquity, it comes to us in relatively late manuscripts which are therefore far removed in time from the originals (sometimes by more than a thousand years). The earliest complete ancient codex which has served as the basis for the text of *Biblia Hebraica*, ed. R.Kittel, Stuttgart ³1937 and reprints, and for the *Biblia Hebraica Stuttgartensia* edited by K.Elliger and W.Rudolph, Stuttgart 1978 (these are the two critical editions generally used today), is the Codex Leningradensis (coll. B 19ª of the Leningrad Public Library), dated according to the colophon in 1008 CE. Another virtually complete codex serves as the basis for the edition of the Hebrew University Bible: this is the Aleppo Codex from the beginning of the tenth century CE which is now in Israel. We also have some earlier codices containing part of the Bible: the Codex Cairensis of 895 and a codex recently discovered in the collection of the Institute for Asiatic Peoples in Leningrad, from 847, both containing only the Prophets. As can be seen, none of these manuscripts is earlier than the ninth century CE. This explains the importance of writings like those at Qumran, which take us back about a thousand years, or of a translation like the Greek of the LXX, a little earlier.

(*b*) The reasons for this apparently disconcerting phenomenon are to be sought in the work of textual criticism and the re-editing of the canonical text of the Hebrew Bible which took place during the second half of the first millennium CE through the work of the scholars who are known as Massoretes (from the Hebrew *massōret*, probably 'tradition').

(*c*) As we have seen, the consonantal text on which they worked was practically complete at the end of the first century CE and indeed probably earlier. The Massoretes were primarily concerned to revise the text and in the case of textual variants to choose the readings which they considered to be most authoritative: they introduced a unitary orthography (their attempts did not always succeed with the coherence that we might expect) which is often better than the somewhat extravagant system existing at the end of the first millennium BCE and the beginning of the first millennium CE. In this system almost only the vowels which are long by nature (that is, those which are not the contingent product of inflections of the root) came to be represented in writing by their nearest consonants: *y* for the sounds *ē/ī*, *w* for the sounds *ō/ū*, *h* for final *ā*. These are the vowels which some modern grammarians transcribe with a circumflex accent or macron. In this way all the more or less precarious systems of representing vowels by means of other consonants (e.g. by *'aleph* and *'ayin*), partially attested also in late Phoenician and Punic, came to be eliminated. The most important work to have been completed by the Massoretes was, however, without doubt that of stabilizing the traditional pronunciation of every word by means of the addition of diacritical signs equivalent to the vowels which the above-mentioned system did not express; and although we cannot affirm with any certainty (or rather, although there are fundamental objections to asserting) that this system always maintained the original sounds, it preserved Hebrew from irremediable confusion with the pronunciation of cognate languages, especially Aramaic and Syriac, and later Arabic.

There were various Massoretic schools: the eastern school, which grew up among the Israelites living in Babylon, and the western school, originating in Palestine, out of which developed the school of Tiberias, which soon achieved the greatest authority. Although the system of this last group was the most complicated, it gained precedence over all the rest, to such a degree that it is still used today in Hebrew Bibles. From the numerous fragments from the other schools which have come down to us we know, however, that there were sometimes notable differences in the pronunciation of the same words among various schools, and this fact is confirmed, albeit in an indirect way, by the Greek and Latin translations of proper names or by fragments of the second column of Origen's *Hexapla*. Here too, then, the tradition appears long and complex, and it is far from certain that the Massoretes always made the best choices.

In any case, from the end of the work of the Massoretes down to the present day the text of the Hebrew Bible has remained the same, even if some mediaeval manuscripts have retained readings which appear either in fragments of the eastern Massoretes or in translations or transcriptions into western languages.

(*d*) One important category of variants is represented by quotations of the Greek Old Testament in the New Testament; the majority of these repeat the text of the LXX, though there are some of them which do not correspond to any Greek version known to us, but differ from the Hebrew text which we have received. It is possible that there were other Greek versions which have not come down to us, but which were used by the writers of the New Testament, unless the quotations are just approximations or have been made from memory.

(*e*) The Massoretes of Tiberias did not have the last word on the pronunciation of Hebrew, although their system soon became dominant. Even now, there are at least three established ways of pronouncing Hebrew: among the Jews of eastern Europe the *a* is pronounced as *o*, the final *t* as *s* and so on; among Jews of Spanish origin, until a few years ago dispersed throughout North Africa, the Near East, some Balkan countries and among those from Italy, we have the pronunciation generally accepted in universities, from which the modern Israeli pronunciation derives. The first is called Ashkenazi, the second Sephardic. A third pronunciation is that of Arabic-speaking Jews and especially Yemenis, which offers the whole range of gutturals and dentals attested in Arabic; it is difficult to establish whether they have maintained the original pronunciation of Hebrew or whether they have adapted it to the pronunciation of the neighbouring Arab population. In any case, the extermination of large numbers of Eastern European Jews and the immigration of Spanish-speaking and Arabic-speaking Jews to Israel has condemned the first and third pronunciations to oblivion in favour of the second. At all events these pronunciations are an important indication that the unifying work of the Massoretes never succeeded in overcoming the traditional differences in pronunciation.

(*f*) It is not therefore surprising that today there are scholars who talk of two original Hebrew dialects, the southern (which then became the sacred language), and the northern, with a remarkable affinity to Moabitic and Phoenician/Punic, and who think even in terms of two Palestinian recensions of the Hebrew text, the southern recension becoming established in Judah and the northern being attested in the Samaritan writings. These are evidently no more than hypotheses, but they offer a very good explanation of the differences of orthography and pronunciation existing in the Massoretic text, notwithstanding the work of unification completed by its editors: sometimes a phonetic tradition may have been so deeply rooted that not even the Massoretes were either able or willing to supplant it.

6. The Greek translations

The attention of scholars had long been directed towards the ancient translations of the Hebrew texts, given their considerable age in comparison with the Massoretic text, and from the publication of the *Biblia Polyglotta Complutensis*, edited by Cardinal F. Xímenez de Cisneros between 1514 and 1517 in Alcala (in Latin *Complutum*) onwards, numerous editions, more or less critical, have sought to compare the Hebrew text with the ancient translations. The chief of these is the *Biblia Polyglotta*, edited by Brian Walton, London 1657.

(*a*) The Septuagint translation is so called because according to a pseudepigraphic Jewish writing composed in Greek towards 100 BCE, the Letter of Aristeas, the work originated from the labours of seventy-two scholars, invited by Ptolemy II Philadelphus of Alexandria to make a Greek translation of the Pentateuch for the library at Alexandria. They were lodged on the island of Pharos so that they could be free to work without interruption and had all the material they needed at their disposal; they worked no more than nine hours a day and attempted by constant comparison to arrive at a uniform text (*Aristeas*, 302). This version of the facts is not intrinsically improbable, as has been authoritatively argued by L.Rost. It later came to be elaborated with legendary elements: after intensive labour, each in utter isolation, the translators arrived at an identical translation. These amplifications were meant to demonstrate the inspired character of the translation as well, and this argument is indirectly put forward towards the end (311) when it is said that anyone who alters the text in any way, by either addition or subtraction, is accursed – a formula used exclusively for works considered to be divinely inspired.

Thus the Letter puts the Greek translation of the Pentateuch at the end of the first half of the third century BCE, but does not explain how the other writings of the Hebrew Bible came to be translated or how what I have called (above, § 3) the Alexandrian collection was formed. Nor does it explain how there are sometimes remarkable differences in the method of translation between one book and another, differences which range from an exact (sometimes literal) translation into tolerable Greek to free translation or bad Greek. It also leaves unexplained the difference between the Massoretic text and that of the LXX in some cases, unless we acceept the most obvious theory, namely that the Massoretic text and that of LXX go back to different archetypes. This theory is now generally accepted, for example in the chronologies and again in the books of Samuel, in which the text of Codex B (Vaticanus) of LXX is better than the Massoretic text; recently Hebrew archetypes have been discovered in the caves of Qumran (4QSam^{abc}) but they are very fragmentary (for the problem see J.H.Hayes*, 58ff.). Moreover the note in the Letter of Aristeas completely ignores the situation in the Greek-speaking Jewish community, which seem to have had more and more difficulties with Hebrew: here the need for a translation must have been felt particularly; the tendency to consider the translation in question also inspired can only be sought, in fact, in the Jewish communities of the Diaspora and obviously not among the authorities of the library of Alexandria. Thus we have two theories, which are not necessarily contradictory, on the origin of the translation.

The best edited part of the LXX is obviously the Pentateuch: it is in the other parts that the difficulties indicated above arise.

One of the problems for the modern student of the translations is the lack of a complete critical edition. Two editions are in course of publication. *The Cambridge Septuagint*, edited by A.Brooke, N.McLean and H.St J.Thackeray, I.1, 1906 – III.1, 1940, covers the historical books. This is a diplomatic edition and uses codex B as a basis. The *Göttingen Septuagint* is edited by J.Ziegler and R.Hanhart; it has been in the course of publication from 1926 on. The problem for the scholar is that the criteria governing the approaches of the two works are different, so that they cannot be considered complementary. Handier editions are those edited by H.B.Swete, *The Old Testament in Greek* (4 vols), Cambridge 1894ff., and by A.Rahlfs, *Septuaginta* (2 vols), Stuttgart 1935. The former also offers a diplomatic edition, based on Codex B.

(*b*) But the Jews felt the need for other translations, especially as the Christian church often made use of the renderings typical of the LXX for its own apologetic and polemic. These translations were primarily meant to be more faithful to the Hebrew text. We know of three of them, though only through fragments of Origen's Hexapla and quotations from the fathers of the church: those of Aquila (A), Symmachus (Σ) and Theodotion (Θ). The three authors are unknown: according to some scholars Symmachus was an exponent of Ebionite Jewish Christianity and thus would be mid-way between the primitive church and Judaism; according to others, he lived in Galilee about 200 CE. It is interesting to note Aquila's method: to avoid errors he tried to be as literal as possible in his translation and chose, where possible, terms which had the same etymology as their Hebrew equivalents. Moreover, there had to be a Greek term to correspond to every Hebrew one. Needless to say, the results are always absurd and sometimes misleading. The fact remains that these three translations did not succeed in taking the place of the LXX, so we have only small fragments of them.

A critical edition of the fragments of the Hexapla was made by F.Field, *Hexaplorum quae supersunt...fragmenta*, 2 vols, Oxford 1875, reprinted Hildesheim 1964. This work, while valuable, needs, however, to be brought up to date in the light of more recent discoveries.

7. The Samaritan Pentateuch

The Samaritan Pentateuch is a unique example of a section of the Hebrew Bible which has evolved in a form independent of the Massoretes, among the Samaritan community. It has about 6,000 variant readings from the Massoretic text, but most of them are only orthographic. In about 1900 cases the Samaritan text agrees with the text of the LXX against the Massoretic text; other variant readings are the product of the theological position of the sect: for example, in Exod.20.17, at the end of the Decalogue, a commandment has been added which calls for the building of a sanctuary on Mount Gerizim, above Nablus, which is still the sacred mountain of the Samaritans. The choice of the place where YHWH will make his name to dwell is often indicated in the past tense and therefore refers to Gerizim, an echo of the old polemic between Jews and Samaritans which was still acute in the New Testament period (cf. John 4). But there is at least one case, Deut.27.4-7, in which the reading 'Gerizim' in the Samaritan Pentateuch, confirmed by Σ and by the Old Latin, seems to be preferable to that of the Massoretic text, which has Ebal, the other mountain standing above Nablus. A critical edition based on more recent research is in preparation; for the moment the edition by A.von Gall, *Der hebräische Pentateuch der Samaritaner*, Giessen 1914-1918, reprinted Berlin 1960, is adequate.

8. Aramaic paraphrases and translations

(a) In the last centuries of the first millennium BCE, Hebrew became less and less a spoken language and more and more a sacred or at best an academic language: it therefore became less and less comprehensible to large areas of the population who either spoke in dialect forms or used Aramaic. Aramaic paraphrases of the biblical text began to arise in the context of synagogue worship, especially during public readings; these translations differed in quality, in method and in aim. They were sometimes literal, sometimes free and sometimes paraphrases which not only translated the original but also interpreted it. They were given the name *targūmīm*, in the singular *targūm* = translation. Given the origin of these writings, the variety of the materials circulating under the name *targūmīm* is not surprising; the Samaritans also found themselves in a similar position to the Jews over language, and the Qumran sect has its own *targūmīm*. Here, too, however, we should also notice the tendency in time to concentrate on an official text; the text now printed alongside the

Hebrew text in rabbinic Bibles is not earlier than the fifth century CE. The *targum* of the Pentateuch came to be attributed, probably wrongly, to Aquila, and is called the Targum Onkelos; that of the prophets was attributed to Theodotion and called the Targum Jonathan, the Hebrew version of this name. A critical edition has been published under the editorship of A.Sperber, *The Bible in Aramaic* (4 vols), Leiden 1959-73.

(*b*) An earlier Syriac translation of the Hebrew Bible than the classic text, the Peshitto (= the simple), has been attested, but we know little about it; some authors even argue that it is of Christian origin. A critical edition of the Peshitto is being prepared in Holland, under the editorship of P.A.H.de Boer and M.J.Mulder. In the Pentateuch and, it seems, Isaiah, it shows strong Targumic influence, which is not surprising in view of the close relationship between Syriac and Aramaic. This appears to prove the Jewish origin of the work, at least in its original form, but does not rule out the possibility of later Christian revisions. We sometimes find readings corresponding to those in the LXX, in contrast to the Massoretic text, but the problem is whether these are authentic variants or corruptions which have entered the two texts.

9. Latin translations

(*a*) The remains of a Latin translation prior to the Vulgate, called the *Vetus Latina* or *Vetus Itala*, have been transmitted through fragments of manuscripts, liturgical works and patristic texts, and by Origen. The work is strongly influenced by the LXX translation, so much so that it was probably based on the Greek text; nothing definite can be said about that, however, until a large part at least of the critical edition which is in preparation at the Abbey of Beuron, under the editorship of B.Fischer, has been published. So far an introductory volume and some volumes of the text have appeared.

(*b*) Much more important, not least because of the canonical position it attained in the West and therefore in mediaeval philosophy, is the translation which derives from the time of St Jerome, widely called the Vulgate (Vg) because it was in common use in the West from the seventh century on. The original translation by Jerome was preceded by a number of introductory studies and revisions of existing material and was finished between 390 and 405. Its importance still lies in the fact that it was made on the basis of Hebrew and Aramaic texts, often in contrast to that of the LXX. This did not fail to arouse hostility among illustrious contemporaries like Augustine. The translation was then revised a number of times in subsequent centuries. Jerome did not hesitate to enlist the help of Jewish scholars, so his work is also important from a technical and critical point of view; also important are the introductions to and the commentaries on individual books, the first example of scientific and critical biblical exegesis known to us in history. From the time of the Council of Trent (session of 8 April 1546, Denzinger, 785ff.) it became the official text of the Roman Catholic Church; in Protestantism, however, it has often been attacked because of some textual variants accepted by Catholicism to support some of its dogmatic positions. It is obvious, however, that the author cannot be considered responsible for this official situation, just as the translators of the LXX are not responsible for the semi-official position which has been conferred on it by the Greek-speaking Orthodox Church after more than a millennium and a half of use.

A critical edition of the Vulgate has been in the course of publication under the editorship of the Benedictine order since 1926, and more than half the Old Testament has already appeared (most recently The Twelve Minor Prophets, 1987). The most recent concise edition, also produced by the same order, is that edited by R.Weber, *Biblia sacra juxta Vulgatam editionem* (two vols), Stuttgart 1969.

BIBLIOGRAPHY

1-2. S.Talmon, 'The Old Testament Text', in *The Cambridge History of the Bible*, Cambridge I, 1970, (159-99) 162ff.; R.Gordis, *The Biblical Text in the Making*, Philadelphia [2]1971; J.A.Sanders, *Torah and Canon*, Philadelphia 1972; id., 'Adaptable for Life. The Nature and Functions of Canon', in *Magnalia Dei... Essays G.E.Wright*, Garden City, NY 1976, 531-60; id., *Text and Canon. Concepts and Method*, Philadelphia 1979; G.Rinaldi, 'Studi italiani sul testo ebraico intertestamentario', *BO* 22, 1980, 55-61; B.S.Childs, 'The Exegetical Significance of the Canon for the Study of the Old Testament', *SVT* 29, 1978, 66-80; and the *Introduction** (for Childs the canon is also a hermeneutical criterion and therefore of basic importance for understanding the texts; this is a theory which so far has not found much acceptance, cf. R.P.Carroll, 'Canonical Criticism. A Recent Trend in Biblical Studies', *ExpT* 92, 1980-81, 73-8). Cf. also J.Weingreen, *Introduction to the Study of the Hebrew Bible*, Oxford 1982; J.D.Kaestli and O.Wermelinger (eds.), *Le canon de l'Ancien Testament*, Geneva 1984; B.J.Diebner, 'Erwägungen zum Prozess der Sammlung des dritten Teils der Bibel', *DBAT* 21, 1985, 139-99; id., 'Zur Funktion der kanonischen Textsammlung im Judentum der vorchristlichen Zeit', *DBAT* 22, 1985 [1986], 568-73; and R.Rendtorff, 'Zur Bedeutung des Kanons für eine Theologie', in *Aufsätze für Hans-Joachim Kraus*, Neukirchen 1983, 3-11. For the problem see the annual *Textus* of the Hebrew University of Jerusalem and the heading 'Il testo dell'Antico Testamento' in the journal *Henoch*, edited by B.Chiesa.

2. For the assembly of Jabneh and the school working in the locality after 70 CE see K.H.Rengstorf, 'Der Glanz von Jabne', in *FS W.Caskel*, Leiden 1968, 233-44; P.Schäfer, 'Die sogenannte Synode von Jabne', *Judaica* 31, 1975, 54-64, 116-24.

5. For a general introduction to the Hebrew text and its problems and to the ancient translations cf. B.J.Roberts, *The Old Testament Text and Versions*, Cardiff 1951; Noth, *OTW*, Part Four; E.Würthwein, *The Text of the Old Testament*, Grand Rapids and London ²1980; P.Sacchi, 'Rassegna di studi di storia del testo del Vecchio Testamento ebraico', *OA* 9, 1970, 221-33; for the terminology see R.N.Soulen, *Handbook of Biblical Criticism*, Atlanta 1976; D.W.Gooding, 'An Appeal for Stricter Terminology in the Textual Criticism of the Old Testament', *JSS* 21, 1967, 15-25.

For the Massoretic text see: C.D.Ginsburg, *Introduction to the Massoretico-Critical Edition of the Hebrew Bible*, London 1897, reprinted New York 1966; P.E.Kahle, *The Cairo Geniza*, Oxford ²1959; G.É.Weil, *Élie Lévite, humaniste et massorète*, Leiden 1964; R.Edelmann, 'Soferim-Massoretes, "Massoretes" – Nakdanim', in *In memoriam Paul Kahle*, Berlin 1968, 116-23. A communication by Dr K.Starkova on the Leningrad Codex containing the prophets was scheduled for the Sixth International Congress for the study of the Old Testament held in Rome in 1968; the communication was never given and it does not seem to have been published elsewhere. The Hebrew University Bible is being published under the editorship of M.H.Goshen-Gottstein, C.Rabin and S.Talmon. Two fascicles of the book of Isaiah have appeared, I, 1974 and II, 1981; the third and last is in preparation.

6. The text of the Letter of Aristeas has been republished in a critical edition edited by A.Pelletier, *Lettre d'Aristée à Philocrate*, SC 89, Paris 1962, and C.Kraus Reggiani, *La lettera di Aristea a Filocrate*, Rome 1979; cf. also F.Parente, 'La lettera di Aristea come fonte per la storia del giudaismo alessandrino durante la prima metà del I secolo a.C', *ASNSP* III.2, 1972, 177-237, 537-67. for the problems connected with it cf A.Pelletier, *Flavius Josèphe, adapteur de la Lettre d'Aristée*, Paris 1962; D.W.Gooding, 'Aristeas and Septuagint Origins. A Review of Recent Studies', *VT* 13, 1963, 356-79; D.Barthélemy, 'L'Ancien Testament a mûri à Alexandrie', *TZ* 21, 1965, 358-70; R.Hanhart, 'Die Bedeutung der Septuaginta für die Definition des "Hellenistischen Judentums"', *SVT* 40, 1988, 67-80. L.Rost, *Vermutungen über den Anlass der griechischen Übersetzung der Tora*, Zurich 1970, accepts the theory that the translation of the Pentateuch came about on an official commission, in the sphere of the unique law which the Jews enjoyed

in Alexandria. Cf. also R.Hanhart, 'Die Septuaginta als Problem der Textgeschichte, der Forschung und der Theologie', *SVT* 22, 1962, 185-20c; P.Walters and D.W.Gooding, *The Text of the Septuagint*, Cambridge 1972. For the LXX and the other translations see A.Fernández Marcos, *Introducción a las versiones griegas de la Biblia*, Madrid 1979; J. Barr, *The Typology of Literalism in the Ancient Biblical Translations*, Göttingen 1979. For the complex relationships between the Massoretic text, that presupposed by the LXX and those of Qumran cf.R.W.Klein, *Textual Criticism of the Old Testament*, Philadelphia 1974; B.Chiesa, *L'Antico Testamento ebraico della tradizione palestinese*, Turin 1978 (where on pp.282 and 327ff. he shows the probability of the theory that the LXX will have worked on a Hebrew text of Palestinian tradition, and therefore deriving from the temple, fragments of which he has collected); F.Vattioni, 'Storia del testo biblico: L'origine dei LXX', *AION* 40, 1980, 115-30; E.S.Frerichs, 'The Torah Canon of Judaism and the Interpretation of Hebrew Scripture', *HorBTh* 9, 1987, 13-25.

For the Qumran fragments which presuppose a text similar to the Hebrew archetype of the LXX cf. F.M.Cross, 'A New Biblical Fragment Related to the Original Hebrew Underlying the Septuagint', *BASOR* 132, 1953, 15-26, and 'The Oldest Manuscripts from Qumran, V', *JBL* 74, 1955, 147-272. While we are waiting for the definitive publication of these fragments the critical edition in *BHS* may suffice: *Liber Samuelis*, curavit P.A.H. de Boer, Stuttgart 1976, who lists many of these variants. Parts of 4QSam have recently been published by E.C.Ulrich, *The Qumran Text of Samuel and Josephus*, Missoula, Mont. 1978. Similar problems have been indicated for fragments of the books of Exodus, Deuteronomy and Jeremiah, cf. F.M.Cross, *The Ancient Library of Qumran*, London 1958, 135 n.30, 137 n.31, 139 n.38.

For the LXX tradition generally see P.Sacchi, 'Il testo dei LXX nella sua problematica più recente', *Atene e Roma* NS 9, 1964, 145-58; J.W.Wevers, 'Septuaginta Forschungen seit 1954', *TR* 33, 1968, 453-75; S.Jellicoe, *The Septuagint and Modern Study*, Oxford 1968; E.Tov, *The Text-Critical Use of the Septuagint in Biblical Research*, Jerusalem 1981. Vol.8 of *Textus* (1973) is devoted to the LXX translation. See also S.Jellicoe, 'Some Reflections on the ΚΑΙΓΕ Recension', *VT* 23, 1973, 15-24; B.S.J.Isserlin, 'The Names of the Seventy-Two Translators of the Septuagint (Aristeas 47-50)', *JANESCU* 5, 1973, 191-7; H.S.Gehman, 'Peregrinations in Septuagint Lexicography', in *A Light unto My Path*, FS *J.M.Myers*, Philadelphia 1974, 223-40; D.Barthélemy, 'Pourquoi la Tora a-t-elle été traduite en Grec?', in *Our Language, Culture and Religion: in Honor of E.A.Nida*, The Hague 1974, 23-41; E.Tov, 'On "Pseudo-Variants" in the Septuagint', *JSS* 20, 1975, 165-77; H.M.Orlinsky, 'The Septuagint as Holy Writ and the Philosophy of the Translators', *HUCA* 46, 1975, 89-114; J.O'Callaghan, 'Lista de los papiros de los LXX', *Bibl* 55, 1975, 74-93; E.Tov, 'Dimensions of Septuagint Words', *RB* 83, 1976, 529-54; id., 'Compound Words Representing Two or More Hebrew Words', *Bibl* 58, 1977, 189-212; J.M.Wevers, 'The Earliest Witness to the

LXX Deuteronomy', *CBQ* 39, 1977, 240-4 (this is Rylands Gk 458 = Gött 957, from the middle of the second century BCE!). For the present state of LXX studies cf. P.M.Bogaert, 'Les études sur la Septante. Bilan et perspectives', *RTL* 16, 1985, 174-200; A.Pietersma, 'Septuagint Research. A Plea for a Return to Basic Issues', *VT* 35, 1985, 296-311; A.Aejmelaeus, 'What Can We Know about the Hebrew *Vorlage* of the Septuagint?', *ZAW* 99, 1987, 58-90.

6b. For Aquila cf. K.Hyvärinen, *Die Übersetzung von Aquila*, Lund 1977: for Symmachus, cf. D.Barthélemy, 'Qui est Symmaque?', *CBQ* 36, 1974, 451-65; A. van der Kooij, 'Symmachus, "de vertaler der Joden" ', *NedTT* 42, 1988, 1-20.

7. For the Samaritans, in addition to the histories of Israel cf. 'Über die ältesten Traditionen über das samaritanische Schisma', *EI*, 1982 , 106*-115*, and R.Pummer, 'The Present State of Samaritan Studies 1', *JSS* 21, 1976, 39-61. For the Samaritan Pentateuch, cf. P.Sacchi, 'Studi samaritani 1', *RSLR* 5, 1969, (413-40) 432ff.

8. Fragments of the Syro-Palestinian Targum have been collected by M.H.Goshen-Gottstein, *The Bible in the Syro-Palestinian Version*, Jerusalem 1973. A manuscript of a hitherto unknown Targum contained in the MS Neophiti 1 of the Vatican Apostolic Library has been published under the editorship of A.Diez Macho, *Ms Neophiti I*, Barcelona I, 1968 – VI, 1980. For the problems connected with the Targum cf. E.Levine, 'La evolución de la Biblia aramea', *EstBibl* 39, 1981, 223-48, and id., 'The Biography of the Aramaic Bible', *ZAW* 94, 1982, 353-79; P.Doron, 'The Methodology of Targum Onkelos', *EstBibl* 43, 1985, 173-87. Levine's *Aramaic Version of the Bible*, Berlin 1988, considers the theological significance of the Targum.

9. This is not the place even to attempt to offer a bibliography on the Vulgate and St Jerome. I shall mention just two titles, J.Barr, 'St Jerome's Appreciation of Hebrew', *BJRL* 49, 1966-67, 281-302, and E.Joussard, 'Réflexions sur la position de Saint Augustin relativement aux Septante dans la discussion avec Saint Jerôme', *Revue des études augustiniennes* 2, 1956, 93ff.

10. For the origins of the Syriac translation see S.R.Isenberg, 'On the Palestinian Origins of the Peshitta to the Pentateuch', *JBL* 90, 1971, 69-81.

For the problem of the progressive growth of the Hebrew Bible by successive re-reading, commentaries incorporated into the text, and explanatory additions, see now the important volume which I have not been able to use: M.Fishbane, *Biblical Interpretation in Ancient Israel*, Oxford 1985. See also the important series edited by D.Barthélemy, *Critique textuelle de l'Ancien Testament*, OBO, of which two volumes have so far appeared.

3

TEXTUAL AND HISTORICAL CRITICISM

1. Introduction

The problems which I have tried to outline in an elementary and simplified form indicate the sometimes extremely complicated factors underlying the process which led to the formation of the texts that make up the Hebrew Bible. No careful reader of the Bible can fail to notice their existence from time to time, and they trouble the scholar and especially the translator constantly. To give a few examples: what if a scholar happens to notice a significant difference between the Massoretic text on the one hand and, say, a Qumran text or an ancient translation on the other? If the Hebrew text is clear, the difference may simply have arisen from an error in copying, orthography or dictation. There are, however, frequent instances in which we find ourselves faced with a genuine textual variant, sometimes preferable to the traditional Hebrew text, either because the latter seems corrupt and even incomprehensible in particular passages or because the former is obviously better. We have already come across the case of LXX codex B in the books of Samuel, the readings of which have now in part been confirmed by Hebrew fragments discovered at Qumran. The text of this codex, as is well known, is better than the Massoretic text. This sort of situation, which is much more common than might be supposed, compels the scholar generally, and especially the commentator and the translator, to make a choice; he or she must necessarily prefer the better text and reject the less reliable one, even if this means an emendation of the Hebrew text on the basis of the textual material indicated.

Now there are some well-tried rules in the field of classical philology which can easily be applied not only to the biblical text but also to Near Eastern texts in general:

(*a*) Prudence and circumspection must come first; textual criticism is not, and never will be, the place for the exercise of individual inspiration.

TEXTUAL AND HISTORICAL CRITICISM

(b) There must be a thorough examination of the value of variants over against the traditional text: the importance of a text is not always established by its antiquity, but rather by the authority of a tradition, even if chronologically the text is relatively late. In our case, a reading attested in a fragment from Qumran or presupposed by a translation in the LXX is not necessarily better than a different reading in the Massoretic text, even if strictly speaking it is earlier; in biblical criticism, rather, the tendency today is to give preference to the Massoretic text.

(c) In any comparison between a shorter and a longer text the shorter text must always be presumed to be the authentic one. In fact it was easy for sacred texts in particular to attract explanations and comments which could sometimes enter the text during their transcription; it would be more difficult to take something away from the text because that would be sacrilege, although we do have omissions through mistakes in transmission.

(d) The more difficult text, not the easier one, is always more likely to be the authentic one. Interventions in the text tend to simplify it rather than to make it more complicated.

The last two principles are called the *lectio brevior* and the *lectio difficilior* respectively.

2. Biblical criticism

In this way we have arrived at the concept of biblical criticism almost spontaneously. As is well known, 'criticism' comes from the Greek *krinein*, the original meaning of which is to separate, distinguish, hence judge. This is the sense of our term 'criticism'. Now because the believer, Jewish or Christian, sees the text as having a sacred and therefore authoritative character, he or she should be able to accept biblical criticism without difficulty in so far as it sets out to present a text which is as close as possible to the original. However, precisely the opposite has happened: among conservative Jews, Protestants and Catholics biblical criticism has often been received with mistrust, as though the discipline set out arrogantly and therefore impiously to set itself above the text to judge it, to criticize it. Such a view of the functions of criticism shows a complete lack of familiarity with the concept, which besides is also valid in music and the arts, so the interpretation cannot be taken seriously. Moreover, conservative but educated religious circles do accept the principle of applying literary criticism to the Bible to a greater or lesser degree, depending on the case in question; it is not in fact a matter of setting oneself above the text, of 'judging' it, but simply of making use of well-tried methods to restore the text as far as possible to the original form from which it has been removed by centuries and even millennia of transmission – first oral and then written. Nor is there any need to go to the opposite extreme: to believe that biblical criticism provides the solution to the majority of problems inherent in the texts. This, too, is an emotional position like its opposite, a position which forgets that the synagogue and the church have read the texts in question for millennia without criticism and have succeeded in capturing the essential part of their message without its help. Thus today we accept biblical criticism simply as one of the many instruments which science has put at our disposal, as biblical scholars, without either unjustified pessimism or exaggerated enthusiasm – and we make use of it with gratitude, and at the same time with freedom.

To understand how it is possible that a text can present sometimes quite notable differences between one manuscript and another, it is enough to remember how a book came into being before the invention of printing. In a modern edition of a work the author reads proofs at least once, so that, leaving a minimal margin for errors and omissions which escape the proof-reader or the type-setter, we may believe the book to accord completely with the text as he or she produced it. But this has happened only since the invention of printing. Up to the middle of the fifteenth century the scholar either personally copied the manuscripts which he needed, or had copies made for him; the bookseller had the books he sold either copied by or dictated to his amanuenses. The works produced by this method were few and therefore extremely expensive; anyone who was writing from dictation or copying from elsewhere in a more or less mechanical fashion could easily make mistakes or misunderstand whole phrases or rarer words. In this way mistakes entered the text, and this danger naturally increased, the more the editions of the same work grew in number. The scholar who copied a text for his own use was less likely to make a mistake; but even he might be distracted, or have to work hurriedly on a book that was available only for a limited period of time. Sometimes he may have had a tendency to 'correct' what seemed to him to be 'errors' in the text or to explain difficult passages (or those he considered difficult) by marginal notes; these notes could easily be introduced into the body of the text by a later copyist.

This general situation will also have applied to the text of the Hebrew Bible with an important qualification; in the last centuries of the first millennium BCE and then especially with the closing of the canon, increasing attention began to be paid to the copying of the sacred texts and to their transmission and this led to the exclusion of almost all the errors. Manuscripts which contained what was considered to be an excessive number of mistakes or which had become illegible through use were taken out of circulation. Before this period, however, even the biblical texts were exposed to the dangers which beset any text transmitted in manuscript form. To begin with, there was no punctuation, which made it possible for the syntax of a sentence to be misunderstood; often so-called *scriptio continua* was used, a form of writing which left no space between one word and another and which encouraged erroneous divisions between individual words. It is not surprising, therefore, that the purely mechanical errors of the kind that are well known to anyone who uses a typewriter found their way even into the text of the Bible. If we add to that conflicts between different textual traditions (we may recall the example of the books of Samuel), we can see that we must reckon with the existence of errors, omissions and confusions even in the Hebrew Bible.

The most frequent mechanical errors, i.e. those due simply to dictation or the copying of texts, are as follows. There is so-called haplography, that is, the failure to repeat a syllable or a word that should have been written twice. Thus if I were to mean to write 'he used no notes' and left out the first or the second occurrence of the 'no', we would have a comprehensible text but one which would not only fail to reflect the author's intention but would even give the opposite sense. However, the literary critic would immediately know how to restore the original form of the text. Another mistake is the opposite of this and is called dittography, i.e. the repetition of a word or a syllable which should only have been written once. If in the phrase 'He used notes' the 'no' is repeated, once again we have a comprehensible text but an incorrect one: again, the expert in textual criticism would know how to restore the original form. A third mechanical error, which is more frequent in copying than in writing from dictation, is homoioteleuton. Here the whole of a phrase lying between two occurrences of the same word or of similar words is omitted because the eye of the copyist jumps directly from the first word to the second. The error can easily be recognized, but it is difficult to correct without the help of a parallel text or a translation. We have a number of obvious examples in the Hebrew Bible, in which the mistake can be corrected only by recourse to an ancient version. In Josh.15.59 part of the list of cities has been omitted, and can only be replaced with the help of the LXX (the omission occurs between two similar phrases); in II Sam.15.20b we have 'So make your brothers return: [the Lord show towards you] faithfulness and truth' (with LXX, Targ, Vg and Syr); in I Kings 19.2 we have the following text: 'Then Jezebel sent a messenger with the following message: "[If you are Elijah I am Jezebel,] so may God do..."' (corrected on the basis of the text of LXX and Vg); there is another instance in II Kings 23.16: 'According to the word of YHWH which the man of God proclaimed [, when Jeroboam was standing by the altar at the time of the feast. As he looked around, Josiah caught sight of the tomb of the man of God] who had foretold these things' (corrected on the basis of LXX). In the second example the Massoretic text, which in the preceding verse explicitly makes reference to the tomb of the prophet in question, is obscure and indeed tautological without the insertion from LXX, which allows us to restore the original text; the reason for the omission is clearly that the eye of the copyist jumped from the first 'man of God' to the second, omitting the intervening phrase. It seems to go without saying that it is necessary to restore the authentic form simply to be faithful to the text, without uselessly tearing one's hair trying to make sense of what is simply a corrupt reading.

3. Textual criticism or 'lower criticism'

Textual criticism or 'lower criticism' is the name of the discipline which sets out to restore, as far as possible, the original form of a text. It therefore works essentially with grammar, syntax and philology, comparing the text with ancient manuscripts and versions. It is required whenever there is uncertainty whether the text that we have correponds to that intended by the author, which is almost always the case before the invention of printing. In the course of the first two sections we have discussed some of its principal elements.

In the study of the Hebrew Bible the tendency of scholars at the end of the last century and at the beginning of this was to mistrust the Massoretic text because of the late date of the manuscripts which have been preserved, and to prefer earlier translations, above all the LXX. In every critical commentary up to the 1930s, therefore, it is easy to find in doubtful or controversial cases a pronounced preference on the part of scholars for the readings of the LXX rather than the Hebrew text. This is, of course, a choice which can rebound against the person who makes it; if the Massoretic text showed a higher incidence of errors or omissions than can be found in the LXX, could this not be a sign, applying the criteria of the *lectio brevior* and the *lectio difficilior*, of so accurate a transmission that no one dared to correct manifest errors or omissions? In this connection one might well recall Jesus' saying in Matt.5.18/Luke 16.17, according to which not a *yod* (or a stroke) of the law will be lost, an all too evident reference to the care taken over the transmission of texts in the first century CE!

Textual criticism today tends to be much more cautious about the traditional Hebrew text than it was some decades ago. It is not that scholars fail to recognize errors of various kinds (I have listed some quite glaring ones), nor is it impossible that in certain cases a parallel text or translation may have preserved a more accurate textual tradition: it is the fundamental attitude to the Massoretic text that has changed. The sole starting-point for the scholar today will always be the Hebrew text, which is accorded a remarkable authority on almost all sides. As we have seen, this does not exclude some blemishes of notable proportions.

4. Historical criticism or 'higher criticism'

Once the scholar has arrived at a text which is as near as possible to the original, a second stage of his or her work begins; we can compare it with that of the engineer who is building a bridge between the two banks of a river, with the reader on the one bank and the text to be examined on the other. The wider and deeper the river bed to be crossed, that is, the greater the chronological and ideological distance which divides us from the times and the setting in which the author of the texts lived or in which the texts, if they are anonymous, came to be written, the more difficult will be the work. In this phase of research the scholar investigates the formal aspects of the text, its contents and hence its literary genre; he or she determines, where possible, the author or at least the period in which it was written, and seeks to discover whether it was used in particular situations in the life of the people: the cult and possibly the particular occasion, the protocol of the court, the wisdom schools, public or private prayer, etc. In this way he or she discovers data which are indispensable for a proper understanding of the text in question. For example, no scholar can be indifferent to the fact that some of the oracles contained in the first chapter of Isaiah were pronounced during the course of Sennacherib's expedition against Judah and Syria-Palestine generally, in 701 BCE; or that Exod.1-15 were probably part of the passover liturgy in the pre-exilic period; or again, that the creation narrative in Gen.1.1-2.4a probably belonged to the liturgy of the New Year Festival, and that this is also probably true of the complex narrative in Exod. 19-34 which records how the *tōrāh* was given to Israel. In this last case the possibility must seriously be considered that the liturgy in question relates to the 'Feast of Weeks', that is, Pentecost. It is not always easy to obtain certain information; in these last lines I have used the word 'probably' three times: too often the elements at our disposal are fragmentary or of doubtful value, so that we find ourselves compelled to work with conjectures and hypotheses.

However, there should be no doubt as to the need to clarify as far as possible the occasion and the milieu in which certain texts came into being: for example, a memorable saying is attributed to one of Leonidas' three hundred Spartans that if the Persians had so many arrows that they obscured the sun, he and his comrades could fight in the shade (Herodotus VII, 226). But what use would this be if we did not know the circumstances in which it was pronounced? This, then, is the principal concern of historical criticism, which forms the greater part of introduction.

BIBLIOGRAPHY

1-2. For textual criticism generally see the now classical manuals by P.Maas, *Textkritik*, Leipzig ²1950, and G.Pasquali, *Storia della tradizione e critica del testo*, Florence ²1962. These are works which are principally concerned with classical literature (to which LXX and Vg in any case belong), but the fundamental problems and the proposed solutions are also essentially valid for the Massoretic text. Pasquali, 241ff., gives a series of examples in which readings attested by Greek papyri reflect a more genuine tradition than the later Alexandrian one and, 261ff., examples of the opposite tendency, where the readings of the *textus receptus* are better than those of the much earlier papyri. The same criterion therefore holds good in both the classical and the biblical worlds; the antiquity of a manuscript does not by itself guarantee, and certainly cannot prove, that it contains a better reading. For the Massoretic text cf. again the bibliography on Chs. 1 and 2; D.R.Ap-Thomas, *A Primer of Old Testament Text Criticism*, Oxford ²1964; and H.Barth and O.H.Steck, *Exegese des Alten Testaments. Leitfaden der Methodik*, Neukirchen ¹²1984. Cf. also J.de Waard, 'The Translator and Textual Criticism', *Bibl* 60, 1979, 409-29; R.P.Carroll, *From Chaos to Covenant*, London and New York 1981, 256, for a case in Jeremiah.

3. For the scope and limits of textual criticism as applied to the Hebrew Bible cf. H.-J.Stoebe, 'Grenzen der Literarkritik im Alten Testament', *TZ*

18, 1962, 385-400; J.Coppens, *La critique textuelle*, Louvain 1960, 260ff. A now classical work, Friedrich Delitzsch, *Die Lese- und Schreibefehler im Alten Testament*, Berlin and Leipzig 1920, has listed the orthographical and mechanical errors found in the Massoretic text. The work must, however, be used with caution, since what in the light of better knowledge of Hebrew and cognate languages are in fact now recognizable as archaic or unusual forms may have been listed as errors. Cf. R.N.Soulen, *Handbook of Biblical Criticism*, Atlanta 1976. Cf. also M.Fishbane, 'Biblical Colophons, Textual Criticism and Legal Analogies', *CBQ* 42, 1980, 438-49; D.Kellerman, 'Korrektur, Variante, Wahllesart?', *BZ* 24, 1980, 57-75; B.Albrektson, '*Difficilior lectio probabilior?*', *OTS* 21, 1981, 5-18; M.H.Goshen-Gottstein, 'The Textual Criticism of the Old Testament; Rise, Decline, Rebirth', *JBL* 102, 1983, 365-99; J.Barton, 'Classifying Biblical Criticism', *JSOT* 29, 1984, 19-35; P.-G.Borbone, 'La critica del testo e l'Antico Testamento', *RSLR* 29, 1984, 251-74; W.H.Schmidt, 'Grenzen und Vorzüge historisch-kristischer Exegese', *EvTh* 45, 1985, 469-81. The whole issue is dealt with in *Semeia* 40, 1987. There is an extreme position which rejects criticism in that it is thought to 'criticize' holy scripture instead of accepting the character of divine revelation, in G.Maier, *Das Ende der historisch-kritischen Methode*, Wuppertal 1974.

4. For historical criticism cf. O.Cullmann, 'The Necessity and Function of Higher Criticism', *Student World* 42, 1949, 117-33; A.Nitschke, 'Historische Wissenschaft und Bibelkritik', *EvTheol* 27, 1967, 225-36. For the basic problem see finally the popular but very well presented explanations by D.Michel, *Israels Glaube im Wandel*, Berlin 1968, chs.1-11. Also A.Stock, 'The Limits of Historical-Critical Exegesis', *BTB* 13, 1983, 28-31; W.H.Schmidt, 'Grenzen und Vorzüge historisch-kritischer Exegese', *EvTh* 45, 1985, 296-71. Cf. also H.Cazelles, 'L'exégèse scientifique au XX^c siècle: l'Ancien Testament', in *Le monde contemporain et la Bible*, Paris 1985.

Some examples of readings which differ between the various textual traditions are given by T.C.Vriezen and A.S.van der Woude*, 95ff.; J.H.Hayes*, 58-81. A very recent introduction to biblical criticism which I have not been able to use is that edited by J.H.Tigay, *Empirical Models for Bible Criticism*, Philadelphia 1985.

4

DESCRIPTION OF THE HEBREW BIBLE

1. The Hebrew Bible as a history book

What kind of a book is the Hebrew Bible? Or better, what kind of a book does the Hebrew Bible consider itself to be? The answers to these questions can vary depending on the standpoint or the aims of the questioner and the person to whom the question is put. For example, there is no doubt that the Hebrew Bible is, *inter alia*, the foundation document for the religion of Israel during the first three quarters of the first millennium BCE, or that ethnologists or sociologists might consider it the principal source for a study of ancient Israel from their particular perspectives. For the comparative philologist it will be the principal source for the Hebrew language in the period mentioned. Similar examples could be multiplied. But one reply which should be obvious and should satisfy the majority of questioners is more simple: the Hebrew Bible is a complex of books which for the most part lay claim to being history books. In other words, the Hebrew Bible professes a very special interest in the history of a specific people in the ancient Near East, the Jews. This interest is not, however, historiographical in the sense that we now give to that expression; it is the history of the people to whom God has spoken and through whom he has acted and, of course, in a more indirect way, of those people who contributed to the formation of the history of Israel. So we are dealing with a historiography which we might call theological.

This statement does not apply only to the historical books proper; it also applies for the most part to the prophetic books, which are continuously in dialogue with the people in particular situations. And to no small degree it applies to the Psalms, even if it is often a difficult undertaking to discover the events underlying their rather nebulous allusions. The one exception seems to be the wisdom literature, which prefers to make generic statements that are always valid and therefore detached from historical problems.

Writers of very different tendencies agree on these points. In 1946 H.W.Robinson wrote that 'the Old Testament is formally a history into which other forms of literature have been incorporated', while Bultmann stated in 1949: 'History is the major theme of the Old Testament literature.' Thus we can see, for example, that collections of legal material in the Pentateuch or in Ezekiel have been inserted respectively either into the account of the journey through the wilderness during the exodus or into the context of the promise of a speedy restoration of the community which was largely destroyed or deported during the events of 587/86 BCE.

Of course, to speak of 'history' introduces some extremely complex problems relating to the meaning of a term which is so controversial today in a philosophical context. The problems involved are impossible to deal with here. I shall therefore content myself with saying that the historical character of the majority of the biblical texts is not constant, as every reader knows: in some cases it does not go beyond the intentions of the authors or those who transmitted certain stories. The authors or transmitters of the creation narratives in Genesis 1-11 clearly located them in time and space and therefore regarded them as history, difficult though it may be to recognize this characterization in the context of modern historiography. The historical character of the patriarchal narratives is different again. Until recently new discoveries from the ancient Near East seemed to have supported their substantial historicity, though they did not make it possible to identify the people involved or to synchronize them with persons or events otherwise known to us. One type of historiography which is almost modern has in the past been thought to exist in the so-called 'succession narrative' (II Sam.9-20, perhaps with the addition of 21.1-14 and I Kings 1-2), but a more accurate analysis of the sections obliges us to revise considerably such a sweeping affirmation. Certain prophetic legends do refer to historical figures and have been collected in contexts the historicity of which is beyond question, but it is quite impossible to verify them in their historical context and they often contain very improbable elements (e.g. II Kings 4). In all these cases we are dealing more with a theology of history; the motive force behind this history is the God of Israel, its sovereign, who through his wisdom and justice rewards the righteous and punishes the wicked on either an individual or a collective basis. Here we can recognize a series of details that make Israelite thought a precursor of the philosophy of history in that it is clearly in search of a principle which unifies certain events and around which particular episodes crystallize. In other words, Israel has already gone far beyond a mere chronicle which narrates facts as such. Israel begins from its present situation and seeks the cause of that situation in the past, choosing only those events and those figures which it considers relevant. Many scholars still affirm that in this way a consciousness developed which, leaving aside the brief episode of the historical prologues to the Hittite treaties in the second half of the second millennium BCE, has few parallels in antiquity in either East or West, but that this is not an element which can be verified by criticism (below, 5.2).

That explains why, contrary to what we might expect in a book which is essentially an expression of the faith of Israel, the Hebrew Bible, like the New Testament, contains very few doctrinal propositions. Accustomed as we are to exact dogmatic formulations, at least in the Western tradition, first from the Hellenistic world, then from the Middle Ages and finally from the baroque period, we are surprised not to find anything similar in the biblical world. Some have sought to see this peculiarity as a typical feature of the semitic mentality, which they understand to be more inclined to proclamation than to reasoning in a systematic form, more prone to dynamic descriptive concepts than to more or less objective accounts in a static form. But the historical approach adopted by the faith of Israel from the very beginning, as expressed in its own writers, would certainly be a better explanation: the faith of Israel is not so much interested in definitions as in history, and it was therefore in history, i.e. in action, that Israel gained its religious experience.

That this history seems substantially different in approach, methods and aims from any form of modern historiography (leaving aside perhaps only political forms of historiography which are highly ideologized) is of course another matter. Thus the fact that the results of modern historical research differ substantially, especially in the earliest period, from the image that Israel had of its own past, is simply the logical consequence of this situation. But Israel is not alone in this situation; we have only to consider the reconstruction that the ancient Romans made of their own past.

God is therefore not defined in formulae of a catechetical kind, but is confessed for what he has done: 'I am YHWH your God, who brought you out of the land of Egypt, out of the house of bondage...' (Exod.20.1); and if the New Testament says at one point that 'God is love' (I John 4.8), it is not so much giving a systematic definition which in any case would be rather vague, as drawing conclusions from the affirmation which is contained in the Fourth Gospel: 'God so loved the world that he gave his only Son' (John.3.16). In other words, even where we would seem to have a definition of a doctrinal kind we really have an association with an element which is firmly bound up with a historical fact. Still in the New Testament, when Hebrews 11.1ff. gives a rather complex definition of faith, it does so only after it has presented the reader with a series of examples which show how faith has been operative in the past (ch.10). None of the more doctrinal passages in the writings of Paul could be understood without the presence of two inescapable historical facts: the crucifixion of Jesus and the apostolic testimony to his resurrection. The choice of examples from the New Testament rather than from the Hebrew Bible was deliberate, to show that even in a period when there were continuous contacts with Hellenistic philosophy, which tended towards abstraction and spiritualization, this form of thinking continued undeterred. So God reveals himself for men and women in the Bible not in doctrines but by acting primarily in history, and secondarily in man and nature. Bultmann, whom I have already cited, continues the discussion by pointing out that contrary to the greater part of Hellenistic philosophy, in which nature with its order and its laws (concepts of which Israel seems to be ignorant) constitute the primary sources of revelation, in Israel, nature, when it appears in this function, does so only in its less attractive, catastrophic forms: storms, earthquakes and so on. These are the phenomena which have historical relevance, and not others. Such an attitude to a natural revelation is certainly negative, but it did not prevent the Israelite believer from showing due wonder and astonishment when confronted with all the marvels of creation (cf. Pss.8; 19; 104, etc.).

Students of Israelite religion will therefore sometimes find themselves confronted with the problem of translating these historical and descriptive forms in which that religion is expressed into categories comprehensible to modern men and women, and in this work Introduction to the Old Testament will provide them with their main tools.

2. For the synagogue and the church the Bible is also the inspired Word of God

This is one of the few points where the course which the arts and theology have so far covered together divides, and we enter, however briefly, the area of the ultimate decision between belief and unbelief.

The Hebrew Bible does not explictly affirm the inspired character of the writings which comprise it, and the New Testament reaches this point only in the final phase of its redaction and then in a somewhat vague and generalized way (cf. II Tim.3.16; II Peter 1.20f.). The late character of these affirmations indicates that the primitive church, still solidly anchored in Hebrew tradition, did not even raise the problem. What God had said and done through human beings and the events which had been singled out for this had normative value. This also means that the concept which later the primitive church felt the need to define in a more or less systematic form (even if it did not specify the nature of inspiration, which is by no means an obvious matter) is also already implicit in the earliest period.

(a) In Protestant orthodoxy between the sixteenth and the eighteenth centuries, in conservative currents within Catholicism and Protestantism to the present day and also in Judaism, the concept of inspiration was understood as special divine aid granted to the biblical authors, by which they were to be kept free from doctrinal and factual error; in this way the normative character of the books in question was justified. This is not the place for the history of a theory which is so complex and controversial; even now it exists in a number of variants and shades of meaning, and there is an apologetic of doubtful effectiveness based on this very presupposition. It is often difficult, therefore, to establish a common denominator between the different concepts of what is sometimes called 'verbal' inspiration, given the differences of culture and social class that frequently exist between the various churches and sects which affirm it. Be this as it may, one element appears with some constancy: the Holy Spirit intervened directly in the production of the sacred writings and particularly in the work of their authors, protecting them from error. However, the same authors reject as mechanistic caricatures of the concept expressions like 'dictated' by the Spirit and similar formulations.

Still, leaving aside the static concept of truth and error which underlies this kind of definition, the problem cannot be defined in terms of truth against error, where inspiration creates the first by excluding the second, which is left to human reason; this is a crudely anti-historical way of stating the problem. Scientific values are quite valid until later discoveries or the perfection of existing methods supersede them, and this applies to all sciences, the humanities as well as the natural sciences. Thus certain statements in the Bible about astronomy, geography, human or animal medicine can hardly be considered true in the present state of the relevant sciences; on the contrary, the geocentric character of the pre-Copernican and indeed pre-Ptolemaean world (Gen.1.1ff.; John 10.12ff.), the flatness of the earth which therefore has 'ends' (Acts 1.8; 13.47), the zoological affirmation that the rock badger and hare 'chew the cud' (Lev.11.5f.) or the astronomical statement that the universe is organized into three superimposed layers (cf. the creed, in which one ascends to heaven but descends to hell), and so on, are statements which do not seem so much to fall into the categories of true and false as into those of what is still valid and what is superseded. For that reason it is impossible to speak of this kind of statement in terms of inspiration, since the texts were composed at particular times, in clearly established ideological contexts which have now been superseded. In the same way, many of our affirmations will be superseded in the future (think only of the advances in natural science, often unknown to the public, from the beginning of the century up to the present day, with the theory of relativity or quantum theory). Terms like truth and error are therefore inadequate to express such a complex reality. Furthermore the opinions in question constitute the common heritage of all the ancient Near East and some of the West, without containing any of the elements which are typical of Israelite faith. Thus an erroneous apologetic attitude has all too often led the synagogue and the church into pointless conflicts with the natural sciences.

A church which takes the incarnation seriously should admit that holy scripture takes human form in particular historical and ideological contexts and should not attempt to reconcile elements that are irreconcilable.

(b) By contrast 'liberal' Protestant theology, in many questions followed at the beginning of the century by Roman Catholic modernism and Jewish groups with similar tendencies, has always professed the utmost openness to natural science and the humanities. Concepts which have been regarded as outdated have been left on one side, and alternative positions have developed with terms which have not always been clearly defined like 'ethical monotheism', 'universalism', 'moral law' on the one hand and 'national god', 'ethnic particularism', 'ceremonial law', etc. on the other, without any concern either for the precise meaning of these expressions or for their capacity to describe an extremely complex reality like that of the faith of the Hebrew Bible and the New Testament. Moreover, the normative character of the Bible has been accepted only in so far as it conforms to certain ethical and scientific canons of a particular age: scripture is no longer scripture, but only a source of inspiration, a (temporary) climax in a process of evolution which is still under way.

(c) As is often the case, neither side is right. The truth lies between. Both positions are the consequence of the same form of rationalism, according to which only what is verifiable or acceptable in the scientific-critical sense is 'true'. Thus the conservative who wishes to safeguard the authority of the Bible has to demonstrate that there is only an apparent difference between science and faith, while the 'liberal' feels obliged to suppress those parts in which the divergence is to be found. However, as we have seen, what we should do is not so much accuse of falsehood a scientific statement made a millennium or so ago, but rather accept the obvious fact of its antiquity. The inadequacy of these formulations never prejudices the validity of the message of the Bible, just as the scientific affirmations of today, which will seem equally inadequate tomorrow, should not condition the validity of our faith. To ask astronauts, if only in jest, whether they have seen God and the angels, is an anti-historical mistake of a certain popular kind of Marxism.

With this proviso, we can now understand what the Hebrew Bible means by inspiration, a concept which, as we have seen, is neither formulated nor described in the Hebrew Bible itself.

(d) Given this absence of formulations, the most adequate way of attempting to describe the concept of inspiration in the Hebrew Bible is probably to ask in what way the biblical narrative differs from other narratives of the same literary genre among neighbouring peoples. As an example we might take the story of the exodus and the settlement in Canaan, events which have been fixed by the general consent of scholars, though hypothetically, in the course of the thirteenth century BCE. I shall deliberately leave on one side the complicated problems connected with the historicity of these events generally and in detail (for more information see my *History*, Chapters VI and VII) and concentrate on the distinctive elements. It is possible to narrate the events in a secular form: a semi-nomadic people, settled for centuries in Egypt in the eastern region of the delta, is unexpectedly considered to be a danger because it has grown in numbers and economic strength. Moreover, because it is close to the frontier, it can make common cause with other peoples of the same extraction who are hostile to Egypt. A series of natural catastrophes makes it possible for the people to escape their oppressors. After a long march across the desert the fugitives succeed in reaching Canaan, having been reinforced along the way by similar groups. At that time the region was in a state of political and economic decadence; Egyptian authority had by now become purely nominal in most cases (that is, with the exception of certain strongholds like

Beth-shean) and counted for almost nothing. By means of a skilful system of alliances through which the invaders succeeded in dividing the enemy (e.g. Gibeon, Josh.9), the ancestors of Israel settled first in the less populated zones, while their ranks were swelled by all those who were discontented with the semi-feudal regime by which the city-states of the region were governed. Then, under David and Solomon at the beginning of the first millennium BCE, the invaders were able to conquer the city states which were still resisting and form a national state.

As can be seen, this interpretation is completely free of any theological and religious elements; it is not wrong according to the biblical text, but merely incomplete. The Hebrew Bible sees in these facts more than just one of the many migrations of peoples which took place at the end of the second millennium BCE; it also sees here the divine action in history for the salvation of a fallen humanity, by means of the election of a people and the fulfilment of the divine promise towards them. In this sense the biblical account comes much closer to stories attested among neighbouring peoples of its time than to modern secular or religious accounts. Be this as it may, this capacity for discerning the divine plan within history beyond events is what distinguishes a 'sacred' author in the Hebrew Bible from any other kind of writer, just as it distinguishes the believing hearer or reader (who therefore accepts this interpretation of events) from any other kind of hearer or reader. But what applies to the text also applies here; ascertaining the nature of the facts is the same for both the believer and the non-believer, and that is why it would be absurd to want to speak of infallibility in the field of history any more than in that of the natural sciences. Historiography, too, progresses, and that is why the reconstruction of the exodus and the settlement which I have just given would no longer be accepted today by any historian, whether he was a believer or not. At the same time, however, the believer can accept the message to which I have referred above, since this is not founded on the detailed verification of the events in question but on the confession of the mighty acts of God.

We can see, then, how stories which were originally rich in legendary and sometimes mythical elements, the primary scope of which must have been to glorify ancestors on a tribal or national level, have been transformed by the biblical narrators into testimonies to the redeeming work of God.

BIBLIOGRAPHY

1. The quotations are taken from the posthumous work of H.W.Robinson, *Inspiration and Revelation in the Old Testament*, Oxford 1946, 123, and R.Bultmann, *Primitive Christianity in its Contemporary Setting*, ET London 1960, 22, cf. 18; cf. N.Lohfink, 'Théologie de l'histoire dans l'ancien Israël', *Archivio di Filosofia*, 1971.2, 189-99; N.W.Porteous, 'Old Testament and History', *ASTI* 8, 1972, 21-77; G.Wallis, 'Die geschichtliche Erfahrung und das Bekenntnis zu Jahweh im Alten Testament', *TLZ* 101, 1976, 801-16. For a criticism of this view, which can be considered to be fairly widespread, cf. G.Fohrer, *Theologische Grundstrukturen des Alten Testaments*, Berlin 1972, 42ff. Fohrer indicates not only the ambiguity of the term 'history' today but also its inapplicability to certain psalms, the wisdom literature and finally, in late Judaism, to the concept of *tōrāh* (usually translated law), which was regarded as being valid above time and history.

For the Hittite treaties cf. A.Malamat, 'Doctrines of Causality in Hittite and Biblical Historiography. A Parallel', *VT* 5, 1955, 1-12; H.Gese, 'The Idea of History in the Ancient Near East and the Old Testament', *Journal for Theology and the Church* 1, New York 1965, 49-64; E.Cancik, *Grundzüge der hethitischen und alttestamentlichen Geschichtsschreibung*, Wiesbaden 1976 (an important work but one which should be used with caution). To assert that in the Hebrew Bible revelation takes place in (rather than through) history is clearly not in any way to assert that other people did not have similar experiences; cf. in this respect B.Albrektson, *History and the Gods*, Lund 1967: all the peoples of the ancient world, both east and west, saw in war, pestilence or earthquake the hand of the God who judged human sin. The difference is that, 'in fact, for the Israelites the recognition of God in history involves the production of a historical programme which is the work of the community (hence it is at a popular level and not the monopoly of the king, as happens in the ancient Near East), seen in a constant hermeneutical tension between paradigmatic saving events and a promise which always awaits fulfilment' (J.C.Croatto, review in *The Ecumenical Review* 28, 1976, 114f.).

For the complex problem of the relationships between biblical historiography and that of other peoples cf. *inter alia* M.Adolfini, 'Storiografia biblica e storiografia classica', *RiBib* 9, 1961, 42-58; id., *Questioni bibliche di storia e storiografia*, Brescia 1969; S.Accame, 'Il problema storiografico e la critica storica', *Teologia* 6, 1981, 243-77; and A.Momigliano, *Biblical Studies and Classical Studies*, ASNSP III.11, 1981, 25-32. There is a recent attempt at a synthesis in J.Van Seters, *In Search of History*, New Haven and London 1983.

2. The concept of verbal inspiration in Protestantism goes back to Matthias Flaccius Illyricus in the sixteenth century. For this theory see still G.L.Archer, *A Survey of Old Testament Introduction*, Chicago ²1971. It has rightly been called docetic by O.Cullmann, 'The Necessity' (cf. the bibliography above, 3.4), 125. That the conservative and the liberal positions

derive from the rationalist Enlightenment has been argued by K.Barth, *Church Dogmatics* III.1, ET Edinburgh 1958, 81ff. For the whole problem and its semantic and hermeneutic ramifications cf. L.Alonso Schökel, *The Inspired Word*, ET New York 1965. For a good account of the applications of structural analysis to texts of the Hebrew Bible see D.Lys, 'Analyse structurale et approche littéraire', *ETR* 52, 1977, 231-53, with a full report on the immense bibliography.

5

MYTH, LEGEND AND HISTORY

In the previous chapter (and here we can rejoin our shared approach with the arts faculty) I spoke of history writing of different kinds in which there are variants between the authors and transmitters of the biblical tradition, though all are equally concerned with writing history. At this point it is necessary to give the reader a number of definitions which aim at distinguishing between the different literary narrative genres. The terms involved are myth, legend, fable and fairy tale, and finally historiography proper. All these genres are present in greater or lesser degree in the Hebrew Bible.

1. Myth

Myth is a narrative literary genre which appears in one form or another in all religions. In biblical and in ancient Near Eastern studies, the genre is used for the deeds of gods or heroes, deeds which are independent of any historical, geographical or chronological context because they are usually, at least in origin, bound up with the cyclical pattern of nature and its fertility (H.Gunkel). Through myth, human beings participate actively in the cult, in the timeless mysteries of birth, life and death, and know the universe as an eternal image of the sacred alternation of light and darkness. These elements are often presented as being *above* and coming *before*: above the world (and therefore transcendent) and before history.

At this point it would be easy to say that myth is therefore the opposite of history: it is cyclical where history is linear; it takes place outside, or perhaps better beyond, time and space, whereas history is deeply and ineradicably rooted in them; it deals with gods and heroes, whereas history has as protagonists human beings like ourselves, although in ancient history there is a manifest tendency to choose the actions of kings and not of commoners. It would, however, be wrong to say that myth belongs to the world of fantasy, whether religious or not; it is still more wrong to say that myth belongs to the world of fable. Myth belongs, rather, to the world of the cult, as I indicated earlier; that is, it provides the *hieros logos* of a rite or a sanctuary and the theme for the liturgical action which the cult sets out to repeat, by actualizing a primordial event for the benefit of those who take part, the community. At this point we could discuss whether myth precedes, and therefore creates, liturgy or whether it is merely the narrative expression of an already existing liturgy of which it is therefore the product. This is a problem which, given the considerable antiquity of both the elements, is impossible to resolve. It is also difficult to say with certainty whether or not a real religious experience lies at the heart of myth.

In any case, there are important limits to be set to the possible historicity of the narrative: these arise from the supra-historical character of the myth itself. That does not mean, however, that a myth is incapable of expressing relevant historical facts, for example in the social sphere (one might think of the caste system in India or the inferior position of women in certain religions and therefore in the social structures to which they relate) and also in politics (see the importance that augurs and soothsayers had throughout the ancient world, in East and West). From the point of view of its specific consequences, then, myth is quite capable of producing tangible historical effects. It is also possible that a mythical narrative may have effectively retained the memory of real religious experiences, but for the reasons mentioned it is usually impossible to verify this. As a general rule it would not be rash to say that the connection of myth with the cycles of nature and with the fertility of the soil, which is particularly evident in myths like that of Persephone (to give a well-known example), robs it of any specific historical or geographical reference: the myth of Persephone happens everywhere and nowhere, eternally and therefore never.

Now it is widely held that because of the monotheistic and historical approach of their thought the biblical writers tried to eliminate the mythical view of the universe from their texts, and that for the most part they succeeded. In other words, God revealed himself, as we have seen, in history and not in mythical narratives, as in all the other religions. Of course one might consider the very notion of a transcendent deity who intervenes in the world of human beings to be mythical, but this is not the problem: religious language of necessity talks about things in categories like the deity, his transcendence and his interventions, the origin of the universe and its eschatological end. In other word, certain forms of myth are by definition part of religious language. The 'demythologizing' which Bultmann and his pupils proposed for the New Testament some years ago would therefore amount to religious thought and language renouncing their very *raison d'être*. The problem is therefore different: namely, whether Israel succeeded or not in its plan, given that intentions are not enough. Now even a superficial reading of the Hebrew Bible will immediately show that obvious elements of myth and a mythical conception of the universe remain. In some cases, certainly, these are only linguistic and do not extend to the content: it emerges clearly from numerous poetical passages that in the first centuries of its existence Israel must have had a remarkably developed mythology. There are myths which speak of the struggles of God the creator and preserver of the world against the forces of chaos, of sacred or semi-sacred marriages. But often we simply have quotations incorporated into quite different contexts, just as a Greek philosopher might cite an ancient text, or just as we might introduce a quotation ourselves, without these texts expressing a particular philosophical, historical or religious faith.

Moreover both the Hebrew Bible and the New Testament have often, if not always, followed a deliberate and coherent practice of demythologization in connection with myth. Ancient mythical themes have thus been taken and inserted into historical contexts, losing the distinctive ahistorical character of myth. The myth of marriages between the gods, which in the Canaanite world was periodically repeated in the cult and which guaranteed the fertility of the family, the soil, the flocks and the herds and which came to be represented under the form of intercourse between the king or a priest and a priestess, became in Israel the marriage between YHWH and his people Israel, a theme particularly dear to the prophets Hosea, Jeremiah and Ezekiel. Granted, this is a mythical theme, but to these relations Israel assigned an origin, a date and a place, the experience at Sinai, which reduces the mythical content of the theme to the inevitable minimum. A myth of Titans who try to scale heaven is now used as an illustration of the arrogance of the king of Babylon and its consequences (Isa.14); the myth of the original man-god and in his fall (which at least in the Christian tradition has hereditary and permanent effects which therefore inevitably affect subsequent generations – typically mythical elements) and which in Gen.2-3 is reduced to a minimum, reappears in Ezek.28 as an example of the pride and punishment of the king of Tyre. The death and resurrection of some gods connected with fertility (Ba'al, Adonis, etc.) are replaced in the New Testament by the unique event of the death and resurrection of Jesus. This, too, has permanent saving effects which are at work now in the cult (in the various Catholic traditions), but the actual event took place in Jerusalem 'under Pontius Pilate' between 30 and 33 and is therefore stripped of the chief elements which characterize myth, even if that of its celebration in the Christian cult has had lasting effects. An ancient myth which spoke of the struggle against chaos has now been inserted into the text of Isa.51.9ff., where chaos has become the image of the enemies of God and Israel, in the form first of Egypt and then of Babylon towards the end of the sixth century BCE. Zaphon, the mythical mountain of the gods, the classical Mount Casius, situated in the extreme north of Syria, must have provided the terminology for Zion: in Ps.48.2 Zion is said to be in the far north, a description which is certainly hyperbole if it is thought only to report the fact that Zion is some tens of metres north of the city of David! We do, however, know the origins and date of the foundation of the sanctuary of Zion: this was under David and Solomon during the first half of the tenth century BCE; its origins are thus quite unmythological, even if part of the terminology applying to the Syro-Palestinian Olympus has come to embellish the traditional description of the Jerusalem sanctuary.

So if we ask whether Israel truly succeeded in demythologizing the universe, we can reply that in some cases it certainly did (for example in connection with nature), but in others, which are rather more numerous, it evidently did not. One need think only of the three-storeyed universe (heaven, earth and underworld); of the constant more or less direct intervention by God in human affairs (here not unlike that element that we find elsewhere for pagan deities); and the concept of recompense, for which piety and justice are rewarded, and impiety and wickedness are punished by means of tangible historical events (famines, earthquakes, plagues, but also foreign interventions and deportations). Moreover we often see the adaptation of these historical data so that they can correspond to the argument which is being put forward. All these are elements which form part of a mythical conception of the universe: it is not possible to jump straight from one century to another but, as I have said, in religion and in faith it is not possible to express oneself without resorting to ideological categories and to concepts which any historian of religions cannot but describe as myth.

Finally, obvious fragments of ancient myth remain which are clearly recognizable: thus in Gen.6.1-4 we have the remains of a myth which originally must have told of the origin of a generation of giants and heroes, offspring of intercourse between divine beings and women.

It is, however, important that the faith of Israel laid the foundation for a separation between faith and myth, that the universe and nature have been so to speak secularized, robbed of any divine immanence and made accessible to scientific investigation. This happened in times which proved incapable of assimilating the consequences, with the result that Jews and Christians soon reverted to the world of myth from which the Hebrew Bible should have excluded them for ever. However, that is another question, and the biblical authors are hardly to blame for the fact.

2. Legend

(a) The term legend may prompt negative reactions from those who are accustomed to the way in which it is used in everyday language, where it is equivalent to a more or less fantastic story (in current understanding, 'legendary' describes an incredible episode) or to the use made of it by mediaeval hagiographers, among whom it serves essentially to refer to edifying episodes drawn from the lives of saints. In ethnology and the history of religions, however, the use of the word is positive: the legend is the record of a fact which could really have happened, of an experience which could have been had or of a person who could really have existed, but in a prehistoric era from which we possess only traditional material of a popular type. Saga is similar but presents more than the individual. Here the tribe, the clan, appear in the figures of their protagonists. Consequently the two genres tend to become intermingled and coalesce. In legend and saga, then, we have the historiography of groups which have not yet reached the stage of mature history writing and which therefore lack the capacity for synthesis and choice which is to be found among those who have arrived historically at a certain level of maturity. In fact (and I do not think that this is a digression from the argument) this maturity is the product of a series of historical, political, cultural and economic coefficients which create the need for a critical examination of a people's past as a condition, a presupposition, for certain present situations. Thus political and economic propaganda, too, can contribute to the formation of legends or of literary genres akin to legends, and still does so today. The two phases, that of the person who remains at the level of legend and that of the person who has arrived at the level of mature history writing, can, however, co-exist peacefully in the same people: in mountain or country areas a whole legendary history can exist as a single relationship between the present and the past.

(*b*) We have various obvious examples of legendary narrative in the Hebrew Bible: in Exod.1 the name of the Pharaoh of the oppression and the exodus is never mentioned (indeed no Pharaoh is named in the Hebrew Bible before the end of the tenth century BCE), but we do have a careful reference to the names of two brave midwives who by their resistance nullified the unjust decree of the Pharaoh aimed at the extermination of the newborn Israelites in Egypt. Now if an interest in these midwives is quite understandable on the level of popular tradition, it is quite lacking on the historical level, while the silence over the name of the Pharaoh makes it impossible to determine with certainty the date of the oppression and the exodus. The patriarchs, too, seem to move in a world populated by only a few phantoms: otherwise it is ethnically void. There is not a single name which allows us to establish any synchronism between their persons and facts contemporaneous to them, despite our considerable knowledge of the latter. The unique episode which seems to put Abraham in the context of international events appears in Gen.14, but in precisely this chapter, which is probably late, there are so many insoluble problems that the chapter might as well not be there. Moreover the various attempts to associate the patriarchal migrations with ethnic movements known to us, around the middle of the second millennium BCE, can be considered failures, as we shall see shortly (below, § 4). In effect Israel achieved mature historiography at the beginning of the period of the monarchy, i.e. during the first decades of the tenth century BCE; before this period, with few exceptions, the sources are inadequate for establishing relevant historical details (names of Pharaohs or other people of some pre-eminence, chronology, and so on) but we do find the names of midwives, nurses and similar people, all moving within a domestic milieu. But already at the end of the eleventh century we have the first hints of a change: interest begins to shift from the anecdote to the relevant historical details, and an example can be found in the older verses of Judg.9. From the time of David and Solomon onwards, we see that in court circles there are not only traces of remarkably developed annals (we have only notes of them; the texts have been lost), but the first lists of provinces and districts, of governors and senior officials, have been preserved, and we are given important information about the administration of the kingdom: forced labour, taxation and other matters. At the same time legend continued to exist, concerned particularly with individuals whose memory must have been particularly alive in the popular tradition: prophets like Elijah and Elisha in the second half of the ninth century BCE. In late Judaism the genre underwent a change: narratives developed around the important figures of antiquity, narratives which are nearer to fairy-tale than to legend, even if they look like legends.

(c) Now – and this is the difference between legend and myth – legend has its setting in a historical experience which can be real and which takes place in time and space; its protagonists are historical (or allegedly historical) people, not gods or heroes. Sometimes it is possible at least in theory to go back from the text of the legend to the experience which underlies it, even if this rarely happens in practice. In the classical world we have some remarkable analogies in this respect: the legend of the *Iliad* takes us back to the Mycenaean and Aegean world, that is, many centuries before the final 'Homeric' redaction; but in the Odyssey the situation is already much more complex because of the variety and intricacy of the traditions, only held together by the figure of the hero.

(d) One particular type of legend, finally, is the so-called aetiological legend – from the Greek *aitia*, cause: this sets out to explain to an audience the origins of a name, a custom or a rite, sometimes a feature connected with a natural element. Gen.32.32 is a typical example; the custom of not eating a certain part of the thigh of an animal is connected with the episode of the struggle of Jacob with the 'angel'; there are numerous etymological aetiologies, i.e. aetiologies which explain a name. These last mentioned rarely have a true historical foundation, but are based on popular etymologies for the names in question, and usually have no value in the linguistic sphere.

3. Fable and fairy-tale

The fable is a narrative literary genre in which the protagonists are usually animals or plants, and more rarely can be humans; it normally ends with a lesson, a 'moral', which is its evident purpose. By definition, then, the fable is not a historical literary genre and does not have any pretensions in that direction, even if on a purely theoretical plane the narrative part could contain historical elements when dealing with people. To arrive at the lesson, the final 'moral', 'a situation is made concrete', as the German historian of religion, A.Bertholet, put it, and in this sense the fable is distinct from the parable, even if it is not always easy to distinguish the two genres in practice. We have at least two examples of the fable in the Hebrew Bible: Judg.9.8ff. and II Kings 14.9. Given the fictitious character of its content, the fable does not present any problems for the historian.

The fable was given its classical form first in Greece by Aesop, then in Rome by Phaedrus, and finally in France by Jean de Lafontaine.

The fairy tale or novella is similar to the fable, and develops out of a delight in story-telling, what the Germans call *Lust zum Fabulieren*. The fairy tale mixes men and animals, the sacred and the profane, and can also include famous historical people, though in obviously fictitious contexts. In it the narrative part does not move towards a moral, while the conflict and the tensions which it contains are not resolved by struggle or compromise, but through the intervention of figures with marked miraculous characteristics similar to the ancient *deus ex machina*, who authoritatively arranges everything to the great satisfaction of all concerned. Late Judaism has a series of rabbinic tales about famous people in the history of Israel: David, Solomon, Elijah, etc. which lie between history and fable: well-known collections of fairy-tales are those by the brothers Grimm in Germany, by 'Mother Goose' in France and by L.Capuana in Italy, all in the past century. No fairy tales exist in their pure state in the Hebrew Bible, although there is no lack of themes that we might characterize in this way: Joseph, who from the deepest humiliation achieves the highest office by virtue of his moral character; Saul, who sets out to look for lost animals and finds a kingdom. The story of Joseph is also typical, because everything is attributed to divine providence and there is no criticism of the injustice with which the story begins.

4. Legend and historiography

I indicated earlier the problems of the relationship between legend and historiography and showed how legend could sometimes provide very important historiographical material. This raises a problem which deserves to be looked at in more detail and which we cannot leave without having posed it properly. For example, consider the mere fact that legend has its roots in historical experience that can be real but has emerged from a people who have not yet reached such historical maturity that they would automatically put it in the category of popular tradition. This results in a markedly dialectical and sometimes ambiguous relationship between it and the historian.

The Enlightenment and the rationalism which developed from it made a notable contribution towards demonstrating the ambiguity of this kind of relationship, and the same is true for historicism and positivism at the end of the last century and the beginning of this. All these approaches accepted the principle that we should take into account only material which could be verified in a historico-critical setting: that is, official documents, contemporary testimony, archive material; but it is obvious that in this way the chronological limit at which historiography begins to operate is notably later and that a considerable amount of material which, if properly studied, could provide valuable information for the researcher, is discarded *a priori*, on principle. This was understood by romantic historiography, which sought to discover what it called the 'soul of the people', and was ready to resort to intuition when material for critical research was lacking. On the other hand, the recourse to intuition and therefore to subjective fantasy has been a serious disadvantage for romantic historiography, and in many cases has prejudiced scientific credibility: the reader will be familiar with the idyllic or violent reconstructions of mediaeval European life written in this vein. It is thus no surprise that this kind of historiography, too, has involuntarily contributed to a devaluation of legend as a historical source.

I think that I am only repeating findings which are now well known if I say that historiography can exist only if a number of conditions are fulfilled. These include (*a*) the existence of sources and (*b*) their adequacy for a critical approach. For legend, the first of these elements does not present any problems: there are as many legends as one could desire; it is the second condition which often presents unsurmountable difficulties. Although the material is abundant, it is rarely adequate, even if, at least in theory, it should be possible to go back from it to facts and people. In practice, however, given the popular character of the traditions in question and hence the uncritical way in which they have been collected and transmitted, the possibility of going back to the events and persons involved is often virtually non-existent, unless we have other more reliable sources which permit of valid comparisons. The patriarchal narratives have thus remained in the limbo of conjecture and the texts found in the Mesopotamian city-states of Mari on the Euphrates and Nuzi east of the Tigris (which we shall be looking at later) have not so far provided material by which to verify them. We would know virtually nothing about the traditions contained in the *Iliad* either, had not H.Schliemann in the second half of the last century carried out his famous investigations and had their results not been continually refined and largely corrected by his successors; the decipherment of Linear B writing in the 1950s then opened up the Myceno-Aegean world for comparison, providing yet further material. In other words, it is sometimes possible to go back from the legend to the individuals and events of which it speaks, but usually that happens only when we have the possibility of comparing it with other more trustworthy literary material: thus at Mari and at Nuzi archive material has been found, i.e. texts which historians can use directly, provided that they take account of the insurmountable difficulties which get in the way of using them to explain the biblical text. In fact, in the light of these texts (which were thought to be the natural background to the patriarchal world where the information on this was historically adequate) from the 1940s to the 1970s many scholars (often well-known ones) sought to explain certain usages, particular customs and some family structures which appear in the patriarchal narratives. But in the meantime the enterprise has proved very doubtful, and the results have proved irrelevant in comparison with the vast effort spent on them. First of all in the field of nomenclature: it is said that names like those of the patriarchs appear in the ancient Near East in the second millennium BCE but become increasingly rare to the point of disappearance at a later stage; or that names like those of the patriarchs in fact appear in northern Syria and in north-western Mesopotamia from the Ebla period about the end of the third millennium BCE to the beginning of the first millennium BCE. However, precisely because of this diffusion (and here we are talking not just of personal names but also of place names) the information is of no use for chronology. Again, the discovery in Mesopotamia (and especially in the city states of Mari on the Euphrates and Nuzi east of the Tigris, which I have already mentioned) of practices, customs and legal norms which would explain or even constitute obvious parallels to certain patriarchal texts like Gen.15.2-3; 16.3ff.; 21.10ff.; 30.1ff. and some others, has meanwhile proved more apparent than real: the ethnic, sociological and legal differences are such as to make any comparison of this kind extremely doubtful and in any case purely formal.

BIBLIOGRAPHY

1. For myth, its nature and its possible historicity, cf. the classical study by R.Pettazzoni, 'The Truth of Myth', in *Essays on the History of Religions*,

Leiden 1954, 11-23; M.Marconi, 'Mito e verità scientifica', *SMSR* 32, 1961, 9-106; U.Bianchi, 'Religione, mito e storia', *Atti del XV Convegno del Centro di Studi Filosofici tra Professori Universitari, Gallarate 1960*, Brescia 1961, 302-15; F.Festorazzi, *La Bibbia e il problema delle origini*, Brescia ²1967, 167ff. For myth in the Hebrew Bible cf. C.Hartlich and E.W.Sachs, *Der Ursprung des Mythosbegriffes in der modernen Bibelwissenschaft*, Tübingen 1952; B.S.Childs, *Myth and Reality in the Old Testament*, SBT 27, 1960; W.H.Schmidt, 'Mythos im Alten Testament', *EvTh* 27, 1967, 237-54; J.Garcia Trapiello, 'Mito y culto en el Antiguo Testamento', *Ang* 44, 1967, 449-77; H.-P.Müller, *Mythos, Tradition, Revolution*, Neukirchen 1973; id., 'Mythos-Anpassung-Wahrheit', *ZTK* 80 1983, 1-25; C.Petersen, *Mythos im Alten Testament*, Berlin 1982; B.Uffenheimer, 'Biblical Theology and Monotheistic Myth', *Immanuel* 14, 1982-83, 7-25; cf. also H.Biezais, *The Myth of the State*, Stockholm 1972; especially the study by L.Honko, 'The Problem of Defining Myth', ibid., 7-19; T.K.Thordarson, 'The Mythic Dimension', *VT* 14, 1964, 212-20; E.R.MacCormack, 'Metaphor and Myth in Science and Religion', Durham NC 1976; M.F.Wiles, 'Myth in Theology', *BJRL* 59, 1976-77, 226-46; S.I.L.Norin, *Er spaltete das Meer*, Lund 1977, 5-9. F.R.McCurley, *Ancient Myths and Biblical Faith: Scriptural Transformations*, Philadelphia 1983, offers an interesting account of the traditional form of the approach to the problem. In his review in *AION* 35, 1975, 287ff., G.Garbini thinks that Israel, rather than demythologizing nature, transferred myth from there to history. For the work of Israel on the deities of Canaan cf. J.Heller, 'Die Entmythisierung des ugaritischen Pantheon im Alten Testament', *TLZ* 101, 1976, 1-10. Cf. also T.H.Gaster, 'Myth and Story', *Numen* 1, 1954, 184-212. For a history of the use of the concept in the interpretation of the Old Testament cf. J.W.Rogerson, *Myth in Old Testament Interpretation*, Berlin 1974. H.Cancik, *Mythische und historische Wahrheit*, Stuttgart 1970, gives the opinion of a scholar in classical history and literature. Cf. also H.-P.Müller, 'Mythos und Kerygma', *ZTK* 83, 1986, 405-35; E.-J.Waschke, 'Mythos als Strukturelement und Denkkategorie biblischer Urgeschichte', *TV* 16, 1986, 9-22; W.G.Lambert, 'Old Testament Mythology in its Ancient Near Eastern Context', *SVT* 40, 1988, 124-43.

For the 'above' and the 'before' see U.Bianchi, *Problemi di Storia delle religioni*, Rome ²1986, 139-45, 147-52.

2. G. von Rad, 'The Beginnings of Historical Writing in Ancient Israel', in *The Problem of the Hexateuch and other Essays*, ET Edinburgh 1966, 166-204. The remarks of E.Meyer, *Geschichte des Altertums* II.1, Munich ³1953, are still valid for the problem of mature history-writing. For the situation in prehistoric Greece cf.A.Lesky, *Geschichte der griechischen Literatur*, Bern 1957-8, 86ff. We also find a remarkable phenomenon of demythologization in ancient Rome: cf. D.Sabatucci, 'Mito e demitizzazione nell'antica Roma', *Religioni e Civiltà* (= *SMSR*) NS 1, 1972, 539-89. For the problem see now J.Van Seters, *In Search of History*, New Haven and London 1983, 221ff. Cf. also J.J.Scullion, 'Märchen, Sage, Legende: Towards a Clarification of

some Literary Terms used by Old Testament Scholars', *VT* 34, 1984, 321-36; G.W.Coats, *Saga, Legend, Novella, Fable*, Sheffield 1985. Scullion would prefer the term 'legend' not to be used in the sense I suggest.

For aetiological legend cf. B.O.Long, *The Problem of Etiological Narrative in the Old Testament*, BZAW 108, 1968, with bibliography; F.W.Golka, 'Zur Erforschung der Ätiologien im Alten Testament', *VT* 20, 1970, 90-8; L.Sabourin, 'L'étiologie biblique', *BTB* 2, 1972, 201-6.

3. For the fable cf. A.Bertholet (ed.), *Wörterbuch der Religionen*, Stuttgart 1952, s.v. 'Fabel'; for the fairy tale the classic work is H.Gunkel, *Das Märchen im Alten Testament*, Tübingen 1917; cf. also E.Haller, 'Märchen und Zeugnis', in *Probleme Biblischer Theologie, Festschrift G.von Rad*, Munich 1971, 108-15; H.-J.Hermisson, 'Altes Testament und Märchen', *EvTh* 45, 1985, 299-322; J.J.Scullion, 'Märchen, Sage, Legende: Toward a Clarification of Some Literary Terms Used by Old Testament Scholars', *VT* 34, 1984, 321-36. For Jotham's apologia in Judg.9 see F.Crüsemann, *Der Widerstand gegen das Königtum*, Neukirchen 1978, 32-42; M.Liverani, 'Partire sul carro, per il deserto', *AION* 32, 1972, has pointed out that fairy-tale elements are often inserted in historical narratives throughout the ancient Near East, and that they often serve to legitimate the succession of an important figure who has taken office in an irregular fashion: cf. in the Hebrew Bible the stories of Joseph, Saul and David. Liverani's researches follow the lines established by the Russian scholar V.J.Propp in the 1920s, cf. *Morphology of the Folk-Tale*, Austin, Texas 1968; P.J.Milne, 'Folk Tales and Fairy Tales: An Evaluation of two Proppian Anayses of Biblical Narratives', *JSOT* 34, 1986, 35-60; D.Irvin, *Mytharion*, Kevelaer and Neukirchen-Vluyn 1978, offers the most recent and up-to-date treatment of the fable and its themes in the Hebrew Bible and in the ancient Near East.

4. For Schliemann and Troy cf. H.Schliemann, *Kein Troja ohne Homer*, ed. W.Schmied, Nuremberg 1960 (a useful popular introduction). For the differences between the world described by the Homeric poems and that which emerges from the texts see now N.P.Lemche, *Early Israel*, Leiden 1985, 361 n.184, and the bibliography there. For comparisons between the patriarchal narratives and the Mesopotamian texts of the second millennium BCE and their limitations cf. C.J.Mullo Weir, 'The Alleged Hurrian Wife-Sister Motif in Genesis', *TGUOS* 22, 1967-68, 14-25; J.Van Seters, 'Jacob's Marriage and Ancient Customs: A Re-examination', *HTR* 62, 1969, 377-95; id., *Abraham in History and Tradition*, New Haven 1975. This last work is very critical. T.L.Thompson, *The Historicity of the Patriarchal Narratives*, Berlin 1974, is also hostile to such comparisons. Despite this essentially negative approach, these are the most important contributions to the study of the problem which have appeared in recent years. Cf. also B.O.Long, 'Historical Narrative and the Fictionalizing Imagination', *VT* 35, 1985, 405-16. The whole of the volume *La storiografia nella Bibbia – Atti della XXVIII Settimana biblica*, Bologna 1986, is dedicated to biblical historiography. For a reconstruction with a conservative but critical approach cf. A.R.Millard and

D.J.Wiseman (eds.), *Essays on the Patriarchal Narratives*, Leicester 1980, passim.

Terminology. A number of scholars have pointed out that terminology is remarkably confused and tends to become even more so with translation. Cf. R.M.Hals, 'Legend: A Case Study in Form-Critical Terminology', *CBQ* 34, 1972, 166-76; P.Gibert, 'Légende ou saga?' *VT* 24, 1974, 411-20; J.Van Seters, op.cit., 131-8; J.J.Scullion, art cit. As a matter of principle it seems necessary to maintain that in Italian, French, English and Spanish the German *Sage* should not be translated by 'saga' and derivatives (a term to be reserved for the Norwegian and Icelandic sagas) but by 'legend' and its derivatives.

For the Pentateuch as a product of the exilic and post-exilic period which is therefore inadequate as a historical source for the second millennium BCE cf.now H.Friis, 'Die Mosebücher als Quelle für die älteste Geschichte Israels', *DBAT* 21, 1985, 5-25, and other writings of the Heidelberg group.

6

THE PRE-LITERARY DEVELOPMENT OF
THE BIBLICAL MATERIAL. THE GENRES

1. The thirteenth to tenth centuries and their importance

As any historical scholar knows, the people of Israel is an inseparable part of the wider context of the peoples of the ancient Near East, and especially of those who speak Western Semitic languages. This is true ethnically, linguistically, historically and culturally; it is also true, within certain limits, of religion, a field in which Israel was soon to represent the exception rather than the rule. However, Israel becomes comprehensible only against the above-mentioned background.

The relationships between the people of Israel and their neighbours are almost comparable to those existing today among people of the same stock: neo-Latins, Germans, Slavs and Anglo-Saxons. The difference is that with the non-Aramaean peoples of the region of Syria-Palestine the relationship is even closer, whether linguistically (in the first millennium BCE, Phoenician, Hebrew and Moabite are dialect variants of the same language rather than three different languages) or on the general level of civilization, with the exception of religion (as I have already mentioned). The rediscovery of the civilization of the city-state of Ugarit, situated in Syria, on the Mediterranean coast, a few miles north of Laodicea, which began in 1929 (excavations are still in progress) has merely confirmed this state of affairs, already known for some decades, although to be exact Ugarit is rather on the periphery of the area. Moreover it is known that at least once the Israelites call their language the 'language of Canaan' (Isa.19.18), so it should not be surprising that the new settlers should also have adopted the language of the region, that is, if they had not always spoken it. Just as the Romanized barbarians adopted Latin in the countries of the Roman empire which had been conquered, though of course at the expense of the original perfection of the language, so in Canaan the Israelites adopted the language of the country and with it its particular genres. So it is not surprising that ancient Israelite poetry, or what is taken for that, e.g. in Gen.49; Exod.15; Num.23-24; Deut.32-33; Judg.5; I Sam.2; II Sam.1.19ff.; 3.1-7; Pss.29; 68 and so on, presents problems which scholars think that they can partially resolve by resorting to the hypothesis that this is Canaanite poetry and treating it as though it were Ugaritic texts. The lines of this study can be traced from the last years of the Second World War onwards from the North American W.F.Albright and down through his disciples, even if the method is now increasingly controversial.

During the last centuries of the second millennium BCE the settlement began in the central and southern hill country and in Galilee, and in this way two groups of tribes, originally separate, came into being. They soon bore the names of Israel and Judah respectively (cf. my *History*, VII). It was then that the first cycles of legends, the first epic and heroic songs began to take shape and were gathered into collections. However, all this material is lost and we know of its existence (no more than that) only from rare mentions here and there in texts. So we can talk of it only by way of conjecture. Nor do we know how these first collections can have come into existence, though some scholars have authoritatively suggested that, following a well-attested practice in the ancient Near East, the sanctuaries were the place where this development took place. Since we are now talking of happenings which antedate even the origins of the earliest writings of the Hebrew Bible, it will be useful to look at this process rather more closely.

2. Oral tradition

Over the preceding pages I have often used the term 'tradition'. I would now like to justify this choice of terminology, since it is by no means obvious.

It is well known that among all peoples oral tradition has preceded the written redaction of ancient texts, sometimes by centuries. This phenomenon should not seem strange to the modern reader, especially in the West: the love which people, especially in ancient times, show for immediate contact with affairs and people in the past is familiar, and this contact seems to many people even today to be better guaranteed through an uninterrupted chain of tradition than by written documents.

We now know that the classical 'Homeric' literature stands at the end of a long chain of bards and poets and therefore that the *Iliad* and the *Odyssey* came to be written down at a relatively late stage after the events which they describe. This did not happen because the Mycenaean-Aegean world was ignorant of writing: the great discoveries of texts in Crete, on other islands and on the mainland show the opposite. But writing served principally for the compilation of archives and inventories, that is, for administrative documents, and not for the transmission of literary texts. We still find the same situation millennia later in the early church, where the community preferred to hear the words of Jesus directly from the mouths of the apostles or indirectly from their disciples rather than to read them in a 'scripture'. The need to set down traditional material in writing usually arises in moments of crisis: for Israel at the time of the exile in 587, or a little earlier when the catastrophe was already beginning to loom; for the church during the persecutions or when heresy threatened to corrupt pure doctrine; for Israel again at a later stage, after the catastrophes of 70 and 135 CE, when tradition which until then had been oral was set down in written documents. The thirteenth to tenth centuries BCE was another of those periods of crisis: the migrants were settling in the hill country and the plains of Palestine; the monarchy was born, presenting us with an institutional change of the kind which was often to be a focal point of crisis during the history of Israel; other peoples with their own traditions began to become part of the group Israel. Moreover the court also needed annals, and on the basis of what we know from elsewhere in the ancient Near East we can infer that the same would have been true of the temple. At all events, in time the various traditions acquired a notable degree of fixity, so that with written redaction the means of transmission changed, but not necessarily the content.

(*a*) We cannot now discover at what point writing became widespread in Israel and Judah. Comparison with peoples in the neighbouring regions, and especially those of the city-states of Ugarit, Mesopotamia and Egypt, and the presence there, as in Israel, of officials who bore the title 'scribe', suggests that not many people will have been able to write: that capability will have been a privilege of specialists who were at the same time senior court officials. So Israel too, before becoming a fully literate people, must have had centuries, if not millennia, of preparation. At all events, with the birth of the state and the foundation of the state temple at Jerusalem, it is reasonable to suppose that administrative documents, collections of laws and religious documents were listed on inscriptions and thus kept, probably in the local temples and in the temple in Jerusalem. But in Israel, as among neighbouring peoples, there must also have been a tendency to maintain the literary and epic-religious tradition in oral form, all the more since their transmission at the various sanctuaries must have been a sufficient guarantee of their conservation.

This principle appears clearly in the two city states that I have already mentioned: the Mesopotamian state of Mari in the eighteenth and seventeenth centuries and the Syrian city state of Ugarit in the fourteenth and thirteenth centuries BCE. The letters which their sovereigns sent are addressed, paradoxically, not to their recipients but to the messenger who delivered them. They follow more or less this pattern: 'To (name of addressee) say: "This is the message of... (name of the sender) your servant..." ', or 'Message of... to...: say thus...' This information would not be so important did we not have an evident parallel in the Hebrew Bible from the second half of the eighth century BCE, in II Kings 19.10ff., where the text of the message of Sennacherib is communicated to King Hezekiah of Judah orally by the messenger: the king reads it and then 'spreads it before YHWH', in other words puts it in the temple archives, which seem also to have been political archives. This is a practice attested to the smallest details in the above-mentioned city states. The function of writing here is solely that of an *aide-mémoire* for the messenger.

We do have a very wide selection of Mesopotamian literature, but we owe it only to the fact that one of the last kings of Assyria, Asshurbanipal, diligently collected a large part of the Mesopotamian literature known in his day through his amanuenses and deposited it in a library. This was then rediscovered in the course of excavations. The Ugaritic literature, on the other hand, was in the temple archives and was discovered by archaeologists at a very early stage.

(b) If we turn to the prophets in the Hebrew Bible, we discover only three cases of writing: Isa. 8.1, which is irrelevant because of the brevity of the text; Hab.2.2, where we do not know exactly what was written; and finally Jer.36, where we have the first and only information about the compilation of a writing of any length. It is, however, significant that when the first document was destroyed by the king, Jeremiah had no difficulty in dictating a second enlarged edition to his amanuensis Baruch (36.32); he knew the text, and more, off by heart. That, at any rate, is what we are told by his biographers (below, 23.1b,d).

Such a love of oral tradition and the memory which naturally goes with it has been maintained in the East down to the present day; even an uneducated but practising Moslem will know a good deal of the Quran off by heart, and among the Jews of Eastern Europe before the Nazi extermination, as among the Yemenis, it was easy to find people, often in menial occupations, who knew off by heart not only the whole of the Old Testament but a large part of the Talmud!

(c) All this has been well known for a long time, but it needed the analyses of H.Gunkel in his comentary on Genesis, the first edition of which came out in 1901 and the third and final edition in 1910, to indicate for the first time the value of oral tradition not only as a formative element in the primitive tradition of Israel but also as a factor which explains certain variants in the texts and certain different texts. This element was then developed in central Europe, especially in Germany, by his pupils M.Noth and G.von Rad, but has been taken to the greatest lengths in Sweden, first by the historian of religion H.S.Nyberg, then by G.Widengren and I.Engnell; the latter in particular very sharply rejected any 'bookish' explanations of the origins and transmission of Israelite literature as modern European interpretation and therefore quite inadequate for explaining a literature which developed on such different premises. We shall see the details in 7.7 below.

Had it not been for oral tradition, the literature of Israel would hardly have been able to survive the catastrophes of 587 BCE and 70 CE, not to mention the other precarious situations which befell the country. It does not in fact take much to imagine how the majority of manuscripts were lost or irredeemably damaged in the pillaging and burning which followed, while the exiles would have been able to carry little or nothing with them. A literature which was exclusively committed to written texts would not have survived. As it was, however, most of this literature could be reconstructed because it had been zealously kept in the minds of those responsible for it, even if the material thus passed through a complex process of redaction.

On the other hand, the many modern references to oral tradition too often have the function of the *deus ex machina* and therefore depart from the time in which they are set as well as being of little use for scientific excavation. So in this case, too, the greatest prudence is advisable: it is probable on the basis of a series of internal indications and the customs of the region that some ancient biblical texts were originally transmitted orally; it is difficult, if not impossible, to get back to this phase, since it was soon replaced by written documents; therefore it is with the latter that we are concerned.

Oral tradition, then, first produced written tradition and then continued parallel to it, so that each exercised a kind of constant control over the other.

3. The genres

Oral tradition tends to fix itself in complexes of identical form and
similar content, called genres. Compositions which display certain
characteristic constants of form (choice of vocabulary, style, etc.),
content or setting in life (the cult, court ceremonial, the prophetic or
wisdom schools) and therefore have a common *raison d'être* belong to
the same genre. To give a modern example: we speak today of a
thriller, of epic poetry, of a leading article, a review; each of these
genres has its own particular language which is easily recognizable,
a similar theme and, in the case of poetry, a consistent metre. Today
there are also marked differences of style caused by the personal
character of individual authors, but this is something which, as we
have seen, is not to be found in the ancient Near East.

Any reader of the Bible is well aware how certain formulae tend
to be repeated at various times and in different books: the style of
the description of a battle in the books of Judges or Samuel is not
noticeably different from that to be found in a report a millennium
later in the books of Maccabees; certain formulae are repeated
constantly in poetry, from the earliest texts, e.g. Judg.5, to the latest,
e.g. the hymn at the beginning of the Gospel of Luke. A similar
problem also arises in the case of earlier classical literature, e.g. the
poems of 'Homer' and Hesiod, as well as in the rest of the literature
of the ancient Near East, so that what we discover is by no means
peculiar to Israel.

A first fundamental division is that between poetry and prose. The
former precedes the latter, just as even today the popular ballad
singer tends to use poetic forms or rhythmic prose rather than
narrative in prose; moreover the epic, which is always in poetry,
precedes any kind of prose narrative, not least because it can be more
easily memorized, a factor which, as we have seen, is important in
the context of oral tradition.

Now one of the most remarkable differences between the literature
of the ancient Near East and first classical and mediaeval literature
and then modern literature is, as we have seen, its anonymity (or
even pseudonymity); in consequence there is a complete lack of any
tendency towards creative originality, which is typical in the West.
Rather, the opposite happens; we find the use of traditional genres
with skill and in constantly new combinations; this is again a situation
which is difficult for the modern Westerner to understand, but it is
well known to experts on the Near, Middle and Far East. The
personality of the author thus completely takes second place and

tends to disappear, which explains the anonymity of such a large number of biblical and oriental writings. The fact that late Hebrew tradition tried to identify the authors of certain books or complexes of books, sometimes attributing them to a fictitious author, makes no difference to this pattern, which in practice continues right through the New Testament period (first century CE) with the exception of the authentic letters of Paul.

This situation presents historians of literature with insurmountable obstacles; they are usually confronted with formulae which are thousands of years old and originate with, or at least are attested among, neighbouring people from an even earlier date. A composition which is itself late can thus conceal its origin behind formulae which are already attested in ancient times, and it is only possible sometimes, and not always, to date the text on the basis of certain indications.

If, for example, we did not know that the compositions contained at the beginning of the Gospel of Luke appeared in the late context of the infancy narratives and were attributed to people closely connected with the birth of Jesus, but had them outside their present context, perhaps even in Hebrew, we would be hardly aware, if at all, of their late origin. Nor can we in fact exclude a priori the possibility that they are early; indeed it is quite probable that the author attributed to the individuals in question traditional liturgical compositions intended for a joyful event and therefore that the whole of the scene is simply made up of ritual components.

Of the genres in poetry, the priests cultivated the psalm. This does not, of course, exclude the possibility that the laity also recited psalms when the ritual provided for it or in private devotion. The tradition which assigns a certain number of psalms to David seems to presuppose that the laity could also compose them. We find a very special genre among the prophets, the oracle in poetry which interprets past history, whether recent or remote, or announces events in the imminent future. They handed down this material to posterity by making use of their disciples and amanuenses (see Isa.8.16; Jer.36). Numbers 21.17 knows of people called *hammōšᵉlīm*, a term which denotes those who pronounced the oracle known as the *māšal*, and is generally translated by an expression like 'gnomic poets'. They were later connected with wisdom in Israel; in an early period they may have been regarded as a kind of ballad-singer. The genre of the funeral lament is often applied in the Hebrew Bible in a sardonic manner to persons or peoples who have fallen under the divine judgment (cf. Amos 5.1-16; Jer.9.17). Legal formulations, on the other hand, are typically in prose and were preserved and handed down at the sanctuaries, if we can apply to Israel well-attested instances from elsewhere in the ancient Near East.

Gunkel also tried to trace the evolution of literary genres, from more simple earlier forms to more complex and developed forms: the shorter and purer forms were taken to be primary and the longer ones, often composed of several literary genres, were taken to be secondary. This is the weakness of his theory. Long and complex forms are to be found throughout the ancient Near East and also in the Old Testament, in passages which are certainly very ancient, like Judg.5 and II Sam.1.19ff.

In the present form of its writings the Hebrew Bible often gives the names of authors who are traditionally connected with the formation of certain groups of books, individual books or sections. Many psalms are attributed to David; part of Proverbs and probably Ecclesiastes to Solomon; a tradition which is now millennia-old tacitly attributes the Pentateuch to Moses; and all the prophetic books are explicitly attributed to the authors whose names they bear. So this seems in marked contrast to the statement made a few pages earlier that the greater part of the Hebrew Bible is anonymous or pseudonymous. However, without wishing to anticipate here the detailed discussion which we shall have later, it may be enough for me to assert that almost all these attributions are later and almost always artificial: originally they were not so much interested in identifying the real author in our sense of the term as indicating the canonical authority of these writings, which was guaranteed by the authority of the 'man of God'.

We perhaps come nearest to reality in the attribution of the prophetic books, but here too there are countless problems, so much so that we should probably consider even a large part of the prophetic books to be pseudepigraphical. There is no lack of books which are not attributed to any author: the 'former prophets', Chronicles, Job, the anonymous psalms and proverbs, and Daniel.

I have remarked that the majority of the literary genres attested in the Old Testament are known in other Semitic literature in the ancient Near East. Given this, it is not surprising to find in the Old Testament compositions reshaped along the lines of other non-biblical patterns. Psalm 104 follows the imagery and perhaps the model of an Egyptian hymn to the sun from the time of Pharaoh Akhenaton (*ANET*, 369ff., below 33.3); Prov.22.17ff. follows, sometimes word for word, a tractate of the Egyptian sage Amenemope (*ANET*, 421ff.) who lived at the beginning of the first millennium

BCE; some of the themes in the story of Joseph have remarkable analogies in the Egyptian story of the Two Brothers (*ANET*, 421ff.), while the whole of the wisdom literature generally has contacts even in fundamental matters with Semitic and non-Semitic Eastern wisdom from Sumerian times on.

The importance of these facts should not be overestimated. Had Israel lived in a watertight compartment, removed from contacts with other peoples, the originality of Israelite faith would not surprise anyone. But it is precisely its continual contact with the whole world of ancient Eastern civilization which makes this independence on the religious plane a unique historical phenomenon. The people with whom Israel had to do were almost always more civilized, technically and scientifically more advanced, and it would therefore have seemed logical that the less advanced group would be absorbed by the more advanced. Moreover this did happen on a very wide scale, but not in the religious field, although, as we shall have occasion to see, conflicts in this area were by no means lacking. Then in the post-exilic period this same people, deprived of political independence (with the exception of a brief interlude under the Maccabees which lasted about a century), autonomous only in the smallest matters, always culturally inferior to the Hellenistic world and very conscious of its inferiority, moved over to the offensive and converted thousands of Gentiles to its beliefs. These are elements which only the richness of the contacts with the surrounding world allows us to appreciate to the full.

4. Genres in poetry

(a) Discussion of the nature and especially the metre of Hebrew poetry, as of western Semitic poetry in general, is not only far from being exhausted but has yet to be correctly framed, even accepting, as we shall see, that such a discussion is possible at all. Apart from a very few instances, e.g. that of the lament, biblical criticism has yet to discover the key to Hebrew metre, always granted that such a thing existed. There are many reasons for this phenomenon. First of all, the revision of texts over the centuries and then the difficulty, and often the impossibility, of distinguishing the authentic parts from additions, make it impossible to determine individual verses exactly. Secondly, the vocalization is that traditionally fixed by the Massoretes and necessarily represents a late stage; we cannot know the original vocalization and accentuation of the texts, the poetic licence allowed, and so on. There are even sound reasons for supposing that as early as the Hellenistic period Hebrew metre was no longer known: otherwise certain additions would be inexplicable.

The most valid criterion for distinguishing poetry from prose remains that discovered by the Anglican bishop Robert Lowth in 1753 and called by him *parallelismus membrorum*, a feature which has its clear parallels in other Semitic literature and also in Egyptian literature; it would be rejected in the West because of its repetitive and therefore aesthetically unacceptable character. It poses a complex problem for translators, bound as they are on the one hand to be faithful to the text which they are translating and on the other to reproduce it in a correct and acceptable form in the language into which they are translating.

The basic characteristic of parallelism is that what is affirmed or denied in the first member is confirmed in the second with an analogous affirmation expressed in a different way. When there are several verses, the process is repeated in each. Depending on the manner in which the repetition is made we have the following varieties:

1. *Synonymous parallelism*, in which the concept expressed in the first line is repeated in the second with different words or concepts which are more or less equivalent (cf. Num.21.28; Ps.2.1-4; Prov.9.10, etc.);

2. *Antithetical parallelism*, in which the concept expressed in the first line is reinforced in the second by means of the introduction of an opposed concept which is negated (cf. Prov.10.11; 11.1);

3. *Synthetic parallelism*, in which the second member complements the first (cf.Ps.1.1-3).

4. *Climactic parallelism*, discovered only recently on the basis of Ugaritic poetry, in which the second member and possibly those following reinforce the theme by comparisons with what was affirmed first (cf. Amos 1.3ff.: 'For three transgressions of Damascus and for four', i.e. 'For the innumerable transgressions of Damascus', or Prov.6.16: 'There are six things which Yahweh hates, seven which are an abomination to him...', i.e. 'There are innumerable...').

The problem whether there can be poetry without parallelism or whether parallelism can also be found in prose may now be considered solved in that there are sentences in rhythmic prose which have forms which are very close to, if not identical with, parallelism (e.g. Gen.21.16; 22.12,17, etc.).

(*b*) A first distinction which modern readers are inclined to make in the context of Hebrew poetry is between secular poetry and religious poetry. In view of the character of the Hebrew Bible, we would not expect to find a great deal of the former, and it should be relatively easy to identify.

1. There are, indeed, many passages in which various scholars have claimed to recognize texts of secular poetry, but as will be seen, the character of these compositions is at least doubtful. I shall list them briefly. In Neh.4.10 a song of unskilled labourers seems to have been handed down, and in Num.21.17 a well-diggers' song. Until recently this latter song was attributed (even in earlier editions of this *Introduction*) to the E source of the Pentateuch (cf. the next chapter), but there are no features which indicate that it should be assigned to any of the earliest sources of the Torah. Isaiah 16.9f.; Jer.24.50; 48.33 refer to harvest songs without giving the words, while Judg.9.27 and Isa.9.3 also allude to the joy which accompanies this occasion. Unlike modern Western peoples, then, Israel will have been a people which was often ready to express its sentiments in song. As we have seen, however, there are fundamental doubts about the secular character of these songs; the first of those mentioned could be the echo of a lament which the poor oppressed labourers were making to God; the second, with its mention of sceptres and staves involved in the activity, could refer to the work of those who make water spring up in the desert (Moses would be a famous precursor here, cf. Exod.17.6 and Num.20.11, so that the diggers in question would be referring to his example and his person). Moreover, from what we know of the religious world of Canaan and the Israelite syncretism which is closely connected with it, the likely explanation of the harvest and vintage songs would seem to be that they were songs of an orgiastic type, to ensure fertility, in origin dedicated to the relevant pagan deities. They will then have come over to Israel in a weaker and perhaps distorted form. The epithet 'secular' cannot obviously be applied to any of these cases, at least in our sense of the word. There are also war songs, banqueting songs and watchmen's songs: fragments of the taunt-song againt Moab which is probably very ancient have been preserved in Num.21.27-30; the satire on the aging prostitute who goes around offering her favours in vain (Isa.23.16, in doubtful taste by modern standards) is now applied to the city of Tyre, a form of historicization similar to what we have seen practised in the case of ancient mythical texts (cf. above, 5.1). Isaiah 22.13 records a fragment of a banqueting song which is again quoted in the New Testament period in I Cor.15.32 and survives with variants in the mediaeval *Gaudeamus igitur*, see also Isa.56.12 and Song of Songs 5.1. Here, too, however, the secular character of many of these songs is open to doubt: the taunt song on

the prostitute, applied to Tyre, would not make sense unless it was a variant of the curse, intended to produce negative effects on the person at whom it is directed. We must take seriously the possibility that the others are secular songs, but they can hardly be said to be numerous. In Isa 21.11f. we have a fragment of a song to a night watchman, which is perhaps also secular, but what it means is doubtful because of the obscurity of the text.

To the modern reader, nothing might seem more secular than a wedding song, and we have a notable example of one in the Hebrew Bible in the Song of Songs. However, the problem is more complex than that, and while I do not want to anticipate what will be discussed in greater detail later (below, 39.2), I should make the following points. Marriage has always had a more or less sacral character in every civilization, if we leave aside the secular Western world, and it has never been a purely secular institution; thus even the marriage song can be considered essentially sacral without resorting to later mystical and allegorical interpretations. Given the importance of wedding feasts throughout the Near East, ancient and modern, there must have been many of these songs: the length of weddings will have been a contributory factor. According to Gen.29.27ff., one lasted seven days. We can see why Jesus often referred to weddings in his parables. However, apart from the Song of Songs, virtually none of these songs has been preserved.

Funeral songs were also frequent; they were often sung by professional singers during funerals (Jer.9.17), and otherwise by relatives or friends of the dead person. We have examples of a funeral song sung by friends in David's elegies in II Sam.1.19ff.; 3.33. Of course these are not secular but religious songs, even if their religion is often not very orthodox; in fact they go back to the celebration of the death of the god of nature, a periodical death which is followed by resurrection, but in the meantime is lamented in ritual. The lament for the death of Tammuz in Ezek.8.14 explicitly attests that these practices will have been known to the Hebrew community at the end of the sixth century BCE. In Israel, such funeral myths rapidly disappeared in more mature theological settings, being confined to the milieu of the underground religion of popular piety, especially in connection with the dead. Even here, however, there is a clear tendency to demythologize and to historicize (Amos 5.1ff.; cf. Jer.9.17ff.; Ezek.19; 26.16-18; 27.3-9; Nahum 3.7). In the first instance the lament is on the fall and death of Israel, and in such cases it is not always easy to distinguish between a funeral song proper and sarcasm. The same literary genre, but not in a sarcastic form, appears in the book of Lamentations, a work which is certainly not secular.

We also have war songs, but given the sacral character conferred on war by traditional popular piety, an element which was inherited millennia later by Islam, even here it is impossible to talk of secular poetry. In the Hebrew Bible we have one almost complete composition of this kind, Judg.5, and important fragments in Josh.10.12-13 and perhaps in the difficult text Ezek.17.9ff. (cf. also II Kings 13.17). We should probably also include in this category the blessings and curses pronounced on occasions of war or battle (Num.23; 24; Ps.68.1; I Sam.17.8-10, 43f., etc.). Here, too, everything already suggests that we should think of religious texts and not yet of secular poetry.

Finally, we must consider briefly a special genre with which we shall be concerned in detail as we go on to examine the texts: the last words of famous people from ancient Israel, eponymous heroes, and so on, in which these delivered to their hearers brief words of blessing or cursing, or sayings connected in other ways with their life. The most important examples are to be found in Gen.49; Deut.33; II Sam.23.1-7, etc., cf. also Gen.9.25ff. In the first two cases the songs presuppose certain political situations which are quite clear and are evidently much later than the speaker. The intention is to give an aetiological explanation of these situations. Often the material is very old and probably originated in the context of the groups to which it refers. The songs of Balaam in Num.23; 24 are similar. While these songs may originally have been secular epics, they certainly are not so in their present context.

Consequently it is easy to end this brief review by pointing out that there are extremely few really secular songs – perhaps only the banqueting songs. Not all the compositions in question have been handed down to us: one example is that of a Book of the Lamentations of Jeremiah which is attested in II Chron.35.25 and was composed on the occasion of the death of king Josiah at Megiddo in 609 BCE. This has nothing to do with the biblical Lamentations, which bears the same name, even if this latter book is traditionally attributed to the prophet. No traces of the former book remain. Other works which have disappeared are a Book of the Wars of YHWH and a Book of the Upright or Jashar, the former attested in Num.21.14 and the latter in Josh.10.13; II Sam.1.18. A Book of Song is attested in the LXX translation at I Kings 8.13 (v.53 in the LXX numbering) and it is possible that this is the same work (metathesis of *yšr* and *šyr*). It was probably an ancient collection which was fundamentally epic, a kind of ancient Hebrew *Iliad*.

In all these cases, given that the subject of the song is Yahweh or that it is addressed to him, we certainly have religious compositions.

(ii) Religious poetry is made up for the most part of the Psalms, but there are indications of it right through the Old Testament from Gen.49 on, especially in the prophets and the wisdom literature, and also in the pseudepigraphical literature, in the Qumran texts and in the New Testament. Here the everyday setting is evidently the cult, in which Yahweh was celebrated; we have seen some examples of less orthodox religious poetry. From the reform of King Josiah (622/621 BCE) onwards, the sanctuary was certainly that of Jerusalem, but we should first allow the possibility that the compositions in question were also used in the liturgy of other sanctuaries.

Because of the abundance of religious poetry contained in the Hebrew Bible (and as has been said, this is what we would expect in a book of this kind) we can, finally, begin to classify it in literary genres, though the majority of the details will be reserved for our discussion of the psalms (below, 33). First of all we have the hymn, a composition primarily in honour of YHWH, but secondarily used for elements closely connected with him; we have a brief liturgical form in the invitation *hal^eluyah*, i.e. 'Praise Yah', from which is derived the Alleluia of Christian liturgy. This and the lament are probably the best-represented literary genres. These compositions are also addressed to others: there are songs in honour of Zion, in which God is celebrated through praise of the sanctuary which he has chosen (Pss.46; 48; 76.18ff.); one variant which has a special theme consists of the hymns for the enthronement of YHWH, which were perhaps connected with a feast in which his eternal kingship was celebrated. This feast was probably observed annually (Pss.47; 93; 96-99, cf.also Ps.24). Songs of thanksgiving are difficult to distinguish from hymns because of their theme and form; they are sometimes accompanied by a confession of sin and a somewhat stereotyped list of the times when the person praying has been delivered (these will have had to serve for a number of different occasions). There is also a sacrifice of thanksgiving, and it is probable that the compositions in question are to be connected with its liturgy (Pss.50.13; 107.12; cf. Joel 2.26). Compositions of this kind are also known from neighbouring countries, cf. the inscription on the sarcophagus of Yehi-milk of Byblos from the fifth century BCE, which reads, 'Yehi-milk, because when I cried to my lady, the *ba'alat* of Byblos, she blessed me' (*KAI*, no.10). This is a prose composition, but the content is identical to that in the biblical compositions – apart, of course, from the deity celebrated; cf. also Isa.38.9; Job 31.19-33. The confession can be one of sin, but more often it protests the innocence of the suppliant. Sometimes his misery is described so abjectly that we seem to have the next genre with which we are concerned, the lament. Often the composition ends with a vow (cf. Ps.66.13-16; 116.14).

The book called Lamentations is only one of a large number of examples of that genre; they have a very close relationship to songs of thanksgiving, to which they often form the introduction. This last literary genre therefore establishes a link between the hymn and the lament. Its particular situation should be obvious enough: collective catastrophes like war, pillaging, plague, natural phenomena (drought, famine, earthquakes, etc.); individual cases like illness, persecution, becoming a social outcast, rejected by the community, outside which the ancient Israelite was unable to live, unjust accusations before judges, and so on. The prophets know the genre and use it frequently, as we shall see in the case of Jeremiah (below, 23). There are also thanksgivings for the community as well as for the individual, but these presuppose that the suppliant has already escaped danger or tribulation.

There are also other literary genres, even if they are not so abundantly attested: Pss.15; 24 list the qualities needed by those who wish to be admitted to the temple precinct; in Pss.20; 85 we have the word of a prophet or priest who proclaims the word of God to the listening community. Formulae of blessing or cursing appear in Pss.1; 32; 112; 128; and perhaps also in 134.3. In Pss.2; 110 we have the divine reply to a petition of the king on the occasion of his coronation or at the feast on which his enthronement was celebrated; these are evidently ritual demands, the situation and content of which we are now told in a prose passage (II Sam.7.17; cf. also Pss.89; 132). While the latter compositions are almost certainly post-exilic, they are rich in earlier material which reflects situations from the period of the monarchy. Finally, Pss.1; 112; 127 are wisdom psalms: Israel knows wisdom poetry which is attested not only in what we are accustomed to call the wisdom literature, but also in the Psalter. This genre was associated by Israelite tradition with the reign of Solomon (cf. I Kings 4.30ff.). We shall meet other details later (below, 35).

5. Remains of ancient Hebrew poetry

Until recently, and even in previous editions of this *Introduction*, a series of texts which were supposed to be ancient were usually attributed either to source J or source E of the Pentateuch (see the next chapter). These attributions were almost never justified by objective criteria, but simply because a parallel passage had been attributed to the other source. So it is not surprising that these attributions have meanwhile proved so problematical that they can no longer be supported in any case. The texts are as follows:

(*a*) The 'song of Lamech' (Gen.4.23ff.). This is the composition of a fierce warrior or bandit, who does not yet seem to know the *lex talionis* which limits personal revenge to the size of the wrong or loss suffered. It has no characteristics which suggest that it should be related to any of the sources of the Pentateuch.

(*b*) The 'words of Noah' (Gen.9.25-27). These seem to refer to the situation in Canaan a little before the institution of the monarchy in Israel, and according to some scholars it is possible that they go back directly to the period in which the Hittites and the Egyptians were fighting over the region, at the beginning of the thirteenth century BCE. The text was then adapted to Israel by means of the insertion of 'YHWH' in v.26. This produces a particularly difficult phrase, 'YHWH, god of Shem', which does not in fact appear elsewhere in the Hebrew Bible. This text has nothing to do with the Pentateuchal sources.

(*c*) 'The blessing of Jacob' (Gen.49.1-27). This does not refer either to groups in the process of formation (as the context would presuppose on the most favourable hypothesis) or to groups which are not yet settled; rather, we are dealing with well-defined ethnic entities which are solidly attested in their own territory and already known for particular characteristics, whether good or bad. Judah has pride of place in the composition; only v.18, an obvious interpolation of a liturgical type, mentions YHWH; otherwise God is called by other quite unusual names and titles (vv.24,25). A similar but not completely parallel composition appears in Deut.33 (cf. below). The attribution of these two blessings to the sources J and E respectively creates more problems than it solves, quite apart from being unnecessary on the philological level. The pre-eminence of Judah in the text would suggest a Judahite source, when the monarchy was still in existence.

(*d*) The oracles of Balaam (Num.23.7-30; 24.7-9, 15-24) traditionally divided equally between J and E. The texts are far less ancient than they might seem to be: 23.9, 23 speak of the particularity of Israel in the religious sphere, vv.21ff. of the divine sovereignty over it, while 24.7 speaks of the episode of Agag at the time of Saul (I Sam.15, a text which is now generally recognized as late). Verses 17-18 speak of the wars of David against Edom and Moab. The assignation to the sources of the Pentateuch is arbitrary.

(e) The song of Moses at the Red Sea (Exod.15.1-18,21). It speaks of Zion in terms attested in Canaan for the mountain of the gods and has until recently been considered very old (as it still is by many scholars), perhaps going back to the pre-monarchical period. However, recent studies have made it probable that this is a Deuteronomistic composition, a type which we shall be considering in due course (below, 12). To separate the so-called Song of Miriam from this composition, as if it were a parallel on a smaller scale, is arbitrary; v.21 is simply the refrain. It is also arbitrary to assign it to one of the sources of the Pentateuch except Deuteronomy or Dtr.

(f) The 'blessing of Moses' (Deut.33), like Gen.49, belongs to the literary genre of the 'last words of the hero', but this text seems to be slightly later than the other: Simeon has already lost its own autonomy and no longer appears; Levi exists only as a priestly caste (vv.8ff., against Gen.49.5f.); Judah seems to bear the blame for the breaking of the union between Judah and Israel (7ff.), while the praises of Joseph are unconditional. The orientation is therefore towards the northern kingdom. The composition is not a unity, and there are no other earlier elements.

(g) The 'song of Moses' (Deut.32) looks back retrospectively towards the founder of the religion, whose age is past. Despite the authoritative attempt by O.Eissfeldt, who tried to demonstrate the antiquity of the composition (he suggested a date probably not later than the eleventh century BCE, to be connected with the events narrated in I Sam.4-5, c.1050 BCE), this is a relatively late text, as is evident from some features to be found in vv.3,7,15,47 etc.; it would not be rash to think of a time just before the exile or even during it.

5. Genres in prose

Hebrew prose, like Western semitic prose in general, has a number of characteristic features which distinguish it not only from classical prose but also from eastern Semitic, Akkadian prose. The sentences tend to be relatively short except when, as in the case of jurisprudence, the material itself requires more developed forms; this also results from the fact that the grammar and syntax of western Semitic languages in general and Hebrew in particular do not have subordinate clauses and therefore use co-ordination, while the verb does not express so much the time of an action as its intensity and its completeness or incompleteness.

The prose contained in the Hebrew Bible can be divided into the following categories. First of all we have the discourse, as it appears in prayer, in religious sermons and in public oratory. Throughout the ancient Near East the word was of the utmost importance, and one of the fundamental criteria for judging the capacity of a person was whether he was able to express himself adequately. A person who was not gifted in this way could thus easily be judged incapable, although there are notable exceptions here also: the person of Moses (Exod.4.1off.) and that of the prophet Jeremiah (Jer.1.69). David, on the other hand, seems to have been a master of the art (I Sam.16.18). The two cases of Moses and Jeremiah show how inability to speak well was considered an insurmountable obstacle to the performance of an office, an obstacle which was either overcome, as in the case of Jeremiah, or circumvented, as in that of Moses.

We should not, however, suppose that a Hebrew speech was similar to the Western speech which is derived from the canons of classical rhetoric. The Greek and Roman speech sets out to convince the audience or adversary by means of arguments, and therefore always has a marked degree of abstraction, even if it can be accompanied by concrete examples; appeal is thus made to the logic of the audience or adversary. As far as we know, a Hebrew speech had a substantially different effect. We are not in a position to know how the audience reacted, but the content of the speech is symptomatic: rather than convince the audience by arguments, the Hebrew speech sets out to impress by its force, by the picturesque character of imagery which we might not necessarily regard as relevant (cf. II Sam.17.8). The truth does not appear as an objective element that the audience has to examine and evaluate peacefully before making a decision; it is something that has to be believed and accepted subjectively through more than argument. A Hebrew speech bewilders and sometimes, it might be said, deafens the audience without leaving any loophole or chance to reflect. The speaker who presented his arguments in the most vivid, indeed violent fashion, in forms which we would restrict to demagogy, was the one to be believed. However, the concept which underlies this form of speech is not negative in itself, as it might seem to be; the Hebrew is convinced that the truth will make itself felt with its own force, and that it does not need to be adorned by argument. We have here, then, a different way of understanding communication which is not necessarily for that reason erroneous or primitive, far less a matter of demagogy. On the contrary, there is no doubt that in the field of the confession of faith this was a means of proven efficacy and as such made more impact than Greek subtlety. However, its value is that much less in the world of thought, where the question is one of doctrine, not faith, and therefore of reasoning, not of confession. In other words, we have two different systems here, each adapted to well-defined situations.

We have political speeches in Judg.9.7-20; and in a text which has been considerably revised at a later date: in Josh.24 where, however, the religious component now dominates; in I Sam.22.6ff.; II Sam.14.1ff; 17.8ff.: II Kings 18.19ff., 28ff.; cf. also I Macc.9.8; 13.2-6. We find sermons or other kinds of religious speeches especially in the prophetic books, for example in Isa.5.1ff.; Jer.7.1f.; 26.1ff. These last, however, have also been considerably revised, although there is every indication that they go back to original episodes: Deuteronomy and parts of Chronicles are presented as religious speeches, the first spoken by Moses. Still, despite the character of the Hebrew Bible as holy scripture, we find relatively few speeches of a religious type and few cases of real preaching apart from the examples of Isaiah and Jeremiah already given. Some scholars have even been led to suppose that it was only with Josiah's reform in 622-21 (II Kings 22-23; II Chron.34-35) that the genre came into current use. Probably, however, this presentation of the facts is an over-simplification of a rather complex situation which we shall examine from time to time in connection with relevant texts. For now, it is enough to point out in anticipation that from the little we know, the ancient Israelite cult must have had a significant space for preaching or for catechetical instruction given in this form.

Prayers, too, are strangely scarce in the Hebrew Bible; we only have a few examples in Gen.32.9-12; Judg.16.28; I Kings 3.6-9; 8.22-52; II Chron.20.6-12, etc. In all these instances only the prayer of Solomon (I Kings 8) is liturgical and could go back to an original source, even if it has been expanded later. Because of its character, it lends itself to historical verification, whereas we could hardly suppose that we could verify private and intimate prayers like that of Jacob in Gen.32. The genre begins to become more frequent in the deutero-canonical and pseudepigraphical books, a phenomenon which coincides in time with the adoption by Israel of certain forms which were well-known in the classical world; in this context they correspond to the public or private discourses given by famous people in circumstances which were considered historically relevant. In this case the prayer is no longer directed by the protagonist to God, but becomes an artificial form of discourse in which the author or redactor puts into the mouth of his hero what he thinks the hero should have said in particular circumstances; his aim is to edify the community or the individual reader, just as happens with classical discourse.

Among the various documents of an administrative kind preserved in the Hebrew Bible we have the texts of contracts in Gen.21.22-32; 23.17-20; 26.26-31; 31.44-54; Josh. 9.15; I Kings 5.10-12 and many others besides. It should be noted, incidentally, that notwithstanding the apparent authenticity of the contracts recorded in Genesis, it seems somewhat improbable that texts of this kind should have come down to us or even down to the time of the redaction of the Pentateuch: that is, centuries after they were created. It is notable that all these texts belong to the sphere of private contracts, whereas agreements between states are included only rarely and at a late date. This is surprising when we think that the ancient Near East has yielded a rich collection of treaties between nations, especially from the Hittite, Aramaean and neo-Assyrian worlds (the first two in the second half of the second millennium BCE and the third in the first half of the first millennium). Only in I Macc.8.22-32 do we have the text of the alliance concluded with Rome by Judas Maccabaeus in the first half of the second century BCE. It is, however, well known that relations between God and his people are expressed in legal categories in the Hebrew Bible (cf. Gen.15.7-20; Exod.19-24; 34; II Sam.23.1-7; II Kings 23, etc.), and the technical term for this relationship is the Hebrew *berīt*. So far there is only one parallel to this term in the linguistic sphere of Hebrew, in a text from Ugarit which has recently been discovered and published. It is traditionally rendered 'covenant, alliance', but there are cases where it has a unilateral significance, i.e. 'obligation' (of God towards the people or of the people towards God; in the latter case it is equivalent to 'law', cf. below, Excursus 1, 137-42).

The Hebrew Bible does, however, provide good information on letters and epistolary correspondence in general. The earliest letter known to us is that sent by David to his generals to arrange for the death of Uriah the Hittite (II Sam.1.14); a similar one is sent by queen Jezebel to the elders of Jezreel on the occasion of the episode of Naboth's vineyard (I Kings 21.8-10); in II Kings 5.5f. we have the letter of an Aramaean king to the king of Israel and, in the same book, a letter sent to Hezekiah by Sennacherib, king of Assyria (19.9-

14, cf. above, § 2). In Jer.29 we have the text (considerably amplified at a later date) of a letter sent by Jeremiah to those deported in 597 BCE, containing an exhortation not to hope for a speedy repatriation; there are fragments of two other letters in vv.24-32. In Ezra 4-6 we have a series of missives which clearly recall the style of the Persian chancellery, and in the books of Maccabees indications of the style of Hellenistic chancelleries. Here, too, as in the classical world, there is no lack at a later date of fictitious letters which imitate the genre at a later date (cf. Dan.4.1ff.; I Macc.10.22ff.).

Throughout the Hebrew Bible there are countless lists of various kinds: genealogies, cities and boundaries, booty taken in battle, and so on. Some which are clearly authentic are out of context, e.g. Num.1; 26; 33; Josh.15-19; 21, etc. We have legal material in the second part of Exodus, throughout Leviticus, in the first part of Numbers and in the central part of Deuteronomy (chs.12-26); there is a ritual and legal programme for the reconstitution of the cult and the community after the exile in Ezek.40-48.

In all these cases we often have archive material which, if we can argue from the example of neighbouring peoples, will have been handed down by priests.

7. Ancient legal texts

Attempts have also been made in the past to attribute to the sources J and E of the Pentateuch the earliest legal texts contained in the Pentateuch (and we shall look at the problem in more detail later: below, 11). The reasons have been not dissimilar to and the criteria identical with those we found in the case of ancient poetic compositions. Here, too, it is not possible to attribute the texts to these sources, since we have no objective basis for this procedure.

(a) In Exod.34.16-26 we have what has been called a 'ritual' decalogue or dodecalogue – to distinguish it from the 'ethical' decalogue in Exod.20.1ff./Deut.5.6ff. (Excursus III below), which in the Exodus version has been attributed to E. It is preceded by a brief Deuteronomistic prologue (vv.10-15). In reality this is a kind of ritual calendar which has its parallel in Exod.23.14-19 (and is traditionally also attributed to E) and in Lev.23 (P), which gives a more extended version of it. The text deals with a series of festivities connected with agriculture, probably of Canaanite origin, which passed from Canaan to Israel. The call to present oneself to YHWH at least three times a year presupposes that the cult was not yet centralized in Jerusalem, so we are certainly in a period prior to that of Josiah. It is not, however, the pre-monarchical period, as some have suggested, since there is no supporting evidence.

(*b*) The so-called 'Book of the Covenant', as Exod.20.22-23.33 is now traditionally called on the basis of Exod.24.7, is a real collection of laws. It contains in 23.14-19 the parallel to Exod.34.16ff. mentioned above. Here too the situation seems to be clearly a sedentary one; there is nothing to suggest that these could ever have been features which were not related to a specific territory, while a number of features tell against this possibility. The object of the legislator's concern is a typical rural society, relatively well-to-do. We shall be looking at this later, in the discussion of law (below, 11).

BIBLIOGRAPHY

1. For the problems of Israel's origins see the histories of Israel listed in the bibliography at the beginning of this book, § 4. For the situation of Canaan at the time of the settlement by Israel and the groups from which Israel arose cf. S.Moscati, *Ancient Semitic Civilization*, London 1957. For the scribes and writing in the biblical period cf. A.R.Millard, 'In Praise of Ancient Scribes', *BA* 45, 1982, 149-53; R.S.Hansen, 'Ancient Scribes and Scripts', *BA* 48, 1985, 83-8; J.Naveh, 'Writing and Scripts in Seventh-Century B.C.E. Philistia', *IEJ* 35, 1985, 8-21 (the last article presupposes a remarkable degree of literacy in the region in the seventh century BCE), and A.Lemaire, *Les écoles et la formation de la Bible dans l'ancien Israël*, Fribourg 1981 (optimistic).

For the reconstruction and textual criticism of the earliest Hebrew poetry begun by W.F.Albright cf. his 'The Old Testament and Canaanite Language and Literature', *CBQ* 7, 1945, 5-31; we have the dissertation of his pupil F.M.Cross, Jr, *Studies in Ancient Yahwistic Poetry*, Baltimore 1950 (Missoula 1975), and I shall be referrring to articles by F.M.Cross and D.N.Freedman from time to time. Although the fundamental basis of this method has been accepted, it is far from producing a unanimous consensus, in view of its inevitable degree of subjectivity and the uncertainty as to the relationship between Canaanite and ancient Hebrew poetry. Albright reaffirmed his own position in *Yahweh and the Gods of Canaan*, London 1968; it has been criticized by D.W.Goodwin, *Text-Restoration Methods in Contemporary USA Biblical Scholarship*, Naples 1969. A collection of relevant materials is being published under the editorship of L.R.Fisher, *Ras Shamra Parallels*, Rome I, 1972; II, 1975; III, 1981.

2. For oral tradition and literary genres cf. E.Nielsen, *Oral Tradition*,

SBT 11, 1954; K.-H.Bernhardt, *Die gattungsgeschichtliche Forschung am Alten Testament als exegetische Methode*, Berlin 1969; K.Koch, *The Growth of the Biblical Tradition*, ET London 1969; id., 'Reichen die formgeschichtlichen Methoden für die Gegenwartsaufgaben der Bibelwissenschaften aus?', *TLZ* 98, 1973, 803-13; R.Knierim, 'Old Testament Form Criticism Reconsidered', *Int* 27, 1973, 435-68; G.M.Tucker, *Form Criticism of the Old Testament*, Philadelphia 1971; cf. also R.C.Culley, 'An Approach to the Problem of Oral Tradition', *VT* 13, 1963, 113-25; A.Haldar, 'Tradition and History', *BO* 31, 1974, 26-37; B.O.Long, 'Recent Field Studies in Oral Literature and their Bearing on Old Testament Criticism', *VT* 26, 1976, 187-98, and recently W.R.Watters, *Formula Criticism and the Poetry of the Old Testament*, Berlin 1976; B.Stolz and R.S.Shannon (eds.), *Oral Literature and the Formula*, Ann Arbor 1976. For an introduction to the problem cf. D.A.Knight, *Rediscovering the Tradition of Israel*, Missoula, Mont.1973. The whole of the annual review *Semeia*, 5, Missoula 1976, was devoted to the problem, cf. also the bibliography to Chapter 3.3. In the first edition of his *Introduction* (1934), O.Eissfeldt was the first to include this material and related considerations in his discussion. For examples of letters which are addressed to the messenger rather than to the eventual recipient see C.H.Gordon, *Ugaritic Literature*, Rome 1949, 116ff.; this material is some centuries earlier than the earliest writings in the Hebrew Bible. The first scholar after H.Gunkel to work out the importance of oral radition in a systematic way was H.S.Nyberg, *Studien zum Hoseabuch*, Uppsala 1935. For the problem of the relationship between Israel and YHWH see D.J.McCarthy, *Old Testament Covenant*, Oxford 1972 (with bibliography) and *Treaty and Covenant*, Rome [2]1978.

3. For a definition of literary genres cf. H.Gunkel, *ZAW* 42, 1924, 162; M.J.Buss, *The Prophetic Word of Hosea*, Berlin 1968, 1f. A recent summary of the problem has been made by J.H.Hayes (ed.), *Old Testament Form Criticism*, San Antonio, Texas 1972; *Introduction**, Chapter IV. For a criticism of method expressed in Crocean terms cf. F.Fubini, *Critica e poesia*, Bari 1956 (= [2]1965), ch.5. However, the criteria put forward do not seem to relate to the literatures of the ancient Near Eastern world. For the Egyptian texts mentioned see the translation by J.A.Wilson in *ANET* [2]1969, 369, 421, 423.

4. For Hebrew poetry the classical work is H.Gunkel and J.Begrich, *Einleitung in die Psalmen*, Göttingen 1933 (= [2]1966); cf. L.Alonso Schökel, *Estudios de poetica hebrea*, Barcelona 1963. The possibility of poetry without parallelism has been examined by G.Fohrer, 'Über den Kurzvers', *ZAW* 66, 1954, 192-236. For Hebrew metre cf. the studies by S.Segert, 'Problems of Hebrew Prosody', *SVT* 7, 1959, 283-91; H.Kosmala, 'Form and Structure in Ancient Hebrew Poetry', *VT* 14, 1964, 423-45; 16, 1966, 152-80. For a critical examination of these positions cf. K.Elliger, 'Ein neuer Zugang?' in *Festschrift L.Rost*, Berlin 1967, 59-65. The fourth form of parallelism was discovered by W.F.Albright, *Yahweh and the Gods*, ch.1. Cf. also D.N.Freedman, 'Acrostics and Metrics in Hebrew Poetry', *HTR* 65, 1972,

366-92; Y.Avishur, 'Addenda to the Expanded Colon in Ugaritic and Biblical Verse', *UF* 4, 1972, 1-10; A.Baker, 'Parallelism. England's Contribution to Biblical Studies', *CBQ* 35, 1973, 429-44; W.G.E.Watson, 'Verse-Patterns in Ugaritic, Akkadian and Hebrew Poetry', *UF* 7, 1976, 483-502; G.N.Schramm, 'Poetic Patterning in Biblical Hebrew', in *Michigan Oriental... Studies G.G.Cameron*, Ann Arbor 1976, 167-81. For a bibliographical study of the problem cf. D.Broadribb, 'A Historical Review of Hebrew Poetry', *AbrNah* 13, 1972-73, 66-87; D.N.Freedman, 'Pottery, Poetry and Prophecy. An Essay on Biblical Poetry', *JBL* 96, 1977, 5-26; M.V.Fox, 'Love, Passion and Perception in Israelite and Egyptian Love Poetry', *JBL* 102, 1983, 219-28. For climactic parallelism see recently H.-P.Rüger, 'Die gestaffelten Zahlensprüche des Alten Testaments und der aramäischer Achikar', *VT* 31, 1981, 229-34. Five recent works provide introductions to Hebrew poetry from various points of view: T.Collins, *Line-Forms in Hebrew Poetry*, Rome 1978; M.P.O'Connor, *Hebrew Verse Structure*, Winona Lake 1978; W.R.Watters, *Formula Criticism and the Poetry of the Old Testament*, 1976; J.-L.Kugel, *The Idea of Biblical Poetry. Parallelism and its History*, New Haven 1981; W.G.E.Watson. *Classical Hebrew Poetry*, Sheffield 1984, the last-mentioned with an exhaustive bibliography. Cf. also A.Berlin, *The Dynamics of Biblical Parallelism*, Bloomington, Indiana 1984; R.Yaron, 'The Climatic Tricolor', *JJS* 37, 1986, 153-9; W.G.E.Watson, 'Internal Parallelism in Classical Hebrew Verse', *Bibl* 66, 1985, 365-84.

5. For these poetical texts see *inter alia*: H.-J.Zobel, *Stammesspruch und Geschichte*, Berlin 1965, which treats them all; for details cf. W.F.Albright, 'The Bible after Twenty Years of Archaeology', *Religion in Life* 21, 1952, 23-50; F.M.Cross and D.N.Freedman, 'The Song of Miriam', *JNES* 14, 1955, 237-50; J.Muilenburg, 'A Liturgy on the Triumph of Jahweh', in *Studia Biblica et Semitica T.C.Vriezen...*, Wageningen 1966, 233-51; F.M.Cross, 'The Blessing of Moses', *JBL* 67, 1948, 191-202; R.Tournay, 'Le psaume et les benedictions de Moise', *RB* 65, 1958, 181-213; O.Eissfeldt, *Das Lied Moses Deut.32.1-43 und Lehrgedicht Asaphs Ps.78...*, Berlin 1958.

I have tried to show the impossibility of attributing ancient biblical poetry and the ancient collections of laws to the sources J and E in my article 'Ancient Israelite Poetry and Ancient "Codes" of Law and the sources J and E of the Pentateuch', *SVT* 27, 1975, 185-95; for the various poetic texts see A.Tosato, 'The Literary Structure of the First Two Poems of Balaam', *VT* 19, 1979, 98-106; A.Rofè, *The Book of Balaam*, Jerusalem 1979 (in Hebrew); L.Schmidt, 'Die alttestamentliche Bileamerzählung', *BZ* 23, 1979, 234-61; H.Rouillard, *La pericope de Balaam (Nombres 22-24)*, Paris 1985; S.I.L.Norin, *Er spaltete das Meer*, Lund 1977; F.Foresti, 'Composizione e redazione deuteronomistica di Ex.15,1-18', *Lat* 48, 1982, 41-69; B.P. Robinson, 'Israel and Amalek', *JSOT* 32, 1985, 15-22; H.Seebass, 'Das Stammessprüche Gen.49,3-27', *ZAW* 96, 1984, 333-91; H.Strauss, 'Das Meerenlied des Mose. Ein Siegeslied Israels?', *ZAW* 96, 1984, 333-50;

A.Caquot, 'Les bénédictions de Moïse', *Sem* 32, 1982, 67-81: 33, 1983, 59-76.

For the genre of the letter in the ancient Near East cf. in addition to the texts translated by Gordon, op.cit. (above, § 2): O.Kaiser, 'Zum Formular der in Ugarit gefundenen Briefe', *ZDPV* 86, 1970, 10-23. For *bᵉrīt* outside the Hebrew sphere cf. E.Lipiński, 'El-Berit', *Syria* 50, 1973, 50f. with bibliography.

Two studies on the problem of oral tradition, R.C.Culley, art.cit., and B.Zuber, *Vier Studien zu den Ursprüngen Israels*, Fribourg 1976, distinguish between a tradition which improvises on pre-existing themes and retains their essential content, adapting it to the circumstances, and a tradition which memorizes an already existing text, developing it in parallel. The former is not 'certain' on the historical level, the latter presupposes a now remarkably fixed text and is therefore necessarily late.

7. Cf. H.Kosmala, 'The So-Called Ritual Decalogue', *ASTI* 1, 1962, 31-61; G.Schmitt, *Du sollst keinen Frieden schliessen mit den Bewohnern des Landes*, Stuttgart 1970, 24ff.; H.Horn, 'Traditionsgeschichten in Ex.23,10-33 und Ex.34.10-26', *BZ* 15, 1971, 293-22; B.Chiesa, 'Un Dio di misericordia e di grazia', *BO* 14, 1972, 107-18; J.Halbe, *Das Privilegrecht Jahwes*, Stuttgart 1975; H.Cazelles, *Études sur le Code de l'Alliance*, Paris 1946; S.M.Paul, *Studies in the Book of Covenant in the Light of Cuneiform and Biblical Law*, Leiden 1970. T.C.Vriezen and A.S.van der Woude*, 178, already consider the assignation to J of Exod.34.10ff. problematical.

PART TWO

THE PENTATEUCH AND
THE FORMER PROPHETS

7

THE PENTATEUCH

1. Introduction

We have already seen that the Jewish tradition considered the first five books of the Bible, commonly designated in the West by the Greek term 'Pentateuch', to be the most important part of scripture. Their Hebrew name is *tōrāh* = 'instruction', and then usually 'law', on the basis of the LXX translation *nomos*, 'law', in the sense of a contrast with the law of the earthly king in the Persian period; so this is instruction *par excellence*. In some languages the section is also called 'Books of Moses', an expression which we already find in the later levels of the Jewish Bible itself: II Chron.30.16; Ezra 3.2; Neh.8.1ff, even if it is not certain, though it is probable, that this is the Pentateuch in its present form. The expression 'the law and the prophets' appears frequently in the New Testament, an evident sign that the Law, Greek *ho nomos*, had already become synonymous with 'Pentateuch'. For other attributions to Moses which raise identical problems cf. II Chron.25.4; 35.12; Neh.13.1. The attribution of the Pentateuch to Moses is generally accepted in the New Testament; cf. Mark 12.26, where Exod.3.6 is cited, and the passages on divorce, where the quotations from the Hebrew Bible are attributed to Moses (Matt.19.3-8 par.). The first certain information comes from Philo and Josephus.

The division into five books is earlier than the LXX translation, which takes it over, but we do not know for how long it had existed or by what criteria it was made. From the middle of the last century the term Hexateuch has often been used for the first six books of the Bible, on the grounds that, as some maintain, Joshua continues the Pentateuch and forms its logical epilogue, as well as displaying many of its characteristics. This term has hardly been used since M.Noth put forward a completely new solution in 1943: the first four books of the Pentateuch form a separate entity, while Deuteronomy and the former prophets are an autonomous history book which, as we shall see (below, 12), is called 'Deuteronomistic'.

In the course of this discussion I shall employ the traditional terminology and therefore use the term Pentateuch; I shall also adopt its traditional divisions. The work covers the period from the creation of the universe to the arrival of the Israelites on the threshold of the promised land; its contents have been formed through an extremely complex history of tradition which it will now be our task to examine.

2. The tradition of authorship

(a) With very few exceptions, it has always been the view of the synagogue and the church that Moses is the author of the Pentateuch. From our point of view this would seem to be an ancient tradition; however, when we consider the time that elapsed between the earliest writings or even the time of Moses and the time which saw the rise of the tradition in question, we need to recognize that the tradition is relatively recent. In the preceding section we saw that we already find the first traces of an attribution of the Pentateuch to Moses in the work of the Chronicler, that is, towards the end of the fourth century BCE, even if it is uncertain whether the attribution refers to the whole of the Pentateuch. However, considering the development of the concept, it is at least probable that the attribution is being stated in these texts as well. The one statement that we can date with certainty is that of Sirach 24.22-39, from the beginning of the second century BCE; and as we have seen, the view is generally accepted without question by the New Testament. In early Christianity, however, the anti-Christian polemists Porphyry and Celsus (for details cf. J.H.Hayes*, 89-91) put in doubt the Mosaic authenticity of the books in question; similar doubts were shown by heretical and especially Gnostic sects; the latter, however, more for dogmatic than for critical reasons. During the Middle Ages there was no lack of suspicion to this effect on the part of Jewish authors who, in the course of their painstaking analyses, had noticed many inconsistencies between the traditional view and what they read in the text. At the time of the Reformation other doubts were raised by Carlstadt in 1520, and, during the Counter-Reformation, by Spinoza (mentioned above) in 1670 and by R.Simon in 1678. It is evident, however, that these were isolated positions, and those who adopted them were soon more or less openly accused of heresy. A discussion of the traditional theory never followed. We must therefore look at the problem a little more closely.

(b) In the Pentateuch itself very few passages are attributed to Moses: Exod.17.14; 24.4; 34.27; Num.33.2; Deut.31.9, 24. In other passages it is said that Moses is speaking: for example throughout Detueronomy, which is regarded as a series of discourses by Moses. Nothing is said here, however, about the editing of the book. In many other cases it is said that 'God spoke to Moses', but here too nothing is said about the editing of the writings which we now possess. In the light of more recent investigations it seems almost certain that the pre-exilic prophets knew at least part of the Pentateuch, and this should not surprise us. However, they never make direct and certain quotations from it, nor do they speak of Moses, though this would have given infinitely more authority to their preaching; indeed, apart from Micah 6.4, a passage of doubtful authenticity, Moses is never mentioned. It seems, then, that the attribution of the Pentateuch to Moses took place between the fourth and the second century BCE and was then generally accepted from the time of the New Testament on, with the few exceptions that I have mentioned. It should, however, be evident that the deutero-canonical books and the New Testament confine themselves to expressing the common opinion of their time and of the world in which they were written, so that their assertions can hardly be considered normative at the level of historical criticism.

To summarize, then, there is no element which allows us to assert that the attribution of the Pentateuch to Moses was known before the fourth century BCE.

(c) It is necessary, however, to make a counter-check, given that much of what I have just said is based on the argument from silence. There are in fact passages in the Pentateuch which were already noted in part by Celsus and Porphyry (mentioned above) in their anti-Christian polemic, and by the mediaeval Jewish exegete Abraham ibn Ezra.

1. The last chapter of Deuteronomy describes the death of Moses and cannot therefore be his work; this is generally recognized even by those who maintain the traditional opinion, though they do not see that this admission jeopardizes the whole theory.

2. In the most varied contexts we often find the formula 'until this day' (Deut.3.14; 34.6, etc.); when as in the second case mentioned we have to do with texts contemporaneous with Moses, the formula evidently indicates a later age and marks a contrast between the later time and that of Moses.

3. We twice read, 'At that time the Canaanites were dwelling in the land' (Gen.12.6; 13.7). This presupposes a period many centuries

after Moses when the Canaanites no longer lived there because the two peoples had been assimilated (to each other). But that was certainly not the situation at the time of Moses' activity.

4. In Gen.40.15 Canaan is the 'land of the Hebrews'. This is evidently an anachronism going back to a time not much earlier than that of the Philistines. We find the same phrase elsewhere in this period (I Sam.13.3ff.); the mention of 'Hebrews' in the traditions of the oppression in Egypt is obviously another matter.

5. We find anachronisms in geographical designations: Gen.14.14 mentions Dan, which has this name only from Judg.18.29; cf. again Deut. 34.1.

6. Genesis 36.31 mentions a king in Israel, which takes us to a period not earlier than that of Saul, in the last decades of the second millennium BCE.

7. Numbers 21.14 mentions a source which contains material on the exodus and the march across the desert.

8. In Genesis 50.10ff.; Num.22.1; 32.32; 35.14; Deut.1.1,5; 3.8; 4.46, etc., the territories east of the Jordan, in which, according to the traditional itinerary, Israel arrived before its entry into Canaan, are regularly called territories on the *other* bank of the Jordan. This presupposes the point of view of an author or tradent who is living in Palestine. Moses, however, as we know, was never allowed to enter it.

9. Finally, we have a series of parallel passages or contradictions in the Pentateuch which rule out a single author and point, rather, to a somewhat complex redaction. In Gen.1.1-2.4a and 2.4b-25 we evidently have two different accounts of the creation, different both in their fundamental approach and in the order in which the elements are created. Exodus 3 and 6 both narrate the revelation of the divine name to Moses; Gen.21.31; 26.33 give two different accounts of the origin of the name of Beer Sheba, making it mean respectively 'well of the oath' and something like the place of 'seven wells'. We now have two recensions of the story of the flood which have been combined: in one the flood lasts for a total of 40 + 21 days, in the other for 12 months and 10 days; in one there are seven of each clean animal (or rather seven pairs of each clean animal) and in the other just a single pair of each animal; in the first recension the flood is the product of a great inundation caused by a tremendous rainfall, while in the other it is 'universal', a cosmic phenomenon which reduces the universe to the situation preceding the creation, which is described in the terms used in Gen.1.1-2.4a. Sinai is called Sinai, but also Horeb (and there is no indication that these are different mountains or

peaks); God is sometimes YHWH and sometimes simply God; in connection with the priesthood there is some discrepancy over such an important question as the age of ordination: twenty-five or thirty years (cf. below, 10.1). Another fact worth noting is that the Pentateuch uses the neo-Babylonian calendar (e.g. Exod.12.2) whereas elsewhere the Hebrew Bible follows the Canaanite calendar (we even know the names of some of the months). Nor is it an accident that the beginning of the year remained in the autumn, thus coinciding with the New Year in Syria and Palestine, whereas the neo-Babylonian New Year began in the spring.

We must therefore conclude that whereas the Pentaeuch does not have any internal elements which prove the truth of the tradition that attributes its redaction to Moses, there are many features which prove incompatible with such an attribution. The Pentateuch was not composed in a single draft; it is the product of a redactional process which proves to be extremely complex. Thus anyone who wishes nevertheless to maintain the traditional view that it was written by Moses would equally have to postulate a long and intricate work of redaction of such a scope that in the end it would no longer be possible to recognize clearly what did in fact go back to Moses.

3. History of the literary criticism of the Pentateuch

The problems posed by the redaction of the Pentateuch on a literary and traditional level had thus already been noted in part by ancient anti-Christian polemicists, by mediaeval Jewish exegetes and by less orthodox Jews, Protestants and Catholics. They were not, however, accepted as such and put in focus. This happened for the first time during the first half of the eighteenth century in the work of the German pastor H.B.Witter (in 1711) and a little later, but independently, in that of the French Catholic doctor J.Astruc (in 1753). Astruc was the son of a Protestant minister who went over to Catholicism in the period of the dragonnades, the persecution directed by Louis XIV. The criterion employed by both was to remain determinative for a long time to come: it was the use made of the divine names in the texts.

(a) *The old documentary hypothesis.* Both Witter and Astruc, quite independently of each other, as we have seen, noted that in Gen.1.1-2.4 God is called by his title *ᵉlōhīm*, whereas in 2.5-3.24 he is called by the title and the name YHWH; the two passages, moreover, reveal clear differences of style and aim. Astruc asserted that there must have been 'notes' of which Moses would have made use in composing the book of Genesis; in other words, he would have worked with earlier sources. Once this criterion had been established at the beginning of the book, it was easy to extend it throughout Genesis, which is the point from which all scholars, even today, begin their analyses. Astruc named the source which calls God by his title the 'Elohist', and that which called him by his name the 'Jahwist', and although the content denoted by these titles has changed, they are still retained today. However, since it was not possible to classify all the material under these two sources, Astruc looked for others, and found about ten of them.

As can be seen, he was not yet concerned with the problem of authorship. He sought, rather, to explain how there could be duplications and discrepancies in the work of a single author. J.G.Eichhorn was the first to pose the problem in the systematic fashion which was necessary.

(b) *The fragmentary hypothesis* was a second attempt to solve the problem. This leaves aside the concept of sources and speaks instead of fragments, which were then brought together by a redactor. Chief among those who put forward this hypothesis was W.M.L. de Wette, to whom we shall return when we consider the book of Deuteronomy (below, 9.2).

(c) *The complementary hypothesis* differed by postulating the existence of a single 'Elohist' source which was then completed by the addition of various texts, for example the Decalogue, the so-called Book of the Covenant and the 'Yahwistic' texts. Its best-known representative was the German H.Ewald. In reality it is a variant of the documentary hypothesis. A most important contribution towards progress was Ewald's discovery that there are two 'Elohist' sources; this laid the foundation for subsequent studies.

(d) *The new documentary hypothesis* is the most important attempt so far at achieving a synthesis along these lines. It therefore forms the necessary starting point even for those who now reject the hypothesis of the existence of sources.

It admits the existence of a Yahwistic source and two 'Elohistic' sources; the problem of the relationship between the two latter was resolved by the Alsatian scholar E.Reuss: he demonstrated that the 'Yahwist' was the earliest source, followed by the Elohist in the strictest sense of the term. The second Elohist, called more appropriately the 'priestly source', was the latest source; it was preceded by Deuteronomy. On the basis of this information the Dutchman A.Kuenen and the Germans K.H.Graf (a pupil of Reuss and his close friend) and J.Wellhausen constructed a system which arranged the sources in chronological order, gathered together the scattered pieces of the other hypotheses and produced a solution which, for those who accept its premises, can still be considered conclusive. It was Wellhausen who gave the documentary hypothesis its definitive form; a brilliant writer and speaker, his influence was immense. He was an acute thinker, and his system can be improved or qualified in detail by those who accept it, or rejected *en bloc*, but it is difficult to ignore it.

4. Wellhausen and his school

The dominant philosophy in German universities in the second half of the last century and at the beginning of this was based in one way or another on the evolutionary dialectic of Hegel. Wellhausen himself had been a pupil of a Hegelian, W.Vatke; Graf's master Reuss, however, was a Kantian, though he too was profoundly influenced by Hegel. So it is not surprising that those who rejected the documentary hypothesis as formulated by Wellhausen sought its weak points in a possible Hegelian derivation, arguing that the system could be explained on the basis of this dependence. In other words, first Vatke and then Graf and Wellhausen are said simply to have applied to the study of the Pentateuch a scheme drawn from the Hegelian philosophy of history. However, the question is not as simple as that. We may begin by noting that to postulate philosophical influences on a scholar is not in itself an argument against the validity of the theory that he is putting forward. We are all children of our age, and absorb certain of its ideological presuppositions. These presuppositions do not necessarily falsify what we put forward. Again, the 'discovery' that Wellhausen's scheme might be of Hegelian origin not only fails to demonstrate its falsity *per se*; there is a further point. It was only made some decades after the master's death, from the 1930s on. Before that it had not occurred to anyone! Nor is this an *argumentum e silentio*, as some might object; in its reply of 27 June 1906 the Pontifical Biblical Commission gave a negative opinion both on the theory according to which Moses could not be the author of the Pentateuch (only allowing the possibility of later additions) and on the possibility that it could be divided into sources. Here we find anti-modernist polemic in full flood, but there is the significant omission that the document does not give a Hegelian origin as a reason for rejecting the documentary hypothesis. In this historical and ideological context that could easily have been a conclusive argument (for the text see Denziger, 1997-2000, and *EnchBibl* n^j, 181-

7; also H.Cazelles*, 135ff., with important clarificatory comments). Again, recent studies have demonstrated without a doubt that with Vatke only the 'outer frame' was Hegelian, while Wellhausen very quickly freed himself from that also. So to speak of this school as Hegelian not only proves nothing but is not even correct from a historical point of view, though we obviously cannot exclude the possibility that Wellhausen and his pupils had unconsciously assimilated Hegelian elements as part of the ideological context in which they lived.

Be this as it may, the hypothesis very soon went from strength to strength, being welcomed by anyone who championed the need for a scientific-critical introduction to the Hebrew Bible. The only exceptions were conservative Jewish Catholic and Protestant circles, which always rejected it.

Wellhausen's system was brilliant in the simplicity of its structure and convincing in the way in which it presented the problems. It can be described briefly along the following lines:

The earliest source is the 'Yahwist' (abbreviated J by scholars, following the German Jahwist), so called because God is always given his name, particularly in the period before the revelation of that name which is made to Moses (Exod.3; 6). It is dated (even now by W.H.Schmidt*, 50ff.) between the tenth and the ninth centuries BCE, and not only for somewhat general reasons like the primitive character of its expression, which has an aesthetic and subjective character which is difficult to evaluate. J is put in that period because the relations with the Aramaeans, with whom Israel and in part Judah were at war during the ninth century, still seem very good. And since the people and places mentioned in J are on the whole to the south of Canaan, it is logical to suppose that the origins of the composition should also be sought there.

The 'Elohist', abbreviated as E, is somewhat later; its material cannot, however, be very much later than that of J. E is less primitive and immediate; for example it feels the need to make use of intermediaries between God and man, or at least not to bring about direct encounters. Thus we have the appearances of angels and dreams. There is a notable tendency to give the title 'prophet' to men who have a special contact with God, e.g. Abraham and Moses. This suggests a redaction at the time when the prophets were regarded as the men of God *par excellence*. The people and localities are mostly in the territory of the kingdom of Israel; when this was destroyed, the material was presumably transferred to the south.

The third source is Deuteronomy (D), which is largely identical with the book of the same name. A school which is dependent on D, whether on the ideological or the linguistic plane, revised the 'Former Prophets', as we shall see (below, 12). According to current opinion, the publication of Deuteronomy coincided with the discovery of a 'book of the law' at the beginning of Josiah's reform in 622-21 (II Kings 22-23), although it is at least probable that there was a second redaction during the exile, in the sixth century. As we shall see, D probably also contains earlier material.

The last source is the 'Priestly Codex', abbreviated as P, which was published at the end of the Babylonian exile or a little later, and which also forms the final framework of the material collected in the sources J and E. It has little narrative material; the greater part is made up of the ritual laws contained in the second part of Exodus, in Leviticus and in the first part of Numbers.

The dates given here clearly refer to the final redaction of each individual source and do not prejudge the possible presence of much earlier material; moreover, these are approximate dates and have been taken as such. Given the principle, the chronological sequence of the sources is generally accepted today. One exception is the Israeli scholar Y.Kaufmann, who has sought to date P before D; we shall see his reasons (below, 10.3), but by way of anticipation it may be said that his principle has not found supporters outside Jewish circles. One basic element of the documentary hypothesis is that the sources J and E can be followed through the first four books of the Pentateuch, thus producing three more or less parallel narratives, despite some obvious gaps which have come about in the course of transmission.

5. Developments of the documentary hypothesis

(a) Once the scholarly world had been presented with a hypothesis which seemed to resolve the problems of the Pentateuch, little or nothing appeared to be left to do in this direction. Wellhausen himself turned to other things, first to Arabic studies and then to the New Testament, but the many attacks made on him in church circles must have contributed in large part to this decision. Reality was soon to show, however, that although an important principle had been discovered, the documentary hypothesis did not exhaust all the material; it was, rather, the initial phase of research. A first attack was made on the criterion of the divine names which had furnished the key for the research of eighteenth-century scholars and which had continued to play an important part. How could the names serve as a criterion, it was asked. if an ancient translation like that of the LXX often presupposed YHWH where the Massoretic text has *'elōhīm* and vice versa, a phenomenon which could be confirmed by reference to the Samaritan Pentateuch? If the criterion of the names was to be considered normative, the recensions and the ancient translations should have disclosed this with some consistency.

(b) A second problem then came to the attention of scholars. E appears only here and there; can one then talk of an independent source? Or does it need simply to be considered as a complement to J, thus becoming a kind of complementary hypothesis? Meanwhile the continual discoveries in the field of ancient Near Eastern studies (frequent in the second half of the past century and the beginning of this) have posed problems for any attempt at dating in view of the tendency of the various literary genres to be repeated over a period of time with stereotyped formulae.

(c) But even in the camp of Wellhausen's disciples things did not go as smoothly as might have been expected; the division into only four sources did not seem an adequate explanation of all the problems which continued to arise, and the addition of a fifth element, the redactor, was not enough to remedy the situation. Hence the need to distinguish various strata of tradition within the various individual sources, a problem which had been raised, but not developed, by Kuenen. So at the beginning of this century E, already much reduced, was subdivided into an E¹ and E² by O.Procksch, while in the 1930s P.Volz and W.Rudolph denied its existence altogether! Again during the 1930s an attempt was made to divide J into a J¹ (or S = southern) and J² (or L = lay) source, the former with a distinct interest in the cult and the latter without this interest; these divisions are still authoritatively maintained today by Eissfeldt* and Fohrer*. P, too, was subdivided into various sub-codices. Analysis became more and more intricate, even taking in quarter-verses or smaller units. In other words, although the documentary hypothesis had resolved a fundamental problem, it had revealed a multitude of others, capable of unexpected developments.

(d) It is not difficult now to establish the reasons for this development of the theories of Wellhausen and his colleagues; the documentary hypothesis grew out of methodology formed from the study of classical texts, and treated the Pentateuch and the other historical books by the same standard. In reality it was a starting point for a series of investigations and not, as some thought, a goal which had been achieved. The isolation of the principal components of a source in fact produced no decisive results (and in this operation it all too often proved impossible to reach even the minimum measure of agreement over a number of passages, while, as we have seen, there was an exaggerated tendency to dissect an individual unit to such a degree as to make ridiculous a method which was quite valid in itself). There was still no knowledge of how the sources had been formed, what scope the redactors felt they had in selection from the material at their disposal, in what circles the collections developed or to what degree and over what period oral tradition preceded written redaction and continued to exist parallel to it. The existence of such oral tradition was admitted on all sides as a matter of principle, but no one was particularly concerned to examine its relation to the text which had been transmitted. And while initially the lack of comparative oriental material could explain this, the abundant discoveries in the course of the second half of the last century and the beginning of this made the existence of a situation of this sort no longer justifiable.

It was with H.Gunkel and his pupils that a large number of these problems came to be tackled in a new way, and even if the proposals of these scholars often did not solve them, they contributed in no small degree towards posing the questions in the right form and indicating the way in which they should be solved.

6. The study of the genres. The history of tradition

(a) Precedents. Foremost among the biblical scholars at the end of the last century and in the first decades of this is the figure of Hermann Gunkel. We have already noted that he was the first to introduce the study of literary genres into Old Testament and Near Eastern studies (above, 6.2c), a method which is appropriate to the anonymous or even pseudonymous character of these writings. Indeed, in the majority of cases it is the only one applicable, if a method is to be used which is not totally alien to the material studied. Gunkel's commentary on Genesis is fundamental to our theme; in the introduction, which is still a classic and can be considered as setting out a basic programme, he established:

1. Genesis is a collection of legends, 2. originally transmitted orally, 3. which had already been collected into cycles at the oral stage. Therefore, 4. the sources are more the production of redactional than of creative work, and simply provided the pre-existent material with a framework and contexts; moreover 5. they are not the works of individuals, whether authors or collectors, but of schools of narrators (scholars now tend to prefer the word 'tradents'). 6. Thus

the individual material in the collections has its own history and its own setting, quite independently of its later position in the sources, so that 7. every lesser unit must first be examined by itself, leaving aside its present context. Gunkel and, as we shall see, his disciples in Germany considered their method quite compatible with the documentary hypothesis; others, especially in Scandinavia, argued that the two methods were incompatible and that a choice had to be made between them.

(b) Meanwhile the documentary hypothesis was subjected to increasing criticism, though it continued to be dominant in the universities. I have already discussed the difficulties caused by the traditional divisions into sources, and shown how the existence of one of these was even denied altogether. I also pointed out that the sub-divisions became increasingly subtle and intricate, sometimes even (if the word may be allowed) impalpable, with the result that the method itself seemed to have been reduced to absurdity and hence implicitly shown to be invalid. Towards the middle of the 1930s Umberto Cassuto, Professor at the University of Rome, demonstrated how the question of the Pentateuch had evolved in parallel to the Homeric question, receiving distinct solutions from different schools in different periods. He also made a rigorous critique of the various theories proposed hitherto in favour of a division into sources, insisting that the data adopted in their support allowed a number of different solutions. This led him to argue that a single redaction took place at the time of David or a little later, on the basis of earlier tradition, i.e. during the time postulated by the supporters of the documentary hypothesis for J. In 1934 Cassuto spoke of a 'master of supreme genius...' a figure who was later suppressed in the successive new editions of his work. In Holland, B.D.Eerdmans was a rigorous critic of the documentary hypothesis, but his argument, culminating in a downright rejection of the hypothesis, ended by destroying the credibility of another series of arguments which are intrinsically valid. At the beginning of the 1930s the Danish scholar J.Pedersen sought to demonstrate that the Wellhausen school was in fact applying Hegelian categories to the study of the Hebrew Bible, but as we have seen, this argument has meanwhile proved to be unfounded, and the accusation was not valid. The arguments used to claim that the documentary hypothesis is invalid are interesting; Pedersen claimed that the origin of the passover narrative, Exod.1-15, was not to be sought in a compilation of various sources, but that the first setting of the passage was an ancient passover liturgy. This origin was, he believed, an explanation of the repetitions and contradictions in the account; consequently it was not only impossible, but completely useless, to look for sources. In 1935 H.S.Nyberg, the Swedish history of religions scholar mentioned above, showed in what was subsequently to be considered a programmatic work how the documentary hypothesis in its classical formulation did not take any account of the primary element, which was oral tradition. Gunkel's best pupil, Hugo Gressmann, had already taken this direction in a series of critical articles, in which he succeeded in isolating a series of complexes of traditions, especially in the Exodus narratives.

Meanwhile a school developed in Great Britain during the 1930s known as the 'Myth and Ritual school', to be followed in the 1940s by the so-called 'Uppsala school' in Sweden. The most distinguished representatives of these schools, S.H.Hooke and I.V.Engnell respectively, stressed the importance of oral tradition and of the setting of this tradition in the world of ancient Near Eastern myth. From this setting could be derived all the ideological constants, which were reducible to a more or less coherent pattern. Of course in a context like this a discussion of sources proved out of the question. In due course (cf. below, § 7) we shall be turning to these problems in greater detail.

In other words, between the middle of the 1930s and the end of the Second World War the documentary hypothesis was attacked at many points and challenged to a considerable degree. This situation did not fail to produce a certain satisfaction in conservative circles associated with the church or the synagogue. The Italian biblical scholar G.Ricciotti openly spoke of a triumph of ecclesiastical tradition (and, he might have added, of synagogue tradition) over literary criticism. In reality the situation was rather more complex: it was not so much a matter of abandoning critical positions in order to return to tradition (besides, it is hard to see how conservative ecclesiastical circles could have accepted the arguments of the Myth and Ritual school or the Uppsala school...), as of criticism rebelling against a method which was considered partly inadequate and partly erroneous. It is, moreover, typical that none of these scholars ever again raised the possibility of attributing the Pentateuch to Moses. This was therefore an attempt to go beyond the documentary hypothesis, not to go back before it.

(c) In Germany in 1938 and 1940 two pupils of Gunkel, Martin Noth and Gerhard von Rad, having refined the historical and geographical method of Albrecht Alt, sought to reaffirm the documentary hypothesis, but at the same time to go back to the oral tradition which underlay it and to look for the reasons which might have led to the formation of the sources. Von Rad's work of 1938 became famous (though the outbreak of war a year later prevented it from being widely known until the end of the war); in it he argued that the collection of material, particularly by J, in the Hexateuch (a term which he continued to accept since he never allowed the existence of a Deuteronomic history school) followed the pattern of ancient 'confessions of faith' or various editions of an ancient 'creed' to be found in passages which, while themselves late, he considered to contain early tradition: Deut.26.5b-6; 6.2off.; Josh.24.2b-13; cf. Ps.136, which was a lyric version of it belonging to the cult. According to von Rad, these confessions of faith provided, in a nutshell, the chronological framework for the events which were narrated, from the time of the patriarchs to the conquest of Palestine, and the material collected by J began progressively to crystallize around them.

From the importance of the confessions of faith in the formation of the earliest sources, especially J, it was easy to infer that in Israel, even in the pre-monarchical period, there was a feast called the 'feast of the covenant', in the course of which this would have been recited; this deduction was made by some authors in the 1950s and 1960s and accepted, though with reservations, by von Rad.

To begin with, this explanation seemed satisfactory to the majority of scholars. It kept very close to the tradition, took account of the religious character of the texts, indeed deeming that to be of fundamental importance, and also recognized a creative element in oral tradition. At the same time, it maintained the documentary hypothesis. It did, however, have two inconvenient features: in the confessions of faith in question there was neither a creation narrative (Gen.1-11) nor any mention of Sinai. Now while the first omission could be explained on the grounds that this was a preface in terms of universal history, added to the original text at a later stage, the question of the absence of a reference to Sinai was more complex, because in a feast of this kind it should have been of fundamental importance.

There have been many explanations of this second feature, which is certainly disconcerting. The explanation which began from literary-critical presuppositions was by no means misguided in arguing that the Sinai pericope was in fact interpolated into its present context: Israel arrives in the region of the sanctuary of Kadesh in Exod.18 and leaves in Num.11; in the middle is the erratic Sinai block. Those, however, who put the emphasis on comparisons between the alleged biblical covenant and oriental vassal treaties preferred to suppose that just as these treaties were often prefaced by historical prologues setting out to explain how their agreements were arrived at, so the facts narrated in the 'confession of faith' constituted the historical prologue to an agreement which was in effect made in the Sinai pericope. Clearly, neither of these explanations is satisfactory; they are merely attempts to explain a situation which was certainly embarrassing for those who accepted the premises which have been set out above. But once these premises were shown to be invalid, the hypothesis that the confessions of faith formed the framework within which the ancient sources, and especially J, came to be formulated, also collapsed. The wheel came full circle, so to speak, in 1966, when it was noted that the confessions of faith, far from representing an early stratum of tradition, in fact consistuted a final stage, a synthesis, for those who presupposed the existence of the sources. With this observation one of the most successful theories of the past twenty to twenty-five years came to an end.

In 1940 M.Noth subjected the legal texts of the Pentateuch to an analogous examination, reaching much more solid results (not least because of the nature of the material which he examined); they were less spectacular and therefore less discussed.

7. The compatibility between the documentary hypothesis and the history of tradition

One problem which does not seem to have preoccupied Gunkel and his disciples H.Gressmann, A.Alt, M.Noth and G.von Rad is that of the compatibility between the documentary hypothesis and the new method of the history of traditions: all seem to have been convinced that the two methods were mutually complementary and therefore did not exclude each other (W.H.Schmidt*, 60, still continues to hold this view). In his other works on the Pentateuch Noth happily worked with the presuppositions of either the documentary hypothesis and that of the study of literary genres, and I do not recall any instance in which the problem seems to have been felt as such. The result was a method which in German is called *Überlieferungsgeschichte* (there are also derivatives), which might be translated 'history of the tradition'. In the Scandinavian countries, however, authors came forward like J.Pedersen and H.S.Nyberg who, precisely because they wanted to carry forward the discussion begun by Gunkel, rejected the documentary hypothesis in the terms in which Wellhausen and his pupils had proposed it, considering it to be incompatible with traditio-historical methods. They were followed by the founder of the Uppsala school, Ivan Engnell, who put forward a new traditio-historical method, in German *Traditionsgeschichte*. The semantic distinction between *Überlieferungsgeschichte* and *Traditionsgeschichte* is difficult to reproduce outside the German language, in which both a Germanic and a neo-Latin term are often available for the same concept. The former term is conventionally used to describe the work of von Rad and Noth, and the latter to describe the work of the Scandinavians mentioned above.

(*a*) For Engnell there were never continuous 'sources' in the first four books of the Pentateuch (Deuteronomy was obviously a separate problem), or, perhaps better, there were no sources as the documentary hypothesis understood them. The presence of doublets and contradictions as well as repetitions could perfectly well be explained on the one hand by oral tradition and on the other by the specific character of Hebrew and other Semitic literature. Many elements introduced to support the documentary hypothesis were said to be simply a product either of our own inadequate Western psychology or – and this is a more serious accusation – of deficiencies on a linguistic and grammatical level. Of course, to sustain this latter charge it would have been necessary to give adequate proof, and that was never forthcoming, though it cannot be denied that Engnell's thrusts sometimes struck home. One example that we can call classic is that of B.Duhm, *Das Buch Jesaja*, Göttingen 1892, ⁴1922. Commenting on Isa.1.10-17, Duhm wanted to delete the expression *miyyedᵉkem*, literally 'from your hands', in v.12; the context in fact speaks of 'treading my (YHWH's) courts', something that one clearly did not do with one's hands. However, he did not take account of the fact that the expression should not be translated literally, but means 'on your part'.

Engnell's proposals, as the reader will note, are not just an academic issue; here is a basic methodological choice which is capable of modifying the procedure substantially and with it the results of the investigation: in fact, once one of the two methods are accepted, Engnell argues, one should automatically exclude the other.

Engnell died prematurely, before he was sixty and after only about twenty years of scholarly activity: this prevented him not only from finishing his own work but also from making a systematic presentation of what he had already accomplished; nor does he seem to have left behind pupils interested in continuing along similar lines the work which he had undertaken. So we have a series of assertions about principles and methods which fall short of even a purely provisional synthesis. Engnell was very conscious of this when he wrote: 'The traditio-historical method [in the sense of *Traditionsgeschichte*, see above] is still in the first stages of its development.' Such a synthesis could have presented an alternative, albeit open to question, to the documentary hypothesis, the methods of which have also been considerably refined, as we have seen. A particularly interesting feature today is the considerable capacity for self-criticism among those who support the documentary hypothesis, a capacity which among other things has developed from constant involvement with ancient Near Eastern literature.

(*b*) In the field of *Überlieferungsgeschichte* too, however, the problem of compatibility with the documentary hypothesis has recently been raised again by R.Rendtorff, a pupil of von Rad. Rendtorff noted the uncritical way in which both von Rad and Noth took for granted the existence of the sources (though this presupposition did not go beyond a purely conjectural stage, a situation which has now lasted for more than a century). He then criticized the vain search for generally accepted criteria of method, style or content by which a passage might be assigned to J or E (for example, there is a widespread tendency to assign to J anything that cannot be assigned to E or P). Rendtorff therefore accused Noth of inconsistency because he accepted both the sources and the method of *Überlieferungsgeschichte*, while arguing that that the validity or otherwise of von Rad's theories was quite independent of their connections with the origins of J. In fact a basic feature of the documentary hypothesis, that the sources J and E can be reconstructed in a more or less organic and parallel way – apart, as we have seen, from gaps here and there because of transmission and redaction – no longer appears anywhere outside Genesis; in the first half of Exodus and in the second half of Numbers the difficulties of distinguishing between J and E are such that it is better to abandon any attempt to identify them with a view to providing support for the documentary hypothesis. For the supporters of *Überlieferungsgeschichte* to accept the documentary hypothesis would then be a sign of inconsistency, not the consequence of a methodological choice. The only reason why this inconsistency has still not been noted properly would be the inadequate development of *Überlieferungsgeschichte*.

(*c*) Still following Rendtorff, all that can be accepted by critics is first the collection of material in larger literary units, within which we should distinguish various narrative cycles; this seems clear in the case of the Jacob traditions, but more problematical in the

Abraham traditions. Only from the cycles can we then go back to the lesser units. But another much more obvious case is that of the Joseph tradition (Gen.37; 39-50, with the exclusion of the hymn in 49.1-28). There can be no doubt that this is a major interpolation, aimed at developing the theme of the emigration of Israel into Egypt, a necessary preliminary to the exodus narrative. But it is also evident that the Joseph story is quite self-contained in itself. In that case, however, what sense does it make to talk of sources? Thus the problem that Pedersen saw in Exodus 1-15 reappears, albeit in different terms. Certainly Rendtorff does not deny the existence of different traditional strata with duplicates and contradictions within these great complexes, but he denies that one can speak of continuous sources, with their own development and their own thought, those features which are an integral part of the documentary hypothesis. The study of the transition from the larger units to our text could possibly also lead to the establishment of the existence of continuous narratives, as the documentary hypothesis would have it, and only in this case would it be legitimate to speak of 'sources'. Rendtorff, however, thinks it more probable that it will be possible only to establish the existence of 'traditional strata', related in style and content, whose position in the wider context of the Pentateuch should also be examined. Thus for example we would have priestly legal material and a priestly redaction, but not a P source.

Studies following Rendtorff's proposals have been continued, and recently a large volume has been published of work by Erhard Blum, one of his pupils. In his discussion of the patriarchal narratives, Blum makes no use at all of the J and E sources, showing how among other things certain attributions have often been made on the basis of alleged duplicates, contradictions and repetitions which in reality to do not exist. He thinks, rather, of originally independent cycles of tradition revised successively; and it is here that Deut or Dtr and later revisions of a priestly type come in.

8. Questions of dating the earliest sources

However, even among those who accept the documentary hypothesis in its traditional form things are far from quiet. Three authors, the North American J.Van Seters, the Swiss H.H.Schmid and the German H.Vorländer, have argued independently of one another and following different methods that J is to be dated in a much later period than that suggested by Wellhausen and his pupils; this is no longer the beginning of the divided monarchy, but shortly before or even during the Babylonian exile. Thus chronologically J would come much closer to Dtn and Dtr. In this way, of course, another pillar of the documentary hypothesis is demolished, while at least two proposals for a new complementary hypothesis have been made in Sweden and in Holland.

So we find ourselves confronted on the one hand with a confluence between German *Überlieferungsgeschichte* and Scandinavian *Traditionsgeschichte* and thus with an outright rejection of the documentary hypothesis. So here it is not surprising that we find even detailed proposals for returning to the complementary hypothesis (S.Tengström and C.Houtman). On the other hand, although the hypothesis is maintained, the distance between the various sources is greatly reduced, so that it does not make much sense to talk about 'ancient' sources of the Pentateuch: the dates of all of them are fixed from the end of the seventh century onwards.

BIBLIOGRAPHY

For the present situation see recently J.van Seters, 'Recent Studies in the Pentateuch. A Crisis of Method', *JAOS* 99, 1979, 663-73; J.Vermeylen, 'La formation du Pentateuque à la lumière de l'exégèse historico-critique', *RTL* 12, 1981, 324-46.

Commentaries

Genesis: H.Gunkel, HKAT, [6]1964; O Procksch, KAT, [3]1924; B.Jacob, *Der Erste Buch der Tora*, Berlin 1934; G.von Rad, OTL [3]1972; U.Cassuto, 2 vols., 1961-4: R.de Vaux, JB, [2]1958: E.A.Speiser, AB, 1964: W.Zimmerli, ZBK I, [3]1967; II, 1976; F.Festorazzi, *La bibbia e il problema delle origini*, Brescia [2]1967 (on 1-11 only); E.Testa, ScBib I, 1969; II, 1974; C.Westermann, ET I, 1983; II, 1986; III, 1987.

Exodus: B.Couroyer, JB, [3]1968; E.Galbiati, *La struttura letteraria dell'Esodo*, Alba 1956; M.Noth, OTL, 1962; U.Cassuto, 1968; J.P.Hyatt, NCB, 1971; B.S.Childs, OTL, 1974; W.H.Schmidt, NK, I, 1988; J.S.Croatto, 1981.

Leviticus; M.Noth, OTL, 1965; K.Elliger, HAT, 1966; N.H.Snaith, NCB, 1967; H.Cazelles, JB, [3]1972; E.Cortese, SacBib, 1982; R.Rendtorff, 1985ff. (one fascicle issued).

Numbers: H.Cazelles, [3]1971; N.H.Snaith, NCB, 1967; M.Noth, OTL, 1968; G.Bernini, SacBib, 1971; J.de Vaulx, SB, 1972.

Deuteronomy: C.Steuernagel, HKAT, [2]1923; H.Cazelles, JB, [2]1958;

P.Buis and J.Leclerq, SN, 1963; G.von Rad, OTL, 1966; A.Penna, SacBib, 1976; A.D.H.Mayes, NCB, 1986.

1. For the 'Deuteronomic history work' (Dtr) see M.Noth, *Überlieferungs-geschichtliche Studien*, Halle 1943; for the Pentateuch in general see M.Noth, *A History of Pentateuchal Traditions*, ET Englewood Cliffs 1972; O.Eissfeldt, *Die Genesis der Genesis*, Tübingen 1961; H.Cazelles and J.P.Bouhot, 'Pentateuque', in *Supplément au Dictionnaire de la Bible* VIII (see general bibliography, § 3); H.Cazelles, 'Positions actuelles dans l'exégèse du Pentateuque', *EphThLov* 44, 1968, 55-78; id., 'Theological Bulletin on the Pentateuch', *BTB* 2, 1972, 3-24. For the figure of Moses and the problems associated with it cf. R.J.Thompson, *Moses and the Law in a Century of Criticism since Graf*, SVT 19, Leiden 1970.

2. For the formula 'until this day' cf. B.S.Childs, 'A Study of the Formula "Until this Day" ', *JBL* 82, 1963, 279-92.

For the calendar cf.S.Mowinckel, *Das israelitische Neujahr*, Oslo 1952.

3. Cf. the works by Diestel, Kraeling and Kraus listed above in the general bibliography, and R.de Vaux, 'Reflections on the Present State of Pentateuchal Criticism', in *The Bible and the Ancient Near East*, London 1972, 31-48.

3c. A modern variant of the complementary hypothesis has recently been put forward by S.Tengström, *Die Hexateucherzählung*, Lund 1976 (a 'basic narrative' supplemented by additions) and by C.Houtman, *Inleiding in de Pentateuch*, Kampen 1980.

4. The main works in which Wellhausen presented his own theories are *Prolegomena to the History of Israel* (ET 1885, reprinted New York 1957) and the article 'Israel' in *Encyclopaedia Britannica*, Vol.16, [9]1883, 86off., which is printed as an appendix to the ET of the *Prolegomena*. On the supposed dependence of Wellhausen and his teacher W.Vatke on Hegel cf. R.Smend, 'De Wette und das Verhältnis zwischen historischer Bibelkritik und philosophischen System im 19.Jahrhundert', *TZ* 14, 1958, 107-19 (esp.112); L.Perlitt, *Vatke and Wellhausen* , BZAW 94, 1965. See also id., 'Wellhausen in Greifswald', *ZTK* 76, 1979, 381-418 (a study in which *inter alia* he defends Wellhausen against the charge of antisemitism). For a sharp criticism of some aspects of Wellhausen's work cf. M.Weinfeld, *Getting at the Roots of Wellhausen's Understanding of the Law of Israel*, Jerusalem 1979. The annual publication *Semeia* devoted the whole of its vol.25, 1982, to Wellhausen.

5. P.Volz and W.Rudolph, *Der Elohist als Erzähler*, BZAW 63, 1933, and Rudolph, *Der 'Elohist' von Exodus bis Joshua*, BZAW 68, 1938, denied the existence of E as an autonomous source. O.Eissfeldt*, [2]1934, and R.H.Pfeiffer*, [2]1948, divided J into two documents, J[1] and J[2] and S (southern) and L (lay) respectively; in both instances the second of the sources is the one that has less interest in theological problems. O.Eissfeldt restated and updated his theory in *Die Genesis der Genesis*, Tübingen [2]1961. Fohrer in his revision of Sellin's *Introduction* takes a similar position. G.von Rad, *Die Priesterschrift im Hexateuch*, Stuttgart 1934, divided P into at least

two sub-codices; for a stringent criticism of his position see P.Humbert, 'Die literarische Zweiheit der Priester-Codex in der Genesis', *ZAW* 58, 1940/41, 30-57.

6a. For Gunkel see his commentary on Genesis (above, 1) and his *Die israelitische Literatur*, Stuttgart 1925 (reprinted Darmstadt 1963). For his personality and academic activity cf. W.Klatt, *Hermann Gunkel*, FRLANT 100, 1969; K.von Rabenau, 'Hermann Gunkel auf rauhen Pfaden nach Halle', *EvTh* 30, 1970, 433-44. There is an evaluation of his programme and methods and of their contemporary relevance in R.Lapointe, 'Les genres littéraires après l'ère gunkélienne', *Église et Théologie* 1, Ottawa 1970, 9-38. Gunkel's method has often been criticized, cf. recently S.M.Warner, 'Primitive Saga Men', *VT* 29, 1979, 325-35, who particularly criticizes his inadequacy on the ethnological level and the fact that in the third edition of the commentary on Genesis he bases himself essentially on the studies of A.Olrik, 'Epische Gesetze der Volksdichtung', *Zeitschrift für deutsches Altertum* 51, 1909, 1-12; but it is easy to see the confusion in Olrik. For U.Cassuto, see his *The Documentary Hypothesis and the Composition of the Pentateuch*, ET, London 1961, cf. also the commentaries cited above (§ 1). The charge of Hegelianism was made against Wellhausen by J.Pedersen, 'Die Auffassung vom Alten Testament', *ZAW* 49, 1931, 161-81; id., 'Passahfest und Passahlegende', *ZAW* 52, 1934, 161-75; cf.H.S.Nyberg, *Studien zum Hoseabuch*, Uppsala 1935; id., 'Die schwedischen Beiträge zur alttestamentlichen Forschung', *SVT* 22, 1972, 1-10. G.Ricciotti, *History of Israel* I, ET Milwaukee 1958, 103ff., describes the triumph of the ecclesiastical tradition. For the person of Pedersen see E.Nielsen, 'Johannes Pedersen's Contribution to the Research and Understanding of the Old Testament', *ASTI*, 1972, 4-20.

6b. G.von Rad, 'The Form Critical Problem of the Hexateuch', in his *The Problem of the Hexateuch and other Essays*, ET Edinburgh 1966, 1-78, accepts the earlier work of M.Noth, *Das System der zwölf Stämme Israels*, Stuttgart 1930; see also Noth's *The Laws in the Pentateuch and other Essays*, ET Edinburgh 1966. For the Exodus and Sinai narratives cf. W.Beyerlin, *Origins and History of the Oldest Sinaitic Traditions*, ET Oxford 1965, and G.Fohrer, *Überlieferung und Geschichte des Exodus*, BZAW 91, 1964; also three recent studies: P.Weimar and E.Zenger, *Exodus*, Stuttgart 1975; R.Schmitt, *Exodus und Passah, ihr Zusammenhang im Alten Testament*, Freiburg CH 1975; B.Zuber, *Vier Studien zu den Ursprüngen Israels*, Freiburg CH 1976. For the J traditions see J.V.Fritz, *Israel in der Wüste*, Marburg 1970. For the problem of the term *bᵉrīt* cf. E.Kutsch, '*bᵉrīt*', *THAT* I, Munich 1971, 339-52; id., *Verheissung und Gesetz*, Berlin 1973, both with bibliography, and M.Weinfeld, '*bᵉrīt*', *TDOT* II, Grand Rapids 1975, 253-79. With good reason Weinfeld maintains an ambivalent position; there are cases in which the term denotes 'pledge' and others in which it can only be translated 'covenant, alliance'.

7. For the problem of the 'confession of faith' see W.Richter, 'Beobachtungen zur theologischen Systembildung in der alttestamentlichen Literatur anhand des "kleinen geschichtlichen Credo" ', *Wahrheit und Verkündigung:*

FS M.Schmaus I, Paderborn 1967, 191-5; B.S.Childs, 'Deuteronomic Formulae of the Exodus Tradition', *SVT* 16, 1967, 30-9; J.P.Hyatt, 'Were there an Ancient Historical Credo in Israel and an independent Sinai Tradition?', in H.T.Frank and W.L.Reed (eds.), *Translating and Understanding the Old Testament. Essays in Honor of H.G.May*, Nashville 1970, 152-70; N.Lohfink, 'Zum "kleinen geschichtlichen Credo"', Deutr.26.5-9', *Theologie und Philosophie* 46, Freiburg im Breisgau 1971, 19-39; R.de Vaux, *The Early History of Israel* I, ET London and New York 1978, 401f.

7b. For I.Engnell see *Gamla Testamentet: en traditions-historisk inledning* I, Stockholm 1945, esp. 189ff. (vol.II was never published). Some of his shorter works have been collected and translated by J.T.Willis: *I.Engnell, Critical Essays on the Old Testament*, London 1970 (US title: *A Rigid Scrutiny...*, Nashville 1969; the quotation given appears on p.11).

For the problem of the 'Uppsala school' and Scandinavian studies generally see now K.Jeppesen and B.Otzen (eds.), *The Productions of Time: Tradition History in Old Testament Scholarship*, Sheffield 1984.

7c. For a possible convergence of *Traditionsgeschichte* and *Überlieferungsgeschichte* cf. R.Rendtorff, 'Traditio-historical Method and the Documentary Hypothesis', *Proceedings of the Fifth World Congress of Jewish Studies 1969*, Jerusalem ²1971, 5-11; id., 'Der "Jahwist" als Theologe? Zum Dilemma der Pentateuchkritik', *SVT* 28, 1975, 158-66; id., *Das überlieferungsgeschichtliche Problem des Pentateuch*, Berlin 1977, and the whole of *JSOT* 3, 1977; F.Crüsemann, 'Die Eigenständigkeit der Urgeschichte', in *Die Botschaft und die Boten – FS H.-W.Wolff*, Neukirchen 1981, 11-29, notes in this connection that there is no link between the creation narratives, Gen.1-11, and the patriarchal narratives, a feature which makes improbable their attribution to the one source J; E.Blum, *Die Komposition der Vätergeschichte*, Neukirchen 1984. There is a review of Rendtorff by G.Garbini, *Hen* 4, 1982, 98-100; of Blum by J.A.Soggin, *Hen* 8, 1986, 245-9. G.A.Rendsburg, *The Redaction of Genesis*, Winona Lake 1986, is also critical of the documentary hypothesis and favours a literary approach.

The following have recently argued in favour of the documentary hypothesis: H.Cazelles, 'Pentateuque', *SDB* 7, 1966, (735-858) 742ff.; A.W.Jenks, *The Elohist and North Israelite Traditions*, Missoula, Mont. 1977; W.H.Schmidt, 'Ein Theologe in salomonischer Zeit. Plädoyer für den Jahwisten', *BZ* 25, 1981, 82-102; S.E.McEvenue, 'The Elohist at Work', *ZAW* 96, 1984, 315-32; L.Ruppert, 'Die Aporie der gegenwärtigen Pentateuchdiskussion und die Joseferzählung', *BZ* 29, 1985, 31-48; G.Larson, 'The Documentary Hypothesis and the Chronological Structure of the Old Testament', *ZAW* 97, 1985, 316-33. See also the bibliographical studies by R.J.Coggins, 'A Century of Pentateuchal Criticism', *CQR* 166, 1965, 149-161, 413-425; E.Otto, 'Stehen wir vor einem Umbruch in der Pentateuchkritik?', *VuF* 22, 1977, 82-97.

The documentary hypothesis has recently been challenged by R.N.Whybray, *The Making of the Pentateuch: A Methodological Study*, Sheffield

1987; he envisages a collector at work not before the sixth century BCE who worked with material from folklore which need not necessarily have been old, and with his own imagination.

7d. For the Joseph narrative cf. G.von Rad, 'The Joseph Narrative and Ancient Wisdom', in *The Problem of the Hexateuch* (see above, § 6b), 292-300, and *Die Josephsgeschichte*, Neukirchen 1954 (he argues that the tradition has the character of wisdom); J.Vergote, *Joseph en Égypte*, Louvain 1959 (cf. the reviews by S.Morenz, *TLZ* 84, 1959, 401-16, and S.Herrmann, *TLZ* 75, 1960, 827-30); L.Ruppert, *Die Josepherzählung der Genesis*, Munich 1965; R.N.Whybray, 'The Joseph Story and Pentateuchal Criticism', *VT* 18, 1968, 522-8; D.B.Redford, *A Study of the Biblical Story of Joseph*, Leiden 1970; G.W.Coats, 'The Joseph Story and Ancient Wisdom', *CBQ* 35, 1973, 285-97; H.Donner, *Die literarische Gestalt der alttestamentlichen Josephgeschichte*, Heidelberg 1975. A Meinhold, 'Die Gattung der Josephgeschichte und des Esterbuches: Diasporanovelle, 1', *ZAW* 87, 1975, 306-24, argues for the late character of the story. Cf. also H.C.Schmitt, *Die nichtpriesterliche Josephgeschichte*, Berlin 1986; L.Schmidt, *Literarische Studien zur Josephgeschichte*, Berlin 1986, which carry on the best traditions of the documentary hypothesis.

J.Van Seters, *Abraham in History and Tradition*, New Haven and London 1975; H.H.Schmid, *Der sogenannte Jahwist*, Zurich 1976; and J.Vorländer, *Die Entstehung des jehowistischen Geschichtswerkes*, Frankfurt-Bern 1978, agree on the late dating of J, though they use different methods. See also the next chapter.

8

THE INDIVIDUAL SOURCES: THE YAHWIST
AND THE ELOHIST

1. Characteristics of the Yahwist

In the classical formulation of the documentary hypothesis, both E
and J stand out from the other sources by virtue of their predominantly narrative character. J is held to differ from E in the relatively
few legal texts which it contains, though as we have seen, the
attribution of legal texts to the two earliest sources cannot be
sustained. God is called by his name YHWH (hence the name given
to the source but with the limitations indicated above, 7.5a) before
the revelation made to Moses, an episode which E narrates in Exod.3,
P in Exod.6. J too seeks to fix a point from which this name was used:
Gen.4.26, that is, after the episode of Cain and Abel; however, the
name of God and his title are already mentioned in the J narrative
of the creation (Gen.2.4bff.), producing the expression *YHWH 'elōhīm*
(all EVV 'LORD God'), which has not been adequately explained.
Of course, after the revelation made to Moses the other sources also
use the divine name, and therefore from then on it is no longer a
distinctive element. Whereas E and P, in connecting the revelation
of the divine name with the beginning of the Mosaic faith, have
certainly handed down a datum which seems very likely in the field
of the history of religion, J insists on the theological concept of
continuity which the other two sources do not know, or express in a
substantially different way: that is to say, for J there is no break
in continuity between the creation narrative and the patriarchal
traditions and that of Moses, whereas E and P prove more interested
in underlining the break between the patriarchal era and its revelation, and that of Moses.

The divine name is a criterion which is always relative and it ends
at the beginning of Exodus. In addition, there is a series of other
elements which allow us to distinguish between J and E. J calls Sinai
by that name, whereas E, followed by Deuteronomy, always uses

Horeb. The native inhabitants of Palestine appear as 'Canaanites' in J and as 'Amorites' in E, which is again followed by Deuteronomy in this respect. The ultimate implications of this latter term escape us, and in any case it does not seem to be connected with the mention of the race of the same name in the ancient Near East. In J Moses' father-in-law (and he is still the father of the same wife) is called Reuel, and in E Jethro. There are other differences of vocabulary, for example the use of different terms for 'maidservant'; and since the reference is often to the same person, it does not seem possible to attach the terminological difference to different functions. However, these are arguments which biblical criticism considers to be indicative rather than definitive; it is their number rather than their quality which makes the division between J and E probable. Therefore, as we saw at the end of the previous chapter, this division continues to be hypothetical. There are, though, certain features of content which, leaving aside the inevitable subjectivity in the evaluation, seem to put the scholar on less shaky ground. For example, J already has a kind of theology of history which sees the work of God developing in the sphere of secular history, of which he is the real motive force. In accordance with this criterion J completely transforms the sense of obviously mythical material like the story of the flood (Gen.6-8), while leaving the component elements formally intact; or it takes over without difficulty material which was originally not Israelite, like the story of Cain and Abel (Gen.4.1ff.). It finds no difficulty in locating the patriarchs near sanctuaries which were originally quite definitely Canaanite, like Shechem, Bethel, Mamre and so on, the use of which was later condemned by the prophets and the Deuteronomic history writing. These elements probably had nothing to do with the ancestors of Israel to begin with, but came to be connected with them through aetiological legends, for example the pillar of salt into which Lot's wife was transformed (Gen.19.26). All these materials have been put in chronological order following first a dynastic scheme (Abraham-Isaac-Jacob-Joseph) and then the itinerary of the exodus and the conquest, and in this form they are brought together in the confession of faith mentioned in the previous chapter. Once the creation story was put at the beginning, the scheme was complete. The result is a remarkably coherent narrative with an ideological content, even allowing that it is incomplete. The creation is followed by a break in relations between God and humankind caused by human sin; the creature wishes to become divine. Following this, it proves impossible to maintain relations within humankind, a development which is illustrated in the story of Cain and Abel.

Humankind degenerates to such an extent that God decides to destroy it by means of a flood, which only a single clan will escape. However, the new humanity which survives the flood is no better, as is shown by the story of the tower of Babel in Gen.11.1ff., originally an aetiology intended to explain the difference in human languages, but now inserted into a much wider context. God remedies this wholesale fall of humankind by choosing the head of a western semitic tribe, Abraham, to be the founder of what will be a new people; cf. his promise to Abraham, 'In you will all the peoples of the earth be blessed' (Gen.12.1ff.). God enters into solemn obligations (better, as we have seen, than 'a covenant') with Abraham (Gen.15.17). Notwithstanding the ingenuous and sometimes simplistic character of this vision of history, it cannot be denied that it is a first attempt at a synthesis, at seeing history as the causal and consistent development of interconnected events which are conditioned by one another and lead to a single goal. J thus forms the point of departure from a legendary and popular cycle of history to more advanced literary history. With J there comes into being the first nucleus of the Pentateuch as we have it today.

2. Reasons for the collection

Is it possible to establish at this point why J wanted to collect together his material in the manner indicated? There is a whole series of indications which allow us to answer this question in the affirmative, even if the circumstantial character of these elements imposes substantial limitations on the work of verification. It should be evident that its aim was not specifically historiographical, at least in the modern sense of the term. Until recently some ancient passages in poetry that we have looked at earlier (6.5), namely Gen.9.25-27; 49.1off.; and Num.24.17, were cited in this context, but we have seen that these poetic compositions cannot be assigned to the sources of the Pentateuch. The passage Gen.12.2 is interesting because it belongs to the material which can be attributed to J and not to the sources that it brought together. Here we find the phrase 'I will make your name great' pronounced by Yahweh to Abraham at the time of his calling. The phrase reappears with slight stylistic variants in II Sam.7.9b, in Nathan's promise to David, whereas the word *goy* used in the first passage, which in this context denotes nation in the political sense of the term, can only refer to the empire of David and Solomon and the Davidic dynasty, since it puts particular stress on its greatness (T.C.Vriezen and A.S.van der Woude*, 163). Again,

Gen.27.40 almost certainly speaks of Edomite attempts to take the Israelite yoke from their necks, which brings us to the end of Solomon's reign (I Kings 11.14-22). At all events, there are many indications that the mind of the redactors was directed towards the empire of David and Solomon, which they considered to be the logical conclusion of the prehistory of their people and the fulfilment of oracles which were either ancient or considered to be ancient.

Therefore, as Cazelles notes, here we have a dynastic document which sees Abraham as the ideal ancestor of David and his house. And in the person of David and in the fortunes of the dynasty all this will be fulfilled. Of course, if we accepted the proposal that J should be dated to a late period, this would have happened shortly before the exile or even during it, when the prospect of the survival of the dynasty seemed increasingly problematical, if not hopeless. At all events, then, it seems that here we have an apologetic political writing the aim of which was to provide theological legitimation for the monarchy and the house of David in the south, and that this legitimation came about through a choice of material which was thought to be ancient, enriched with prophecies, probably for the most part *ex eventu*, and the insertion of comments (like Gen.12.1ff.) by J into the whole. This gives rise to the theory according to which not only was the institution of the monarchy fully in conformity with the divine will, but David and his successors were also rulers by divine grace, to whom had been promised the eternal kingdom.

3. Date and composition

According to the founders of the documentary hypothesis, the earliest collection of these texts dated from shortly after the united monarchy, the end of the tenth and beginning of the ninth century BCE; recently it has even been suggested that a small part of it should be dated to the time at which David was king only over Judah, at Hebron (II Sam.1-4). That does not, of course, exclude the possibility of later material, or material which was revised at a later stage; it was thought that such a revision could be found in Gen.18.22-33, in which Abraham discussed with YHWH the influence of the possible presence of righteous men in Sodom and Gomorrah on the fate of the two places. This is a passage which is notably remote from the main theme of J and could reflect later thought on the fate of the righteous and their beneficial influence on their wicked neighbours.

The material which we find in J is decisively orientated on the south, i.e. on the kingdom of Judah. Not only does its obvious sympathy for the cause of David give it an important slant in this direction; the patriarchs make their home in the south where their sanctuaries are to be found, and turn their attention northwards only as to an inevitable staging area. There is now a certain consensus to this effect among scholars.

As far as the composition of J is concerned, I shall limit myself to those passages which are generally considered certain, leaving aside controversial sections. It will still be necessary to confine ourselves to Genesis: the situation in Exodus is so complex that it is impossible to assign material to sources with any degree of certainty. Following these criteria we have: Gen.2.4b-4.26; 6.1-8; 9.18-24; 10.8-19, 28-30; 11.1-9, 28-30; 12.1f. (each with what is probably a small insertion from P); 18.1ff.; 28.13-16; 29.2-19, 31-35; 43.1ff.; 50.1-11. Chapters 6-8 and 37 are particularly interesting and are used as examples in introducing the principle of division into sources.

4. Characteristics of the 'Elohist'

The chief difficulty confronting the scholar in a study of E is the fact, indicated above, that only a few fragments of this source have come down to us. Here, of course, I am referring only to those passages which can be assigned to E with a reasonable degree of certainty. As we have seen, there are many scholars who have denied the existence of E, regarding the material of which it is composed merely as a complement to J. Today those who work with the documentary hypothesis generally accept the existence of E as an autonomous source, but its sparseness remains, and constitutes the principal problem. The 'Uppsala school' would regard E simply as a rather later phase of the redaction of the material contained in J, but this explanation does not seem convincing, because of the clearly contradictory material which is contained in the two sources. We saw in § 1 above the lexicographical characteristics which distinguish E from J; moreover, E has no creation narrative, unless the term 'elōhīm attached to YHWH is an indication that the two sources are combined, at least in Gen.2.4b-3.24; there is no trace in the rest of the narrative. Until recently people thought that E began in Gen.15, where it would provide a parallel to Gen.12, but the difficulties of dividing this chapter into the traditional sources are such that virtually all modern scholars have given it up. In other words, in the present state of research we cannot even say where E begins.

5. Scope of the collection

The few passages which we can assign with a greater or lesser degree of probability to E immediately show characteristic traces of its redaction. First of all, there is no trace of any discussion of the kind of historical and political problems that we found in J, and this does not fail to have a positive influence on the manner in which the ancient traditions were handed down: almost all of it is characterized by a greater freshness and an absence of extraneous preoccupations. But the religious situation is different. J did not have any problems in presenting the patriarchs as being in direct contact with YHWH, but E prefers contacts through intermediaries, by the intervention of angels or through dreams. J occasionally reports miraculous occurrences, whereas E abounds in narratives of this kind for the greater glorification of the God of Israel. E's discussion of theological problems is pronounced, whereas this happens only rarely in J (cf. Gen.18.22ff., a passage which I have already mentioned and which is probably late); cf. Gen.20.4ff.; 31.5. Its psychological subtlety has been generally reecognized: Gen.22 is sufficient evidence in this respect. Whereas J is indifferent to or equivocal about the Canaanites and their cult (which fits in perfectly with what we know of the policy of David and Solomon towards the non-Israelite population in their empire), E is negative. (Cf. Gen.35.1ff; Exod.32; Josh.24.24ff.) This attitude recalls that of the great prophets from the end of the ninth century to the beginning of the sixth century BCE. The title 'prophet' attached to men who have a particularly close relationship with God is also reminiscent of the prophetic movement (Abraham in Gen.20.7; Moses in Deut.34.10, even if, historically speaking, neither of these two were prophets). On the other hand, this criterion is quite untypical, given that a passage like Num.11.16-30, which speaks of the inspiration of the seventy elders of Israel and imagines all the members of the community to be divinely inspired, is generally assigned to a late phase of J. E shows a greater sensitivity to moral problems: J has no difficulty in recounting the misadventure which befell Abraham and Sarah in Egypt (Gen.12.10ff.), whereas E tries to show that no irreparable harm was done and that Abraham's lie was not really a lie, since Sarah was his half-sister (Gen.20.12). Another expresion of this sensitivity, which is by no means purely rhetorical, is the remark made by Joseph to his master's wife in Gen.39.9.

6. Date, place and composition

Here we find ourselves almost certainly at a period in which the prophet had a place of the utmost importance in Israelite religion and in which relations with the indigenous population of Canaan were particularly strained, especially in the religious sphere. The struggles of Exod.32 are not unlike those experienced by Elijah in I Kings 18, an episode which is immediately followed by a pilgrimage to Mount Horeb (ch.19). Thus everything seems to indicate that we are now in a period which reflects the struggle of the prophets: the *terminus ante quem* for the earliest phase is the fall of the kingdom in 722/21, since after that the material would have been transferred to the south to be further developed there. The places mentioned are predominantly in the north, and the cult of the golden 'calves' had its home there (cf.Exod.32 with I Kings 12).

Reasonably certain passages are; Gen.20.1ff.; 21.10-14; 22.1-19; 27.1ff. (combined with J); 28.10-12, 17-22; chs.29-34 (with J elements); 35-37 (with J and P); Exod.3.1ff. (with J); 11.1-3; 18.1ff.; 19.1ff. (with J, but generally doubtful); 32.1ff.; Num.12.1ff.; Deut.32.1ff.; 34.1ff. (with J).

BIBLIOGRAPHY

1. Cf. the bibliographies to the previous chapters and H.W.Wolff, 'The Kerygma of the Yahwist', *Int* 20, 1966, 129-58; W.Brueggemann, 'David and his Theologian', *CBQ* 30, 1968, 156-81; L.Schmidt, 'Überlegungen zum Jahwisten', *EvTh* 37, 1977, 230-47.

Cf. also F.García López, 'Del "Yahwista" al "Deuteronomista"'. Estudio crítico de Genesis 24', *RB* 87, 1980, 242-73; M.Rose, *Deuteronomist und Jahwist*, Zurich 1981; J.Van Seters, 'The Place of the Yahwist in the History of Passover and Mazzot', *ZAW* 95, 1983, 167-82; J.R.Lundbom, 'Abraham and David in the Theology of the Yahwist', in *The Word of the Lord Shall Go Forth. Essays... D.N.Freedman*, Philadelphia 1983, 203-9; F. Kohata, *Jahwist und Priesterschrift in Exodus 3-14*, Berlin 1986, offers a new attempt to divide this difficult pericope of Exodus into sources.

2. For the reference to Cazelles cf. the review in *OA* 15, 1977, 354-7.

3. W.Resenhöff, *Die Genesis im Wortlaut ihrer drei Quellenschriften*, Berne 1974, has re-examined the individual sources in Genesis. One proposal which would date J even later is that by F.H.Cryer, 'On the Relationship between the Yahwistic and the Deuteronomistic History', *BN* 29, 1985, 58-

74, who would like to believe that Dtr (below, 12) has been subjected to a J redaction; that would also explain why in the past so many authors have thought that they can rediscover J in the 'Former Prophets'.

4-5. There is a bibliographical study by J.F.Craghan, 'The Elohist in Recent Literature', *BTB* 7, 1977, 23-35; see also the texts quoted in the previous chapter. Also H.W.Wolff, 'The Elohistic Fragments in the Pentateuch', *Int* 26, 1972, 158-73; H.Klein, 'Ort und Zeit des Elohisten', *EvTh* 37, 1977, 247-60. For Gen.15 cf. *inter alia* J.Ha, *Genesis 15: A Theological Compendium of Pentateuchal History*, Berlin 1988, where there is also a bibliography with comments relating to this important chapter.

5. For Gen.22 cf. the classical study by E.Auerbach, *Mimesis*, ch.1.

6. K.Jaroš, *Die Stellung des Elohisten zur kanaanäischen Religion*, Göttingen and Freiburg CH 1974; J.Schüpphaus, 'Volk Gottes und Gesetz beim Elohisten', *TZ* 31, 1975, 193-210.

9

THE INDIVIDUAL SOURCES:
DEUTERONOMY

1. Characteristics

The name of the book is derived from that borne by the LXX translation: 'second law'. The early translators thus seem to have been aware of the fact that the fifth book of the Pentateuch constitutes a later phase in the redaction of the whole work, even if they attributed this phase to the last period of the life of Moses. From the standpoint of the documentary hypothesis, D coincides for the most part with the book of Deuteronomy: only the poems Deut.32 and 33 and the last chapter do not belong to the source.

Deuteronomy has a style which is easy to recognize. There are many stereotyped phrases like 'With all your heart and with all your mind', a formula which describes love towards God; or 'The place which YHWH has chosen, to make his name dwell there', for the central sanctuary, implicitly the temple of Jerusalem; 'With powerful hand and outstretched arm', as a description of the power of God. The form is almost always homiletical, and in fact the work is presented as a speech made by Moses to the Israelites on the plains of Moab, in front of the Jordan, before the entry into the promised land. Exhortations in the second person abound, either in the singular or in the plural; there are repetitions typical of direct speech, intended to make it easier for the listeners to remember. There are a number of typical theological concepts: predominant among these is that of reward, in which the sinner goes to ruin and the righteous receives material well-being and spiritual blessings; there are particularly humanitarian touches, for example in chs.20; 22; 23, or the position of the woman in the Deuteronomic version of the Decalogue. Some passages are duplicates or updatings of legal texts contained in the 'Book of the Covenant' (cf. above, 6.7b) and it has some lexicographical characteristics in common with E (cf. above, 8.1). And although it is easy to divide the work into different sections, its linguistic and ideological characteristics give it a marked uniformity, which is also recognizable in a good translation.

In his 1971 study S.Herrmann noted that Deuteronomy and the Deuteronomistic work are clearly the central element of the Hebrew Bible; in them, in fact the pre-exilic material comes together, whereas the whole of the post-exilic development emanates from them. It is also interesting to see that in Deuteronomy the celebration of the passover and the theme of the exodus are central elements, unlike the situation in P, where the stress falls on the great autumn festival and its elements. Moreover the divine presence in the sanctuary is seen as that of the name, YHWH, a feature which cannot easily be assessed and probably did not antedate the work.

2. The problem of origins

(a) Among the various problems in the higher criticism of the Hebrew Bible, that of the origins of D seems to have been stated best. Some fathers of the church – Athanasius, Jerome, Procopius of Gaza and John Chrysostom – already related the content of the book to the religious reform carried out by Josiah, king of Judah, in the years 622-621 BCE, which is noted in II Kings 22 and 23, and also in II Chron.34 and 35. But the critical presentation of this theory of the origins of Deuteronomy was only made at the beginning of the last century by W.M.L.de Wette (already mentioned above), though it soon became one of the axiomatic components of historical criticism. Of course differences continued to exist over the dimensions of the book discovered in the temple and how far this book had in fact become part of Deuteronomy. But there is no doubt that de Wette's theory still dominates the field and that it provides one of the few virtually certain dates in the literary history of the Bible.

De Wette's work, with its somewhat prolix title, thus marks a memorable development not only in connection with the fifth book of the Pentateuch but also in the whole history of the Pentateuch.

In his argument de Wette began by noting that, as is obvious to those who accept the tradition, the narrative of the Pentateuch refers, or means to refer, to people and events earlier than the conquest of Canaan by Israel or its ancestors. However, a critical examination of this starting point shows:

(i) That there is a very close connection between the Deuteronomic legislation and the 'book of the law' discovered in the Jerusalem temple about 622-21 BCE in the reign of Josiah, and that it constituted the basis for the religious reform carried out under the auspices of the sovereign.

(ii) That particular features of style and content which are partly attested in the 'former prophets' appear in Deuteronomy.

Only the first of these two questions had been noted by the ancient writers and formulated with a flash of intuition: it was for de Wette to present the whole matter in critical and systematic form, thus providing, as we have seen, the first relatively certain data for historical criticism.

What was the basis on which de Wette presented his arguments? One incontrovertible fact for him was that the threats which appear in II Kings 22.13-17 are to be connected with the curses contained in Deut.27; 28. Furthermore, the implementation of Josiah's reform follows themes which are not only present in Deuteronomy but typical of it: the centralization of the cult in Jerusalem (II Kings 23.5-9/Deut.12; 16, and other minor passages; of course Jerusalem is not mentioned, for that would be too gross an anachronism, but there is mention of the 'place which Yahweh will have chosen to make his name to dwell there'); condemnation and extermination of pagan and syncretistic cults, especially astral cults (II Kings 23.4-11/Deut.17.2ff.); the cults on the so-called 'high places' coupled with sacral objects like the *maṣṣēbōt* (sacred stones) and the *ᵃšērīm* (sacred posts or trees) (II Kings 23.4f., 13-19//Deut.12.2f.; 16.21f.); sacral prostitution (II Kings 23.7/Deut.23.18f.); the cult of '*molok*', divination, spiritualism, etc. (II Kings 23.10,24//Deut.18.10f.); and yet other elements.

(*b*) There is no doubt that de Wette succeeded in establishing a series of relevant parallels, which were sufficient to prove beyond any question the existence of a relationship between the book and Josiah's reform. But this relationship does not exist in every case; at least once we may note a remarkable discrepancy between the former and the latter. In Deut.18.6ff. the levites are in all respects equivalent to the priests of the temple, after being concentrated there; in II Kings 23.9, however, they are assigned a markedly subordinate position equivalent to that of the priests from the suppressed sanctuaries, provided that the II Kings passage can be interpreted in this way. Such an interpretation has been authoritatively rejected by J.Lindblom in his study; he observes with strong arguments that the limitations in question are not imposed on the levites, but on the priests from the dismantled 'high places'. Now if it is true that this discrepancy can be explained in the context of possible struggles and jealousies among the various categories of priests, each one concerned to maintain his vested interests, it would seem very strange that Josiah's reform should be allowed to diverge from what should have been its written programme in a point of such great importance. Furthermore, the two texts which narrate the implementation of the reform differ markedly: II Chron.34.2-7 makes the reform begin a few years before the finding of the 'book of the law' and puts it in the context of the attempts of Josiah (or better of his ministers – at that time the king was only sixteen years old) to shake the Assyrian yoke off his neck, and this note is more trustworthy than that in II Kings, which presents the events in perhaps rather a simplistic way, as if it had been the finding of the book which had moved the king's heart towards reform. For this reason, too, the classic theory about the origin of Deuteronomy is now being subjected to critical verification, as it presents some elements which are difficult to reconcile.

(c) The matter-of-factness of de Wette's work should certainly be noted. This is a feature which distinguishes it from some later studies. He might have established the existence of close connections between the 'book of the law' and Deuteronomy, but he did not accept that the two were identical. It is also interesting that he never pronounced on the origins of either the book of the law or of Deuteronomy (except to admit the relationship indicated above); he simply raised the possibility that the work had been composed by Hilkiah the priest, a theme which was to appear constantly from the last century onwards, sometimes paraphrased in a more or less elegant manner with the expression *pia fraus* (pious fraud). However, he never followed up the hint; he felt that it was enough to have found a kind of critical Archimedean point on which he could hinge all the traditions of the church and the synagogue about Pentateuchal origins, an opinion which one cannot but accept.

I shall limit myself here to giving some of the salient data in the development of the literary criticism of Deuteronomy, drawing heavily on the works of M.Weinfeld and S.Loersch, which should be consulted for all questions of detail.

For almost a century the question of Deuteronomy remained at the point where de Wette had left it. His theory was generally accepted: Wellhausen established agreements between J and E and Deuteronomy, and between this and the account of Josiah's reform in the books of Kings and Chronicles, but still did not see what Loersch called the 'distinctive problem' of the book, a problem which is expressed in a fact which should have been obvious after de Wette's discovery, namely that 'the problems of Deuteronomy are substantially different from those of the other sources of the Pentateuch' (Loersch, 24).

3. The revival of studies

From the end of the last century to the beginning of the 1930s we witness a revival of studies. Among the most important works the commentary by C.Steuernagel should be singled out. It is a book which even today is the starting point for anyone setting out to work on the theme, in that it collects together the results of the author's studies from 1894 on. For Steuernagel, chs.1-4; 5-11; 28ff. were a later framework for the central body of legislation (chs.12-26). This situation provided the proof that Deuteronomy could not have been written down all at once, but was rather the product of complex editorial work. It was also Steuernagel who drew the critics' attention to the distinction between the passages in the second person singular and those in the second person plural, a criterion by which he thought it possible to establish the original texts in comparison with later redactional additions, which he did with what Loersch has aptly called 'what seems to us a bewildering certainty'. He distinguished four later redactional additions.

Another extremely important work, because of its pioneering character, is that of A.Klostermann. In his second volume he showed how Deuteronomy is at the same time both 'law' and a commentary on laws, independent of them and presented as oral instruction. Having established this, he arrived at the important hermeneutical conclusion that Deuteronomy is the product of the 'living practice of public teaching about the law'. As Loersch rightly points out, he was the first to see that an oral tradition of a catechetical type was the basis of Deuteronomy, and with this anticipated by many years the study of literary genres in the book.

In the wake of the Wellhausen school it is not surprising that there were attempts to discover sources, or at least sub-sources, within Deuteronomy. J.Hempel made an attempt in 1914, but the matter was not followed up, at least along the lines which he indicated.

Critics of de Wette's thesis, up to that point accepted without further discussion, are also important. In 1922, G.Hölscher argued that Deuteronomy was in fact a post-exilic work about a century later than Josiah's reform; negative arguments of a similar kind were put forward by T.Oestreicher in 1923 and in various studies which came from the pen of A.C.Welch. With marked differences of detail, these authors maintained that Deut.12.14 and all the similar phrases scattered through the book should not be translated 'In the place which YHWH shall have chosen... to make his name dwell there', but 'In every place which YHWH has chosen, in each one of his tribes...', arguing from this that the work does not fight for a centralization of the cult as in Josiah's reform, but on the contrary for a plurality of sanctuaries. They also noted that, as we have already seen, the chronology of events given by II Kings 22; 23 is qualitatively inferior to that of II Chron. 34; 35, insisting on the basis of the latter that Josiah's aim was not so much a reform in the religious field as a political liberation from the Assyrian yoke. Now while the first affirmation will not hold up under criticism, the second seems to be extremely probable, again as we have already seen.

4. The genres and Deuteronomy

With the progressive application to the Pentateuch of the methods inaugurated by Gunkel, Deuteronomy too began to be analysed in terms of the history of the traditions and the material which it contained, rather than in more narrowly literary terms. The method opened up completely new prospects. Among its precursors we find F.Horst and A.Alt, who has already been mentioned. For Horst, the starting point is the varied terminology which Deuteronomy adopts for the laws which it contains: *ḥuqqīm* and *mišpāṭīm*, terms which refer respectively to sacral law and the norms for everyday life. On the basis of this classification, Horst attempted to assemble the former in a decalogue of five pairs of laws, arguing that this decalogue would have constituted the nucleus from which the central section, chs.12-26, emerged. Its origin was to be sought among levitical circles in the north, cf.Deut.27, which describes how it was promulgated at Shechem. As we have seen, Shechem was the site of a most important sanctuary in the pre-monarchical period and certainly continued to be extremely important even after the founding of the Jerusalem sanctuary and the other sanctuaries in the north after the division of the empire of David and Solomon. On the fall of the northern kingdom in the eighth century these norms then, it is argued, passed to the south. Horst did not have a classification to propose for the regulations concerned with everyday life, which in any case consisted of material which was partly parallel to other material attested in the earlier sources (above, 6.7). On the other hand, it could be argued against Horst's theory that while such a neat distinction between sacral law and secular law comes readily to the modern Western mind, on the most favourable of hypotheses it seems extremely doubtful in a society which did not recognize distinctions of this kind. Worship and everyday life were an integral and indivisible part of one and the same reality, and the violation of a ritual regulation was treated with the same strictness as that of an ethical regulation. The penalties for sacrilege and for homicide were precisely the same, since sacrilege destroyed the stability of the community, and homicide was an offence directed against God, the giver of life. The formal distinction between laws formulated in apodeictic terms and those formulated in casuistic terms proposed by Alt was much more apposite; we shall return to it (below 11.4) when discussing law in Israel and in the Ancient Near East.

5. The studies of von Rad and Noth

On the premises of Gunkel, Horst and Alt, von Rad and Noth (already mentioned above) constructed an edifice the foundations - and to a great extent the structure – of which must be taken into account even by those who have a critical view of them. This appears clearly in the work of L.Perlitt, who is extremely critical of the work done in recent decades and especially over the last ten years, but hardly ever attacks the two authors in question, to whom he declares himself to be much in debt, even if he makes some criticism of details here and there.

Von Rad's first monograph dates from 1929. In it, he applies Gunkel's methods consistently to Deuteronomy, seeking a way out of the vicious circle in which studies seemed to have become inextricably involved. Comparisons between Deuteronomy and Josiah's reform come to an end and so do attempts at dividing up Deuteronomy (apart, of course, from those which arise naturally from the text). The starting points are, rather, on the one hand the formal characteristics of the text and on the other its content, while von Rad again examines the relationship between the parallel laws in the 'Book of the Covenant' (above, 6.7) and in Deuteronomy, seeking to establish the modifications in form or substance which were made in the course of transition from one to the other. Von Rad's discovery here is of crucial importance: Deuteronomy is addressed to Israel both as people of God and as a nation in the ethnic and political sense of the term. The people are called the 'am qādōš (= holy people) or denoted with semantically similar phrases; Deuteronomy is addressed to them with a preaching or catechesis which has still not been clearly defined. This discovery explained some of the central concepts in Deuteronomy: the centralization of the cult, the particular sense of responsibility towards neighbours (understood, again, in the ethnic categories which I have indicated), the doctrine of reward, the theology of the divine name which dwells in the temple (a valid way of confessing the divine presence in the sanctuary without binding it to the sanctuary as a complex of buildings). Nor were von Rad's discoveries exhausted by establishing this relationship between God and his people and the key importance that it has in Deuteronomic theology. The significance attached to the concept of the people of God in Catholic theology during and after the Second Vatican Council is well known.

In his work published in 1938, which we have already examined (above, 7.6c), and in which he put forward his theory about the ancient confessions of faith (though this, as we have seen, has meanwhile proved to be untenable), von Rad proposed as a working hypothesis the existence of an ancient 'covenant festival' originally celebrated in the sanctuary of Shechem and connected with a festival of the conquest celebrated at Gilgal. The earliest part of the Pentateuch would have been formed around these two liturgies. Now according to this theory, Deuteronomy will have been the product of such liturgies, which are thought to be still clearly visible at salient points; in chs. 1-12 we have a summary of the events which took place between the departure from Sinai and the arrival before the Jordan, a summary followed by an exhortation; in 12.1-26.15 we would have the proclamation of the law (or perhaps better, following the etymology of *tōrāh*, the divine 'instruction'); in 26.16-19 we would have the obligation of the people to obey the divine will, while in chs.27; 28 we would have a series of blessings and curses, depending on the attitude of the people towards the obligations they had undertaken. Moreover, von Rad believed that he could discover some of these elements in the section of the Sinai pericope attributed to E, but we have seen the difficulty created by such an attribution and will be examining other elements below (11.9). Von Rad therefore concluded that the origins of Deuteronomy are to be sought in the liturgy indicated and in its four constituent parts, supplemented of course by successive amplifications; this also explains the substantially unitary character of the composition, despite the sections into which it can obviously be divided. There would be sections which would correspond to the various stages of the liturgy,

In a third work on the question, written in 1948, von Rad brought out the essentially 'lay' character and orientation of the preaching and instruction in Deuteronomy. In other words, more than being divine 'law', Deuteronomy is preaching to the people on the divine law. In this way von Rad took up again a theme which had earlier been put forward by Klostermann (mentioned above), but which contrasted with elements of Horst's theory.

Von Rad believed that the theme of the centralization of the cult in the sanctuary of Jerusalem, which was identified by the generic phrase 'the place which Yahweh has chosen, to make his name dwell there', and which was usually attributed to the last phase of the Deuteronomistic tradition, that of Josiah's reform, has very old roots. The first central sanctuary of Israel would in fact have been the ark, which would take us back into the pre-monarchical period, to the last two centuries of the second millennium BCE; and the ark would have had this function in the sacral tribal league, a concept which, as we have seen, von Rad took over from Noth. This is therefore probably an element which the reformers of the seventh century wished to restore, together with that of the holy war (with which it was intimately involved) and other ancient institutions which had fallen into disuse or had been distorted. In contrast to Horst, von Rad sees the country levites of the north behind this movement towards restoration. These levites will have been estranged from the cult soon after the division of the kingdom of David and Solomon under Jeroboam I (I Kings 12.31), but will have been supported by the strictly Israelite population against the Canaanites. We also find this population as supporters of orthodoxy in the south during the same period; it is known as the 'am hā'āreṣ (= 'people of the land'), an expression which is not to be confused with the same term in late Judaism, though it is lexically identical. In the later period it is used disparagingly. This last explanation was developed in 1956 by H.-W.Wolff and in 1958 by F.Dumermuth, but was not new in itself; it had already been proposed in 1926 by A.Bentzen.

The question whether Deuteronomy originated at Shechem or more generally in the north has been the subject of a number of studies following the work of Alt in 1953. Authors have included G.E.Wright (who laid special stress on the role of the levites) in 1954, J.L'Hour in 1962, N.Lohfink in 1963 and G.Schmitt in 1964. In addition to refining the proposals put forward by von Rad, thes works confirmed the theory proposed earlier by Klostermann, according to which Deuteronomy was the product of a homiletical and catechetical public proclamation. Von Rad then confirmed and developed his own position in the first volume of his *Old Testament Theology* in 1957 and his 1964 commentary.

On the other hand, despite these attempts to argue otherwise, it is clear that Deuteronomy originates from Jerusalem, in the sphere around the temple and perhaps even in the last years of the palace; this is all that we can establish by critical means. It is not possible to establish whether there are sections or fragments which arose elsewhere and in earlier periods.

Martin Noth made an important contribution to the solution in 1943 by putting forward the hypothesis of a continuous 'Deutero-nomistic' history work (Dtr, cf. below, 12). As far as Deuteronomy is concerned, he assigned to Dtr chs.1-2 and perhaps also 4, along with 31.1-13, 24-26a and sections from ch.34. Taking up earlier suggestions, he regarded the passages formulated in the second person singular as the earliest, and those in the second person plural as the product of later amplifications, which arose through the need for public reading and explanation, together with interpretation of the law.

6. The last quarter of a century

In the course of recent years the discussion thus begun has been effectively carried forward in a series of monographs. Particularly important are the writings of N.Lohfink (1962, 1963 and 1964) on chs.29-30, chs.5-11 and the relationship between Deuteronomy and Josiah's reform respectively; of J.G.Plöger (1967) on 1.6-3.29 and on ch.28; and of R.P.Merendino (1969) on chs.12-26. Thus, as can be seen, virtually the whole book has been re-examined.

Basing his study on the above-mentioned works of Steuernagel, Klostermann and von Rad, Lohfink sees chs.5-11, on the basis of an analysis which uses techniques drawn from modern linguistics, as a section juxtaposed with the material contained in 12.1-26.16; this last section is in fact a collection of commandments and prohibitions, while the first is centred on the 'great commandment', for which it acts so to speak as a framework in presenting primary and secondary material. The change from the second person singular to the second person plural is not in every case indicative of different strata but is only an important stylistic element which serves to intensify the effect of the discourse. Deuteronomy 5-11 is neither preaching nor catechesis, but contains liturgical texts intended to be repeated periodically. Their archetypes go back to the earliest period in Israel, probably to the end of the second millennium BCE. It is therefore by no means strange that Deuteronomy has been connected with the person of Moses and that from its origins it has consisted of written material. Lohfink summarized his position in the argument again in

1965. Continuing his researches he showed how the Deuteronomist, to whom we shall return later (below, 12) built on this basis, introducing the work with Deut.1-4 and putting it as a prologue to the 'former prophets'. The process of growth will thus have followed more or less these lines: first of all the liturgy of the pre-exilic cult; then, during the exile, the insertion of Deuteronomy into the Deuteronomistic history work; and finally, in the post-exilic period, its addition to the Pentateuch as a conclusion.

To avoid misunderstanding, however, in a 1964 study Lohfink attempted to make it clear that if the concept of the 'covenant' is central in Deuteronomy (as God's obligation towards the people and the people's obligation towards God), and this element has its logical consequence in the Deuteronomistic history work, it does not appear without a break. The reasons for this phenomenon seem to be essentially theological: there is a danger that the legal categories in which relations between God and the people are expressed will end by obscuring YHWH's special character; that fulfilling the commandments wil create a sense of personal righteousness, of moral self-sufficiency, with the consequence of making a claim on God. In the end, given this approach, which argues in terms of blessing and cursing, fulfilment and violation, the concepts of grace and forgiveness will be completely absent. The concept of *berīt* is thus an inadequate category for denoting relationships between God and the people and therefore must be constantly brought up to date and even corrected.

The works of Plöger and Merendino are also important, but as they are very technical, it is enough to give a brief account of them. Plöger clarifies both the origins of the material contained in the section 1.6-3.29 and the blessings and curses of ch.28. He shows how these last originally belonged in autonomous lists, each one characterized by particular stylistic characteristics (use of the participle, etc.). Merendino distinguishes in the central section (chs.12-26) a pre-Deuteronomic stratum of tradition, a second stratum of Deuteronomic redaction and finally a post-Deuteronomic redaction: the parallel passages to those contained in the 'Book of the Covenant' do not depend on that book but are the product of an autonomous tradition; nor are the passages which speak of the centralization of the cult always unitary and consistent, seeing that they seem to be governed by such different criteria. This is also indicated by the diversity of the phraseology used (cf.12.1ff.; 14.23-27; 15.19-23; 16.1ff.; 17.8-11; 18.6; 26.1ff.).

The approaches of the two most recent works, by J.Lindblom and

M.Weinfeld, are different again. Both again see the origins of Deuteronomy in terms of a compilation by scribes or priests during the beginning of the seventh century (Lindblom stresses the period of persecution under king Manasseh). The former, however, does not see any affinity between Deuteronomy and the prophets, a problem which we shall discuss below (17); the latter takes a similar position, but does note the existence of marked affinities to the prophet Hosea. Weinfeld believes that the composition by scribes will have been influenced by the wisdom movement and the Assyrian vassal treaties. This would explain, first, the didactic character of the work and, secondly, the presence of elements which we shall examine shortly in Excursus 1.

7. Perplexities and problems

As we saw earlier (above, § 2), the problem of the discovery in the Jerusalem temple of the 'book of the law', a feature which is one of the hinges on which discussion of 'Josiah's reform' in II Kings 22-23 turns, has perplexed scholars for many decades; a number of them have even spoken, as we have seen, of a pious fraud. Two features cause this perplexity; the first is the theme of the discovery of the work. More or less miraculous discoveries are common throughout antiquity, including classical antiquity, and set out to give authority to a work which otherwise would not have it, or to justify unusual provisions which could not be justified in any other way. Another problem is that raised by the 'reform' in itself, in other words that of the transition to the centralization of the cult in the temple and the open struggle with Cannaanite religion on behalf of the oneness of Judah's own national god YHWH (this last feature was taken over by the prophets in particular, especially from Elijah onwards, if we can trust the sources). Are these unexpected provisions, coming from on high, a few years before the exile? We now know (as has been stressed particularly in the study by H.-D.Hoffmann) that the Deuteronomistic history work (cf. below, 12) sees the political and religious history of Judah as an alternation between pious and reforming rulers and wicked and anti-reforming (as we might put it) rulers, the latter always ready to re-establish good relations with Canaanite religion. This being the case, does it still make sense to talk about a reform which is said to have taken place following the discovery 'by chance' or by a miracle of a text which would have formed the basis for the reform? Let us remember here that the version in II Chron.34-35 certainly takes up the theme of the discovery of the scroll but does not attach a great deal of importance to it! There is clearly no question here of fradulent attitudes, nor is it worth raising the problem whether the content is more or less old (naturally, in the sense of material existing before the 'reform'). The whole narrative seems rather to be an artificial construction, an ideological product conceived of in the study, of which it is difficult to say whether and to what point it contains the recollection of real events. So the situation is not very different from that of the inter-testamental pseudepigrapha.

In conclusion, then, it is possible to state that although the problem of Deuteronomy is far from being resolved, it is certainly (as I have already said) the best defined of the questions about the Pentateuch. This is all the more so since the problematical character of the sources J and E has recently been reinforced. However, a complete and satisfactory solution to the problem is not to be expected in the near future, seeing that studies proceed with noteworthy circumspection.

BIBLIOGRAPHY

1. Bibliographical studies: M.Weinfeld, 'Deuteronomy – the Present State of Inquiry', *JBL* 86, 1967, 249-62; S.Loersch, *Das Deuteronomium und seine Deutungen*, Stuttgart 1967; cf. also E.W.Nicholson, *Deuteronomy and Tradition*, Oxford 1967. For Deuteronomy generally now see the work edited by N.Lohfink, *Das Deuteronomium*, Louvain 1985.

2. W.M.L. de Wette, *Dissertatio critica exegetica qua Deuteronomium a prioribus Pentateuchi libris diversum, alius cujusdam recentioris auctoris opus esse monstratur*, Halle 1805, republished in a German translation in *Beiträge zur Einleitung in das Alte Testament*, Darmstadt 1970; for the relation between the 'book of the law' and Josiah's reform on the one hand and Deuteronomy on the other cf. N.Lohfink, 'Die Bundesurkunde des Königs Josias', *Bibl* 44, 1963, 261-88, 461-98. Cf. also A.Rofè, 'The Strata of the Law about the Centralization of Worship in Deuteronomy and the History of the Deuteronomic Movement', *SVT* 22, 1972, 221-6; J.R.Lundbom, 'The Law Book of the Josianic Reform', *CBQ* 38, 1976, 293-302; E.Würthwein, 'Die Josianische Reform und das Deuteronomium', *ZTK* 73, 1976, 396-423.

3. C.Steuernagel, *Das Deuteronomium*, HKAT, ²1923; A.Klostermann, *Der Pentateuch*, two volumes, Leipzig 1893 and 1907, esp. II, 348ff.; J.Hempel, *Die Schichten des Deuteronomiums*, Leipzig 1914; G.Hölscher, 'Komposition und Ursprung des Deuteronomiums', *ZAW* 40, 1922, 161-255; T.Oest-reicher, *Das deuteronomische Grundgesetz*, Gütersloh 1923; A.C.Welch, *The*

Code of Deuteronomy, London 1924; id., 'When was the Worship of Israel centralized in the Temple?', *ZAW* 43, 1925, 250-5; id., *Deuteronomy, the Framework to the Code*, London 1932.

F.Foresti recently suggested in the course of preparing his doctoral thesis to the Pontifical Biblical Institute that 'the place which YHWH has chosen' has been deliberately kept anonymous because during the exile the worship in the ruined temple at Jerusalem was reduced to a minimum (cf. Jer.41.4ff.). From this it is possible to deduce that the demand for the centralization of the cult cannot be earlier than the exile and that it arose among the exiles (contrary to the theory of G.von Rad, above, p.130). F.Foresti, 'Storia della redazione di Dtn. 16, 18-18, 22 e le sue connessioni con l'opera storica deuteronomistica', *Teresianum* 39, 1988, 1-199. Fr Foresti died before he could discuss his dissertation.

4. F.Horst, *Das Privilegrecht Jahwes*, FRLANT 45, 1930 (= *Gottes Recht: Gesammelte Studien*, Munich 1961, 17-154); A.Alt, 'The Origins of Israelite Law', in his *Essays on Old Testament History and Religion*, ET Oxford 1966, 79-132.

5. L.Perlitt, *Bundestheologie im Alten Testament*, WMANT 36, 1969. See G.von Rad, *Das Gottesvolk im Deuteronomium*, Stuttgart 1929; id., 'The Form-Critical Problem of the Hexateuch', in his *The Problem of the Hexateuch and other Essays*, ET Edinburgh 1966, 1-78; id., *Studies in Deuteronomy*, ET SBT 9, 1953; J.A.Soggin, 'Der judäische *'am hā'āreṣ* und das Königtum in Juda', *VT* 13, 1963, 187-95; H.W.Wolff, 'Hoseas geistige Heimat', *TLZ* 81, 1956, 83-94 (= *Gesammelte Studien*, Munich 1964, 323-50); F.Dumermuth, 'Zur deuteronomischen Kulttheologie', *ZAW* 70, 1958, 59-98; A.Bentzen, *Die josianische Reform und ihre Voraussetzungen*, Copenhagen 1926; A.Alt, 'Die Heimat des Deuteronomiums', *Kleine Schriften* II, Munich 1964, 250-75; G.E.Wright, 'The Levites in Deuteronomy', *VT* 4, 1954, 325-30; J.L'Hour, 'L'Alliance de Sichem', *RB* 69, 1962, 5-36, 161-84, 350-68; G.Schmitt, *Der Landtag von Sichem*, Stuttgart 1964; M.Noth, *Überlieferungsgeschichtliche Studien*, Halle 1943; N.Lohfink, *Das Hauptgebot*, Rome 1963; id., 'Die Wandlungen des Bundesbegriffes im Buch Deuteronomium', *FS Karl Rahner* I, Freiburg 1964, 43-44; id., *Höre Israel!*, Düsseldorf 1965 (a synthesis of his views); J.G.Plöger, *Literarkritische, formgeschichtliche und stilkritische Untersuchungen zum Deuteronomium*, Bonn 1967; R.P.Merendino, *Das deuteronomische Gesetz*, Bonn 1969; J.Lindblom, *Erwägungen zur Herkunft der josianischen Tempelurkunde*, Lund 1971; M.Weinfeld, *Deuteronomy and the Deuteronomic School*, Oxford 1972; A.D.H.Mayes, 'Deuteronomy 4 and the Literary Criticism of Deuteronomy', *JBL* 100, 1981, 23-51. Cf.also G.Seitz, *Redaktionsgeschichtliche Studien zum Deuteronomium*, Stuttgart 1971. The study by S.Herrmann is 'Die konstruktive Rekonstrution', in *Probleme biblischer Theologie. FS Gerhard von Rad*, Munich 1971, 155-70. For the theology of the 'name' cf. T.N.D.Mettinger, *The Dethronement of Sebaoth*, Lund 1982, esp. 77ff., 124ff.; in an unpublished lecture given in the University of Rome in 1981 P.A.H.de Boer argued similarly about the importance of passover and the exodus in

Deuteronomistic thought. See also R.E.Bell, 'A Study of Deuteronomy based on Statistical Properties', *VT* 29, 1979, 1-22; H.Weippert, ' "Der Ort, den Jhwh erwählen wird, um dort seinen Namen wohnen zu lassen." Die Geschichte einer alttestamentlichen Formel', *BZ* 24, 1980, 76-94 (for the centralization formula); B.Halpern, 'The Centralization Formula in Deuteronomy', *VT* 91, 1981, 20-38; J.G.McConville, *Law and Theology in Deuteronomy*, Sheffield 1984. R.Albertz, *Persönliche Frömmigkeit und offizielle Religion*, Stuttgart 1978, 169ff. sees the change of person as the sign of a transition from collective religion to individual piety; cf. already G.Minette de Tillesse, 'Sections "tu" et sections "vous" dans le Deutéronome', *VT* 12, 1962, 29-87, for an examination of the phenomenon, and C.T.Begg, 'The Significance of Numeruswechsel [sic!] in Deuteronomy. The Pre-History of the Question', *ETL* 55, 1979, 116-74. For the problem of relationships with the other Pentateuchal sources cf. M.Rose, *Deuteronomist and Jahwist*, Zurich 1981, and N.P.Lemche, *Early Israel*, Leiden 1985, 372-7. An unconvincing attempt to date the language of Deut. to the earliest period of the monarchy has been made by C.Rabin, 'Discourse Analysis and the Dating of Deuteronomy', in *Interpreting the Hebrew Bible. Essays... E.I.J.Rosenthal*, Cambridge 1972, 171-7.

For the problem of reform and anti-reform in the Deuteronomistic history cf. H.-D.Hoffmann, *Reform und Reformen*, Zurich 1980, esp. 169ff. and passim. M.Smith, 'Pseudepigraphy in the Israelite Literary Tradition', *Pseudepigrapha* 1, Geneva 1972, (189-215) 203, regards the information about the discovery of the scroll as part of biblical pseudepigraphy (however, the term that he uses, a 'forgery', does not seem to me to be adequate: the problem of pseudepigraphy is much more complex, and modern criteria of professional ethics canot be applied to other periods and situations). Y.Yadin, *The Temple Scroll*, Jerusalem 1983, I, 82 n.76, has argued recently against the application of modern ethical criteria to ancient authors. W.Speyer, *Bücherfunde in der Glaubenswerbung der Antike*, Göttingen 1970, has an exhaustive discussion of the problem of the apparently casual discoveries of books in antiquity; cf. also B.J.Diebner, 'Gottesdienst II – Altes Testament', *TRE* 14, 1985, 5-28, esp.21-3, for the theme of the 'discovery' of objects, relics, etc., in antiquity.

Excursus I

COVENANT OR OBLIGATION AND DEUTERONOMIC THEOLOGY

1. A formulary

We have seen that one of the principal elements in the theology of Deuteronomy, which then went on to be an integral part of Deuteronomistic theology, is that of the *bᵉrît*, a word traditionally translated by 'covenant', 'alliance' or similar terms. In recent years the argument has increasingly been put forward that the word really means unilateral obligation (and in this sense it often appears in parallelism with the word 'oath'). This obligation may be of God towards his people or of the people towards God. Of course where we have a reciprocal obligation between two parties, for example of God towards the people and of the people towards God, the term 'covenant' is admissible, though not 'alliance', since there is obviously no notion of a bilateral agreement because of the qualitative difference betwen the two contracting parties. Human beings can only reject what God has promised them; otherwise what remains for them is to accept and act accordingly.

In recent years, a two-sided approach to the problem implicit in the term 'alliance' has led to a study of political alliances in the ancient Near East, to see if this might not also be the setting for the biblical concept, and the results of researches have been surprising. The vassal relationship in ancient Near Eastern treaties was grossly unequal when we consider the status of the parties involved, the great king and the vassal, and these treaties have provided an extremely useful collection of material for comparative purposes, even if it is not permissible to draw from it the extreme conclusions favoured by some scholars. These treaties range from the second half of the second millennium BCE down to the sixth century BCE.

The starting point was provided by the young Yugoslav scholar V.Korošec in his work on Hittite treaties in 1931, which was not concerned with possible biblical parallels; E.Bickerman in 1951 and

G.E.Mendenhall in 1954 made independent researches in this field. The discussion was then broken off for a few years until in 1960 a young German scholar, K.Baltzer, followed soon after by the American D.J.McCarthy, took it up again with important monographs. The German scholar R.Smend was more critical, but not necessarily opposed. Baltzer concentrated essentially on the biblical material in his study, which soon appeared in a second edition with an extended bibliography, while McCarthy collected all the available ancient Near Eastern parallels, as well as subjecting the biblical material to a new examination. An important series of studies by the South African F.C.Fensham appeared from 1960 on. The bibliography has meanwhile grown quite terrifyingly and has been collected in a critical study by F.Vattioni; it ends provisionally with a book by Perlitt published in 1969 which questions the whole validity of the enterprise, and some studies and a book by E.Kutsch in which the meaning 'obligation' rather than 'covenant' or 'alliance' is established for *berīt*.

2. Ancient 'vassal' treaties

The arguments put forward by Baltzer, independently of those formulated ten years earlier by Bickermann and five years earlier by Mendenhall, which were endorsed by McCarthy, may be summarized as follows. The structure of the vassal treaties of the ancient Near East, which begin with the Hittite treaties described by Korošec and go down to the Assyrian and Aramaean treaties from the first half of the first millennium, follows a constant pattern, so that it is legitimate to talk in terms of a 'vassal treaty formulary' or a 'formulary of alliance', depending on whether or not the parties are of equal status. There is substantial agreement over their composition, which follows this pattern:

(*a*) A preamble which introduces the great king who initiates the relationship in vassal treaties, which binds the two parties in an agreement between equals. In the first case (and this is more interesting in the present context), it can be a real Great King, like the king of the Hittites, of Assyria or Babylon, or a lesser ruler dealing with a still more minor figure or one who is for the moment in an inferior position. The vassal treaty is evidently more an imposition of the stronger on the weaker (though the former voluntarily limits his power) than a bilateral agreement with equal laws and duties for both parties: it is not difficult to see that the more powerful party had almost all the rights, the weaker one almost none.

(*b*) The preamble is followed by the history of the relationship between the two parties, written for obvious reasons in a way which demonstrates the generosity and the magnanimity of the stronger party.

(*c*) There follows a basic declaration of the features which will in future determine relationships between the parties, indicating the duties and the rights of each.

(*d*) This declaration of principle is followed by a detailed listing of the rights and duties of each party, which at first had been expressed only in general terms.

(*e*) There follows an invocation of one or more deities as witnesses and possibly guarantors of the pledges made.

(*f*) The document concludes with a series of blessings and curses, the former on those who are faithful to the obligations contracted, the latter on anyone who violates them.

When the treaty has been drawn up, it is notified to the vassal in terms fixed by custom and the relationship is completed. The text is transcribed in duplicate and deposited before the principal deity of each party, i.e. in the temple, and in some cases provision is made for it to be read periodically in public by the vassal. Having established this, Baltzer proceeded to review the Old Testament texts to see if it was possible to find a similar situation. The result of his research was positive, even if it was put in extremely cautious terms. 'On the basis of the texts that have been studied, I think it is possible to say that the covenant formulary, as a literary type, was familiar in Israel' (p.38). Baltzer shows similar prudence towards the vassal treaties and the formulae which govern the relationship between Yahweh and his people in the Hebrew Bible: 'on a strictly formal level these relations seem very close, but the difference seems all the greater at the level of substance' (p.91). Moreover, the Old Testament does not have any complete version of the 'formulary', whereas it is Deuteronomy and its dependent literature which make predominant use of it. Finally, on the basis of Deut.31.9ff., Baltzer conjectures a public reading of the texts at regular intervals in Israel also.

3. Treaties and 'covenant' or 'obligation'

McCarthy's work, which has now been published in a second completely revised edition, is much broader in its general approach and in its choice of comparative material; the Near Eastern texts cited run from the third millennium to the middle of the first, with special emphasis on western Semitic texts, which are geographically and ideologically closer to the biblical environment than the others. The results at which he arrives are important: 'I believe that, notwithstanding the more or less significant variations in the different manifestations of the treaty, there was in fact a formulary used by international agreements for the greater part of the history of the ancient Near East in the pre-Hellenistic period' (7). For the Hebrew Bible he arrived at similar results to those of Baltzer: the writings of Deuteronomy and the Deuteronomists are those where the best results are to be found, whereas the earlier strata of the Sinai pericope produce more negative results. In Deuteronomy, as has been indicated, we do in fact have an introduction with strong historical elements (chs.5-11), followed by a collection of laws (chs.12-26); the section ends with a series of blessings and curses. However, as we have seen, Plöger has demonstrated that the history of this last element contained in chs.27 and 28 is very complex and that, ruling out a composition at a single point in time, the pattern in question can be attributed to the redactional phase rather than to the original formulation.

4. Criticism

These relationships between Deuteronomy and the 'covenant formulary' in its variant of the vassal treaty have not, however, been accepted by all scholars in the past, and are now considered even less probable, if only for reasons of dating. Authoritative criticisms were made of the theory by G.Fohrer in 1964 and by F.Nötscher in 1965; Perlitt's work of 1969 then denied the antiquity of the concept, affirming that it was a theological creation of Deuteronomy or at best of the period immediately preceding, which came about under the impact of the preaching of the prophets. The texts regarded by some scholars as pre-Deuteronomic are: Gen.15.18; Deut.33.9; Josh.24.25; II Sam.23.5; I Kings 19.10, 14; Hos.6.7; 8.1; Pss.44.18; 89.7,35,40; 132.12, though for some of these a late date seems likely. In Deut.33 the mention of berit is generally recognized to be late; a Deuteronomic redaction seems obvious for Josh.24 and I Kings 19; Gen.15 is a very difficult passage throughout and at all levels, and it too is probably Deuteronomistic and therefore late, while the Psalms mentioned present complex problems of dating, as we shall see (below, 34.3). Only II Sam.23 and Hos.8.1 are dated to an early period and to the eighth century respectively, the former by the majority of scholars and the latter by almost all. So despite Perlitt's acute analysis it is impossible to demonstrate that there is no evidence at all for the term *bᵉrīt* in the period before Deuteronomy. Rather, the result of the examination suggests that the use of the term is rare in the time before Deuteronomy and that it is only with Deuteronomy that it came to represent a central concept.

BIBLIOGRAPHY

Bibliographical study: E.W.Nicholson, 'Covenant in a Century of Studies since Wellhausen', *OTS* 24, 1986, 34-69; cf. also his *God and His People*, Oxford 1986.

1. V.Korošec, *Hethitische Staatsverträge*, Leipzig 1931; E.Bickerman, 'Couper une Alliance', *Archives d'Histoire du Droit Oriental* 5, Brussels 1950 I, 133-56; G.E.Mendenhall, 'Ancient Oriental and Biblical Law' and 'Covenant Forms in Israelite Tradition', *BA* 17, 1954, 26-46, 50-76 (also published separately as *Law and Covenant in the Ancient Near East*, Pittsburgh 1955); K.Baltzer, *The Covenant Formulary*, ET Oxford 1971; D.J.McCarthy, *Treaty and Covenant*, Rome ²1978; id., *Old Testament Covenant*, Oxford 1972; R.Smend, *Die Bundesformel*, Zurich 1963; L.Perlitt, *Bundestheologie im Alten Testament*, WMANT 36, 1969; E.Kutsch, opp.citt. (see bibliography to 7.6b); M.Weinfeld, 'Covenant Terminology in the Ancient Near East and its Influence upon the West', *JAOS* 93, 1973, 190-9. For a critical bibiography see F.Vattioni, 'Recenti studi nell'alleanza nella Bibbia e nell'Antico Oriente', *AION* 27, 1967, 181-232 (cf. above, 7.6b). The relevant Near Eastern texts have recently been collected with commentaries by P.Kalluveetil, *Declaration and Covenant*, Rome 1982.

2. For the neo-Assyrian treaties cf. R.Frankena, 'The Vassal Treaties of Esarhaddon and the Dating of Deuteronomy', *OTS* 14, 1965, 122-54.

3. Cf.G.Fohrer, 'Prophetie und Geschichte', *TLZ* 89, 1964, 481-500 (= *Studien zur alttestamentlischen Prophetie*, BZAW 99, 1967, 265-93), esp. 488ff. (= 274ff.); F.Nötscher, 'Bundesformular und "Amtsschimmel" ', *BZ* 9, 1965, 182-214; L.Perlitt, op.cit. (above, § 5); D.J.McCarthy, *'Bᵉrīt* and Covenant in the Deuteronomistic History', *SVT* 23, 1972, 65-85; E.Kutsch, *'Karat bᵉrīt*, Eine Verpflichtung festsetzen', in *Wort und Geschichte. FS K.Elliger*, Neukirchen-Vluyn and Kevelaer 1973, 121-7; L.Wächter, 'Die Übertragung der Beritvorstellung auf Jahwe', *TLZ* 99, 1974, 801-16; E.Kutsch, ' "Ich will euer Gott sein": *bᵉrīt* in der Priesterschrift', *ZTK* 71, 1974, 361-88; C.Westermann, 'Genesis 17 und die Bedeutung von *bᵉrīt*', *TLZ* 101, 1976, 161-70; R.E.Clements, 'Covenant and Canon in the Old Testament', in *Creation, Christ and Culture. FS T.F.Torrance*, Edinburgh 1976, 1-12; P.Buis, *La notion d'Alliance dans l'Ancien Testament*, Paris 1976; J.Barr, 'Some Semantic

Notes on the Covenant', in *Beiträge zur alttestamentlichen Theologie. FS W.Zimmerli*, Göttingen 1977, 23-38; H.Cazelles, 'Alliance du Sinai, Alliance de l'Horeb et renouvellement de l'Alliance', ibid., 69-79; P.Sacchi, 'La legge e il patto nell'Antico testamento', *Hen* 7, 1985, 129-49.

In favour of the relatively late character of the concept (Deut. and Dtr) see now B.J.Diebner, 'Gottesdienst II – Altes Testament', *TRE* 14, 1985, 5-28, esp. 13f.

In favour of the antiquity of the concept of covenant and the term *berīt* cf.recently K.A Kitchen, 'Egypt, Ugarit Qatna and the Covenant', *UF* 11, 1979, 453-64; J.Day, 'Pre-Deuteronomic Allusions to the Covenant in Hosea and Psalm LXXVIII', *VT* 36, 1986, 1-12. The argument of the former, a distinguished Egyptologist, is that the concept is present in antiquity among other peoples, so it is not strange also to find it in Israel; but the question here is not that of the political concept but of the theological one. The latter complains about what he calls the 'pan-Deuteronomism' of Perlitt and thinks that he can find the concept in the passages cited. I have discussed these problems in the text.

Excursus II

DEUTERONOMIC OR DEUTERONOMISTIC PASSAGES IN THE OTHER BOOKS OF THE PENTATEUCH

1. The problem

Along with studies of Deuteronomy and the Deuteronomist, in recent years Deuteronomic or Deuteronomistic (in some cases a distinction between the two is difficult or even impossible) passages have been discovered in the books from Genesis to Numbers. The starting point for investigations has been a remark by Wellhausen, that in these books there are passages which cannot be assigned to any of the sources J, E or P, while their style recalls that of Deuteronomy or the Deuteronomist: these are passages which appear particularly in Exodus. Various authors have returned to this problem from time to time, but without resolving it or arriving at any significant results. It was the formation of Noth's hypothesis of the existence of a Deuteronomistic history work, in 1943, which restated the problem in new terms. Denying outright that the books in question could have undergone a Deuteronomistic revision, Noth suggested that in passages like Exod.23.20ff.; 34.10ff. 'the old text has been elaborated in Deuteronomistic style', whereas Num.21.33-35 would have been revised secondarily on the basis of Deut.3.1-3. This remark did not seem to raise problems of any importance, but the question changed once the number of passages involved proved to be greater and their content to be relevant from a historical and religious point of view. In this case we find ourselves confronted with a problem of undeniable importance, which is certainly not marginal and therefore cannot be brushed aside, as Vriezen* already pointed out in 1961.

Now in the calculation of these passages made by Perlitt, the number seems to have grown to such a point that they no longer represent merely a marginal phenomenon. Perlitt in fact mentions, among others, Exod.13.5,11; 19.3-6,11; 24.3-8; 32.9-14; 33.1; 34.10ff.: Num.11.12, 14.(16), 23; and in addition Gen.15.7, 18b, 19-21; 26.3b-

5; 50.24 and the Decalogue in its two versions, Exod. 20.1-17//Deut 5.6-21. If this list is correct, we find ourselves confronted with a situation like that of the Deuteronomistic insertions in Joshua and I and II Samuel.

2. Criteria of evaluation

One thing is certain. There are various criteria of evaluation and therefore it is extremely uncertain whether the description 'Deuteronomic' or 'Deuteronomistic' should be applied to some passages in Genesis-Numbers. To avoid this difficulty, the problem has been the subject of several studies. C.H.W.Brekelmans, who has studied the problem and presented his conclusions in monographs, rightly laments the lack of any objective criteria for recognizing the passages in question, and therefore assigning them to sources. In this connection he cites the perplexity of authors like S.Mowinckel in 1927 and more recently A.Weiser and H.Cazelles. A purely stylistic criterion is evidently not sufficient, given that a Deuteronomistic style could have existed even before the book itself, which we know to have been the product of a complex redaction, continuing the work of E, as the lexicographical affinities show. For Cazelles, typical elements of Deuteronomistic thought need to be present as well as affinities on a stylistic level; but, he continues, since these elements are absent from the passages in question, these are neither Deuteronomic or Deuteronomistic. The argument is developed by Brekelmans: in addition to stylistic affinity and the presence of elements attested in Deuteronomistic thought, it is also necessary that there should not be elements absent from Deuteronomistic thought, but attested in other Pentateuchal sources. Only when these three features are present can the material be assigned to Deuteronomy or to a kindred source.

Applying these criteria consistently, Brekelmans comes to the conclusion that only Exod.23.20-23 has contacts with Deut.7; with Vriezen* he then accepts that E, which we have seen to have contacts on an ideological level with the great prophets, and on the lexicographical level with Deuteronomy, had a continuation which we might call 'proto-Deuteronomic'. Other authors have come to similar conclusions with regard to Gen.50.24 and Exod.13.3-16. On the other hand, the information noted by Perlitt and especially the list of passages to which he refers cannot be put aside so easily; it is in fact evident that the verses which he cites from Gen.15 are also Deuteronomic or Deuteronomistic, and the same goes for the

Decalogue, to which the next excursus is devoted. So we should conclude that during the Babylonian exile or immediately afterwards there was a Deuteronomic or Deuteronomistic redaction of J and E; this is the only explanation for the presence of this material in the first four books of the Pentateuch.

BIBLIOGRAPHY

C.H.W.Brekelmans, 'Éléments deutéronomiques dans le Pentateuque', *Recherches Bibliques* 8, 1967, 77-91; id., 'Die sogenannten deuteronomistischen Elemente in Genesis bis Numeri', *SVT* 15, 1966, 90-6; M.Caloz, 'Exode XIII, 3-16 et son rapport au Deutéronome', *RB* 75, 1986, 5-62; B.S.Childs, 'Deuteronomic Formulae of the Exodus Traditions', *SVT* 16, 1967, 30-8; L.Perlitt, op. cit., 65ff., 71, 83, 90f., 169ff., 193, 197, 205ff.; J.G.Plöger, op.cit. (see above, 9.5), 69ff.; T.C.Vriezen*, 1961, 131; H.Cazelles, 'Connexions et structures de Gen.XV', *RB* 69, 1962, 321-49, esp. 334 n.5; W.Fuss, *Die deuteronomistische Pentateuchredaktion in Exodus 3-17*, BZAW 126, 1972; A.Reichert, *Der Jahwist und die sogenannten deuteronomistischen Erweiterungen im Buch Exodus*, Diss. Tübingen 1972.

Excursus III

THE DECALOGUE

The texts

The Decalogue, which is contained in Exod.20.1-17 and Deut.5.6-18 with some significant variations to which we shall return later, has a particular importance not only for the position which it occupies in Jewish and Christian catechesis but also as an example of a text with a remarkably complex tradition, which has been handed down in a number of recensions. It, too, has been assigned to E for purely conventional reasons: T.C.Vriezen and A.S.van der Woude*, 178ff., already considered it doubtful. We need to look at two main problems:

(a) That of the relationships between its two recensions within the Hebrew Bible and with the other two outside it;

(b) That of authorship and the date of its composition.

(a) The recensions of the Decalogue. We have seen that the Hebrew Bible gives two parallel recensions of the text; these are two versions of identical substance, though there are some remarkable divergences. Here I shall list only the most obvious ones. The commandment to observe the sabbath (Exod.20.8-11; Deut.5.12-15) differs completely in motivation and length of text. In the first instance, in Exodus, it is taken from the creation in the P version (Gen.1.1-2.4a); in the second, in Deuteronomy, from the theme of slavery in Egypt. Again, the length of the text is different in the commandment to honour father and mother (Exod.20.12: Deut.5.16). In the commandment about bearing 'false witness' (Exod.20.16; Deut.5.20) in the first case we have the expression *'ēd šāqer*, i.e. false witness, and in the second *'ēd šāw*, i.e. vain witness. Now whereas the first expression is legal, the second, even if its meaning is not completely clear, probably refers to gossip, a form of conduct which is particularly destructive in the sphere of the community, but which is difficult to identify and suppress on the legal level. In the last commandment Deuteronomy puts the woman at the head of the list, while in Exodus she is simply classified as one of the goods not to be coveted, between the animals and property generally; this element makes the Deuteronomistic version look rather more advanced on a social level, while in the case of the observance of the sabbath the theme of slavery in Egypt belongs to Deuteronomy and is therefore earlier than the creation narrative according to P. This analysis based on the content of the two recensions already biasses us towards a recognition of the greater antiquity of that attested in Deuteronomy. This conviction is reinforced by the fact that it has a precarious position in the context of Exodus; there is no doubt that it is out of context. Exod. 19.25 in fact ends with the words 'Moses came down to the people and said to them'. After that we would expect his speech in 20.1ff.; instead we have 'Then God spoke all these words', and there follow those of the Decalogue. But the sequel (20.18ff.), with which the so-called 'Book of the Covenant' also begins, does not have any relationship to the Decalogue. In other words, in Deuteronomy the Decalogue is in its proper place and contains elements which suggest a recension which from a literary point of view is earlier, even if it is sociologically more advanced.

There is another recension of the Decalogue in the Samaritan Pentateuch; in addition to this we have two more outside the Hebrew Bible: that of the LXX translation in which the commandments appear in a different order, which is also attested in the New Testament in Luke 17.20, and that of the so-called Nash Papyrus, a manuscript from the second century CE (and until the discoveries of the Qumran texts the earliest ancient manuscript of a biblical text) which is based on the Deuteronomic text, though it shows some variants from it.

(b) The problem of the authorship and date of the composition seems particularly complex in the light of the various recensions of the text: a long history runs from the first author of the Decalogue to its final redaction. The differences in the order of the commandments and the variants in the text show that for a long time the final redaction was doubtful about which form was to be chosen. The text contained in Deuteronomy shares in the problems of this book, which we examined in the previous chapter, whereas that of Exodus is, as we have seen, an interpolation: so it seems clear that the Decalogue, too, cannot in any case go back to Moses, and that on the contrary it shares in the problems of the Pentateuch as a whole. In fact for the most part the individual commandments presuppose a settled life in the territory of the population to whom it is addressed (cf. the mention of the ox, a typically agricultural animal, of regular work, of slavery, of the gates of the city). And that applies even to an abbreviated form of the commandments stripped of what are obviously additions of a clarificatory or casuistic kind, or even of a homiletic nature:

Exod.20.2; Deut.5.6: 'I am YHWH your God, who brought you out of the land of Egypt, from a state of slavery' (prologue, perhaps late);
Exod.20.3; Deut.5.7: 'You shall not have other gods than me' (first commandment);
Exod.20.4; Deut.5.8: 'You shall not make any sculpture or image' (second commandment);
Exod.20.7; Deut.5.11: 'You shall not take the name of YHWH in vain' (third commandment);
Exod.20.8; Deut.5.12: 'Remember and keep holy the day of rest' (fourth commandment);
Exod.20.12; Deut.5.16: 'Honour your father and mother' (fifth commandment);
Exod.20.13; Deut.5.17: 'Do not kill' (sixth commandment);
Exod.20.14; Deut.5.18: 'Do not commit adultery' (seventh commandment);
Exod.20.15; Deut.5.19: 'Do not steal' (eighth commandment);
Exod.20.16; Deut.5.20: 'Do not bear false witness' (ninth commandment);
Exod.20.17; Deut.5.21: 'Do not covet' (tenth commandment).

Of course the division or the numberings made of the Decalogue in Israel and in the Christian churches are unimportant because the commandments have all been handed down and a preface was added, without which the Decalogue risks becoming an arid list of commandments and prohibitions without any motivation and lacking that breath of the gospel which alone can serve as a foundation for the divine order; since in fact God has chosen and liberated his own people, he cannot bear that this community which he has formed should be dissolved or corrupted because of human weakness or evil. But these are already reflections which presuppose a late stage of the tradition. At all events, only in this way does the Decalogue differ from the basic commandments of other religions, the content of which is often very similar.

If the Decalogue were reduced to these dimensions, it would be possible, in the view of some scholars, that it went back to the pre-monarchical period; however, the reality is that the Decalogue now appears in Deuteronomic garb, nor are there any indications of its greater antiquity.

BIBLIOGRAPHY

H.H.Rowley, 'Moses and the Decalogue', *BJRL* 34, 1951-52, 81-118 = *Men of God*, London 1963, 1-36; J.J.Stamm, *The Ten Commandments in Recent Research*, SBT II.2, 1967; H.Reventlow, *Gebot und Predigt im Dekalog*, Gütersloh 1962; E.Nielsen, *The Ten Commandments in New Perspective*, Copenhagen 1965; W.Richter, *Recht und Ethos*, Munich 1966, 101ff.; H.Gese, 'Der Dekalog als Ganzes betracht', *ZTK* 64, 1967, 21-38; A.Phillips, *Ancient Israel's Criminal Law. A New Approach to the Decalogue*, Oxford 1970; E.W.Nicholson, 'The Decalogue as Direct Address of God', *VT* 27, 1977, 422-33; A.Lemaire, 'Le Décalogue: Essai d'histoire de la rédaction', in *Mélanges bibliques et orientaux... H.Cazelles*, Neukirchen 1981, 159-95. A work which has stimulated modern studies is that of S.Mowinckel, *Le Décalogue*, Strasbourg 1926. The text of the Nash Papyrus is accessible in E.Würthwein, *The Text of the Old Testament*, Grand Rapids ²1979 and London ²1980; cf. also A.Jepsen, 'Beiträge zur Auslegung und Geschichte des Dekalogs', *ZAW* 79, 1967, 277-304, with a very good comparative study of the relations between the two Massoretic recensions and that of the LXX. For the tradition history of the Decalogue cf. W.H.Schmidt, 'Überlieferungsgeschichtliche Erwägungen zur Komposition des Dekalogs', *SVT* 22, 1972, 210-20. Also M.Lestienne, 'Les "dix paroles" et le décalogue', *RB* 79, 1972, 484-510. H.Schüngel-Straumann, *Der Dekalog, Gottes Gebote?*, Stuttgart 1973, offers an explanation. The supposed antiquity of the basic or reduced form of the Decalogue has been subject to criticism in many circles, cf. O.Kaiser, review, *ZDPV* 93, 1977, 309f.

The recent study by C.Levin, 'Der Dekalog am Sinai', *VT* 35, 1985, 165-91, is important for the Decalogue and the whole of the Sinai pericope. Cf. also L.Perlitt, *Bundestheologie im Alten Testament*, Neukirchen 1969, 77ff.; H.H.Schmid, *Der sogenannte Jahwist*, Zurich 1976, 95ff.; F.-L.Hossfeld, *Der Dekalog*, Freibourg CH 1982; A.Phillips, 'Ancient Israel's Criminal Law', *JJS* 35, 1985, 1-20; C.M.Carmichael, *Law and Narrative in the Bible*, Ithaca, NY 1985; A.Grampner, 'Zum Verhältnis der beiden Dekalogfassungen Ex 29 und Dtr 5. Ein Gespräch mit Frank-Lothar Hossfeld', *ZAW* 99, 1987, 308-29. For two recent works see A.Grampner, 'Zwei Arbeiten zum Dekalog', *VuF* 31.1, 1986, 87-9.

10

THE INDIVIDUAL SOURCES:
THE PRIESTLY CODEX (P)

1. Characteristics

Of the sources of the Pentateuch scattered through the first four books of the work, P is the easiest to recognize because of its relatively consistent vocabulary, its solemn style tending towards pomposity, its love of elements connected with the cult (liturgy, ritual, institutions) and its genealogies. P's chronology sets out to be very precise, and it seeks to include a history of the world from its origin. However, we may say in anticipation, the result does not correspond with the intentions, since the chronology in question is clearly artificial, not in the sense that it is an imaginary creation by redactors, but because it is inspired by criteria which are not really historiographical. We shall return to this subject a little later. P should thus be a unitary source almost by definition, but it also contains contradictory details in areas which scarcely allow of contradictions. In Lev.4.4-16 only Aaron and the high priest are presented as 'anointed ones', whereas in Exod.28.41 and 29.29 all the priests have this character; in Num.4.23ff. the service of the levites does not begin before they are thirty, but in 8.24 it begins when they are twenty-five. Moreover, the offerings required for the sacrifices are not always the same: in Lev.4.14 the situation is different from that attested in 9.3 and in Num. 15.24. On the subject of altars, in Exod.27.21ff.; 38.1ff.; 30.29 (cf.Lev.8; 9) we have one for whole burnt-offerings; in Exod. 30.1-10 another appears which is intended for incense. Moreover, some sections seem to have been interpolated in their present context: Lev.1-7 and 11-15 and 16 clearly interrupt it, while chs.17-26 are evidently an independent entity with its own vocabulary and stereotyped phraseology. All this is enough to demonstrate that P, too, has experienced a somewhat eventful history, probably quite a long one, before being accepted as the final source of the Pentateuch. However, attempts to separate more or less continuous subsidiary sources or strata within P have not been successful: others have attempted in the past to distinguish between a narrative P and a legal and ritual P, but here too the legal and ritual sections have been inserted into the context of a historical narrative, following the characteristic criterion of the Hebrew Bible which I have already mentioned, i.e to consider only what has been realized in history as relevant for faith. In other words, contrary to Dtr (below, 12.1) P would seem to be a redactor. This opinion has, however, been challenged in a recent article by K.Koch: the autonomous creation narrative and the revelation of the divine name show that P could also be a creative writer.

2. Chronology

The chronology of P is one of the most characteristic elements of the whole source. It begins with creation (Gen. 1.1-2.4a), and the modern calculation of the Jewish year still in use in the synagogue (1988-89 corresponds to 5749 'from the foundation of the world') is a direct continuation of this chronology. The exactness and precision of the figures were a source of certainty for biblical scholars down to the beginning of scientific biblical criticism (the biblical chronologies by Bishop Jacob Ussher of Armagh, composed in the first half of the seventeenth century, still appear in many Bibles), so much so that only towards the middle of the last century, culminating with the studies of Wellhausen and his school, did it become possible to demonstrate their artificial character. There is, however, no justification for the assertion to which I have alluded briefly that the chronological system of P is fictitious only because it cannot be reconciled with that of historical or natural science (Charles Darwin's difficulties, it may be remarked in passing, stemmed from the fact that he began by attempting to confirm the chronology which we know to be that of P in terms of natural science, and succeeded in arriving at diametrically opposite results). The figures given in P express theological and ritual criteria which in some cases are clear and in others have still to be discovered: for example, that a fundamental divine act in the history of salvation stands at the beginning of each new period of human history. Matters of particular importance are accompanied by the celebration of a *berīt*, in which God incurs obligations towards humankind and humankind towards God. This takes place in two instances. Thus we have a constant relationship between the division of human history into periods (which P of course saw and recognized) and its chronology. After the flood we have a divine pledge to Noah (Gen.9.1-17) followed by a divine command to humankind over food (see below, 4b); at the election of Abraham in P (Gen.17.1ff.) we have further divine obligations to which Abraham is to respond by adopting circumcision. The sources J and E did not know such an ancient institution of this rite. Indeed we find in Exod.4.24-26 what is apparently a very ancient text which originally was intended to narrate the institution of circumcision; now, however, it has been harmonized by the redactors so that it seems like a repetition. The chronology of P has not only been developed with great care, but was quickly inserted into an organic structure which continues through the Hebrew Bible right down to the book of Daniel (cf.below, 41), and this organic structure would seem to have been composed with a view to the expectation of the end of time. According to it the world will finish 4000 years after its creation, i.e. after four millennia. In the Massoretic text the exodus takes place in the year 2666 of creation, i.e. around two-thirds of the 4000 years; then follow 480 years from the exodus to the building of the temple (I Kings 6.1), a figure which is no longer that of P; 410 years from the building of the temple to the exile according to I-II Kings, and finally 490 years, i.e. the 'seven weeks of years' of Dan.9.24, of which 1334 years form the other third of the 4000 years, and 46 years which are not explained. That seems to be one approach to the discussion, a discussion which, however, is far from being exhausted. First of all this chronology contrasts with that which we can calculate today; secondly it can be sustained only on the basis of the figures in the Massoretic text: those of the Samaritan text, the LXX, the pseudepigraphical text of Jubilees and Flavius Josephus are different and obviously match other criteria, even if we do not know what these criteria are. In any case, the fact that this chronology is continued in the book of Daniel (which, as we shall see, cannot be older than the first half of the second century BCE) and thus forms an organic whole with it, favours a late dating of the whole system.

But what seems to interest P more than anything else is the constitution of the legitimate cult and its priests, and of the people among whom it is practised. Thus whether in the case of Noah or in that of Abraham, we have the celebration of a *berît*: in the former we find the first dictary laws, and in the latter the election of Israel through Abraham and the institution of the rite of circumcision, which was its distinguishing mark over the centuries. Various names for the God of Israel correspond to these periods: until he discloses himself to all humanity he bears the name *'elōhīm* = God; he presents himself to Abraham as *'ēl šaddai*, a term which has yet to be explained adequately, but which appears often in the inscription of tell Deir 'Alla (cf. below, Appendix 1.11) in parallelism with *'elōhīm*, and only with Moses is his real name, YHWH, revealed (Exod.6), a theory which is shared, as we have seen, with E. At the same time, from the creation of the world onwards there is a degeneration of the human vital force; a man's life declines from almost a thousand years (a figure which is never reached, Gen.5.1ff.) to a little over a century with the patriarchs, then soon arriving at normal limits, all under a century. In other words, P does not hand down a story of the 'fall' of humankind as does J (Gen.3), but it does show a very similar belief about the human tendency to sin which is only mitigated by the fact that humankind can adopt the ritual practices which have been commanded. For P the climax of history is the theophany on Sinai, to which half Exodus, all Leviticus and a third of Numbers are devoted: in the course of this the basis for later Hebrew worship is established, along with some of its details. Anyone who wished to be particularly precise and rational in his or her observations would be reduced to the absurd conclusion that there was no form of true worship before the theophany on Sinai, with the exception of the laws about food, the sabbath and circumcision, the first and third of which are given to Noah and Abraham respectively.

In a source like P it is not surprising to find an exalted concept of divine transcendence: only Moses is allowed to see God and then only from behind (Exod.24.16ff.; 33.18ff.), and the figure of the mediator between God and man becomes a necessity. J does not seem to be excessively preoccupied with the problem, though in E we already see a tendency in this direction. The 'glory' (Hebrew *kābōd*) of God is present in the sanctuary, a glory which in particularly serious circumstances (for example shortly before the exile in Babylon, Ezek.1; 10) can abandon the Jerusalem temple and therefore God's people. The concept is connected with the tradition which sees YHWH as king of the universe. The divine 'glory' is soon replaced by the expression *YHWH šebā'ōt*, 'of hosts', and is a characteristic feature of the post-exilic temple. The difference from Deuteronomy and Dtr is evident; these latter, as I have indicated (above, 9.1) see the presence of God realized in the dwelling of the holy name. We no longer find the familiar form in which the patriarchs intercede with their God in J and, with greater limitations, even in E (for this latter source see Gen.22): now we have to do with YHWH, God of Israel, in all his majesty, in all his transcendence and therefore in all his remoteness. Though it may seem paradoxical, this does not exclude the presence of numerous anthropomorphisms and anthropopathisms: P too is concerned to proclaim a personal God, removed but not detached from humankind and the world, and it tries to indicate this with all the means at its disposal.

3. Date and place of composition

(a) Once H.Ewald (cf. above, 7.3c) had ascertained that there were two 'Elohistic' sources in the Pentateuch and that one was later than the other, discoveries in the material followed with remarkable speed: it was E.Reuss (mentioned above, 7.3d) and his pupil K.H.Graf who placed P at the end of the development of the Pentateuch. The correspondence between the two shows clearly that it was Reuss who first made this discovery, although Graf was the first to publicize it. This completely overturned the chronology which had been hitherto accepted and, as we have seen, laid the foundations for the definitive construction of the documentary hypothesis.

(b) Over recent decades only a few objections of any weight have been made to what so far has been the dominant theory. In 1929 A.Jepsen argued that the starting-point of the chronology of P was the construction of the temple in Jerusalem and that therefore the constitutive elements of the source must necessarily be prior to the exile. This argument was certainly not without its force, but one would have to ascertain to which temple P referred, whether to the temple of Solomon or, rather, to the second, post-exilic temple. In any case, one thing is clear: the chronological relationship between P on the one hand and Deuteronomy and the Deuteronomistic history work on the other would have to be subjected to a thorough examination to discover whether P presupposed the existence of the other two, and if so at what point. We find a similar problem in the case of the Israeli scholar Y.Kaufmann, whose theory we touched on at the beginning of our examination of the sources. He argues for the priority of P over Deuteronomy, a theory which had already been put forward by De Wette. This is because, as he argues, there is no proof that P presupposes Deuteronomy; moreover, for this author P cannot be post-exilic and it therefore has the temple of Solomon in mind. The first theory is valid only if we consider the centralized cult in the single sanctuary as presented by P not as the consequence but as the presupposition of Josiah's reform, an evaluation in which considerations of a subjective kind have a by no means unimportant role; the second is based on the generally accepted fact that there are certainly important pre-exilic sections in P (a problem to which we shall return), whereas not a few elements of P are incompatible with a post-exilic date. For example, there is constant mention of the ark, but it is unanimously said by tradition to have been made in the desert period, disappearing at a date which cannot now be determined, probably in the seventh or the sixth century BCE, and certainly not later than the fall of Jerusalem in 587. How could a post-exilic text show so much interest in an object of this kind? The school of Kaufmann has now shaped two generations of Israeli scholars, and his work is highly valued in Jewish circles outside Israel.

(c) A third theory was developed in 1964 by the American orientalist E.A.Speiser: according to this, P is the work of a school with roots in the earliest history of Israel, which continued to work throughout the history of Israel before and immediately after the exile. Again, Speiser is on target when he indicates the complex history of the P tradition or when he demonstrates the existence of what are certainly pre-exilic elements, but there is no proof of a school of this kind.

(d) A fourth theory was presented in the same year by J.Hempel: he discovered in Gen.17.6 an evident allusion to the monarchy and believed that the roots of P are to be found in the milieu of the ancient sanctuary of Hebron, David's capital when he was king only of Judah (II Sam.1-4). But what has already been said still holds true: the presence of ancient material does not imply anything about the date of the final redaction of the sources, nor is it evident why this redaction should be dated back to such a remote period, the last years of the second millennium. Moreover, we know nothing of any sanctuary at Hebron.

(e) It seems that none of these arguments, apart from that of Kaufmann, touches on the fundamental problem; the date of the final redaction of P and its relationship to the other sources of the Pentateuch. They deal only with peripheral elements. All that they show is that in P, as in all the other sources, there are elements of tradition which are much earlier than the final redaction. But here too the last word does not seem to have been said, if a recent introduction like that of W.H.Schmidt* considers the problem not yet resolved (60).

(f) The discussion so far and the objections which have been indicated invite us automatically to consider the problem of the dating of P or of its final redaction, or, finally, that of a possible earlier dating of some of its sections, and if so, which. A *terminus ante quem* here is obviously given by the definitive breach between Jews and Samaritans, at a time when the Pentateuch was evidently complete, since it is common to both; the date of this breach is uncertain, but it is generally put towards the end of the fourth century BCE and not later, during the transition from Persian to Macedonian rule (cf. my *History*, XIII.4).

(g) First, however, it will be necessary to examine the text of P rather more closely. The problem of the relationship between the historical texts and the legal texts, which we have seen to be particularly acute in the J and E sources, seems to be much simpler in P: in the two categories of texts there are lexical, stylistic and ideological constants which make them an undoubted unity, leaving aside some differences of detail and an exception which we shall examine a little later. Now we have seen that the Sinai pericope, with its narrative of the institution of the legitimate cult, indubitably forms the climax of P: the material which follows is essentially connected with the continuation of the journey through the wilderness before the arrival in the Promised Land. Moreover, the Sinai pericope contains the greater part of the material which has been assigned to P. It would not therefore be illogical to argue that the narrative sections also tend towards this high point: the proclamation of the *tōrāh* on Sinai and the foundation of the cult. Paradoxically, however, what would be a climax from the narrative point of view does not constitute the central element of the source on an ideological and theological plane. In this area the centre of the source is to be found in three elements: the institution of the sabbath, of the dietary laws and of circumcision, which are now to be found respectively at the beginning, a quarter of the way and half way through P. These results have been achieved through laborious investigations which we shall attempt to follow, though only in their main points.

4. Component elements

(a) We have already seen in 2 that even at the heart of P we have contradictions, duplicates and interpolations of compositions which clearly show signs of being of autonomous origin. A solution had been sought up to the beginning of the 1930s in the possibility that there were subsidiary sources in P. This had been postulated for J and E and was now being argued for by some scholars in the case of P too. Wellhausen thought of two sources and of a work of a genealogical character (*tōlʿdōt*); this principle was taken up again in 1934 by von Rad, who sought to divide the fundamental writing (Pg – from the German *Grundschrift*) into two subsidiary sources, Pa and

Pᵇ, to which various supplementary elements were then added, indicated by Pˢ. The hypothesis of the existence of a genealogical source received the authoritative endorsement of O.Eissfeldt, but as early as 1940 the Swiss scholar P.Humbert, followed by Weiser*, demolished the theory of two subsidiary sources. In 1948 Noth had proposed the theory that P is an essentially historiographical work, culminating, as we have seen, in the Sinai narrative. Other materials of diverse character were then incorporated into this work. This is the theory which has a majority of adherents today. Of course, if we allow that P is essentially a historiographical work, though with various types of material, it is necessary to study the nature and the scope of P's historiography.

(b) More than twenty years ago an important work on this theme by K.Elliger was published, while other authors have also been occupied with it in a more or less direct way. Meanwhile Elliger has produced an authoritative commentary on Leviticus in which his theory has again been tested. He accepts that P has a composite character, but sees only the possibility of distinguishing between a Pᵍ (basic document) and Pˢ (later supplements). Many legal and ritual passages are assigned to Pᵍ because they are held to belong there without a shadow of doubt; the difficulty in attributions of this kind, however, rests in the fact that they cannot be made without introducing subjective elements on which others can cast doubt simply because they have a different sensibility. According to Elliger, Pᵍ begins with Gen.1.1-2.4a, a narrative which concludes with the creation of humanity but in reality culminates in the divine institution of the sabbath, one of the key elements in the theology of P. The first section of the work ends with the genealogy of the Sethites or antediluvian patriarchs (ch.5). The second section begins with the flood and ends with the institution of the first dietary laws (Gen.8.3f.): the prohibition against eating flesh with blood, which is considered the seat of life. With the table of peoples we have a transition to the patriarchal section (chs.10ff.), in which the narrative is distinguished by its dry and sometimes pedantic style, stripped of all elements of folklore (with one exception: the dealings over the purchase of the case of Machpelah, Gen.23) and of any narrative which might put the protagonists in a less flattering light. The culminating point is given with the institution of circumcision (Gen.17), another key element in the theology of P which, as we have seen, sets the introduction of the rite with the ancestors of Israel at a time which is notably earlier than that attested in J and E. In reality, the account of Sinai which, as we have seen, forms the logical goal of P, only takes up themes which are already present in the narration: the sabbath, food laws, circumcision. It is interesting that the regulations seem to presuppose a public confession of faith, and therefore a situation of contact with other people; in other words, it is a post-exilic situation, even if the institutions described can be very much older.

(c) I have already spoken generally about the chronology. It is intended to displace all earlier chronology in the Pentateuch, thus giving rise to interesting discrepancies with the chronology of J and E (cf. Gen.16; 21).

(d) The intertwining becomes complex in the narrative of the exodus from Egypt and the march across the desert. The revelation of the divine name (Exod.6) and the liberation from oppression in Egypt restore the equilibrium between the ancient promises and their fulfilment, which seemed to have been irremediably compromised. For P, however, the revelation of the divine name does not seem to have had the importance which it has, for example, in E: P seems to consider the name or title Shaddai (see above, § 2) more important. This is already attested in the ancient songs Gen.49.25 (in a conjecture which is generally accepted, cf. *BHS*) and Num.24.4,16; from Gen.17 it becomes a name that is typical of P. During the march through the desert the culminating episode is obviously that of Sinai, where the people receive, through the mediation of Moses, a series of laws which make them a holy people *par excellence*, set apart by YHWH. The narrative breaks off on the soil of the Promised Land, to which Moses is not admitted. According to Noth and Elliger, and probably rightly, as we shall see (below, 13.1a), P is continued in Joshua only in a number of fragments: Josh.1.1; 18.1; 19.51a; 22.9-34, and it does not seem that more recent studies, taking up hints made by Wellhausen, have been able to demonstrate the contrary. We shall return to the subject in ch.12 when we look at the problems of the Deuteronomistic history work.

(e) It is thus interesting to note that the Sinai pericope for the most part does no more than amplify themes and institutions which are already present in the more strictly narrative section, so much so that Elliger can assert that the various passages in the pericope in question never belonged to P^g: the laws about the altar of incense, the holy oil, the thurible, sacrifices, the ritual calendar and perhaps even the legislation about the levites. It was only later that P felt the need to add this material, which would have been lacking in its original redaction. The sections involved are especially Lev.1-7; 8-10; 11-15, a series of codices the themes of which are sacrifices, the priesthood and ritual impurity respectively; ch.16, which deals with the Day of Atonement; and chs.17-26, already mentioned, a collection usually called the 'Holiness Code' because its regulations are motivated by the holiness of God: the majority of scholars have no difficulty in accepting a pre-exilic origin. A special position is also occupied by Num.33, an itinerary, and 35, the list of levitical cities and cities of refuge (for these latter see what will be said in connection with the book of Joshua, below 13.3). To what degree these texts can be attributed to P is debatable; however, the question is not of great importance. This, then, would be an excellent explanation of the contradictions, inconsistencies and duplications which we have noted so far.

(f) The P Sinai pericope is dominated by a particular kind of theological dialectic: on the one hand God lives, dwells in the midst of his own people (root *škn*, whence *miškān* = dwelling), in the temple, by means of his own 'glory' in the sense of dwelling in a tent, and thus indicates, at least in origin, the provisional, precarious character of this dwelling (cf. the analogous *skēnoō* in John 1.14 in the New Testament); on the other hand, he 'meets' with the people in the tent of meeting (*'ōhel mōʿēd*), an artefact also mentioned in J and E and which, like the ark, disappeared in the pre-exilic period. Now in this dialectic the theme of meeting plainly prevails over that of dwelling, however precarious the latter may be, and in this way one of the principal elements of the promises made to Abraham is achieved. This also explains a theory put forward a few years ago according to which the tent of meeting is not so much a projection of the Jerusalem temple into the past as a real, more provisional sanctuary, the importance of which will have been stressed by opponents of the party which wanted to rebuild the temple. Of course the temple was built nevertheless; this, it is argued, was the consequence of a compromise with the priesthood. This theory appears untenable in such a neat form, but if it were toned down more and re-expressed in less extreme terms it could explain the insistence on the tent at a time when there were animated discussions about the rebuilding of the temple, as we shall see (below, 26).

There seems no point in calling the attention of the modern reader to the fact that, regardless of the *intentions* of those who compiled it, this kind of narrative cannot now be considered historical. As Elliger puts it, the primary interest is in the 'truth of faith', to which the redactors testify with due certainty. But, continues Elliger, such a testimony was persuasive to the age of the exile or immediately afterwards, when this kind of certainty tended to recede following the catastrophe that had befallen the nation, in the train of real historical events which theological speculation could not change. This chronological situation would explain the contacts which P has with Ezekiel and Deutero-Isaiah: the reference to the temple in Ezek.40-48 as a prophetic vision, in P as a reference to the tent of earlier times, but in both cases the sign of a totally new beginning. Authors like Roth, Cazelles and Kapelrud, working with different methods, agree in dating P^g at a time not earlier than 562 and not later than about 550.

A recent work moves on a completely different plane. Its starting point is Gen.17, with the institution of circumcision, a feature which, as we have seen, is fundamental for P along with the observance of the sabbath and the dietary laws. It would assign an early date to this chapter on the basis of the vassal treaties mentioned in Excursus 1 above, but since the existence of these treaties is attested right down to the neo-Assyrian period, there are problems in using them to date a passage which could refer to them. Moreover, the work argues that after Gen.17 other passages speak of circumcision, thus presupposing that it has already been instituted: Gen.21.4; 34.15; Exod.12.44; Lev.12.3; Josh.5.2-9. This fact had also been noted by Graf, when the documentary hypothesis was taking its first steps, and he had arrived at similar conclusions. However, the situation is already different: all the texts mentioned, with the exception of Gen.34 and Josh.5, belong to P and therefore must be ruled out as proof. Nor is it possible to argue that Gen.34, a passage which presents notable difficulties on the historical level, refers to Gen.17, even if it knows the practice of circumcision. In Josh.5, vv.5-7 are Deuteronomistic, as is the conclusion of v.2 ('a second time'); only the part which makes a general reference to circumcision is original. Even here, then, given that the passage refers to Egypt and not to Gen.17, it is more obvious to relate it to Exod.4.18-26. Elliger's theories can thus be defended much better. We therefore have to deal with two strata in P, but not in the sense argued by Wellhausen and by von Rad in 1934: a basic element, P^g, has been supplemented in various ways, P^s, some of which may be earlier than the basic element.

5. Composition

The following passages are usually assigned to P: Gen.1.1-2.4a; 5.1-27, 30-32; 9.1-7, 28f.; 11.10-27, 31f.; 17.1ff.; 23.1ff.; 25.7-20; 27.46-28.9; 35.9-13, 15, 22-29; 46.6-27; Exod.1.1-7, 13f.; 6.2-30; 7.1-13,

19f., 23; 8.1-3, 12-15; 11.9-12, 20, 28; 12.40-51; chs.25-31; 34.29f.; all Leviticus; Num.chs.1-10; 13; 14; 16.1-19; 20 (in part); 22.1ff; chs.28-30 (?) and 33-36. It should be noted that the last two sections are traditionally assigned to P, but that this is probably independent geographical material, certainly parallel to Josh.13-21.

6. The final redaction of the Pentateuch

Those who have followed the discussion so far will have realized how complex was the process which led to the redaction of the Pentateuch, and what the fundamental points are which remain obscure. We know so little of what has happened to other literature in similar situations that we do not even have the possibility of comparative study. It is possible to note a certain consensus at most on the following points: J and E must have existed in parallel forms for some years until on the fall of the northern kingdom the E material passed to the south, where it was fused with that of J; this would explain why E exists in such a reduced form. JE will soon have been subjected to a Deuteronomic or Deuteronomistic redaction (cf. above, Excursus II). Deuteronomy will have taken a similar course. This would give us a combination of J and E plus Deuteronomy/Dtr; the earlier traditions of P developed in parallel to this, probably in the Jerusalem sanctuary. At the end of the exile and during the restoration this material will have been brought together again along the chronological and historiographical lines of P. The result was a composition similar to, if not identical with, the Pentateuch as we now have it. This composition must have been finished before the final break with the Samaritans.

We shall be concerned a little later with the problem of a continuation of J, E and P in Joshua (below, 12) when we study the problem of the Deuteronomistic history work.

BIBLIOGRAPHY

1. Bibliographical studies: J.Roth, 'Thèmes majeurs de la tradition sacerdotale dans le Pentateuque', NRT 90, 1958, 696-721; J.G.Vink, 'The Date and Origin of the Priestly Code in the Old Testament', OTS 15, 1969, 1-144; cf. also H.Cazelles and J.P.Bouhot, art.cit. (see bibliography to 7),

28off.; D.Kellermann, *Die Priesterschrift von Numeri 1.1 bis 10.10*, Berlin 1970. For Lev.1-7 cf. K.Elliger, HAT 1966, 21 (with bibliography); A.van den Branden, 'Lévitique 1-7 et le tarif de Marseille, CIS 1,165', *RSO* 40, 1965, 107-30, and A.Capuzzi, 'I sacrifici animali a Cartagine', *Studi Magrebini* 2, Naples 1968, 45-76. For Lev.11-15, cf. Elliger, ibid. For Lev.17-26 see Elliger, 23, with bibliography; K.Koch, 'P – Kein Redaktor!', *VT* 37, 1987, 446-67. For the relationship between the 'Holiness Code' and Deuteronomy, cf. now A.Cholewinski, *Heiligkeitsgesetz und Deuteronomium*, Rome 1976.

2, 3, 4. For the chronology of P see D.S.Russell, *The Method and Message of Jewish Apocalyptic*, London and Philadelphia 1964, esp. ch.8. K. von Rabenau, in an unpublished communication to the Fifth Congress of the International Organization of the Study of the Old Testament, Geneva 1965, argued for the possibility of a fall of humankind as part of the P account. For the theology of P cf. recently T.N.D.Mettinger, *The Dethronement of Sebaoth*, Lund 1982, esp. ch.III.

3, 4. E.Reuss, *Geschichte der Heiligen Schrift des Alten Testamentes*, [2]1890; K.H.Graf, 'Die sogenannte Grundschrift des Pentateuchs', *Archiv für wissenschaftliche Erforschung des Alten Testaments* I, Halle 1869, 466-77; A.Jepsen, 'Zur Chronologie der Priesterkodex', *ZAW* 47, 1929, 251-5; Y.Kaufmann, 'Probleme der israelitisch-jüdischen Religionsgeschichte', *ZAW* 48, 1934, 23-43, esp.28-32; *Tōlᵉdōt hā'ᵉmūnāh hayyis'rā'ēlīt*, Vol. 1, Tel Aviv 1937 (English abridgment by M.Greenberg, *The Religion of Israel*, Chicago 1960, 208f.); id., 'Der Kalender und das Alter des Priesterkodex', *VT* 4, 1954, 307-13 (in support of Kaufmann's thesis cf. recently A.Hurvitz, 'The Evidence of Language in Dating the Priestly Code', *RB* 81, 1974, 24-45); S.Mowinckel, *Erwägungen zur Pentateuchquellenfrage*, Oslo 1964, 44-6; J.G.Vink, art.cit. (above, § 1), 9f.; E.A.Speiser, *Genesis*, AB, xxvi; J.Hempel, *Geschichten und Geschichte im Alten Testament*, Gütersloh 1964, 113ff., 200ff.; G.von Rad, *Die Priesterschrift im Hexateuch*, Stuttgart 1934; O.Eissfeldt, 'Biblos Geneseos', in *Gott und die Götter. Festgabe für E.Fascher*, Berlin 1958, 21-40 (= his *Kleine Schriften* III, Tübingen 1966, 458-70); P.Humbert, 'Die literarische Zweiheit des Priester-Codex in der Genesis', *ZAW* 58, 1940-41, 30-57; A.Weiser*, 135-42; M.Noth, *A History of Pentateuchal Traditions*, ET Englewood Cliffs 1972, 8ff.; K.Elliger, 'Sinn und Ursprung der priesterlichen Geschichtserzählung', *ZTK* 49, 1952, 12-43 (= his *Kleine Schriften*, Munich 1966, 174-98); S.R.Külling, *Zur Datierung der Genesis P-Stücke*, Kampen 1964; for P in Exodus see P.Weimar, *Untersuchungen zur priesterschriftlichen Exodusgeschichte*, Würzburg 1973; cf. also Cazelles and Bouhot, 289ff., and Vink, 8off. For the revelation of the name in P cf. Lohfink, 'Die priesterliche Abwertung von der Offenbarung des Jahwenames an Mose', *Bibl* 49, 1968, 1-8. For P in Joshua see J.A.Soggin, *Joshua*, ET OTL 1972, on individual passages; it does not seem that Vink, art.cit., 63ff., has succeeded in demonstrating the existence of more extended passages in Joshua. For the tent-temple polemic cf. T.E.Fretheim, 'The Priestly Document: Anti-Temple?', *VT* 18, 1968, 313-29; cf. also A.S.Kapelrud, 'The Date of the Priestly Code (P)', *ASTI* 3,

1964, 58-64 and Cazelles and Bouhot, 301ff.; S.McEvenue, *The Narrative Style of the Priestly Writer*, Rome 1971; R.E.Friedman, *The Exile and Biblical Narrative*, Chico, Cal, 1981, ch.II. For the chronology, J.Barr, 'Why the World was Created in 4004 BC - Archbishop Ussher's Biblical Chronology', *BJRL* 67, 1984-85, 575-608, is a basic and largely definitive study. M.Haran, *Temples and Temple Service*, Oxford 1978, and recently Z.Zevit, 'Converging Lines of Evidence Bearing upon the Date of P', *ZAW* 94, 1982, 381-511, have argued, the former for the pre-exilic composition of a number of elements of P and the latter for a dating of much of the document in the pre-exilic period (from the eighth century onwards). At this point we are agreed on the question: a complex ritual like that of P, supported by an ideology and a theology which is far from simple, will not have come to be formed from nothing nor in a relatively short time. Therefore the presence of pre-exilic material, sometimes in whole sections, cannot be excluded *a priori*, and the task of identifying it must be left to scholars. But as a finished product P is clearly post-exilic; G.-F.Ravasi, 'Una comunità santa, sacerdotale, pura', *RiBib* 36, 1988, 1-27. See also P.Weimar, 'Struktur und Komposition der priesterschriftlichen Geschichtsdarstellungen', *BN* 23, 1984, 81-143. S.Tengström, *Die Toledotformel*, Lund 1981, has tried to see P not as a source but as a revision of earlier materials. For the problem of the relations between P and the account of the settlement cf. E.Cortese, *La terra di Canaan nella storia sacerdotale del Pentateuco*, Brescia 1972. For the orientation on post-exilic Judaism in P cf. W.Brueggemann, 'The Kerygma of the Priestly Writers', *ZAW* 84, 1972, 397-414.

Cf. also N.Lohfink, 'Die Abänderung des priesterlichen Geschichtswerks im Segen des Heiligkeitsgesetzes. Zu Lev.29.9,11-13', in *Wort und Geschichte*, *FS K.Elliger*, Neukirchen-Vluyn and Kevelaer 1973, 129-36; J.Blenkinsopp, 'The Structure of P', *CBQ* 38, 1976, 275-92; and E.Cortese, 'Dimensioni letterarie e elementi strutturali in P^s. Per una teologia del Documento Sacerdotale', *RiBib* 25, 1977, 113-41, and 26, 1978, 113ff. For the dating cf. B.J.Diebner, 'Gottesdienst II – Altes Testament', *TRE* 14, 1985, 19-21.

6. There is a chart setting out a possible outline of the way in which the Pentateuch reached its present form in C.R.North, 'Pentateuchal Criticism', in H.H.Rowley (ed.), *The Old Testament and Modern Study*, Oxford 1951, 81.

I I

ISRAELITE LAW

1. Introduction

The specifically legal parts of the Pentateuch are a particularly important part of it. I have classified some elements as 'ancient Israelite law' (above, 7.7), but the majority of it belongs to P. This attribution is simple, even if we must allow for interpolations and additions of material which was probably autonomous in origin. In § 9 of this chapter we shall return to the problem in more detail. It goes without saying, given the context, that legal material in the strict sense is mixed with material which we would tend to regard as liturgical: the world of the ancient Near East did not distinguish between the regulations of the cult and those of civil life.

Whereas the synagogue has drawn important elements for its cultic and social life from this material, in the context of the Christian church it has usually been neglected or at most read in the light of the Epistle to the Hebrews in the New Testament. However, it is of special importance not only for the study of law in general and of oriental law in particular, but also to anyone who is interested in the way in which the theological and ethical principles of the Hebrew Bible worked out in practice. This is the case even though it is not always easy to discover whether particular laws were actually applied and at what point, or whether they were simply programmatic.

After what I have just said, it will not seem strange that even biblical law belongs in the wider context of the law of the ancient Near East. Thus we find resemblances and sometimes remarkable parallels. For this reason we shall note the points at which the differences in approach are particularly evident.

2. Law and faith

Leaving aside some countries which have Islamic law, today the laws of the various developed countries have an essentially secular perspective: they are not inspired by religious principles and only deal with religious matters where these matters have become the object of public and private law. There are, of course, instances of state religion in which we have the acceptance of religious norms in the regulation of certain institutions in the political sphere. For example, there are the norms of rabbinic jurisprudence in the state of Israel, and in other nations in the case of marriage, whether it is indissoluble or whether divorce is allowed is influenced, rightly or wrongly, by biblical thought. Again, a church or a religious community can in some cases enjoy considerable privileges compared with ordinary people who have a normal legal status. These instances, however, are fairly rare, and authoritative currents in jurisprudence consider them to be anachronistic survivals, incompatible with the demands and the principles of a modern state, which is regarded as having an essentially secular basis, like the philosophies which underlie it. The state may have an underlying philosophy, but not a theology: with very rare exceptions, modern philosophies are lay, regardless of the personal faith of their major representatives.

Of course this does not mean that religious law no longer exists: every Christian religious confession, and Judaism too, has its own traditional laws, whether or not they are in codified form. These laws regulate relations within the community in question, whether on a public, personal or cultic level. Thus we have the canon law of the Catholic church, the *ḥalakāh* of Judaism, and certain regulations and constitutions of the Protestant churches. But these are norms which do not have any validity outside the community in which they have been formed, except where a special arrangement has been made with common law (for example, until recently marriage under the concordat in Italy); therefore the power behind their application is extremely limited. In other words, their value on the practical plane does not transcend that of the statutes and regulations of an ordinary party at law.

If we turn now to the situation in the ancient Near East (which, moreover, is also largely that of the classical world), we seem to find exactly the opposite. The law is always sacral, whether it refers to the cult or to elements of social life; this is because it has been given either directly by the deity or indirectly with his approval. A dualism between 'church' and state is inconceivable, since religion is one of the principal foundations, if not *the* principal foundation, of the constituted order. As might be expected, the result is a series of extremely conservative societies. In many respects Israel is an exception here, because at least some prophets can visualize a separation between 'church' (that is, the believing people) and state (that is, the people in an ethnic and political sense). In a few cases, indeed, they actually proclaim this. Speaking of the prophets, we shall also see how the concept of the 'elect remnant' began to give form to this distinction, though still in a very rudimentary manner.

The sacrality of the law is shown by the fact that there were always gods to mediate the law to man, usually in the person of the monarch, even when that law was merely a new compilation of earlier norms. The best-known example is the stele of Hammurapi surmounted by a representation of the sun in the act of delivering the royal insignia to the monarch, his vassal. It should be noted, however, that the situation is not substantially different in the Hebrew Bible: YHWH delivers the law to Moses on Mount Sinai. We now know (and in the case of Israel we were occupied with this question in earlier chapters) that the process was much more complex. The most obvious consequence of this approach to the law is that every law has a sacral character and that all violations are thus automatically sacrilege; this explains in turn the frequency with which the death penalty was inflicted for crimes for which one might have expected short periods of imprisonment or even a fine.

In Israel this emphasis on the sacral character of the law is evident from the beginning of the Decalogue: 'I am YHWH, your God, who brought you out of the land of Egypt, out of slavery' (Exod.20.1; Deut.5.6; above, Excursus III). Considering this sacral character of the law it is likely that, as among so many other peoples in the ancient Near East, it was handed down by priests in the sanctuaries, especially and later exclusively in the sanctuary at Jerusalem. There is also a less obvious consequence for modern Westerners, except perhaps for those who live in the area of Anglo-Saxon law: the state is not the source of the law, since in general the existence of the law is anterior to the formation of the state. Outside Israel, the principle remains that the law comes from the deity and finishes in practice by deriving from the person of the monarch or from instruments chosen by him.

Like all the other problems of biblical criticism, the question of the relationship between biblical and Near Eastern law has only been raised in modern times. This, too, is because only from the beginning of this century, with the discovery of the codex of Hammurapi, has such a comparison been possible. As we have seen, this document, which is cut on a stele with phallic form, has a representation on its upper part of the delivery of royal insignia to the king by the sun. One particular reason for its importance is that it is almost complete, unlike the collections discovered at later times which have all been more or less fragmentary. It is also important that these later discoveries, fragmentary though they are, allow us to recognize the composite character of the codex, which thus appears to be the result of complex work with already existing material. The discovery of the Hammurapi codex was very soon followed by that of early Assyrian, Hittite, Babylonian and Sumerian laws; all, as we have seen, more or less incomplete. This has sometimes made it difficult to understand individual passages or to determine the principles which have shaped the collections. In all these laws we often have striking parallels to the laws of the Hebrew Bible, as we shall see in due course; in other cases we have complete independence and sometimes a remarkable contrast. In other words, on the one hand Israel draws on the vast legal tradition of the ancient Near East; on the other, in some quite significant cases, as we shall see, it maintains a remarkable independence.

In the Pentateuch we have the following collections of legal texts which we could call codices had their content been arranged in a more systematic way. We have already examined some of them:

1. The 'Book of the Covenant', Exod.20.22-23.33 and perhaps the beginning of ch.24;
2. The Decalogue, Exod.20.1-17//Deut 5.6-21;
3. The Decalogue or Dodecalogue of Exod.34.10-26;
4. The twelve curses of Deut.27.14-26;
5. The main body of Deuteronomy, chs.12-26;
6. The 'Holiness Code', Lev.17-26;
7. Various codices: on sacrifice, Lev.1-7; on the priesthood, Lev.8-10; on ritual purity, Lev.11-15; on the Day of Atonement, Lev.16.

Other sections seem too fragmentary to allow a classification.

3. Characteristics of the biblical collections of laws

It is impossible here to enter in detail into the problems about the legislation of the cult, of the priesthood and of sacrifice, and the regulations for the ritual calendar and the fasts which it covers. I shall limit myself to dealing with those passages which are more concerned with everyday life, those which we would now call secular.

The way in which the laws are scattered over the Pentateuch means that here, too, it is impossible to attribute their range to a single author or redactor; that therefore completely cuts the ground from under the traditional opinion which derives the laws from Moses. Here a knowledge of the classical world, and especially of Justinian's collections (sixth century CE) in which it is possible to distinguish the authentic texts from later elaborations, sometimes with remarkable clarity, has provided specific help for studying biblical law. However, we should immediately note that the normal distinctions of modern jurisprudence, between public law and private law, between penal, civil and administrative law, are impossible to apply because of the common denominator of sacrality, which makes all the laws qualitatively alike. Here, too, it is only possible to proceed by literary genres and to make inferences from them. Thanks to Alt in 1934, a formal classification has been established once and for all, and has also been accepted as applying to the majority of the laws of the ancient Near East: there are laws framed in apodeictic form and laws framed in casuistic form. We shall begin with the latter, as they present fewer problems.

4. Laws in casuistic form

(a) Characteristic of the law formulated casuistically is its attempt to provide for every kind of situation which could arise as the result of an action or an omission, adapting the norm to each one of them. The description of these laws arises from this interest in the specific 'case' in which the law finds its application. In the 'Book of the Covenant', about half the laws are formulated in this fashion. They have a characteristic beginning, always with a conditional formula: 'If...' or 'Whenever...' or 'Given that...', etc. This beginning describes the essential characteristics of the action or omission. An analogous formulation is well known in a Mesopotamian milieu in the formula *šumma awīlum...* = 'Whenever a man...' The description of the fact is then followed by a list of aggravating or mitigating factors or simply points of explanation. The style is normally objective; the discourse is in the third person; in the few cases where the second person appears we probably have explanations or comments on the law given to the community assembled in the sanctuary, sometimes in reply to questions about specific facts. The style is often prolix, as the material requires; it has been said to be 'non-Hebraic' in comparison with other specimens of biblical prose.

(b) We do not need to go far for the origins of casuistic law; all the ancient Near East knows norms formulated according to these criteria from the earliest period. Thus Israel did not invent them but took them over from its environment. However, we may notice two peculiarities of the genre in Israel, though they are purely negative.

1. The casuistic formulation is never used in laws connected with the cult or with ethics. It is therefore at this point that perhaps a distinction between sacral and secular law might begin.

2. These laws are therefore neutral in the religious field. A typical example comes from the 'Book of the Covenant', which has already been mentioned. In Exod 21.6; 22.8 we twice read *ᵉlōhīm* = God (one of the reasons, perhaps, for attributing these passage *en bloc* to the E source, cf. above, 6.7b). But it becomes obvious to anyone who sets out to make a translation that, although it would be possible to render the term by 'God', it could also be translated as 'the deity', without any specific reference to the faith of Israel. In other words, the text considers situations relating to a temple, but not typical of the faith of Israel.

Alt thought that these laws were taken over by Israel in the process of settling in Canaan, not least because the situations presupposed are typical of agriculture in a village setting. We shall see later how this theory has recently been modified.

5. Laws in apodeictic form

These are the laws which contain a commandment or a prohibition, with or without a sanction against the transgressor, and with no provision for mitigations or special emergencies. As we have seen, in the 'Book of the Covenant' they appear mixed in with the others, but in Deut.27 or in Lev.17-26 they are collected together exclusively. In Exod.21.21ff. [EVV 21.22ff.] we have an instance of a law which was originally formulated in apodeictic form and was then attenuated by additions of a casuistic type.

These laws immediately give the impression, to those used to modern law, of a primitive harshness, as though they had been made by a society which was not interested in assessing degrees of culpability, criminal intention or the pressure of circumstances; the commission or omission of the act seems sufficient reason for the implementation of the penalty which, when it is provided for, is almost always capital punishment. The shedding of innocent blood (it does not matter whether the homicide was premeditated, voluntary or just manslaughter) cries aloud to God (cf. Gen.4.10, where the blood of Abel cries out to God) and demands adequate expiation. It might be concluded that the society which regulates itself by this kind of law is necessarily a society at the beginning of its development;

and it does not seem to be fortuitous that these laws have for the most part been replaced in everyday matters by laws formulated casuistically. However, such an evolutionary valuation of this kind is simplistic; we are not dealing with a still semi-barbaric society but with laws whch affect religious and therefore ethical questions. Homicide is an offence against the God who gives life, and therefore it can only be expiated by the death of the offender, regardless of the degree of his culpability. Only a certain move towards secularization will introduce other elements of evaluation. Meanwhile, however, when an act which offended God in this way was discovered within a community, this community had no alternative but to eliminate the guilty one from its midst. This was usually achieved by executing him; on other occasions he was banished, which in practice was an equivalent penalty.

Alt's hypothesis, taken up by some of his pupils, was that these laws reflect the 'primitive' and therefore harsh situation of Israel in the nomadic period, but from what has been said this is no longer acceptable. Nor can it be argued, as it could be in the time of Alt, that law framed in an apodeictic form was a prerogative of Israel, and was not to be found among other peoples of the Near East. Alt went so far as to suggest that these laws went back to Moses, and thus formed the beginning of the collection of the 'law of Moses'.

6. Criticism of Alt's theories

I have just attempted to show that the evolutionary approach of Alt's theory is untenable, but there is yet more to be said. I begin by repeating that the criterion of distinction, although essentially formal (it is not completely formal, as we have seen, since the content of the two categories of laws is different), not only remains valid but is the starting point for any investigation of ancient Near Eastern law. What made possible the evolutionary explanation of the two types of the law was the fact, to which I drew attention above, that laws formulated apodeictically were not known elsewhere in the Near East. Now the situation is different; laws of this type have been discovered in Mesopotamia and among the Hittites: the best-known collection is the edict of Ammi-ṣaduqa, king of Babylon, of the dynasty of Hammurabi, in the second half of the eighteenth century BCE, which was published at the end of the 1950s (cf. $ANET^3$, 526ff.).

Even before the publication of this document, however, doubts had already been raised about Alt's distinction by G.E.Mendenhall (see above). He began by indicating that it is impossible to relate

Israelite law framed in casuistic terms to Canaanite law; as far as the latter is known from Ugaritic texts, it either reveals a direct Mesopotamian influence and therefore does not constitute an original element, or, if it is autochthonous, does not display any parallel features to those of the Hebrew Bible. Moreover, the discovery of law formulated apodeictically among other peoples in the ancient Near East robs Alt's theory of another of its foundations. But Mendenhall does not limit himself to criticism; he offers his own solution to the problems. The laws formulated apodeictically are only guiding principles, whereas those formulated casuistically reflect legal practice, the specific decisions of tribunals. Mendenhall finds such a system in Mesopotamia and among the Hittites. He goes on to argue that the system of law formulated apodeictically, the principles, will have reached Israel through the patriarchs; the earliest collections of Israelite laws will then have developed on this basis. He sees his view supported by the fact that every substantial change of régime finds it necessary to codify the law afresh; he cites as examples Hammurapi's accession to the throne of Babylon, the Napoleonic era in Europe, and so on; something similar, he argues, will have happened in Israel on its settlement in Canaan.

Mendenhall's theory represents notable progress, but leaves doubts on at least one point: Alt rightly observed that the laws in apodeictic form have ethical or religious elements as their content, whereas those formulated casuistically contain secular material. It is therefore difficult to see in the latter the concrete application of the former, because of the difference in content. Moreover to attribute to the patriarchs the function of being carriers of ancient laws from country to country is manifestly naive in the present state of research, all the more since the texts never say that the patriarchs had contacts with people in the cities of the two regions.

E.Gerstenberger and W.Richter both came to the same conclusion independently of each other: laws in apodeictic form did in fact contain principles, directives, but rather as ethical and religious imperatives addressed to the ruling class and for the instruction of those aspiring to join it. Once this material had been published, it would be supplemented by material drawn from ancient Near Eastern legislation concerned with everyday life. What we have now is simply a synthesis of the two, which has left intact the religious and ethical legacy of Israel.

Two further studies have taken the discussion forward. The first shows that laws formulated apodeictically can be classified as:

(a) 'Prohibitive' laws (so called from Akkadian grammar), which in place of the usual imperative negated by *'al* use the ordinary imperfect with *lō'* and relate to matters of principle, generalizing from specific situations;

(*b*) The counterpart of these is normally a law which threatens the death penalty for the offender;

(*c*) A third category includes the various laws of retaliation, which limit the right of revenge by the victim on the guilty to the loss which has been suffered.

The second study seeks, on the basis of these features, to eliminate the distinction between laws formulated casuistically and laws formulated apodeictically, considering it to be purely formal and therefore invalid for distinguishing two literary genres. By the nature of things, it is argued, a legitimate distinction should consider content as well as form. In the present state of research it is difficult to come to a decision on this latter suggestion. The problem is the greater because the distinction proposed by Alt has been used with profit, as we have seen, not only in the study of Israelite law but also in the study of collections of ancient Near Eastern laws generally.

7. Lawsuits in the Hebrew Bible

The best way of seeing how the law functions in practice is to observe the course and conclusion of a trial. Nowadays the course of such a trial in the world of the Bible seems extremely simple, with a series of pragmatic and patriarchal connotations: a kind of 'rough justice' of the sort to be found in ancient Anglo-Saxon law. The difference in this case is that the place of meeting was the gate of the village, through which all those going out to work had to pass. The themes are also extremely simple and cover only relatively minor problems of the kind which can arise in an essentially agricultural community, no matter how harmonious it may be: quarrels, woundings, incidents of various kinds, especially involving other people's animals; thefts, runaway slaves and so on. In this sense Hebrew law and legal processes are clearly different from Roman ones: there is no theory or even philosophy of law, but simply the most rapid solution possible of conflicts that arise.

Ruth 4 is a relatively late passage and certainly post-exilic, but it does seem to reflect the very old usages preserved in the countryside, which are probaby not very different from those of the period we are considering (cf. below, 38.1). Here we have the account of what we would now call a civil case: the renunciation of title to a right in a case of redemption and its transference to the party with the nearest claim, Boaz. The plaintiff sits at the only gate of the village, waiting for the arrival of those who constitute the tribunal. When the court is constituted, it hears the cases of the parties (here the declaration of the parties) and passes sentence. In Jer.26 we have a more complex case: this is a criminal trial of the prophet, who is accused of blasphemy, a crime punishable by death. Here we do not have the simple conditions prevailing in the village, but a tribunal constituted with much greater formality. Here, too, the prosecution and the defence are heard: the latter invokes a 'precedent', that of the prophet Micah who, about a century earlier, had spoken in similar terms (3.12) without being prosecuted. Therefore the prophet is completely acquitted: as we would say, there is no case to answer. The verdict is given: 'This man does not deserve the sentence of death' (26.16). The tribunal is said to be composed of 'the princes and all the people'. This suggests a kind of jury composed of the elders, and a public debate.

The lack of a basic theory of law does not prevent the Hebrew Bible from formulating the scope of the law with remarkable clarity. Deuteronomy 25.1 asserts that the law is concerned with 'acquitting the innocent and condemning the guilty'. This statement is of the utmost simplicity, but is an effective guide for the judge.

The death penalty is invoked on the responsibility of the whole community in whose name it is pronounced and executed: sometimes the entire community has to take part in the execution, which is carried out by means of stoning. Justice is therefore speedy and public, cheap if not free, and all assume their own responsibility without delegating it to others. Only with the monarchy do we see a new institution arise: appeal to the king (II Sam.14.1-25; 15.2-3). In this way cases of greater importance are taken to a superior authority, independent of the local situation. Because of the silence of the sources, however, we do not know how this institution developed or what functions it had.

In many ways the older system might seem to have had advantages, but it was too simple to be capable to operating effectively in more complex political situations. The relative size of the country; its composite ethnic structure, in which the indigenous Canaanite people were accustomed to the supreme power of the monarch and an assembly with an aristocratic composition; the complication of social relationships in an economic and political structure which was continually tending to evolve, hindered its functioning and sometimes paralysed it – or worse. We can see, for example, illicit interventions by the court in the local administration of justice and the monarch's unwillingness to submit to decisions of the tribunal. One example is that of Naboth's vineyard (I Kings 21; cf. also the accusations against judges made by the prophets), even if this is extreme and therefore uncharacteristic. Here the local tribunal, as a result of court pressure, pronounces an unjust sentence on the basis of testimony which the judges know to be in bad faith. On the other hand, the late date and romance-like character of the account get in the way of an adequate legal evaluation of the facts and the specific case presented in it (cf. below, 15.3d). This is the explanation of the law in Deut.17.8ff., which centralizes in the central sanctuary all cases of particular importance, and especially those which carry the death penalty. This is to guarantee a debate which is as free as possible from outside interference.

8. Israelite law and that of the ancient Near East

From what has been said, it should be obvious that there are many parallels between Israelite law and that of the ancient Near East. Rather than indicate these, however, it seems better to highlight the differences between Israelite law and that of the Near East, seeking where possible to elucidate the reasons for them.

Ancient Assyrian law is renowned for its harshness. The penalties inflicted on the guilty party are extremely cruel: physical mutilation for crimes which today would seem to be far from serious (cf. artt. 5, 7, 8, 15, 16-21, 24, 44, 49, 54, etc.): in contrast, the codex of Hammurapi is more progressive – generally more so even than the Israelite collections of law. In art. 117 we have the institution of slavery for debt (cf. Exod.21.1-11; Deut.15.12-18): on the one hand the codex of Hammurapi is more favourable to the debtor in that it limits his stay in the house to three years; on the other, Israelite law stipulates that the slave shall not be set at liberty without means. In art. 250 we have an important parallel to Exod.21.28ff. in the case of damage to persons and property caused by a goring ox. For all its progressiveness from a legal point of view, however, even this collection deliberately accepts a class justice in which the penalty for the same crime varies depending on the status of the offender (free or slave, etc.). Finally, Hittite law seems particularly mild: every misdemeanour committed by a free man can be expiated by a fine, although for slaves the law is as cruel as that in Assyrian law (cf. I, artt. 5, 7, 79ff.; II, artt. 73-76, etc.).

I have pointed out that Israel does not stand out from its neighbours for the progressive character of its law, and indeed it was often retarded in this respect compared with neighbouring peoples. The absence of any physical penalty involving mutilation or torture should, however, be noted, despite the sometimes great intrinsic severity of Israelite law: the death penalty is called for in connection with offences in the religious and moral sphere, the penalty for which among other peoples can be commuted to a fine. The law of retribution is known in Israel only in a direct form; that is, it applies solely to the guilty party and not to a third person. Moreover the death penalty is never exacted for crimes against property, a concept which at the beginning of the last century had not been accepted among all the more progressive Western nations! There is no deliberately class justice in Israel; the only difference is that between slave and free, but Exod.21.20ff., 26ff., know significant limitations to the master's right to dispose of his slaves at his own whim. This last element might not seem particularly progressive today, but it is remarkable for its time, especially when we consider the evolution in the institution of slavery in a legally more progressive area like that of Rome and Greece centuries later. But Israel is also unaware of the exaggerated mildness of Hittite law, another way of devaluing the rights of the human person, this time the victim.

I have already pointed out that we have no way of knowing how these norms will have functioned in practice, and that is an inevitable lacuna. But the legal principles are those that we have been able to see. The question now arises whether there is a way of explaining these notable differences between Israelite law and that of the more advanced neighbouring peoples. One explanation has been proposed by W.Eichrodt, and in the present state of research it seems to be the most probable: the particular respect for the human person which emerges from a comparison between Israelite law and other laws is the product of a religion which put the human person above every legal norm and therefore rejected every penalty which infringed on his dignity. We have only one case in which this valuation seems to be contradicted: Lev.20.14, where the penalty of burning is provided for a particularly grave and scandalous case of incest. This is probably, however, a very isolated relic of an ancient rule which is perhaps connected with certain very early forms of tabu.

176   THE PENTATEUCH AND THE FORMER PROPHETS

BIBLIOGRAPHY

1. Cf. the bibliographical study by W.Schottroff, 'Zum alttestamentlichen Recht', *VuF* 22, 1977, 1-29. The legal material relevant to the present discussion is collected in a work which, though old, is still valuable: G.Furlani, *Leggi dell'Asia Anteriore antica*, Rome 1929; cf. also H.A.Brongers, *Oud-oosters en bijbels recht*, Nijkerk 1960. Neither of these works has received the attention they deserve, on account of the languages in which they were written. The interdependence between the Old Testament material and that of the ancient Near East has been examined by W.F.Albright, 'The Old Testament and the Archaeology of the Ancient East', in H.H.Rowley (ed.), *The Old Testament and Modern Study*, Oxford 1951, 27-47. For cultic law cf. H.Reventlow, 'Kultisches Recht im alten Testament', *ZTK* 60, 1963, 267-304, and R.Hentschke, 'Erwägungen zur israelitischen Rechtsgeschichte', *Theologia Viatorum* 10, Berlin 1965-6, 108-33 (a basic study). Cf. also P.E.Dion, 'Une inscription araméenne en style *awilum ša* et quelques textes bibliques datant de l'exil', *Bibl* 55, 1974, 399-403; D.Patrick, 'Casuistic Law Governing Primary Right and Duties', *JBL* 92, 1973, 180-4.

4. For these problems cf. M.Noth, 'The Laws in the Pentateuch', in his *The Laws in the Pentateuch and Other Essays*, ET Edinburgh 1966, 1-107; H.Rückert, *Die Begründungen der Weisungen Jahwes im Pentateuch*, Leipzig 1973; H.-J.Boecker, *Recht und Gesetz im Alten Testament und im alten Orient*, Neukirchen 1971; G.Liedke, *Gestalt und Bezeichnung alttestamentlicher Rechtssätze*, Neukirchen 1971. For an attempt to distinguish between penal law and civil law cf. M.J.Buss, 'The Distinction between Civil and Criminal Law in Ancient Israel', in *Proceedings of the Sixth World Congress of Jewish Studies* 1, Jerusalem 1977, 51-62.

3. A.Alt, 'The Origins of Israelite Law', in his *Essays on Old Testament History and Religion*, ET Oxford 1966, 79-132.

6. G.E.Mendenhall, 'Ancient Oriental and Biblical Law', and 'Covenant Forms in Israelite Tradition', *BA* 17, 1934, 26-46, 50-76 (also published separately as *Law and Covenant in the Ancient Near East*, Pittsburgh 1955); R.Kilian, 'Apodiktisches und kasuistisches Recht im Licht ägyptischer Analogien', *BZ* 7, 1963, 185-202; E.Gerstenberger, *Wesen und Herkunft des apodiktischen Rechts*, WMANT 20, 1965; W.Richter, *Recht und Ethos*, Munich 1966. Some of the apodeictic laws now appear in poetic form, the most obvious example being the *lex talionis* in Gen.9.6, cf. B.Schulz, *Das Todesrecht im Alten Testament*, BZAW 114, 1969. A proposal to abandon Alt's classification was made by V.Wagner, *Rechtssätze in gebundener Sprache und Rechtssatzreihen im israelitischen Recht*, BZAW 127, 1972. The legal character of norms formulated apodeictically was denied by G.Fohrer, *Theologische Grundstrukturen des Alten Testaments*, Berlin 1972, 166ff., but without sufficient reason. M.Weinfeld, 'The Origin of the Apodictic Law', *VT* 23, 1973, 63-75, supported Alt's theory, adducing comparisons with other legal material from the ancient Near East which had not previously been cited. For other information cf. S.M.Paul, 'Studies in the Book of the Covenant in the Light

of Cuneiform and Biblical Law', *SVT* 18, 1970, 112-24; cf. also J.Bright, 'The Apodictic Prohibitions: Some Observations', *JBL* 92, 1973, 185-240; A.Phillips, 'Another Look at Murder', *JJS* 28, 1977, 105-26. For the Edict of Ammi-ṣaduqa see the critical edition by F.R.Kraus, *Ein Edikt des Königs Ammi-Ṣaduqa von Babylon*, Leiden 1958.

7. L.Köhler, *Hebrew Man*, ET London 1956, 149-75; G.C.Macholz, 'Zur Geschichte der Justizorganisation in Juda', *ZAW* 84, 1972, 314-40 (important for royal justice in the south and for the legal reform of Jehoshaphat); E.Otto, 'Kultus und Ethos in Jerusalemer Theologie', *ZAW* 98, 1986, 161-79; H.Nier, *Rechtssprechung in Israel*, SBS 130, Stuttgart 1987. For trials in the Hebrew Bible see now the recent exhaustive study by P.Bovati, *Ristabilire la giustizia*, Rome 1986.

8. W.Eichrodt, *Theology of the Old Testament* I, ET, OTL, 1961, 74-97. Cf. also G.Gardascia, 'Droit cunéiforme et droit biblique', in *Proceedings of the Sixth World Congress* (above, § 2), 63-70; F.C.Fensham, 'Extra-biblical Material and the Hermeneutics of the Covenant Code', *Proceedings of the Oudtestamentiese Werkgemeenskap van Suid Afrika* 20/21, 1977-78, 53-65 and recently R.Westbrook, 'Biblical and Cunciform Law Codes', *RB* 92, 1985, 247-64. For the various Near Eastern laws see T.J.Meek in *ANET*[3], 217, 163ff. for Mesopotamian law; A.Goetze, ibid., 188ff. for Hittite law. This is of course a small selection of the vast amount of material which is now available to scholars, and a comparative study taking account of all of it would be very useful.

1 2

THE DEUTERONOMISTIC HISTORY WORK

1. Character

With the first of the 'former prophets' there begins what I have called in previous chapters the Deuteronomistic history work (abbreviated Dtr). From what we have seen, its prologue would have been made up of the brief historical summary in Deut. 1-4, while its name derives from the fact that at least two books, Judges and Kings, have been edited in such a way that time after time an early episode or an early note has been inserted into a context which clearly displays the lexical and ideological features of the fifth book of the Pentateuch. The other two books, Joshua and Samuel, have not been subject to revisions of this kind, but present large sections, often entire chapters, which are the work of the redaction in question and have been inserted into the text at key points in such a way as to give an explanation, usually of subsequent and sometimes of previous events. For Noth in his work of 1943 the result of this redaction was a continuous historical text in which the key for understanding was given by the redactors, although they included the ancient sources of which they made use. At the same time, similar results were arrived at independently by A.Jepsen, but his work only saw the light in 1953 because of the war.

Discussion about Dtr does not therefore centre on its existence within the 'former prophets', which is universally recognized, but on just how much work was involved in it. Is it a question of scattered interpolations and revisions which take on a certain organic character only here and there (in Judges and Kings), or do we have a history which is unified in scope and ideology, as Noth and Jepsen would prefer?

An answer to this question is far from easy: while it is true that the theories of Noth and Jepsen have found widespread acceptance, we cannot ignore the few voices which deny their validity, particularly as these are the voices of scholars of great prestige: among others we may cite O.Eissfeldt, G.von Rad and G.Fohrer. But whereas Eissfeldt, it should be noted, with due caution keeps the question open, von Rad and Fohrer, having noted that Noth's and Jepsen's observations allow of other explanations, consider the hypothesis that the sources of the Pentateuch continued in the book of Joshua to be more probable. In other words, they maintain the theory of the existence of a 'Hexateuch', asking how Deuteronomy could ever have been detached from Dtr had it formed its beginning. The last question can, however, be turned against those who raise it: how could Joshua ever have been detached from the Pentateuch if it had formed its conclusion? However, for M.Noth, followed by T.C.Vriezen and A.S. van der Woude*, 196, there can be no doubt that Dtr was an author. He had his own thought and was not just a collector or a compiler of pre-existing material.

It is certain that the hypothesis of the existence of Dtr, while resolving a series of problems, also explains a certain unitary character in the 'former prophets' and gives a clear reason for the otherwise strange title that is applied to them. Of course we must also allow for the interpolation into Dtr of material which originally had little or nothing to do with it, but it is certain that once the existence of large Deuteronomistic sections has been accepted, whether interpolated among early episodes or as an interpretative framework with which the early episodes were surrounded, it is easier to allow in consequence the existence of a unitary work of revision (which may have taken place in stages) than to stop without drawing what would seem to be the obvious conclusion. Of course it is necessary to recall that this is a working hypothesis and not an established theory.

Another difficulty is raised by the dimensions of Dtr. Giovanni Garbini points out that it would have been a much larger work than anything contemporary. So it seems, as is also shown by analysis, that Dtr grew progressively larger, and began from markedly more modest proportions. In the various editions of this Introduction, I too have accepted the hypothesis of a Deuteronomistic history work and will try to demonstrate in each instance what material has been left intact and what has never belonged to the work in question.

2. The aim of the work

What is the aim of Dtr? The most adequate answer was given some years ago by Perlitt in these terms: 'The authors of the Deuteronomistic history work were not moved by a passion for writing history but by the need to give a theological explanation of the fall of the two kingdoms.' In other words, divine promises and oracles seem to have been addressed to the Davidic dynasty in the course of the first half of the first millennium BCE which announced that the reigning house would last for ever. But not only were these prophecies not fulfilled, they were even proved wrong by the fall of the house of David, the exile and the loss of political independence. Having been frustrated on the earthly level, the oracles were very soon to reappear in an eschatological mode; at the end of time, when God himself restored all things, a descendant of David, an 'anointed', would reign, and his reign would have no end. Meanwhile, however, Dtr explained that what had in fact happened was none other than divine judgment on the reigning house and its people, both of which were sinful. In fact the ancient prophecies had not been unconditional: they depended for their fulfilment on the fidelity of the king and the people to certain demands of a theological kind. The people and its ruling house should have put into practice from time immemorial the principles of Josiah's reform; this had in fact been done by the fathers of the earliest period, and a small number of just and righteous kings had attempted to follow them. It is here that one of the most characteristic theological theses of the Hebrew Bible appears: that of an originally pure and uncorrupt religion which progressively became contaminated by the sin of the people and its contacts with the Canaanite population. Deuteronomy explicitly forbade these contacts and Josiah had been the one who restored this purest faith.

Beginning from the Babylonian exile (the last date in II Kings 25.27-30/Jeremiah 52.31-34 is that of the pardon given to Jehioachin about 561 by Evil-Merodach [Amel-Marduk] king of Babylon), the school thus sought to give the people of Israel a series of retrospective historical reasons, beginning from the settlement in Canaan and going down to the exile, to explain how the political destruction of the people was the result not of the weakness but of the power of YHWH. He had warned the people for many centuries through the prophets, exhorting them to conversion. Failure to respond to this appeal had brought divine judgment upon the people, and oracles announcing judgment through the prophets were strictly fulfilled; the north had fallen between 722 and 720 BCE (II Kings 17); the south suffered two exiles, one in 597 and the other, which was definitive, in 587/6. In other words, Dtr recalls the prophetic preaching, if only implicitly, though we also note in it a tendency to give a legalistic stamp to what the prophets had presented as a possibility.

3. Sources

Dtr tends generally to present its sources in an objective fashion, but the mere fact that they are almost always incomplete and that Dtr puts them in a different context, interpolating comments of its own which are meant to be the key to reading them, clearly shows that the various texts have developed considerably from their original form and context. In all instances the original points of reference have been suppressed and new ones have been created. The Deuteronomistic texts now no longer have their original function, that is, supposing that they *are* traditional texts and not *ad hoc* creations of the authors. Here are some examples of what I mean (cf. below, 16.1,3).

Two kings of the dynasty of Omri of Israel in the ninth century BCE, Omri himself and his son Ahab, were probably not the pious and devoted kings that the Deuteronomistic authors would have liked, so they are judged harshly – much more so than the other kings of Israel who were guilty of having caused or continued the breach with Judah, the southern kingdom. However, we know that in the political field they were both prominent figures (as also was Jeroboam II, just under a century later, who was also judged harshly). As far as we know, these were the two most notable rulers that the region produced in the first half of the first millennium BCE, and their work was crowned with success. They succeeded in forming a coalition which united Israel, Judah, and some of the Aramaean and Phoenician city states; it resisted and fought off the advance of Assyria westwards during a good part of the ninth century BCE. Only thanks to a series of *coups d'état* in Israel, Judah and Damascus did Assyria succeed in eliminating the ruling house of Israel and replacing it with an administation which toed the line. In this way Assyria overthrew the coalition from within, reached the Mediterranean and thus made the peoples of the region vassals (see my *History*, X. 3 and 4). The Assyrians continued to call the new ruling house of Israel 'kings of the country of Omri', although Omri's dynasty had fallen.

Now the political work of these two kings is simply ignored, and it is only from the Assyrian annals that we know, for example, of the battle of Qarqar on the Orontes in 853 in which Ahab is a prominent figure; the Assyrians claimed the victory, but they did not succeed in advancing any further west. By contrast praise is heaped on monarchs who adopted an orthodox religious position like Hezekiah and Josiah, but the attentive reader of the Bible will immediately see that their policies resulted in a series of catastrophes.

The position of Dtr is sometimes ambiguous towards other monarchs: it first makes a prophet announce that Jeroboam I of the north will be invested by God with ten tribes, but it then feels constrained to condemn him, as it condemns all the kings of Israel, for theological reasons (cf. I Kings 11 with ch.12). Perlitt is right, then, in seeing that what we have here is not what he has called a 'passion for writing history' but a history which is clearly written from a theological perspective and never seeks to disguise its aim. Moreover the schematization of political history in categories of 'reform' (modelled on that of Josiah) and 'anti-reform' (i.e. the negation of what has been done to approximate to Josiah's reform) is so clearly artificial that it does not need any other explanation: I have already discussed it above (9.7). But here, too, the historiographical element comes in, because the school sets out to explain the present situation (in this case, the political destruction of the people and the exile) as the result of past choices, choices which Dtr obviously considers to have been wrong. But the choices which have brought down the divine judgment on the people are theological: they are not choices in the economic and political field. In this sense, then, Dtr is a history, but the criteria for the choice and collection of its material are substantially different from those that a modern historian would consider suitable for corroborating his theories. We must therefore accept the accusation of tendentiousness, though the charge should not be dramatized. It is important to know the tendency of an author in order to be able to neutralize it as far as possible. At the same time we should remember that all history is tendentious in that it presupposes certain conditioning factors in history writing (no historian starts from an ideological void) and also certain features which it seeks to prove and certain aims which it seeks to achieve.

4. Place and date of composition

(a) It is not easy to establish where the Deuteronomists composed their work: whether in Babylon during the exile, which is a minority opinion, or in Palestine, among the survivors of the catastrophe, as most suppose. I personally tend towards the former alternative, at least for the latest phase, while accepting that other redactions (for which see the bibliography) may have originated in Canaan. (Here it is difficult to establish how far they took place before the exile, during the last years of the monarchy, and how far afterwards). The inclusion of the unitary narrative of the conquest in Josh.1-11 and the material relating to the division of the promised land in Josh.13-21 (even if this is not Deuteronomistic in origin), the concentration on the reign of David (II Sam.5-12 – though his sins are not glossed over) and other elements seem to indicate that Dtr does not limit itself to criticism of the people's past but also sets out to reinforce the old traditions. The choice that Dtr makes of some of these traditions is an important indication that it seeks also to strengthen and revive the people. If this theory is accepted, we should also allow that the aim in view was the restoration of the people, as with Ezekiel and later with Deutero-Isaiah.

For Dtr as for Deuteronomy the key point for assessing people and events is, as I have already said, Josiah's reform; the past history of the people is judged on the basis of the degree of faithfulness on the part of kings and people to the precepts of the reform in question. As we have seen, the whole Deuteronomistic history is interpreted as an alternation of reforms in a Deuteronomistic direction and anti-reforms which restore everything to its former state. The words of the prophets, fulfilled by the exiles, are also seen as pointing towards a conversion of both the community and the individuals who make it up, along the lines sought by the reform. But here, too, despite the obvious and consistent tendentiousness of a judgment basically formulated on a requirement established later than the persons or events described, Dtr is relatively objective: none of the kings, even Josiah, succeeded in fulfilling all the requirements in question. Thus the judgment acquires a remarkably relative character. However, it is interesting and disconcerting that, despite the implicit reference to the prophets and their message, virtually none of the prophets who have given their names to books of the Hebrew Bible are mentioned in the work. And this is even more disconcerting when we reflect that the majority of the prophetic works have passed through a process of Deuteronomistic redaction, as we shall also see.

(b) I spoke earlier about phases of redaction. Here, in a debate which took place some years ago in a somewhat listless fashion, at the beginning of the 1970s, a new note was struck. In 1971 Rudolf Smend of Göttingen demonstrated in a monograph how there are quite evident traces of a later Deuteronomistic redaction in the books of Joshua and Judges; he calls it DtrN ('nomistic') because it lays stress on observing the Law. In 1972, his colleague W.Dietrich pursued the study of DtrN and at the same time pointed to the existence of a further redactional phrase which came between DtrH and DtrN; he calls this DtrP because it incorporates material which either is prophetic or has a prophetic tendency. Another Old Testament scholar, T.Veijola of Finland, followed this up with two successive studies in 1975 and 1977: in the first he re-examined passages in Samuel and Kings and in the second, passages in Judges and Samuel, arriving at the conclusion that whereas DtrH is well-disposed or indifferent to the monarchy, DtrN seems anti-monarchical. However, these attributions to the various sections of Dtr are so specific that the result sometimes leaves one perplexed, because of the fragmentation of the texts to which it leads. It is therefore probable that although these suggestions are valid in principle, they will prove controversial for some time yet.

A last word. 'Deuteronomistic phraseology is only apparently a unitary language, with always the same patterns. Those who read it will find it full of nuances and surprises. So-called Deuteronomism had a long and extensive history, research into which is still only just beginning' (C.Levin). This is an element to take into account, one which may further studies which are now only in their beginnings.

BIBLIOGRAPHY

There is a bibliographical study in H.Weippert, 'Das deuteronomische Geschichtswerk', TR 50, 1985, 213-49. For the Deuteronomistic history work cf. M.Noth, Überlieferungsgeschichtliche Studien, Halle 1943 (there is a partial ET of 1-10 in The Deuteronomic History, Sheffield 1981; A.Jepsen, Die Quellen des Königsbuches, Halle ²1956; H.-W.Wolff, 'Das Kerygma des deuteronomistischen Geschichtswerks', ZAW 73, 1961, 161-86 (= his Gesammelte Studien, Munich ²1972, 308-24); J.A.Soggin, 'Deuteronomistische Geschichtsauslegung während des babylonischen Exils', in Oikonomia. Festschrift O.Cullmann, Hamburg 1967, 11-17; id., Joshua, ET, OTL, 1972, 3ff.; J.M.Schmidt, 'Vergegenwärtigung und Überlieferung', EvTh 30, 1970, 196-200. For an evaluation of Noth's work cf. G.Minette de Tillesse, 'Martin Noth et la Redaktionsgeschichte des livres historiques', in Au grands carrefours de la révélation et de l'exégèse de l'Ancien Testament, ed. C.Hauret, Tournai and Paris 1967, 51-75. The Perlitt quotation comes from Bundestheologie im Alten Testament, WMANT 36, 1969, 7. For a bibliography on the 'former prophets' cf. E.Jenni, 'Zwei Jahrzehnte Forschung an den Büchern Josua bis Könige', TR 27, 1961, 1-32, 97-146. For the passages about the prophets within Dtr cf. W.Dietrich, *Prophetie und Geschichte*, FRLANT 108, 1972. For the problem of the place of origin of Dtr cf. my 'Der Entstehungsort des deuteronomistischen Geschichtswerkes', *TLZ* 100, 1975, 3-8. The scholarly theory is that the work came out in Babylon, among the exiles, a theory which I would now want to make more specific: only the parts from the exilic period originated there, for example DtrN, for which abbreviation see above. Cf. also the 1972 Mainz dissertation by A.N.Radjawane, *Israel zwischen Wüste und Land*, which contains a full critical bibliography on the theme. A series of studies has allowed us to be clearer about the number of Deuteronomistic historians: R.Smend, 'Das Gesetz und die Völker', in *Probleme biblischer Theologie: Festschrift G. von Rad*, Munich 1971, 494-509; T.Veijola, *Die ewige Dynastie*, Helsinki 1975, and *Das Königtum in der Beurteilung der deuteronomistischen Historiographie*, Helsinki 1977; and W.Dietrich, op.cit. DtrN is the latest, DtrG (= *Geschichtswerk*, historical work) or DtrH is the earliest. For the divisions suggested for Dtr see the bibliographical study by W.Dietrich, 'David in Überlieferung und Geschichte', *VuF* 22, 1977, 44-64, especially 47-9.

Cf. also J.Rosenbaum, 'Hezekiah's Reform and the Deuteronomistic Tradition', *HTR* 72, 1979, 23-43; H.-D.Hoffmann, *Reform und Reformen*, Zurich 1980; R.E.Friedman, 'From Egypt to Egypt', in *Traditions in Transformation*, ed. B.Halpern and J.D.Levenson, Winona Lake, Indiana 1980, 167-92; R.P.Carroll, *From Chaos to Covenant*, London and New York 1981, 13ff. (in this important work the author shows how the theory of cognitive dissonance can explain the fact that many ancient prophecies were either not fulfilled or else became true in quite a different way. For a definition of 'cognitive dissonance' see J.S.Kselman in *RSR* 11, 1985, 120-9; it is 'inconsistency (or 'dissonance') experienced by a person holding conflicting beliefs or assumptions ('cognitions')'; R.E.Friedman, *The Exile and Biblical Narrative*, Chico, Ca. 1981; G.Garbini, review in *AION* 32, 1982, 497f.; A.D.H.Mayes, *The Story of Israel between Settlement and Exile*, London 1983; Z.Zevit, 'Deuteronomistic Historiography in I Kings 12', *JSOT* 32, 1985, 57-73; H.Weippert, 'Das deuteronomistische Geschichtswerk', *TR* 50, 1985, 213-49 (a bibliographical study); B.Peckham, *The Composition of the Deuteronomistic History*, Atlanta 1985; and T.Römer, 'Israël et son histoire d'après l'historiographie deutéronomiste', *ETR* 61, 1986, 1-19. For the problem of the absence of any mention of the prophets in the work cf. K.Koch, 'Das Prophetenschweigen des deuteronomistischen Geschichtswerks', in *Die Botschaft und die Boten. FS H.-W.Wolff*, Neukirchen 1981, 115-28; I.W.Provan, *Hezekiah and the Book of Kings*, BZAW 172, 1988; for the problem generally see J.Van Seters, *In Search of History*, New Haven and London 1983, 337ff. For the thought of Dtr cf. also S.Amsler, 'La motivation de l'étique dans la parénèse du Deuteronome', in *Beiträge zur biblischen Theologie. FS W.Zimmerli*, Göttingen 1977, 11-22; R.Rendtorff, 'Die Erwählung Israels als Thema der deuteronomistischen Theologie', ibid., 75-86; N.Lohfink, 'Kerygmata des deuteronomistischen Geschichtswerkes', in *FS Wolff*, 87-

100. The quotation at the end of the chapter is from Christoph Levin, *Die Verheissung des neuen Bundes*, FRLANT 137, Göttingen 1985, 18.

13

JOSHUA

1. Division and characteristics

(*a*) We can now go on to examine the first of the 'former prophets' and the first complete book of Dtr, Joshua. We must leave aside the opinion expressed in the Babylonian Talmud (Baba Bathra 14b) that Joshua himself was the author of the work: in that case the author would be describing his own death in ch.24.

The problem of the authorship of Joshua does not seem to be very different from the problem of the authorship of the Pentateuch which we have considered, with the difference that here there is no tradition about the author. Apart from the untenable Talmudic attribution, Joshua is anonymous. The person of Joshua is only the protagonist of the book. The expression 'until this day' appears often (4.9; 5.9, etc.), which is the sign of a later revision; we often have cross-references to the Pentateuch, the promises of which are 'fulfilled' in Joshua, but these are passages from Deuteronomy fulfilled in Deuteronomistic passages (8.30-35 and ch.23); moreover, the narrative of the conquest is the obvious conclusion not only of the journey through the wilderness after the exodus but also of the many indications scattered through the Pentateuch. It is thus quite understandable that in the past, as today, from Wellhausen onwards the book of Joshua has been seen as the logical conclusion of the Pentateuch, which has thus been expanded into a Hexateuch. However, the situation seems more complex because of the presence of numerous Deuteronomistic texts, whereas in the Pentateuch outside Deuteronomy, as we have seen, these are reduced to a relatively small number (see above, Excursus II). Even for those who do not accept the hypothesis of an organic history work, the problem of Joshua thus seems substantially different from that of the Pentateuch. At all events, the final Deuteronomistic revision has not completely concealed the presence of sources which could be closely connected with the Pentateuchal sources even by those who accept the Deuteronomistic hypothesis. Chapter 2 (leaving aside some of the dialogues, where we have a good deal of Deuteronomistic material); 6.25; 11.13; 15.13-19, 63; 16.10; 17.12f., 14-18; 19.42, some of which has an obvious parallel in Judg. 1 (see below) seem similar to J (and Noth himself accepts the existence of this kind of material, which he attributes to a 'collector', German *Sammler*). The non-Deuteronomistic part of ch.24 is usually attributed to E, while a few scattered verses (14.1a; 17.4 and 19.51) seem to belong to P. At all events, the tone of the book is now determined by the Deuteronomistic insertions (chs.1; 23 and part of ch.24), which virtually form the beginning and the end of the book. The second of these chapters is important because it often speaks of divine judgment and of exile, should the people not accept and observe certain obligations towards YHWH. Here, then, we seem to have the reason why the whole book has been handed down.

(b) The book of Joshua naturally falls into three parts. The first comprises a unitary account of the conquest by the twelve tribes of Israel under the leadership of Joshua: they cross the Jordan, pitch camp in the region of Gilgal near to Jericho, occupy successively Jericho and Ai, make a first expedition towards the south and then head north. This narrative leaves many areas unsecured, while others are occupied without our knowing how Israel could have crossed the intervening territory. This is particularly evident in the expedition northwards: how did they arrive there without having occupied the central zone to make the journey possible? We hear only that Israel had control of Shechem and its sanctuaries (cf.8.30ff. and ch.24), but not how this was obtained: was it by an arrangement with the people of the place, by conquest or in some other manner? All this, of course, presupposes that we start from the actual biblical narrative, according to which all Israel crossed the Jordan near Jericho and succeeded in conquering the greater part of the country under the leadership of Joshua, so that it could be divided between the tribes. The second part, chs.13-21, speaks of this division of the country. Only the tribes west of the Jordan are considered: the others had already received what was promised them before crossing the Jordan. To show solidarity with the others, however, they also shared in the expedition; they are present in ch.22 but then cross the Jordan to return to their own land. The third and last part relates to the assembly at Shechem (chs.23 and 24), which has already been mentioned several times: ch.23 is the purely Deuteronomistic version, while ch.24 is a version revised by the Deuteronomist.

(c) A last point of interest is the break in continuity between Joshua

and Judges: twice we have a note about the leader's dismissal
(Josh.24.28; Judg.2.6) and twice a note of his death (Josh.24.29f.;
Judg.2.8-10). It is easy to see that we have the same texts in each
case. The explanation is simple. This is the same narrative which is
now interrupted by Judg.1.1-2.5, a passage which belongs to J or to
the source which Noth calls 'the collector'. It is a text which, as I
have pointed out and will go on to note in more detail, has remarkable
parallels with Josh. 15-17. Here is an almost typical example of texts
interpolated into Dtr with which the work itself has nothing to do.

Judges 1 is one of the more important texts for anyone concerned
with the study of the 'conquest' of Palestine. Leaving aside the
problems of the individual sections, which we cannot examine here,
this text gives a picture of the conquest which is markedly different
from that attested in Josh 1-12:

1. According to this earlier tradition, there was no unitary conquest
of Palestine under a single leader. On the contrary, there was a
settlement made by individual tribes or the nuclei of tribes or other
groups in succession, especially in the wilderness and in mountain
country which was thinly populated and therefore particularly
suitable for movements of this kind. The text also shows that when
the invaders attempted to settle in the fertile plain they were routed.

2. In its initial phases the settlement was an essentially peaceful
operation on the part of non-sedentary elements in the territories
mentioned above. When it came to armed encounters, the technically
more advanced Canaanites found no trouble in getting the upper
hand. In territories with little or no population, however, there was
no opposition. Genesis 34, a text which is difficult to interpret
historically, certainly late, and independent of the book of Joshua,
clearly shows that the rulers of the Canaanite city-states did not see
any objection to groups like those of the ancestors of Israel settling
in areas of their territory since they brought with them abundant
herds and at the same time populated uninhabited areas.

3. In any case, the conquest was not over with Josh.12, since 13.1ff.
and Judg.1 list a series of city states and their territories which Israel
did not succeed in conquering. On the contrary, Israelites were
sometimes forced to become their subjects.

These considerations, which actually arise out of the biblical book,
make it impossible to accept the account in Josh.1-12 according to
which the country was conquered by a united Israel under one
commander, composed of a federation of the traditional tribes. This
also takes the ground from under the theory that after it had been
conquered the country was divided (cf. chs.13-21) by drawing lots

for the parts which each tribe was to occupy. The institution of drawing lots, quite apart from being impossible on the political level, also appears extremely problematical in purely technical terms: how would it be possible to draw lots for a territory of hundreds of thousands of acres which was for the most part only just occupied and therefore almost totally unknown? A division of the land by lot would, however, fit in with the earlier period, as being the rotation of tribal lands between the various clans or families, an institution which then began to die out under the impetus of the political and economic situation.

The list of groups to whom the land is assigned is interesting: we have Caleb, Judah, Ephraim, Manasseh, Benjamin, Asher, Simeon, Zebulun, Issachar, Naphthali and Dan; Levi, the priestly tribe, receives forty-eight places for its support, six of which are also cities of sanctuary for those guilty of homicide, whose blood cannot be shed within their walls. As has been noted, as well as tribes in the traditional sense of the term, descended from Jacob, we also have other groups which were later absorbed into the tribes, like Caleb. The total number is twelve, but the two Transjordanian tribes of Reuben and Gad are missing. That makes a total of fourteen (or thirteen if Caleb is considered as a group which receives land but is not a tribe in the strict sense; the figure twelve can be obtained only by counting Ephraim and Manasseh as a single group, that of Joseph). Be this as it may, the enumeration of the twelve tribes of Israel constitutes a separate problem, to which we shall return in our discussion of Judg.5 (cf. below, 14.3). If we were then to add Machir (presented in ch.16 as a 'son' of Manasseh) and the Kenites (Judg.1.16), a group similar to Caleb, we would have an even larger number. Thus we have a series of ethnic and geographical problems to which we must soon return. Van Seters regards this as a late text, probably P.

I referred earlier to promises or commandments contained in the Pentateuch which are fulfilled or carried out in Joshua. Some of the most important and best known of these are: Exod.13.19// Josh.24.32ff.; Deut.11.29//Josh.8.30ff. with 18.28; 23.8 with 24.14. Deuteronomic influence or interpolations can be seen clearly in chs.1 and 3 and in the speeches in chs.2; 10 and 24. I cannot go into more detail here; cf. my *History*, VII.

2. The problem of the book

The problems that I sketched out in the previous section can thus be posed in the following terms: first there is the problem of the relationship between the unitary narrative of the conquest (Josh.1-12) and the fragmentary account (Judg.1); secondly there is the problem of the territory assigned by lot, although part of it had not been conquered and the rest was scarcely known.

Judges 1 shows clearly, as we have seen, that the 'conquest' took place in a fragmentary way, in stages, and was limited to certain regions in which the indigenous populations had no interest: desert, steppe, mountains and wooded country. This made the settlement of the new arrivals automatically either a matter of no interest to the city state or in some cases even desirable. The settlement took place, but only in small groups. The same chapter shows how most of the time the attempts of the invaders to occupy better territory (usually in the plains or at any rate in the more densely occupied areas) came up against the resistance of the inhabitants, who almost always proved victorious. In this Judg.1 agrees with the parallel passages of Joshua, both probably fragments of J or of the 'collector' (cf. Josh.15.13-19 with Judg.1.8; Josh.16.19 with Judg.1.29; Josh.17.11-18 with Judg.1.27ff.). Joshua 19.47 and Judges 17-18 belong in the same category, but the two narratives are now too different for us to be able to examine them together.

Now there is a substantial difference between the 'unitary' narrative of the conquest and the fragmentary account, a form of incompatibility which can be overcome only if we admit that we have to do with two different phases of the 'conquest'; but this last possibility is excluded by the fact that the 'unitary' narrative precedes the other. Another difficulty is presented by a feature to which I have drawn attention, that Judg.1.1-2.5 interrupts the narrative of the final dismissal given by Joshua and his death and burial, thus clearly revealing its character as an interpolation into Dtr. But the fact that the same material is to be found partly in Joshua immediately suggests that here we have a source which the Deuteronomistic narration wanted to replace but which later, in circumstances of which we know nothing, managed to find its way into its Deuteronomistic context. However, it resisted harmonization with this context and was simply ignored. Comparison with patterns of settlement in the ancient Near East certainly makes the fragmentary version of the settlement more likely in both geographical and ethnic terms, whereas the other has every appearance of being a later

'official' version. For the problems see my *History*, VII and Appendix
1.

Credit for having demonstrated this state of affairs goes to A.Alt
and his pupils, principally Noth. Given the premises, they developed
the theory that the settlement would originally have been presented
in a fragmentary fashion with scattered theological elements: later
the new version was superimposed, replacing these elements with a
rich unitary version. Continuing the investigation, they established
that in Josh.1.1-10.15 almost all the occupied territories (with rare
exceptions) correspond to those of Benjamin. The sanctuary of Gilgal
also belonged to Benjamin up to the beginning of the period of the
monarchy (I Sam.11). The obvious conclusion, though it has still to
be universally accepted, is that the version of the conquest which
ended by becoming 'canonical' for the whole of Israel was that of
Benjamin, handed down through the Gilgal sanctuary, though it is
impossible to establish the process by which this happened.

In other words, whereas J or the 'collector' still had the fragmentary
account of the conquest which had been preserved in fragments of
Joshua and Judg.1, the unitary version, which was of considerable
theological importance because it shed light on the great acts of God
of which the conquest was the most miraculous sign, very soon
became the official and canonical version, replacing the other. It is
also difficult to say here how that happened and through whose
work: it is possible that there was a pre-Deuteronomistc redaction,
and one's mind turns immediately to E, but it is impossible to go
beyond sheer conjecture. For Van Seters, however, all this section
should be attributed to J, with P additions here and there; there
never will have been a 'collector' in the sense of the term given to it
by Noth.

3. Geographical texts

Chapters 13-21 are a separate problem. They obviously do not belong
to the Deuteronomistic redaction in either style or content; in their
present position they follow on the whole-hearted acceptance of the
theory of the unitary conquest of the country. Otherwise, their
inclusion in the present context would be obscure. Their insertion
into Joshua is thus obviously later than the substitution of the
'unitary' theory for the 'fragmentary' theory. On the other hand the
composition of these texts, which are of importance generally for
students of the geography of the Bible or of the ancient Near East,

and for the historian, presents such special problems that it is obviously necessary to devote independent study to them.

Here too we begin with the studies of A.Alt. In 1925 and 1927, he arrived at the conclusion that in these texts we have two different literary genres: the description of a series of boundary lines between the various tribes obtained by means of a consecutive listing of places which serve as fixed points of reference, and a system of provinces essentially connected with Judah. The first system reflects the situation of the country between the settlement and the institution of the monarchy and is therefore very old, still in the last years of the second millennium BCE; the second, on the other hand, reflects the reorganization of Judah under Josiah after his conquests (but see the problems discussed in my *History*, XI.4f.), and cannot therefore be earlier than the second half of the fifth century BCE. The validity of this distinction can now be considered to have been generally accepted, and the same is true for the dating of the lists of boundaries, which in fact could be very old. The situation over the districts of Judah is rather different: the studies of the Americans F.M.Cross and G.E.Wright and of the Israelis Y.Aharoni and Z.Kallai in the 1950s and 1960s proposed that the dating of these districts should be moved considerably further back in time, in some cases as far back as the tenth century BCE! However, this is a theory which shares the problems of all the sources which are supposed to be 'ancient'.

Until recently there was some agreement over the details of the levitical cities in ch.21 and the cities of refuge in ch.20. The majority felt that the list in Josh.21, to which we have parallels in Num.35 and I Chron.6, also reflects a historical situation certainly not earlier than the time of David and Solomon, since many of the areas mentioned were conquered under them. However, opinions differed over the dating of the institution. A.Alt again thought of the time of Josiah; W.F.Albright, on the contrary, of the earliest period of the monarchy. The opinion of the Israeli B.Mazar was not very different; he put it some decades earlier still. The same problem also arises over the cities of refuge, which are all contained in the earlier list. F.Horst, following the lines traced by Alt, also suggested the time of Josiah here: once the sanctuaries in which the guilty party could find refuge had been abolished, it was necessary to institute the cities in question. However, R.de Vaux, after an examination of the passages, argued that this was an institution independent of the tribes and not earlier than the time of Solomon; he was also strictly against dating the institution any later. In any case we know as little about it as about the levitical cities. This problem too may be resolved in the next few years: a recent archaeological surface examination of almost all the tells involved has shown that a large number of these places was not inhabited before the eighth century BCE. This is powerful support of the dating suggested by Albrecht Alt (cf. my *History*, VII.3.5).

5. The thought of the book of Joshua

The thought of the book of Joshua is obviously that of the successive editors and redactors of the material collected in it, and is thus in a special way that of Dtr. Thus we find a rigid separation from Canaanite elements and descriptions of the massacre of those indigenous populations with which Israel was not to come into contact. That the massacres of the kind described in the book of Joshua never happened is sufficiently demonstrated by the presence of a numerous Canaanite population during the whole of the first half of the first millennium BCE, especially in the kingdom of Israel. This population several times succeeded in getting the upper hand over Israel. Thus we have a theory typical of Deuteronomy and Dtr, intended to underline the need for the people of God not to accept the customs of these peoples and sometimes to avoid all contact with them. Only once in Joshua do we have the concession of the report of a 'vassal' relationship between indigenous populations and the invaders, that of the Gibeonites in ch.9 (there should be no doubt as to its essential historicity, since the theme reappears in II Sam.21.1ff, where the house of Saul is punished for having violated this agreement). Here Dtr constructs a theme in the narrative according to which Israel had been deceived by the Gibeonites, who claimed that they had come from a long way away. No notice is taken of the incongruity of the fact that in that case there was no reason why they should ask to be 'vassals', an incongruity which 'Israel' should have noticed. Jericho (ch.6), Ai (chs.7-8), places in the south (ch.10) and the north (ch.11) are given over to extermination. For the crime committed by an Israelite during the conquest of Jericho, all Israel suffers a defeat before Ai, a place which Israel succeeds in conquering only after the guilty person has been identified and punished. This is an interesting narrative variation on the Deuteronomic and Deuteronomistic doctrine of reward and punishment. The strength of the combatants has little or nothing to do with their victories: these are the work of God. Jericho (ch.6) falls after a complex cultic act; the narrative about the sending of spies in ch.2 suggests that a text now lost would have spoken of an attack in force against Jericho, and this is presupposed by a variant attested in LXX 2.18, cf.24.11; the battle in ch.10 is won by Israel following the well-known miracle which caused Galileo Galilei so much difficulty and which has at least one notable parallel in the *Iliad*. The events at Shechem in ch.24 are centred on the recitation of the confession of faith and the renewal of the people's obligation, which is just what Josiah sought in his reform. In this way history is simplified and reduced to a great schematic unity: the conquest of practically all the country *en bloc* by 'all Israel' with Joshua at its head, but in reality led by YHWH; once occupied, the territory could be easily divided, and as material Dtr or possibly others afterwards used ancient texts which spoke of frontiers and districts. It is evident that the theological element, the preaching and the instruction, finished by in fact having almost absolute dominance over history; and it is the latter which reappears, almost on the sly, in Judg.1 and the parallels in Joshua. Of course Dtr was not created out of nothing; it made use of already existing liturgies and tried to historicize them. Instead of looking, then, for possible agreements between the narrative and the results of archaeological excavations, it is necessary rather to start from the principle that Dtr (or possibly others even earlier) historicized pre-existing liturgical material and used it for its preaching.

BIBLIOGRAPHY

Commentaries

D.Baldi, SacBib, 1952; M.Noth, HAT, [2]1953; H.W.Hertzberg, ATD, 1957; F.-M.Abel, JB, [2]1958; J.Gray, NCB, 1967; J.A.Soggin, ET, OTL, 1972; R.G.Boling, AB, 1982; T.C.Butler, Word, 1983.

For a critical text of LXX (as far 19.38) see M.A.Margolis, *The Book of Joshua in Greek*, Paris 1931-9. The missing leaves were rediscovered a few years ago and should soon be published. For an examination of the problems of this text cf. recently L.J.Greenspoon, *Textual Studies in the Book of Joshua*, Chico, Cal. 1983.

2. A.Alt, 'The Settlement of the Israelites in Palestine', in his *Essays on Old Testament History and Religion*, ET Oxford 1966, 133-69; id., *Erwägungen über die Landnahme der Israeliten in Palästina*, Berlin 1939 (= his *Kleine Schriften* I, Munich [3]1963, 126-75). His theories have often been contested by archaeologists, especially in the United States, cf. W.F.Albright, 'The

Israelite Conquest of Canaan in the Light of Archaeology', *BASOR* 74, 1939, 11-23; J.Bright, *Ancient Israel in Recent History Writing*, SBT 19, 1956. The whole question is discussed in M.Weippert, *The Settlement of the Israelite Tribes in Palestine*, ET, SBT II 21, 1971; R.G.Boling, 'Levitical History and the Role of Joshua', in *The Word of the Lord Shall Go Forth. Essays... D.N.Freedman*, Philadelphia 1983, 241-61; C.T.Begg, 'The Function of Josh.7.1-8.29 in the Deuteronomistic History', *Bibl* 67, 1986, 320-34. For the problem of the presence of J in Joshua cf. S.Mowinckel, *Tetrateuch-Pentateuch-Hexateuch*, BZAW 90, 1964, 17ff., 33ff.; for the 'collector' see M.Noth's commentary (above). For the topographical details of the campaigns in Joshua and Judges see the important study by H.Rösel, 'Studien zur Topographie der Kriege in den Büchern Josua und Richter', *ZDPV* 91, 1975, 159-90; 92, 1976, 10-46. Cf. also J.Van Seters, *In Search of History*, New Haven and London 1983, 324ff. See also A.G.Auld, *Joshua, Moses and the Land*, Edinburgh 1975, passim, esp.107ff.; id., 'Judges 1 and History', *VT* 25, 1975, 261-85 (in this last study see also the problems posed on a historical level by Judg.1); id., 'Joshua: The Hebrew and Greek Texts', *SVT* 30, 1979, 1-14; G.W.Ahlström, 'Another Moses Tradition', *JNES* 39, 1980, 65-9; L.L.Thompson, 'The Jordan Crossing, *ṣidqōt* YHWH and World Building', *JBL* 100, 1981, 343-58; R.D.Nelson, 'Josiah in the Book of Joshua', ibid., 531-40; (G.)R(inaldi), 'Jehosua', *BeO* 24, 1982, 80; J.Sanmartín, *Las guerras de Josué*, Valencia 1982. For Van Seters the texts would be P texts, following the theory of S.Mowinckel, op.cit., and *Zur Frage nach dokumentarischen Quellen in Josua XIII-XIX*, Oslo 1946. For Judg.1 see also E.T.Muller, 'Judges 1.1-36', *HTR* 77, 1984, 33-54. H.Seebass, 'Josua', *BN* 28, 1985, 53-65, has argued that an original P version in the book of Joshua will have been suppressed, because it was eminently peaceful and therefore in contrast with the official Dtr version. For the literary genre of the book see now G.W.Coats, 'The Book of Joshua: Heroic Saga or Conquest Theme?', *JSOT* 38, 1987, 15-32.

3. A.Alt, 'Das System der Stammesgrenzen im Buche Josua' (1927), and 'Judas Gaue unter Josia', *PJB* 1925 (= his *Kleine Schriften* I, Munich [3]1963, 193-202 and II, Munich [3]1964, 276-88; F.M.Cross, Jr, and G.E.Wright, 'The Boundary and Province Lists of the Kingdom of Judah', *JBL* 75, 1956, 202-26; Z.Kallai-Kleinmann, 'The Town Lists of Judah, Simeon, Benjamin and Dan', *VT* 8, 1958, 134-60; Y.Aharoni, 'The Province-List of Judah', *VT* 9, 1959, 225-46. For the levitical cities and the cities of refuge cf. W.F.Albright, 'The List of Levitical Cities', in *L.Ginzberg Jubilee Volume*, New York 1945, 49-73 (a fundamental study); B.Mazar, 'The Cities of the Priests and Levites', *SVT* 7, 1960, 193-205. The position of F.Horst appears in 'Recht und Religion im Bereich des Alten Testaments', *EvTh* 16, 1959, 49-75 (= his *Gottes Recht*, Munich 1961), 260-91, esp. 59 = 273f.; R.de Vaux, *Ancient Israel*, ET London 1961, 160ff.; id., *The Early History of Israel* II, ET London 1978, 523ff. For the geographical and topographical passages in the Hebrew Bible and especially in Josh.15-21 see now Z.Kallai, *Historical*

Geography of the Bible, Jerusalem and Leiden 1986, Parts II and III (I have not been able to consult this work, which has a solidly conservative approach).

4. For the 'holy war' and the massacres of the indigenous population see my article 'Krieg, Altes Testament', *TRE* 16, 1988.

14

JUDGES

1. Title and contents

The title of the book derives from the figures who are the protagonists in the greater part of it, called in Hebrew *šōpᵉṭīm*, from the root *špṭ* = normally 'judge'; it is therefore logical that the word has always been translated 'judges'. However, the root also has an archaic sense, attested in Ugaritic and in some passages of the Hebrew Bible, in which it means 'govern'; this meaning also appears in Phoenician and Punic, cf. the well-known Carthaginian *suffetes* during the Punic wars. The meaning is attested in the Hebrew Bible among other passages in Pss.96.13; 98.9, where the rule of YHWH is mentioned. It is therefore likely that this is the sense to be preferred and that we should not translate the word 'judges' but 'rulers' or something similar. Moreover, if we are looking for a cross-check, we never see the 'judges' exercising any kind of judicial function; the only exception is that of Deborah (4.4-5), but here her function precedes her call to be a 'judge'. This is therefore a title assigned to someone who exercised particular powers within the tribal alliance of Israel before the monarchical period.

The 'judges' may be formally divided into 'major' or 'minor' judges; the former are called by YHWH to deal with situations of especial danger, usually enemy attacks, and are sometimes called 'saviours', which was probably their original title. In the case of the latter, on the other hand, we only have notes of an anecdotal kind, but a particularly detailed chronology. They could have had functions similar to those of the Assyrian 'eponyms' in the official measuring of time, but we have no certain information about them. We shall return to this problem later.

As it is, the book is divided into three parts: the beginning comprises the section 1.1-2.5 which we discussed in the previous chapter (13.1,2); this speaks of two expeditions, one by the tribes of the south, i.e. Judah, and the other by the tribes from the centre and the north, i.e. Israel in the strict sense. We have also seen that the information given here has handed down an echo of the difficulties encountered by individual groups whenever they attempted to occupy territories which were not more or less uninhabited. The second part makes up the body of the book, and here we have information about the 'judges' (2.6-16.31). In it we have an account of the prowess of five or six 'major judges', figures who now appear to be operating on a national scale (this is once again the theme of 'all Israel' with which we are already familiar from Joshua), though a closer examination shows that they work within well-defined territories. We cannot therefore exclude the possibility that, contrary to the theory of the book, which has them acting in chronological succession, they could sometimes also have been active to some degree simultaneously. There is also mention here of the 'minor judges'. Their title was probably extended at a later stage to the 'major' judges, who, as we have seen, were perhaps originally called 'saviours'; no important historical narratives about them have been handed down to us. The 'major judges' are: Othniel (3.7-11); Ehud (3.12-20); Deborah and Barak (chs.4-5); Gideon (chs.6-8); Samson (chs.13-16); the 'minor judges' are: Tola and Jair (10.1-5); Ibzan, Elon and Abdon (12.8-15). Jephthah is a figure who seems to combine the characteristics of both (10.6-12.7), while Shamgar ben 'Anat (3.31; 5.6) and Abimelech (ch.9) have nothing to do with the 'judges'. The third part of the book, finally, presents two episodes; the conquest of the land in the extreme north by Dan (chs.17;18) and a civil war against Benjamin (chs.19-21). The body of the book poses a series of problems which we shall examine briefly.

2. The body of the book

The variety of narratives contained in 2.6-16.31 does not prevent the 'body' of the book from having an internal unity which is immediately apparent to the reader. This is disconcerting: it is a quite singular phenomenon, given the diversity of the narratives which the book contains. This diversity would rather lead one to expect some lack of unity in this section. Instead, we have a reduction to schematic categories which stands out clearly; every episode is preceded by an introduction in which it is reported how the people have sinned, how God, to punish them, has sent particular enemies against them (or has delivered them into the hands of particular enemies), how the people has repented and how God has sent them a 'saviour' in the person of a leader who has guided them to victory and thus liberated them. In this way each of the 'major judges' is dealt with in turn.

This schematic form has every appearance of being artificial, especially when it is repeated a number of times, as happens in this case. It is the product of a later organic rethinking which sets out to use an ancient episode to instruct audience or readers. In this case the instruction is offered in a theological key: sin causes ruin on the historical plane also, and repentance leads to salvation. However, it is these introductions, which are all followed by episodes dealing with individual judges, which confer on the book the unitary aspect of which I have been speaking; thus the redactors can allow themselves to report the ancient traditions about their heroes almost entirely intact, since the introductions give the reader the key to the way in which they are to be interpreted. Now these introductions prove to be Deuteronomistic in both style and content: among other things, the formulation of the doctrine of retribution and the criteria for judgment, inspired by Deuteronomy, seem to be typical. The chronology of the 'major judges' is also stereotyped: it always speaks in terms of forty, twenty or eighty years, and this does not happen with the 'minor judges'. It would seem, then, that Dtr had at its disposal the ancient narratives about the saviours, but that they had no chronology, or the chronology did not fit in with that of Dtr. In the second case apparently the opposite happened: there were no relevant historical narratives, but the chronology was that much more exact; perhaps the redaction, which was not Deuteronomistic, found here notes of an annalistic type which included a precise chronology, as we shall soon discover in the books of Kings. In any case, given that we have no other chronological material available for comparison, this chronology is now of little use.

I have referred to the fact that the redactors, faithful to their ideal of 'all Israel', wanted to extend the activity of the 'major judges' to the whole nation, but that their theory would not hold up geographically. And indeed it is not difficult to see that the 'major judges' operate in regions which are geographically limited to the abode of a particular group or the area immediately adjacent to it. Thus, in the very important Song of Deborah (see the next section), only the tribes directly interested take part in the battle, while the rest either prevaricate or do not reply at all. This process is particularly clear in the story of Gideon. It begins with 'all Israel' and finishes with 300 men of Abiezer (7.1ff.), that is, members of Gideon's clan; the inconsistency is obvious from the fact that all Israel is said first to have been sent home, having been discharged so that the smallness of the number of combatants can shed a brilliant light on the divine work (another theme which appears in Joshua): they are then recalled after a few days or even after a few hours. Samson is another figure who is active in a limited area: the description of his work is embroidered with legendary elements which sometimes come from folklore. It is limited to the region of the boundary between the Philistines and Dan which at that time was to the west of Benjamin: the struggle probably ended in the defeat of Dan, as we see them looking for new territory in chs.17-18. Jephthah, on the other hand, works essentially in Transjordan. Dtr has no chronology for the last two heroes, and it is possible that to begin with, attempts were made to exclude them from the work as being ethnically and morally inadequate: they will have found their way back into it later. The episode of Abimelech in ch.9 also stands outside the scheme. It is a text of considerable importance and is basically authentic; it is connected with the destruction of Shechem, which on the basis of excavations carried out in the area has been dated at the end of the twelfth century BCE.

3. The 'Song of Deborah' (Judg.5)

This is considered to be the earliest poetical composition in the Hebrew Bible: the text does not show signs of Deuteronomistic revision, but it is not a unity. There is a Yahwistic framework to a central corpus which does not mention the God of Israel and has clear pagan connotations (for example, the struggle of the stars alongside the tribes, v.20); in this way the song has been made orthodox (cf. vv.6-8 [12?], 14-22, 24-30 with vv.2-5, 9-11, 13, [23?], 31a). The first part seems to be the earlier of the two, but not so much earlier as has been supposed in the past. The language is in fact later than that found in the so-called agricultural 'calendar' of Gezer (below, Appendix 1.2) which is usually dated towards the end of the tenth century BCE; it would not therefore be rash to conjecture the early monarchical period, soon after the division of the kingdom. The Yahwistic redaction does not have the vocabulary typical of Dtr, so it could be dated between the eighth and seventh centuries BCE. The language of the song poses its main problem. Whereas the grammar is regular, albeit archaic, the lexicography presents many difficulties and G.Garbini points out that a high percentage of the terms used is of doubtful meaning or are even unknown; moreover LXX[A] already transliterated many words because it did not know how to translate them.

The theme of the ancient song is how Israel, in the course of a battle, succeeded in vanquishing a coalition of Canaanite city states situated around the plain of Jezreel and here assembled under the leadership of a certain Sisera. This is one of the regions which according to Judg.1 Israel did not succeed in occupying because it was tenaciously and skilfully defended by its inhabitants. YHWH is presented here as coming forth from Seir (cf. Deut.33.2; Ps.68.8; Hab.3.3, all very ancient or archaizing compositions). Seir is in the region of Edom, situated in southern Transjordan, and the mention of the name is often used to attribute to Sinai a location in north-western Arabia, thus different from the traditional location in the peninsula which bears its name. Verse 14 shows that the invitation to take up arms was issued to all the tribes, but that only Ephraim, Benjamin, Machir (Manasseh?), Zebulun, Issachar and Naphtali joined in the battle. Those who did not take part, probably because they were far removed from the sphere of operations and consequently were less interested, and who thus attract taunts from the singer, are Reuben, Gilead (the territory inhabited by Gad), Dan and Asher. Levi, Judah, Simeon and Caleb are completely missing, while the Kenites appear at the end, in a markedly odious role. This suggests an obvious conclusion which I have hinted at earlier: the constitution of the tribal league must have been extremely weak, if such an organization existed at all, since each of the tribes acted exclusively in its own immediate interests. It is probable that Judah did not yet belong; the absence of Levi might be explained by the fact that it was not (or was no longer) an ethnic entity.

The historical basis of this epic is relatively easy to discover. It is an attempt to eliminate or at least neutralize the Canaanite enclaves which divided the central tribes – Ephraim, Manasseh and Benjamin – from those in the north of the country, by virtue of their domination of the plain of Jezreel. So we find that only those tribes were involved whose territory bordered on the plain and who had a direct interest in either eliminating this situation or at least modifying it substantially in their own favour. With good reason, the Israelite victory is felt to be an extraordinary event: up till then Israel had always been defeated in struggles against the Canaanite city-states. It was therefore celebrated in epic style, even if it did not lead to the occupation of the region in question: it was enough that communications had been secured between the northern central area and the north. Thanks to parallels from the ancient Near East, we know that the miraculous element, testimony to an intervention by YHWH, was provided by a torrential rainfall which made the battlefield impossible for the horses and chariots of the Canaanite armies, whereas the light infantry of the Israelite were not substantially impeded. Now given that fighting tended to take place in the spring and the summer, no rain should have fallen in this season. Rainfall would have been a quite extraordinary event in the eastern Mediterranean, where there is usually no rain from April to September (the last rainfall recorded there in this season was in August 1957, cf. my *History*, VIII.3.2.3). This is the origin of the statement in the poem (vv.20ff.) that the stars joined in the battle.

4. Chapters 17-21

Chapters 17-21 are important, not because they have not been subject to Deuteronomistic redaction, as was supposed, but because they testify to situations existing before the institution of the monarchy. In general the phrase 'In those days there was no king in Israel...' (17.6; 18.1;19.1, 25) is seen as a criticism of the political situation obtaining under the tribal alliance, a situation which is thus seen as one of open disorder. The Deuteronomistic history work, on the other hand, tends to exalt these times and the mode of government then prevailing. However, other explanations of the phrase are quite possible: traces of a Deuteronomic revision have recently been found (cf. the works by T.Veijola cited in ch.12).

(a) Chapters 17-18 narrate some episodes in the migration of Dan towards its definitive abode in the north of Canaan, after having left its original abode to the west of Benjamin. Joshua 19.47 also alludes to this migration (Leshem is only a variant of Laish, the place called Dan by the Danites). This place, treacherously attacked by Dan, became their capital and the site of their sanctuary, whose priests boasted Mosaic descent. The present redaction of the story (18.30 speaks of the conquest of the region and the deportation of its population under Tiglath-pileser III of Assyria in the second half of the seventh century BCE, cf.II Kings 15.27) is obviously later than the events to which it refers, and the polemical note against the sanctuary and those who founded it cannot be ignored. The reader must necessarily receive an unfavourable impression. So this is polemic against the sanctuary from within the northern kingdom or an argument used by the south to disqualify the north in this field also.

The presence of this polemical element is particularly interesting in a text which is not prophetic and which, as we have seen, is partly free from Deuteronomistic revisions.

(*b*) In chs.19-21, on the other hand, we have an episode which narrates the causes and course of a holy war followed by the ban. This institution is also attested outside ancient Israel: we have an example of it among the Moabites in the second half of the ninth century BCE on the stele of King Mesha (lines 15f., *KAI* no.181; *ANET*³, 320ff.; below, Appendix 1.3). At the end of the battle, everything belonging to the vanquished enemy – people, animals and possessions – was consecrated to the deity in one great barbarous extermination: the victor was not to stain his hands with the spoil. Now these chapters present a situation which at first sight we might consider different: the object of the holy war is not a people hostile to Israel nor are they defeated; they are one of the tribes of Israel, Benjamin. This tribe is accused of having given refuge to the perpetrators of a savage crime (to which we have a partial parallel in Gen.19) and therefore of complicity in it. Since it has rebelled against the dictates of the tribal alliance, the tribe is attacked and exterminated, to such effect that to repopulate the region it is necessary to resort to a stratagem which has notable parallels in the history of religions and ethnology, among other events in the rape of the Sabine women. The friendship which linked Benjamin with the central and northern region of Transjordan, Gilead, and which so notably helped Saul some time later (cf.I Sam.11; 31), seems to date from this time. Excavations at Gibeah (present-day Tell el-Ful, a few miles north of Jerusalem to the east of the main road), later the site of Saul's fortress, have unearthed clear evidence of violent destruction towards the end of the twelfth century, which could well be connected with the episode recorded here. We would thus seem to have archaeological evidence of the substantial historicity of the acts narrated. But on closer examination the text reveals a series of inconsistencies: first of all the disproportion between the crime and the punishment; then the indication of a situation of anarchy (as in the preceding passage) but at the same time the presence of the tribal alliance, a proper organ of government, a kind of central authority which maintains public order even at the cost of applying extreme penalties, penalties which moreover weakened Israel in the face of its enemies. The framework outlined here evidently arises from a highly romanticized approach and presupposes a later redaction of the tradition (exilic or post-exilic) – that is, if there ever was a tradition at all. In a late period, in which the hierocracy has now taken the place of the monarchy, the reference to the tribal alliance seems particularly pertinent.

Could this sort of thing have happened in reality? Atrocities committed by a people can serve as a pretext for war, but are rarely its cause, particularly if, as in this case, it is a civil war. The historian may find a more prosaic explanation of the real facts. Both Ephraim and Benjamin were engaged in vigorous expansion. Conditions for the latter were particularly disadvantageous, squeezed as it was between its powerful neighbour to the north and the territory of the city-state of Jerusalem and part of Judah to the south. This, rather than failure to observe the laws of the sacral alliance, seems to have been the real reason for the conflict which led to the extermination of Benjamin. Judg.12 also speaks of a civil war, again with Ephraim, but this time against the population of Transjordan whose friendly relations with Benjamin we now know.

5. The origins of the book

Underlying the book, then, and especially the main body of it, we have narratives which originally told of the deeds of Israelite heroes who had saved their people from distress, heroes working in a limited geographical and ethnic sphere. Dtr has made them heroes of 'all Israel', or perhaps this had already happened in an earlier redaction. It was, however, Dtr which gave the body of the work its present character, with an introduction to each episode containing the doctrine of reward and punishment. The heroes in question were in all probability originally called 'saviours', and if we leave out of account the Deuteronomistic redactional material it is in fact possible to discover what has been called a 'book of saviours', in which the early traditions were probably collected together before the final Deuteronomistic redaction. Chapter 1 has a history of its own, as we have seen, while chs.9; 17-18; 19-21, the first of which shows signs of strong Deuteronomistic redaction, give information which is remarkably useful. The same goes for the 'minor judges', the chronology of whom appears in chs.10 and 12.

The Hebrew text seems in good condition, but there are virtually two versions of the LXX: Codex B (Vaticanus) and Codex A (Alexandrinus) have so many variants that the critical edition by Rahlfs reproduces them both side by side. This allows us to conclude that a much more complex textual tradition underlies the book than the Hebrew text might lead us to suppose.

6. Thought

As in the case of Joshua, the thought of Judges is above all that of the Deuteronomistic redactor, who has revised ancient tradition according to his doctrine of retribution, making use of it as proof for his theory. The original traditions have been well preserved, at least in part, and we can see that much of them is made up of epic material and folklore. This does not mean that we do not have testimony here to quite a mature Yahwistic faith: the problem of religious syncretism is raised by the Gideon narratives in terms of the alternative YHWH or Ba'al, even if the stratification of these traditions is extremely complex. The first redaction cannot be earlier than the eighth century BCE; a distinct preference for the theocratic régime over against the monarchy is expressed in 8.22f., but here too there is already a mention of 'all Israel', a concept which, as we have seen, also belongs to a late stage of redaction, even if it was still pre-Deuteronomistic. Taunts against the monarchy as an institution also appear here and there in ch.9, especially in Jotham's fable (9.7ff.), though this may have been inserted into the passage at a secondary stage and thus may be no more than a wisdom-type interpolation against abuses of power. But even in the revision of the early song of Deborah (ch.5), as in the narratives about Gideon, the real victor is YHWH. God can choose even equivocal people like Jephthah for his own purposes (11.1f.). Through all the ancient narratives, even those like that of Ehud (ch.3), which seems to have no theological content at all, there is an expression of faith in the God of Israel which can make good all human deficiencies.

A particularly lofty ethic appears in passages like chs.19-21, when the reprehensible act against the protégés of the Benjaminites is judged with the words, 'Was ever such a thing seen in Israel?', and followed by the punishment of those responsible and their accomplices, even though this operation weakens the ranks of the new arrivals. The fact that criticism may then show this event to stem from very different motives does not affect this basic position.

BIBLIOGRAPHY

Commentaries

C.F.Burney, [2]1920 (reprinted 1970); H.W.Hertzberg, ATD [2]1959; A.Vincent, JB, [2]1959; A.Penna, SacBib 1963; J.Gray, NCB [2]1986; R.G. Boling, AB 1975; J.A.Soggin, ET, OTL [2]1987.

1. E.Täubler, *Biblische Studien*, Tübingen 1958; W.Richter, *Traditionsgeschichtliche Untersuchungen zum Richterbuch*, Bonn 1963; id., *Die Bearbeitungen des 'Retterbuches' in der deuteronomistischen Epoche*, Bonn 1964; id., 'Zu den "Richtern Israels" ', *ZAW* 77, 1965, 40-71; D.M.Gunn, 'Narrative Patterns and Oral Traditions in Judges and Samuel', *VT* 24, 1974, 286-317; A.J.Hausch, 'The "Minor Judges" – a Re-evaluation', *JBL* 94, 1975, 190-200. S.Abramski, 'On the Kenite-Midianite Background of Moses', *EI* 12, Jerusalem 1975, 35-9 (in Hebrew with an English summary) studies the mentions of Moses in Judges. For various problems cf. W.Brueggemann, 'Social Criticism and Social Vision in the Deuteronomistic Formula of the Judges', in *Die Botschaft und die Boten. FS H.-W.Wolff*, Neukirchen 1981, 101-24; D.W.Gooding, 'The Composition of the Book of Judges', *EI* 16, 1982, 70*-79*. For the 'minor' judges cf. J.A.Soggin, 'Das Amt der "kleinen Richter" ', *VT* 30, 1980, 245-9. For 1.1-25 see G.E.Wright, 'The Literary and Historical Problem of Joshua 10 and Judges 1', *JNES* 5, 1946, 105-14; S.Mowinckel, *Tetrateuch-Pentateuch-Hexateuch*, BZAW 9, 1964, 17ff. For the chronology cf. G.Sauer, 'Die chronologischen Angaben in den Büchern Deut. bis 2.Kön', *TZ* 24, 1966, 1-14, and my commentary, 6ff. For the topograpical problems see now H.Rösel, 'Studien zur Topographie der Kriege in den Büchern Josua und Richter', *ZDPV* 91, 1975; J.Van Seters, *In Search of History* (above, p.196), 342ff.

2. For the Gideon cycle cf. W.Beyerlin, 'Geschichte und heilsgeschichtliche Traditionsbildung im Alten Testament', *VT* 13, 1963, 1-25; L. Schmidt, *Menschlicher Erfolg und Jahwes Initiative*, WMANT 38, 1970, ch.2; for that of Samson, J.Blenkinsopp, 'Structure and Style in Judges 13-16', *JBL* 82, 1963, 65-76.

3. The bibliography on this important document is vast. Cf. *inter alia* W.F.Albright, 'The Song of Deborah in the Light of Archaeology', *BASOR* 62, 1936, 26-31; A.Weiser, 'Das Deboralied', *ZAW* 71, 1939, 67-97. Albright, 'Jethro, Hobab and Reuel in Early Hebrew Tradition', *CBQ* 25, 1963, 1-11, esp. 9ff., holds that the song belongs to the J tradition. See my 'Il cantico di Debora, Giudici cap.V', *RANL* VIII.32, 1977, 97-112 and 'Bemerkungen zum Deboralied, Richter Kap.5', *TLZ* 106, 1981, 625-39. G.Garbini, 'Il canto di Debora', *Il parola del passato* 178, Naples 1978, 5-31, is important for the philological aspect. Cf.also C.Grottanelli, 'L'inno a Hermes e il canto di Debora: due facce di un tema mitico', *RSO* 56, 1982 [1985], 27-37; B.Halpern, 'The Resourceful Israelite Historian; the Song of Deborah and Israelite Historiography', *HTR* 7, 1983, 279-401; A.Caquot, 'Les tribus d'Israël dans le cantique de Débora (Juges 5, 13-17)', *Sem* 36, 1986, 47-70.

4. For chs.17-18 see M.Noth, 'The Background of Judges 17-18', in B.W.Anderson and W.Harrelson (eds.), *Israel's Prophetic Heritage*, London 1962, 68-85. For chs.19-21 see A.Besters, 'Le sanctuaire central dans Jud.XIX-XXI', *EphThLov* 41, 1965, 20-41; J.Muilenburg, 'Mizpah of Benjamin', *StTh* 8, 1954, 25-42. The historical background to the civil war is illustrated by K.-D.Schunck, *Benjamin*, BZAW 86, 1963, 57-79 (with

bibliography). For an investigation of the fortress of Gibeah cf. L.A.Sinclair, 'An Archaeological Study of Gibea (Tell el-Ful)', *AASOR* 34, 1960, 1-52, with Noth's very favourable review in *ZDPV* 78, 1962, 91-4. For the formula 'there was no king...' cf.S.Talmon, 'In those days there was no king in Israel', *Proceedings of the Fifth World Congress of Jewish Studies* 1969, I, Jerusalem 1971, 135-44 (in Hebrew: English summary, 42f.); he takes *melek* to stand for *šōpēṭ*, so that the phrase is simply a reference to a vacancy beween the rule of two judges. Cf. also the recent works by T.Veijola (cited above, p.185) and H.-W.Jüngling, *Plädoyer für das Königtum, Richter 19*, Rome 1981, and my commentary ad loc.

6. For the content of Judges cf. E.Jenni, 'Vom Zeugnis des Richterbuches', *TZ* 12, 1956, 257ff.; A.Ibáñez Arana, 'El deuteronomismo de los marcos en el libro de los Jueces', in *Palabra y vida – homenajes a J.Alonso Díaz*, Madrid 1984, 55-65; F.E.Greenspahn, 'The Theology of the Framework of Judges', *VT* 36, 1986, 385-96.

15

THE BOOKS OF SAMUEL

1. Introduction

Eusebius of Caesarea (*HE* VI, 25.2) quoting Origen, and Jerome in his *Prologus Galeatus* (his preface to the books of Samuel in the Vulgate), report that originally the two books of Samuel and the two books of Kings were a single work. The division into four books has been attributed by some scholars to the LXX: with written vowels the LXX will have needed more scrolls than the one or two used in Hebrew. And in fact in the LXX the books in question are called I, II, III and IV Kingdoms or Kings, names and divisions which have passed over to the Latin Bibles and which therefore still appear today in some Roman Catholic translations of scripture. In any case, the question is purely one of form: the content remains the same whatever the divisions. These divisions have certainly been made in a quite illogical way, almost haphazardly, which could justify the empirical criterion put forward above. Only I Samuel has a logical conclusion, with the death of Saul and some of his sons; II Samuel should end with the death of David, but his death appears only in I Kings 2. In turn the division between I and II Kings splits at least two episodes between one part and the other, as we shall see in the next chapter.

In the Babylonian Talmud (Baba Bathra 14b) Samuel himself is said to have been the author of I and II Samuel, but there is no foundation to the note: the prophet dies and his death is described twice (I Sam.25.1; 28.3), a typical case of duplication. What we have here, therefore, resembles (though in lesser degree) what we have seen in the case of Joshua: Samuel is the protagonist of the first book (not of the second), but certainly not its author, and his role is sufficient explanation of the book's title.

2. *The content of the book and its textual problems*

In the 'former prophets' Samuel precedes Kings and follows Judges; Ruth belongs with the Writings (cf. below, 38.1). It is perhaps possible to connect Judg.17-21 with the beginning of Samuel, to which it might form an introduction intended to explain why it became necessary to introduce the monarchy in Israel. However, this does not particularly affect the interpretation of the book.

The first seven chapters speak of Samuel's youth: of his birth in circumstances which are at least remarkable, of his service in the temple, of the tribal alliance in Shiloh, of the defeat of Israel in its struggles against the Philistines, culminating in the capture of the ark (a kind of mobile sanctuary), and of Samuel's activity as judge and prophet. At first sight the narrative has certain unitary and coherent characteristics, but on closer examination it can immediately be divided into a number of units, though these are connected together in quite a harmonious way. The text presents some irregularities: for example, in 1.20-27 we have a play on words around the verb *šā'al* = 'ask' and its passive participle *šā'ûl* = the one who is asked for. This, however, is referred to the person of Samuel, whereas etymologically (and these plays on words are always centred on an aetiological etymology of names) it should be connected with Saul and not with Samuel. For that reason, it has even been supposed that the narrative originally told of the birth of Saul and at a later date was revised in a polemical fashion in such a way as to glorify his opponent Samuel, but there are strong arguments against such a conjecture – for example, the name of Saul's father, which we know to have been Kish and not Elkanah. Chapters 8-15 refer to the first phase of relationships between Samuel and Saul, and tell of the institution of the monarchy. We have three versions of this event, which differ in detail although they have many elements in common: (*a*) ch.8 + 10.17-27 and ch.12; (*b*) 9.1-10.16; 13.5-15; (*c*) ch.11; 13.1-4, 16-23; ch.14. The first version is very much against the monarchy, though some scholars have felt that this tendency is the consequence of a later interpolation. This tendency reflects the last phase of Dtr, DtrN, now fundamentally critical of the monarchy, which is held to be the cause of the catastrophe of 587/6. This perspective is evidently that of the post-exilic hierocracy, for which the ideal regime is that of the tribal league; the institution of the monarchy was a mistake or even a sin. The other two accounts are favourable to the monarchy, but the description in the last account of the process by which Saul became the first king seems to be closer to events. The theory has been proposed that each of the three narratives will originally have been an account of how Saul was elected king in one of three different tribal groups; the three narratives would then have been extended to 'all Israel' in the way with which we are familiar from Joshua and Judges. This suggestion is not viable: the first version is clearly late, as we have just seen; the second is legendary with some elements of fable. Only the third, which is also full of later insertions, might preserve the record of the political and military difficulties which would have led to the institution of the monarchy in Israel, here originally probably only the north. But here, too, the theme of the lowly figure who rises to the highest position of rule recalls stereotyped narratives from antiquity, while the dialogue between the besieger and the Jabeshites has something unreal and fantastic about it.

It should also be noted that chs. 7, 8 and 12 have been considerably revised by Dtr, whereas in 13.5-15 and ch. 15 the circumstances of the rejection of Saul are rather obscure but apparently connected with what prerogatives the king should have in the cult. The majority of scholars believe that the latter of the two chapters is late, since it also reflects the message of Dtr.

Chapters 16-31 describe the conflict betwen Saul and David, interpreted by the redactors as the consequence of rejection by YHWH. The narrative shows the progressive decline in the mental health of the first king, while at the same time his general David moves about in circumstances which are more than equivocal. The heroic death in battle of Saul and some of his sons (ch. 31) serves almost to resolve a tension which has become intolerable.

In II Samuel, chs. 1-4 show the difficulties under which the country struggled after the death of Saul. In the south, David, a vassal of the Philistines, had assumed rule over Judah and had a capital of his own, Hebron; in the north Abner, commander of Saul's surviving troops, was de facto king, while the institutional figurehead was the weak and insignificant Eshbaal, surviving son of Saul: his name is regularly distorted to Ishbosheth, but it can be reconstructed from Chronicles. In chs. 5-8 David, elected king of Israel after Eshbaal's death, founds a real empire. After conquering the city-state of Jerusalem, which is promptly elevated to become the capital, he defeats the Philistines and occupies or makes vassals of all Transjordan and Syria. At the same time he establishes the best of relations with the great Phoenician city-states of Tyre and Sidon. Chapters 9-20 speak of the difficulties encountered by the king in his domestic policy, difficulties which involved his own family; he only escaped by a miracle when his son Absalom revolted. Finally, an appendix, chs.21-24, reports some isolated episodes from the life of the king: 21.1-14 seems to be the prelude to ch.9, which begins with David's question whether any survivors of Saul's family are still alive.

The ordered and coherent appearance of the narrative, especially from a chronological point of view, has already been noted; it does not, however, succeed in concealing some less coherent elements. We noted above the position of the first part of II Sam.21, but it is also obvious that chs.9-20 have their logical continuation and conclusion in I Kings 1-2. Further, we have seen that there are three narratives about the institution of the monarchy, which we may either regard as parallels or take to have arisen successively in three different areas and then to have been extended to 'all Israel'. The anti-monarchical narrative begins in I Sam.7, in which Samuel achieves a notable victory over the Philistines, and ends in ch.12, where Samuel takes leave of the people. As we have seen, however, both chapters have clearly been revised by Dtr, which in ch.7 evidently wanted to demonstrate that the situation was not as grave as the people made it out to be in ch.8, since Samuel had defeated the Philistines. In fact this note is tendentious, and we now know that it was the danger from the Philistines which accelerated the institutional move towards monarchy in Israel, even though in any case the time was ripe. It is certain that the royal prerogatives listed by Samuel in 8.11ff., which correspond to those of the sovereign in a Canaanite city-state, and which in Israel and in Judah presuppose a considerable experience with the monarchy, do not reflect an ancient document but are part of the negative judgment on the monarchy mentioned above. The narrative in ch.11 is generally considered to be closer to events; Saul was proclaimed king of the people once his longed-for victory over the Ammonites and the liberation of the territory of Jabesh-Gilead in Transjordan had revealed to all that God was with him and that therefore he would from then on be the leader of Israel. This interpretation of the institution of the monarchy is substantially different from the one we know to have existed among neighbouring peoples. But even in this case we could be dealing with interpolations which seek to present the monarchy in Israel as a singular development, though there is no way of proving this. Probably here, too, we have the product of later re-reading (cf. what I have already said above).

There are a number of doublets: in I Sam.10.11 and 19.24 we have a double explanation of the proverb 'Is Saul also among the prophets?'; the first occurrence is probably the earlier and authentic one. There are also a number of contradictions: in I Sam.16.23 David comes to court as an expert musician, while in vv.18ff. he is described as a mighty warrior; however, in the story of his fight with Goliath in ch.17 he appears as a youth who is presented to Saul for the first time (v.55, see below, § 3f.). We also have different narratives about David's flight and the change of side in which he becomes a Philistine vassal (21.11-16; 27.1ff.), while we have two accounts of the death of Goliath (ch.17; II Sam.21.19, where he is killed by a different hero, cf. also I Chron.20.5). The circumstances of Saul's death also differ: in I Sam.31 he kills himself by falling on his own sword, whereas in II Sam.1 an Amalekite mercifully kills him when he is seriously wounded so that he does not fall into enemy hands alive. As we have seen, the death of Samuel is narrated twice (I Sam.25.1; 28.3), while chs.24 and 26 give duplicate versions of the episode in which the fugitive David generously spares the life of Saul. The relationship between the sanctuaries of Mizpah and Gilgal, both mentioned in connection wih Saul, is not clear, unless the theory which would make them regional sanctuaries in which each group of tribes will have elected Saul king is viable – and we have seen that that is not the case.

It is therefore evident that here, too, we have the product of a union of various traditions and later re-readings, though any attempt to distinguish sources, as in the Pentateuch, must be considered unsuccessful. All that can be recognized is a discreet Deuteronomistic redaction; this has affected the text very little. The theory is more plausible which sees Samuel as a series of different cycles and scattered traditions, assembled by a redactor who was not of the Deuteronomistic group and was certainly earlier than Dtr. He will have followed a scheme which Dtr was able to take over, limiting its revision of the material to minimal interference. Anyone who accepts the hypothesis of a continuous Deuteronomistic history work will therefore have no difficulty in allowing that the final Deuteronomistic redaction accepted *en bloc* this material which had already been shaped by previous redactions, only adding its own retouchings here and there.

3. Independent units

The units, originally independent and clearly identifiable in the work, are not always very different from those into which the book naturally falls. They can, however, be classified by distinct criteria, generally by themes.

(a) A first narrative is that about the ark and its vicissitudes, from the time when it falls into the hands of the Philistines up to its triumphal entry to Jerusalem through the work of David (I Sam.4-6; II Sam.6). More or less a generation elapsed between its capture and its triumphal return to Israel, during which time it stood for many years in a domestic sanctuary only a few miles away from the future capital. P.D.Miller and J.J.M.Roberts have, however, criticized the imposition of these limits on the 'narrative': this presupposes the texts which speak of the impiety of the sons of Eli and must include other texts which speak of the sacred object. We should also note the differences in topography and nomenclature between I Sam.6 and II Sam.6, as a result of which it is not even clear 'how the narrative finishes'. For Van Seters, this is again a Deuteronomistic theme: the ark appears here as a precursor of the centralization of the cult, and therefore of the post-exilic hierocracy. The narrative now appears to have been inserted into the wider context of the struggles between the Israelites and the Philistines. The beginnings of these struggles were narrated in Judg.13-16 (above, 14.2), in the story of Samson, and they developed under Saul down to his heroic death, coming to a provisional end under David (II Sam.5.17ff.), who defeated the Philistines. The story of the ark has its own stylistic and lexicographical peculiarities (it has some humorous touches, as for example when it relates how the statue of Dagon, god of the Philistines, was found one morning face downwards before the ark which, though in captivity, is still a sign of the presence of YHWH, or when it describes the humiliating illness with which the Philistines were afflicted, so that they were persuaded to abandon the ark). Its aim is simply to show how the ark reached Jerusalem under David, having been captured a number of decades earlier by the Philistines. The importance of the ark cannot have been particularly great, since later references are extremely rare (I Kings 8.1, 6, paralleled in Chronicles; Jer.3.16, on its destruction, a note which it is difficult to evaluate historically).

(b) Another section is made up of the narratives about relationships between Samuel and Saul (chs.8-15). We have already seen that these are the result of a redactional work which did not avoid duplicates, contradictions and incongruities. It is probable that underlying this collection is an attempt at a biography of the unfortunate first king of Israel, but it seems clear that the materials involved were not used objectively. It is certain that whoever saw to the redaction of these episodes supported first Samuel and then David against Saul. Another fact indicating the composite character of this material is that we have a neat break at the end of ch.14. The

chapter clearly concludes a literary unity; as we have seen, ch. 15 is
a late construction in which we cannot see whether and up to what
point ancient traditional material may have been used. The historical
value of the material also varies; we have seen that ch. 11 is old and
relatively close to the events narrated, and the same also applies to
chs. 13 (not vv. 5-15) and 14. The reason given for the break between
Samuel and Saul is interesting: in 13.5-15, when Samuel is late for
his appointment and the army is about to fall apart because of its
inactivity, the king himself offers a sacrifice; in ch. 15 a variant of the
LXX at 15.12f. provides a similar motive, but it is by no means
certain that it is original over against the Massoretic text. In any
case it seems possible that the ancient redactor saw the reason
for the breach between Samuel and Saul in a dispute over the
prerogatives of the king in the cult. Be this as it may, although the
redactor of the history favours first Samuel and then David, he does
not keep silent about the military exploits of Saul and his son
Jonathan. He recognizes their considerable achievements in the field
and in civil affairs.

(c) Another unit which, however, is directly linked to the preceding
section, is concerned with the relationship between Saul and David
up to the former's death in battle (cf. my *History*, III.3,4). This is a
sometimes ruthless chronicle of the fluctuating relationship between
these two heroes of ancient Israel, and there is nothing to prevent
our thinking that the same hands are at work here as revised the
previous section. This narrative, too, is clearly in favour of David:
Saul is now robbed of the divine blessing which had been at the heart
of his earlier success. Moreover, he gives signs of mental unbalance
with a progressive form of persecution mania. It would certainly not
have improved the king's mental state to hear the women singing
under his window, 'Saul has slain his thousands, but David his ten
thousands' (I Sam. 18.17; 21.11; cf. 29.5), but Saul's reaction was
clearly pathological. This is confirmed by the homicidal gesture with
which he turns against his general in 18.10f. The redactor calls this
pathological state 'an evil spirit from YHWH', a concept which is
also attested in classical literature, except that in the Hebrew Bible
the place of fate is taken by YHWH. Quite apart from the mental
health of the king, the fact remains that achievements in the military
field were the one incontrovertible sign that God was with the person
who could boast them, and the situation evidently put a serious
question-mark against the king's future. The fact that the narrator
clearly took the part of David against Saul does not, however, mean
that he has unconditionally defamed the latter, or that he has

particularly embellished David's deeds. David is presented here as a man with a great personal ascendancy, an ascendancy which did not spare even Jonathan, the heir to the throne. Forced to flee from Saul, David now becomes leader of a band of outlaws (22.2 describes David's troop as composed of 'people who were in distress and every one who was in debt and every one who was discontented') and collaborates with the Philistines. Indeed, the text does not hesitate to declare that it was quite by chance that David did not take part in the battle in which Saul and his sons died brave deaths (I Sam.29.1ff.): the Philistines did not trust David and preferred to send him against their and his enemies in the south. And while part of the responsibility would fall on the persecution inflicted by Saul on David, David's position was difficult to justify – so much so that he gave up being a vassal of the Philistines as soon as possible.

In this narrative we also have two quotations from the 'Book of the Upright' which has already been mentioned (cf. above, 6.4.1): II Sam.1.19ff.; 3.33. These are compositions which some scholars do not hesitate to attribute to David himself.

The author or redactor of the history in its earliest form may have been an official at the court of David or Solomon, with a knowledge of events and access to all the available material, well disposed to the ruling house without making partisan judgments on its adversaries or favouring his own side uncritically. Now, however, the narrative is an integral part of the Deuteronomistic history work. The one objection that should be made to it is perhaps that it has not presented Saul in all his greatness; he was, after all, the first king, that is, the first person who succeeded in giving political unity to Israel and in defeating the Philistines and enemies coming from Transjordan, an achievement which he accomplished in an almost desperate situation. And if one can talk of mistakes – here was a man who paid for them in person.

(d) The 'succession narrative', II Sam.9-20 (perhaps preceded by 21.1-14 and ch.24, cf. the question in 9.1, which is probably a reference to the episode described in 21.1ff., and the beginning of 24.1ff., the form of which is similar to that of 21.1ff.) and I Kings 1-2 is a work of remarkable importance. After the classic study by L.Rost, the narrative has often been considered to be one of the earliest history writings in the world, if not the earliest. The author is a supreme storyteller and sees history as a series of interconnected events linked by a chain of cause and effect, and at the same time dominated by the concept of divine recompense. In this sense, then, we have a precursor of Dtr. The narrative begins with a few factual details: David sought to possess the wife of one of his generals, Uriah the Hittite, and did not hesitate to have the latter killed to remove the impediment to his marriage. Now comes retribution: as David has destroyed the family of Uriah, so his own family is to be destroyed by the divine judgment (cf. the speech by the prophet Nathan in II Sam.12.7-21). The criterion which unites this history is thus the hand of God, who is the real protagonist in it: he guides it even in its less edifying aspects (cf. also II Sam.11.27; 17.14). For the rest, however, we have a secular history and a principle of approach which is basic to any scientific history. On the other hand it has been noted that the narrative is rich in elements which by their nature cannot be subjected to historical investigation: not only the concept of divine reward and punishment, an anticipation of Dtr and a feature common to all Near Eastern and Israelite wisdom (which believes in a cosmic order of which YHWH is the guarantor in Israel) but also other aspects cannot be verified in any way. A typical example of this is the conversation between Amnon and his half-sister Tamar (II Sam.13.1ff.) in the bedroom where the former is pretending to be ill; there cannot have been witnesses, as v.9b says explicitly, but the conversation is reported in its entirety. Thus although the narrative refers to historical events, it is not properly historical, but rather a historical novel which attempts to penetrate into the make-up of the people it describes and bases its approach on a fundamental theme of wisdom: no one can escape the laws of the world order which is guaranteed by YHWH. Furthermore, it is a story with an obvious message: Solomon is the legitimate successor to David, willed by God, and it is good that he ascended the throne, albeit at the cost of a *coup d'état* and the cruel measures which followed. Despite these reservations, however, it is difficult to deny that the account bears witness to the way in which Israel struggled to gain an understanding of history as a world-wide phenomenon, an interest which we do not find among any other people at this time (with the brief exception of the Hittites).

(e) This material, then, was collected together on two successive levels; the first comprised the various units which I have described, and involved several redactors, each operating in his own field, concerned to combine and co-ordinate the traditions (or complexes of existing traditions) dealing with a particular theme; the second comprised Dtr. On the first level we are probably dealing with court chroniclers, a theory which has already been put forward. They will have had access to all the traditional material and to the existing archives. It was certainly in the course of this work of redaction that the narrative of the ark was divided into two pieces, each of which was inserted in the position in which it now stands: I Sam.4-6 and II Sam.6. Other material, however, will have remained outside the general treatment: see II Sam.21-24, of which we have noted that at least 21.1-14 almost certainly belongs before II Sam.9.

The result was that the Deuteronomistic historiographers found Samuel in part already finished: only I Sam.7-12 were revised, and then Nathan's oracle in II Sam.7, a text which possibly contains a historical nucleus, though in detail it is not always easy to separate the original parts from the revision. However, the general approach of the books was such that the Deuteronomistic historians in their various redactions found that they had predecessors. For those who accept the hypothesis, this explains why they limited themselves to rearranging the material, and why their revisions are so scattered and insignificant ideologically.

(f) The text of the LXX also comes under the heading of an independent unit, especially in Codex B (Vaticanus). This is a text which in many cases is not only remarkably different from the Hebrew text, but is almost always considered by critics to be better. Some fragments from Qumran (and we have already alluded to the problem: above, 2.6a) now confirm at least in part the variants with which it has been customary to emend the Massoretic text; they thus prove that LXX[B] also had a Hebrew archetype and is not therefore a creation of the translators in question. In other cases, however, the same fragments support the variants contained in the text of Chronicles, so that the problem is not limited to the text of I and II Samuel and therefore proves to be more complicated than might appear at first sight. Here once again is a problem of a most technical kind; the extremely fragmentary character of these texts which are known by the sigla 4QSam[a,b,c] has made possible the publication of only a few verses in the last twenty years; questions of detail and the bibliography have been discussed above (2.6).

4. Thought

(a) The theology which underlies the books of Samuel before their final redaction by Dtr is, given the content of the work, a pre-Deuteronomistic theology of history, but similar to it in many respects. It is customarily called 'prophetic', since in its later texts, e.g.I Sam.15, it draws widely on the thought of the prophets of the eighth and probably the seventh centuries BCE. However, this thought is not only indicated in texts like the one mentioned above;

it also appears in some questions of detail, which are none the less significant for that. For example, there is the polemical form in which the theophoric names compounded with Baal are reported. In I Chron.8.33 and 9.39; 8.34 and 9.40, we read of Eshbaal and Merib-baal respectively; in I Sam.2-4 and 9 these are distorted into Ishbosheth and Mephibosheth, and the polemic is carried on with such consistency that in II Sam.11.21 the Jerubbaal of Judg.8-9 has become Jerubbesheth! *Bōšet*, with its orthographic and phonetic variants = 'shame, abomination', is the term often used to transcribe the Canaanite term *ba'al*, the name of the principal god of Canaan, and also of other deities. Now as we have seen in connection with E, anti-Canaanite and anti-syncretistic polemic began at the end of the ninth century BCE and became acute during the eighth and seventh centuries, following the prophetic preaching; it is addressed more to élite groups than to the masses, whereas we have clear indications that it was not acute at the beginning of the tenth century and immediately afterwards. In other words, without at all wishing to cast doubt on what our texts relate, we should remember that their definitive formulation, especially in the realms of ideology and theology, reflects a complex of problems from a time some centuries later, and this complex is also likely to be reflected in the first attempts at history writing.

(b) One of the fundamental theological problems which appears right through the work is that of the election and the rejection of particular people. Quite apart from any expectation of personal merit, and often choosing men whose morals are at least doubtful (David is the most impressive example of this), God directs human history by making use of individuals whom he elects and whom he endows with particular gifts in view of their vocation. To the modern reader Saul might hardly seem to be a 'sinner', and we might doubt whether his 'sin' made more of an impression on the post-exilic reader. There would not seem to be any basis in reality that at the heart of the conflict between Saul and Samuel there were questions like that of the prerogatives of the monarch in the cult: only decades after Saul, David and Solomon intervened directly in the affairs of the cult, the first bringing the ark to Jerusalem with a solemn procession in which the king officiated, and the second building a temple, sacrificing, blessing the people and pronouncing prayers of intercession, with hardly anyone making any objection or finding anything to complain about. Moreover, the religious reforms laun-ched by Hezekiah and then especially by Josiah were praised (with a few reservations) by the Deuteronomistic historian and were not attacked by the prophets, who were often very polemical in their encounters with the monarchy. More than dwelling on facts, then, the redactors were concerned to make an intensely theological presentation of two paradigmatic cases. In the case of Saul we have a man who was elected by God for a specific task but could not surrender his office once that task had been accomplished and could not see that others, more gifted than himself, were ready to succeed him. From this spiritual insensitivity there arose an inner conflict which led the protagonist to pathological forms of mistrust, hypochondria and persecution mania which would have proved suicidal for one who had been (and remained to the end) a prince without fault or fear had not his glorious death on the battlefield (to put it in pious terms) liberated him. In the case of David the situation is substantially different: here we have a most able and somewhat unscrupulous politician (the texts faithfully admit these qualities), a superb leader endowed with a special capacity for dealing with those like himself: so able that even Jonathan, the prince and heir, remains fascinated, although it becomes obvious that David has conspired against his interests. But again following this description, David is never deaf to the word of God and thus appears to the redactor in an exemplary form as a person who is capable of overcoming the many negative elements in his personality. These evaluations, then, are later theological ones; they are intended to provide examples, and certainly go far beyond any historical investigation. The starting point of such considerations is, of course, the fact that Saul and his house lost the throne while David and his gained it. This fact 'should' have matched some divine intention (and here the interpretation of the facts leaves the sphere of secular history, to enter the purely theological sphere) which the explanation given seeks to discover. And this is the weakness of such an approach on the level of history writing. But it cannot be denied that the authors – whether deliberately or not we do not know – succeeded in presenting at least in the person of Saul a figure who anticipates the protagonists of Greek tragedy; this explains why for centuries, down to a few decades ago (see André Gide's play), the unhappy first king of Israel has been the protagonist of tragedies. He remains the hero, the loyal warrior incapable of taking part in a political game which is both refined and brutal, an art in which David, by contrast, was master. And the fact that David's work was crowned with success while that of Saul ended gloriously, but tragically, on the heights of Gilboa, does not prevent us from considering Saul to be the more sympathetic and the more upright of the two, even if in

THE BOOKS OF SAMUEL

the intention of the redactors of the texts this is evidently a wrong view.

BIBLIOGRAPHY

Commentaries

S.R.Driver, *Notes on the Hebrew Text of the Books of Samuel*, Oxford ²1913; W.Caspari, KAT, 1926; G.Bressan, SacBib, 1954; H.W.Hertzberg, ET, OTL 1964; J.Mauchline, 1971; H.-J.Stoebe, KAT (NS), I, 1973; F.Stolz, ZBK, 1981; P.K.McCarter, AB, I, 1980; II, 1984.

For the problems of the origins of the monarchy and of the relation between Saul and Samuel and Saul and David cf. J.A.Soggin, *Das Königtum in Israel: Ursprünge, Spannungen, Entwicklung*, BZAW 104, 1967, I, chs.1-2 (with bibliography); T.N.D.Mettinger, *King and Messiah*, Lund 1976; T.Ishida, *The Royal Dynasties in Ancient Israel*, Berlin 1977, and 'Solomon's Succession to the Throne of David. A Political Analysis', in id. (ed.), *Studies in the Period of David and Solomon and Other Essays*, Tokio 1982, 175-87; J.P.Fokkelman, *Narrative Art and Poetry in the Books of Samuel*, Assen I, II, 1981-1986; J.Conrad, 'Der Gegenstand und die Intention der Geschichte von der Thronfolge Davids', *TLZ* 108, 1983, 161-76. For Saul see F.Langlamet, 'David et la maison de Saul', *RB*, 1979, 194-213, 481-516; 87, 1980, 161-210; W.L.Humphreys, 'The Tragedy of King Saul', *JSOT* 18, 1980, 18-27, and 'From Tragic Hero to Villain', *JSOT* 22, 1982, 95-117. For the individual and his elevation to the throne cf. D.M.Gunn, *The Fate of King Saul*, Sheffield 1980; J.V.Fritz, 'Die Deutungen vom Königtum Saul in den Überlieferungen von seiner Entstehung, I Sam.9-11', *ZAW* 88, 1976, 346-62; H.Donner, *Die Verwerfung des Königs Saul*, Wiesbaden 1983; T.R.Preston, 'The Heroism of Saul', *JSOT* 24, 1982, 27-46; T.Seidl, 'David statt Saul. Göttliche Legitimation und menschliche Kompetenz des Königs als Motive der Redaktion von I Samuel 16-18', *ZAW* 98, 1986, 35-56; G.Bettenzoli, 'Samuel und das Problem des Königtums', *BZ* 30, 1986, 222-36; id., 'Samuel und Saul in geschichtlicher und theologischer Auffassung', *ZAW* 98, 1986, 338-51.

2. I. Mendelsohn, 'Samuel's Denunciation of Kingship in the Light of the Accadian Documents from Ugarit', *BASOR* 143, 1956, 17-22, has tried to demonstrate the antiquity of the content of I Sam.8.11ff. For the question of the three accounts of the election of Saul see G.Wallis, 'Die Anfänge des Königtums in Israel', *WissZ Univ.Halle* 12.3-4, 1963, 239-47, amplified in his *Geschichte und Überlieferung*, Berlin 1968, 45-66, where the theory is put

forward that Saul was elected as king by three different groups, each at its own sanctuary. There is a not dissimilar situation for David: he is succesively crowned king of Judah (II Sam.2), then of Israel (II Sam.5), and in II Sam.3.19 reference is also made to negotiations with Benjamin. For the figure of Saul cf. recently C.Grottanelli, 'Possessione charismatica e razionalizzazione statale nella bibbia ebraica', *SSR* 1, 1977, 236-88. For DtrN cf. T.Veijola, op.cit. (above 13.1).

3a. A.F.Campbell, *The Ark Narrative*, Missoula 1975; P.D.Miller and J.J.M.Roberts, *The Hand of the Lord: A Reassessment of the 'Ark Narrative'*, Baltimore and London 1977; G.W.Ahlström, 'The Travels of the Ark. A Religio-Political Composition', *JNES* 43, 1984, 141-9; K.A.D.Smelik, 'De ark in het filistijnse Land', *Amsterdamse cahiers* 1, 1980, 42-50; T.N.D.Mettinger, *The Dethronement of Sebaoth*, Lund 1982, 50ff., 128ff.; J.Van Seters, *In Search of History*, 397ff.

3b. The figure of Samuel in all its complexity is analysed by J.L.McKenzie, 'The Four Samuels', *BiblRes* 7, 1962, 3-13, and A.Weiser, *Samuel; seine geschichtliche Aufgabe und religiöse Bedeutung*, FRLANT 81, 1962. For the origins of the monarchy cf. H.-J.Boecker, *Die Beurteilung der Anfänge des Königtums in den deuteronomistischen Abschitten des I.Samuelbuches*, WMANT 31, 1969; L.Schmidt, *Menschlicher Erfolg und Jahwes Initiative*, WMANT 38, 1970, chs.3-4, 6.

3c. David's initial period is analysed by H.U.Nübel, *Davids Aufstieg in der frühe israelitischer Geschichtsschreibung*, Bonn Dissertation 1959; L.Schmidt, op.cit., ch.5.

3d. For the figure of David cf. R.A.Carlson, *David. The Chosen King*, Stockholm 1963; this illustrates the schematic nature of the Deuteronomistic redaction and shows that the life of David is presented in two clearly distinguishable periods: the king under the blessing and the king under the curse. Although its details cannot always be accepted, this thesis is of interest since the redactors seem to have used similar criteria in the cases of Saul and Solomon. The classic study of the 'succession narrative' is that of L.Rost, *The Succession to the Throne of David* (1926), ET Sheffield 1982; cf. also W.Brueggemann, 'David and his Theologian', *CBQ* 30, 1968, 156-81; R.N.Whybray, *The Succession Narrative*, SBT II 9, 1968, which emphasizes the novellistic elements in the story and its derivation from a wisdom milieu. For the nature of doctrinaire narratives cf. E.Lipiński, *Le poème Psaume LXXXIX 1-5, 20-38*, Paris 1967, 83-6. J.Van Seters, 'History and Historians of the Ancient Near East: the Israelites', *Or* 50, 1981, (137-85) 166f.; id, *In Search of History*, New Haven and London 1983, 277-91; O.Kaiser, 'Beobachtungen zur sogenannten Thronnachfolgeerzählung Davids', *ETL* 64, 1988, 5-20. Van Seters dates the 'Court History' in post-Dtr times with most interesting arguments; Kaiser tries a more subtle approach, which would see the original stratum of the 'History' as being more ancient, but certainly not before the reigns of King Hezekiah and King Jehoiakim, i.e. between the eighth and seventh/sixth centuries BCE. The traditional, more

THE BOOKS OF SAMUEL

ancient datings (e.g. just after the death of Solomon) have generally been abandoned today. Cf. also J.W.Flanagan, 'Court History or Succession Document? A Study of II Samuel 9-20 and I Kings 1-2', *JBL* 91, 1972, 172-81; E.Würthwein, *Die Erzählung von der Thronnachfolge Davids – theologische oder politische Geschichtsschreibung?*, Zurich 1974. Cf. also J.Kegler, *Politisches Geschehen und theologisches Verstehen*, Stuttgart 1977; D.M.Gunn, *The Story of King David*, Sheffield 1978; C.Conroy, *Absalom, Absalom! Narrative Art and Language in 2 Samuel 13-20*, Rome 1978; N.P.Lemche, 'David's Rise', *JSOT* 10, 1978, 2-29; P.R.Ackroyd, 'The Succession Narrative (So-Called)', *Int* 35, 1981, 383-96; J.P.Fokkelman, op.cit., I, passim; W.Brueggemann, '2 Samuel 21-24: An Appendix of Deconstruction?', *CBQ* 90, 1988, 383-97. For David and Solomon see now G.Garbini, *History and Archaeology in Ancient Israel*, London and New York 1988, ch.2; for David as the paradigm of believed and imagined history cf. W.Brueggemann, *David's Truth*, Philadelphia 1985.

3e. There have been continuing attempts to rediscover the sources of the Pentateuch in Samuel, none of them convincing. The most recent is H.Schult, *...Bis auf diesen Tag*, Hamburg 1967.

3f. For the text of Samuel cf. F.Langlamet, 'Les divisions massorétiques du livre de Samuel', *RB* 91, 1984, 481-519. For the text of LXX cf. T.Muraoka, 'The Greek Texts of Samuel-Kings: Incomplete Translations or Recensional Activity?', *AbrNah* 21, 1982-3, 28ff.; S.Pisano, *Additions and Omissions in the Books of Samuel*, Freiburg CH 1984; R.Althann, 'Northwest Semitic Notes on Some Texts in I Samuel', *JNWSL* 12, 1984, 27-34. For the textual problems of I Sam.17 cf. now D.Barthélemy et al., *The Story of David and Goliath*, Freiburg CH 1986.

16

THE BOOKS OF KINGS

1. Introduction

(*a*) We have seen that in the Greek Bible the first and second books of Kings are called III and IV Kingdoms, a numbering which is retained in the Latin translations and which has found its way from there into some modern translations. We have also seen that the division between II Samuel and I Kings is artificial: the story of David, the end of which should have constituted the logical point of division, is concluded in I Kings 1-2. However, the division between I and II Kings also leaves much to be desired; the narratives about Ahaziah and Elijah and Elisha respectively are both split in two. The Babylonian Talmud identifies their author as Jeremiah, but here too we have an untenable attribution: the prophet is not named at all. However, the attribution could originate in the Deuteronomistic revision, which dates from the time of the prophet onwards.

(*b*) The two books can easily be divided into four parts, each distinct from the other:

1. The epilogue to the 'succession narrative' (I Kings 1 and 2);
2. The history of the reign of Solomon (I Kings 3-11);
3. The history of the two divided kingdoms down to the fall of the kingdom of Israel (I Kings 12-II Kings 17);
4. Finally, the history of the kingdom of Judah down to the second fall of Jerusalem and the final deportation (II Kings 18-25).

One of the principal problems of the books is that of their chronology, for the details of which the reader must be referred to the histories of Israel and the monographs on the subject. An eloquent proof of the complexity of the problem is the fact that scholars have often arrived at very different results, sometimes differing only by a matter of a few years, but in no case reaching unanimity except from the time of Josiah onwards (end of the seventh century BCE). The difficulty is that the chronology of the kings of Israel is calculated on the basis of that of the kings of Judah and vice versa, without our knowing the starting date or the criteria used. Were it not for the Assyrian annals and the mention of phenomena like earthquakes and eclipses, we would have no firm point at all (cf. especially Appendix 2 by H.Tadmor in my *History*, 368-84, and the recent works indicated in the bibliography). Another difficulty arises from the fact that whatever the criterion used to calculate the years of a reign, in at least one case we find a monarch whose chronology has not been calculated on the basis of the years in which he effectively reigned, but starts from the beginning of his co-regency with his father. Therefore the chronology of at least two kings partially overlaps. This happens in the case of Uzziah/Azariah and Jotham of Judah (II Kings 15.5//II Chron.26.21), and we cannot exclude the possibility that there are other cases of this kind which are not recorded.

(c) These fundamental difficulties are far from being resolved, but they do not prevent the books of Kings from also disclosing a certain internal unity and a constant ideology which recall the pattern in the body of Judges: the rise and then the decline of the united kingdom under Solomon, the end of the united monarchy, the alternating political and religious fates of the two kingdoms up to their falls at the end of the eighth and the beginning of the sixth centuries respectively, are explained by commentaries which illustrate the religious position adopted by each individual monarch. The kings who acted as 'precursors' to Josiah, the obvious model for the redactors, are praised and considered 'just', despite possible imperfections in their work which are also mentioned. Those, on the other hand, who followed syncretistic tendencies in the religious field are severely condemned and considered 'impious', even though it is obvious that they could not foresee that they would be judged by the standard of persons who lived some centuries after them. The texts are almost always silent about the political importance of the kings; the redactors were only concerned with the work of each king in the religious field. Thus it happens that politically less able kings with 'orthodox' theologies (according to Deuteronomistic criteria, e.g. Hezekiah and Josiah) receive unconditional praise, whereas other monarchs, who were politically very able, but in religious terms failed to keep up with the requirements of the redactors, are severely censured. For example, Omri was in fact so important a king that the Assyrian annals continue to call the reigning house of Israel the 'house of Omri' for decades after his fall (above, 12.3).

The judgments in question, whether positive or negative, are formulated in stereotyped phrases which, without being the same as those that we find prefaced to every narrative in the body of Judges, certainly recall their content and follow the same criteria: the difference is that in Judges we have a *people* which sins, whereas here we have individual *kings*, even if the results are more or less the same. Thus beginning from I Kings 14.21ff., we have a typical formula with the following structure: the monarch in question is mentioned with the years of his reign (calculated within the parameters which I have mentioned); then comes the name of his mother and, if it is important, the name of his wife. Finally there is a judgment on his reign in accordance with the criteria mentioned above. Thus Dtr has adapted its criteria to a different subject, while the evaluations remain substantially the same.

The reader may therefore begin from the presupposition that the criteria by which the person and work of a king are judged are not political or economic, but theological. These theological criteria are formed from the parameters laid down by Josiah's reform: the rejection or suppression of the syncretistic or Canaanite sanctuaries (sometimes called 'high places' because they stood above the level of their surroundings, not because they were necessarily on peaks or in hill-country), a foreign policy which would be more a testimony of faith, first for the two small kingdoms and then for the one that remained, than a viable form of steering between the great empires of the age. It is not surprising, therefore, that some have called the criteria in question anachronistic, because they take as a model the work of a king who lived at the end of the period of the monarchy. Others have called them unrealistic because they ignore the existence of an economic and political situation of which even a king with deep religious concerns could not fail to take account if he wished to keep his kingdom alive. The situation is presented in particularly crude forms in the case of the kingdom of Israel, whose monarchs without exception are summarily judged to be guilty of the 'sin of Jeroboam' I, described in I Kings 12.25ff. Jeroboam I set up and maintained in the sanctuaries of Bethel and Dan a cult separate from that of Jerusalem, in which YHWH was celebrated in some connection (precisely what is obscure) with a golden bull (the so-called 'golden calf'). This was probably the pedestal of the God of Israel, who was set invisibly above it, just as he sat enthroned, equally invisibly, above the ark in the temple of Jerusalem. According to Exod.32.1ff., this form of cult was instituted by Aaron himself. Contrary to the view of the later redactors, this gave it an obvious claim to orthodoxy. Moreover the relevant passage in Exodus in its primary form does not condemn the cult in question; the condemnation enters with an evident revision of the text (cf. Exod.32.1-6 with 32.7-10).

Thus we have, once again, valuations of a strictly theological character which find their ideological expression, but also their limitation, in this characteristic: on the one hand they in fact tell us precisely how during and after the exilic period Israel judged its past, but on the other hand they are difficult to sustain on the level of pure historiography, even if the historian can find a mine of historically relevant information in the material they present. For the Deuteronomistic historian, the destruction of Jerusalem and the deportation were important elements of proof that what had been proclaimed was an effective explanation of history, and they became the occasion for announcing that what had happened was not due to the weakness of the God of Israel when confronted first with the gods of Assyria and then with those of Babylon (as non-Israelites of the period might have supposed), but was a product of the judgment of God against the kings and the people of God, who were guilty of not having listened first to the preaching of the prophets and then to the decrees of Josiah's reform. Seen in this context, the message of Kings acquires a new value, though not really from a historiographical point of view; on the other hand, the insistence with which it points to the intervention of YHWH in human history instead of making him work in the sphere of myth (battles and victories or defeats of gods, etc.), is already a significant fact when we consider the period in question. In short, Dtr preaches, announces, comments on well-known historical facts and seeks to look so to speak behind the scenes.

The homiletical and catechetical character of Dtr would much reduce the value of these texts for the historian did the texts in question not continually contain references to sources which the redactors suppose to be easily accessible, or the content of which would have been in the public domain: the 'Chronicles of the Kings of Israel' or 'of Judah', preceded by a 'Book of the Acts of Solomon', works from which a few extracts are cited. It thus seems possible to recognize that it was not the desire or the intention of Dtr to produce history or chronicle so much as to comment on known facts and to 'explain' them in a theological context. What have come down to us are only the commentaries, and none of the original texts on which the commentaries were made. We may think that this is an irreparable loss, but it is in any case not the fault of Dtr but can be attributed to the historical vicissitudes through which the people of God passed. These considerations give a completely different significance to the historical labours of Dtr, and almost automatically refute the criticisms which have been usually directed against the work. Thus the annals mentioned above will certainly have recorded that Omri and Ahab were great kings, even if they appear as impious men in the Deuteronomistic evaluation. We also know from the prophets Elijah, Amos and Hosea that certain social conditions in the north were quite insupportable and that their negative judgment, for strictly theological reasons, was by no means unfounded, even if there seems to be no reason for it on the political plane.

(d) To return to the problem of chronology. At present three main hypotheses dominate the scene. The first, which came out of Germany on the basis of a work by J.Begrich in 1929 and was taken up again by A.Jepsen, is used in the works of A.Alt and M.Noth; the second is that formulated by W.F.Albright in the United States in 1945 and developed by his pupils; the third is that put forward by H.Tadmor and included in my *History* as Appendix 2. Studies on this subject keep coming out and I have listed some of them in the bibliography.

For the earlier period the two chronologies show differences of about a decade, but from the time of Josiah on they tend, as I have said, to coincide.

2. The sources of Kings

Three sources are mentioned explicitly by name in the books of Kings, as we have seen:

(a) The 'Book of the Acts of Solomon' (I Kings 11.31);

(b) The 'Book of the Chronicles of the Kings of Judah' (I Kings 14.29 and about fourteen times elsewhere);

(c) The 'Book of the Chronicles of the Kings of Israel' (I Kings 14.19 and about sixteen times elsewhere).

It is obvious that there is no reference here to the books of Chronicles, which the Hebrew Bible places among the Writings, and which LXX puts after Kings. There is no reason to suppose, as some writers have in the past, that the Pentateuchal sources J and E appear, at least up to I Kings 12: in fact there is no continuous element in the scattered quotations that we have. The one certain thing is that the Deuteronomists, whose redaction is generally accepted here, even by those who do not accept a continuous historical work, have made use (as I said in the previous section) of what are probably official sources (though see the critical comment by G.Garbini), on which they have made an interpretative commentary. The only fragment of any length which survives from these ancient sources is I Kings 4.7-19, which describes the administrative system introduced by Solomon (or perhaps already by David) in the north. But the Deuteronomistic revision is substantial as early as chs. 6-8, which narrate how the temple came to built, even if there is no reason to doubt the historicity of the facts related. In any case, the first part of the narrative is extremely favourable to Solomon, at some points amounting to adulation, while in the second part it is strongly critical. It notes the progressive degeneration and decadence of the kingdom, seeing religious syncretism as the primary cause but not concealing other causes: unpopular fiscal policy and even harsher forms of tyranny.

(d) According to the LXX, the prayer of consecration for the temple, pronounced by Solomon in I Kings 8.12ff. (8.53ff. LXX), has been taken from a certain 'Book of the Song', perhaps the same as the 'Book of the Upright' which we have already found mentioned in Josh.10.13ff.; II Sam.1.19ff. (see above, 6.4b1); this phenomenon could be explained by a metathesis from *yšr* to *šyr*. If the notice given in the LXX is correct (and scholarly opinion is almost unanimous on this point), there is an authentic kernel in the long prayer which was then considerably revised by Dtr.

(e) The epilogue to the 'succession narrative', with which we were concerned in the previous chapter.

(f) The traditions about the prophet Elijah, though they lack a beginning: I Kings 17-19; 21; II Kings 1-2, which are now interpolated with notes on the reign of Ahab of Israel. There are various episodes: the drought (ch.17); the divine judgment on Carmel, probably the aetiological legend on the end of the Canaanite sanctuary and the substitution of an Israelite sanctuary for it (ch.18); the theophany on Mount Horeb, in which we note a theological reflection on the relationship between the physical phenomena caused by the presence of YHWH and YHWH himself (ch.19); the episode of Naboth's vineyard, an example of the way in which the monarchy intervened in a destructive way in the popular justice of the villages and of the conflicts which arose in the encounter between Canaanite concepts of landed property and the ancient Israelite tribal tradition which is still attested in Lev.25.23ff. (ch.21). From a stylistic point of view these episodes are written in the best Hebrew known to us. Discussions of important themes appear: monotheism, the toleration of other cults alongside that of YHWH, relationships between the citizen and the state and the conflict which could arise from different interpretations of the law, and the position of the prophet in the context of these relationships. I Kings 17.24; 18.21,39: 19.1ff., 9ff., etc. give solutions which demonstrate the existence of a remarkable maturity. The redactional elements from Dtr are sparse: almost the only appearance is in 19.10,14. At the beginning of the narrative (17.1) the Massoretic text reads, 'Elijah the Tishbite, one of the inhabitants of Gilead', but the LXX reading 'the Tishbite, from Tishbe in Gilead' seems better: the consonantal spelling of the two terms is practically identical.

(g) The traditions of Elisha (I Kings 19.19-21; II Kings chs.2; 4-10). These contain traditions which are often parallel to those of Elijah, whose pupil Elisha was (but in some cases are considered to be inferior: cf. I Kings 17 with II Kings 4; II Kings 2.12 with 13.14). In I Kings 19.15ff., Elijah receives the order to anoint Hazael king of Damascus and Jehu king of Israel, and it is Elisha who carries out the charge which he receives from his master (II Kings 8.7; 9.1ff.; for the background, the implications and the historical problems of this twofold political act see my *History*, IX.3.6). These passages, too, are almost completely free of Deuteronomistic redaction; their origin is generally sought in different circles from those in which the traditions of Elijah arose. They are thought to be probably more 'popular' because of the miracles they contain, which sometimes have a crude and anecdotal character, though they are also influenced by the preaching of Elijah. This establishes a *terminus post quem* for their dating. It is interesting to note that, less than a century later, Hos.1.1ff. severely condemns the *coup d'état* organized by Elijah and Elisha because of the bloodshed which it caused. O. Eissfeldt and others have argued that the traditions about Elisha are prior to those about Elijah.

(h) Ahab's Aramaean wars (I Kings 20; 22) are mixed in with episodes from the life of Elijah and the prophet Micaiah ben Imlah, who is not to be confused with the eighth-century minor prophet of the same name (known to us as Micah). The narratives are free from Deuteronomistic revisions and would be an important historical source – even though they only illuminate a few aspects of the life of Ahab, who, as we have seen, was a remarkably capable king – if only the information given could be verified with any degree of precision. It seems strange that there were wars between Israel and Damascus at the very time of the great anti-Assyrian coalition. This has led to the putting forward of many conjectures.

(i) Traditions of Isaiah parallel to Isa.36-39 are to be found in II Kings 18.13-20.19. They are interesting because, like every doublet, they give an opportunity to make a synoptic study of the transmission of an identical text by different agents and of the difficulties which could arise.

(*j*) We have traditions about various prophets: in I Kings 11.29-39; 14.1-18 and 15.29 about Ahijah of Shiloh; in I Kings 12.21-24 about Shemaiah; in I Kings 12.32-13.32 about an anonymous prophet who comes from the south to curse the sanctuaries of Bethel and Dan, an episode often related to the ministry of the prophet Amos (though in 13.2 we have an explicit reference to Josiah's reform, so that this is probably a *vaticinium ex eventu* interpolated by Dtr). In II Kings 21.10-15 an anonymous prophet attacks Manasseh of Judah, while in 22.14 the prophetess Huldah plays an important part in Josiah's reform, even if this is difficult to assess because of the inadequacy of the sources. Deuteronomistic revision is evident in the last three instances.

(*k*) Until a few years ago it was held that the Deuteronomistic material had been composed and edited in at least two stages, which could also be distinguished chronologically. There was no complete agreement among scholars. For example, Noth was doubtful about such a double redaction. In any case, the first stratum would have been inspired by the precepts of Josiah's reform: centralization of the cult and therefore elimination of the local sanctuaries (the so-called high places), fundamental hostility to any Canaanite or syncretistic elements. A second and later stratum sought on the other hand to interpret the tragedy which befell Judah and Jerusalem in 597 and 587-6, but which had already hit Israel in 722/21. The explanation follows the well-known lines of reward and retribution: the prophets had announced judgment again and again, and look – it had happened, first in the fall of the northern kingdom, Israel, then in the first deportation in 597 and finally, in the second, followed by the destruction of Jerusalem, the fall of the dynasty and the loss of political independence.

At all events the problem of the various stratifications of Dtr seems to have been removed thanks to the studies of the Göttingen group; it sees an original DtrH revised with a DtrP and DtrN (above, 12.4).

Despite the fundamental pessimism of its considerations Dtr, and with it the book of Kings, ends with an optimistic note. In II Kings 25.27ff. Jehoiachin, the last legitimate king of Judah, deported in 597, is pardoned by the king of Babylon and admitted to his table in 561.

3. Thought

The North American scholar J.A.Bewer regarded Dtr as a philosophy of history; I would prefer to call it a theology of history. In the books of Kings it presents a period which it considers crucial: first for Israel and Judah and later only for Judah. Before the reform of Josiah the scene is one of struggle and polemic between those who want to worship the only God of Israel, YHWH, and those who prefer to continue along the course of assimilation to Canaan. Alongside these religious struggles the texts give us some glimpses of an almost desperate political problem; the two Hebrew states were two fragile entities, caught between two dominant and powerful ones: Egypt on the one hand and first Assyria and then Babylon on the other. This gave them very little, if any, room for manoeuvre. They tried to maintain their independence, but then succumbed one after the other to the overwhelming power of Mesopotamia.

In such a situation, it was easy to interpret the history of the two peoples in categories like that of divine retribution. Using modern criteria of assessment, we may find these categories philosophically and historically inadequate, but there were certainly attempts to understand destiny and the reasons for the catastrophe which befell the people in an organic way.

The Deuteronomistic redactors had some facts which provided useful support for their thesis: the end of the kingdom of Israel and the deportation of some of its inhabitants in the second half of the eighth century; the first fall of Jerusalem and the deportation of some of its inhabitants in 597; and the second, definitive fall of the capital after the deportation. Moreover, almost all the prophets had proclaimed the end of the people as a divine judgment. Thus verification in the light of the facts seemed to confirm the Deuteronomistic valuation completely, and Dtr could solemnly declare that God did not allow himself to be mocked.

Hence Dtr with its critical discussion of the past history of the people became an important link in the chain which led to the post-exilic restoration. Even if this restoration succeeded in removing once and for all the dangers of paganism and syncretism, however, it introduced regimented ways of conceiving the faith, thus giving the religion of Israel a new face. It was no longer influenced by the animated polemic of the prophets, which was to be rapidly extinguished in the course of little more than a century of restoration. The place of the prophet was taken by the apocalyptist and the doctor of the law: in the post-exilic theocracy the priests are in charge. The problematical but lively circumstances which preceded the exile were replaced by the tranquillity of a religious orthodoxy. Whether or not this was an advantage, the reader will have to judge, while at the same time asking whether there was any alternative, since there was no political independence.

BIBLIOGRAPHY

Commentaries

C.F.Burney, *Notes on the Hebrew Text of the Books of Kings*, Oxford 1905 (reprinted 1970); S.Garofalo, SacBib, 1951; J.A.Montgomery and H.S.Gehman, ICC, 1951; R.de Vaux, JB ²1958; M.Noth, BK, 1968 (to I Kings 16 only; the work is to be completed by R.Smend); J.Gray, OTL, ²1970; E.Würthwein, ATD, I, 1977; II, 1984; G.Henschel, 1984.

1. For the structure of I & II Kings see now *JSOT* 40, 1988, 39ff. For the chronology of the period of Kings cf. J.Begrich, *Die Chronologie der Könige von Israel und Juda*, Tübingen 1929 (reprinted 1966); A.Jepsen and R.Hanhart, *Untersuchungen zur israelitisch-jüdischen Chronologie*, BZAW 88, 1964; D.N.Freedman and E.F.Campbell, 'The Chronology of Israel and the Ancient Near East', in G.E.Wright (ed.), *The Bible and the Ancient Near East: Essays in Honor of W.F.Albright*, New York 1961, 203-28; J.Finegan, *Handbook of Biblical Chronology*, Princeton 1964; E.R.Thiele, *The Mysterious Numbers of the Hebrew Kings*, Grand Rapids ³1983, and 'Coregencies and Overlapping Reigns among the Hebrew Kings', *JBL* 93, 1974, 174-200 (he works with the theory that in more than one case a king of Israel or Judah will have ruled in association with his successor, thus having a 'co-regency' and causing an 'overlap' of chronology). Cf. further H.Tadmor, Appendix 2, in my *History*, 368ff. On the same theme cf. P.K.McCarter, ' "Yaw, Son of Omri": a Philological Note on Israelite Chronology', *BASOR* 216, 1974, 5-7, on the problem of the mention of this name in the Assyrian annals; V.Pavlovsky and E.Vogt, 'Die Jahre der Könige von Juda und Israel', *Bibl* 45, 1964, 321-74; G.Sauer, 'Die chronologischen Angaben in den Büchern Deut. bis 2.Kön', *TZ* 24, 1968, 1-14; A.Laato, 'New Viewpoints on the Chronology of the Kings of Judah and Israel', *ZAW* 98, 1986, 210-21; N.Na'aman, 'Historical and Chronological Notes on the Kingdoms of Israel and Judah in the Eighth Century BC', *VT* 37, 1986, 71-92; A.Lemaire, 'Vers l'histoire de la rédaction des livres des Rois', *ZAW* 98, 1986, 221-36; H.N.Wallace, 'The Oracles against the Israelite Dynasties in 1 and 2 Kings', *Bibl* 67, 1986, 21-40; E.Nobile, 'Un contributo alla lettura sincronica della redazione Genesi – 2 Re, sulla base del filo narrativo offerto da 2 Re 25, 27-30', *Ant* 61, 1986, 207-24. For a synopsis of all the chronologies proposed up to the end of the 1950s cf. H.Tadmor, 'Kronologia', in *EncBibl* IV, 1962, 254-310, esp.259ff. (in Hebrew) and 'The Chronology of the First

Temple Period' in *WHJP* IV. 1, Jerusalem 1979, 44-60, 318-20, reprinted as Appendix 2 to my *History*.

2. For the value of these references to earlier official sources cf. recently G.Garbini, 'Le fonti citate nel "Libro dei Re" ', *Hen* 3, 1981, 26-46; O.Kaiser*, 164f. For a history of the Assyrian empire and its relations with Israel see W.W.Hallo, 'From Qarqar to Carchemish', *BA* 23, 1960, 34-61; H.Spieckermann, *Judah unter Assur in der Sargonidenzeit*, Göttingen 1982.

2c. For Solomon's districts see F.Pintore, 'I dodici intendenti di Salomone', *RSO* 45, 1970, 177-207; T.N.D.Mettinger, *Solomonic State Officials*, Lund 1971.

2f-g. For Elijah and Elisha cf. J.J.Stamm, 'Elia am Horeb', in *Studia biblica et semitica T.C.Vriezen dedicata*, Wageningen 1966, 327-34; O.H.Steck, *Überlieferung und Zeitgeschichte in den Elia-Erzählungen*, WMANT 26,1968; H.Schweizer, *Elischa der Krieger*, Munich 1974; G.Henschel, *Die Eliaerzählungen*, Erfurt 1974; H.C.Schmitt, *Elisa*, Gütersloh 1972; G.Fohrer, *Elia*, Zurich ²1968; R.P.Carroll, 'The Elijah-Elisha Sagas', *VT* 19, 1969, 400-15; O.Carena, *La comunicazione non verbale nella bibbia*, Turin 1981; B.J.Diebner, 'Überlegungen zum "Brief des Elia", 2 Chr.21, 12-15', *Hen* 9, 1987, 197-228. The priority of the Elisha traditions over the Elijah traditions has been argued by O.Eissfeldt, 'Die Komposition von I Reg.16.29-II Reg.13.24', in F.Maass (ed.), *Das Ferne und Nahe Wort. FS L.Rost*, BZAW 105, 1967, 49-58 (= his *Kleine Schriften* V, Tübingen 1973, 21-30).

2h. Many scholars have denied that Ahab originally appeared in these two narratives; cf. e.g. E.Lipiński, 'Le Ben Hadad II de la Bible et de l'histoire', in *Proceedings of the Fifth World Congress of Jewish Studies*, 1969, 1, Jerusalem 1972, 157-73; others favour an identification with different enemies.

2i. The parallels between I Kings 18-20 and Isa.36-39 have been studied by e.g. B.S.Childs, *Isaiah and the Assyrian Crisis*, SBT II 3, 1967; M.E.W.Thomson, *Situation and Theology*, Sheffield 1982. For Assyria see H.Spieckermann (op.cit., section 2c above). The material and the studies have recently been discussed in the monumental volume by F.J.Goncalvez, *L'expédition de Sennacherib en Palestine dans la littérature hébraïque ancienne*, Louvain-la-Neuve 1986.

2k. For DtrH, DtrN and DtrP cf. above, 12.4; for the problem of the reform see the above mentioned work by H-D.Hoffmann, *Reform und Reformen*, Zurich 1980.

For the problems of the text and translation of the LXX cf. the article by Muraoka mentioned in the previous bibliography, § 3f.

PART THREE

THE PRE-EXILIC PROPHETS

I 7

THE PROPHETS OF ISRAEL

1. Etymology and use of terms

(*a*) Our term 'prophet' derives etymologically from the Greek *prophētēs*. This is a word attested in classical Greek from the time of Pindar and Herodotus (for whom it denotes a temple official), i.e. from the fifth century BCE onwards. It denotes 'one who announces, proclaims something'. The accent is thus on the public character of the communication or message. The preposition *pro-* with which the term is compounded thus primarily indicates the position in which the message is given: 'before' an assembly, a group, a person. The chronological connotation 'before' an announcement is fulfilled, which the preposition also has, seems still to be extraneous to the term, at least in this phase. On the other hand the twofold significance of the preposition, both local and temporal, favoured a connection with oracular praxis, for example in the oracle of Zeus at Dodona in Epirus. This is the origin of the significance that the term has today. However, apart from oracular practice, the term has the meaning of proclaiming someone's will, someone's message, before groups or individuals, independently of its content.

(*b*) In Greek Egypt in the Hellenistic and Roman period the term was used to denote a high religious official called the 'servant of the deity' (*ḥm nt̲r*). The translators of the LXX version (from the middle of the third century BCE onwards) thus wanted to identify the prophet with this figure. In the New Testament the use is ambiguous: on the one hand, the 'prophets' of the primitive church announced the divine will in assemblies for worship and during the agapes; on the other hand the prophets of the Hebrew Bible were said to have predicted the coming of the Messiah, prophecies which were then 'fulfilled' in the person and ministry of Jesus of Nazareth. However, the former of these two meanings shows that the original sense of the term was still in use at the time when the New Testament was written. With the progressive extinction of prophecy in the primitive church, the temporal, futuristic significance survived and the term increasingly acquired the significance which it has today; it denotes the prophet as the person who has the capacity to predict the future or to practise clairvoyance, naturally in the name and with the help of God.

The concept which underlies this semantic development is not, however, characteristic of the biblical prophets: these rarely announce the future proper, and when they do so it is in vague and general terms which are often idealized. They concentrate, rather, on the interpretation of the past and the present, and for the present they proclaim the divine will, as we shall again see. The concept which underlies the supposed futurological function of the prophet does not come from the Hebrew Bible but from intertestamental apocalyptic and from the two canonical apocalyptic books: Daniel and the New Testament Apocalypse of John. Here the course of future events seems to be fixed from the beginning to the end of time and recorded in the heavenly books. Someone who has been taken up into heaven can have had access to these books and relate their content; others can recognize certain aspects by means of direct divine revelation, and finally both can reveal things of which they have thus gained knowledge. It is in precisely this perspective that the New Testament sees one of the functions of the prophet of the Hebrew Bible: he has seen in anticipation that which must be fulfilled in Jesus Christ. This element can thus be regarded as being an integral part of the apocalyptic element in the New Testament. For details the reader should refer to the monumental article in *SDB* (a book in itself); its one defect seems to be that in listing the parallels from the ancient Near East it dwells too much on manticism, divination and predictions, elements which when they appear in the biblical prophets have only secondary functions.

(c) In the Hellenistic world the term has yet another meaning, with little or no importance for the study of biblical prophecy, which was also borrowed from Pindar: the prophet as inspired by the muses, whose herald he becomes. We too have similar expressions, as for instance when we speak of the inspiration of an artist.

2. Origin and derivation

(a) In the LXX version the Greek *prophētēs* always translates the Hebrew *nābī'*, and on a very few occasions also the less frequent terms *ḥōzeh* and *rō'eh* (the respective meanings of which are 'he who has visions' and 'seer'). The two latter terms are often used as synonyms, the former sometimes with disparaging connotations (e.g. in Amos 7.14), almost as though it were the negative counterpart of the prophetic ministry. In comparison to *nābī'* they are often used to put the stress on the visionary element, which is not necessarily present in *nābī'*.

We do not know what led the LXX to choose the term *prophētēs*; at all events the reason does not seem to have been theological or apologetic. Evidently this was thought to be the most suitable Greek word for translating the Hebrew term. However, if we think how substantially different oracles and ecstatic phenomena within the historical and religious sphere of the Greek and Hellenistic world were from the character and message of the biblical prophets, we may have doubts about the adequacy of the chosen term – all the more so because as a result of the twofold meaning of the preposition, it also opened the way to an interpretation of their message in terms of the future. And although it is impossible to suggest a more adequate word (which in any case would do little to clarify matters in the situation), one cannot avoid the suspicion that this translation ended up by distorting the meaning of the original term, beginning the development which was to make the prophet a kind of futurologist of his time.

(*b*) A derivative of the term *nābī'* is the verb *nb'*, used only in the *niphal* and *hithpael* (sometimes to indicate an ecstatic condition which resembled madness: II Kings 9.11; Jer.29.26). The origin of the term, which only appears in Western Semitic in the Lachish ostraka (below, Appendix 1.9), i.e. in Hebrew texts, is almost certainly to be sought in Akkadian, as W.F.Albright argued many years ago. He derived it from *nabīum* and *nabū(m)*, 'the one who is called', 'the one who has received a commission' (*AHw* II, 697f.), root *nb'*, already apparently attested at Ebla during the last centuries of the third millennium BCE. There are also attestations of it in Egyptian (for a complete discussion cf. *SDB* X, 812-68); for the very special case of Mari see below.

In Hebrew, nouns of the *qātīl* type (that is, with the vowel sequence *ā-ī*) also often have a passive meaning (*SDB* X, 921f.; Gerhard von Rad, *Old Testament Theology* II, Edinburgh 1965 reissued London 1975, 7ff., is still doubtful). From Hebrew the term was then transferred to Aramaic and Syriac, to Arabic and Ethiopian. However, it is interesting to note that despite this obvious etymological relationship with Akkadian, that language does not use derivatives of the root to describe people who exercised functions similar to those of the biblical prophets, whom instead it terms *maḥḥū(m) (AHw* II, 582), 'prophet', 'ecstatic'.

(*c*) In Canaan we have a classical example of ecstatic possession in the story of the Egyptian official Wen-Amon (*ANET*, 25-29: 26b); during his stay at Byblos, where he had gone to get wood for building the sacred boat of the god Amon, he was present at a sacrifice in the course of which the deity took possession of a man (the term is not clear), throwing him to the ground in ecstasy and making him pronounce an oracle. At Hamath in Syria, in the Aramaic inscription of Zakir (*KAI* 202, A-12 and *ANET*, 655f.), from the first quarter of the first millennium BCE, we find the title *ḥzyn*, etymologically equivalent to the Hebrew *ḥozeh*, 'seer', attributed to the person through whom he received his message from the deity.

(*d*) It seems legitimate to conclude from all this that the Hebrew term, which also has a feminine form *nᵉbī'āh*, is the product of a development in the autonomous technical theological sense of a root attested elsewhere. In Israel, it took on a special significance connected with a calling by the deity. In fact we have some cases in which the term still has a generic sense: Aaron is the *nābī'* of Moses, who is unskilled in speaking (Exod.7.1; and this is the only case attested in which the prophet represents a human being); the title is also used of king Saul (I Sam.18.10); of Pashhur, a priest (Jer.20.6); of the women of Israel (Ezek.13.17); and of the elders in the wilderness (Num.11.25). In the eschatological age the young men and the women will prophesy (Joel 2.28); some figures bear the title, especially the singers (I Chron.25.1-3). There are also prophets of Baal (I Kings 18.20ff.; II Kings 10.18ff.).

(*e*) This development from a more general meaning to a specialized one would become even clearer if we accepted the theory of A.G.Auld that it is probable that the title *nābī'* was applied to the prophets of Israel at a relatively late stage, after the exile (the same also applies to *rō'eh* and *ḥozeh*).

(*f*) So it seems clear that the prophet considered himself to be (and indeed was considered to be) someone who was 'called', 'sent' by the deity, whoever this deity might be, and that in Israel his particular function was that of delivering a message by word of mouth. This relationship with the deity also appears in other terms: *'īš (hā-) 'ᵉlōhīm*, man of God; *mal'āk*, 'messenger', and others. Sometimes he was considered 'mad', 'fanatical', *mᵉšugga'* (Gen.29.26; Hos.9.7), an evident sign of the ambiguous and contradictory character which attached to the interpretation of his ministry.

(*g*) Given the oral character of their message, we find in the prophets the following literary genres: 'the messenger saying' (German *Botenspruch*); 'invective' or 'rebuke' (German *Scheltwort*); the threat (German *Drohwort*); the 'announcement of judgment' (German *Gerichtswort*) and the *tōrāh*, i.e. announcement, instruction, teaching in oracular or catechetical form.

(*h*) Anyone studying biblical prophecy is therefore confronted with an initial difficulty: in the Hebrew Bible *nābī'* and its derivatives indicate functions and institutions which to our way of thinking should be kept distinct, whereas the biblical books lump them together under the same terminology. It is true that Hebrew distinguishes between two types of 'seer', at least on the theoretical level, but as I have indicated, the two terms often occur in synonymous parallelism with *nabī'*; and even ecstatic, mantic and paranormal phenomena generally can be included under this term, phenomena which in some cases we would consider typical of sorcerers or 'medicine men'. We have also seen some cases in which the term, conjugated in the *hithpael*, can take on the meaning of 'fall into ecstasy'. This is also a well-known phenomenon in the Hebrew Bible, cf. I Sam.10.5ff.;19.18ff; cf. Saul's homicidal ecstasy, a form of *amok*, in 18.10ff.; and the prophets of Ba'al also seek to fall into ecstasy, though by means of artificial techniques (I Kings 18.28). The mention of the 'prophet' as *mᵉšugga'* in Hos.9.7 is also, as we have seen, an interesting piece of information about the way in which the *vox populi* reacted to certain phenomena, regarding them as the product of exaltation, of madness. If we leave aside the historical-critical problems of the chapter for a moment, I Sam.9 is the interesting case of a person who is given the title 'man of God'; Saul and his companions resort to him to discover the asses of Kish, Saul's father, which were lost, and for his advice the person in question receives payment. This 'man of God' is then explicitly identified with the *nābī'* of the time of the redactor. This is a significant identification when one thinks that at the time of the redactor biblical prophecy must have arrived at its fullest development. We can draw only one conclusion from this: even at the height of the development of their ministry the prophets were neither felt nor understood to be in any way fundamentally different (as we might suppose) from the complex world of soothsayers, magicians, sorcerers, necromancers and others of this kind.

(*i*) In the Hebrew Bible, as we have seen, no distinction is made on the semantic level between the prophets of YHWH and those of Ba'al (cf. I Kings 18; II Kings 10.18), to whom what I have said above also applies. Nor does the Bible distinguish on a semantic level between those prophets who tell the truth and those who announce falsehoods (the latter are divided into two categories: those who act in good faith, inspired to tell falsehoods for some divine reason, and those who act in bad faith, i.e. those who speak falsehoods knowing that they are lying). We find the title *nābī'* used for all these. It was the LXX which introduced the category of *pseudoprophetes*, false prophet, which then appears in the New Testament. However, here we have an important lexical change: whereas in Hebrew the accent falls on the falsehood of the message, in Greek it falls on the falsehood of the person, which is not necessarily the case in Hebrew.

3. Prophets among neighbouring peoples

(*a*) To investigate the complex historical and religious problem of prophecy generally, among all peoples, would take us very far afield. Here I shall therefore limit myself to Israel's neighbours, where in some cases we find kindred phenomena of great interest. I shall not, however, take account of all the paranormal phenomena which have been mentioned and which are well attested in Israel. I want to point out, rather, that in some cases the people of God has in common with neighbouring peoples phenomena which belong to prophecy at its highest stage, phenomena which until a few decades ago seemed to be the monopoly of Israel. First among the peoples who show notable affinity with prophecy is the city-state of Mari on the Euphrates, towards the thirtieth parallel, which flourished between the eighteenth and seventeenth centuries BCE. It was discovered by French archaeologists towards the end of the 1930s and the texts from there are still being published (so far, around twenty volumes have appeared). However, given that other parallels which were thought to have been discovered with the texts of this city and those of the city-state of Nuzi, especially in connection with the patriarchal narratives, have meanwhile been proved either slight or non-existent (above 5.2,4), here too it is well to proceed with caution.

(*b*) Parallels between biblical prophecy and that of Mari do not exist just on a formal level: the use of the same literary genres and the same forms, the presence of particular people, the existence of privileged relationships between the deity and his emissaries and the calling of these latter. There are also parallels on a more substantial level, where the analogies are more than remarkable. The initiative in the oracle belongs exclusively to the deity; techniques of consultation are therefore extremely rare, or absent altogether. The 'prophet' is legitimated in his own ministry by signs and wonders, and his messages are sometimes open criticism of the policy pursued by the court or the state cult. There are also promises in both the religious and the political fields for the present and the future, oracles against the nations and other features. As among the prophets of Israel, in Mari use is rarely made of ecstasy and incomprehensible oracles; the choice falls primarily on the announcement of the divine word to the interested party or parties through the man who is chosen beforehand as prophet.

The implications and the consequences to be drawn from this information, which I have only summarized briefly, are still uncertain, and the problem of possible relationships between the Mesopotamian city-state of the second quarter of the second millennium BCE and the Hebrew world of the first half of the first millennium (note the interval of just under a thousand years) cannot be satisfactorily resolved in the present state of research. It is not easy to conjecture any type of relationship, nor would such a conjecture be very useful. At most it is possible to note the parallel development of a phenomenon which began in analogous circumstances and was developed with similar results: a stage which was highly mature in theological, sociological and political terms. And in this case to suppose the existence of relationships on an ideological and material level becomes useless.

(c) We have important prophetic material from Assyria, dating from the seventh century BCE, mostly published at the end of the last century in editions which are now partially obsolete and therefore not easy for the non-specialist to study. In the bibliography I list three introductory studies to these materials: M.Weippert has promised a major publication on the subject. There is no doubt that here we have true prophecy, often oracles of salvation addressed to the king (rare in the Hebrew Bible, where they are usually addressed to prophets and charismatics).

(d) The phenomenon of Islam is also particularly interesting, but Islam came into being more than a thousand years after biblical prophecy. I hope that we have abandoned for ever the traditional Christian polemic against Islam, and all attempts either to deny the originality of Mohammed's prophecy and his message or to question his good faith and intellectual honesty. Modern scholarship has tried to put aside prejudices and to study the most important features of what is one of the most important faiths in the world. Various elements come together in the person of Mohammed, as they did centuries earlier in the person of Moses. Mohammed is the founder of the religion, the prophet, the statesman, the charismatic leader (endowed with the rare ability to transmit his own charisma to his immediate successors); moreover in the political field he has been a focal point for various peoples who were originally enemies fighting among themselves, and this function partly endures in Islam down to the present day. There remains one basic problem the ultimate implications of which are difficult to evaluate: that of the conditioning of Islam by Judaism and Christianity and therefore, in a more or less open and conscious form, by biblical prophecy. Both are certainly present, given the frequent contacts of the Prophet with Jews and Christians whom (with some exceptions) he respected and to a certain point tolerated, though he sought their conversion. At all events the development of Islam has been so original, so new, that the problem is ultimately only of relative importance: on the phenomenological level Mohammed was something like a biblical prophet.

(e) To conclude this all too brief review, it seems clear that we cannot establish any assured link between ancient Near Eastern prophecy, whether earlier or later than biblical prophecy, and that of the prophets of the Bible. One thing remains certain. This did not arise in an ideological void. It does not start from nothing and end in nothing, as is shown by the primitive church and later by Islam; so it has predecessors and successors. However, the relationships seem constant and obvious in the case of ecstatic prophecy, the popular forms of soothsaying and divination.

4. Sources of biblical prophecy

(a) The sources for the study of prophecy are exclusively the biblical narratives on the prophets and the prophetic books. The one exception is that referred to above, the twofold mention of an anonymous prophet (nb') in the Lachish ostraca (3.20; 16.16, Appendix 1.9); the latter text is so damaged that it is practically incomprehensible (ANET, 321f.; KAI, no.193). A prophet is mentioned in the first text (below, 23.4b), but no functions are indicated other than that of being a messenger. The use of the term nābī' and derivatives is therefore limited to the Bible. However, several prophets are not even mentioned in Dtr.

(b) We do not have any writing attributed to the two great prophets Elijah and Elisha; we do, however, have a series of narratives which deal with episodes in their lives (I Kings 17-19; 21; II Kings 1; 2.1-18 for Elijah; II Kings 2.1-18; chs.4-9 for Elisha). However, these are episodic accounts, often only anecdotal, from which it is difficult to obtain a coherent picture of the lives of these two figures whom the biblical and post-biblical tradition has always regarded as very important – especially Elijah. It therefore becomes difficult, not to say impossible, to establish a difference between the two and other similar forms attested both within and outside Israel, or the prophets who exercised their ministry in Israel after them (above, 9.2f-g).

(c) Some prophets have given their names to biblical books. We have more or less important biographical data about some of them, depending on circumstances. In Amos, 7.10-17 tells us about Amos's occupation before he was called and therefore about his economic position. In Hosea we have information about one or two unhappy marriages, ending with the repudiation of his wife; however, in the book they are elevated into a paradigm for the relations between YHWH and his people. In Isaiah 6-7 we have information about his vocation in general or his call to a particular ministry, followed by information about his contacts with the court and with king Ahaz on the occasion of the so-called 'Syro-Ephraimite' war, which is supposed to have happened around 734 BCE. Finally the book of the prophet Jeremiah gives us a series of pieces of information which allow us to reconstruct a fairly complete biography. He was born into a priestly family and lived at Anathoth; his calling took place when he was still a young man, in the reign of Josiah (the thirteenth year is mentioned, which puts it around 627). We hear that he had a timid and reserved character, which proved an obstacle to the consistent practice of his ministry; we hear of the difficulties that he had to confront, which culminated in a plot against his life; and we hear how his preaching unmasked the unbelief, impiety and vice of his contemporaries which were skilfully hidden under the mask of faith, piety and virtue. We hear of his growing and increasingly dramatic isolation, aggravated by the divine prohibition against entering into marriage, the final break with his fellow-citizens and his imprisonment, his encounters with king Jehoiakim and the ups and downs of his relationship with the last ruler, Zedekiah. Then there is his imprisonment and liberation by the Babylonians as soon as Jerusalem is captured, the situation after the occupation and his deportation to Egypt by a group of rebels opposing the Babylonian occupation and its Judahite officials. In short, for Jeremiah the amount of evidence seems quite encouraging when compared with other similar figures inside and outside Israel; after all, it seems possible to extract something from the documentation in our possession, and this something ought to be enough to reconstruct a fairly complete framework.

(*d*) However, the overall situation for the prophets is neither as simple nor as clear as it might appear at first sight. The biographical information to which I have referred does not in fact derive from what we could call critical historical biographical studies, nor are the texts even like the Lives attested in the late classical world, but are what Baltzer has called 'model biographies'.

This is already evident in the brief text of Amos 7.10-17: here the prophet appears as one who 'breeds cattle and prepares sycamore fruit'; he is taken by 'YHWH from following the flock' and sent to prophesy 'to my people Israel', i.e. to the northern kingdom.

Schult's study, which passed almost unobserved, began from the observation that Amos' occupation before his call was not as obvious as it might seem. His work with the sycamores presents no problems; what seems strange, rather, is that the prophet is presented simultaneously as a 'breeder of cattle' and a shepherd of the 'flock' (*sō'n*), a term used exclusively for small cattle, i.e. sheep and goats. But these are two different forms of rearing animals: the cattle breeder is resident in one place, whereas the shepherd moves with his flock from one pasturage to another. And to say that Amos had both a herd of cattle and a flock of sheep and goats is no explanation, because the two forms of rearing were incompatible, and moreover are still not compatible even today, at least in the context of the small family farm. So according to Schult it is impossible to extract any trustworthy information from this note about Amos' occupation. However, things do not end here. The account copies stereotypes which are also well known from elsewhere: a shepherd or countryman or other person in modest, though not straitened, economic conditions is called by the supreme authority – God, the king, the people – to undertake a charge of great importance, that of political ruler, poet or prophet. Schult lists a series of examples of this down to the present day, of which I shall mention only some.

1. David, the youngest of Jesse's sons, 'was looking after the flock' (I Sam.16.11), as his father says to the prophet Samuel, while in II Sam.7.8 God says to David through the mouth of Nathan: 'I took you from the pasture, from following the sheep, that you should be prince over my people Israel.' Both are Deuteronomistic texts.

2. Moses was tending his father-in-law's flock when he was called near the 'mountain of God' (Exod.3.1ff.).

3. Saul is returning from ploughing in the fields behind the oxen with the plough (this time it is not the pasture, I Sam.11.5ff.), defeats the enemy and is proclaimed king to popular acclaim.

4. Elisha is ploughing with twelve oxen, Elijah calls him and he becomes a prophet (I Kings 19.19-21).

5. Gideon is threshing in the wine-press and the 'messenger' calls him to become leader against Midian (Judg.6.11ff.).

6. In the New Testament some disciples are summoned from their menial labour and called to be disciples (Mark 1.16ff.; 2.14).

7. Various figures in the ancient world, Sargon I of Akkad and others, down to Cincinnatus in the West and Christian heroes, are the object of similar treatment.

Thus the theme of the 'calling of the shepherd' or 'the countryman' is not so much a factual description as a literary theme, though of course that does not exclude the possibility that historical reality and motif can coincide. However, in the cases I have cited that seems improbable: David made his way because he was brave and politically able, and the same was certainly also true of Saul, at least at the beginning of his career. Where accession to the position takes place in the usual way, the presence of the theme does not seem necessary; but where we find it in connection with a seizure of power in a non-traditional way, the theme appears and has legitimating functions: it serves to eliminate or at least to weaken any opposition, which in fact more often than not did not then materialize. The function of the theme is also obvious in the case of Amos: it is meant to legitimate the stranger, the one who 'does not belong to the trade', the one who has no authorization. In the particular case of Amos it is certainly possible that though the information about the occupation of the prophet has been presented in the stereotyped terms of the theme, in fact it also forms part of the original biography and therefore corresponds to reality, and until recently this possibility used to be taken into account; however, it is clear that for the authors and the redactors the stress is not so much on the work by which Amos once lived as on the demonstration of the divine calling. Amos is shown, in following the call, to have left work which, while it did not put him in the category of the prosperous, enabled him to have a decent life with economic independence.

(e) The case of the prophet Isaiah is different, though it has some affinity to that of Amos. In chs. 6 and 7 we find some biographical information: Isaiah's call, followed by the encounter and confrontation with King Ahaz at the outlet of the aqueduct, shortly before the 'Syro-Ephraimite' war. The theory is increasingly gaining ground that in ch.7 we have a narrative of past events, written in the late exilic and post-exilic period, with marked Deuteronomistic elements, or elements which recall this school. At all events the chapter was composed a long time after the events, as is evident from 7.1, a text which simply copies II Kings 16.5. However, it follows from 7.8b that the north had also fallen some time before, so whoever was writing lived after 722/20. The author or redactor now has the catastrophe of 587/6 behind him and is asking himself why it happened; he examines the options that the court had and sees the person of the prophet as the divine emissary, the inspired interlocutor, who tried to convert the people and the king by dissuading them from taking a step like a request for Assyrian intervention. He rightly saw this step as the beginning of a process which was to prove irreversible and lead Judah to become a vassal first of Assyria and then of Babylon (cf. my *History*, X.3.1ff.). What disturbed the redactors of these chapters was the fact that the dynasty which had been declared to be eternal by the dynastic oracles had fallen; in other words, that the oracles had not been fulfilled. And here was the explanation: it was true that the oracles had not been fulfilled; but it was also true that the king had refused to make the choices which the word of God required of him and which was a condition of the fulfilment, and therefore it had been impossible for the monarchy to survive.

If there is any viable historical information in the text, it is that which originally may have been an oracle of salvation, an authentic fragment of which could be concealed in 7.16. However, the redaction has transformed this into an oracle of judgment, because of the attitude adopted by the court (Dietrich, 73; Carroll, 139; Kaiser, commentary *ad loc.*). So here we have what Carroll has called, perhaps somewhat cryptically, 'cognitive dissonance'. Instead of talking of unfulfilled prophecies, of a lack of connection between what is proclaimed and what happens, of a divergence between promise and fulfilment, the authors introduce the conditional element: the ancient oracle was valid only to the degree that those to whom it was addressed observed certain conditions absent from the original and introduced subsequently, sometimes by themselves. We should not be surprised at this procedure, since it is well known that Dtr judged the various kings in accordance with criteria drawn from Deuteronomy and which underlay Josiah's reform (above, 12.3). In all this it remains extremely difficult, if not impossible, to separate the authentic material (the little remaining – that is assuming that there is any at all) from that interpolated by the redactors.

(*f*) The case of Jeremiah is on a larger scale. It is particularly worth noting because, as we saw above, we have a substantial amount of biographical material from Jeremiah, which hitherto has led the majority of scholars to make optimistic comments. Among autobiographical sketches and biographical sections that have been transmitted it seems that we have a remarkable, albeit incomplete, quantity of data available to us. This series of materials seems incomplete because we have no information about basic issues like that of the relationship between the prophet and Josiah's reform (on which every scholar tries to present his own conjectures); we also lack any information about Jeremiah's youth and his education, or about his death. Again, the relationship between Jeremiah and Baruch is unclear. Baruch is presented as Jeremiah's amanuensis, and modern scholars have often readily attributed the redaction and editing of the first text of the book to him. That there was then a second redaction during the lifetime of the two men is expressly stated at the end of ch. 36. The history of the text in general also bears witness to a constant process of growth; the development most worth noting, because it can be assessed objectively, is that between the LXX translation and the Massoretic text.

Be this as it may, there is an official biography of the prophet, if only a partial one, which is interested more in the ministry of the prophet than in his actual life (Baltzer, 128); as we have seen, there are substantial gaps in it here and there, even in questions relating to Jeremiah's ministry. The information that can be recovered from the biography of Jeremiah was brought together and developed in a now classic study by J.Skinner in 1922; almost all scholars refer to this study in its various reprints, whether explicitly or implicitly (as did the previous editions of this *Introduction*).

However, a deeper study of the situation, like that made recently by Robert Carroll, reveals a series of disconcerting facts. First of all, as has now been noted for some decades, we cannot treat the sentences in prose and those in poetry on the same level: there are in fact remarkable differences in language and concepts between these two genres, and the presence of sentences in prose contrasts markedly with our knowledge that the prophets were poets. Furthermore, within the sections in poetry it is easy to identify generic, stereotyped, relatively impersonal texts like the so-called 'confessions' (12.1-13; 15.10-21; 18.19-23; 20.7-18), impersonal in that they copy themes, vocabulary and styles characteristic of the Psalms and Job. One passage of the 'confessions' (16.1-13) is even in prose, which means that it must have undergone a special revision. Again, it has long been accepted that the majority of the material in prose is the product of the Deuteronomistic redaction, though there are those who would want to see a substantial reassessment of the amount of this material (recently H.Weippert, 1973). However, there is no question here, of course, of a mechanical legalistic application of specific categories and fixed criteria; the term 'Deuteronomistic' is used 'in a broad connotation' (Carroll, 14). Moreover it is well known that the Deuteronomistic sections form one of the most important components of the book, in that they contain a large number of the key passages.

If we want to draw the obvious conclusions from this state of affairs, it seems that the 'Deuteronomists' wanted to make Jeremiah the standard-bearer and especially the spokesman of their thesis, so that the book is one more case of pseudepigraphy. The fact that such an important role in the work is attributed to Baruch is an evident sign that the memory of scribal redaction had not been completely lost. That appears clearly from ch.36; it has in fact been noted for some time that this is not a factual account of the meeting between the amanuensis and king Jehoiakim, but a literary creation intended to dramatize the event, which set out to legitimate the function of the scribe in the process of creating and passing on the account, just as the discovery of the book of the *tōrāh* legitimates Deuteronomy and Josiah's reform in the account in II Kings 22-23. II Chronicles 34-35, of course, has a substantially different account at precisely this point (above, 9.7). So it is that the prophet is in fact presented as one who proclaims the message of Deuteronomy and Dtr, in other words in a ideological key – though I do not intend the term 'ideological' to have the negative sense which it has in popular Marxist thought (a system of thought which legitimates the interests of a class or social group over against third parties and one's own unquiet conscience). By calling the message 'ideological' I mean that it is related to 'a body of ideas or a coherent set of political beliefs' (Carroll, 17).

In this way there comes into being a figure of the prophet utterly intent on serving the aims of Deuteronomy and of Dtr as these took shape during and after the exile, to explain the fall of the two Hebrew kingdoms and a new existence in a much reduced territory, shorn of any political independence. In other words the reconstruction of the life of Jeremiah is not very different from that of the life of Jesus; in both cases any attempt comes up against insurmountable difficulties, given the 'kerygmatic' character of the texts. The result is the figure of a prophet in constant conflict with his own era and with its representatives: kings, priests, other prophets, the people; these are individuals and institutions who were unwilling to receive the message, though if they had listened to the message, it would have much reduced, perhaps even prevented, the catastrophe. This is the theory of the redactors, and throughout the book the prophet becomes their herald.

(g) We also know a good deal about Ezekiel, though not as much as about Jeremiah. He came from a priestly family and was one of the Judahites deported in 597. He kept in constant touch with the home country, indeed he harried the survivors with messages of judgment. But when he received news of the final destruction of Jerusalem in 587/6 and of the deportation of another group of its inhabitants, he became the herald of reconstruction (chs.33ff.; cf. chs.40-48). He had succeeded (as had quite a few of the deportees) in achieving a certain degree of well-being, and in 3.23 and 8.1 we are told that he had a house of his own in which he received the elders of Judah; his wife died there (24.16ff.). However, this framework has been elaborated by visions verging on the extravagant and symbolic actions at the fringe of normality. Moreover the spirit appears as the means by which Ezekiel travels from Babylon to Judaea (8.3) and, presumably, returns. It is clear that these are not data that we can use historically; various suggestions have been made to explain the phenomena, but none of them is very satisfactory. In Ezekiel, too, the Deuteronomistic redaction seems very consistent.

(h) We shall be taking up the themes of this short account again when we come to look at individual prophets. To conclude it, we may note some clear negative factors. For the most part it is impossible to get back to the prophets as historical figures; rather, we are dealing with literary stereotypes (Amos) or with late reconstructions on the part of persons or schools which made the prophet the heroic proclaimer of their own theories, which they thought should have been observed in the past and which were the necessary and probably also sufficient condition of the salvation of the people. It is only through the mediation of these individuals and groups, which act as a filter, that we can approach the prophets. The consequences for a study of their message should be obvious, and we shall consider them in due course.

5. The periods in which the prophets were active

(a) The Hebrew Bible clearly distinguishes three periods in the history of prophecy. The earliest period begins with the foundation of the state and runs to the end of the eighth century; a second begins with the eighth century and ends after the exile of 587/86-539; the last runs from the end of the exile to the end of the movement a century or two later. During the last two periods we have a series of books which bear the name of the prophets to which they are traditionally attributed. During the phase in which prophecy is coming to an end a series of new movements come into being, all denoted generically as 'apocalyptic'. These movements lasted more or less up to the catastrophes of 70 and 135 CE; they have many features in common with prophecy, but are also quite clearly distinct from it.

(b) It is interesting to note that the bibical tradition has prophecy appearing only with the beginnings of the state or at least immediately before that. Saul appears surrounded by ecstatic prophets, and is first supported, then rebuked and finally rejected by Samuel. David has frequent encounters with Nathan which are sometimes confrontations. In the northern kingdom Elijah and Elisha were active in the ninth century BCE. Many other prophets are mentioned in episodes of an anecdotal kind, often anonymous, from the beginnings of the monarchy onwards, and this is a phenomenon which lasts up to and beyond the exile. Jonah, whose book is certainly post-exilic, appears among the twelve minor prophets, but is not treated in the same way as the others: as in the case of Elijah and Elisha, we are given an episode from his life which is rich in fantastic elements, but are not told anything about the content of his preaching.

We are told of episodes from the life of quite a number of these prophets, especially their encounters with public powers, in particular with ruling sovereigns; the substance of their interventions is often a defence of the poor and the oppressed, but here too it is impossible to check the episodes against a historical setting. At all events a figure like that of Elijah must have been much more important than the texts suggest, seeing that in the post-exilic period he becomes the main character in some apocalyptic books; in the Hebrew Bible cf. already Mal.3.23/4.5 and in the New Testament Matt.16.14, where Elijah appears as the eschatological prophet, the precursor of the coming of the Messiah and of the end of time; his assumption into heaven seems justified only if he had such a position of pre-eminence.

(c) In the second period the situation becomes more complicated. In the previous paragraphs we have seem the difficulties posed by the biographical data given in the books of Amos, Isaiah, Jeremiah and Ezekiel. This automatically raises the questions: Is it possible to reconstruct anything of their original message, and if so how much? How much, rather, is to be attributed to the redactors who have sought to make the prophet their spokesman? Clearly the problem must be examined in isolation in the case of each individual prophet; for the moment, however, one thing alone seems relatively easy, namely to isolate the texts which have a Deuteronomistic redaction. In the case of the others we have to attempt an always complex history of the redaction, a work which is usually barren. The result of this work is very often disappointing: very little remains of the *ipsissima verba* which the prophets uttered and we can know very little of the circumstances in which these words were in fact pronounced. All this usually tends to contrast with the role which the redactors have wanted to assign to the individual prophets.

(*d*) The post-exilic prophets are a minority. Moreover it is easy to see a remarkable decline in the quality of their message. Now questions relating to the rebuilding of the temple (Haggai and Malachi), marriage (Malachi), and various ritual matters are the order of the day. We find prophecies interwoven with apocalyptic themes which are not always easy to understand (Deutero-Zechariah); the one post-exilic prophet who recalls the glories of the pre-exilic prophets on a literary level in both form and content seems to be Joel. Moreover, many scholars have asked whether in the case of these prophets we can speak of the continuation of a movement which reached notable heights before and during the exile which have rarely been equalled in the history of religion. However, it is evident that the circumstances in which the prophets worked after the exile were substantially different from those before. On the one hand political independence was at an end and the ruling house had fallen; on the other hand the people was in constant contact with the local populations were now constant, and the texts from Judah suggest that these populations were always hostile. In these circumstances the prophetic preaching also became different: it took on routine tones and was occupied with a variety of things which were not very 'prophetic'. Now the movement seems to be in sharp decline, on the way to extinction. Very soon it was to be allied with and then replaced by apocalyptic.

(*e*) The distinction between these periods in biblical prophecy, which is apparently so clear in the Hebrew Bible, becomes much less so when we subject the texts to a detailed examination; as we can immediately see, there is no more than a formal difference. In reality it derives solely from the way in which the accounts of their lives have been handed down. It is also said of Samuel, Nathan, Elijah and Elisha that they were profoundly interested in the political and economic life of their nation; we know of the second and third that they did all they could towards the solution of social problems, and in all of them we find a criticism of worship as it was practised in Israel and in Judah. So it seems clear that the prophets earlier than the eighth century BCE had interests similar to those whose books have been handed down under their own name.

(*f*) Some of the earliest prophets, for example in the time of Samuel those ecstatics in whose actions Saul too was caught up, often (though not necessarily always) seem to have been gathered in groups and in schools, and are often connected with a sanctuary. This is a matter that we shall be dealing with later (below, 7). Elijah had a disciple, Elisha, and he in turn had followers (II Kings 4.38ff.). Amos, however, denied in his prophetic biography that he had been part of a prophetic school (7.14); his calling is presented as something which came about without intermediaries, and was a matter directly between himself and his God. However, there are scholars who do not discount the possibility that he too had been the disciple of a prophet, and in any case his situation seems to be somewhat unusual. Isaiah is said to have had disciples (cf. 8.16); it is also said that there was a time when he limited his activity to this circle of disciples, instead of seeking the greatest possible publicity, which seems to have been his practice in ordinary conditions (cf.5.1ff.). It is on the basis of the mention of these disciples that some scholars have sought to attribute the compilation of Deutero- and Trito-Isaiah to disciples of Isaiah. That would be a reasonable explanation of how the name of Isaiah came to be attributed to texts which in no case can go back to the eighth century BCE, as we shall see when we come to discuss them (below, 20.1). Again, the existence of an 'Isaiah school' which operated over many centuries would also explain the inclusion in the text of chs.24-27, a writing of an apocalyptic kind, which is even later. Of course these are no more than hypotheses, but they are hypotheses which have made possible significant progress in discovering how the redaction of at least one prophetic book took place. As we have seen, we know that Jeremiah had a disciple, Baruch, who also acted as a secretary.

(*g*) On the problem of the possible connection between the prophet and certain sanctuaries, which we shall be occupied with below (§ 7), it is enough to note that although Amos came from the south, he preached freely in the sanctuary of Bethel, the national temple of the north (7.10ff.); it is also probable that he preached mainly there. He was expelled only when he made a personal attack on King Jeroboam II, who exercised something like a right of patronage over it. Isaiah received his visions when he was in the temple of Jerusalem (6.1ff.) and probably in the inner sanctuary, the second hall which only the priests could enter. Moreover a real theology of Zion and its sanctuary is attributed to Isaiah, although there are scholars (nowadays the majority) who would prefer to attribute these elements to later redaction (they are probably right). Jeremiah, too, preached freely in the temple, as is shown by the speech which he made according to chs. 7 and 26, two parallel texts; the difficulties began only when he announced its destruction (again according to the model biography which I have mentioned), a statement which amounted to blasphemy. The knowledge that Hosea seems to have had of the priesthood has led some scholars to suppose that he came from priestly stock, as we are told Jeremiah and Ezekiel did. This produces on the one hand a very close relationship between the prophets and the priesthood, contrary to what a superficial observer might deduce from the texts, if he or she went only by the criticism which the prophets direct at the ruling cult.

(h) I have referred to the distinctions between the pre-exilic and the post-exilic prophets. At least in the biographies which have been handed down to us, the former were occupied with almost every field of life, whether religion, or civic and political affairs: the cult, foreign and domestic policy, social problems, the fate of non-Israelite peoples. Among the post-exilic prophets this universal interest is much reduced: their preaching is predominantly about matters domestic to the Judahite community, with an emphasis which sometimes resembles legalism. There is no criticism whatsoever of the cult, the priesthood and sacrifice, except as concerns their degree of perfection. There is no challenge, but a desire that everything should be done in order and with the greatest possible perfection. Ethical problems are also seen in a narrower perspective; we might almost call it provincial. Of course it is easy to make criticisms here, to pass disparaging judgments, and this has been done. It is also easy to note the lower level of the themes dealt with by the prophecy of these years, and to point out its basically introverted character. It is easy to highlight a set of problems which could seem petty to anyone measuring these prophets by the standard of the pre-exilic giants, and to criticize a certain nationalistic note which was lacking at first. But we should also remember here that before the rise of a vast diaspora the Judahite community was very small indeed and primarily provincial; that the economic and political situation was very serious, and that the work of the spiritual and material rebuilding of the community, which risked irretrievably losing its spiritual heritage, compromised by the serious disruption of the exile, could only be done with difficulty. We should also remember that everyday life consisted in a constant confrontation with the neighbouring peoples, now no longer held at bay by any kind of army, under a régime which, however liberal it might have been, was foreign.

This was the case in the Persian period; later, in Macedonian and Hellenistic times, we have the alternation of relative freedom and oppression, followed by the Maccabaean revolt and the brief national interregnum of around a century (167-63 BCE). By now prophecy had been finished for some time and had been replaced by apocalyptic. It is not surprising, therefore, that during the few centuries that prophecy continued to exist, it was occupied with problems which might seem insignificant to us, but which acquired a crucial value for those who had lost everything.

However, even granting all these features, there is no doubt that we now have a movement which had exhausted itself, a phenomenon which was clearly decadent both on a spiritual and an intellectual level. Only eschatological speculations developed in this period, soon gaining the upper hand and then turning into apocalyptic. But at that stage we have a phenomenon which is no longer, strictly speaking, prophetic, even if it is derived from prophecy and perpetuates quite a number of its features. Be this as it may, the transition takes place without a break, in a gradual way. This is a problem which I cannot deal with here; for it I would refer to my study mentioned in the bibliography.

Thus in the course of the sixth and fifth centuries prophecy was gradually in process of exhausting itself, and finally disappeared, although 'prophets' still emerged here and there.

6. Characteristics of the prophetic ministry and unsolved problems

(a) At the end of the last century and the beginning of this, scholars were concerned not only with the question of the Pentateuch but also with the problem of prophecy and the prophets: who precisely were they and in what did their ministry consist? I have already pointed out that in the traditional exegesis of the Christian church the prophets appeared essentially as those who proclaimed the Christ who was to come, in whose person and whose work, crowned with the cross and resurrection, their prophecies had been fulfilled, and it is also possible to encounter messianic interpretations in Jewish exegesis. It is possible to find not dissimilar attitudes in Jewish and Christian circles even today. Of course, once the prophets had been assigned this task, it was easy to extend it throughout the Old Testament, and to multiply to infinity the number of messianic prophecies, interpreting 'prophetically' material which had nothing to do with the prophets. A typical example of this attitude is the treatment of Gen.3.15, which was given the title 'protevangelium', as though it announced the definitive victory of the woman and her progeny over the serpent. The whole approach was based on a saying attributed to Jesus 'You search the scriptures... it is they that bear witness to me' (John 5.39).

(b) Historical criticism has put an end to this kind of exegesis once and for all, but of course that affects only those who accept the method; although this exegesis reached high levels of spirituality, it opened the door to extremely subjective speculations. In the light of a more objective approach, only a few texts can be considered applicable to the expected Messiah: Isa.8.23-9.6 [EVV 9.1-7]; 11.1-9; Micah 5.1-4 [EVV 5.2-5]; Zech.9.9 and perhaps also, with major qualifications, Isa.7.10-17. Moreover, here too the primary reference of the texts of Isaiah and Micah is to persons and events of their own time, while the messianic application draws essentially on later interpretations. What the primitive church made of these interpretations is another problem, and an integral part of the history of the thought of the primitive church and the history of exegesis. As I have already mentioned, at a later stage messianic exegesis was also extended to the rest of the Bible, in fact leading to an impoverishment of the prophetic message, whether for the historian of religions, the believer or the theologian.

(c) After centuries of research in a christological vein in the sphere of the Christian church, research which was carried out along impersonal lines and according to criteria which were often mechanical, in terms of promise and fulfilment, towards the end of the nineteenth and the beginning of the twentieth centuries research came to be centred more on the personalities of the prophets, their religious experiences, the comparison of these experiences with kindred phenomena in other religions, the prophets' struggles with the situation of their time and with power. In this way the human dimension of the prophets was recovered after a neglect lasting many centuries. Study began of the historical context of the prophets, the economic and social problems which they faced, and the political situation within which they found themselves working. Two German scholars, Bernard Duhm and Gustav Hölscher, particularly distinguished themselves here: the former was a colleague of Wellhausen in his struggles and continued his work; the latter was a rather isolated figure. Though their works have nowadays largely been superseded, they remain valid as evidence of a historical shift and also of a series of questions which were addressed for the first time to biblical science, and are still partly valid.

(d) We have already encountered Bernhard Duhm (above, 7.7d); his first work was *Theologie der Propheten als Grundlage für die innere Entwicklungsgeschichte der israelitischen Religion* (Theology of the Prophets as the Basis for the History of the Inner Development of Israelite Religion), Bonn 1875: this was followed by commentaries on Isaiah (*Das Buch Jesaja*, Göttingen 1892, [4]1922, reprinted 1967, in which he proposed the separation of chs.56-66 from Deutero-Isaiah), and Jeremiah (*Das Buch Jeremia*, Tübingen 1901), and finally the synthesis, *Israels Propheten* (Tübingen 1916, [2]1922). Duhm's intention was finally to let the prophets themselves speak at last after having been overshadowed by pre-existing theories for so many centuries; moreover, he thought that in this way he could reconstruct the development of Israelite religion. At all events he did not want to start from what it was thought that the religion of Israel or the prophets should have been, preferring rather to gather his information from the prophetic books and the texts which described the activity of the prophets. He intended the term 'theology', which he used in his first work, to denote an ideal interest in the historical continuity between the religion of Israel and Christianity, but totally avoided concepts like revelation and inspiration. For Duhm the significance of the prophets in the sphere of the history of Israel lay in their break with the natural forms of religion, with Canaanite religion: they raised religion to an ethical level. The prophetic contrast was thus between natural or naturalistic religion and ethical religion; however, this did not prevent Duhm from taking the visionary and clairvoyant element seriously. Thus for example he regarded Jeremiah's announcement of the imminent death of the false prophet Hananiah as a historical episode, as is evident from his comment on Jer.28.15ff. It is, of course, easy to criticize the concept of ethical religion, a concept which Duhm did not regard as a prejudice, and I shall attempt to do that briefly in due course; however, the fact remains that he had a correct view of the break with natural, i.e. Canaanite, religion.

(e) The perspective of Gustav Hölscher, *Die Profeten*, Leipzig 1914, is different. He too wanted to use the prophets to reconstruct the history of religion, but he was particularly interested in the psychological side of the prophetic experiences. He thought a certain knowledge of psychology and its more technical bibliography necessary for an appreciation of these experiences. In this sphere his model was the 'physiological psychology' and the 'psychology of peoples' put forward by Wilhelm Wundt. Hölscher's reflections relate particularly to para-psychological phenomena like ecstasy (especially catalepsy) and hallucinations, which he describes with precision and exactness.

(f) These two works, which we may consider to be pioneering, bring together elements of idealistic philosophy and German romanticism (see the stress in Duhm on the *ethical* character of religion), the history of religions, German historicism, ethnology and psychology, and their merit is essentially that they are one of the first attempts at inter-disciplinary analysis. Here the prophet, then, is examined primarily as an individual and as a religious personality, whose experiences can be considered typical and paradigmatic. The one concession made to the idea of community was to see the prophet as the head of a school, and of course he preached to crowds or cultic gatherings. In a historiography which attached fundamental importance in the political, economic, social and ideological spheres to the work of the individual genius, disregarding for the most part the factors without which the 'genius' could not have succeeded or perhaps would not even have existed, an approach to the problem on these lines should not be surprising; if in principle we are forced to reject it as inadequate, we should at least recognize that it was a valid alternative to the disembodied, impersonal approach through which the prophets had hitherto been studied. Suddenly, in fact, the prophet appeared to his modern audience as a man of flesh and blood, situated in a particular ideological, social, economic and political context, with all the conflicts which that normally involved. According to this new evaluation, confronted with a predominantly conservative or conformist people or ruling group, the prophet emerged as a spiritual giant, often forced to fight on two fronts: against an audience which was uninterested, if not hostile, and against his own God, who sometimes did not hesitate to overwhelm the prophet's will. Thus Amos 7.14 asserts that God 'seized' (root *lqḥ*) him; in Jer.1.4ff. at first the prophet does not want to accept the divine call, but he is constrained by God who sweeps all his excuses aside. Ezekiel is even overwhelmed by a tremendous vision (1.1ff.) which leaves him very little space for a decision. Where, as in the case of Jeremiah, the theme of direct compulsion appears, we of course have inner insecurity and conflict: the so-called 'confessions' (or better 'laments') of Jeremiah which we shall be looking at in due course (below, 23.1) and to which I have already referred. Conflict could also arise over certain tasks which were considered to be too hard, as in the case of Isa.6.1ff., and only a symbolic action on the part of God could convince the prophet that he should announce to his people their irrevocable destruction. The application of the term 'confessions' to these passages of Jeremiah is already itself indicative of the personalistic and sentimental approach made to the problem; so much so that it was rejected in the classic study of the problem by W.Baumgartner, *Die Klagegedichte des Jeremia*, Giessen 1917 (ET forthcoming Sheffield 1988), who suggested rather 'laments in poetry'. For the figure of Ezekiel there is no lack of texts which suggest psychopathological or perhaps even parapsychological phenomena: abnormal visions (chs.1 and 10); speechlessness (3.26); catalepsy (4.4-8); and ch.8 with the transportation of the prophet in the spirit from Babylon to Jerusalem.

(g) As individualists, then, whether by nature or vocation, the prophets were said to have rejected the form of cult current in their time in favour of a more spiritual piety with more social commitment, of the kind that was recommended to the faithful in the circles of bourgeois Victorian Protestantism. They were even thought sometimes to have foretold the abolition of absolutely every form of worship, of public piety, in favour of an ethically exalted life, pledged to the struggle against the injustices which plagued society. In a context of this kind public worship was an unnecessary superstructure. Typical positions of the 'liberal' or 'pietistic' Protestantism of the period were thus anachronistically projected back by the writers on to the prophetic message: the triumph of the moral law, ethical monotheism (whatever the exact meaning of this expression might have been – it was far from obvious), contempt for any external form of cult. Nor can it be asserted that these views are superseded today; they still appear, paradoxically, among some 'progressive' Christian groups in the uncritical rejection of public worship, which is replaced with personal and collective commitment in the sphere of social ethics and politics, which is no better, or just as vaguely defined – and their advocates claim the support of the prophets for them.

There are still approaches of a psychological kind today, as for example in the basic work of the Swedish scholar J.Lindblom, *Prophecy in Ancient Israel*, Oxford 1962.

(h) Although they keep reappearing every now and then, all these ways of approaching the problem can now be considered superseded from a scientific point of view, though they have the undisputed merit of having helped to open up a set of problems which has proved stubborn for some time. Nowadays, as we saw earlier (above, 4d), we know that the lives of the prophets or the few pieces of information available to us allow only a minimum of reconstruction of a biographical kind. So it is difficult to say what a prophet 'felt', what he tried to do, what moved him to act in a particular way; the history of the redaction by which a prophetic book reached its present form also seems to have been complex.

One thing that remains certain is that many of the questions raised by scholars over the last century and at the beginning of this have yet to be answered satisfactorily, and that the majority of the problems remain unsolved, precisely because the sources present a framework which is that of the later redactors and not that of the real protagonists. So here we have a set of open questions, which will have to be tackled with the new methods now at our disposal. This has been argued for some years now by G.von Rad, *Old Testament Theology* II, Edinburgh 1965 (reissued London 1975), 299, who is followed by M.-L.Henry, *Propheten und Tradition*, Berlin 1969, 3ff.; moreover, Henry, having noted the unique character of biblical prophecy in the history of religion, asks how it could be that these words, always spoken in relation to particular situations and problems, could have survived and come down to our day as authoritative words for situations which no longer have anything to do with those in which they were originally spoken. This problem too must be tackled and, if possible, resolved. And it is evident that criticism directed at unsatisfactory approaches cannot be used as an excuse for not responding to the questions which have been raised. I shall list some of these in the next sections.

7. Prophets and cult

(*a*) This topic can be dealt with from three distinct perspectives: 1. the activity of the prophets in the sphere of the cult; 2. their activity outside the cult and their frequent criticism of it; 3. words which refer indirectly to the cult (Murray, 1982).

In the pre-exilic prophets the following passages refer directly to the cult, all in a polemical manner; they therefore belong to category 2. Amos 4.4f.; 5.21-25; Hos.6.6; 8.11-13; Isa.1.11-17; Micah 6.6-8; Jer.7.1-11, 21-23. I shall mention only the most important and the most explicit of them here. First of all, it should be noted that none of these passages is polemic against the cult as such; only some of its features are mentioned as they were to be found in northern sanctuaries (Amos and Hosea), in the Jerusalem temple (Isaiah, Micah and Jeremiah), or in other sanctuaries in the south (Amos 8.14 refers to an unknown cult, practised at Beersheba). The chief concern is with sacrifices: of the eight passages mentioned, six refer to this practice, which must have led to many abuses. The other features of the cult are significantly much rarer: there are two mentions of festivities, two of different sanctuaries and one each of pilgrimages, altars and prayer. Despite these criticisms, as we have seen (above, 5g), the prophets were frequently connected with a sanctuary, so much so that this is almost the rule.

(b) As we have already seen, in the literature of some decades ago one might often read that the prophets sought the abolition of the ritual cult in favour of a more 'spiritual' cult which, in the intention of the scholars in question, would have anticipated Jesus' words to the woman of Samaria in John 4.23, understood idealistically. It would be without sacrifices, without ceremonies, without sanctuaries and composed exclusively of songs, prayers and meditations. As well as being untenable, this explanation has the defect of simplifying complex problems. The fact of the matter is that this was not the sphere of the confrontation; that should be sought rather in the struggle between Yahwistic faith and Canaanite religion, between two positions which for some time had been apparently in accord, but which the prophets saw to be really incompatible.

(c) It is far from easy to establish precisely what the prophets were referring to: we have only sparse and fragmentary knowledge of the nature of Israelite religion and therefore of Israelite cult in the pre-exilic period. However, from the little that we have managed to discover it is possible to infer that this was a religion and a cult very much closer to the religion of Canaan than the official sources, the majority of which are late exilic or post-exilic, would have us believe. A series of features which appear here and there is evidence of that: the abundant use of Ba'al in nomenclature, the presence of a royal ideology hardly different from that of neighbouring peoples and bound up with the fertility of the soil, the family, the flock and the herd, in which the king took over the office and exercised the functions of the priest (Ps.110.4) and was adopted by the deity (Ps.2.7). It seems increasingly evident that YHWH was only one of the deities worshipped in the context of a more numerous pantheon, even if he was the national deity of the two kingdoms and also the dynastic deity in the south. As a working hypothesis it is possible to suppose that the concept which made YHWH first the one national God of Israel and Judah and therefore the one absolute God was put forward for the first time by the prophets, later to become one of the foundations of Josiah's reform, then of Deuteronomy and of Deuteronomistic historiography.

However, the argument of the Hebrew Bible is a different one: the religion of Israel was originally already monotheistic, pure and incorrupt; it would then have been contaminated in contact with that of Canaan, giving rise to unacceptable forms of syncretism (this is also the theory of the Israeli Y.Kaufmann). But this concept is based on the presupposiition of a glorious past which gave way to decadence, and thus on a variant of the myth of the golden age, so it cannot be sustained on a historical-critical level. If we can trust the few pieces of information at our disposal, the process must have been precisely the opposite.

Like the other peoples of Syria, Canaan and Transjordan, Israel and Judah also lived in a territory which was for the most part infertile, without any water other than the winter rains. Thus in contrast to the peoples of Egypt and Mesopotamia, they depended on the caprices of the climate and on other factors which were beyond their control. In such conditions it is not surprising that Israel, too, felt the need of those rites and beliefs which, without evidently providing an absolute guarantee, at all events secured the good will of the gods and could therefore lead to hopes of at least a sufficient harvest.

However, as far as we can establish, it was the prophets who posed the alternative of either YHWH or Ba'al and the other deities. In that case, however, the question arose: how much in the cult was addressed to other deities and how much to the God of Israel? Where could one draw a dividing line? Where had the characteristics of the other gods been attributed to YHWH? How was it possible to make YHWH also responsible for fertility? And was it possible to do so without attributing sexual characteristics to him? Again, the ethical character that the religion of the prophets soon attributed to YHWH (and it is here that the otherwise vague and imprecise expression 'ethical monotheism', so dear to scholars at the end of the last century and the beginning of this, has some validity) was incompatible with the use of rituals and religious practices which replaced a covenant that covered all spheres of life. The practice of sacrifice, in particular, lent itself to all sorts of abuses, offering the possibility of an easy expiation of one's guilt by means of something very similar to an oblation pure and simple which dispensed the guilty one from specific restitution of the loss incurred and the pledge not to commit the same faults again.

(d) So it seems clear that the prophets adopted a critical attitude towards the cult and especially towards sacrifices. However, this argument must not be exaggerated; in his important 1963 study E.Würthwein preferred to speak of 'opinions on the cult' rather than polemic against the cult; at all events, there is no rejection in principle here. That is confirmed by the fact that, as we have seen, the prophets were allowed to speak freely in the cult, and one might also suppose that the liturgy explicitly provided for their interventions. So it does not seem rash to argue that if Amos could speak at Bethel and Jeremiah in the temple of Jerusalem, they did so with full justification. Thus they did not voluntarily exclude themselves from a cult which they felt ought to disappear, nor even, as many Scandinavian scholars asserted in the 1930s and 1940s, were they necessarily functionaries in the state cult: the words attributed to Amos in 7.10ff. in his exchange with the priest Amaziah rule out an interpretation of this kind, though there is clearly nothing here to cast doubts on the existence of such functionaries, who were also denoted by the title *nābī'*.

8. Prophets and politics

(a) One field in which the prophets are presented as having been active from the beginning of the movement is that of politics, both domestic and foreign. Samuel and Nathan stand by kings, the former by Saul and the latter by David; Ahijah of Shiloh promises Jeroboam that he will reign over the ten northern tribes (I Kings 11.31f.); Elijah plots and Elisha organizes a revolution, or rather a *coup d'état*, which overthrows the house of Omri in Israel, replacing it with a general, Jehu (II Kings 9); and one of the first acts of the new sovereign was the extermination not only of the survivors of the deposed dynasty but also of those who were faithful to Ba'al (II Kings 10.18ff.); soon after that we see him pay homage to Shalmaneser III, king of Assyria (*ANEP*, 351-5). The narrative attributes to Elisha a similar operation against Damascus, but the note seems historically improbable, unless we think of a *coup d'état* favourable to Assyria in the two states, intended to eliminate the coalition which until that point had succeeded in containing the Assyrian advance westwards (cf. my *History*, IX.4.1ff.). Be this as it may, it remains remarkable that the narrator does not find it strange for a prophet to intervene in a revolt followed by a *coup d'état* not only in his own country, but also in a foreign one. However, later generations did not accept these actions uncritically: Hosea 1.4 dissociates itself from them with hard words, and the prophets in general, while often severely criticizing the monarchy and its institutions, were never ready to back violent actions of this kind with their participation. At this point the fact that this framework is often the product of the way in which later generations, under the stimulus of Dtr, understood the figure of the prophet as the man of God *par excellence*, is no longer relevant.

(*b*) In the prophetic books Amos and Micah do not take up any position in the political field, unless we want to put the attack against the person of the king which Amos 7.10ff. attributes to the prophet or the oracles against the nations in this category. Hosea, however, attacks the politicians of the north and especially the monarchy; cf. Hos.5.13, where there is a reference to attempts at an alliance with Assyria (but in that case, following a generally accepted conjecture, we should read 'to the Great King', a title frequently borne by the kings of Assyria, and not the Hebrew 'to king Jareb': the correction leaves the consonantal text intact); cf. also 7.3 and 8.10. The theme is much more developed in Isaiah and we have a real political theology: in 2.12-22 and 20.1ff. the support given to political alliances is considered evidence of lack of faith, whereas in Isa.7.1ff. two alternatives are considered by the court: to surrender to the coalition troops of the north and Damascus or to call on the help of Assyria against them (which was in fact the policy adopted). The prophet proposes a third possibility: to trust in YHWH and his promises that the attack by the allies will not be carried out. Behind the apparent quietism we have here an exhortation to take the divine promises seriously and to act in conformity with this faith. But in this third text, too, we are faced with the problem whether such standpoints were those of the prophet himself or the product of the reflection of later generations, as we saw earlier (above, 4d), and also of what specific political option arose from them. Throughout his book Jeremiah calls for an attitude of faith, and especially in the reign of Jehoiakim and Zedekiah urges the people to submit to Babylon and not to trust in the help of Egypt. For this stand he is imprisoned for high treason.

(*c*) In Israel, of course, as with the majority of the peoples of the ancient world, eastern and western, national community and religious community coincided, as we saw when considering Israelite law. Consequently this political involvement of the prophets seems conditioned by particular circumstances which had already been superseded at the time of the return from exile and which certainly can no longer be established today. Be this as it may, the fact remains that the tradition is almost unanimous in presenting the figures of the prophets as being intent on reminding even the monarchy and the organs of state of the divine order. This attitude was not without its dangers, as the case of Jeremiah shows.

9. Prophets and social problems

(*a*) II Samuel 12, which I have already mentioned, presents the figure of the prophet Nathan pleading the cause of the victim of a serious abuse of power on the part of the king; I Kings 21 is comparable, with the episode of Naboth and his vineyard, in which again the interests of the crown or the personal interests of the monarch had been maintained at the expense of a poor citizen of Israel. In the two cases the king accepts the reproach and repents of his evil deed, though the death of the victim makes it impossible for him now to make adequate reparation. The two cases seem historically improbable: it is in fact difficult to outline a period in the history of Israel and Judah in which the individual, even if he were a prophet, could have argued publicly with a monarch, let alone have the monarch listen to him and repent. In the former of the two episodes we have an idyllic description of the situation at court, in which anyone can take the king to account over his acts of government and the actions of his subordinates. This is what the *vox populi* considered to have been the good government of times past, to which every monarch should have conformed, and a society which was still basically healthy, in which abuses only took the form of individual acts of dishonesty, which were immediately condemned by a powerful public opinion. In the second case the situation already seems less idyllic: the pressures of the court succeed in intimidating the village tribunal composed of the elders. These elders should have come together as one man in defence of the rights of their fellow citizen; here, however, public opinion is now silenced and the tribunal condemns an innocent person in sheer bad faith. The golden age is thus over, and we find ourselves in more evil times in which the powerful can do virtually anything; neverthelesss protest was still possible. In this second case biblical historiography notes, as elsewhere, a retrogressive process and sees its ominous consequences; according to its theory the blame for this is to be attributed to the influence of the religion and culture of Canaan on Israel. In this case, too, the reality is probably different, namely that the monarchy produced a situation of increasing inequality, creating structures of power concentrated around the palace instead of in the local organs of Israel and Judah; and these structures worked with a perverse mechanism which made the rich increasingly rich and the poor increasingly poor. However, it is impossible to analyse the structures thoroughly, given the present state of the evidence.

(*b*) The invective of the prophets, especially in the eighth century

BCE, thus presents a social structure which has deteriorated; it is even necessary to speak of a system which is at the same time corrupt and repressive, one that H.Donner has been able to compare with that of early capitalism in Europe and North America in the last century, while Fohrer speaks of the transition from a closed, patriarchal economy to a kind of market economy, a transition which the prophets did not reject *per se*, but only in so far as it led to distortions in the economic and social sphere. And this system is said to have taken the place of the relative equality distinctive of patriarchal societies.

As we have seen, the prophets attributed this retrogressive development to Canaanite society. However, this theory presents a series of problems quite apart from the difficulties already mentioned. We have noteworthy evidence of ideals of good government from Ugarit at the time of its greatest prosperity. There were features which, even in a society ruled by absolute and authoritarian systems, guaranteed the administration of justice in accordance with certain canons of equity and therefore the protection of the weakest members in society. A legendary king like Keret was accused of having omitted through negligence to judge the cause of the widow and to do justice to one who had suffered unjustly, and of not having exiled one who enriched himself at the expense of the poor. Another legendary king, Daniel, 'judged the cause of the widow and did justice to the orphan'. So towards the end of the second millennium Canaan knew what we call good government and what the prophets looked for from their own rulers. This means that arguments based on a corrupt Canaanite society, whether social or religious (the latter, as we have seen, is difficult to sustain since it involves the concept of a regression from a pure religion to a corrupt and syncretistic religion), prove to be unfounded. If anything, one might think of a decadent stage of Canaanite civilization, but with a hypothesis of this kind we come up against the absolute silence of the sources. Moreover, even if we could accept these observations, they would not be enough in themselves to explain the phenomenon. It is evident, rather, that the patriarchal structures, based on village economy, proved inadequate for a confrontation with a different economic and political situation, namely that of the centralized state, and along with their inadequacy went the loss of any possibility of offering effective opposition to new developments, even where the old order formally remained intact. The building of the temple of Jerusalem by Solomon and the restoration of worship at the northern sanctuaries by Jeroboam I at the end of the tenth century BCE had put the cult, too, under the patronage of the crown, whereas the inclusion of the tribal territories in a system of districts, attested for the first time under Solomon (I Kings 4.7ff.), had in turn weakened the traditional economy, also leading on an ethnic level to an integration of the Israelites and the populations of the Canaanite city-states, a process for which Israel and Judah do not seem to have been ready. The palace formed a centre from which royal power emanated, and a text which the redaction puts in the time of Saul (I Sam.22.7) attributes to the king the practice of recompensing his faithful followers with land and other benefits. This favoured the rise of a new social class tied to the court instead of to the original order of society, precisely following the pattern among neighbouring peoples. The new class had been assigned large pieces of land in competition with tribal property, and sometimes in conflict with it, and in those days to have land was to have economic power. The ancient society had little chance of survival in such conditions.

Finally, the process seems to have been accelerated by the Aramaean wars which particularly afflicted Israel, the northern kingdom, during part of the ninth century. In the course of these conflicts the great landowners, while sometimes of course also suffering losses, were easily able, unlike the poor, to make them good on the battlefield by gaining plunder, since because their lands were so extensive, at least some of them could be saved. By contrast owners of tribal property, concentrated as this was in relatively restricted areas, were more exposed to pillage and destruction, and without the support of capital they almost inevitably ended up having to resort to loans at high rates of interest and were therefore soon swallowed up by the great landowners.

This reconstruction, which we must consider purely hypothetical, poses one difficulty. Until a few years ago archaeology was preoccupied more with literary and religious phenomena, for which it sought confirmation or explanation, still looking for information which would help towards a reconstruction of the history of Israel. The modern historian therefore had no other choice than to accept the historical theories of the Hebrew Bible, which could be summed up in two terms: progressive 'Canaanization' and religious 'syncretism'. However, it is proving increasingly necessary for archaeology to investigate the economic and social causes of this contrast between rich and poor by discoveries providing evidence of material culture, seeking to distinguish changes especially in the economic field. In the United States this task of the so-called 'new archaeology' has already been pursued for some years.

(c) Prophetic invective in the social field, then, should be seen against the background of this social change of which I have tried to make a conjectural reconstruction. The principal texts are as follows: Amos 2.6ff.; 3.9ff.; 4.1-3; 5.7-10f.; 6.4ff.; 8.4; Isa.1.10-17 (which we have already examined in connection with the question of the prophets and the cult); 1.23; 2.7; 3.13-15; 5.11ff., 22ff.; 29.21; Micah 2.1-5; 3.1-4; 6.6-8; cf. also Ezek.22. The theme is, however, absent in Hosea and is rarely discussed by Jeremiah.

The chief faults are indicated with tragic monotony: the corruption of the courts, which prevented anyone with right on his side or who had suffered a wrong from obtaining what he was owed by law, especially if he was poor; violence used on the economically weak; the plundering of the poor, which often happened in a way which kept to the letter of the law (for example, through loans given at high rates of interest); money-making that was illegal or at any rate disproportionate to the capital invested and the risks run, all followed by the ostentatious luxury which is typical of the *nouveaux riches*.

We should look in vain, however, among the prophets for an analysis of the socio-economical and political factors which underlay these developments; what I have just put forward is in fact, as we have seen, a modern conjecture. For the prophets – and here we are at the limit of their protest – the problem is of an essentially theological kind. The population has abandoned the Yahwistic faith of its ancestors, and therefore it has become corrupt. This is a theory which recalls the similar theories of Deuteronomy and Dtr: the people should not have abandoned their ancestral faith, and should have been able to discover new structures adapted to the different situation in which Israel now found itself. The recollection of the past and its purity, and of laws which were thought then to have been in force, subsequently to be abrogated or consigned to oblivion, of course runs contrary to history, and therefore could not resolve the problems which it faced.

(d) We also look in vain among the prophets for an integrated plan for reform; still less is there any hint of the possibility of a revolution. The experience of Jehu's *coup d'état* which had been sponsored by Elijah and Elisha had not in fact been encouraging: after the overthrow of the house of Omri and the beginning of a kind of bloody religious reform (at least as the sources describe it), everything had remained just as it was, and a prophet like Amos preached in his day to a great ruler of the house of Jehu, Jeroboam II. For the prophets it is not a matter of reforms or revolutions, but rather of conversion: if only the people had 'returned' to YHWH and lived in accordance with their faith, the problems would at least have been markedly reduced, even if they might not have been resolved. The austere dignity which the prophets attributed to the pre-monarchical period would have returned and the poor would no longer have been needy. The land would again belong to everyone and everyone would cultivate it in turn, by means of a system of rotation. So it is not surprising that, given the impossibility of realizing plans of this kind, the accent fell on eschatological hope, which in fact envisages a return to the time of paradise.

The modern reader, especially the reader with social commitment, might be disappointed by the lack of a constructive programme, in other words suggestions of alternatives to the prevalent system. However, this should not be surprising: the economic and social structure of Syria and Canaan at that time did not offer real alternatives. Nor do the prophets, as is shown by their surrender to eschatological hope, seem to have been capable of offering any. It is clear that the recollection of ancient structures was anachronistic and utopian: it is impossible to see whether these structures ever worked, and if they did, how. At the same time, however, we do get an answer to the question why such words, pronounced in specific circumstances, kept their validity down the centuries: this was not just because of the sympathy that part of the population of Judah seems to have had with nomadism (as appears clearly from Jer.35), but also because of the eschatological hope which developed increasingly with time. In the structures of the semi-nomads who moved around the cultivated land and with whom the patriarchs of Israel were associated, the prophets had found a parameter of judgment in the ethical and social field: the structures of these populations had (and in part still have) a marked element of democracy. In this confrontation the prophets did not pursue immediate aims, but pointed towards an element which was to bear its fruits centuries later.

10. The prophets and history

(a) Among the prophets we see the rise of a special kind of historiography (or theology of history) which was to be the model for the Deuteronomistic history. For all its limitations, this is a feature of remarkable originality; its one negative aspect is that, as we have already seen, we do not always know precisely what goes back to the original prophet and what belongs, rather, to the later specifically

Deuteronomistic revisions, so that all too often we are groping in the dark.

(b) The prophets tend to evaluate the past history of their people – individuals and events – in a very critical way. Even the traditions about the prehistory and protohistory of the people do not escape this judgment, though the prophets sometimes recall them in their criticism of the cult and the social situation. On other occasions, however, though less frequently, they idealize the past.

In what we might call the 'critical' category we find almost all the rare mentions of the patriarchs which are made outside the Pentateuch. Jacob is mentioned in Hos.12.3b-5 and severely censured and accused of the same fault as the people; he seems to have been their precursor, if not their inspiration. The passage is interesting because it indicates the existence of different traditions from those handed down in the Pentateuch. In Hos.9.10-11; 11.1-4; cf. Amos 9.7 we find a critical evaluation of the exodus, while Hos.9.9; 10.9 probably allude to the events reported in Judg.19. The cult of Bethel and Dan is judged severely in Hos.8.5; Amos 4.4; 7.10ff. Prophetic historiography resembles that of Dtr, albeit here on a smaller scale, in looking for the origins of the situation in which the people now find themselves in past history; it is not that there are no instances in which the people did what they should have done, but these are scanty. The verdict is generally negative: on the most favourable of hypotheses the attitude of the people and its rulers has been inadequate. For this reason YHWH punished them by means of catastrophes for which they were to blame: wars, enemy invasions, drought and famine. This historiography also significantly expanded the horizons of the people, to include their immediate neighbours and, more rarely, distant peoples in their message. In this way there comes into being something like an attempt at universal history, and with this arises the awareness that history, and therefore the fate of the people of God, are intimately connected with those of other peoples.

Passages like Isa.9.3 [EVV 9.4]; Jer.2.2-3 come within the sphere of the most optimistic evaluations of Israel's past; in them the exodus is evaluated in an extremely positive way as the ideal period for relations with God.

These forms of thought are important because they show that by means of the prophets, as well as discovering monotheism, Israel also liberated itself from the concept that the fate of the deity is closely bound up with that of the people or peoples who worship him; this concept appears clearly in the Mesopotamian and Hittite practice of deporting the statues of their deities along with the peoples, so as to bring out the 'metaphysical' character of their defeat. However, in 597 and 587/6 the Babylonians instead carried off the sacred vessels of the temple in Jerusalem, vessels which Cyrus, king of Persia, restored after 539. YHWH thus exists independently of the people who worship him, nor is he conditioned by them: he can reject them and choose others, all at his pleasure. Ezekiel was deported in 597 after the first siege of Jerusalem and therefore, along with his older contemporary Jeremiah, had an unparalleled experience of the drama of his own people; he does not hesitate to overturn the traditional categories of election which were the inspiration of Israel (cf. chs. 16; 22; 23). Later, however, when news of the fall of Jerusalem arrived (24.1ff.), restoration began to be preached, followed some years later by the message of Deutero-Isaiah. This preaching also freed Israel from the idea that there is a fate which is sovereign over all and in the face of which not only human beings but even the gods are impotent. YHWH is and remains the sole motive power behind history, and all is subject to him. These categories are evidently mythical, even if now everything takes place on earth, among and by means of human beings.

(c) A particularly disconcerting element reappears in the context of this problem: that of prophecy which the texts call 'false'.

'False' prophecy is opposed to 'true' prophecy; this is a phenomenon to which I have already referred (above, § 2d). The phenomenon may be disconcerting for us, but it must have been even more so for the audience of that time, who were often compelled to choose between two substantially different messages, both of which laid claim to being divine revelation.

The search for an objective criterion of evaluation therefore began quite soon, and Deut. 18.21-22 is evidence of this search: prophecy which is fulfilled is true and the rest is not. This was apparently a simple and obvious solution, but in fact it was simplistic, first of all because it transformed the figure of the prophet into one who proclaimed the future, a role which the prophets originally did not have, and then because the choice between the two or more messages had to be made immediately, without the possibility of waiting for verification.

An important difference appears here between two kinds of 'false' prophecy: the first, which we shall consider in the following example, is subjectively in good faith; the second is in bad faith. Jeremiah 23.30 accuses these prophets of 'stealing' the word of God.

The character of the problem appears clearly in two cases. The first is that of Micaiah ben Imlah, towards the middle of the ninth century BCE (I Kings 22.6, 16-23); here the prophet announces that God himself has put a lying spirit in the mouth of the prophets consulted by King Ahab precisely so that they shall not tell the truth. So objectively speaking they are 'false' prophets, though subjectively they are not, in that they limit themselves to proclaiming the message that they have received.

The second case is the more complex one of the confrontation between Jeremiah and Hananiah (Jer.27-28: the chronology of the text is in disorder; in 27.1 'Jehoiakim' should be corrected on the basis of the information given in vv.3, 12, 16 to 'Zedekiah', while in 28.1 we should follow LXX in reading 'In that same year, the fourth of Zedekiah...', i.e. 594 BCE, cf. *BHS*). Hananiah announces the inviolability of Zion and its sanctuary, one of the themes of the preaching attributed to Isaiah, though some scholars think that this is a later addition; another passage, Micah 3.12, which many people also think to be late, casts doubts on this relationship between the holiness of the place and the need for divine protection. In itself the preaching of Hananiah would seem to be the most orthodox possible, so that the message would have all that was necessary for it to be considered 'true'. And indeed that is so much the case that Jeremiah himself (28.11b) initially prefers to withdraw, not knowing whether he should respond, and if so how. But having soon afterwards received a clarificatory message from YHWH, he returns to his task and pronounces a stern indictment against Hananiah, who is guilty of having pronounced a false prophecy, and against the people who have listened to him.

The two cases seem to me to be typical illustrations of the complexity of the phenomenon and the impossibility of putting forward objective solutions: these are cases in which the believer has to make choices, which will be all the more difficult and deeply felt, the more risky and less clear the alternative. So we need to beware of studies which seek to propose simple solutions. Moreover these problems are typical of any proclamation of the word of God, a proclamation which takes place by means of men and women who are also necessarily conditioned by contingent factors and by their environment.

(*d*) However, the prophets were occupied not only with the near future but sometimes also with a more distant future, though much more rarely than used to be believed. That already appears in a second phase of their preaching: after the inevitable judgment, pardon is often announced. For some prophets this is limited to a 'remnant'.

This 'remnant' is imagined as having been converted after escaping the judgment, which is embodied in the historical invaders of the country. As to the antiquity of the concept, there is a degree of unanimity that it is exilic and post-exilic, but a study by O.Carena has made possible a dating as early as the Assyrian period, since the concept appears among the Assyrians, but not among the Babylonians and the Persians. The concept seems to lead to a clear distinction between Israel as an ethnic and political unity and Israel as a community limited to believers. For other prophets, however, the situation has deteriorated to such a degree that only a direct intervention on the part of God can remedy it: thus Jer.31.31, a Deuteronomistic text, speaks of a 'new covenant' which is to replace the early one, made inoperative by the prevarications of the people. This is still the Sinai covenant, but the ways in which it is applied are new; some scholars think that it even refers to the institution of the synagogue. In Ezek.36-37 God himself is to create 'a new heart and a new spirit in the people'. Again, Deutero-Isaiah announces the coming of the 'servant of YHWH', who will bear the weight of the sins of the people in his own sufferings. This is a concept which the primitive church then used for its own earliest christology. Now we are moving in a metahistorical sphere, even if, contrary to the message of the apocalyptists, for the prophets everything is to take place in the sphere of history. Human beings have to be converted, but though the conversion is brought about by God, there will be no transformation of all things ordained from on high and a sudden transformation of humankind.

BIBLIOGRAPHY

Commentaries on all the prophetic books:

J.A.Bewer, *The Prophets*, New York and London 1949-54; G.Fohrer, *Die Propheten des Alten Testaments* (7 vols), Gütersloh 1964-78.
   Bibliographical studies: G.Fohrer, 'Neue Literatur zur alttestamentlichen Prophetie', *TR* 40, 1975, 193-209; 41, 1976, 1-12; 45, 1980, 1-39, 109-32; 47, 1982, 105-35; G.Bernini, 'Rassegna sui Profeti', *RiBib* 23, 1975, 175-215; J.M.Schmidt, 'Probleme der Prophetenforschung', *VuF* 17.1, 1972,

39-81, and 'Ausgangspunkt und Ziel prophetischer Verkündigung im 8.Jahrhundert', *VuF* 22.1, 1977, 65-82, and recently, E.Osswald, 'Aspekte neuerer Prophetenforschung', *TLZ* 109, 1984, 641-50.
Select general bibliography: C.H.Cornill, *Der israelitische Prophetismus*, Berlin [13]1920; E.Sellin, *Der alttestamentliche Prophetismus*, Leipzig 1914; H.Gunkel, *Die Propheten*, Göttingen 1917; B.Duhm, *Israels Propheten*, Tübingen [2]1922; A.Jepsen, *Nabi*, Munich 1934; P.Volz, *Prophetengestalten des Alten Testaments*, Stuttgart [3]1944; M.Buber, *The Prophetic Faith*, ET New York 1949; T.H.Robinson, *Prophecy and the Prophets in Ancient Israel*, London [2]1953; A.Neher, *The Prophetic Existence*, ET Cranbury and London 1969; C.Kuhl, *The Prophets of Israel*, ET Edinburgh 1960; E.Balla, *Die Botschaft der Propheten*, Tübingen 1958; G.von Rad, *Old Testament Theology* II, ET Edinburgh 1966, reissued London 1975; J.Lindblom, *Prophecy in Ancient Israel*, Oxford 1962; A.J.Heschel, *The Prophets*, New York 1962; J.Scharbert, *Die Propheten Israels*, 2 vols., Cologne 1965-7; W.H.Schmidt, 'Die prophetische "Grundgewissheit" ', *EvTh* 31, 1971, 630-50; K.Koch, *The Prophets*, two vols., ET London and Philadelphia I, 1982; II, 1983; E.W.Davies, *Prophecy and Ethics*, Sheffield 1981; D.L.Petersen, *The Role of Israel's Prophets*, Sheffield 1981; A.G.Auld, 'Prophets through the Looking Glass', *JSOT* 27, 1983, 3-23, and 'Prophets and Prophecy in Jeremiah and Kings', *ZAW* 96, 1984, 66-82; cf. also P.D.Miller, *Sin and Judgement in the Prophets*, Chico, Cal. 1982; W.McKane, 'Prophet and Institution', *ZAW* 94, 1982, 251-66; F.Ahuis, *Der klagende Gerichtsprophet*, Stuttgart 1982; G.Wallis (ed.), *Von Bileam bis Jesaja*, Berlin 1985. A.Rofè, *The Prophetical Stories*, Jerusalem 1988, is also important.

2. For the problem of the prophetic visions cf. B.O.Long, 'Reports of Vision among the Prophets', *JBL* 95, 1975, 353-65; for the literary genres represented among the prophets cf. R.Rendtorff, 'Botenformel und Botenspruch', *ZAW* 74, 1962, 165-77; Rendtorff shows that one of the most widespread literary genres is that of the 'messenger speech'; cf. A.Rofè, 'Classes in the Prophetical Stories: Didactic Legenda and Parable', *SVT* 26, 1974, 141-64; N.H.Ridderbos, 'Einige Bemerkungen über den Propheten als Boten von Jahwe', in *Travels in the World of the Old Testament. Studies presented to M.A.Beek*, Assen 1974, 211-16; S.Amsler, 'Le thème du procès chez les prophètes d'Israël', *RTP* 111, 1974, 116-31; A van den Toorn, 'From Patriarchs to Prophets. A Reappraisal of Charismatic Leadership in Ancient Israel', *JNWSL* 13, 1987, 191-218; for the problem of ecstasy see B.Uffenheimer, 'Prophecy, Ecstasy and Sympathy', *SVT* 40, 1988, 257-69.

2a. W.F.Albright, *From the Stone Age to Christianity*, Baltimore [2]1957, 303ff., esp. n.37; H.M.Orlinsky, 'The Seer in Ancient Israel', *OrAnt* 4, 1965, 153-74; A.Jepsen, 'Gottesmann und Prophet', in H.-W.Wolff (ed.), *Probleme biblischer Theologie. G. von Rad zum 70.Geburtstag*, Munich 1971, 171-83; W.W.Müller, 'Sudsemitische Marginalien zur Etymologie von *nābī*', *BN* 32, 1986, 31-7. K.Koch, 'Die Briefe "prophetischen" Inhalts aus Mari', *UF* 4, 1972, 53-77. For Zakir, see J.F.Ross, 'Prophecy in Hamath, Israel and

Mari', *HTR* 63, 1970, 1-28. The basic study on the literary genres used by the prophets is C.Westermann, *Basic Forms of Prophetic Speech*, ET Nashville and London 1967; id., *Prophetische Heilsworte im Alten Testament*, Göttingen 1987; cf. also S.Herrmann, *Ursprung und Funktion der Prophetie im alten Israel*, Opladen 1976.

3. F.Ellermeier, *Prophetie in Mari und Israel*, Hertzberg am Harz 1968, is a basic work which presents the material available up to the date of publication (some unpublished or only partially so) and discusses this bibliography. However, cf. the review by J.G.Heintz, *RHPR* 51, 1971, 165-8. See also H.B.Huffmon, 'Prophecy in the Mari Letters', *BA* 31, 1968, 101-24; W.L.Moran, 'New Evidence from Mari on the History of Prophecy', *Bibl* 50, 1969, 15-56; J.F.Ross, art.cit. For the origins of the prophets and parallels with other neighbouring peoples cf. V.W.Rabe, 'The Origin of Prophecy', *BASOR* 221, 1967, 126-8; M.Weinfeld, 'Ancient Near Eastern Patterns in Prophetic Literature', *VT* 27, 1977, 178-95; A.R.Millard, 'La prophétie et l'écriture, Israël, Aram, Assyrie', *RHR* 202, 1985, 25-145 (advances the theory that the prophecies in these countries will have been written down immediately to make them capable of verification, so that from then on they were not changed; clearly this theory cannot apply to the Bible).

On Assyria see M.Dietrich, 'Prophetie in den Keilschrifttexten', *Jahrbuch für Anthropologie und Religionsgeschichte* 1, 1973, 15-44; M.Weippert, 'Assyrische Prophetien der Zeit Asarhaddons und Asssurbanipals', in F.M.Fales (ed.), *Assyrian Royal Inscriptions: New Horizons in Literary, Historical and Ideological Analysis*, Rome 1981, 71-115; id., 'Die Bildsprache der Neuassyrischen Prophetie', in *Beiträge zur prophetischen Bildsprache in Israel und Assyrien*, Freiburg CH 1985, 55-93.

3b. For the general problems relating to Mari cf. *inter alios* H.Cazelles, 'Mari et l'ancien Testament', *XVᵉ Rencontre assyriologique internationale Liège 1966*, Paris 1967, 73-90 and bibliography; A.Petitjean and J.Coppens, 'Mari et l'Ancien Testament', in *De Mari à Qumrân: Hommage à Mgr Coppens* I, Gembloux 1969, 3-13; A.Malamat, 'Mari', *BA* 34, 1971, 2-22, and 'A Mari Prophecy and Nathan's Dynastic Oracle', in *Prophecy. FS G.Fohrer*, Berlin 1980, 68-82; J.G.Heintz, 'Oracles prophétiques et guerre sainte selon les archives royales de Mari et l'ancien Testament', *SVT* 17, 1969, 112-38; E.Noort, *Untersuchungen zum Gottesbescheid im Mari*, Kevelaer-Neukirchen/ Vluyn 1977. He proves sceptical about the existence of such relationships. T.W.Overholt, 'Prophecy; The Problem of Cultural Comparison', *Semeia* 21, 1981, 55-78, also warns of the dangers of these comparisons.

3c. T.Andrae, *Mohammad, the Man and his Faith*, ET London ³1960 (a classic biography); B.Spuler, 'Muhammed', *RGG* IV ³1960, 1187-9; G.Widengren, *Religionsphänomenologie*, Berlin 1969, analytical index s.v. See also T.Kronholm, 'Dependence and Prophetic Originality in the Koran', *Orientalia Suecana* 31/32, 1982/83, 47-70; T.Polk, *The Prophetic Persona*, Sheffield 1984 (who considers the prophets to be literary figures created by the redactors rather than historical persons); H.Ringgren, 'Israelite Prophecy: Fact or Fiction?', *SVT* 40, 1988, 204-10.

4a. C.Begg, 'The Non-Mention of Amos, Hosea and Micah in the Deuteronomistic Historian', *BN* 32, 1986, 41-53.

4b. For the prophetic traditions recorded in the books of Chronicles cf. R.Michel, *Die Seher- und Prophetenüberlieferungen in der Chronik*, Frankfurt 1983; C.T.Begg, 'The Classical Prophets in the Chronistic History', *BZ* 32, 1988, 100-7.

4d. P.R.Ackroyd, 'A Judgement Narrative between Kings and Chronicles. An Approach to Amos 7, 9-17' (1977), in his *Studies in the Religious Tradition of the Old Testament*, London 1987, 196-208; H.Schult, 'Amos 7.15 und die Legitimation des Aussenseiters', in *Probleme biblischer Theologie. FS G.von Rad zum 70.Geburtstag*, Munich 1971, 462-78.

4e. For the problems of these texts see the commentaries by R.E.Clements, 1980, and O.Kaiser, OTL (2 vols.), ²1983, 1974, and the monographs by W.Dietrich, *Jesaia und die Politik*, Munich 1976, 62ff.; R.P.Carroll, *When Prophecy Failed*, London 1979, 40-5.

4f. For Jeremiah cf. J.Skinner, *Prophecy and Religion*, Cambridge 1922 and reprints; R.P.Carroll, *From Chaos to Covenant*, London 1981. For the Deuteronomistic redaction of the book see W.Thiel, *Die deuteronomische Redaktion von Jeremia 1-25*, Neukirchen 1973, and *Die deuteronomistische Redaktion von Jeremia 26-45*, Neukirchen 1981; against this, however, cf. H.Weippert, *Die Prosareden des Jeremiasbuches*, Berlin 1973. For the model biographies of the prophets cf. K.Baltzer, *Die Biographie der Propheten*, Neukirchen 1975.

5. H.-C.Schmitt, 'Prophetie und Tradition', *ZTK* 74, 1977, 255-72, and M.Haran, 'From Early to Classical Prophecy', *VT* 27, 1977, 385-97. For apocalyptic, see D.S.Russell, *The Method and Message of Jewish Apocalyptic*, OTL, London and Philadelphia 1964; K.Koch, *The Rediscovery of Apocalyptic*, SBT II 22, 1972. For the relationship between prophecy and apocalyptic cf. the studies by C.R.North, 'Prophecy to Apocalyptic via Zechariah', *SVT* 22, 1972, 47-71; B.Corsani, 'L'apocalittica fra Antico e Nuovo Testamento', *Prot* 27, 1972, 15-22; J.A.Soggin, 'Profezia ed apocalittica nel Giudaesimo postesilico', *RiBib* 30, 1982, 161-73; R.R.Wilson, 'From Prophecy to Apocalyptic', *Semeia* 21, 1981, 79-95.

6a. For the character of the prophetic ministry cf. G.Wallis, 'Prophet und Ämter', in *Weg und Gemeinschaft. FS H.Urner*, Berlin 1976, 271-82. For the prophets as announcers of disaster cf. E.Cortese, 'Le sventure annunciate dai profeti preesilici e l'escatologia dell'Antico Testamento', *Teologia* 2, 1977, 91-108; O.Keel, 'Rechttun oder Annahme des drohenden Gerichts?', *BZ* NF 21, 1977, 200-18; G.von Rad, *Old Testament Theology* II, 299; J.Muilenburg, 'The "Office" of the Prophet in Ancient Israel', in *The Bible in Modern Scholarship*, ed. J.P.Hyatt, New York and Nashville 1965, 74-97; M.L.Henry, *Prophet und Tradition*, BZAW 116, 1969. There is a complete collection of the material traditionally considered messianic in E.König, *Die messianischen Weissagungen des Alten Testaments*, Stuttgart ², ³1925; for the current position see my article *mlk* in *THAT* I, Munich 1971, 913f. with bibliography. Cf. also C.H.J.De Geus,'Wie waren de profeten?', in *Profeten en profetische geschriften, FS A.S.van der Woude*, Nijkerk and Kampen no date [1986], 20-7; beginning with the affirmation that the prophets seemed like experienced poets, he concludes that they must have belonged to the educated classes.

6b-h. For the individuals mentioned see H.-J.Kraus, *Geschichte der historisch-kritischen Erforschung des Alten Testaments*, Neukirchen ³1982, 65 and 75. See also J.Muilenburg, 'The "Office" of the Prophet in Ancient Israel', in *The Bible and Modern Scholarship*, ed.J.P.Hyatt, Nashville 1965, 74-97; H.B.Huffmon, 'The Origins of Prophecy', in *Magnalia Dei... In Memoriam G.E.Wright*, Garden City, New York 1976, 171-86; G.Wallis, 'Prophet und Ämter', in *Weg und Gemeinschaft. FS Hans Urner*, Berlin 1976, 271-82; R.P.Carroll, *When Prophecy Failed*, London 1979, 21ff.; W.Wifall, *Israel's Prophets. Viziers of the King*, BTB 10, 1980, 169-75. For the problem of the relationships between prophecy and apocalyptic and the transition from the former to the latter cf. R.R.Wilson, 'From Prophecy to Apocalyptic', *Semeia* 21, 1981, 79-95; M.A.Knibb, 'Prophecy and the Emergence of the Jewish Apocalypses', in *Israel's Prophetic Tradition. Essays... P.R.Ackroyd*, Cambridge 1982, 155-80; J.A.Soggin, 'Profezia ed apocalittica nel Giudaesimo postesilico', *RiBib* 30, 1982, 161-73; P.Sacchi, 'Riflessioni sull'essenza dell'apocalittica: peccato di origine e liberta dell'uomo', *Hen* 5, 1983, 31-61; J.M.Schmidt, *Die jüdische Apokalyptik*, Tübingen 1969; W.Schmithals, *The Apocalyptic Movement*, ET Nashville 1975, and the contributions in *Apocalypse et Théologie de l'Espérance. Congrès de Toulouse*, Paris 1977. The nature of apocalyptic is a problem which cannot be explored here.

7. Select bibliography: R.Hentschke, *Die Stellung der vorexilischen Propheten zum Kultus*, BZAW 75, 1957; E.Würthwein, 'Kultpolemik oder Kultbescheid?', in Würthwein and O.Kaiser (eds.), *Tradition und Situation. FS A.Weiser*, Göttingen 1963, 115-31 (= Würthwein, *Wort und Existenz*, Göttingen 1970, 140-60). For cultic prophecy: G.Quell, 'Der Kultprophet', *TLZ* 81, 1956, 401-4; J.Jeremias, *Kultprophetie und Gerichtsverkündigung in der späten Königszeit*, WMANT 35, 1969; G.Fohrer, 'Priester und Prophet – Amt und Charisma?', *KuD* 17, 1971, 15-27; H.Schüngel-Straumann, *Gottesbild und Kultkritik vorexilischer Propheten*, Stuttgart 1972. Cf. also R.P.Carroll, *When Prophecy Failed*, London 1979, 61-5; H.-J.Boecker, 'Überlegungen zur Kultpolemik der vorexilischen Propheten', in *Die Botschaft und die Boten. FS H.-W.Wolff*, Neukirchen 1981, 169-80; R.Murray, 'Prophecy and the Cult', in *Israel's Prophetic Tradition. Essays... P.R.Ackroyd*, Cambridge 1982, 200-16.

7c. For the problem of the religion of Canaan and its relations with that of Israel cf. E.Jacob, 'L'héritage cananéen dans le prophète Osée', *RHPR* 43, 1963, 250-9; O.Eissfeldt, 'Israels Religion und die Religionen der Umwelt', *Neue Zeitschrift für die systematische Theologie* 9, 1967, 8-27 (= his *Kleine Schriften* V, Tübingen 1973, 1-20). Cf. also the analytical index in my *History*.

7d. That almost all Israel's prophets were cultic figures is argued by S.Mowinckel, *Psalmenstudien* III, Oslo 1923 (reprinted Amsterdam 1961); A.Haldar, *Associations of Cult Prophets among the Ancient Semites*, Uppsala 1945; A.R.Johnson, *The Cultic Prophet in Ancient Israel*, Cardiff [2]1962; B.O.Long, 'The Social Setting of Prophetic Miracle Stories', *Semeia* 3, 1975, 46-63.

8. Select bibliography: K.Elliger, 'Prophet und Politik', *ZAW* 53, 1935, 3-22 (= his *Kleine Schriften*, Munich 1966, 118-40); H.-J.Kraus, *Prophetie und Politik*, Munich 1952 (with an important bibliography); E.Würthwein, 'Jesaja 7, 1-9, Ein Beitrag zu dem Thema: Prophetie und Politik', in *Theologie als Glaubenswagnis. FS Karl Heim*, Hamburg 1954, 47-63 (= Würthwein, *Wort und Existenz*, Göttingen 1970, 127-43); E.Jenni, *Die politischen Voraussagen der Propheten*, Zurich 1956; H.Donner, *Israel unter den Völkern*, Leiden 1964; L.Rost, 'Das Problem der Weltmacht in der Prophetie', *TLZ* 90, 1965, 241-50; R.Martin-Achard, 'Esaïe et Jérémie aux prises avec les problèmes politiques', *RHPR* 47, 1967, 208-24; J.A.Soggin, 'Profezia e rivoluzione nell'Antico Testamento', *Protestantesimo* 25, Rome 1970, 1-14; E.Jacob, 'Prophètes et politique', *Parole et Société* 80, 1972, 3-19; B.Albrektson, 'Prophecy and Politics in the Old Testament', in H.Biezais (ed.), *The Myth of the State*, Stockholm 1972, 45-56. For the attitude of the prophets towards the monarchy in Judah cf. K.Seybold, *Das davidische Königtum im Zeugnis der Propheten*, FRLANT 1972; W.Dietrich, *Jesaia und die Politik*, Munich 1976 (a basic study). Cf. also B.Janecko, 'Israel, Prophecy, Politics', *BTB* 8, 1978, 177-83; C.H.J.de Geus, 'Die Gesellschaftskritik der Propheten und die Archäologie', *ZDPV* 98, 1982, 50-7; B.Uffenheimer, 'Ancient Hebrew Prophecy. Political Teaching and Practice', *Immanuel* 18, 1984, 7-21; W.Dietrich, *David, Saul und die Propheten*, Stuttgart 1987.

9. Select bibliography: H.-J.Kraus, 'Die prophetische Botschaft gegen das soziale Unrecht Israels', *EvTh* 15, 1955, 295-307 (= his *Biblisch-theologische Aufsätze*, Neukirchen 1972, 120-33); H.Donner, 'Die soziale Botschaft der Propheten im Lichte der Gesellschaftsordnung in Israel', *OrAnt* 2, 1963, 229-45; K.Koch, 'Die Entstehung der sozialen Kritik bei den Propheten', in H.-W.Wolff, (ed.), *Probleme biblischer Theologie. G.von Rad zum 70.Geburtstag*, Munich 1971, 236-57; O.H.Steck, 'Die Gesellschaftskritik der Propheten', in *Christentum und Gesellschaft*, ed. W.Lohff and B.Lohse, Göttingen 1969, 46-62; for the economic sitation cf.G.Pettinato, 'Is.2,7 e il culto del sole in Giuda nel sec.VIII a.Cr', *OrAnt* 4, 1965, 1-30; H.Bardtke, 'Die Latifundien in Juda während der zweiten Hälfte des achten Jahrhunderts v.Chr. (zum Verständnis von Jes.5.8-10)', in *Hommages à A.Dupont-Sommer*, Paris 1971, 235-54; O.Loretz, 'Die prophetische Kritik des Rentenkapitalismus. Grundlagen. Probleme der Prophetenforschung', *UF* 7, 1975, 271-8 (this is an important study which takes account of the resistance movements against the ruling powers and the social problem in the ancient Near East); cf. also M.Schwantes, *Das Recht der Armen*, Frankfurt 1978; J.Pons, *L'oppression dans l'Ancien Testament*, Paris 1981; B.O.Long, 'Social Dimensions of Prophetic Conflict', *Semeia* 21, 1981, 31-53; J.L.Sicre, *Con los*

pobres de la tierra, Madrid 1985; J.S.Kselman, 'The Social World of the Israelite Prophets', *RSR* 11, 1985, 120-9 (examines the most recent bibliography); for archaeological features and discoveries see C.H.J.de Geus, 'Die Gesellschaftskritik der Propheten und die Archäologie', *ZDPV* 1982, 50-7. For the whole problem see finally: G.Wanke, 'Zur Grundlagen und Absicht prophetischer Sozialkritik', *KuD* 18, 1972, 2-17; S.Holm-Nielsen, 'Die Sozialkritik der Propheten', in *Denkender Glaube. FS K.H.Ratschow*, Berlin 1976, 7-23. For an analysis of the social problem in ancient Israel and the sparseness of the evidence cf. I. Schiffmann, 'Die Grundeigentumsverhältnisse in Palästina in der ersten Hälfte des 1.Jahrtausends v.u.Z', *Acta antiqua Academiae scientiarum Hungaricae* 22, 1973, 457-71. I have attempted my own examination of the relevant economic texts in 'Ancient Israel: An Attempt at a Social and Economic Analysis of the Available Data', in *Text and Context... Studies for F.C.Fensham*, Birmingham 1988, 201-8.

9b. For the Ugaritic texts mentioned cf. the translation in C.H.Gordon, *Ugaritic Literature*, Rome 1949, 82 (translation corrected according to E.Hammershaimb, *SVT* 7, 1960, 89) and 88; for the first text see also J.Gray, *The Krt Text in the Literature of Ras Shamra*, Leiden ²1962, 28 and 77; for the second P.Fronzaroli, *Leggenda di Aqhat*, Florence 1955, 36. These texts are Gordon no.127, 45 and 2 Aqht Vff. Cf. also G.Fohrer, *Theologische Grundstrukturen des Alten Testaments*, Berlin 1972, 235ff. (an important discussion of the problem).

10. Select bibliography: G.von Rad, 'Les idées sur le temps et l'histoire en Israel et l'eschatologie des prophètes', *Hommage à W.Vischer*, Montpellier 1960, 198-209; S.Herrmann, *Die prophetischen Heilserwartungen im Alten Testament*, Stuttgart 1965; P.R.Ackroyd, 'Historians and Prophets', *SEÅ* 33, 1968, 37-54; P.Grech, 'Interprophetic Re-Interpretation and Old Testament Eschatology', *Aug* 9, 1969, 235-65; J.Vollmer, *Geschichtliche Rückblicke und Motive in der Prophetie des Amos, Hosea und Jesaja*, BZAW 119, 1971; K.-H.Bernhardt, 'Prophetie und Geschichte', *SVT* 22, 1972, 20-46. For an examination of unfulfilled prophecies cf. R.P.Carroll, 'Ancient Israelite Prophecy and Dissonance Theory', *Numen* 24, 1977, 135-51.

10c. Select bibliography: J.Hempel, 'Vom irrenden Glauben', *Zeitschrift für systematische Theologie* 7, Berlin 1930 (= *Apoxysmata*, Berlin 1961, 174-97); G.Quell, *Wahre und falsche Propheten*, Gütersloh 1952 (a basic work); E.Jacob, 'Quelques remarques sur les faux prophetes', *TZ* 13, 1957, 479-81; H.-J.Kraus, *Prophetie in der Krisis*, Neukirchen 1964 (on Jeremiah); T.W.Overholt, 'Jeremiah 27-29: The Question of False Prophecy', *JAAR* 35, 1967, 241-9; C.R.North, 'Angel-Prophet or Satan-Prophet', *ZAW* 82, 1970, 31-67; J.L.Crenshaw, *Prophetic Conflict*, BZAW 124, 1971; F.L.Hossfeldt and I.Meyer, *Prophet gegen Prophet*, Fribourg CH 1973; I.Meyer, *Jeremia und die falschen Propheten*, Fribourg 1977; R.P.Carroll, 'A Non-Cogent Argument in Jeremiah's Oracle against the Prophets', *StTheol* 30, 1976, 43-51; W.Vogels, 'Comment discerner le prophète autentique', *NRT* 99, 1977, 681-701; S.J. De Vries, *Prophet against Prophet*, Grand Rapids 1978; R.P.Carroll, *When*

Prophecy Failed, London 1979, 184ff. For the criteria of distinction between true and false prophecy see now G.Münderlein, *Kriterien wahrer und falscher Prophetie*, Berne ²1979; the work concludes that there are no objective criteria of distinction; see further A.Schenker, 'Gerichtsverkündigung und Verblendung bei den vorexilischen Propheten', *RB* 93, 1986, 563-80.

10d. Select bibliography: W.E.Müller, *Die Vorstellung vom Rest im Alten Testament*, Leipzig dissertation 1938, republished Neukirchen 1973 (ed. H.D.Preuss); P.Zerafa, 'Il resto di Israele nei profeti preesilici', *Ang* 49, 1972, 3-29, with bibliography; G.F.Hasel, *The Remnant*, Berrien Springs 1972; G.Gerleman, 'Rest und Überschuss eine terminologische Studie', in *Travels in the World of the Old Testament. Studies presented to M.A.Beek*, Assen 1972, 71-4, which examines the terminology and the concepts used. Cf. finally O.Carena, *Il resto di Israele*, Bologna 1985 (with extensive bibliography); J.Hausmann, *Israels Rest*, Stuttgart 1987. Cf. also below, 20.4.

18

AMOS

1. Person and origins

(*a*) We find some important biographical information in the passage Amos 7.10-17; however, since it is in the third person it is to be attributed to the redactors. Here the prophet appears as someone who did not originally exercise the prophetic ministry and did not belong to an association of prophets; he devoted his life, rather, to rearing cattle and sheep and goats, and was involved in agricultural activity which consisted in the preparation of sycamore fruit as fodder (v.14). For the problems connected with an evaluation of this biography at the historical level cf. above, 17.4d. The reply given by Amos to the priest in charge of the temple of Bethel, who had told him to go and earn his living in his homeland, in Judah, stresses the prophet's original economic independence; therefore he did not belong to a deprived social class. The story also says that one day YHWH took (root *lqḥ*) him from his everyday activities and sent him to preach to the people of the north, Israel.

However, the phrase which Amos uses is not completely clear: the Hebrew is *lōʾ nābī ʾanōkī weʾlōʾ ben-nābīʾ ʾanōkī*, a noun sentence which, detached from its particular context, can be interpreted either in the present or in the past (in Hebrew, as in the other semitic languages, the copula was unknown and the tense of a noun sentence without a verb was determined by its context). Thus we can render it either 'I am not a prophet nor do I belong to an association of prophets', or 'I was not a prophet nor did I belong...' Those who accept the first possibility sometimes do so to demonstrate a polemical attitude on the part of Amos to the title *nābīʾ* which he is said to have rejected for himself, thus producing on the conceptual plane that distinction which we have seen to have been absent on the lexicographical plane. But the context only has verbs in the past, so that it seems necessary to translate this phrase also in the past, despite authoritative opinions to the contrary. In that case Amos is not contrasting himself with other similar phenomena of his time, and is saying simply that he was originally a 'layman' who lived, not at all badly, by his own labours, and that he was then called to exercise the function of a prophet.

(*b*) According to 1.1 his homeland was the district of Tekoa (coord.170-115); from the Talmud we hear of a place with the same name in Galilee (coord.265-191), but we know virtually nothing about it. Therefore the traditional identification with the place southeast of Bethlehem, facing the desert, is preferable. According to the superscription, his ministry took place under Uzziah, king of Judah, and Jeroboam II, king of Israel; the latter is mentioned in the biographical passage 7.10ff. to which I have already referred. In 1.1 an earthquake is said to have taken place two years before the year in which Amos began his ministry, and there are allusions to it in various other passages of the book. This must have been a very serious earthquake, since it is taken some centuries later, in Zech.14.4ff., as a model for eschatological catastrophes. Now obvious traces of an earthquake which scholars tend to identify with this one have been found during the excavations at Hazor, in upper Galilee, a little south of Lake Huleh (coord.203-269), and these traces are dated towards the end of the first half of the eighth century BCE. So we can affirm that the redaction puts the ministry of Amos around 760 BCE. Nothing is said about the duration of his ministry; if we go by what the texts say, it seems to have been of short duration. But the mention of exile for the northern kingdom could also suggest that Amos preached up to this event.

When Amos began to preach, the economic situation seems to have been relatively favourable: the Aramaean wars which had devastated the border regions for some years had finished because of the pressure exercised on the Aramaeans by the Assyrians, but the latter had not yet appeared on the Palestinian scene. The high military expenditure had therefore ceased, and so had the destructive invasions. On the other hand, as tends to happen in cases of this kind (and I discussed this in the previous chapter, § 8), economic prosperity seems to have been limited to particular groups, without raising the standard of living of the population generally: they continued to live in conditions of abject poverty and oppression.

Some scholars would like to connect the calling of Amos with the visions listed in 7.1-9; 8.1-3; 9.1-4. That is a possible conjecture, but we have no proof. In any case, here the figure of the prophet appears as a 'mediator' between YHWH and his own people, as an intercessor.

Because we no longer have the visions together, but they have been split up, it is impossible to determine their original association.

Many scholars accept that the ministry of Amos ended with his expulsion from the sanctuary of Bethel, but that cannot be demonstrated, since it is impossible to date any of the passages apart from 1.1.

2. Divisions and principal problems of the book

As we saw in the previous chapter, the criteria which governed the redaction of the prophetic books are not always clear. For our modern mentality, two criteria would be the most obvious: a chronological and biographical classification, or a systematic classification; however, these are the ones which are manifestly absent from the books. To complicate an already difficult situation, there has been a series of Deuteronomistic insertions (below, § 3). At all events, all the books give the modern reader of the prophets an impression of disorder.

Amos is no exception: 7.10-17 interrupt the context of the visions, a theme which we would expect at the beginning of the book if it is true that these visions were connected with his calling. Chapters 5 and 6 are also in disorder. Moreover, the first, second and third person alternate in the texts. The texts which speak of the visions and which therefore present themselves as autobiographical have been edited in the first person; they are followed by an explanation of what each vision signifies. We have in succession locusts, fire, a plumb-line (not that of the builder but that of the demolisher, if we can understand in this way a passage in which the technical terms are not always clear), a basket of ripe fruit (because the people is ripe for their end), and then YHWH himself appears, standing upright in his sanctuary, in order to judge. It is possible to note a degree of rhetorical progression in the visions, and from a literary and logical point of view they form a closed unity, artificially interrupted by the biographical narrative. It is probable that their roots are to be found in the prophet's own vocation; he uses them to legitimise his own authority and the negative content of his preaching in the hearing of the community to whom he speaks.

In 1.3-2.16 we have a collection of oracles against the nations, culminating in 2.6-16 in an oracle against Israel, which has in part been revised by Dtr. As the Danish scholar A.Bentzen pointed out at the beginning of the 1930s, the literary genre of the 'oracle against a nation' could have its roots in the Egyptian practice attested in the so-called execration texts; in them the name of an enemy prince or people was written on a vessel or a potsherd which was then broken, a symbolic action which indicated the destruction of the adversary. In the biblical prophets these actions would then have been replaced by preaching: given the efficacy which was attributed to the word in both the Hebrew Bible and in the Near East, the effect would not have been dissimilar. This explanation is interesting and could allow us to get back to the origin of a genre which is well attested among the prophets, an origin which would then need to be placed around the nineteenth century BCE. However, the connection has rightly been challenged independently by H.-W.Wolff and M.Weiss, who do not want to go beyond the formal similarity: there is not only a significant gap of more than a millennium on the chronological level, but we also find marked differences both on the religious level and on that of topographical criteria.

It is possible that before reaching their present form the prophecies of Amos circulated orally, certainly in fragments. In many passages we find characteristics which indicate a Deuteronomistic revision, as we shall see in the next section; in 9.11-13 we find the oracle on the 'booth of David which has fallen', an expression unparalleled in the Hebrew Bible. Now while it is possible that the text refers to the break of the personal union at the end of the tenth century BCE which put an end to the empire of David and Solomon, it is more plausible that this is an announcement of the restoration of the house of David as a ruling house, in which case we find ourselves in the post-exilic period. For details I would refer to my commentary cited in the bibliography, where I discuss the various aspects of the problem.

3. Deuteronomistic redaction

One of the most interesting discoveries about the book is the existence of some passages of Deuteronomistic redaction: 1.9-10; 2.4-5, 10; 3.1, 7; 5.25-26. 1.1-2; 2.11-12; 9.7-8a are doubtful. It seems that in many cases these are insertions made, as in the first four books of the Pentateuch, at key points in the context, in order to show how they should be interpreted.

4. Thought

In its present form the book of Amos presents us with a clear and simple thinker; the thought is not speculative, and perhaps its content is not particularly original. The life of the prophet, divided by his calling into two clearly separate periods, bears the mark of a direct and probably violent divine intervention; as we have seen, we know nothing of any third period, after Amos is driven out of the north. We should not exclude *a priori* the possibility that he witnessed the fall of the north, even if that was after his return to his homeland.

His encounter with his God appears in his book as the measure of all things: people and events, and therefore also ethics, the cult, respect for the authorities. These are elements which are all judged by the standard of the sovereign divine will and found wanting. In the visions this judgment is expressed in a vivid form, taking its cue from objects in everyday life; and in them every element moves inexorably towards judgment. It is said that twice the intercession of the prophet succeeds in making YHWH desist from carrying out the sentence, but the other times the announcement remains in all its force. In 5.1ff. the prophet intones a funeral lament: the dead person is 'the virgin Israel', fallen not to rise again; so the north is already condemned and will not be able to survive for many more years. Without repentance there is no hope for it. In 5.18ff. the prophet announces the coming of the 'day of YHWH': the people apparently expected it as a day of joy, of national triumph over their enemies, but the prophet declares that instead it will be a day of darkness and not light, a day on which the people will not only be unable to realize their aspirations but will experience harsh judgment.

For Amos, God makes himself felt in every area of the society of his people: law, ethics, everyday life all become subject to the divine sovereignty and thus rule out any other field of lordship. The God of Israel is not like the Ba'al of Canaan; he cannot be placated by the offering of sacrifices; he cannot be propitiated by the practice of particular rites, like those of fertility. And it is precisely at this point that the criticism of the cult begins; since things were as they were, the cult practised by Israel was not a support to the community; rather, it contributed towards destroying it, in that it left unchanged the negative social conditions which had come to be established. In 2.10ff.; 3.2; 9.7 we have a markedly polemical attitude to the doctrine of the election of the people of God that had been developed in Israel; this is not a privilege received once for all, but a heavy responsiblity. It is true that most of these texts are Deuteronomistic, but that is not to say that they do not reflect the original thought of the prophet. So election is seen as a mission the scope of which seems to have been formulated in the Hebrew Bible once for all by J in Gen. 12.3b: to be a blessing for all the peoples of the earth.

BIBLIOGRAPHY

Commentaries

On the twelve minor prophets: E.Sellin, KAT, 2,3 1929-30; G.Rinaldi, SacBib, I-III, 1953-69; T.H.Robinson and F.Horst, HAT ²1954; A.Weiser and K.Elliger, ATD I, ³1956; II, ⁴1959; E.Jacob, C.A.Keller, S.Amsler, R.Vuilleumier, CAT, 3 vols, 1965ff.; W.Rudolph, KAT (NS) (4 vols), 1966-76.

On Amos: E.Osty, JB ²1958; K.Koch et al. (3 vols), 1976; H.-W.Wolff, Hermeneia, ET 1977; J.A.Soggin, *The Prophet Amos*, ET London 1987.

Bibliographical studies: J.F.Craghan, 'Amos dans la nouvelle recherche', *BTB* 2, 1972, 243-62; A. van der Wal and E.Talstra, *Amos. Concordance and Lexical Surveys*, Amsterdam 1984 (enlarged edition); G.Pfeifer, ' "Ich bin in tiefe Wasser geraten, und die Flut will mich ersäufen" (Psalm LXIX 3) – Anregungen und Vorschläge zur Aufarbeitung wissenschaftliche Sekundärliteratur', *VT* 37, 1987, 327-39. For the whole book cf. further H.Weippert et al., *Beiträge zur prophetischen Bildsprache in Israel und Assyrien*, Fribourg CH 1985, 1-29; R.Martin-Achard, *Amos*, Geneva 1984; A.G.Auld, *Amos*, Sheffield 1986. On the composition of the book see now J.Limburg, 'Sevenfold Structures in the Book of Amos', *JBL* 106, 1987, 217-22.

1. On the problem of Amos 7.14: for the rendering in the present tense cf. H.H.Rowley, 'Was Amos a Nabi?', in *FS O.Eissfeldt*, Halle 1947, 11-18; H.Reventlow, *Das Amt des Propheten bei Amos*, FRLANT 80, 1962, 7ff. According to N.H.Richardson, 'A Critical Note on Amos 7.14', *JBL* 85, 1966, 89, the *lō'* would in fact be an emphatic *lamed*, a form attested in Ugaritic. This seems improbable, first because there is argument even as to whether such a form appears in Hebrew at all, let alone over its meaning; secondly, 'Certainly I am a prophet, certainly I belong to a prophetic association' is nonsense, at least for the second part of the parallelism: Amos was never a member of a such a school. The commentaries by S.Amsler and J.L.Mays also support the rendering 'I was not'. In favour of 'I am not' cf. O.Eissfeldt*, § 51.1; G.Fohrer*, 432f.; the latest supporters of what is the majority rendering are R.R.Wilson, *Prophecy and Society in Ancient Israel*, Philadelphia 1980; B.J.Diebner, 'Berufe und Berufung des Amos (Am 1,1 und 7.14f.)', *DBAT* 23, 1986, 97-120; cf. further H.Utzschneider, 'Die Amazjaererzählung (Am 7.10-17) zwischen Literatur und Historie', *BN* 41, 1988, 76-8. For the earthquake cf. Y.Yadin et al., *Hazor I. An Account of the*

First Season of Excavations 1955, Jerusalem 1958, 22ff.; for the date see my 'Das Erdbeben von Amos 1,1 und die Chronologie der Könige Ussia und Jotham von Juda', *ZAW* 82, 1970, 117-21; for the historical events at the time of Amos and Jeroboam II cf. J.García Trapiello, 'Situación histórica del profeta Amos', *EstBibl* 26, 1967, 249-74; C.Sansoni, 'Amos, uomo del suo tempo', *BeO* 10, 1968, 253-65, and my 'Amos VI, 13-14 und I, 3 auf dem Hintergrund der Beziehungen zwischen Israel und Damaskus im 9. und 8. Jahrhundert', in H.Goedicke (ed.), *Near Eastern Related Issues. Studies in Honor of W.F.Albright*, Baltimore 1971, 433-41; H.F.Fuchs, 'Amos 1,1', in *Bausteine biblischer Theologie. FS G.Botterweck*, Cologne 1977, 271-89. For the social problem, the economic situation and related issues cf. L.Randellini, 'Ricchi e poveri nel libro del profeta Amos', *SBFLA* 2, 1951-2, 5-86, and H.Donner, 'Die soziale Botschaft der Propheten im Lichte der Gesellschaftsordnung in Israel', *OA* 2, 1963, 229-45; these put forward the theory of a particularly favourable economic situation, but one from which only a few privileged people will have benefited. However, G.Pettinato, 'Is.2,7 e il culto del sole in Giuda nel sec.VIII av.Cr', *OA* 5, 1965, 1-30, is critical of this; he comes to the conclusion, which he supports both by texts and by archaeological discoveries, that the Israelite society of the time was in fact poor and that only a few people succeeded in achieving a degree of prosperity. For the profession exercised by Amos before his vocation cf. H.-J.Stoebe, 'Der Prophet Amos und sein bürgerlicher Beruf', *WuD* 5, 1957, 160-81; H.Schult, 'Amos 7, 15a und die Legitimation des Aussenseiters', in *FS G.von Rad*, Munich 1971, 462-78, and T.J.Wright, 'Amos and the "Sycomore (sic) Fig" ', *VT* 26, 1976, 362-86. For the origins of Amos cf. S.Wagner, 'Überlegungen zur Frage nach den Beziehungen des Propheten Amos zum Südreich', *TLZ* 96, 1971, 653-70. For the vocabulary, typical concepts and so on cf. V.Maag, *Text, Wortschatz und Begriffswelt des Buches Amos*, Leiden 1951; cf. also A.Szabo, 'Textual Problems in Amos and Hosea', *VT* 25, 1975, 500-24; I.Willi-Plein, *Vorformen der Schriftexegese innerhalb des Alten Testaments*, Berlin 1971 (for Amos, Hosea and Micah); W.Berg, *Die sogenannten Hymnenfragmente im Amosbuch*, Berne 1974. T.Overholt, 'Commanding the Prophets; Amos and the Problem of Prophetic Authority', *CBQ* 41, 1979, 517-32, considers the possibility that the activity of the prophets in the sanctuary was subject to periodic control, which would have led to the discovery of the preaching against the king by Amos. Cf. also H.M.Barstad, *The Religious Polemics of Amos*, SVT 34, 1984; A.Bjørndalen, *Untersuchungen zur allegorischen Rede der Propheten Amos und Jesaja*, BZAW 165, 1985.

2. For the oracles against the nations cf. A.Bentzen, 'The Ritual Background of Amos 1,2- 2,16', *OTS* 8, 1950, 85-99; M.Weiss, 'The Pattern of the "Execration Texts" in the Prophetic Literature', *IEJ* 19, 1969, 150-7; S.M.Paul, 'Amos 1,3-2,3, a Concatenous Pattern', *JBL* 70, 1971, 397-403; also K.N.Schoville, 'A Note on the Oracles of Amos against Gaza, Tyre and Edom', *SVT* 26, 1974, 55-63; M.L.Barré, 'The Meaning of *l' šybnw* in

Amos 1:3 – 2:6', *JBL* 105, 1986, 611-31; V.Fritz, 'Die Fremdvölkersprüche des Amos', *VT* 37, 1987, 26-38 (he finds only a couple of verses which he believes to go back to Amos!); B.Gosse, 'Le receuil des oracles contre les nations du livre d'Amos et l'"histoire deutéronomique" ', *VT* 38, 1988, 22-40; G.Pfeifer, 'Die Fremdvölkersprüche des Amos – spätere *vaticinia ex eventu?*', *VT* 38, 1988, 230-3 (against V.Fritz). B.Gosse attempts to demonstrate which parts may belong originally to Amos and how much has been edited by Dtr. The authenticity of the oracles against the nations has been defended with strong arguments by W.Rudolph, 'Die angefochtenen Völkersprüche in Amos 1 und 2', in *Schalom. FS A.Jepsen*, Berlin 1971, 45-9. For 9.11-15 cf. the works cited above by Kapelrud, op.cit., 53ff.; Reventlow, op.cit., 90ff.; both favour authenticity. For arguments against cf. my commentary *ad loc.*

3. For the topic see W.H.Schmidt, 'Die deuteronomistische Redaktion des Amosbuches', *ZAW* 77, 1965, 168-93; G.Vermeylen, *Du prophète Isaïe à l'apocalyptique*, Paris I, 1977; II, 1978: II, 519-69. Cf. also R.B.Coote, *Amos among the Prophets*, Philadelphia 1981.

4. For the lament in these circumstances see the recent study by C.Hardmeier, *Texttheorie und biblische Exegese*, Munich 1978. For the doxologies 4.13; 5.8-9; 9.5-6 cf. W.Berg, *Die sogenannten Hymnenfragmente im Amosbuch*, Berne and Frankfurt 1974.

19

HOSEA

1. The person and his time

The name of this prophet paradoxically means 'YHWH helps', whereas his life as it is outlined in the book which bears his name seems to indicate precisely the opposite. The superscription (1.1) presents him as a contemporary of Isaiah, but this information causes a number of problems: in 1.4 his own ministry begins under the last kings of the dynasty of Jehu, i.e. at the latest under Zechariah, son of Jeroboam II, to whom I referred in the previous chapter, but 7.7; 8.4 and 10.3,5 seem to allude to the disorders which followed Zechariah's assassination. In 5.13; 7.15ff.; 8.8f.; 10.5ff. and 12.2 it would seem that he knows of the tribute sent to Tiglath-pileser III of Assyria in 738 BCE (II Kings 15.19-20), and the relations between the two countries which followed this action. According to Alt's 1919 study, 5.8-6.6 would allude to the so-called 'Syro-Ephraimite' war with which we shall be concerned in the discussion of the prophet Isaiah; on another occasion there is talk of relations with Egypt (7.11; 9.6; 12.2), probably at the time of his namesake, king Hoshea. However, there is no reference to the events after the fall of the kingdom of Israel in 722-20, so that the period of his ministry can be put between the middle of the century and about 725. If Hosea, then, was a contemporary of Isaiah, he was an earlier contemporary, while the names of the later kings could have been added by the redaction (we do not know why): we have a similar case in Isa.1.1.

In the proclamation of his message the prophet refers continually and exclusively to the situation in the kingdom of Israel, so that it is probable that he always worked in the north. His knowledge of the historical and political situation, the effectiveness of his imagery and his elevated language (but see below on the problems of the text) are a mark of education, a feature which seems to distinguish Hosea from his earlier contemporary Amos. Hosea 5.2ff. shows that he was familiar also with the situation of the priesthood, which has suggested to some that he himself was a priest; however, there is no proof for this claim. On the basis of 9.7 it has also been supposed that he was part of a prophetic school in which ecstasy was practised, but here too, quite apart from the difficulties of distinguishing clearly between the various categories of prophets, a question with which we have already been occupied (above, 17.2), this is a problem which has yet to be resolved.

2. His marriage

We know little or nothing of the prophet's life. We have his father's name, and we are told the story of his unhappy marriage (chs 1; 3). His matrimonial problem is one of the most obscure matters in the Hebrew Bible, and a satisfactory solution has yet to be found. These are the possibilities:

(a) That the whole matter is simply a poetic and prophetic fiction, a kind of metaphor for the relations between YHWH and his people.

(b) That this was a real experience, through which the prophet had to drag himself laboriously during his life, and that it then became the symbol of his own prophetic vocation and his message. On the one hand we are certainly given the name of the wife, which is a normal if not frequent one; on the other hand, however, the names of the children are clearly symbolic, like those of Isaiah's children, and it seems hard to suppose that anyone ever really bore them. In 3.2 there is a mention of the dowry, another realistic element. So it is not surprising that scholars are divided between those who accept the reality of the experience and those who consider the whole matter, rather, as a metaphor. The former accept what Paul Humbert said in 1918: 'It would have been ridiculous if he had presented himself as the fictitious victim of adultery while at the same time living happily in the bosom of his family.' For the latter the reality is more complex, especially if we take into account the Deuteronomistic redaction to which the book has been subjected, a problem with which we shall be dealing later (below, § 4). To speak of 'spiritual fornication' might seem a third solution, but it ends up by making the narrative quite pointless. We also need to establish what precisely is meant by the expression *'ēšet zᵉnūnīm*, which is commonly rendered 'prostitute': was this a prostitute in our sense of the term, or a 'sacred prostitute'? For this last interpretation see Wolff's commentary. A.J.Heschel, *The Prophets*, 52 n.8, proposed instead '...a person who is disposed to become a harlot, a woman filled with the spirit of whoredom', but intention in itself clearly cannot be taken as guilt. A recent study has suggested that the woman was really an image for the Canaanite goddess Astarte.

A second problem in connection with Hosea's marriage has attracted the attention of scholars for some time: do we have marriages with two different women, or two successive marriages to the same woman? The character of symbolic action or even metaphor in the marriage episode might suggest the same woman, first driven out and then forgiven and accepted back again. This conclusion also commends itself after the study made by Borbone in 1985, which demonstrates that we do not have to translate 'a woman loved by another', in other words what the scholar calls 'the odd man out' (thus already the mediaeval Jewish exegete Ibn Ezra), but rather correct the term *rē'*, 'friend' to *ra'*, 'evil', thus producing 'a woman loving evil'. Mediaeval Jewish exegetes like Rashi and Kimchi, who kept 'the friend', suggested that this was the prophet himself and not a third party (cf. moreover already A, Σ and Tg). Borbone arrives at his conclusion on the basis of the LXX reading, which is an obvious *lectio difficilior*. In this way the developed symbolism of the metaphor seems clear: just as the prophet drives out the unfaithful wife but then pardons her and takes her back, so YHWH rejects his unfaithful people but then pardons them and takes them back. The problem of how to reconcile what is said here with the law in Deut.24.1-4 (cf. Jer.3.1ff.) does not even arise. We find similar imagery in Ezek 16; 20, and we have another instance in the New Testament, this time positive (Eph.5.21ff.). The obviously metaphorical character of these images is one more pointer towards the need to regard this episode, too, as metaphorical. The image is made even more evocative if we remember that the biblical world laid down the death penalty for adultery (Lev.20.10; cf. John 8.3ff.).

If all the narrative is understood metaphorically, the names of the children, too, are also clearly symbolic and need not necesarily correspond to real names. In 1.9 there is a reference to the breaking of the covenant: the people has violated the pledges made, and even God no longer feels bound by his own promises. The name of the second son is also probably meant in this sense. The name of the first son has a more contingent character: it is judgment on the revolt organized by Elijah and brought to a conclusion by Elisha against the house of Omri, utilizing the work of the general Jehu, who then becomes king and founds a dynasty (1.4). We also find names of this kind in Isaiah's family (7.3; 8.1). In any case, in the book of Hosea this conclusion from the first part of the imagery does not bode any good; judgment is imminent. Or, if this is a *vaticinium post eventum*, it serves to explain the reason for the catastrophe.

3. Divisions and text

(*a*) It seems clear that the first three chapters are an independent unit the theme of which is the matrimonial misadventures of the prophet; ch.2 then expounds the theme of the unfaithful spouse, but presupposes chs.1 and 3. In chs.4-14 we have, by contrast, a collection of very varied material which apparently has no internal unity and is not always easy to divide. However, it does seem probable that there is a break between chs.4-11 and 12-14. Each group is centred on a particular theme and seems to be independent of the others. The theme which seems to dominate all others is that of the religious decadence of the kingdom of Israel, a topic dear to the prophetic preaching; this decadence largely explains the situation not only in the sphere of faith but also in the ethical, legal and social spheres. According to this thesis religious decadence also had catastrophic consequences in other spheres of life, especially in the social field, in that the basic foundations were destroyed. So it could come about that despite the favourable economic situation the rich were becoming increasingly rich and the poor increasingly poor, because the ancient tribal solidarity had diminished. This theory is practically identical with that formulated by Dtr on the past faults of the people. The monarchy proved incapable of dealing with the situation: the country, an earthen vessel squeezed between two iron vessels, was concerned to steer a middle course between the great powers of the time, and lacked any government capable of coping with an emergency. The prophet's invective shows the seriousness of the situation, even if it does not give us sufficient information to analyse it and understand it precisely. That is a further difficulty in understanding the book.

(*b*) Another difficulty is posed by the state of the text and the prophet's language. Everything conspires to persuade us that here we have one of the most difficult texts in the Hebrew Bible. Because the text abounds in corrupt passages or because an unfamiliar terminology is used (there are many *hapax legomena*), or because this is a different dialect of Hebrew, the difficulties sometimes seem insurmountable. A linguistic examination carried out on the basis of the new knowledge that we have acquired of Western Semitic in the last few decades would prove useful, though it has to be said that these studies are only just beginning. Difficulties are further increased by the presence of difficult plays on words, unusual or only approximate parallelisms, and references to and associations with features which were evidently known to the audience but are no longer known to us, popular etymologies, assonances and so on. These are elements which at present largely evade a critical study, so that we shall remain at sea until we have a thorough critical examination of them.

4. Hosea, Deuteronomy and the Deuteronomist

F.I.Andersen and D.N.Freedman point out in their 1980 commentary: 'However, the discourses of Hosea are interwoven with Deuteronomic concepts in such a way as to show that Deuteronomy already had authority in Israel. Whether it already existed in an earlier written form or was largely in oral form, the Deuteronomic material served as a basis for much of the thought of Hosea' (75). This statement, also supported indirectly by Jeremias, is interesting, but it seems to me that it starts off on the wrong foot. Why speak of *pre-existing* Deuteronomic and Deuteronomistic material which the prophet is said to have used and not rather of a Deuteronomic or Deuteronomistic redaction? The same problem arises in Zobel's recent study: he too talks of pre-Deuteronomic material. On the basis of what has happened with other prophets – Amos, perhaps Isaiah and certainly Jeremiah and Ezekiel – it seems more plausible to argue the other way round: that there was a later Deuteronomic or Deuteronomistic revision. The later Judahite additions also point in this direction, and the problem of the presence of unusual expressions is similar. It will be the task of scholars over the next few years to try to resolve the problem: what texts can be attributed at least hypothetically to the prophet himself and what are to be classified under the category of Deuteronomic or Deuteronomistic redaction? It can be said that once this problem has been resolved, many expressions which are so far obscure and many texts which so far are considered untranslatable will unexpectedly become clearer.

5. Thought

The message of Hosea has many points of contact with that of Jeremiah around a century later and then with Deuteronomy and the Deuteronomistic work. We have seen that it is probable that this similarity is to be sought not so much in the use of pre-existent material by the prophet as in a Deuteronomic and Deuteronomistic revision in the post-exilic period. The following lines can be brought out, of course, in the book as it appears in its final redaction:

(a) The theme of the marriage with an unworthy woman and of her forgiveness. This suggests the love and the depth of feeling which bind YHWH to his people, if we take this metaphor seriously. This seems evident not only in chs. 1-3 but also in 9.15; 11.1ff.; 14.4ff. and yet other passages. Again, it is the divine love which becomes the criterion for evaluating the past history of the people: in 1.1 YHWH appears as a father, and in the other passages as a husband for Israel. The judgment then appears as the reaction of disappointed love, of frustration (13.7ff.), which explains why this judgment tends not to be definitive, but one to be served out: according to the harsh pedagogy of the time, to be a necessary lesson from a father to a son who was unwilling to listen. So the aim seems to be more the conversion than the destruction of the people: it is intended to bring about the re-establishment of the original relationship of reciprocal love and affection. This approach to the problem is not unlike that of the Deuteronomistic history. A love of this kind is presented, with another bold anthropomorphism, as jealous; in fact on the other hand it calls for total commitment, without hesitation or compromise (4.1ff.; 6.6).

(b) A second element, which is a consequence of the first, is the unremitting struggle against paganism and syncretism. Still keeping to the image of matrimony (cf. especially ch.2, which presupposes the existence of chs.1 and 3 since it comments on them), paganism and syncretism are simply the adultery of the spouse Israel towards her spouse YHWH, and therefore constitute fornication. And if we bear in mind that in Israel the death penalty was attached to these offences, the generosity of the second offering should be clear, as well as confirming that basically the people has what it deserves. On the other hand, even if the prophet shared the theory of religious decadence with his fellows, this theory shows that this was not a sudden acceptance. Just like Dtr, it indicates that this attitude on the part of the people has deep roots: in 12.3f. the patriarch Jacob is described in far from flattering terms, and this is one of the few mentions of the patriarchs outside the Pentateuch. Other episodes from the past are described in a critical key, indicating Israel's guilt (cf.9.10ff. with Num.25; 9.15ff. with the history of the Gilgal sanctuary, where there was a celebration of the crossing of the Jordan and where Saul was crowned, Josh.3-5; I Sam.11). Again, the monarchy is one of the features which led to religious decadence and therefore the decadence of the whole of civil life, a process begun by

Saul (10.9ff.; 13.10ff., cf. I Sam.8, one of the late Deuteronomistic texts, probably DtrN).

(c) Hosea has a distinctive eschatology. Some of its features reappear about a century later in Jeremiah. Only one road is open to the people, that of returning to the desert, the symbol of a new beginning, a starting from scratch (2.14ff.; 12.10ff.). The optimistic evaluation that Hosea gives of the desert seems to exclude the theme of murmuring, of the hard-necked people; the only negative element is the episode described in Num.25; otherwise this is the ideal period of the people in its relationships with God. However, the return to the desert does not come about through any human initiative, a kind of colossal rite of purification; it is rather the work of God himself. The exile and deportation, mentioned many times in the text, therefore seem to constitute an updated form of this return to the desert and to serve as a purification of the people, which will present itself afresh before God as in a new exodus. The theme is typical of Deutero-Isaiah, as we shall soon see. God is disposed to do even this for the love of his people (2.1-3; 3.1-5; 5.15-6.5; 11.8-11; 12.7ff.; 14.10).

This is a feature which Hosea has in common with Jeremiah, and it, too, could be part of the Deuteronomistic redaction; at all events it is an impressive testimony to the realism with which either the prophet evaluated his own present or his redactors considered the people's immediate past.

BIBLIOGRAPHY

Commentaries

On the twelve minor prophets see the bibliography to the previous chapter. On Hosea: E.Osty, JB, ²1958; H.-W.Wolff, ET, Hermeneia, 1974; W.Rudolph, KAT, 1966; J.L.Mays, OTL, 1969; F.I.Andersen and D.N.Freedman, AB, 1980; J.Jeremias, ATD 1983.

Cf. also W.Kuhningk, *Nordwestsemitische Studien zum Hoseabuch*, Rome 1974; J.Mejia, *Amor, pecado, alianza. Una lectura del profeta Oseas*, Buenos Aires 1975.

Bibliographical study: J.F.Craghan, 'Le livre d'Osée et la recherche récente', *BTB* 1, 1971, 150-172.

For the prophet generally cf. G.Emmerson, *Hosea. An Israelite Prophet in*

Judean Perspective, Sheffield 1984; H.Utzschneider, *Hosea. Prophet vor dem Ende*, Fribourg, CH 1980.

1. For Hosea 5.8-6.6 cf. A.Alt, 'Hosea 5.8-6.6. Ein Krieg und seine Folgen in prophetischer Beleuchtung', *Neue kirchliche Zeitschrift* 30, Erlangen 1919, 537-68 (= his *Kleine Schriften* II, Munich ³1964, 163-87) and the opposing view of E.M.Good, 'Hosea 5.8-6.6. An Alternative to Alt', *JBL* 85, 1966, 273-86; id., 'The Composition of Hosea', *SEÅ* 31, 1966, 21-63.

2. Discussion of the problem of Hosea's marriage is centuries old. There is now a report on the solutions put forward in S.Bitter, *Die Ehe des Propheten Hosea*, Göttingen 1975; it begins with the Targum and goes down to the eighteenth century. Cf. *inter alia* P.Humbert, 'Les trois premiers chapîtres d'Osée', *RHR* 77, 1918, 158-71; R.Gordis, 'Hosea's Marriage and Message: A New Approach', *HUCA* 25, 1954, 1-35; H.H.Rowley, 'The Marriage of Hosea', *BJRL* 39, 1956-7, 200-33 (= his *Men of God*, London 1963, 66-97). Pfeiffer*, 569, and J.Coppens, 'L'histoire matrimoniale d'Osée. Un nouvel essai d'interprétation', in *FS F.Nötscher*, Bonn 1950, 38-45 supports an interpretation along the lines of 'spiritual fornication'. For the difficulties of drawing any kind of specific conclusion from the information in chs.1,3 cf. J.Schreiner, 'Hoseas Ehe. Zeichen des Gerichts', *BZ* NF 21, 1977, 163-83. For the use of the verb *nkr* in Ugaritic cf. J.Gray, *The Krt Text in the Literature of Ras Shamra*, Leiden ²1964, 13 (= 1, 101f.) and 44f., and the article by Rowley cited above, 203 n.1. H.Balz-Cohois, 'Gomer oder die Macht der Astarte', *EvTh* 42, 1982, 37-65. For the text of 3.1ff. cf. the recent study by P.-G.Borbone, 'Il terzo incomodo. L'interpretazione del Testo Massoretico di Osea 3, 1', *Hen* 7, 1985, 151-60.

3. For the text of the book see the introductions and I. Willi-Plein, op.cit. (above, 18.1), and P.-G.Borbone, 'Reflessioni sulla critica del testo dell'Antico Testamento ebraico in riferimento al libro di Osea', *Hen* 8, 1986, 281-309; cf. recently P.-G.Borbone and F.Mandracci, *Concordanze del testo siriaco di Osea*, Turin 1987.

4. M.Weinfeld, *Deuteronomy and the Deuteronomic School*, Oxford 1972, index s.v. Hosea; H.-J.Zobel, 'Hosea und das Deuteronomium', *TLZ* 110, 1985, 12-24. A similar proposal has recently been made by E.Kragelund Holt, '*'lhym, d't* und *hsd* im Buche Hosea', *SJOT* 1.1, 1987, 87-103.

5. Cf. Behler, art.cit.; H.-W.Wolff, ' "Wissen um Gott" bei Hosea als Urform von Theologie', *EvTh* 12, 1952-3, 533-54 (= his *Gesammelte Studien*, Munich 1964, 182-205); E.Baumann, ' "Wissen um Gott" bei Hosea als Urform von Theologie?', *EvTh* 15, 1955, 416-25 (who warns against reducing Hebrew *yd'* to intellectual categories); H.-W.Wolff, 'Erkenntnis Gottes im Alten Testament', *EvTh* 15, 1955, 426-31; G.Fohrer, 'Umkehr und Erlösung beim Propheten Hosea', *TZ* 11, 1985, 161-85 (= his *Studien zur alttestamentlichen Prophetie*, BZAW 99, 1967, 222-41); J.M.Ward, 'The Message of the Prophet Hosea', *Int* 23, 1969, 387-407; W.F.Stinespring, 'A Problem of Theological Ethics in Hosea', in *Essays in Old Testament Ethics. J.P.Hyatt in Memoriam*, New York 1974, 131-44; M.J.Buss, *The Prophetic Word in Hosea*,

BZAW 111, 1969 (a basic study); A.Gelston, 'Kingship in the Book of Hosea', *OTS* 19, 1974, 71-85, for his attitude to the monarchy, and I. Cardellini, 'Hosea 4.1-3, eine Strukturanalyse', in *Bausteine Biblischer Theologie, Festgabe für G.J.Botterweck*, Cologne 1977, 259-70. Cf. also F.Dietrich, *Die Anspielungen auf die Jakob-Tradition in Hosea 12.1-13.3*, Würzburg 1977. For the prophet's own traditions cf. H.-D.Neef, *Die Heilstraditionen Israels in der Verkündigung des Propheten Hosea*, BZAW 169, 1987; M.Köchert, 'Prophetie und Geschichte im Hoseabuch', *ZTK* 85, 1988, 3-30. Also M.De Roche, 'The Reversal of Creation in Hosea', *VT* 31, 1981, 200-9; J.Lundbom, 'Poetic Structure and Prophetic Rhetoric in Hosea', *VT* 29, 1979, 300-8; W.G.E.Watson, 'Reflexes of Akkadian Incantations on Hosea', *VT* 34, 1984, 242-7; H.-J.Zobel, 'Prophet in Israel and Juda', *ZTK* 82, 1985, 281-99; J.Day, 'Pre-Deuteronomic Allusions to the Covenant in Hosea and Psalm LXXIII', *VT* 36, 1986, 1-12. For the foreign policies criticized by the prophets cf. J.A.Soggin, 'Hosea und die Aussenpolitik Israels', in *Prophecy. Essays... G.Fohrer*, Berlin 1980, 131-6. For the eschatology cf. J.Jeremias, 'Die Eschatologie des Hoseasbuches', in *Der Bote und die Boten, FS H.-W.Wolff*, Neukirchen 1981, 217-34.

20

ISAIAH

1. The book and its problems

Isaiah, with 66 chapters, is one of the longest of the prophetic books. However, the attentive reader will find it easy enough to see that it is composed of different parts and that there are considerable differences between them. A first part is made up of chs.1-39, which are clearly distinct from chs.40ff., as J.G.Eichhorn already noted in the eighteenth century. Chapters 40ff. do not in fact refer to people and events of the eighth century BCE, but to those of the sixth century, that is, during and after the Babylonian exile. Even within chs.1-39, however, there is an erratic block made up of what is commonly considered to be the apocalyptic section chs.24-27. Chapters 56-66 for the most part no longer address the exilic community but the community of the restoration, and are therefore to be assigned to the last quarter of the sixth century BCE. So we have at least three, if not four, distinct collections, and we therefore speak of 'Isaiah' (eighth century), 'Deutero-Isaiah' (middle of the sixth century) and 'Trito-Isaiah' (in the last quarter of the sixth century). It would seem necessary to date the apocalyptic section in an even later period, as we shall soon see. We shall only examine Deutero- and Trito-Isaiah in any detail when we come to consider the exilic and post-exilic prophets.

Here we might ask how three or four such different writings came to bear the name of the eighth-century prophet. It is not easy to give an answer: in the past some scholars thought of the survival of a school of the prophet which would have continued to operate for some centuries and then gave all its work the master's name; recently, however, R.Rendtorff (1984, below, § 3), while maintaining the tripartite division of the work, has noted a series of references and correlations between the parts of the book. He argues that 40-55 is its dominant central core. The standpoint of W.Brueggemann (cf. below, § 3), arrived at independently, is similar.

At all events, the first time that Isaiah is mentioned as being complete, i.e. with its 66 chapters, is in the deutero-canonical book of Ecclesiasticus (48.20ff.), at the beginning of the second century BCE.

We also have the two manuscripts of the book, one almost complete, discovered in Cave I of Qumran in 1947; they are indicated by the sigla 1 QIs^a and 1 QIs^b respectively.

2. The prophet and his age

The biography and hence the person of the prophet Isaiah are better known than those of his predecessors Amos and Hosea. As well as being given his patronym we are told that in the year of the death of king Uzziah/Azariah (though the exact chronology of this period is at present unknown) he received a special charge: he was to announce inexorable judgment to the people of Judah and Jerusalem. The text of Isa.6 has traditionally been understood as an account of the prophet's vocation, but it is more the confirmation of a particular charge. That evidently presupposes that by that date the prophet had already been at work for some time. The date of the death of Uzziah/Azariah is fixed between 742 and 736, depending on the chronology adopted. We shall examine a little later the problem whether Isaiah's was a vocation or a charge (below, §§ 3a, 4). His ministry lasted up to the Assyrian expedition against Judah and the siege of Jerusalem in 701 (the hypothesis of a second expedition on the part of Sennacherib seems increasingly improbable; those who still accept it put it around 688), and we have no evidence that Isaiah was active outside this period.

Isaiah was married, and his wife bore the title $n^e b\bar{i}\,'\bar{a}h$, 'prophetess'. We do not know whether this reflected her husband's profession or whether she also had a prophetic role. We are told that she bore him two sons: in 7.3 we find $\check{s}^e\,'ar\ y\bar{a}\check{s}\bar{u}b$ = 'a remnant will return (to YHWH)' or 'be converted'; in 8.3 we have $mah\bar{e}r\ \check{s}\bar{a}lal\ h\bar{a}\check{s}\ baz$ = 'speedy spoil, hasty prey'. As in the case of Hosea, these are symbolic names, which the book itself explains in 10.6 and which announce what the fate of the people will be: for the wicked, judgment and destruction; for the 'remnant', conversion and salvation. It is probable that these names, too, are not real names, as is also the case with Hosea's children. For this biographical information cf. above, 18.4b.

If we look for the circle in which the prophet moved, we may infer that he must have belonged to the ruling class: he dealt with the king

face to face, even when the king was outside the palace (7.1ff.); in
37.1ff. the king sends for him. Therefore both Dietrich and Schoors
independently call him a court prophet. He does not seem to have
encountered opposition to his preaching of the kind which Amos and
later Jeremiah suffered. A person of the rank of Isaiah was evidently
allowed to express himself without reticence.

Isaiah's ministry is said to have taken place essentially in Jerusalem: we do not hear that he travelled elsewhere. The first date
given is that of the death of King Uzziah/Azariah; there is also
mention of the kings Jotham, Ahaz and Hezekiah. A pseudepigraphical book, The Ascension of Isaiah, from the first or second century
CE (cf.Heb.11.37), has him die under King Manasseh, whom
Deuteronomistic historiography considered to be the prototype of
the wicked monarch; it is not easy to check the reliability of this
information but it seems to seek to continue the hagiographical
tradition.

Isaiah's preaching took place during a particularly troubled period
in the history of Israel, and this is one of the reasons why such a
major part of it is devoted to political themes (cf. my *History*, XI.2).
He witnessed the so-called 'Syro-Ephraimite' war (as it has been
generally termed from Luther onwards) of 735-734, during which
Israel and the kingdom of Damascus tried first to persuade and later
to constrain Judah to join in as part of the anti-Assyrian coalition;
when Judah refused, they moved against Jerusalem to impose the
alliance by force. Isaiah also witnessed the fall of Damascus in 732
and of the kingdom of Israel in 722-20. The various anti-Assyrian
rebellions of 713-11 and 705 took place during his ministry, the latter
being overcome by the expedition of Sennacherib in 701. So it is not
surprising that the message of Isaiah was taken up little more than
a century later to exemplify the exile in Babylon and the destruction
of Jerusalem.

As a writer, Isaiah is matter-of-fact. Only once do we find any
symbolic action which seems bizarre: this is in 20.1ff. when he appears
naked before the foreign ambassadors assembled at Jerusalem to
show them their potential future as deportees and thus to dissuade
them from taking up arms against Assyria. We never see him in a
situation like that of Hosea's marriage or performing symbolic
actions like those attested in Ezekiel. The motive of the preaching
common to all the prophets appears particularly in Isaiah. As I have
already indicated, it appears from 8.16 that he had a school, and it
will not be far from the truth to suppose that it is to this school that
we owe a first transmission of his words. It is possible that the school

also collected some texts of doubtful authenticity and its own products, combining these under the name of the master; as we have seen, similar theories have been proposed to explain the existence of Deutero- and Trito-Isaiah. One difficulty remains: we do not know for how long the school of Isaiah continued to operate, nor is it clear whether 8.16 presupposes the existence of written material; finally, we do not even know whether the school may not be a creation of later redaction.

3. Divisions and content

It was the achievement of the German B.Duhm, professor at the University of Basel until his death, to have argued for the first time in his commentary (first edition 1892) that Isaiah is composed of six originally independent units: chs.1-12; 13-23; 24-27; 28-33; 34-35 – chapters 36-39 are a special case, since they are a historical text parallel to II Kings 18-21. Duhm showed a marked tendency to assign the texts which he examined to a late date, a tendency which we shall examine in more depth in the Psalms (below, 34.1, 3). In some cases he went down to the second century BCE, the necessary *terminus ante quem* because of the mention of Isaiah in Ecclesiasticus. On the other hand the Qumran texts, which also date from this period, know the book of Isaiah in its present form (at least that is true of the first and most complete text; in the other the many gaps prevent us from making a definitive judgment); and they were certainly copied from earlier manuscripts.

O.Procksch also made such divisions in his commentary, but in conformity with the more conservative approach of his commentary series, he traced back the individual collections to the prophet himself or to his disciples. According to him chs.1; 2-6; 9.7-10.4; 28-32 can be attributed to the prophet; 7.1-9.6; 11.1ff., 15-23 are to be attributed to the disciples. The suggestion made by K.Budde and S.Mowinckel was on essentially similar lines, but in less detail. According to them Isaiah simply consisted of three parts: chs.1-12: oracles against Judah and Jerusalem; chs.13-23: oracles against the nations; chs.28-33: oracles of salvation. Chapters 24-27 remain outside this scheme; they are later because they are apocalyptic. This division has the advantage of simplicity; sometimes, however, that seems excessive: for example in 1.1; 2.1 and 13.1 we have three superscriptions which were added to the text not earlier than the exile, and the second of these demonstrates that at least traditionally there was a caesura between chs.1 and 2. In 13.1 we have the term *maśśa'* = literally 'burden', hence 'charge, oracle'; this often appears in this sense in chs.13-23, but otherwise it is frequent in post-exilic times. The verb *ḥāzāh* (= 'see') and the derivative *ḥāzōn* (= 'vision') also belong to post-exilic language, though the scarcity of the material at our disposal counsels caution here.

G.Fohrer suggests a much more detailed division of the book, but its extreme complexity makes it difficult to work with, regardless of its merits. He has the following division:

A. 1.2-28; 1.29-31 (fragments) and 2.2-5 (promises);

B. 2.6-4.1 (in 3.25-4.1 fragments) and 4.2-6 (promises);

C. 5.1-23; 10.1-4 (5.14-17, 24 fragments);

D. 6.1-8.18 (8.19-22 fragments) and 9.1-6 (EVV 2-7) (promises)

E. 9.7 (EVV 8)-20; 5.25-30; 10.5-15, 27b-32 (fragments); 11.1-9, 10-16 (promises);

F. Chs.13-23; 28.1-4, 5f., 17f. (promises);

G. 28.7-32.14; 32.15-20 (promises).

However, the studies by H.Barth, R.E.Clements, A.G.Auld and R.Rendtorff, along with the second edition of Kaiser's commentary (for which see my review, *VT* 34, 1984, 496-9) have taken up the question of dating again, and with it the division of the book, in new terms which recall, rather, the approach to the problem made by Duhm. For Barth a good part of the book is to be dated to the time of Josiah, while other elements are dated even later, after the catastrophe of 587/6. First Clements' study and then his commentary take this line: 1.9; 2.18-31; 6.12-13; 8.21-22; 17.7-9; 22.5-11,24-25; 23.13 belong to the later redaction. And it is to this redaction that we owe the present position of 2.6-4.1. The aim of the redactors was to reinterpret the references to Assyria in terms of Babylon, and it is also to them that we owe the connection with chs.40-55. Kaiser goes much further than this; he denies that the majority of the book is authentic Isaiah material, attributing it to a later redaction, post-exilic but pre-Hellenistic, aimed at commenting on, and applying to, the contemporary situation 'a small collection of words of the prophet'. The theology of this redactor is Deuteronomistic. Authentic parts are to be found only in chs.1; 28-31; and the 'memorandum' of the prophet (following the happy definition made by Budde) in 6.1-8.18 refers to them.

Here I follow the division put forward by Duhm and in essence continued by other scholars; that suggested by Fohrer in fact differs only formally from the others. As was the practice some decades ago, A.Lods*, 277ff., attempted to give a date for each individual section, but the problems are such as to make an enterprise of this kind inadvisable even for those who accept the authenticity of the bulk of the text.

(a) *Oracles against Judah and Jerusalem* (chs.1-12). In this first part of the book we have a collection of oracles which until recently were considered largely authentic. The section ends in ch.12 with a doxology, which suggests that this part was an independent unity from a relatively early period and that it was used in public worship. We have seen that chs.1 and 2 each begin with a superscription, so originally they must have been two separate entities. Anyone who considered ch.6 to be an account of the calling of the prophet was surprised not to find it at the beginning of the work, and moreover 6.1-9.6 [EVV 9.7], which is a unity (often called Isaiah's memorandum, at least as far as 8.18), interrupt a lament in three stanzas (5.25-30; 9.7-20 [EVV 9.8-21]; 10.5-15), recognizable by a refrain which keeps recurring. On the other hand, since the criteria followed by the redactors of the prophetic books are obscure, we cannot be surprised that if ch.6 is the account of the prophet's calling it is not at the beginning of the book. Be this as it may, in this first part of the book we have the following sections: chs.1; 2-4; 5.1-24; 6.1-9.6 [EVV 9.7]; 5.25-30; 9.7-20 [EVV 9.8-21]; 10.5-15; 9.21[EVV 9.22]-11.16, and finally the doxology, ch.12.

1. The first chapter presents a series of texts of the prophet which deal with different themes. They date from different periods of his ministry. Fohrer put forward the hypothesis that this is a selection of various texts, forming a kind of summary and programmatic presentation of the whole of Isaiah's preaching. That would also explain why this chapter is put at the beginning of the book. 1.2-3 is an invective against the people which cannot be dated; it seems to presuppose that the prophet had some kind of experience with his audience, in which case it cannot belong at the beginning of his ministry. 1.4-9 describes the situation in Jerusalem during or a little after the invasion by Sennacherib in 701, now revised in terms of the events of 597/587-6. The other passages cannot be dated, but they probably belong to the earliest period of the prophet's ministry. 1.10-17, which is attached to the previous pericope only by the repetition of the words Sodom and Gomorrah, is a prophetic invective in the form of instruction (*tōrāh*) against the degeneration of the cult in Judah and castigates social and moral evil, thus having links with similar passages especially in Amos, but also in Hosea. However, this time it is addressed to the south. 1.18-20 announces YHWH's forgiveness by means of the image of the legal argument (cf. the use of the root *ykḥ* = try); the majority of modern scholars would see the

passages as in fact a rhetorical question which presupposes a negative reply. This is one of the m st interesting examples of the ambiguity of certain texts, which gives a great deal of trouble to both exegetes and translators. 1.21-26 is a unit discovered by Duhm: it stands out by ending in the same way as it began, and takes the form of a lament against the sin of Jerusalem. In 1.27-31 we have a series of sayings on the theme of redemption and judgment, without any logical unity.

The compiler of the chapter must therefore have followed certain criteria in the collection of this material, connecting the various oracles together either by means of similar words which would serve as mnemonics or by similar ideas: thus 1.4-7 follows 1.2f., where the mnemonic is 'sons', and 1.9 is connected to 1.10, as we have seen, by the mention of the two accursed cities.

The text has the following order: sin, judgment, discussion of possibilities which are still open, decision, possibilities of redemption.

2. Chapters 2-4 are a collection of sayings from the prophet's first period, but were probably put in this position by a later redactor. At the beginning we find 2.2-5 (which Fohrer considers to be the conclusion of the preceding collection), a text which is also transmitted in Micah 4.1-4. With the information at our disposal it is impossible to establish which of these two versions is the earlier, whether both depend on an earlier prototype or whether, again as Fohrer indicates, they are post-exilic texts or at most to be dated in the late exilic period. We do not have decisive evidence for any of these possibilities, but if we take into account the eschatological character of the text, the probability tends towards lateness. In 2.6-22 we have a threat in poetic form and with regular strophes (though there are also later additions). Its theme is the catastrophes which will accompany the 'day of YHWH', a theme which we have already examined in Amos. In 3.1-15 we have threats against the rulers of Jerusalem because of their misgovernment (vv.1-9 are perhaps an independent unit). In 3.16-24 (vv.18-21 are probably late) the object of the invective is the women of Jerusalem, especially those of the ruling class: here too the context is that of the 'day of YHWH'. The passage is difficult because of the many technical terms used for the jewellery; for that see the study by van den Branden mentioned in the bibliography. In 3.25-26 we have a terrible vision of judgment which has already taken place: the corpses of the fallen lie in the middle of the streets and the women are sold as slaves. 3.27-4.1 is probably an incomplete oracle, perhaps a fragment of an old collection, while 4.2-6 stands out so markedly from its present context that many authors do not consider it to be authentic. Fohrer thinks that

it was put here as an introduction to the third section, but it is not easy to come to a decision. In any case, the oracles that are probably authentic can all be dated to the period before the Syro-Ephraimite war.

3. In 5.1-24 we have another collection of sayings which most scholars consider early. 5.1-7 is particularly interesting because it provides an example of the prophet's preaching (or what the redactors thought was his preaching). His method is first to gain the assent of his audience on a non-controversial matter, here the sentence pronounced by the friend on the vineyard (the same method that Nathan used with David in II Sam.12) and then to identify the audience with the party condemned. In 5.8-24 we have a lament-invective the stanzas of which begin with 'Woe to...', a formula which normally introduces ordinary invective. In 5.25-30 we have reflections on the wrath of YHWH which manifests itself in political catastrophes; the main cause of the anger is the social situation in the country, and the text continues in 9.7-21 [EVV9.8-22]; 10.1-4, as appears from the refrain which is constantly repeated (5.25d; 9.11,16 [EVV 9.12,17]; 10.4): 'For all this his (YHWH's) anger is not turned away and his hand is stretched out still.' The structure recalls that of the visions of Amos, and perhaps both follow the same liturgical pattern, which was probably one already in existence. There is no positive element, no possibility of forgiveness. Most scholars regard the passage as early: G.Fohrer even thinks of the period of the 'Syro-Ephraimite war', but here too we should note that the second part of the refrain uses a typically Deuteronomistic expression, so Kaiser supposes that the exile has already come about. The collection ends with a messianic passage (11.1-16), but only the first part of it (vv.1-9) can be authentic. For Fohrer the whole section is inauthentic because of the gift of the spirit in v.2: this is a feature which appears only with Ezekiel; v.1, however, seems to be connected with Isa.65.25; Hab.2.14. On the other hand this is not a conclusive argument: the gift of the spirit does not appear here in relation to prophecy, but as an attribute of the king for good government; the passage may be connected, rather, with the ceremonial and ritual of the coronation of the monarch in Judah; there is a similar instance in 9.5bff [EVV 9.6bff.], even if there is no mention of the Spirit. The passages in Habakkuk and Trito-Isaiah could well be quotations of this one. The problem therefore remains open, and it is important because it concerns whether we have a first messianic text with Isaiah, i.e. in the second half of the eighth century BCE, or whether this is a concept which emerged later. From a purely logical point of

view, it would seem natural to think that the expectation of a coming Messiah began only with the fall of the earthly monarchy. 11.10-16, however, make explicit mention of 'the dispersed of Judah' (v.12), and therefore presuppose that the exile has taken place (either that of 597 or that of 587/6) and so cannot be the work of Isaiah.

4. The collection 6.1-9.6 [EVV 9.7] now interrupts the previous collection; this shows it to be a separate composition, interpolated later. It is usually called 'Isaiah's memorandum' (German *Gedenkschrift*), following Budde's suggestion, on the basis of 8.16.

The section is dominated by the narrative in 6.1ff., of which vv.12-13 are certainly late, and by successive narratives, especially by ch.7 which gives an account of the dialogues between the prophet and King Ahaz at the time of the Syro-Ephraimite war. This chapter is later, as is clearly evident from the beginning (v.1), where the events are described as belonging to a remote past. The chapter deals with the discussions which preceded Amos' decision to turn to Assyria for help against the coalition between Damascus and Israel, who were on the march against Jerusalem to force it to enter into an anti-Assyrian alliance, and possibly to replace Ahaz with another ruler to their own liking. According to the text Isaiah was opposed to the project: the remedy proposed would in fact have been more serious than the danger, as indeed it was; rather, he counselled the king to have faith (7.9), difficult advice to evaluate politically, though later facts were to confirm its validity. After this intervention at court the prophet seems to have had to limit his preaching to his own disciples (8.16), in whose circle the memorandum will have been composed. In 8.19-23 (of which vv.21-22 are certainly late), we have various additions which lead into another messianic text (8.23-9.6 [EVV 9.7]). Here there are two possibilities: either this is an oracle pronounced in the closer circle of the disciples, or, as Fohrer indicates, it is an exilic or post-exilic oracle; this latter alternative seems more probable, in that the eschatological expectation of a king presupposes the end of the earthly monarchy.

The beginning of the section, ch.6, is particularly important. Traditionally it has been considered the autobiographical account of the prophet's call, accompanied by the features of a theophany similar to that on Sinai (Exod.19). As to the phenomena, it is enough to note that this particular parallel seems suspect: Exod.19 is a late text, certainly post-exilic, with its reference to a 'kingdom of priests' and 'holy nation' (v.6), which reflects the post-exilic hierocracy. To speak of Deuteronomistic redaction does not, however, seem relevant since Dtr does not make use of visionary elements. The interpretation of the vision as a calling has also recently been put in doubt after some earlier attempts in Steck's study, to which I have already referred briefly. The passage is about more than a calling; it deals with legitimation to a particular onerous charge, the announcement of the destruction of the prophet's own people. The passage is formulated, again, in such harsh terms that the LXX gives a watered-down version of it (possibly without modifying the consonantal text), and this version then appears in the New Testament (Matt.13.14-15). Chapter 12, the final doxology, is composed of an introduction and two songs: in vv.1-2 we have the introduction with a hymn of thanksgiving, and in vv.3-6 a psalm of action and thanksgiving which in turn ends with a doxology.

(b) *Oracles against the nations* (chs.13-23). These chapters all contain material of the same literary genre; they are 'oracles against the nations', a theme with which we dealt when discussing Amos. They are a form of curse. The majority of scholars are now agreed on which passages may be authentic and which are not.

1. The following passages are probably authentic (with the reservations made by Kaiser in his commentary): 14.24-27, an oracle against Assyria; 14.28-32, an oracle against Philistia, dated in the year of the death of King Ahaz (715 or 729/25 BCE, the exact date is uncertain): 17.1-11, against Damascus, earlier than 732, again 'fulfilled' in the conquest of the place by Assyria. Fohrer considers only vv.1-6 to be authentic; vv.7-8 will be a later addition and 9-11 a second appendix, polemic against idolatry, not composed before 600 BCE. 17.12-14 is a lament on 'many peoples' which some scholars would like to connect with the arrival of Sennacherib's army at the walls of Jerusalem in 701 (cf. II Kings 19). Chapter 18 could be an oracle directed against the Egyptian ambassadors at the court of Judah, with the aim of warning them in the light of a possible anti-Assyrian alliance; the allusion is to the twenty-fifth 'Nubian' dynasty, ruling from 751 BCE to 656, and the occasion would have been that of the preparation of the revolts of 713-11 or 705, both of which ended catastrophically. Chapter 20 mentions the one symbolic action of the prophet, probably performed during the preparation of the revolt in 713-11; it symbolizes the way in which the survivors will have to go off to be deported. Some scholars regard 22.1-14 as an exhortation to the inhabitants of Jerusalem after the end of the siege in 701 not to let themselves be carried away by facile optimism (v.13); in 22.15-25 we have oracles against two palace officials, Shebna and Eliakim, which were elaborated at a later date. For the first see Appendix 1.6; perhaps 28.1-5 may be additions.

2. The following oracles are of doubtful authenticity or certainly not authentic: 13.1-14.23 is a taunt song against the king of Babylon with threats of the final destruction of his kingdom. This includes elements of a myth about the Titans who wanted to scale heaven and were hurled down to the depths (14.13); now the myth serves as an example of the present attitude and the future destiny of the king of Babylon. Its inauthenticity is obvious: at the time of Isaiah Babylon was not an enemy, but rather Judah's ally against Assyria (cf. II Kings 20.12-21/Isa.39.1-8: Merodach Baladan = Marduk Apal Iddina II), in the revolt of 713-11 or 705, whereas the text announces events which took place at the beginning of the second half of the sixth century BCE. Chapters 15-16 contain an oracle against Moab divided into three sections; part of it also appears in Jer.48.29. It is probably an early oracle, but not by Isaiah; Fohrer regards it as post-exilic. Chapter 19 records a post-exilic oracle which some scholars would date to around 550 BCE because they think it reflects the hope of Deutero-Isaiah. In 21.1-10 we have an oracle which again seems to refer to the fall of Babylon; 21.11f. talks of Edom in terms which seem exilic, while 21.13-15, which is also post-exilic, deals with Dedan, an Arabian tribe. In ch.23 the situation is complex: the fall of Tyre is mentioned, but we are not told at whose hands. History records the following falls of Tyre: one by Tiglath-pileser III or Shalmaneser V of Assyria in the second half of the eighth century; another at the hands of Nebuchadnezzar II of Babylon in the second quarter of the sixth century; and a third under Alexander the Great at the end of the fourth century BCE. It is not possible to determine to what the text relates; it is enough to point out that only in the first case could the author be Isaiah.

(c) Chapters 24-27 are *a collection of apocalyptic fragments* the theme of which is the end of the world.

Features which are certainly late in this context include the resurrection of the dead, a concept which so far has been attested only in late statements, even if attempts have been made by M.J.Dahood and his pupils to show that it is much earlier. The text is 26.19. The same goes for the developed angelology of 24.21. So the critics oscillate between the fifth and second centuries BCE! In 24.10 there is another mention of an unknown city, probably Jerusalem.

(d) For the most part chs.28-33 contain *authentic words of the prophet*; that is even true for Kaiser, who finds the bulk of the original material here.

The tone is generally negative. The whole passage is directed against individuals who are only partly known, connected with the anti-Assyrian rebellions of 713-11 and 705-01. G.Fohrer would like, probably rightly, to put 28.1-5 among the oracles against the nations (chs.13-23), also because it is stylistically and significantly different from the context. Chapter 33 is a prophetic liturgy the theme of which is the future; Fohrer does not want to date it before the post-exilic period, probably rightly.

(e) Chapters 34-35 are another *short apocalypse*, the theme of which is the liberation of Zion and the destruction of Edom.

There are references in the text here to the Jewish diaspora, which only came into being with the exile, and the exile itself is explicitly mentioned in ch.35 in the description of countries abandoned by their inhabitants. In 34.16 there is mention of a book, with the use of the term *sēper*; this is generally considered a sign of late redaction, but in international treaties prior to the exile it often denotes a stele, so the usage cannot be taken as support for a late dating. For the term *sēper* see my 'Osservazioni a due derivati della radice *spr* in ebraico', *BeO* 7, 1965, 279-82 = *OTOS*, 184-9.

(f) Isa.36-39 is a *narrative section* parallel to II Kings 18.13-20.18 (cf. above, p.230).

This section, the bulk of which is to be considered a product of later reflection (for Clements it is to be dated at the earliest to the time of Josiah, and Garbini and Ackroyd date it in the post-exilic period), has therefore been added by the redactors to the eight-century prophet's work, that is, if it is not an introduction prefixed to chs.40ff. R.F.Melugin and P.R.Ackroyd have put forward that theory, and there is much in its favour.

So in conclusion we can argue that the genesis of the book was very complex, and this is accepted even by those who think that the majority of the material is to be attributed to the prophet, as tradition has it. Up to what point we can still trace the authentic words of the figure who lived in the second half of the eighth century BCE is doubtful, and authors range from a maximalist position (H.Wildberger) to a minimalist one (O.Kaiser). At all events it is certain that the starting point must have been Isaiah's preaching. The book was probably not finished before the fifth century, perhaps not before the fourth (that explains why it was possible to add Deutero- and Trito-Isaiah), and it is possible that chs.24-27 take us down to an even later date.

According to our classical and western criteria, revisions of a work in the course of transmission are the sign of inaccurate activity which does not distinguish between original elements and later additions; in reality the phenomenon bears witness to a living tradition ready to update itself over the centuries without ever raising the problem of literary originality as we might do today. This has obviously made the work of the critic difficult, but it also attests the living character of the tradition.

4. Thought

Studying the thought of an author when some scholars tend to disown his paternity of the writings traditionally attributed to him is clearly not an easy task; the fact of the matter is that whether we like it or not we are studying more the thought of the various redactors than that of the prophet of the eighth century BCE. This is a fact that we have to live with, in this case as in the case of so many other prophets, so we must be content to expound the thought of the book as we now have it.

All through his long and brilliant scholarly life K.Budde had always argued that there was some relationship between Isaiah and Amos, though he never went into the matter more deeply. That was done in the study by R.Fey (1963). He demonstrated the existence of a parallel between Amos 6.1-7 and Isa.5.11-13; as well as the use of the same technical terms with the same meaning, like *ṣdāqāh*, 'justice', and *mišpāṭ*, 'law', there is the similarity of style in the construction of the various articles, themes and motives like the identification of pride as the root of sin, and concepts, like for example that of the divine holiness. We should not therefore be surprised if in the study of the book of Isaiah we find concepts and forms that we have already examined in connection with Amos. However, that does not mean literary dependence: we have, rather, the same literary genres, each of which develops in its own way, and a common ideological and theological basis: that of the south. But what appears only sketchily in Amos because of the brevity of his text, and is sometimes presented in rather a rough form, is taken to perfection of form and substance in Isaiah, a person of considerable education. Not for nothing is it said that Isaiah is the first Israelite theologian whose name we know. That is certainly the case, provided that we take into account the complex origin of the book.

Isaiah appears as a theologian in the scene narrated in ch.6, in which he was an active witness: the famous *trisagion* is nothing other than the proclamation of the absolute holiness of the God of Israel, a theme which echoes throughout the book with a special emphasis. In it God is given a special predicate, that of the 'Holy One of Israel' (*qᵉdoš yiśrā'ēl*), a definition which at the same time dialectically underlines the distance which separates God from humankind (in origin 'holy' means 'separated from', 'set apart by God'), but also the relationship of communion which binds him to his people, to the believing and praying community. Directly face to face with this holiness the prophet can only exclaim 'Woe is me! I am undone' (6.1ff.) and wait for God to put him in a position to bear the divine presence. For human beings confronted with this God their attitude can only be one of trust. Nor is it simply an inner attitude; it is a matter of specific decisions of faith, of taking each case by itself, as is shown by 7.9; 30.15 and other passages. So we do not have here anything so intellectual as the struggle between orthodoxy and heterodoxy or heresy; it is a matter of taking the attitude called for in any eventuality. The believer is not assailed with a norm, with casuistry, but is called on for active commitment in a particular situation. Chapter 7 is typical in this respect, even if this is an instance of late redaction: the prophet exhorts the king not to play a political game which will be beyond him and in which he can only be the loser, but to 'trust' in the Lord. This advice was certainly impracticable in an emergency situation, but it was borne out by the facts and proved ultimately to be realistic, in contrast to the attitude of so many politicians. Isaiah denies that Judah can trust in armies or astuteness (double-crossing policies and so on). As we have seen, ch.19 criticizes the foreign policy of the kingdom of Judah, while ch.31 condemns both foreign politics generally and recourse to military strength: not only are these sacrilegious positions because they deprive God of his sovereignty in history, but they have no concrete effect on the practical level. Because it is in history that God is at work, as 10.5ff. shows, Assyria is a pawn in his game, a pawn which will rapidly be taken as soon as it makes claims. However, the prophet is not presented as a utopian or a fatalist, nor does he expect that things will settle themselves. Human beings are enjoined to practise justice (1.16ff.); Ahaz is given the alternative of trusting in YHWH or in himself and in politics, in the choices of his bureaucracy (ch.7).

For Isaiah, too, human sin consists in a refusal to recognize divine sovereignty in the whole of life. Dishonesty, corruption, immorality, the thirst for riches and luxury, irresponsibility or downright oppression in the social sphere, syncretistic worship are all aspects of a basic attitude of human rebellion against the divine will. And confronted with this position, God can go to the opposite extreme, hardening the mind (literally 'heart') of the people and thus making them blind and deaf to the prophetic preaching, impeding their understanding and therefore their conversion. That appears clearly in the second part of chapter 6: man here is compelled to run the course that he has chosen right to the end, and suffer its extreme consequences (6.9ff.; 29.9ff.; cf. similarly I Kings 22 and the exodus narrrative, where the same thing happens to Pharaoh). This hardening of the mental faculties does not, however, excuse man from his own responsibilities; it is an integral part of the divine punishment, not an excuse to enable him to escape. In this way God triumphantly sets himself against all those who think that they can oppose him or slow down the realization of his plans (2.12ff.). These are features which evolve over the decades, but in essence they remain the same, and they are taken forward by the redaction of the book, which sees in the Babylonian exile the fulfilment of the ancient threats and invectives. That also happens with the announcement of salvation: the details may change, but the basic question remains the same in its almost incredible magnitude (cf. 2.1ff.; 9.1ff. [EVV 9.2ff.]; 11.1ff., provided that we accept that these still reflect something of the original message of the prophet).

One of the principal concepts of salvation is that of the 'remnant'. I spoke of this at the end of ch.17. Until recently it was considered one of the earliest elements in the preaching of Isaiah (cf. also the name of one of his two sons, who was certainly born before 734, 7.3). The catastrophes which successively struck the region – the fall of the north and then the two sieges and the two deportations in Judah – must have convinced the people of Judah that they were the 'remnant', and later this was also felt by those among them who returned from Babylon. All this, however, serves to bring out the antiquity of the concept, at least in the book of Isaiah, even if, as we have seen, it seems that we should take seriously the possibility that the concept already emerged in the Assyrian period.

Another characteristic feature of the book is what has been called the 'theology of Zion'. This appears throughout the work from 2.1ff. onwards; however, here too there are doubts as to whether the concept is authentic Isaiah. At all events here are elements, especially the idea of the remnant, which begin to show that the idea was making ground that the people of God could also be just a part of Israel or Judah. This was the line which was to be followed by the messianic hope, though these texts too are probably also not the work of the eighth-century prophet.

BIBLIOGRAPHY

Commentaries

B.Duhm, HKAT, [4]1922 (reprinted 1967); O.Procksch, KAT, 1930; V.Herntrich, ATD, 1950 (on 1-12 only and replaced in the series by O.Kaiser); J.Steinmann, Lectio Divina, Paris 1950; A.Penna, SacBib 1968; E.J.Kissane, Dublin [2]1960; G.Fohrer, ZBK, 2 vols, 1960-2; H.Wildberger, BK I, 1972; II, 1978; III, 1982; R.E.Clements, NCB, 1980; O.Kaiser, ET, OTL, 2 vols, [2]1983, 1974; F.Montagnini, *Il libro di Isaia* (1-39), Brescia [2]1982. The monograph by J.Vermeylen, *Du prophète Isaïe à l'apocalyptique*, Paris I, 1977; II, 1978, is not strictly a commentary. Lesser commentaries are P.Auvray, 1972; P.Auvray and J.Steinmann, 1972. R.Kilian, *Jesaja 1-35*, Darmstadt 1983, and J C.Hardmeier, 'Jesajaforschung im Umbruch', *VuF* 31.1, 1986, 3-31, are bibliographical studies.

1. For Isaiah generally see the now classical study by K.Budde, *Jesajas Erleben*, Gotha 1928; cf. also F.Huber, *Jahwe, Juda und die anderen Völker*, Berlin 1976; K.Nielsen, 'Das Bild des Gerichtes (*Rib* Pattern) in Jes I-XII', *VT* 29, 1979, 309-24; J.Koenig, *L'herméneutique analogique du Judaisme d'après les témoins textuels d'Isaïe*, Leiden 1982, 117ff.; J.C.Exum, 'Of Broken Pots, Fluttering Birds and Visions in the Night', *CBQ* 43, 1981, 331-52; W.Brueggemann, 'Unity and Dynamic in the Isaiah Tradition', *JSOT* 29, 1984, 89-107; cf. also A.G.Auld, 'Poetry, Prophecy, Hermeneutics. Recent Studies in Isaiah', *SJT* 33, 1980, 567-81; R.Rendtorff, 'Zur Komposition des Buches Jesaja', *VT* 34, 1984, 295-320. Against this classification of Isa.6ff. as 'memorial' see recently H.Graf Reventlow, 'Das Ende der sogenannten "Denkschrift" Jesajas', *BN* 38/39, 1987, 62-7. For the structure of the book see further A.E.Evans, 'The Unity and Parallel Structure of Isaiah', *VT* 38, 1988, 129-47; E.W.Conrad, 'The Royal Narrative and the Structure of the book of Isaiah', *JSOT* 41, 1988, 67-81.

The two manuscripts discovered at Qumran were published respectively by M.Burrows, *The Dead Sea Scrolls of St Mark's Monastery* I, New Haven, Conn. 1950, and E.L.Sukenik, *The Dead Sea Scrolls of the Hebrew University*, Jerusalem 1955; it is not possible here to go into details or mention the publications which refer to them.

The threefold division of the book, proposed by Duhm at the end of the last century, has been confirmed by a computer study, cf. Y.T.Radday, 'Vocabulary Eccentricity and the Unity of Isaiah', *Tarbiz* 39, 1969-70, 323-41; id., 'Two Computerized Statistical-Linguistic Texts concerning the Unity of Isaiah', *JBL* 89, 1970, 319-24.

2. The text of *The Martyrdom and Ascension of Isaiah* can be found in J.H.Charlesworth, *The Old Testament Pseudepigrapha*, London and New York 1985, 143-76. For the problem of the campaigns of Sennacherib see J.Bright, 'Le problème des campagnes de Sennacherib en Palestine', in *Hommage à W.Vischer*, Montpellier 1960, 20-31, and id., *A History of Israel*, Philadelphia and London [3]1980, 286ff., where he argues for *two* Assyrian campaigns

against southern Syria. The difficulty with this theory, which would resolve quite a few problems in the Hebrew text, is that there is no information about them or hint of them in the Assyrian annals; the theory has therefore been rejected by almost all scholars. See also B.S.Childs, *Isaiah and the Assyrian Crisis*, SBT II, 3, 1967; H.Barth, *Israel und das Assyrerreich in den nichtjesajanischen Texte des Protojesaja*, Hamburg dissertation 1974; id., *Die Jesajaworte in der Josiazeit*, Neukirchen 1977: G.T.Sheppard, 'The Anti-Assyrian Redaction and the Canonical Context of Isaiah 1-39', *JBL* 104, 1983, 193-216; M.A.Sweeney, *Isaiah 1-4 and the Post-Exilic Understanding of the Isaianic Tradition*, Berlin 1988. For the person of the prophet cf. W.Dietrich, *Jesaja und die Politik*, Munich 1976, 200, and A.Schoors, 'Isaiah. The Minister of Royal Anointment', *OTS* 20, 1977, 85-107.

The very existence of the Syro-Ephraimite war has been challenged by R.Bickert, 'König Ahas und der Prophet Jesaja. Ein Beitrag zum Problem des syrisch-ephraimitischen Krieges', *ZAW* 99, 1987, 361-83. He argues that there was no more than a plan.

3. For the composition of the book cf. J.L.Liebreich, 'The Compilation of the Book of Isaiah', *JQR* 46, 1955-56, 259-77; 47, 1956-57, 114-38; G.Fohrer, 'The Origin, Composition and Tradition of Isaiah I-XXXIX', *ALUOS* 3, 1961-2, 3-38 (with bibliography), a theory which is taken up again in his *Introduction**; H.W.Hoffmann, *Der Intention der Verkündigung Jesajas*, Berlin 1974; W.H.Schmidt, 'Die Einheit der Verkündigung Jesajas', *EvTh* 37, 1977, 260-2 (deals with the problem of the oracles of salvation); H.Barth, the two volumes cited in the previous section; R.E.Clements, 'The Prophecies of Isaiah and the Fall of Jerusalem in 587 B.C.', *VT* 30, 1980, 421-36; id., 'The Unity of the Book of Isaiah', *Int* 36, 1982, 117-29; G.T.Sheppard, 'The Anti-Assyrian Redaction and the Canonical Context of Isaiah', *JBL* 104, 1985, 193-216; the commentary by O.Kaiser cited above and his *Introduction**, 224f.; and recently M.A.Sweeney, *Isaiah 1-4 and the Post-Exilic Understanding of the Isaianic Tradition*, Berlin 1987, a volume which I have not been able to use. Cf. also K.Nielsen, 'Isa. 6:1-8:18* as a Dramatic Writing', *StTheol* 40, 1986, 1-10 and A.J.Bjørndalen, *Untersuchungen zur allegorischen Rede der Propheten Amos und Jesaja*, BZAW 165, 1985.

3a1. G.Fohrer, 'Jesaja 1 als Zusammenfassung der Verkündigung Jesajas', *ZAW* 74, 1952, 251-68 (= his *Studien zur alttestamentliche Prophetie*, BZAW 99, 1967, 148-66).

3a2. A.van den Branden, 'I gioielli delle donne di Gerusalemme', *BeO* 5, 1963, 87-94.

3a3. G.R.Williams, 'Frustrated Expectations in Isaiah V 1-7', *VT* 35, 1985, 459-65; H.Nier, 'Zur Gattung von Jesaja 5, 1-7', *BZ* 30, 1986, 99-104; K.Budde, *Jesajas Erleben*, Gotha 1928; E.Jenni, 'Jesajas Berufung und der neueren Forschung', *TZ* 15, 1959, 321-39; R.Knierim, 'The Vocation of Isaiah', *VT* 18, 1968, 47-68. Doubts on the character of the experience described as a calling were already expressed by M.M.Kaplan, 'Isaiah 6, 1-11', *JBL* 45, 1926, 251-9, and more recently by J.Milgrom, 'Did Isaiah

Prophesy during the Reign of Uzziah?', *VT* 14, 1964, 164-72, a conclusion at which I also arrived in my 1960s lectures. The final proof has been provided by O.H.Steck, 'Bemerkungen zu Jesaja 6', *BZ* 16, 1972, 188-206, and 'Rettung und Verstockung', *EvTh* 33, 1973, 77-90. See also R.Kilian, 'Der Verstockungsauftrag Jesajas', in *Bausteine biblischer Theologie. FS J.G.Botterweck*, Cologne 1977, 209-26 and K.Nielsen, 'Is. 6:1 – 8:18* as Dramatic Writing', *StTh* 40, 1986, 1-10. For Isa.7 cf. J.Lindblom, *A Study of the Immanuel Section of Isaiah*, Lund 1958; C.Dohmen, 'Das Immanuelzeichen. Ein jesajanisches Drohwort und seine intertestamentliche Rezeption', *Bibl* 68, 1987, 305-29; A.Laato, *Who is Immanuel?*, Åbo 1988. Cf. also B.Oded, 'The Historical Background of the War between Rezin and Pekah against Ahaz', *Tarbiz* 38, 1969, 205-24 (in Hebrew with an English summary); id., 'The Historical Background of the Syro-Ephraimite War Reconsidered', *CBQ* 34, 1972, 153-65; W.Zimmerli, 'Jesaja und Hiskia', in *Wort und Geschichte. FS K.Elliger*, Kevelaer-Neukirchen 1973, 199-208 (= his *Gesammelte Studien* II, 88-103); W.Berg, 'Die Identität der "jungen Frau" in Jes 7.14, 16', *BN* 13, 1980, 7-13; M.Görg, 'Hiskija als Immanuel. Plädoyer für eine typologische Identifikation', *BN* 22, 1983, 107-25. For 8.21-22 cf. K.T.Jeppesen, 'Call and Frustration. A New Understanding of Isaiah VIII 22-23', *VT* 32, 1982, 145-57. For 8.23-9.6 cf. A.Alt, 'Jesaja 8,23 -9,6', in *FS A.Bertholet*, Tübingen 1959, 29-45 (= his *Kleine Schriften* II, Munich [3]1964, 206-55); H.Reventlow, 'A Syncretistic Enthronement Oracle', *UF* 3, 1971, 321-5; with Alt, he argues for the antiquity of the pericope.

3a. For Isa.23 cf. G.Chiera, 'Isaia 23: l'elegia su Tiro', *RSF* 14, 1986, 3-19.

3b. For Isa.13.2-14.23 cf. S.Erlandsson, *The Burden of Babylon*, Lund 1970; B.Gosse, 'Un texte apocalyptique du règne de Darius; Isaie XIII,1- XIV, 23', *RB* 92, 1985, 200-22; id., *Isaïe 13,1-14.23*, Fribourg CH 1988; for Isa.19 cf. J.F.A.Sawyer, ' "Blessed Be My People Egypt", Isaiah 19,25', in *A Word in Season. FS W.McKane*, Sheffield 1986, 57-71; O.Loretz, 'Das ugaritische Topos *b'l rkb* und die "Sprache Kanaans" in Jes 19, 1-25', *UF* 19, 1987, 101-12; for Isa.21 see B.Gosse, 'Le "moi" prophétique de l'oracle contre Babylone d'Isaïe XXI, 1-10', *RB* 93, 1986, 70-84, which shows how ch.21 has been re-used in various contexts. For the whole section see G.R.Hamborg, 'Reasons for Judgement in the Oracles against the Nations of the Prophet Isaiah', *VT* 31, 1981, 145-59.

3c. G.Fohrer, 'Der Aufbau der Apokalypse des Jesajabuches (Jesaja 24-27)', *CBQ* 25, 1963, 34-45 (= his *Studien...*, 170-81; he dates the apocalypse in the fifth century); M.-L.Henry, *Glaubenskrise und Glaubensbewahrung in der Dichtung der Jesaja-Apokalypse*, Stuttgart 1967; R.J.Coggins, 'The Problem of Isaiah 24-27', *ExpT* 90, 1978-79, 328-33; J.Day, 'A Case of Inner-Scriptural Interpretation', *JTS* 31, 1980, 309-19. For the identification of the cities cf. R.Hanhart, 'Die jahwefeindliche Stadt', in *Beiträge zur alttestamentlichen Theologie, FS W.Zimmerli*, Göttingen 1977, 152-63. For the problem of the resurrection in this section cf. J.F.A.Sawyer, 'Hebrew Words for the Resurrection of the Dead', *VT* 23, 1973, 218-34.

3d. J.C.Exum, 'Of Broken Pots, Fluttering Birds and Visions in the Night...', *CBQ* 83, 1981, 331-52.

3f. B.S.Childs, *Isaiah and the Assyrian Crisis*, SBT II 3, 1967; R.F.Melugin, *The Formation of Isaiah 40-55*, BZAW 141, 1976; G.Garbini, 'Il bilinguismo dei Giudei', *Vicino Oriente* 3, Rome 1980, 209-23; R.E.Clements, *Isaiah and the Deliverance of Jerusalem*, Sheffield 1980; P.R.Ackroyd, 'Isaiah 36-39: Structure and Function' (1982), in his *Studies in the Religious Tradition of the Old Testament*, London 1987, 105-20; A.Catastini, 'Le varianti greche di Isaia 36-39', *Egitto e Vicino Oriente* 6, Pisa 1983, 209-34; K.A.D.Smelik, 'Distortion of Prophecy. The Purpose of Isaiah xxxvi and xxxvii', *OTS* 24, 1986, 70-93. Cf. also J.Begrich, *Der Psalm des Hiskia*, Göttingen 1926; J.A.Soggin, 'Il "Salmo di Ezechia" in Isaia 38,9-20', *BeO* 16, 1974, 177-81.

4. K.Budde, 'Zu Jesaja 1-4', *ZAW* 49, 1931, 16-40, 182-211; T.C.Vriezen, 'Essentials of the Theology of Isaiah', in B.W.Anderson and W.Harrelson (eds.), *Israel's Prophetic Heritage*, New York and London 1962, 128-46; R.Fey, *Amos und Jesaja*, WMANT 12, 1963; G.Fohrer, 'Wandlungen Jesajas', in *FS W.Eilers*, Wiesbaden 1967, 58-71 (= his *Studien 1966-72*, 11-23); W.Zimmerli, 'Verkündigung und Sprache in der Botschaft Jesajas', in *Fides et Communicatio*, *FS M.Doerne*, Göttingen 1970, 441-54 (= his *Gesammelte Studien* II, 73-87); R.L.Melugin, 'The Conventional and the Creative in Isaiah's Judgement Oracles', *CBQ* 36, 1974, 301-11; for the 'remnant' cf. above 17.9d.

21

MICAH

1. The name and the man

The name of the prophet, in Hebrew *mīkā-yāhū*, means 'Who is like YHWH?' It occurs relatively frequently in the Hebrew Bible: we know of at least one other prophet of the same name, Micaiah ben Imlah (I Kings 22; cf. above, 17.9c). There are some variants of the name; the prophet usually appears under the short form *mīkā'*. He came from Moresheth Gath, present-day *tell el-jehudeide* (coord.141-115), south-west of Jerusalem, according to the most common identification. According to the superscription he lived under kings Jotham, Ahaz and Hezekiah (1.1), and was thus a contemporary of Isaiah. That he lived under the last of these kings is confirmed by Jer.26.18, a passage intended to clear the prophet of the charge of blasphemy, though it is a redactional passage. The argument here cites the 'precedent' of Micah, who also preached against the temple. But the authenticity of this passage is in question (below, 23.1b).

The considerable proportion of messages about social problems, a feature which is not absent from Isaiah, even if it is not of primary importance there, has suggested the possibility that Micah originally belonged to the class of free Israelite countryfolk who lived on tribal lands and then fell on hard times following the new economic situation which came into being with the rise of the monarchy (above, 17.8aff). In that case there would be some points of contact between Micah and Amos: both come from an agricultural setting, and both have a strong social element in their message. Micah's ministry seems to be directed exclusively towards Jerusalem, and contemporaneity with and geographical closeness to Isaiah could explain certain similarities in the language and message of the two prophets; both know the oracle in Micah 4.1-4/Isa.2.2-5 and the idea of the 'remnant', but there are also real parallels: Micah 2.1-5 and Isa.5.8ff.; Micah 5.9-14 and Isa.2.6ff., etc.

The object and audience for Micah's invective, in addition to the rich oppressors, are the priests and the prophets who exercise their ministry unworthily, the Canaanite element in state religion and the false security which it helped to create: the feeling of having done one's duty and therefore being able to contemplate the future with equanimity.

2. Content

The text of Micah can readily be divided into four parts: chs.1-3, threats; chs.4-5, promises; chs.6.1-7.6, more threats; 7.7-20, more promises. This form is sufficient evidence of a redaction. For a long time there was a tendency to consider the oracles of salvation inauthentic because, it was argued, a prophet could not logically first announce judgment and then contradict himself by announcing salvation. On the other hand, if we reflect that we have a collection of oracles which probably extend over many years, the argument does not have the strength that it might seem to have at first sight. In reality the problem is much more complex, as we shall see in the next section, and the Uppsala school rightly asked whether the distinction between authentic and inauthentic oracles still has any meaning.

(a) Judgment (chs.1-3). In 1.2-7 we have a threat against the kingdom of Israel, later adapted to Judah by means of an addition (v.5b). We might therefore think, at least in principle, of a text earlier than 722-720, which was then adapted to the situation in Judah after the fall of the north. In 1.8-16 we have a lament against Judah, probably on the occasion of the Assyrian invasion under Sennacherib in 701. Chapters 2-3 which give the reasons for the judgment are more difficult to date: 2.1-5 is addressed to avaricious landowners, 2.6-11 to the enemies of the prophet, while 2.12-13 speaks of the assembling of the scattered exiles of Israel and their return and is therefore an exception in a context which speaks throughout of judgment. 3.1-4 is against unjust judges, and 3.5-8 against false prophets. In 3.9-12 the priests and prophets are the object of Micah's invective, and there is a divine threat to destroy the temple of Jerusalem; however, this passage is doubtful, as I have already indicated: Jer.26.18 dates it in the time of Hezekiah. Those who accept its authenticity note the great impression it must have made, since around a century later it could be quoted in a court as a reason for acquittal in such an important case.

(b) Promises, chs.4-5. In 4.1-5, as I have already indicated, we have a passage parallel to Isa.2.1-4 with an additional verse. 4.6-8 speaks of the return from the diaspora and the inauguration of the kingdom of God in Jerusalem, cf. *inter alia* Ezek.34; this is therefore certainly a passage later than the eighth century BCE and is not to be dated before the exile. 4.9-14 speaks of the destruction of the enemy before Jerusalem and v.10 is an insertion which identifies these enemies with the Babylonians; that it is an insertion emerges clearly from the fact that 'there' in the second half does not refer to Babylon but to the 'fields' which precede the mention of it. Discounting v.10, it would not be at all strange for the text to contain a reference to the headlong retreat of the Assyrians from Jerusalem in 701; but if v.10 is an integral part of the context, we would have a section which could not be dated before the exile. In 5.1-5 [EVV 2-6] we have a famous passage which speaks of the birth of the Messiah at Bethlehem; however, the locality cannot be identified clearly, as the text is uncertain. Most authors in fact suggest that the term *leḥem* should be deleted and that we should simply read *bēt 'eprāt*. In any case, it would seem certain that the author meant to speak of Bethlehem and that the addition, if that is what it is, is at least correct. Because of the explicit mention of Assyria in vv.4-5, the passage presents a problem not unlike that of Isa.9.1ff.; 11.1ff. 5.6-8 [EVV 7-9] is a promise of victory for the remnant of Jacob; it is probably exilic (it is difficult to date it before that), while 5.9-14 [EVV 10-15] speaks of the elimination of the horses, the magic and the syncretistic cult which, like Isa.2.7; 31.1ff., this text considers to be symbols of human rebellion against God. It is possible that this too is an oracle against Judah, adapted at a later time to a new situation and therefore perhaps originally authentic: could it refer to Hezekiah's reform and then have been adapted to that of Josiah?

Both the authenticity and the chronology of this section in particular are problematical. The main difficulties were noted for the first time in two articles by B.Stade, 'Bemerkungen über das Buch Micha', *ZAW* 1,1881, 161-72 and 'Weitere Bemerkungen zu Micha 4.5', *ZAW* 3, 1883, 1-16. He denied that any of the text after ch.4 was authentic. B.Renaud has more recently argued that the whole of this section should not be dated earlier than the fifth century BCE, thus making it a 'Deutero-Micah'. There are stylistic and lexicographical reasons for assigning the section to this period, though it should be noted that the text is too short for an in-depth examination. So it is not surprising that other modern scholars have defended the authenticity even of much of this section. For details see the bibliographical studies of K.T.Jeppesen, cited at § 1 below; it is enough to mention here the commentary by W.Rudolph (who considers only 4.1-4; 5.7-9 [EVV 8-10] and 7.8-20 inauthentic) and the study by A.S.van der Woude, cited below, § 2, who considers chs.1-5 to be substantially authentic; according to him chs.6-7 are inauthentic in that here we have an anonymous prophet from the kingdom of Israel who will have worked a few years before the fall of Samaria in 722-20. At all events the divergence among so many authors cannot be taken lightly, and is one element against an automatic acceptance of authenticity.

(c) Judgment (6.1-7.6). 6.1-8 is a speech by YHWH in the course of a trial of his people, an image dear to many prophets. Like a great Eastern king, and in a trial quite unlike any modern legal proceedings, YHWH combines in his person the functions of prosecutor, plaintiff and judge. In the course of the speech he argues that the people have violated their pledges, while he, Yahweh, has kept them faithfully. The term b⁽rīt does not appear, but the concept of covenant seems to be present. Verse 7 could allude to the practice of human sacrifice, that is if the question is not meant purely rhetorically. Biblical historiography connects the practice of human sacrifice with the reign of Manasseh, but we have no indication that Micah's ministry extended into the seventh century. So this feature, along with the presupposition of the concept of covenant implicit in the text, could be the sign of a late redaction, in the exilic or post-exilic period. In 6.9-16 we have a tirade against the avarice and dishonesty prevalent in Jerusalem, while 7.1-6 laments the decadence of the people of God.

(d) Promises (7.7-20). This passage brings the book to an end with what has been called a 'prophetic liturgy'. There are many features in it which take us far beyond the time of the prophet: in v.11 the walls of Jerusalem have fallen in ruins, and that would take us beyond 587/6, if not down to the time of Nehemiah (cf.Neh.1.1ff; 2.1ff.). Scholars have also tried (T.Lescow, art. cit.) to date this section to the time of the Samaritan schism, thus producing even a 'Trito-Micah'.

3. Thought

The complexity of the redaction of a relatively brief work and the difficulties of dating a number of passages, some of which are certainly late and others of which are the subject of argument, makes it difficult to identify a single line of thought. As J.L.Mays rightly observed in his commentary, the treatment of which I am following here, determining Micah's thought clearly depends on whether or not particular sayings are attributed to the prophet. These difficulties have been common knowledge since they were pointed out for the first time in 1881 and 1883 by B.Stade, but they have not been unanimously accepted by all scholars, as we saw in the previous section. At the beginning of the 1940s and then at the beginning of the 1950s two distinguished scholars, T.H.Robinson and A.Weiser, came to the conclusion that despite everything the greater part of the material had to be considered authentic. However, for Mays there is a criterion for the evaluation of the authenticity of the various texts which was put forward by the prophet himself in 3.5-8, the last verse of which reads: 'But as for me, I am filled with power, with the Spirit of the Lord, and with justice and might, to declare to Jacob his transgression and to Israel his sin.' In this text the mention of the 'spirit of the Lord' is usually considered a later addition in that it interrupts the list of the properties which the prophet claims to possess, among which it is impossible to number the spirit. According to Mays, none of this can be reconciled with this declaration, so virtually all chs.4-7 must be considered inauthentic. If this criterion proved valid, it would simplify hypotheses like 'Deutero-Micah' (not to mention 'Trito-Micah'). As for the authentic material, this would then have been partly reused during the Babylonian invasion (we have seen one example of that already), while chs.4-5 contain oracles of salvation which came into being during the exile. By contrast chs.6-7 are different collections of various sayings which also are not prior to the exile.

Here, too, we see applied to God the categories of justice which we already know from the books of Amos and Isaiah; this is justice not understood as a philosophical or theological ideal but as a specific element in the sphere of inter-personal relationships. Historically it is expressed in the pledges which bind one person to another, even if the term *berit* is not present. That such motives are present to a greater degree in Micah than in the other prophets was argued in 1959 by Beyerlin, and his reasons are impressive. However, the argument seems to point, rather, to a late dating of the sections in which these elements appear.

In the book of Micah, too, social injustice appears as the most obvious evidence of the spiritual situation in which the people find themselves, and to them the prophet proclaims the divine judgment which is a consequence of God's justice (3.8); again, in this passage the prophet introduces himself as one aware of being the representative of this just and judging God. The people delude themselves that they have done their duty, and that therefore God is automatically with them (3.11), aided in this belief by the preaching of the 'false' prophets. But since it should be evident to anyone that the situation is the opposite of what God desires for his people, the prophet is called to pronounce the only message possible, that of judgment. Confronted with an announcement of this kind, the only attitude of the people can be (or better, should have been, since these are probably later reflections) that indicated in 6.8ff.

For the prophet the events of 701 BCE must have been historical verification of his own message; for the later redaction the events of 597 and 587/86 must have been the final proof: that the end was near and that the insights of the prophetic preaching had been correct.

BIBLIOGRAPHY

Commentaries

Cf. the commentaries on the twelve minor prophets listed under Amos, along with A.George, JB, ³1960; J.L.Mays, OTL, 1976; D.R.Hillers, Hermeneia, 1984.

1. For the whole work: J.T.Willis, 'The Structure of the Book of Micah', *SEÅ* 34, 1969, 5-52; K.T.Jeppesen, 'New Aspects of Micah Research', *JSOT* 8, 1978, 2-32, and 'How the Book of Micah Lost its Integrity', *StTh* 33, 1979, 101-31; J.de Waard, 'Vers une identification des participants dans le livre de Michée', *RHPR* 59, 1979, 509-16.

2. For the text cf. I.Willi-Plein, *Vorformen der Schriftexegese innerhalb des Alten Testaments*, Berlin 1971. For 'Deutero-Micah' see B.Renaud, *Structure et attaches littéraires de Michée IV-V*, Paris 1962, and *La formation du livre de Michée*, Paris 1977; for chs.6-7 an early date has been defended by A.S.van der Woude, 'Deutero-Michea; ein Prophet aus Nordisrael', *NTT* 25, 1971, 365-78 (note the different use of the term Deutero-Micah by these two scholars); a late date has been argued for by T.Lescow, 'Redaktionsgeschichtliche Analyse von Michea 6-7', *ZAW* 84, 1972, 182-212. See also the article cited in the previous paragraph by J.de Waard and that of van der Woude, along with W.R.McFadden, 'Micah and the Problem of Continuities and Discontinuities', in W.W.Hallo et al. (ed.), *Scripture in Context* II, Winona Lake, Ind. 1983, 127-46. Cf. further C.S.Shaw, 'Micah 1:10-16 Reconsidered', *JBL* 106, 1987, 223-9. For Micah 3.12 see now J.M.Vincent, 'Michas Gerichtswort gegen Zion (3, 12) in seinem Kontext', *ZTK* 83, 1986, 167-87. He agrees that it is a late text.

3. W.Beyerlin, *Die Kulttraditionen in der Verkündigung des Propheten Micha*, Göttingen 1959 (who argues for a decidedly early date and defends the

authenticity of the whole book); J.L.Mays, 'The Theological Purpose of the Book of Micah', in *Beiträge zur alttestamentlichen Theologie. FS W.Zimmerli*, Göttingen 1977, 276-87; A.S.van der Woude, 'Three Classical Prophets: Amos, Hosea and Micah', in *Israel's Prophetic Tradition. Essays... P.R.Ackroyd*, Cambridge 1982, 48-53.

22

NAHUM, HABAKKUK AND ZEPHANIAH

1. Nahum

(*a*) The individual and the content of his work. The name Nahum could be theophoric in origin: *neḥūm-yāh, 'the one comforted by YHWH'; the prophet is connected with Elkosh, but we do not know where it was or even whether it was his home (1.1). From Hellenistic times onwards a number of places and tombs have been associated with the name of the prophet (the best-known of these is the Capernaum of the time of Jesus): this is a sign that even then nothing was known about his origins, his life and his death.

The book bears the superscription *maśśāʿ*, which was examined in 20.3 above. In the intention of the redactor, therefore, it is a 'charge', an oracle against someone, in fact the city of Nineveh, capital of Assyria. Indeed the whole book is a collection of invectives against Assyria, beginning with the alphabetic acrostic in 1.2-10, which can be followed accurately only down to the letter *lamed*. In 1.10-2.3 [EVV 2] we seem to have two compositions which are different and yet complementary, and have now been combined: an oracle of salvation for Judah (1.12-13; 2.1,3 [EVV 2]) and an announcement of judgment on Assyria (1.10-11,13; 2.2 [EVV 1]). The two compositions are different literary genres, but they fit together, since the liberation of Judah, which at that time was a vassal of Assyria, was only possible once Assyria had been considerably weakened. The announcement of judgment on Nineveh follows in 2.2-14 [EVV 3-15]: the imagery chosen is that of an enemy attack on the place. 3.1-7 gives a second oracle against Nineveh; the city will be destroyed because of its many sins. This attitude recalls that adopted, albeit in a more general way, by Isa.10.5ff. In 3.8-17 a similar fate is announced for Nineveh to that of No-amon in Egypt: this last name is the contemporary Hebrew term for Thebes, which was conquered and sacked by the Assyrians in 663. The prophecy ends with a sarcastic funeral lament on the situation of Nineveh after its destruction, a cause of joy for the people who had been oppressed or terrorized by Assyria.

(b) The date and period of Nahum are therefore easy to determine: the time is after 663, the year in which the Assyrians sacked Thebes (3.8f.); on the other hand, while Assyria is decadent and considerably weakened, it has not yet fallen, even if it is severely threatened. The situation is such that the prophet can announce its fall any minute. This puts us either in 625, when the city was invested and besieged by the Medes, or in 612, when it fell after being besieged by a coalition of Medes and Babylonians.

(c) The text is of remarkable quality in chs.2-3, but falls off in ch.1, which, as we have seen, is also incomplete; here the style, too, is very different. This might seem disconcerting in such a short work, and various explanations have been sought for it, but none of them commands general approval. Until relatively recently many scholars denied the authenticity of the acrostic, and R.H.Pfeiffer* even dated it in the second century BCE. The Scandinavian school tried to discover in the book a ritual for the mythical struggle between YHWH and Tammuz, which ended with the victory of the former; the whole passage would thus be constructed from formulae and expressions taken from the liturgies of the two deities. However, here too we have no more than pointers.

(d) The thought of Nahum has always been of particular interest. Following the studies of P.Humbert, it has been considered almost unanimously to be the isolated expression of one of those prophets who proclaimed an optimistic nationalist message and gave so much trouble to their colleagues, who were more critical and therefore more pessimistic about the future of the people. Micah, whom we have already examined, and (as we shall see) Jeremiah and Ezekiel in particular fall into the latter category. This theory, as we have seen, recalls Isa.10.5ff., so that it is not clear whether that passage should be the key to reading the text. Jeremias has taken a different course and suggests that the second part of the work should be considered to be dependent on Deutero-Isaiah, while the first, which is probably the fragment of a psalm, escapes all investigations. That would also substantially change the dating of the work, which, while it makes reference to events in the Assyrian period, was composed long afterwards. Moreover Nahum, too, whether we regard him as a 'nationalistic' prophet or understand the book as the product of later composition, takes up a theme dear to the prophets, that of divine intervention in history, and in this sense it bears witness to the work of YHWH, which embraces the actions of the great powers of the period: Assyria, Media and Babylonia, and also Egypt, which is mentioned indirectly. In any case the problem of the book cannot be said to have been resolved; even the character of the work is not clear, since the acceptance of Humbert's theory is no longer as general as it once was. In this area a decision has to be taken which will only be possible after further studies.

2. Habakkuk

(a) The name of the prophet has not been transmitted in an agreed form: in Hebrew it appears as $ḥ^abaqqūq$ (perhaps from the Akkadian *habbaqūqu*, a garden plant, maybe *Cassia tora*, cf. *AHw* I, 304), but in Greek as *Ambakoum*; we know nothing about his person, nor is anything known about the origin of this important document. Be this as it may, here we have a visionary prophet whose relationship with the word of God, whether perceived or preached, appears somewhat tenuous (Keller); 2.1-3 give some important details about the circumstances connected with the visionary inspiration of the prophet, while 3.16 mentions physical phenomena which accompanied the vision. According to Jeremias's study, which I mentioned in connection with Nahum, Habakkuk will have been the true cultic prophet.

The book readily divides into two parts: chs.1-2 and ch.3. In 1.2-4 we have a lament by the prophet (according to some, by the community, but that seems improbable) over the problem of the power of the wicked; this is the ancient problem of theodicy which we shall examine in more detail when studying the book of Job (below, 37). In 1.5-11 it is announced that YHWH is stirring up the Chaldaeans (a term used for the Babylonians from the first quarter of the first millennium BCE onwards), and their irresistible power is described. A second lamentation begins in 1.12-17: despite God's judgment on the wicked, he will allow them to act evilly against the just. In 2.1-3 there is a description of the prophet's preparations to receive a vision, followed by an order to write it down; 2.4-5 contains a new curse against the wicked, followed by the famous phrase which has perhaps been the object of more passionate theological discussion than any other, and is quoted by Paul in Rom.1.7; Gal.3.11. However, while Paul's interpretation (which follows the LXX translation) is limited to considering faith as the proper attitude towards God, the present text goes further: it also describes the waiting in trust which is prompted by God himself. 2.6-20 contains a threat in five strophes, each introduced by 'woe to', a formula typically used to introduce this literary genre. It does not appear clearly from the text what the prophet's aim is in pronouncing this invective; therefore some scholars see it directed against the corrupt ruling classes of Jerusalem, while others regard it as oracles originally directed against Assyria and then re-utilized against Babylon. The text concludes with a liturgical composition.

The second part of the book is composed of ch.3, a hymn which is no different from similar compositions in the Psalter, with strong archaic or archaizing features. The theme is an appearance of YHWH and the description recalls similar compositions like Deut.33.1; Judg.5.1; Ps.68.1. YHWH is acclaimed as he comes to the help of his people and destroys the wicked. As in the Psalms, the term *selāh* appears in the composition; it is of uncertain meaning and could be evidence of the liturgical use of the text. According to W.F.Albright, the work is divided into four originally independent parts. Verses 1-2 are a very old prayer for the preservation of life, perhaps that of the king, with a Yahwistic-type addition by means of which the text will have been adapted to the faith of Israel. This is a text which might be argued to be of Canaanite origin. We also already have compositions of this kind in Mesopotamia, at the time of the Third Dynasty of Ur (beginning of the second millennium BCE). Verses 3-7, too, are a very old text: they speak of the appearance of YHWH who comes from the desert in the south-east, as already in Deut.33.2ff.; Judg.5.3ff. Again according to Albright, the date should be put around the eleventh century BCE. The third part, vv.8-12, is the Israelite adaptation of a Canaanite poem which celebrated the victory of Ba'al over River and Sea (primordial chaotic elements, cf. in Israel Gen.1.2) and Death (which in the summer, after the death of Ba'al, takes control of the world and reigns in his stead). But now everything seems to be applied to the person of YHWH, who is also victor over these elements, and there is no sign that the final redactor was aware of these adaptations. It is interesting to note that the storm which, as elsewhere, accompanies the manifestation of YHWH, does not come from the south-west, as is usual in the region, but from the north-west, and is therefore an unusual phenomenon. For vv.10ff. cf. Ps.77.17ff. Verse 13 mentions the king as the 'anointed' of David, which shows that the final redaction comes from a relatively late stage of the tradition, even if it is certainly earlier than the exile. Finally, from v.14 to the end we have a composition which recalls those of the pre-exilic prophets and therefore has no particular archaic features. The Norwegian scholar S.Mowinckel has opposed this division and evaluation of Hab.3, arguing that the composition is a unitary one. Some comments at least need to be made on Albright's evaluation of the composition: first of all the archaic language is typical of all kinds of poetry (in Israel this can continue down to Ecclesiasticus, at the end of the second century BCE), so it need not be an indication of antiquity; again, the presence of Canaanite elements is quite obvious throughout the pre-exilic period and even later, so that this element, too, cannot be used for dating the text; finally, the divisions suggested produce a series of texts so short that it becomes problematical to use them for any purposes at all. So the whole question needs to be studied again, and some scholars have already produced works on parts of the composition.

(b) The time of Habakkuk. It is not easy to date a book like this, where even the precise name of the supposed author has not been clearly transmitted, and in which there is no reference to specific historical events, which is what we have in Nahum. Even the category of the wicked and the impious, mentioned many times, cannot be identified – there are those who think of people in Judah and others who consider the wicked to be the Assyrians: logically one explanation does not exclude the other. The mention of the Chaldaeans is particularly interesting: first of all, if we leave out the late topographical mention in the Abraham cycle (Ur of the Chaldaeans, Gen.11.28-31; 15.7) this is the first mention of this people in the Hebrew Bible; moreover, it appears on the horizon of Israel and Judah for the very first time after the brief episode of the embassy to Hezekiah (II Kings 20.12-19/Isa.39.1ff.). This mention could be a useful feature for dating the book did not the passage give the clear impression of having been interpolated into its present context (cf. 1.5-11 with 1.2-4,12-17); besides, there is no reason to suppose that what goes for the other prophets does not go for Habakkuk, namely that the books attributed to individuals are anthologies of originally independent texts. The vision announced by ch.2 could describe the annihilation of the wicked, but that does not happen; A.Weiser felt this so strongly that he argued that ch.3 could only be the conclusive intervention of YHWH in this sense. Be this as it may, if the mention of the Chaldaeans can be used as an element in dating, it would point to the second half and probably the last quarter of the seventh century BCE and make it probable that the wicked are in fact the Assyrians. However, we cannot exclude the alternative, that the Babylonians are those who are charged to exercise judgment on the wicked of Judah, which would put the passage between the two extremes of 612 and 587/6 BCE. The theory of B.Duhm, who wanted to put the whole book in the time of Alexander the Great, i.e. towards the end of the fourth century BCE, is no longer taken up: first of all it is based on an emendation of *kaśdīm* (Chaldaeans) to *kittīm* (Westerners generally, first the Hellenists, then the Romans) in 1.6; however, quite apart from being arbitrary interference with the text, this emendation does not solve anything: the name is attested on the ostraka of Tell 'Arad, cf. below, Appendix 1.10, and could therefore well refer to facts of the period to which the prophet is traditionally dated.

(*c*) The thought of Habakkuk is similar to that of Nahum. Here the divine justice appears as the motive force in history and is vividly represented at work in ch.3. The problem of theodicy appears on the periphery, but without being dealt with in depth. The theophany is clearly the central element of the text. The fact that other peoples are mentioned, but not Judah, could be a nationalistic feature, as has been recently argued; in any case, however, this is not chauvinism, nor is there the note of false optimism which we know to have been typical of some of those who were considered 'false' prophets.

3. Zephaniah

(*a*) The individual and his time. A genealogy at the beginning of the book traces the prophet back over four generations to a certain Hezekiah. Is this the king of the same name, and does it mean that the prophet will have belonged to the royal house of Judah? It is impossible to say. Now a superscription dates the book to the time of Josiah. But this dating presents problems: the religious situation presented by the book is catastrophic; hence we can either date the book to the time of Josiah but before the reform, or we can assign it a date under his successor Jehoiakim under whom much of the reform was reversed. In any case, the prophet is to be put between Nahum and Jeremiah, or is a contemporary of the second period of the latter's activity.

(*b*) Content and composition. Chapter 1 speaks of the judgment which is coming on Judah because of its sin. We have two narratives on the coming of the 'day of the Lord', which has already been mentioned: 1.7,14-18, a text which forms the basis for the mediaeval hymn *Dies irae*, in use in the Roman Catholic liturgy, and 2.1-3, where the just are exhorted, rather, to seek Yahweh, to repent and be saved 'in that day'. 2.4-15 contains threats and curses against neighbouring peoples, while 3.1-13 is directed against Jerusalem and its leading class, the object of imminent judgment, the instrument of which will be the pagan nations. Only a 'remnant' of the humble will escape, while the proud will perish. 3.14-20 is an exhortation to Jerusalem to strike up a hymn of joy to YHWH, the king who will restore the scattered people of Judah.

The pattern of the book is therefore identical to what we have seen in other prophetic books: judgment against Judah and Jerusalem, oracles against the nations and finally an announcement of salvation. This schematic character suggests a redaction, but we have no information about it. In 3.15ff. we have elements which reappear in Ezek.34; 35; 37. Here and there we have traces of revision, but much of the book seems to be authentic, except for 3.14-20, which presupposes the diaspora.

(c) The thought of Zephaniah follows the patterns detected in Amos and Isaiah: at its centre is the expectation of the coming of the terrible 'day of YHWH' (cf. Amos 5.18ff.; Isa.2.7ff.); the doctrine of the remnant also has precedents in Amos, Isaiah, and Micah, to which the reader should refer.

BIBLIOGRAPHY

Commentaries

In addition to the commentaries on the twelve minor prophets listed under Amos see M.Bič, *Trois prophètes dans un temps de ténèbres: Sophonie – Nahum – Habaquq*, Paris 1968.

1. On Nahum

Commentary: A.George, JB ²1959. Cf. also K.J.Cathcart, *Nahum in the Light of North West Semitic*, Rome 1973 (only philological).

Monographs: P.Humbert, 'Essais d'analyse de Nahoum 1,2-2,3', *ZAW* 44, 1926, 266-80; id., 'Essai d'analyse de Nahoum 2,4-11', *AfO* 5, 1928-29, 14-19; 'Le problème du livre de Nahoum', *RHPR* 12, 1932, 1-15; these articles have been influential in study of the book right down to the present day. Cf. also C.A.Keller, 'Die theologische Bewältigung der geschichtlichen Wirklichkeit in der Prophetie Nahums', *VT* 22, 1972, 399-419; H.Schulz, *Das Buch Nahum*, Berlin 1973. For the myth and ritual interpretation cf. A.Haldar, *Studies in the Book of Nahum*, Oslo 1947. Humbert's interpretation is criticized by J.Jeremias, *Kultprophetie und Geschichtsverkündigung in der späten Königszeit*, Neukirchen 1970, 11ff., 48ff. Cf. also A.S.van der Woude, 'The Book of Nahum: A Letter Written in Exile', *OTS* 20, 1977, 108-26, who argues that the work will have been written in the north under Assyrian occupation; also K.J.Cathcart, 'More Philological Studies in Nahum', *JNWSL* 7, 1979, 1-12; B.Renaud, 'La composition du livre de Nahum', *ZAW* 99, 1987, 198-219; D.L.Christensen, 'The Acrostic of Nahum Once Again. A Prosodic Analysis of Nahum 1, 1-10', ibid., 409-15; C.Begg, 'The Non-Mention of Zephaniah, Nahum and Habakkuk in the Deuteronomistic History', *BN* 38/39, 1987, 19-35.

2. On Habakkuk

Commentaries: B.Duhm, 1906; J.Trinquet, JB²1959. Monographs: P.Humbert, *Problèmes du livre de Habacuc*, Neuchâtel 1944 (a basic study); J.Jeremias, op.cit, 55ff., 108ff.; P.Jöcken, *Das Buch Habakkuk*, Cologne and Bonn 1977 (a bibliographical study); cf. also C.A.Keller, 'Die Eigenart der Prophetie Habakuks', *ZAW* 85, 1973, 156-67 (on its visionary character); W.M.Brownlee, 'The Composition of Habakkuk', in *Hommages à M.André Dupont-Sommer*, Paris 1971, 255-75; E.Otto, 'Die Stellung der Wehe-Worte in der Verkündigung des Propheten Habakuk', *ZAW* 85, 1973, 73-107 (both on the 'woes' announced); for the text 2.4-5 cf. S.Schreiner, 'Erwägungen zum Text von Hab.2.4-5', *ZAW* 86, 1974, 538-42; J.A.Emerton, 'The Textual and Linguistic Problems of Habakkuk II 4-5', *JTS* 28, 1977, 1-18; for 2.2-4 cf. J.G.Janzen, 'Habakkuk 2,2-4 in the Light of Recent Philological Advances', *HTR* 73, 1980, 53-78; for ch.3 cf. W.F.Albright, 'The Psalm of Habakkuk', in H.H.Rowley (ed.), *Studies in Old Testament Prophecy presented to T.H.Robinson*, Edinburgh 1950, 1-18; S.Mowinckel, 'Zum Psalm des Habakuk', *TZ* 9, 1953, 1-23 (against Albright); J.H.Eaton, 'The Origin and Meaning of Habakkuk 3', *ZAW* 76, 1964, 144-71; S.Margulis, 'The Psalm of Habakkuk: A Reconstruction and Interpretation', *ZAW* 82, 1970, 409-42; S.I.L.Norin, *Er spaltete das Meer*, Lund 1977, 159-61. For various topics cf. also J.G.Janzen, 'Eschatological Symbol and Existence in Habakkuk', *VT* 35, 1985, 274-95; B.Peckham, 'The Vision of Habakkuk', *CBQ* 48, 1986, 617-36; A.H.J.Gunneweg, 'Habakkuk und das Problem des leidenden *ṣdq*', *ZAW* 98, 1986, 400-14. For the Akkadian etymology see J.Hobbins, 'Il nome del profeta Abacuc', *RiBib* 35, 1987, 307-11. Cf. also the article by C.Begg cited above. For the Qumran text (1 QpHab) cf. M.Burrows, *The Dead Sea Scrolls of the St Mark's Monastery* 1, New Haven 1950.

3. On Zephaniah

Commentaries: A.George, JB ²1959; L.Sabottka, *Zephanja. Versuch einer Neuübersetzung mit philologischem Kommentar*, Rome 1972 (philological).

Monographs: G.Langohr, 'Rédaction et composition du livre de Sophonie', *Le Muséon* 89, Louvain 1976, 51-73; A.M.Gozzo, 'Il profeta Sofonia e la dottrina teologica del suo libro', *Angelicum* 52, Rome 1977, 3-37; K.Seybold, 'Die Verwendung von Bildmotiven in der Prophetie Zefanjas', in H.Weippert, K.Seybold and M.Weippert, *Beiträge zur prophetischen Bildsprache in Israel und Assyrien*, OBO 64, Fribourg CH 1985, 30-

54; D.L.Christensen, 'Zephaniah 2:4-15: a Theological Base for Josiah's Program of Political Expansion', *CBQ* 46, 1984, 669-82; R.Gordis, 'A Rising Tide of Misery; A Note on Zephaniah II 4', *VT* 37, 1987, 487-90; and the article by C.Begg cited above.

23

JEREMIAH

1. Life and work

Jeremiah stands out among the prophets, as we have already seen (above, 17.4e), for the number of biographical notes in the text. Some of them appear to be autobiographical and some are collected by third parties. The information which is given is also concerned with the inner conflicts of the prophet, and at first sight this seems to give us a privileged view of the personal, inner element which went with the prophetic ministry and sometimes conditioned it. These latter passages are sometimes called, improperly, 'Jeremiah's confessions'; in reality, they are material which, as we shall see, has been evaluated in different ways.

Traditionally three periods are distinguished in Jeremiah's life. The first is during the reign of Josiah, in the thirteenth year of which the prophet is said to have received his calling; depending on the chronology followed, this is either 626-5 or 627-6. This period must have lasted more or less up to the period of the reform, 622/21. The second period was in the reign of Jehoiakim, probably from its beginning, i.e. from 609 onwards. The last period was in the interregnum between the first fall of Jerusalem in 597 and the second fall in 587 or 586, with the events which followed: a group of rebels against the Babylonian occupation of the region, having killed the governor appointed by the occupying power, carried Jeremiah off with them when they took refuge in Egypt. For want of any other information, it is assumed that he must have died there.

During the Second World War the North American scholar J.P.Hyatt put forward a different theory on the beginning of the prophet's ministry and this has been taken up in modified form by some modern scholars: the prophet is said to have been *born* in the thirteenth year of King Josiah, which would make his ministry begin only around 615. And according to N.Lohfink and C.Levin, Jeremiah's ministry will have begun under King Jehoiakim, while the previous period is only a creation of the redaction. If this theory holds, as seems to be increasingly probable, a series of problems which we shall consider in due course would be automatically resolved.

(a) The first period (under Josiah)

Jeremiah was born into a family of priests at Anathoth, near present-day 'anāta, a few miles north of Jerusalem; the place has kept its old name in Arabic. There is no information about the date of his birth, but it is traditionally put around the middle of the seventh century. An indirect piece of information that we have is the prophet's youth at the time of his calling: when the call comes the prophet replies 'I am too young' (better than 'I am a boy', though that rendering is philologically possible). However, this information is rather vague, since rather than speaking of his age the prophet is evading the call by saying that he is not mature enough for his words to be listened to; the theme is therefore his authority as a preacher. We know nothing of his family, but the mention of the priesthood of Anathoth suggests that he is descended from those priestly followers of Abiathar whom Solomon had confined to that area because they had supported his rival Adonijah (I Kings 2.26). So it is not strange that the prophet was destined for the priesthood from his childhood: that would also explain how he could speak freely in the Jerusalem temple. The thirteenth year of Josiah is given as the date of his calling in 1.1 and 25.3 and seems to be an element attested by the tradition, though it does cause the problems indicated earlier.

The words addressed to the prophet in the act of his calling characterize well enough what his ministry is to be in the years to come: he is to 'pluck up and break down, to destroy and to overthrow, but also to build and plant' (1.10), in other words principally to announce judgment (four verbs out of six) but also to proclaim an alternative to destruction. We know nothing about the relationship between the prophet and Josiah's reform, and we shall return to the subject in due course.

A mission like that of Jeremiah must necessarily have made many enemies, and the prophet is presented as a person who had to suffer in a particular way. Twice we hear of conspiracies against him (11.19ff.; 18.18ff.) with the aim of eliminating him, and from these passages we can deduce that there were nests of opposition in his own village which did not hesitate to resort to murder to do away with an inconvenient preacher. Another time he is brought before a tribunal on a charge of blasphemy, following the announcement of the destruction of the temple, a crime which carried the death penalty (7.1ff.; 26.1ff., 8ff.). The superstition and corruption which he saw in the countryside were not just limited to it, but extended to the ruling class in the capital, a well-educated group (5.1ff.).

In various passages, all traditionally dated to the beginning of his ministry, the prophet announces the execution of judgment by means of an unspecified people from the north (4.5-31; 5.15-17; 6.1-8, 22-26; 8.14-17; 10.18-22). B.Duhm tried to identify this people with the Scythians, who are reported by Herodotus (1.103-6) as having reached the borders of Egypt during the last quarter of the seventh century and who contributed markedly to the weakening of the Assyrian empire, destroying its bases and disrupting the system of communications and administration in the northern and western territories. Having been discarded for many years, this theory has now reappeared in the study by Cazelles cited below.

According to the traditional chronology of the life of the prophet, he seems to have interrupted his ministry during Josiah's reform, resuming it only after Josiah's death. Nothing is said about the reasons for the silence over the reform; those who accept the traditional reconstruction think that he unreservedly approved the work of the reformer king, so that the main element, the announcement of judgment, diminished. In fact we find a positive evaluation of the work of Josiah in 22.15, where it appears in the context of invective against his successor Jehoiakim. Again, for some authors chs.30-31, along with the first chapters of the book, would be an indication of the utmost support for this king's policy of reformation and reconquest. However, these are no more than conjectures. All the problems are resolved if we make the ministry of Jeremiah begin at the time of Jehoiakim, because in that case they do not even arise.

(b) The second period (under Jehoiakim)

On the accession of Jehoiakim both the political and the religious situation deteriorated rapidly. The new king had been installed by Pharaoh Necho II of the XXVI Dynasty, who had annulled the coronation of Josiah's first son carried out by the popular assembly, replacing him with another son, whose name he changed as a sign of vassalage (II Kings 23.30ff.). This condition of vassalage to Egypt must be kept in mind if we are to understand the policy of support for his overlord maintained by this king. However, this was a policy which at the same time set Judah on a collision course with Babylon. If we take what is said in 22.13 as true, Jehoiakim must have reigned unscrupulously on the political level, while at a religious level he seems to have wanted to annul Josiah's reform. Jeremiah must have wanted to preach against these elements in his speech in the temple (chs.7, 26), and his position immediately became an affair of state. The announcement of the destruction of the temple put the prophet in a position of being within a hair's breadth of the death sentence (26.18, where the defence quotes Micah 3.12, though it is unlikely that this passage is authentic, above 21.1). So it is not surprising that quite apart from attempts to remove the prophet physically, there were also campaigns aimed at discrediting him and bringing about his moral destruction.

The real break with his fellow-citizens took place after a symbolic action which at this time appears to be a replica of the ancient Egyptian ritual of the 'execration texts' in 19.1ff. (cf. above, 18.2). Jeremiah breaks a potter's flask, a sign of the forthcoming 'breaking' of Judah by the divine judgment. The act and particularly its implications cannot have escaped anyone, all the more so as the prophet made no secret of what was involved; the aggravation was evidently that while in Egypt the ceremony was used against the enemies of the country, here the symbolic action was directed against Judah itself. Jeremiah was imprisoned, put in the stocks and flogged (20.1ff.); he was forbidden to enter the temple. The void around him increased: to the people he seemed to be a blasphemer and to the politicians a defeatist and a potential traitor; it was better for everyone not to be seen in his company. The so-called 'confessions' are seen as an expression of his solitude and the despair which often seized him; the passages involved are 12.1-3; 15.10ff.; 16.1ff. (from which we learn that God had even forbidden him to enter into marriage, an unheard-of condition for Israelites of the time); 18.19ff.; 20.7ff.

However, the power of Egypt, the nation whose vassal Jehoiakim had become, did not last long; in 605 the Egyptian troops were defeated in the battle of Carchemish on the Euphrates by those of Nebuchadnezzar, still heir apparent to the throne of Babylon (the Vulgate called him Nabucodonosor, a word that is nearer than the Hebrew to the original). While a victory of Necho II in the winter of 601-600 near the frontier between Judah and Egypt, followed by the occupation of Gaza, seemed to augur well, there was no Egyptian recovery, and in this situation prudence must have counselled Jehoiakim to adopt a more or less ambivalent position to the two contenders, avoiding any commitment in a situation which was still confused. Jeremiah, however, saw matters clearly (as did Isaiah in his day): there was a need for immediate submission to the king of Babylon, and an abandonment of Egypt. The 'enemy from the north' announced in the first period now took on very precise connotations in the person of the king of Babylon, who had meanwhile ascended the throne as Nebuchadnezzar II. According to ch.36 it was in this period that the prophet received the order to have the words spoken so far written down and read before the people, the authorities and then the king. Jeremiah dictated a scroll to his amanuensis Baruch and soon afterwards sent it to the temple (which he had been forbidden to enter) to be read before the people and the authorities on a fast day in December 604. The leading men brought the matter to the king, so great was the impression made by the reading, but he would not listen to the reading, cut the scroll in pieces and threw them on the brazier which was burning in the room. Immediately afterwards he ordered the arrest of Jeremiah and his secretary. However, after being warned by a court official, they succeeded in saving themselves: the prophet dictated a second scroll to Baruch to replace the one that had been destroyed, adding other material to it.

(c) The third period (under Zedekiah and down to his death)

In the year 598 the oracles pronounced by Jeremiah against the people seemed to be coming true. Nebuchadnezzar, who could not allow on his south-west frontier a vassal of an enemy who a short time before had defeated him and occupied Gaza, set out on an expedition against Judah and laid siege to Jerusalem. Jehoiakim died during the last month of the siege, leaving the throne and a burdensome legacy to his son Jehoiachin (II Kings 24.6ff.). When the city fell, some of the nobility and the royal family were deported to Babylon, while Nebuchadnezzar replaced Jehoiachin with Mattaniah, one of his brothers, whose name he changed to Zedekiah (II Kings 24.17f.) to indicate the vassal relationship. Zedekiah's position was complex from what we would now call a constitutional point of view: on the one hand the legitimate sovereign was alive, though he was prevented from exercising his functions, so that the new king was no more than a regent; on the other hand the Babylonians considered him a king in every respect. Moreover he seems to have had a weak character, being the pliable victim of a number of pressure groups: on the one hand were the priests and prophets who in the time of his father had announced that YHWH was with Judah and therefore there was nothing to fear; these, given the fact that Jeremiah's words seemed to have been verified, found themselves called on to demonstrate that what had happened was a temporary set-back, intended merely to be a kind of test to which God was subjecting his people. On the other hand there were political and military groups which kept faith with the alliance with Egypt in the hope that it would soon come to their aid – evidently they tended to overestimate its impetus. Yet others tried to steer a course between the two great powers, between which the room for manoeuvre tended increasingly to diminish. All these groups found Jeremiah's preaching an evident danger.

Now the prophet attacks all these positions, instead advising submission to Nebuchadnezzar. Three times Nebuchadnezzar is called 'my servant' in the name of YHWH (25.9; 27.6; 43.10, albeit only in passages with a Deuteronomistic revision); this is an interpretation of the foreign ruler which closely resembles the characterizations of Assyria in Isa.10 as instruments of the divine judgment; the same will later be true of the characterization of Cyrus in Deutero-Isaiah, this time the architect of the restoration of Judah. In 594, during an attempted rebellion, some prophets exhorted the people to make common cause with the rebels. Chief among them was a certain Hananiah, whose preaching took up a theme dear to Isaiah, that of the inviolability of Zion (chs.27-28). Jeremiah fought tenaciously against them. Similar voices also made themselves heard among the exiles of 597, and an echo of them comes through Ezekiel, who was probably one of them. However, in ch.29 we have the text of a letter (with considerable Deuteronomistic revisions, though its substance may be authentic) in which Jeremiah exhorted the exiles to settle in the new land without being misled by those who promised them liberation too soon and too easily. The text of this letter gave rise to a work included in the Alexandrian collection, *The Epistle of Jeremiah* (cf. below 49.4).

In 588 Nebuchadnezzar again moved against Jerusalem, laying siege to it for a second time. Jeremiah, who was considered a potential traitor, was subjected to all kinds of vexations and was finally accused of communicating with the enemy. He was imprisoned in an empty cistern where he certainly would have died had not the king given help to him in secret (chs.37-39). The king did not have the courage, or perhaps even the material means, for helping the man under his protection more effectively. Jeremiah was freed on the storming of the city by the Babylonians; the conquerors treated him with respect and allowed him to stay, together with the governor Gedaliah, to begin the reconstruction. However, a conspiracy organized by nationalist elements and outlawed soldiers did away with the governor and the rebels took the prophet with them to Egypt (chs.42-43). It was here that he died, without having ceased to preach.

According to a legend which we cannot check, Jeremiah too died a martyr death.

(d) Model biography and critical biography

As I have already indicated (above, 17.4), this is the information which we can glean from the biography of Jeremiah, as it has come into being through the various redactions of the work. There are a number of inconsistencies in this biography, for example the positive evaluation of the Babylonians indicated above, contrasting with a markedly negative evaluation in chs.50-51; the harsh judgment on Judah and Jerusalem throughout the work contrasting with the favourable attitude in chs. 30-31; 32-33 (for other features see the commentary by Carroll already cited), and these have been noted for some time. It is also well known, however, that the book does not give information about very important matters (for example the relationship of the prophet to Josiah's reform, which is basic for anyone who puts the beginning of his ministry under this king). Carroll infers from this that the biography is the product of the redactors, intended, as in the case of Isaiah, to make the prophet the man of God who was the instrument for calling the people to penitence and conversion. However, no notice was taken of his message, with consequences that all the people experienced in harsh reality. The story thus makes him a martyr, who by the proclamation of his word had to suffer all kinds of troubles and abuses. The whole matter is further complicated by the history of redaction which, as in Isaiah and Ezekiel, is so complex as to be practically inexplicable. So we need at least to assess this biography critically if we do not want to run the risk of simply taking over the theories and theses of the redactors (cf. above, 17.4f.).

2. The text

(a) The complexity of Jeremiah's biography and the disconcerting features in it thus indicate that the redaction of the book which bears his name must also have been very complex. Even those who for the most part accept the prophet's biography agree that it is impossible that he and his disciples completed the redaction. That is not only because of the troubled times in which he lived, which were hardly favourable to the creation of literary works, or because of the misadventures and persecutions of which Jeremiah and Baruch were the object; it is evident that many hands contributed to the work over a considerable period.

An obvious starting point might be the information given in ch.36, about the dictation of the two scrolls, the second destined to be kept; the redactors date this episode in 604 BCE. It is certain that the first scroll cannot have contained much material, and this is even more obvious to anyone who accepts a late date for the beginning of the prophet's ministry: it was in fact possible to read it aloud three times in the course of a day. But even those who accept the basic historicity of the episode recognize the impossibility in the present state of research of determining what texts the second scroll included, though it is obvious that not all the passages dated after 604 cannot have been part of it. Every now and then someone attempts a reconstruction of the content of the second scroll, in which some scholars have wanted to recognize passages contained in chs.1-6. But so far this theory has not commended itself to scholars.

The personality of the prophet, understanding of which until recently seems to have been conditioned by an autobiographical view of the 'confessions' (in the previous section I, too, have drawn abundantly on this) was put in a new dimension as the result of a book by H.von Reventlow (1963). He criticized the personalistic approach of exegetes to these passages which began from a characterization of Jeremiah as having been sensitive and fragile, forced against his will to embark on adventures for which he had neither the strength nor the courage. Hence the drama of which the 'confessions' would be the evidence. The reality, however, is different and the problem is more complex. The 'confessions' belong to the literary genre of the 'individual lamentation', well attested in the Psalms (we have already touched on this in passing, above 6.4, 11, and will be returning to it in due course, below, 34.5b), and we cannot simply consider them as personal emotive outbursts; rather, we have laments of a liturgical kind which the redactor puts in the mouth of the prophet speaking in the name of his people, whose mediator he is before God. On the other hand a re-reading of these texts shows that there is an undoubted autobiographical note; it could be that Jeremiah is repeating traditional liturgical material, but it is also obvious that he chose passages the content of which corresponded to his own situation (cf. above, 17.6f.).

(b) In 1923 the Italian scholar G.Ricciotti defined the book of Jeremiah as a 'miscellany', and this is an appropriate description. We find a certain systematic unity on a small scale, in particular passages; but the whole book gives the impression of having been assembled with what to our way of thinking is an almost complete lack of criteria. This immediately raises the problem of the classification of the texts, since the book is fifty-two chapters long.

A first classification seemed to be gaining acceptance at the end of the last century and the beginning of this, that of verse passages and prose passages. For B.Duhm in his now classic commentary of 1901, only the verse passages could derive from the prophet's preaching; the others would be more or less apocryphal additions. However, Duhm himself soon noted that an attempt at classification along these lines was too formal and therefore simplistic: in fact there was no reason why the prose material should not be the product of redactional work on the original texts. Duhm therefore soon proposed a new system of classification which was accepted in 1914 by Mowinckel and re-presented by him in an improved form in 1946 with, among other things, the substitution of 'cycles of tradition' for 'sources'. In this classification we have:

1. Authentic oracles of Jeremiah (for Duhm, those in poetry);
2. The 'biography' of Jeremiah, attributed by some to Baruch, though there is no certain information about this: it is, of course, in prose;
3. Finally, secondary revisions of the work by various authors, usually identified with Dtr (W.Rudolph prefers to speak in terms of 'words of Jeremiah, revised by the Deuteronomistic writers'), though other scholars have recently denied the redaction attributed to Dtr.

This threefold classification is generally accepted today, though a recent study has cast doubt on the existence of a biography by Baruch (for which, as we have seen, there is no evidence); the fact is that the writings which are classified in this way do not have a unitary character, and a thorough analysis indicates that they are the product of the fusion of at least three independent complexes of tradition. In any case, Reventlow's warning against being too influenced by the distinction between poetry and prose seems to be valid. The latter is certainly the style preferred by preaching of the Deuteronomistic type, the former that preferred by the prophets, and the relationships between Jeremiah and Deuteronomy and the Deuteronomistic school are, as we shall see, so complex that it is inadvisable to keep too closely to purely formal questions.

The book can then be sub-divided into five parts: (a) 1.1-25.14; (b) chs.26-36: (c) chs.37-45; (d) 25.15-38 and chs.46-51; (e) ch.62.

(a) In 1.1-25.14 we have a series of oracles arranged according to the three periods of the prophet's life.

1. Chs.1-6: under Josiah;
2. Chs.7-20: under Jehoiakim;

3. Chs. 21-24: generally belonging to the last period. 25.1-14 is attached to the second section. In this part one may note a tendency to regroup the oracles according to a particular theme: sin, judgment, the temple, laments and invective especially against the prophets. It is here that we find most of the 'confessions'.

(*b*) Chapters 26-36 are generally written in the third person and are a report of the prophet's life. It is interesting to compare two texts which narrate the same episode (chs.7 and 26). With the exception indicated, this material and especially chs.37-45 has been considered for the most part the work of Baruch. In chs.26-29 there is an attempt to follow a chronological order, and in chs.30-31 and 34-35 a thematic classification appears again.

(*c*) Chapters 37-45 narrate the activity of the prophet during the last years of his ministry, especially during the siege of the city in 588-87. For those who accept the validity of the theory, the hand of Baruch will have been at work here.

(*d*) 25.15-38 and chs.46-51 are the oracles against the nations, which LXX puts together immediately after the second half of ch.25; the result is a different numbering in the LXX text. Opinions are divided over the authenticity of this material and it is impossible to make a generalized judgment. In any case we know that the literary genre is attested for the majority of the prophets.

(*e*) Chapter 52 is a historical appendix parallel to II Kings 25; it is therefore a similar, though shorter, instance of what we have seen in connection with Isa.36-39 and II Kings 18-20. There is no reason to attribute this passage to the work of Jeremiah or to circles in any way connected with him.

The book may therefore have taken shape more or less in the following way: first of all came the second edition of the scroll dictated by the prophet to Baruch, then a collection of sayings of the prophet and material about him (whether or not the latter was the work of his amanuensis), then revisions (Deuteronomistic?) of various materials and finally some additions of different kinds. This work evidently extended over many years.

3. The LXX text

The statements made in the previous section seem to be verified as soon as we turn our attention to the LXX translation. We have already seen that this presents a different division of the material, but here we have only a problem of classification and not one of content. However, there is a problem of content when we compare the LXX text with the Massoretic text: the former is notably shorter, by about 2800 words. Now there are cases in which it is clear that the translator wished to summarize texts which he considered to be prolix or of little interest to his readers; at other times we have the errors and omissions which are typical of translations and transcriptions. But there are a number of passages of major importance which LXX omits: Jer.33.14-26 is a typical case. One of the conclusions we might arrive at is that the LXX will have been translated from an original text which was in fact shorter than the present Massoretic text, implicit evidence that even after the second century BCE the book continued to be expanded with various additions. A Qumran fragment offers partial help in this direction: it is that indicated by the siglum 4Q Ier[b] and gives a fragment of 9.22-10.18. Here the Hebrew follows the order of the LXX, which differs from that of the Massoretic text, and offers at least one reading which is exclusive to the Greek text and is not attested in the Hebrew. Thus the LXX seems to have been derived from a Hebrew archetype which differs in some respects from our Massoretic text. After the important study by Janzen, it looked as if the problem of the dimensions of the original text should be resolved in favour of the LXX, which as we have seen in the case of the books of Samuel (above 2.6a) seems to be in a better state. In that case it would be the Massoretic text which has expanded at a later stage, becoming a 'mixed text'. However, the recent works by Soderlund and Stulman have again challenged this assumption, so that the situation is again fluid.

4. Jeremiah and contemporary sources

(a) One important problem, though it is far from a satisfactory solution, is that, as I indicated above, of the relationship between Jeremiah and Josiah's reform, i.e. Deuteronomy and Dtr. We have already seen that the book contains texts in a Deuteronomistic redaction or, to put the problem in a different way, passages which have strong affinities of style and content with the products of these schools. The existence of the problem is generally admitted, but there is no agreement among scholars over its implications. For example, ch.11 is typically Deuteronomistic, but when we say that what do we mean? For H.H.Rowley, passages like Jer.3.1ff.; ch.34; 44.24ff. demonstrate clearly that the prophet knew Deuteronomy. 34.9 in fact shows that women, too, were included in the wholesale liberation of slaves which took place as the end drew near, and this agrees fully with the amplification of Exod.21.2ff. made by Deut.15.1,16. Jeremiah 3.1ff. is very closely connected with Deut.24.1ff., while in Jer.11.5 we seem to have allusions to Deut.8.18 and 6.3. Rowley concludes that Jeremiah must have known the reform and that he restated some of its demands; on the other hand, if this is in fact the case, we do not know how far his support extended. It is no surprise to find a certain similarity in language or in the discussion of problems among authors of the same period. I continue to maintain the theory of Deuteronomistic redaction, which remains the most convincing explanation.

(*b*) In the Lachish letters, with which we shall be concerned in Appendix 1.9, there is an allusion which some writers have wanted to connect with the person of Jeremiah. Letters 3.20 and 6.4 in fact mention 'the prophet' and 'a man' respectively, who would seem to have much in common with the characterization which the heads of the people make of Jeremiah in 38.4. Some scholars therefore seek to identify the figure with him. Attractive though this identification may be (and it would be the only case where a person formerly attested only in the Bible now appeared in extra-biblical sources), it is simply an indication and not a proof, and since we do not know the name of the person mentioned in the letters in question, identification cannot be established.

5. Jeremiah the thinker

We have already seen the apparently personal character of the book of Jeremiah, though this feature lends itself to differing judgments. In any case, it is a factor which gives Jeremiah a special character in comparison with other prophetic books. Jeremiah shares with his predecessors his ministry as a herald of YHWH to his people, even if he was almost always ignored. He seems to have been unwilling to fulfil this function: one has only to compare the bold 'Here am I, send me...' with which Isaiah (6.8b) responds to YHWH's question whether anyone is prepared to go in his name, with the continual wavering of Jeremiah which is already evident at the moment of his call (1.6); this attitude of perplexity and reticence was to continue for a good part of his ministry, cf. the 'confessions'. There are many instances in which Jeremiah feels that violence has been done to his own will and that his power of decision has been unjustly nullified; in one case he goes so far as to say that he has been 'seduced', deceived. He is thus anything but a passive instrument in God's hands, a person who goes his own way doing his duty without looking either to right or to left. On the contrary he struggles to understand; he does not accept anything without being convinced, or at worst being constrained or deceived; where possible he seeks to halt the disaster which he sees pressing in on the future of his people (20.7ff.). There is thus a marked tension between the personality of the prophet and his ministry, between his own inclinations and his own vocation. Left to himself, he would have been a good citizen by the standards of his age: honest, hardworking, quiet in his everyday life, ready to avoid any violent emotion or particularly prominent standpoints; in practice he saw himself compelled to act continually against his own character. Even if the confessions are liturgical material and nothing more, they are an excellent expression of his state of mind.

In this spiritual situation the prophet finds himself driven to cope with problems like those of theodicy (ch.12), predestination (1.5) and sin (13.23). But his approach to these problems is always very specific; he does not elaborate theories but lives by what is proposed to him and what he proposes. And the most adequate solution always seems to him, as to his predecessors, to be obedience to the divine will (15.19). His office as mediator puts him in a difficult situation: on the one hand he feels his solidarity with his people, whom he defends before YHWH until his God has to prohibit him from interceding for his nation (7.16; 11.4; cf. Isa.1.15); on the other hand he has to act as a crucible to purify the people in the name of YHWH (6.27ff.). The drama of a man who seems in this respect to be extraordinarily modern derives from this inner conflict.

(a) The testimony about God has remarkable points of contact with that of Hosea, as I have indicated above (Chapter 19). Like Hosea, Jeremiah proclaimed the divine love and grace, often represented by the image of marriage (2.1ff.; 3.1ff.; 31.20ff.; cf. Hos.1-3; 11.8). For Jeremiah, too, at the beginning of relationships between God and the people stands the pledge of the former to which the latter responds (11.1ff.); the future of these relationships can only be seen in terms of a 'new covenant', 31.31-34 (as I have already said, with Jeremiah the use of *berīt* becomes frequent, whereas previously it was limited to Hosea), and this is a theme which reappears in different ways in the exilic prophets Ezekiel and Deutero-Isaiah. As with Amos and Isaiah, God is also the Lord of history and makes use of foreign rulers and peoples (recall 'my servant' Nebuchadnezzar) to carry out his plans; but if this is the task of the king of Babylon, all opposition to him becomes opposition to YHWH's plans and therefore sacrilege. This theological clarity is here united with a political realism to which Jeremiah's contemporaries would have done well to listen. Eschatology does not seem to be very developed in Jeremiah: in addition to the concept of the 'new pledge, covenant' which replaced the old one that had been violated (31.31-34), in 33.14ff. we have a sketch of a messianic figure. As well as presenting textual difficulties, the two passages (and especially the second) are obscure on a conceptual level and are regarded by some scholars as inauthentic.

(b) For Jeremiah too, as I have indicated, the only possible attitude that human beings can adopt to God is one of absolute obedience. This takes specific form in love and faithfulness (5.11f.; ch.35). The cult is only the expression of an attitude of gratitude and obedience, not a substitute for them (7.1ff., 26ff.; cf. 6.20). This is especially true in the field of social ethics, in which Jeremiah follows the lines marked out by his predecessors, even if, as we have seen (above, 17.7c), the theme is not so basic to his message as it is to that of other prophets (2.34; 6.7; 7.5ff.; 21.11; 22.3ff.; 34.8ff.). It is true that human sin is expressed in individual conscious acts, but in Jeremiah more than in any other prophet it appears as something more profound, as the result of a basically wrong attitude, which in fact is now part of human nature (4.22; 5.3 and especially 13.23, where we have the tragic assertion that just as the negro cannot change the colour of his skin nor a leopard that of his coat, a man cannot but be a sinner). This situation cannot, however, serve as a moral excuse for human beings, so that they can ignore appeals for conversion: chs.1-6 are full of these appeals; cf. also 8.4ff. This dialectic, which is part of any authentic theology, expresses the difference which exists between the human situation on the one hand and human power to overcome its effect on the other. However, the solution is not found within the context of this dialectic, but in God himself, who forgives men and women out of his love and resumes with them the relationships which they have broken off (31.31-34).

BIBLIOGRAPHY

Commentaries

B.Duhm, KHC, 1901; G.Ricciotti, Rome 1923; P.Volz, KAT, ^{2}1928; A.Penna, SacBib, 1952; J.Steinmann, Lectio Divina, 1952; A.Aeschimann, Neuchâtel 1959 (a popular work); A.Gelin, ^{2}1959; A.Weiser, ATD, ^{4}1962;

J.Bright, AB, 1965; W.Rudolph, HATR, [3]1968; J.A.Thompson, 1980; R.P.Carroll, OTL, 1986; W.McKane, ICC, I, 1986; W.L.Holladay, Hermeneia 1, 1986. O.Loretz, 'Die Sprüche Jeremias in Jer.1.17-9.25', *UF* 2, 1970, 109-30, is an important philological study.

Bibliographical studies: S.Herrmann, 'Forschungen am Jeremiabuch', *TLZ* 102, 1977, 481-90; J.L.Crenshaw, 'A Living Tradition. The Book of Jeremiah in Current Research', *Int* 37, 1983, 117-29; W.Brueggemann, 'The Book of Jeremiah', ibid, 130-5; P.R.Ackroyd, 'The Book of Jeremiah. Some Recent Studies', *JSOT* 28, 1984, 47-59; W.Thiel, 'Ein Vierteljahrhundert Jeremiaforschung', *VuF* 31.1, 1986, 32-52.

Monographs: J.P.Hyatt, 'Jeremiah and Deuteronomy', *JNES* 1, 1942, 156-73 and *IB* V, 779ff.; in his shadow C.F.Whitley, 'Carchemish and Jeremiah', *ZAW* 80, 1968, 38-49, who puts the beginning of Jeremiah's ministry at the end of the seventh century; C.Levin, 'Noch einmal: die Anfänge des Propheten Jeremia', *VT* 31, 1981, 428-40; id., *Die Verheissung des Neuen Bundes*, FRLANT 137, 1985; he thinks of the period of Jehoiakim. The prophet is dated in an unspecified late period by N.Lohfink, 'Der junge Jeremia als Propagandist und Poet', in *Le livre de Jérémie*, ed. P.-M.Bogaert, Louvain 1981, 351-68; this approach is continued by U.Schröter, 'Jeremias Botschaft für das Nordreich', *VT* 35, 1985, 312-19. For the traditional dating see T.W.Overholt, 'Some Reflections on the Date of Jeremiah's Call', *CBQ* 33, 1971, 165-82; W.L.Holladay, 'The Years of Jeremiah's Preaching', *Int* 37, 1983, 146-59. For the biography of the prophet and his age cf. J.Skinner, *Prophecy and Religion*, Cambridge 1922; A.C.Welch, *Jeremiah*, Oxford 1928; S.H.Blank, 'The Prophet as Paradigm', in *Essays in OT Ethics. J.P.Hyatt in Memoriam*, New York 1974, 111-30; R.P.Carroll, *From Chaos to Covenant*, London 1981, and his commentary; also J.Unterman, *From Repentance to Redemption*, Sheffield 1987. For Jeremiah's call see D.Vieweger, *Die Spezifik der Berufungsberichte Jeremias und Ezechiels*, Frankfurt 1986.

1a. For the Scythians cf. H.Cazelles, 'Zephaniah, Jeremiah and the Scythians in Palestine', in L.G.Perdue and B.Kovacs (eds.), *A Prophet to the Nations. Essays in Jeremiah Studies*, Winona Lake, Ind. 1984, 129-49.

1b. For the two scrolls of Jer.36 cf. W.L.Holladay, 'The Identification of the Two Scrolls of Jeremiah', *VT* 30, 1980, 452-67; R.L.Hicks, '*Dēlet* and *m^egillāh*, A Fresh Approach to Jer XXXVI', *VT* 33, 1983, 46-66.

1c. For the problem of false prophecy cf. T.W.Overholt, *The Threat of Falsehood*, SBT II, 16, 1970; I.Meyer, *Jeremia und die falschen Propheten*, Fribourg CH 1977; cf. above 17.9c. For ch.29 cf. W.L.Holladay, 'God Writes a Rude Letter (Jeremiah 29:1-23)', *BA* 46, 1983, 46-66.

1d. R.P.Carroll, *From Chaos to Covenant*, London 1981, and his commentary.

2. The text. For the 'confessions' see the classic study by W.Baumgartner, *Die Klagedichte des Jeremias*, Giessen 1917 (ET forthcoming, Sheffield 1988); a liturgical interpretation of them has been proposed by H.Reventlow, *Liturgie und prophetisches Ich*, Gütersloh 1963. Cf. also H.-J.Stoebe, 'Jeremia.

Prophet und Seelsorger', *TZ* 30, 1964, 385-409; id., 'Geprägte Form und geschichtliche, individuelle Erfahrung im Alten Testament', *SVT* 17, 1969, 212-19; J.M.Berridge, *Prophet, People and the Word of Yahweh*, Zurich 1970; P.Welten, 'Leiden und Leiderfahrungen im Buch Jeremia', *ZTK* 74, 1977, 123-50; W.Zimmerli, 'Frucht der Anfechtung des Propheten', in *Die Botschaft und die Boten, FS H.-W.Wolff*, Neukirchen 1981; T.Polk, *The Prophetic Persona. Jeremiah and the Language of the Self*, Sheffield 1984. For other redactional problems of the book cf. W.L.Holladay, 'Prototype and Copies: A New Approach to the Poetry-Prose Problem in the Book of Jeremiah', *JBL* 81, 1961, 44-5; id., 'The Background of Jeremiah's Self-Understanding. Moses, Samuel and Psalm 22', *JBL* 83, 1964, 153-64; id., 'Style, Irony and Authenticity in Jeremiah', *JBL* 81, 1961, 44-54; id., 'The Recovery of Poetic Passages in Jeremiah', *JBL* 85, 1966, 401-6; A.H.J.Gunneweg, 'Konfession oder Interpretation im Jeremiabuch?', *ZTK* 67, 1970, 395-416; O.Eissfeldt, 'Unheils- und Heilserwartungen Jeremias als Vergeltung für die ihm erwiesenen Weh- und Wohltaten', *WissZ Univ.Halle* 14.3, 1965, 181-6 (= his *Kleine Schriften* IV, Tübingen 1968, 181-92); T.R.Hobbs, 'Some Remarks on the Composition and Structure of the Book of Jeremiah', *CBQ* 34, 1972, 257-75; T.W.Overholt, 'Remarks on the Continuity of the Jeremiah Traditions', *JBL* 91, 1972, 457-71; W.Thiel, *Die deuteronomistische Redaktion von Jeremia 1-25*, Neukirchen 1973; id., *Die deuteronomistische Redaktion von Jeremia 26-45*, Neukirchen 1981; H.Weippert, *Die Prosareden des Jeremiabuches*, Berlin 1973; W.Brueggemann, 'Jeremiah's Use of Rhetorical Questions', *JBL* 92, 1973, 358-74; W.L.Holladay, 'A Fresh Look at "Source B" and "Source C" in Jeremiah', *VT* 25, 1975, 394-412; A.van Selms, 'Telescoped Discussion as Literary Device in Jeremiah', *VT* 26, 1976, 99-112; A.H.J.Gunneweg, 'Heil im Gericht', in *Tradition, Krisis, Renovatio. FS W.Zeller*, Marburg 1976, 1-9; J.R.Lundbom, *Jeremiah*, Missoula, Mont. 1975; T.R.Hobbs, 'Some Proverbial Reflections in the Book of Jeremiah', *ZAW* 91, 1979, 62-72; A.Marx, 'À propos des doublets du livre de Jérémie', in *Prophecy. Essays... G.Fohrer*, Berlin 1980, 106-20; J.V.M.Sturdy, 'The Authorship of the Prose Sermons of Jeremiah', ibid., 143-50; R.J.Van den Busch, 'Jeremiah: a Spiritual Metamorphosis', *BTB* 10, 1980, 17-24; H.Migsch, *Gotteswort über das Ende Jerusalem*, Klosterneuberg 1981; W.McKane, 'Relation between Poetry and Prose in the Book of Jeremiah', *SVT* 32, 1981, 220-37; R.Albertz, 'Jer 2-6 und die Frühverkundigung Jeremias', *ZAW* 94, 1982, 20-47; W.Zimmerli, 'Visionary Experience in Jeremiah', in *Israel's Prophetic Tradition. Essays... P.R.Ackroyd*, Cambridge 1982, 95-118; R.M.Paterson, 'Reinterpretation in the Book of Jeremiah', *JSOT* 28, 1984, 37-46. For the 'new covenant', cf. S.Böhmer, *Heimkehr und Neuer Bund*, FRLANT 137, 1976; C.Levin, *Die Verheissung des Neuen Bundes*, Göttingen 1985; M.S.Moore, 'Jeremiah's Progressive Paradox', *RB* 93, 1986, 388-75; U.Schröter, 'Jeremias' Botschaft für das Nordreich', *VT* 35, 1985, 312-29 (for relations with the north).

2b. For a literary and structural analysis of Jer.27-29 cf. T.Seidl, *Texte und Einheiten in Jeremia 27-29* (2 vols), St Ottilien 1977-78; C.de Jong, *De volken bij Jeremia*, Franeker-Kampen 1978; R.Liwak, *Der Prophet und die Geschichte*, Stuttgart 1987 (examines chs.1-6). The possibility that pupils of Jeremiah worked on his text and that this work influenced the book of Ezekiel has been considered by D.Vieweger, 'Die Arbeit des jeremianischen Schülerkreises am Jeremiabuch und deren Rezeption in der literarischen Überlieferung der Prophetenschrift Ezechiels', *BZ* 32, 1988, 15-34.

2d. P.Höffken, 'Zu den Heilszusätzen in der Völkerorakelsammlung des Jeremiahbuches', *VT* 27, 1977, 398-412.

3. The special features of the LXX text can be examined in the critical edition edited by J.Ziegler, *Ieremias...*, Göttingen 1957, in the commentaries and in the monograph by J.G.Janzen, *Studies in the Text of Jeremiah*, Cambridge, Mass. 1973. For 4QIer[b] cf. F.M.Cross Jr, *The Ancient Library of Qumran*, London 1957, 139 n.38.

However, S.Soderlund, *The Greek Text of Jeremiah. A Revised Hypothesis*, Sheffield 1985, and L.Stuhlman, *The Greek Text of Jeremiah*, Sheffield 1985, have cast doubt on Janzen's theory, pointing out that rather than putting forward global solutions it is important to go back to examining each text on its merit. For the problem of detail cf. E.Tov, *The Septuagint Translation of Jeremiah and Baruch: A Discussion of an Early Revision of Jeremiah 29-52 and Baruch 1.1-3-8*, Missoula, Mont. 1976.

4a. H.H.Rowley, 'The Prophet Jeremiah and the Book of Deuteronomy', in *Studies in Old Testament Prophecy presented to T.H.Robinson*, Edinburgh 1950, 157-74; O.Eissfeldt, 'The Prophetic Literature', in H.H.Rowley (ed.), *The Old Testament and Modern Study*, Oxford 1951, 152ff.; S.Herrmann, *Die prophetischen Heilserwartungen im Alten Testament*, Stuttgart 1965, 162-95 (esp. 188ff., where the conclusion is reached that the Deuteronomistic-type passages are simply later revisions); cf. E.W.Nicholson, *Preaching to the Exiles*, Oxford 1970; E.Tov, 'L'incidence de la critique textuelle sur la critique littéraire dans le livre de Jérémie', *RB* 79, 1972, 189-99.

4b. D.W.Thomas, 'Again the "Prophet" of the Lachish Ostraka', in J.Hempel and L.Rost (eds.), *Von Ugarit nach Qumran. FS O.Eissfeldt*, Berlin 1958, 244-9.

5. J.Swetnam, 'Why was Jeremiah's New Covenant New?', *SVT* 26, 1974, 11-15. Swetnam's argument is important because he sees the 'newness' of the 'new covenant' in the foundation of the synagogue, the means by which the word of God, first limited to the temple, arrives in the midst of the people. R.P.Carroll, 'A Non-Cogent Argument in Jeremiah's Oracles against the Prophets', *StTh* 30, 1976, 43-51; S.Herrmann, 'Die Bewältigung der Krise in Israel', in *Beiträge zur alttestamentlichen Theologie. FS W.Zimmerli*, Göttingen 1977, 164-78. R.E.Winkle, 'Jeremiah's Seventy Years for Babylon: A Reassessment', *AUSS* 25, 1987, 201-14, 289-99, is a study of the term 'seventy years'.

For the social problem cf. L.Wisser, *Jérémie, critique de la vie sociale*, Geneva 1982. Relations with the book of Amos have been found by J.M.Berridge,

'Jeremia und die Prophetie des Amos', *TZ* 35, 1979, 321-41. For the prophecies of destruction, especially of the capital, cf. H.Migsch, *Gotteswort über das Ende Jerusalems*, Klosterneuburg 1981.

PART FOUR

THE EXILIC AND POST-EXILIC PROPHETS

24

EZEKIEL

1. Name and person

If Jeremiah can be considered the last of the pre-exilic prophets, although he personally suffered the consequences of the political catastrophe which befell his nation, Ezekiel appears as the first of the exilic prophets. According to the biographical details in the work he was in fact deported to Babylon after the siege of 597 and exercised the greater part of his ministry in that country. The Hebrew name *yᵉḥezqē'l* means 'God strengthens', and that is appropriate if we consider the circumstances in which the prophet who bore it had to work; the LXX transcribes it as *Iezekiel* and the Vulgate as *Ezechiel*, hence our Western transcriptions. Like Jeremiah, Ezekiel belonged to the priestly class; we know the name of his father (1.3) and he had a good knowledge of the temple, its topography and the rituals practised there (1.1; 33.21; 40.1); in Babylon he lived in a place called Tel-Abib (3.15), which was situated near the Kebar canal (1.1: the name is still preserved in the *naḥr el-qebir*), not far from the city of Nippur in the southern part of the country. Like many of the exiles, he had achieved a reasonable standard of living; among other things he was the owner of a house in which the elders of Judah were accustomed to meet (3.23; 8.1). In 24.16ff. we are told that Ezekiel was married, but that his wife had died suddenly. According to the chronology of the book, his call to be a prophet came in the year 593; the beginning of the book (1.1ff.) has a rather obscure text, but the number five in 1.2 seems to be that of the years which have elapsed since the deportation of 597, while the enigmatic 'thirty' probably refers to the age of the prophet at the time of his calling. It is certainly not by chance that this was one of the ages laid down for taking up the levitical ministry (cf. Num.4.23 and above, 10.1). Ezekiel enjoyed a great deal of respect among the exiles (8.1; 14.1). According to A.Bertholet in his 1936 commentary, however, Ezekiel will have worked in Jerusalem down to the exile of 587, arriving in Babylon with the second and not the first deportation; in this way Bertholet tries to explain the wealth of information that we find in the book about the situation in the capital between the two exiles. Howevei, this is an explanation which clearly presupposes the revision of an original text of which we have no knowledge, before it achieved its final form. It would be disconcerting that this work had complicated the contents of the book rather than simplifying them. To explain the presence of Ezekiel in Jerusalem for the period before 587, which would have been clearly attested in the primitive form of the book, the redactors would have had to introduce the theme of the transportation of Ezekiel from Babylon to Jerusalem by the hand of the spirit. It is clear that while this explanation solves the problem of the presence of Ezekiel in Jerusalem at a certain time, it creates considerable problems in the rest of the book. The solution of the problem is probably again to be sought in the literary genre of the 'model biography': the information that we obtain is not objective biographical information, but is part of the edifying legend, the theme of which is the prophet's life. And that is also true of the paranormal features which we shall be discussing shortly (§ 2). Note, too, that Ezekiel is the first prophetic book in which the work of the spirit is of basic importance. For this type of 'biography' cf. above, 17.4f-g.

According to this biography, Ezekiel's work falls into two clearly distinct periods: the first extends from his calling to the fall of Jerusalem in 587 (chs.1-24); the second includes oracles which go from the fall of Jerusalem onwards. During the first period Ezekiel preached judgment, taking up more or less the lines followed by Jeremiah in 593 (cf. Jer.27; 28 and the argument of ch.29): all hope of an imminent return of those who have been deported and thus of a speedy restoration is false. In the second period, on the other hand, Ezekiel preaches God's grace and becomes the herald of the restoration of his people (chs.33ff.; 40ff.), since the people have accepted the judgment that was announced and have shown themselves ready to be converted. The last oracle is dated to 571 (29.17), so that Ezekiel's ministry will have lasted at least twenty-five years.

2. Visions and symbolic actions

(a) A first distinctive feature of the book of Ezekiel is the quantity and quality of the visionary elements, with a very marked tendency towards excess, towards the bizarre. This is a feature which is virtually absent from the books of Hosea, Micah and Jeremiah, and which takes a very sober form in Amos; it is present in Isa.6.1ff., but there it is because of the importance and the unprecedented character of the message which Isaiah was to pass on and which the vision was meant to justify. In other words, whereas for Ezekiel's predecessors visions were an unusual feature, and often involved everyday things, in Ezekiel their contents verged on the grotesque and were the forerunners of the kind of vision which was to be a feature of the apocalyptic style of certain pseudepigraphical books at the end of the first millennium BCE and the beginning of the common era; we find an example in the book of Daniel (cf. below, 41).

(b) A second feature to note is the ecstatic character that some of Ezekiel's experiences take on: the prophet is really 'outside himself' when the phenomena in question occur. In ecstasy he is transported by the spirit from Babylon to Jerusalem (8.1ff.), as we have already seen; other phenomena can be described as cataleptic (3.15; 4.4; 24.27; 33.22). On the other hand, leaving aside any hasty diagnosis in the medical or the psychiatric fields (and there was no lack of attempts in this direction in the first half of our century), medical answers to questions in this area have always indicated due reserve towards classifying the phenomena in question under this aspect, and especially towards admitting the existence of pathological phenomena: first of all, the material at our disposal is too sparse for us to be able to risk a diagnosis, and secondly, these are phenomena which almost by definition cannot be investigated by research of this kind, especially at such a distance in time.

(c) A third feature is the frequency and the character of Ezekiel's symbolic actions. While these are rare and matter-of-fact among his predecessors (cf. Isa.20; Jer.19; 27, where only the first case is at all bizarre) and therefore relatively simple to interpret, they seem to become the rule with Ezekiel, and also show a marked tendency towards the bizarre and the grotesque.

There are no obvious explanations for the transportation of Ezekiel in ecstasy from Babylon to Jerusalem: we have seen Bertholet's attempt to set the first part of Ezekiel's ministry in Jerusalem; R.H.Pfeiffer*, 536f., makes a similar proposal. He argues that Ezekiel, deported in 597, will have returned home following the order which he received in 3.4 and will have then been deported a second time in 587/6; the redactors will have attributed his activity to the work of the spirit. But although this proposal has better foundations than that of Bertholet, it only avoids the problem and does not overcome it: Ezekiel is and remains an out-of-the-ordinary prophet, often disconcerting, and in any case different in character from his predecessors and also to a great extent from those who came after him.

So the explanation suggested above, connected with the 'model biography', remains the most reasonable one (cf. above, 17.4d).

3. The book

One particularly striking characteristic of Ezekiel is that the book appears to be in relatively good order – so good, that down to the end of the last century it was presented as a model, apart from a text which in many places is far from easy. It is in fact remarkably easy to make a division: (a) oracles against Judah and Jerusalem in chs. 1-24; (b) oracles against the nations in chs.25-32; and finally (c) oracles of salvation in chs.33-48. The last section is subdivided into two parts: the preparation in chs.33-39 and its programmatic realization in the restoration of the temple and the cult in chs.40-48. Once again, then, we would seem to have the tripartite scheme that we have also found in other prophets, but which we have seen to be almost certainly the work of the redactors. So even in the apparently perfect Ezekiel we have signs of a redaction, and there are in fact many others: too often the chronology, which we have seen to be so exact (and it is worth noting that in this period, with the first, tentative hints in Jeremiah, the prophetic oracles begin to be dated, a system dropped in Deutero-Isaiah and then taken up on a large scale by Haggai and Proto-Zechariah), appears valid essentially for the verses which immediately follow the chronological note, but stops there: there are a good many contradictions and repetitions, passages edited in the first and the third person, and so on. This has suggested at least two redactions. Others have wanted to make a distinction beween passages in poetry and passages in prose, a criterion which, as we have seen, is also followed in the case of Jeremiah but has been shown to be too simplistic. On the basis of the apocalyptic elements present in the book, yet others have come to see it as having been written by an anonymous prophet who lived towards the third century BCE and who will have projected his work back to the time of the exile in order to make it comply with the criteria established in the first century CE for the place of a book in the canon, namely that it should have been composed at a time earlier than that of Ezra and Nehemiah (cf. above, 2.1a-b). In reality these attempts are simply the result of a swing of the pendulum in opposite directions: whereas Ezekiel was first cited as an example of systematic redaction (or what was thought to be systematic redaction), at a later stage the

truth seemed to be precisely the oppposite, and Ezekiel therefore *had
to* become an artificial work at a stroke, possibly put together with
scissors and paste, with a fictitious order and fictitious chronology.
Today, however, as with the other prophets, the tendency is to
examine each passage in Ezekiel on its own merits, deciding on the
authenticity, the inauthenticity or the dubious character of each one
of them in turn. Thus it is possible to find some interpolations in
27.2-9a, 25-37; in ch.38 and in chs.40-48; and in some further cases.
We have seen that this situation also exists among many of the
prophets who preceded him. 27.12-24 is an interesting case: here
G.Garbini has suggested that we have Phoenician material. It is not
possible to establish who has been at work. We do not hear of any
disciples whom Ezekiel may have had, but since he regularly received
the elders of Judah, a school or at least a circle could (this of course
is only a possibility) have arisen which transmitted his words and
meditated on them. In any case, the inauthentic material is difficult
to recognize in Ezekiel because we have fewer external points of
reference with him than with others.

A theory has been put forward recently which seeks to provide an
explanation of the presence of material which does not tally with the
prophet's work. It is contained especially in chs.5; 11; 12; 13; 16; 21;
23; 34, while chs.20; 33-34 are entirely composed of such material,
so that they have been called 'Deutero-Ezekiel'. It is in them that we
find the majority of parallels to the 'Holiness Code ' in P (cf. above,
10.1,3). Only an initial analysis has been made of the problem, and
it is therefore too early to pass judgment, but it is certain that the
proposed solution would resolve adequately a problem which has
always given scholars a great deal to think about, that of the
relationship between certain sections of Ezekiel (which then would
not come from Ezekiel) and the relevant material in P.

Another problem in Ezekiel is that of the relationship between the
Massoretic text and that of the LXX. It is generally recognized that,
leaving aside some wrong or tendentious translations, the Greek text
goes back to an archetype which is better than the Massoretic text;
it is therefore a regular practice to seek to correct the latter on the
basis of the former. In particular, it is a fact that even LXX[A], which
usually represents an LXX text adapted to the Massoretic text by
means of the elimination of some of the material which differs from
it (and which is preserved, e.g., in LXX[B]), presents remarkable
differences from the Massoretic text. However, the extent of the
phenomenon is not obvious; no Hebrew document has emerged from
Qumran which bears any trace of these recensions, as happened, e.g.

in the case of the books of Samuel and Jeremiah (only partly, in the latter case), so that we can do no more than note their existence. This explains why the most recent commentary, by M.Greenberg, limits itself to examining the Massoretic text on its merits.

4. Ezekiel the thinker

(a) Jeremiah and Ezekiel are the bridge by which we pass from the pre-exilic period to the exile and the post-exilic period. In Ezekiel priest and prophet meet, as clearly appears from the programme of the renewal of the cult in chs.40-48. A critic of the cult would certainly have been out of work after 587/86, when it now existed in the most limited form in the ruins of the temple. But in every case in which Ezekiel gives his opinion, he always considers it an essential element of the community, whether past or future. This explains his work aimed at a restoration of the cult purified of the abuses which his predecessors had pointed out. But Ezekiel is still the theologian, the ecstatic, the organizer of the exiles, beginning with the semi-official meetings in his home. The vision which marked his call almost overwhelmed him, and the divine power excited in him phenomena which were at the same time both mysterious and disconcerting. The originality of his thought is not affected by these elements: Ezekiel has a message of his own to give and it is by no means inferior to the message of those who preceded him. Decades ago he was criticized for a supposed 'coldness' and for particular characteristics which were thought to prove that his writing was only theoretical, and did not therefore have any contact with real life. But the categories which underlie such evaluations are aesthetic, and they are irrelevant because they have only a very limited bearing on Ezekiel's thought. We may leave aside the criticism that Ezekiel did not have a prophetic 'personality', as this arises from the romanticizing assessment of the prophets which we have seen not to be valid (recall what was said in the previous chapter about Jeremiah's 'confessions'). It is obvious that in Ezekiel elements of remarkable complexity existed side by side on the personal level and in the area more closely connected with his ministry. We have seen that attempts have been made to give a psychopathological evaluation of certain aspects of his ministry; the weakness of this approach does not do away with the fact that it has been possible in the case of Ezekiel where it has not worked with his predecessors and his successors, thanks to the presence of certain objective data which cannot be denied. From what we can deduce from the texts, he is a complex personality, who is sometimes contradictory, full of disconcerting characteristics, deeply tormented but in a very different way from e.g. Jeremiah, and endowed with a remarkable capacity for organization (we need only think of the circumstances which governed his ministry).

For Ezekiel, too, the axis around which the history of the world and of his people turns is the holiness of God. He refers to this explicitly when he speaks to his audience, as he does often, with the phrase 'That they may know that I am YHWH'. For Ezekiel, too, it was the case that what happened to Judah was the consequence of divine judgment. However, once the news of the fall of Jerusalem had arrived, his negative message could immediately be reversed. Since the people had now been freed from all false security, and now seemed ready to listen, the reconstruction could begin, starting first of all with the discouraged figures whom he had in front of him. However, the prophet's fundamental experience always remains that of the divine power which overwhelms him: this is tersely expressed in the form of address which YHWH most often uses towards him: 'Human being...' (literally, 'Son of man'). For the prophet, the recognition of this divine sovereignty is also the basis and the foundation for the message of reconstruction. Since God is sovereign, after judgment and destruction he can build on a completely new basis. Thus the strict censor becomes the pastoral counsellor, if it is permissible to use this modern expression, and in this new guise he visits, exhorts, organizes to such a degree that he is sometimes dubbed 'the father of post-exilic Judaism'. In his teaching he appropriates the doctrine of Deuteronomy and Dtr on reward, which is the key by which the people are to understand what has happened to them. Here, however, he comes up against individual guilt and responsibility which transcend collective guilt and responsibility (14.12ff.; 18.2-20). In any case, like Jeremiah before him, Ezekiel refutes the easy excuse of collective guilt as a disguise for individual faults: although the responsibility of the individual is closely bound up with that of the community, it is not done away with, and human beings are presented as being completely responsible for their own actions.

Concerned as he is to lay the foundations for the reconstruction of his people, Ezekiel does not show any particularly universalistic features, even if the oracles against the nation clearly reveal that he knew that the destiny of the people of God was irrevocably bound up with that of other peoples. It is certain that the temple against which he himself had preached down to 587 now becomes the place for the final gathering of his people, the future centre for the new community (chs.40-48).

(b) The vision of the final assault of the peoples on Jerusalem, where they meet with destruction, and the visionary character of such a notable part of his own prophetic experience have earned Ezekiel the title 'father of apocalyptic', a title which until a little while ago sounded like a reproof. It is a precise evaluation so long as it is not used as a reproof against the prophet but as a statement of fact pure and simple; it does seem that the apocalyptic genre is inspired by all kinds of thoughts and expressions first found in Ezekiel. But Ezekiel nevertheless remains a prophet in all that he does and despite everything (for the difference between the prophets and apocalyptic see above, 17.5h). It is even possible to set the futuristic elements in his preaching alongside the preaching of Deutero-Isaiah: concepts like those of the 'new exodus', the 'new covenant', the 'new people' are common to the two prophets, despite the fundamental difference between them on the stylistic level. Like Jeremiah, Ezekiel sees that the ancient exchange of pledges between God and his people and between the people and their Lord has been annulled by the prevarications of Judah. It is therefore necessary for God himself to put this relationship on a new basis (cf. the end of ch.16 and chs.34; 36-37). This is the only perspective in which it is possible to look to the future with a certain optimism – otherwise (cf. ch.13) not. The prophet himself defined his ministry with the appropriate simile of the watchman who warns his people of the coming of the enemy (ch.33) so that they can be saved, and announces the coming liberation, so that they can make it their own (ch.37).

BIBLIOGRAPHY

Commentaries

R.Kraetzschmar, HKAT, 1900; J.Herrmann, KAT, 1924; G.A.Cooke, ICC, 1936; A.Bertholet and K.Galling, HAT, 1936; F.Spadafora, SacBib, 1948; G.Fohrer and K.Galling, HAT, 1955; P.Auvray, JB ²1957; W.Eichrodt, ET, OTL, 1970; J.W.Wevers, NCB, 1969; K.W.Carley, Cambridge, 1974; W.Zimmerli, ET, Hermeneia (2 vols.), 1979, 1983; M.Greenberg, AB, I, 1983.

M.Nobile, 'Ezechiele nella ricerca contemporanea', *Ant* 60, 1985, 664-9, is a bibliographical study; J.Lust, *Ezekiel and His Book*, Louvain 1986, is a collection of papers on the prophet.

Again on the order of the book cf. U.Cassuto, 'The Arrangement of the Book of Ezekiel', in *Miscellanea Giovanni Mercati*, Vatican City 1946, 40-55 (= *Biblical and Oriental Studies*, Jerusalem 1973, 227-40; G.Fohrer, *Die Hauptprobleme des Buches Ezechiel*, BZAW 72, 1952; K.von Rabenau, 'Die Entstehung des Buches Ezechiel in formgeschichtlicher Sicht', *WissZ Univ. Hall.* 5.4, 1955-56, 659-94; J.Garscha, *Studien zum Ezechielbuch*, Berne 1974. Cf. also H.Reventlow, *Wächter über Israel*, Berlin 1962; W.Zimmerli, *Gottes Offenbarung*, Munich 1963 (a collection of essays mainly concerned with Ezekiel); F.Hossfeld, *Untersuchung zu Komposition und Theologie des Ezechielbuches*, Würzburg 1977; H.Simian, *Die theologische Nachgeschichte des Propheten Ezechiel*, Würzburg 1974; A.Bettenzoli, *Geist der Heiligkeit*, Florence 1979; L.Boadt, 'Textual Problems in Ezekiel', *JBL* 97, 1978, 489-99; B.Lang, *Kein Aufstand in Jerusalem*, Berne 1978; id., 'A Neglected Method in Ezekiel Research: Editorial Criticism', *VT* 29, 1979, 39-44; E.Vogt, 'Die vier "Gesichte" (*panim*) der Cheruben in Ezechiel', *Bibl* 60, 1979, 327-47. For the inaugural vision see now D.I.Block, 'Text and Emendation: A Study in the "Corruptions" in Ezekiel's Inaugural Vision', *CBQ* 50, 1988, 418-42; cf. also W.Zimmerli, 'Das Phänomen der "Fortschreibung" im Buche Ezechiel', in *Prophecy. Essays... G.Fohrer*, Berlin 1980, 174-91; H.V.Parunak, 'The Literary Architecture of Ezekiel's *mār'ōt 'elōhīm'*, *JBL* 99, 1980, 61-74; J.Lust, 'Ezekiel 36-40 in the Oldest Greek Manuscripts', *CBQ* 43, 1981, 517-33; R.Wilson, 'Prophecy in Crisis. The Call of Ezekiel', *Int* 38, 1984, 117-30; G.Garbini, *I Fenici*, Naples 1984, ch.6; T.N.D.Mettinger, *The Dethronement of Sebaoth*, Lund 1981, 97ff.; E.Kutsch, *Die chronologischen Daten der Ezechielbuches*, OBO 62, Fribourg CH 1985. For the problem of the dates in Ezekiel cf. K.S.Freedy and D.B.Redford, 'The Dates in Ezekiel in Relation to Biblical, Babylonian and Egyptian Sources', *JAOS* 90, 1970, 426-85. In this study the authors argue for the substantial authenticity and organic nature of the chronological system in the book. Cf. also K.W.Carley, *Ezekiel among the Prophets*, SBT II 31, 1975, for the problematical relationships with the other prophets. For the LXX text see L.J.McGregor, *The Greek Text of Ezekiel: An Examination of its Homogeneity*, Atlanta, Ga 1985.

2. K.Jaspers, 'Der Prophet Ezechiel. Eine pathographische Studie', in *Arbeiten zur Psychiatrie, Neurologie, und ihren Grenzgebieten. FS K.Schneider*, Heidelberg 1947, argued against the detection of pathological states in Ezekiel. Cf. also R.R.Wilson, 'An Interpretation of Ezekiel's Dumbness', *VT* 22, 1972, 91-104. For the 'symbolic actions' in the prophets cf. G.Fohrer, 'Die Gattung der Berichte über symbolische Handlungen bei den Propheten', *ZAW* 64, 1952, 101-20 (= his *Studien zur alttestamentlichen Prophetie*, Berlin 1967, 92-112), and recently T.Overholt, 'Seeing is Believing', *JSOT* 23, 1982, 3-31. There is an interesting comparison between the norms of P and those of Ezekiel in M.Haran, 'The Law Code of Ezekiel XL-XLVIII and its Relations to the Priestly School', *HUCA* 50, 1979, 45-

71. Cf. also A.Hurvitz, *A Linguistic Study of the Relations between the Priestly Source and the Book of Ezekiel*, Paris 1982; for the historical problems see E.Vogt, *Untersuchungen zum Buch Ezechiel*, Rome 1981. On relations with other oriental sources see Y.Avishur, 'The "Duties of the Son"', the "Story of Aqhat" and Ezekiel's Prophecy of Idolatry', *UF* 17, 1985, 49-60.

3. For chs.26-28 cf. H.J. van Dijk, *Ezekiel's Prophecy on Tyre*, Rome 1968; B.O.Pennacchini, *Temi mitici in Ezechiele 28, 1-19*, Assisi 1973; L.Boadt, *Ezekiel's Oracles against Egypt*, Rome 1980; G.Garbini, op.cit. For 'Deutero-Ezekiel' cf. H.Schulz, *Das Todesrecht im Alten Testament*, Berlin 1969, 163ff.; but cf. W.Zimmerli, 'Deutero-Ezechiel?', *ZAW* 84, 1972, 501-16, who presents valid arguments against separating out a Deutero-Ezekiel. For the oracles against the nations see B.Gosse, 'Le recueil d'oracles contre les nations d'*Ezéchiel* XXV-XXXII dans la rédaction du livre d'*Ezéchiel*', *RB* 93, 1986, 535-62. For chs. 40-48 cf. S.Niditch, 'Ezekiel 40-48 in a Visionary Context', *CBQ* 48, 1986, 208-24.

4. W.Zimmerli, 'The Message of the Prophet Ezekiel', *Int* 23, 1969, 131-57; J.Lust (ed.) *Ezekiel and his Book*, BETL 74, 1986. For the relations between Ezekiel and Deutero-Isaiah cf. D.Baltzer, *Ezechiel und Deuterojesaja*, BZAW 121, 1971; E.Vogt, op.cit. Cf. also W.Zimmerli, 'Jerusalem in der Sicht des Ezechielbuches', in *The Word of the Lord Shall God Forth... FS D.N.Freedman*, Winona Lake, Ind. 1983, 415-26; R.Bartelmus, 'Ez. 37, 1-14, die Verbform *w^{e}qātal* und die Anfänge der Auferstehungshoffnung', *ZAW* 97, 1985, 366-90; F.C.Fensham, 'The Curse of the Dry Bones in Ezekiel 37, 1-14 changed to a Blessing of Resurrection', *JNWSL* 13, 1987, 59f.

25

DEUTERO-ISAIAH

1. The prophet and his age

The second prophet to exercise his ministry among the exiles was an anonymous figure whose words have been collected in Isa.40-55 and who is therefore often called 'Deutero-Isaiah'. Along with the preaching of Jeremiah, with which it has a number of features in common, his message is classified in Christian tradition as one of the climaxes of Old Testament thought. At least this was the view of the earliest Christian church, which cited it frequently in New Testament texts. A central feature of this prophet's thought, the message of the 'servant of YHWH', very quickly achieved the status of one of the earliest christological formulations in the primitive church.

Today no scholars, apart from some who belong to conservative circles in Catholicism, Judaism and Protestantism, and who adopt their position because of preconceived dogmatic reasons, attribute Isa.40-66 to the eighth-century prophet. Although the attribution to Isaiah has been generally accepted over the centuries, the reasons against it are too many. It is enough to list the chief of them:

(*a*) In these chapters the exile is not presented as a threat, as the announcement of judgment in the more or less imminent future, but as an event which has already taken place. The people are in exile, and the author addresses the community of those who have been deported, and not the community in Judah. Palestine, however, has remained the prey of the surrounding peoples, who have not hesitated to divide up the lands which formerly belonged to Judah (42.22-25; 43.5-7, 28; 44. 26-28; 45.13, etc.).

(*b*) The enemy is no longer Assyria, as in the eighth century and at the beginning of the seventh, but Babylon; at the time of Isaiah, on the other hand, Babylon, too, was oppressed and therefore entered into more friendly relations with Judah (II Kings 20.12-19; Isa.39.1ff.; II Chron.32.31). Besides, at this time Babylon did not even have the power to invade and to oppress Judah. Moreover, Assyria is not even mentioned in Isa.40-66.

(c) On the other hand, the people of Judah who live in exile are no longer a prey to discouragement, as we saw in the second period of Ezekiel's preaching, nor in a euphoric state, as Jeremiah and Ezekiel show to have been the case between the two exiles. Deutero-Isaiah begins by announcing that their bondage is over (40.1f.), that the armies of liberation are now on the march and are encircling Babylon (41.2-4; 45.13; 46.11; 48.14-16), and these events are not described in the nebulous form typical of prophetic announcements about the more or less distant future, but with the precision that one would expect from the eyewitness to an event. Babylon is now faced with defeat (41.25-27; 42.9). But this is evidently the situation at the middle of the sixth century and not in the second half of the eighth.

(d) Cyrus, king of Persia, victor in the year 539 BCE, is twice mentioned explicitly in the text (44.28; 45.1-8). This never happens with other prophets in the case of a future figure, even in messianic prophecies. That applies even if the name was added later.

(e) In many passages the prophet refers to the fulfilment of ancient prophecies against Babylon and in favour of Judah (41.21-29; 42.9; 43.8-13; 44.8; 45.21; 46.8-12). None of these would make any sense to anyone living in the second half of the eighth century or at the beginning of the seventh, but they take on special significance if, as is said at the beginning of the book (40.1ff.), they are intended to console the people of YHWH between 547 and 546, the year of Cyrus' victory over Croesus, king of Lydia, and 539, the year of the fall of Babylon.

(f) There is a marked difference of style between the book of Isaiah from the eighth century and the passages under consideration, discernible even in a good translation: Isaiah has been edited according to the pattern and in the style of a prophet of his time, whereas Deutero-Isaiah is marked by a style which we might call 'epic', with a particularly elevated and flowing manner.

(g) A new vision of history begins with 'Deutero-Isaiah'. There is a clear distinction between the past and the present, which are full of calamity, and the coming era, that of salvation. There is no parallel to this kind of thought in pre-exilic prophecy, but it does appear with Haggai and Zechariah (cf. below, 26, 27) and will then be a characteristic feature of the apocalyptic books.

With few exceptions, virtually all these facts, which are now obvious to anyone with a critical approach, were only noted from the eighteenth century on: and only at the end of the last century did they become assured results of criticism. A computerized statistical check carried out at the University of Haifa confirmed what critics had said earlier about Isaiah (above, 20.2). There is still room for doubt and controversy over these results, but they do give scholars an objective basis for coping with the problems. Our starting point, too, will therefore be the acceptance of a Deutero-Isaiah whose ministry took place around the middle of the sixth century BCE. However, recent suggestions that the editing of Proto-Isaiah should be dated in the exilic period, shortly before or shortly afterwards, have brought the two books of Isaiah much closer together chronologically, and as we have also seen, a number of authors recognize the similarity of the basic problems between the two works. That could explain why they were combined (cf. above, 20.5).

Once this basic division between chs.1-39 and 40-66 has been made, a second problem immediately arises: is 40-66 a literary unity or a collection of fragments; and if the latter alternative is accepted, what are these fragments? There are various possible solutions.

1. Chapters 40-66 are a collection of fragments connected only by key-words or similar means.

2. Chapters 40-66 can be divided into the following units: chs.40-48; 49-55; and 56-66. The theme of the first unit is the action of Cyrus against Babylon, and is therefore to be placed between 550 and 539 BCE; the second speaks of the new community which came into being after the liberation and is therefore dated a little after 539; chs.56-66 constitute a 'Trito-Isaiah' and need to be studied separately: in fact we have a series of fragments most of which can be dated and located in the Jerusalem community in the last quarter of the sixth century.

3. Yet others would see 'Deutero-Isaiah' (chs.40-55) as a basic unity, the internal breaks within which coincide perfectly with the progress of the author's thought from the period preceding the liberation to that immediately afterwards. Chapters 56-66 then again constitute the 'Trito-Isaiah' mentioned in the previous paragraph. The discovery of 'Trito-Isaiah' is the work of B.Duhm, who proposed it in the first edition of his 1892 commentary on Isaiah. I too shall therefore be discussing 'Trito-Isaiah' among the post-exilic prophets (below, 28).

Most scholars regard the so-called 'Servant Songs' as a special category; I shall deal with them in § 3 below.

2. Analysis and content

Deutero-Isaiah can be divided easily into two large units, as we have already seen: chs.40-48 and chs.49-55. In the first part the dominant theme is that of Cyrus, king of Persia, whom the anonymous author supports with great enthusiasm, seeing him as the realization of YHWH's plan in history. The people of God, who have now paid the penalty for their guilt, are on the verge of liberation. This brings us down to the last years before the fall of Babylon, when Cyrus was ably forging the pincers which were soon to squeeze the Babylonian empire on many sides and the jaws of which would snap shut in the year 540-539, ending with the fall of the capital, Babylon. As we have seen, it is reasonable to date this unit between 547-46, the year in which Cyrus conquered Lydia, and 539. It is perhaps possible to be more exact: one study beginning from the phrase attested in Isa.40.2, '…the time of her servitude (lit. 'of her military service') is fulfilled', and from the fact that such military service lasted forty years, arrived at about 547 BCE from a starting point of 587. For some scholars (most recently R.P.Merendino), only this first part can be attributed to Deutero-Isaiah.

In the second unit there is none of the epic character which marks the first, and little or nothing is said of political events of any importance. The conquest of Babylon by Cyrus must therefore have taken place, and politically we are now in a static period. However, 40.8; 50.11 indicate that there is a clear relationship between the two parts.

3. The 'servant songs'

The most mysterious part of the book consists of the songs of the Servant of YHWH: 42.1-9; 49.1-6; 50.4-9; 52.13-53.12. They are marked out not only by a special theme, independent from that of the rest of the work, but also by the fact that they have evidently been interpolated into their present context, from which they can be removed without any resultant damage or interruption. They also have their own linguistic characteristics and their own theological content, which is independent of that of the other passages in the work. Collected together in a separate unit, they present a logical progression, culminating in the expiatory death of the servant and also in his triumph. That is the traditional Christian interpretation, from the earliest church onwards. However, I have expressed my own doubts about this interpretation of the last song, and these doubts have recently been taken up by Whybray and Mettinger: according to the text of Isa.53, the servant almost certainly was not killed, and in any case he was not raised. The text is unusual for being in the third person, but its hyperbole is familiar from the individual lament. Moreover, as we shall also see, some scholars no longer accept that the songs have an independent existence apart from the rest of the work.

One obvious question arises: is it possible to identify the servant, and if so to say who he was? Was he a tangible historical individual? The question is an old one; we find it put in the New Testament by the Ethiopian eunuch of Acts 8.34 to the apostle Philip. Philip's reply is well known, but it is a product of about five hundred years of reflection on the theme. Even within the last century, every possible answer has been given and every conceivable person has been identified with the servant. I, too, shall therefore attempt to answer the question, with the difference that, in contrast to specialist works or studies, I shall have to be content to keep to the main headings.

(a) If the author of the songs were the anonymous author of the book, as has been affirmed by Muilenburg and Fohrer, it would be natural for us to consider the songs in which the servant speaks in the first person as autobiographical (49.1ff.; 50.4ff.). This solution of the problem has again received authoritative support and has much to be said for it. On the other hand, to anyone who knows oriental literature it seems unreal, quite apart from the fact that the prophet or the redactor could very well have quoted a series of songs in the first person. We would then have a similar problem to that of the 'confessions' of Jeremiah. So the solution is implausible; it is not only unnecessary, but also by no means the only one that can be put forward.

(b) Another direction in which research has turned has been a consideration of the great figures of the history of Israel who pass through particularly serious trials, from Moses to Jehoiachin or later Zerubbabel, a figure to whom we shall return (below, 27.2). The various attempts and figures have been listed by the commentators, who also give reasons for their choice of one figure rather than another.

(c) The collective interpretation is also important. This theory was particularly acceptable among Jewish scholars, and is based on 49.2-5, where the servant is understood as 'Israel'. The theory was already put forward by the LXX and the Targum, so it may be based not only on a text but also on a very ancient exegetical tradition.

(d) Attention should also be paid to Engnell's theory. He has connected the figure of the servant with that of the king. According to the ritual of the *akītu* festival (the Babylonian day of expiation celebrated during the New Year festival), it appears that the monarch vicariously took on himself the guilt of his people, sometimes even suffering death (in this case it seems certain that in Babylon a temporary king was elected and sent to his death in place of the real king). With this expiatory act the people would then be freed from their guilt. The ritual of the festival would thus be an adaptation of the liturgy of the death of the god Tammuz, whose cult we have seen even to have been practised in the Jerusalem temple before 587 (Ezek.8). For Engnell there is no doubt that the figure of the Servant was originally a royal figure (and his theory has been confirmed indirectly by the fact that in the ancient Near East only royal inscriptions are written in the first person). This would justify either an individual (the king clearly was an individual) or a corporate interpretation (the king *was* his people according to the theory of 'corporate personality' developed by Wheeler Robinson in 1936). Therefore although the messianic interpretation of the figure of the servant is not attested in the Jewish writings of the period (with a single exception which is difficult to evaluate and which we shall be examining shortly), in the New Testament period it would be completely legitimate, indeed the only truly legitimate interpretation. However, the centrality of the *akītu* festival in the Babylonian New Year Festival has recently been questioned in the study by P.Welten, on the basis of new texts, so that Engnell's theory now seems doubtful.

Be that as it may, the term 'servant' supports Engnell's interpretation rather than ruling it out. The Hebrew *'ebed* is not necessarily a title of humiliation. It has the same ambivalence as our 'minister', a word which originally had clearly servile connotations. The 'King's Servants' are his ministers or at any rate high officials in I Sam.16.15ff.; the title is used for the prophets in Amos 3.6: YHWH consults with 'his servants the prophets' before doing anything. The title is thus one of exaltation rather than humiliation. In Gen.40.20ff. the ministers and other dignitaries at Pharaoh's court bear this title, as does the major-domo of the patriarchs (Gen.15.1ff; 24.1ff.), to whom are entrusted extremely confidential matters, like that of looking for a wife for the heir. P.Volz in his commentary (p.18) could therefore rightly speak of a 'favourite minister'. The title is also used of the monarch in his relationships with YHWH (cf. Pss.89.21; 132.10 for David), and while here (but not necessarily elsewhere) it could also indicate the king's relationship of inferiority with YHWH, the attribution of the title to David makes its connection with the monarchy obvious. That would also explain the universalistic elements which are to be found in the servant songs, like those that we encounter in the royal psalms 2 and 110. J.Morgenstern has attempted to reconstruct a servant ritual, but as Muilenburg rightly observes, this is to go too far: too many links are still missing in such a chain. Moreover, as the studies by Bonnard and Mettinger have shown, it is not in fact legitimate to detach the servant songs from the rest of the book. Why, Bonnard asks, take only four songs and not use all the texts in the book which mention the term *'ebed* and its cognate verb? In this case, the danger is that Christians allow themselves unconsciously to be influenced by the first christology of the earliest church.

It is certain that once we put the problem in such terms, markedly individual elements (cf. the suffering described in Isa.53, which is difficult to apply to a collective figure) and collective features (e.g. 'Israel' in 49.2ff.) can alternate without any incongruity.

I said earlier that Judaism never knew a messianic interpretation of the person of the servant. A variant to Isa. 52.14a does, however, appear in 1QIs[a] (but not in Is[b]) which might argue to the contrary. There we read: *kēn mšhty mē'īš mar'ēhū* (that is, the text has the root *mšḥ*, 'anoint', instead of *šḥt*), giving the translation (the variants from the Massoretic text are in italics): 'As many were astonished at him, so *I have anointed* his face beyond human semblance... [15]and as many nations are startled *because of him...*' Provided that we do not have a copyist's error here, this shows that in circles a little earlier than, or contemporary with, the New Testament there was a serious proposal of the alternative of a messianic interpretation, even if we do not know whether and to what degree it was accepted.

4. Thought

The prophet presents five principal themes in his first message:

(a) YHWH is the Lord of history. This is a theme common to all the prophets, but in Deutero-Isaiah it reaches a climax, all the more so since the times and the condition of the people had led them to doubt. But the defeat of the people had not been a defeat for YHWH. And whereas with the prophets who had preceded Deutero-Isaiah it had been a sign of divine judgment announced centuries earlier by other prophets and again by Dtr shortly before the exile, it was now to become impressive testimony to a new creative act by God through which Judah would rise again from its ruins. Now that the phase of judgment was terminated, the very people who had first been used to chastize Judah would be the instrument for its rehabiliation. God had rejected his people, but now he re-elected them: a new exodus had brought Judah back to its native land. The warning signs of what was about to happen were given by the slow but certain erosion of the security of the Babylonian empire, which was being undermined by the Persians (43.4ff.). Israel is again the elect people of God; the election has never been nullified but only suspended (43.22-28: 48.1-11; 54.10), a theme which the apostle Paul also takes up in Rom.9-11.

On this basis the people will set out on the march home. They will be liberated, and will be led by the very God who in Ezek.10.18ff. had abandoned Jerusalem. Things will again be as they were at the time of the exodus (40.3ff.; 49.25ff.; 51.9). For this reason some scholars have wanted to see the servant as a kind of Moses of this new exodus. The themes of creation and exodus are key elements in understanding Deutero-Isaiah; this is a *creatio ex nihilo* of a people who were no longer a people, the exodus of a prostrate people and their settlement in the promised land.

(*b*) YHWH reveals himself as the one God. It is not that Israel had not known forms of monotheism before this period, but rather that only with Deutero-Isaiah was the faith changed to certainty. Israel had reckoned with the possibility of the existence of other gods, at least as far as other nations were concerned, but now they are revealed for what they really are: non-existent, creations of man's hands in wood, metal and stone (40.18f.; 41.6f.; 42.17; 44.6; 45.5,15,18; 46.9). In some cases these passages are interpolations, but when they are authentic, they show for the first time a polemical attitude towards polytheism even on a theoretical level. In his comparisons Deutero-Isaiah, followed much later by the deutero-canonical Wisdom of Solomon (cf. below, 47.2d), chs.13-15, does not hesitate to use heavy irony and sometimes harsh sarcasm, with obvious signs that the prophet not only does not understand his opponent but is not even concerned to understand him. We also find a similar criticism of the cult of divine images much later, in Western paganism. It is enough to recall the lines written by Horace (*Satires* I, 8, 1-3):

Olim truncus eram ficulnus, inutile lignum,
cum faber, incertus scamnum ʾfaceretne Priapum,
Maluit esse deum; deus inde ego...

('In Days of Yore our Godship stood
A very worthless Log of Wood.
The Joiner doubting, or to shape Us
Into a Stool, or a Priapus,
At length resolv'd, for Reasons wise,
Into a God to bid me rise.

ET by Philip Francis, *A Poetical Translation of the Works of Horace*, London [5]1853, III, 125.)

We shall return to the subject when speaking of the Wisdom of Solomon, whose polemic repeats these texts of Deutero-Isaiah.

(c) Another characteristic of the prophet is his universalism: as Lord of history and creator of the universe, God must necessarily be the God of all nations, a concept which is expressed in a particularly clear way in the servant passages (42.1-6; 49.6). A critical reading of this material, however, leads to a disconcerting conclusion: in this passage it is not easy to see what the position of the Gentiles will be. This leads us to the question of:

(d) The mission to the Gentiles. The problem, it must be said from the start, is far from being resolved, and it may be put in the following terms: do we or do we not have in Deutero-Isaiah an exhortation to his people to begin the mission among the Gentiles? We know that later the Pharisees in particular had a strong missionary and proselytizing concern, a characteristic of which Jesus reminds them in his polemic (Matt.23.15), and it could well be that if the reply to the question is in the affirmative, they drew from Deutero-Isaiah the inspiration for what must certainly have been a revolutionary attitude. In general the reply is affirmative, on the basis of passages like 42.1ff.; 49.6, which are parts of the servant songs, mentioned above. On the other hand, as R.Martin-Achard has recently pointed out with some acuteness, these passages do not mention any kind of mission or proselytism among the Gentiles. 'The Chosen People's business is to exist; its presence in the world furnishes proof of Yahweh's divinity; its life declares what He means for Israel itself and for the universe. The mission of Israel consists in reflecting the glory of God by accepting His gifts and His judgment alike. When they contemplate the singular destiny of the Chosen People, the heavens and the earth find Him who has wrought it.' It is obvious that the idea of mission could be drawn with logical consistency from an interpretation of this kind, but it is another matter to affirm that it was in the intentions of the preaching of the prophet himself.

(e) Another element of considerable importance is one which

appears in the servant songs, the new evaluation of suffering. While Dtr or Wisdom (as we shall soon see) had unfailingly considered suffering to be a punishment for sins, here it acquired the value of vicarious expiation for the sufferer and those closest to him, and is not the object of mournful laments, as happens in certain psalms. In earlier times there had been men who had suffered for their people: Moses, Jeremiah, perhaps Isaiah and later Zerubbabel, and towards the end of the first millennium BCE the Teacher of Righteousness at Qumran; in the New Testament Paul also applied this concept to himself, though in a rather obscure context (Col.1.24). The depth of thought shows clearly that explanations of an individualistic or a collective type are not sufficient here. This overturning of values in a case like the suffering of the righteous appears to be a fundamental stage in the development of the thought of the Hebrew Bible.

(d) Finally, it is characteristic of the thought of Deutero-Isaiah that he often uses feminine attributes and titles for God (cf. 42.13-14; 45.10; 45.19a).

5. The text

Despite the differences from the Isaiah of the eighth century which were indicated at the beginning of this examination, there are notable analogies; the two authors have many elements of vocabulary in common, and in both books the designation of YHWH as 'the Holy One of Israel' is important. In any case, the question arises how these chapters could have been put together in one book; it is certain that the fusion is a relatively early one. Ecclesiasticus 48.23ff. explicitly identifies the Isaiah at work in the time of Hezekiah as the one who consoles the afflicted, and he is writing at the beginning of the second century BCE. There is a sign betwen chs.39 and 40 in 1Q Is[a] which some scholars interpret as a sign of separation, but in fact it has not been explained. The situation in the fourth to third centuries BCE is confused: II Chron.36.22ff.//Ezra 1.1-3 attribute Isa.44.28 to Jeremiah, which is perhaps an indication that at this time at least part of the book was attributed to that prophet. An explanation deduced from the Babylonian Talmud does not seem satisfactory: arranging the books by size, Isaiah comes after Jeremiah and Ezekiel, which would only be possible if it had less than forty-eight chapters... The argument is too vague for us to be able to draw any conclusions from it.

The solution put forward by the various Scandinavian schools seems more attractive: Bentzen supposed that the school which arose around the prophet of the eighth century had continued to work for a long time afterwards, maintaining certain ideological elements and terminological constants; I have already called attention to these in speaking of Isaiah. Of course, if the redaction of Isa.1-39 and 40-55 took place more or less at the same time, a notion which has been gaining ground increasingly in recent times (above, 20.3), this problem would be considerably reduced.

In any case, the difference between Isaiah, Deutero-Isaiah and Trito-Isaiah is now accepted by practically everyone, whatever the explanation may be. The only dissenters are those in very conservative Jewish and Christian circles.

BIBLIOGRAPHY

Commentaries

Cf. on Isaiah, above, 20. Also P.Volz, KAT, 1932; E.J.Kissane, Dublin ²1962; G.Fohrer, ZBK, 1965; C.R.North, Oxford 1964; G.A.F.Knight, New York and Nashville 1965; C.Westermann, ET, OTL, 1969; J.L.McKenzie, AB, 1968; R.N.Whybray, NCB, 1975; K.Elliger, BK I, 1978, continued by H.-J.Hermisson, 1987ff.; P.-E.Bonnard, *Le Seconde Esaie, son disciple et leur éditeur, Ésaïe 40-66*, Paris 1972 (this is important because it rejects the detachment of the servant songs from the rest of the prophet); Bonnard reviewed his position in an article, 'Relire Esaie 40-66', *ETR* 50, 1975, 351-9; H.D.Preuss, *Deuterojesaja*, Neukirchen-Vluyn 1976; C.Stuhlmueller, 'Deutero-Isaiah. Major Transition in the Prophet's Theology and in Contemporary Study', *CBQ* 42, 1980, 1-29; H.-J.Hermisson. 'Deuterojesajas Problem', *VuF* 31.3, 1986, 53-84. All these studies provide up-to-date bibliographies.

Monographs on the whole book: L.Köhler, *Deuterojesaja (Jesaja 40-55), stilkritsch untersucht*, BZAW 37, 1923; J.Begrich, *Studien zu Deuterojesaja*, Stuttgart 1938, reprinted Munich 1963; J.Morgenstern, 'The Message of Deutero-Isaiah in its Consequential Unfolding', *HUCA* 29, 1958, 1-67; 30, 1939, 1-102; id., 'Isaiah 49-55', *HUCA* 36, 1965, 1-38; M.Haran, 'The Literary Structure and Chronological Framework of the Prophecies in Is.XL-XLVIII', *SVT* 9, 1963, 127-55. For relations with Jeremiah and with other prophets cf. the old article by U.Cassuto, 'On the Formal and Stylistic Relationship between Deutero-Isaiah and Other Biblical Writers' (1911-13), in *Biblical and Oriental Studies* I, Jerusalem 1973, 144-66; S.M.Paul, 'Literary and Ideological Echoes of Jeremiah in Deutero-Isaiah', in *Proceedings of the Fifth World Congress of Jewish Studies, Jerusalem 1969*, 1, Jerusalem

1972, 102-20; Y.Gitay, *Prophecy and Persuasion*, Bonn 1981; C.Westermann, *Sprache und Struktur der Prophetie Deuterojesajas*, Stuttgart 1981; R.P.Carroll, *When Prophecy Failed*, London 1981, 150ff.; A.S.Kapelrud, 'The Main Concern of Second Isaiah', *VT* 32, 1982, 50-8; E.W.Conrad, 'Second Isaiah and the Priestly Oracle of Salvation', *ZAW* 93, 1981, 234-46; W.Zimmerli, 'Jahwes Wort bei Deuterojesaja', *VT* 32, 1982, 104-24; M.C.Lind, 'Monotheism, Power and Justice. A Study in Isaiah 40-55', *CBQ* 46, 1984, 432-46; D.W.Van Winkle, 'The Relationship of the Nations to Yahweh and to Israel in Isaiah XL-LV', *VT* 35, 1985, 446-58. For particular topics cf. K.Kiesow, *Exodus-texte im Jesajabuch*, Fribourg CH 1972; H.C.Schmitt, 'Prophetie und Schultheologie im Deuterojesajabuch', *ZAW* 91, 1979, 43-61; R.P.Merendino, *Der Erste und der Letzte. Eine Untersuchung von Jesaja 40-48*, Leiden 1981; R.J.Clifford, 'The Function of the Idol Passages in Second Isaiah', *CBQ* 42, 1980, 450-64; H.M.Barstad, 'The So-Called Babylonian Influence in Second Isaiah', *JSOT* 2,2, 1987, 90-110.

1g. For the division into two eras in Deutero-Isaiah see G.Fohrer, 'Die Struktur der alttestamentlichen Eschatologie', *TLZ* 85, 1960, 401-20 (= his *Studien zur alttestamentlichen Prophetie*, BZAW 99, 1967, 32-58), suggesting that the term 'eschatology' may only legitimately be used where a separation is implied between an evil past and present age and a blessed future age. Cf. also Haran, art.cit. K.Baltzer, 'Jes 40,13-14 – ein Schlüssel zur Einheit Deutero-Jesajas', *BN* 37, 1987, 7-10, argues for the substantial unity of Deutero-Isaiah.

2. For the date cf. A.Schreiber, 'Der Zeitpunkt des Auftretens von Deuterojesaja', *ZAW* 84, 1972, 242f. For the structure of the work cf. R.F.Melugin, *The Formation of Isaiah 40-55*, Berlin 1976; R.Lack, 'La struttu-razione di Isaia 40-55', *La scuola cattolica* 101, 1973, 43-58, and for the text C.F.Whitley, 'Further Notes on the Text of Deutero-Isaiah', *VT* 25, 1975, 683-7. For a collective rather than an individual interpretation of the person of the author cf. recently D.Michel, 'Das Rätsel Deuterojesaja', *Theologia Viatorum* 13, 1975-76, 115-32; T.N.D.Mettinger, 'In Search of the Hidden Structure: YHWH as King in Isaiah 40-55', *SEÅ* 51/52, 1986-7, 148-57.

3. There is an immense literature on the Servant Songs. For bibliographical information see H.H.Rowley, 'The Servant of the Lord in the Light of Three Decades of Criticism', in his *The Servant of the Lord and Other Essays*, London [2]1965, 1-57; C.R.North, *The Suffering Servant in Deutero-Isaiah*, London [2]1956. Among other writings note especially I.Engnell, 'The 'Ebed Yahweh Songs and the Suffering Messiah in "Deutero-Isaiah" ', *BJRL* 31, 1948, 54-93; J.Lindblom, *The Servant Songs in Deutero-Isaiah*, Lund 1951; J.Muilenburg, introduction to the commentary in IB V, 1956, 381-415; O.Kaiser, *Der königliche Knecht*, Göttingen 1959; J.Morgenstern, 'The Suffering Servant, a New Solution', *VT* 11, 1961, 292-320, 406-14; G.Kehnscherper, 'Der "Sklave Gottes" bei Deuterojesaja', *FuF* 40, 1966, 279-82 (a Marxist interpretation of the problem; though its basic thesis is invalid, it is a stimulating viewpoint); G.R.Driver, 'Isaiah 52, 13-53,12: the Servant

of the Lord', in M.Black and G.Fohrer (eds.), *In Memoriam Paul Kahle*, BZAW 103, 1968, 90-105; P.E.Dion, 'Les chants du Serviteur de Yahweh et quelques passages apparentés d'Is.40-55', *Bibl* 51, 1970, 17-38; K.Baltzer, 'Zum formgeschichtlichen Bestimmung der Texte vom Gottesknecht im Deutero-jesajabuch', in H.-W.Wolff (ed.), *Probleme biblischer Theologie. G. von Rad zum 70.Geburtstag*, Munich 1971, 27-43; G.Fohrer, *Theologische Grundstrukturen des AT*, Berlin 1972, 22f., with bibliography; E.Kutsch, *Sein Leiden und Tod, unser Heil*, Neukirchen-Vluyn 1967; L.Ruppert, *Der leidende Gerechte*, Würzburg 1972. The theory of parallels from the ancient Near East has been questioned by H.M.Kümmel, 'Ersatzkönig und Sündenbock', *ZAW* 80, 1968, 289-318. H.M.Orlinsky, *The So-called 'Suffering Servant' in Isaiah 53*, Cincinnati 1964 (reprinted in *Interpreting the Prophetic Tradition*, New York 1969, 225-73), has argued that the servant is neither a particular individual nor Israel, and that his person is never interpreted in terms of vicarious expiation; vicarious messianic interpretations only arose in circles associated with the New Testament writers. Orlinsky's views have not won general acceptance. An attempt to place the figure of the servant, taken as an individual, within the context of events begun by Cyrus' movement has been made by G.Sauer, 'Deuterojesaja und die Lieder vom Gottesknecht', in G.Fitzer (ed.), *Geschictsmächtigkeit und Geduld*, Munich 1972, 58-66. P.-E.Bonnard in his commentary denies that the servant passages can be detached from their present context; they should be regarded as an integral part of Deutero-Isaiah, and the servant must be considered in terms of the total presentation. Consequently the identification has several dimensions: usually the people as a whole is meant, sometimes the people as an élite, at other times the prophet himself or Cyrus. T.N.D.Mettinger, cf. below, denies that the songs have an independent existence. Other studies of the theme are R.N.Whybray, *Thanksgiving for a Liberated Prophet. An Interpretation of Isaiah Chapter 53*, Sheffield 1978; H.-J.Hermisson, 'Israel und der Gottesknecht bei Deuterojesaja', *ZTK* 7, 1982, 1-24; T.N.D.Mettinger, *A Farewell to the Servant Songs*, Lund 1983, thus also R.Rendtorff*, 195f.; P.R.Raabe, 'The Effect of Repetition in the Suffering Servant Songs', *JBL* 103, 1984, 77-84; O.H.Steck, 'Aspekte des Gottesknechtes in Deuterojesajas "Ebed-Jahwe-Lieder" ', *ZAW* 96, 1984, 372-90; H.-E.von Waldow, 'Der Gottesknecht bei Deuterojesaja', *TZ* 41, 1985, 201-19.

For the concept of 'corporate personality', cf. H.W.Robinson, 'The Hebrew Conception of Corporate Personality', in P.Volz (ed.), *Wesen und Werden des Alten Testaments*, Giessen 1936, 57ff. (reprinted Philadelphia 1964); R.de Fraine, *Adam et son Lignage*, Louvain and Bruges 1959. For the idea of the substitute king in Mesopotamia cf. Kümmel, art.cit.; P.Welten, 'Königsherrschaft Jahwes und Thronbesteigung', *VT* 32, 1982, 297-310; J.A.Soggin, 'Tod und Auferstehung des leidendes Gottesknechtes', *ZAW* 87, 346-55, presents my own view.

For Qumran and the New Testament cf. H.-W.Wolff, *Jesaja 53 in*

Urchristentum, Berlin ²1950; W.H.Brownlee, *The Meaning of the Qumran Scrolls for the Bible*, New York 1964, chs.9-10.

3b. H.Cazelles, 'Le roi Yoyakin et le Serviteur du Seigneur', in *Proceedings of the Fifth World Congress of Jewish Studies...*, 121-6.

3c. L.E.Wilshire, 'The Servant City: a New Interpretation of the "Servant of the Lord" in the Servant of the Lord Songs of Deutero-Isaiah', *JBL* 94, 1975, 356-67, suggests that Zion/Jerusalem are the 'servant' (against this cf. J.Coppens, 'L'identité du Serviteur de Yahvé', *ETL* 52, 1976, 344-6).

4. H.-E.von Waldow, 'The Message of Deutero-Isaiah', *Int* 22, 1968, 259-87; O.H.Steck, 'Deuterojesaja als theologischer Denker', *KuD* 15, 1969, 180-93; C.Stuhlmueller, 'Yahweh-king and Deutero-Isaiah', *BiblRes* 15, 1970, 32-45; D.Baltzer, *Ezechiel und Deuterojesaja*, BZAW 121, 1971.

4a. S.Porúbčan, *Il Patto Nuovo in Is.xl-xlvi*, Rome 1959; W.Zimmerli, 'Le "nouvel exode" dans le message des deux grands prophètes de l'exil', in *Hommage à W.Vischer*, Montpellier 1960 (= 'Das "neue Exodus" in der Verkündigung der beiden grossen Exilspropheten', in his *Gottes Offenbarung*, Munich 1963, 192-204); R.N.Whybray, *The Heavenly Counsellor in Isaiah xl, 13-14*, Cambridge 1971; A.Schoors, *I am God Your Saviour*, Leiden 1973; A.Lauha, 'Der "Bund des Volkes" ', in *Beiträge zur alttestamentlichen Theologie. FS W.Zimmerli*, Göttingen 1977, 257-62; B.W.Anderson, 'Exodus and Covenant in Second Isaiah and Prophetic Tradition', in *Magnalia Dei. Essays... G.E.Wright*, Garden City 1976.

For the creation cf. T.M.Ludwig, 'The Tradition of the Establishing of the Earth in Deutero-Isaiah', *JBL* 92, 1973, 345-57; D.M.Gunn, 'Deutero-Isaiah and the Flood', *JBL* 94, 1975, 493-508; R.Albertz, *Weltschöpfung und Menschenschöpfung*, Stuttgart 1974 (who distinguishes between the creation of the universe, an element of invocation to YHWH, and that of humankind, an element of prayer: on the basis of creation, humankind can reproach itself for the tolerance of features which seem to deny it).

4d. R.Martin-Achard, *A Light to the Nations*, ET Edinburgh 1962, 31; A.Schoors, 'L'eschatologie dans les prophéties du Deutéro-Isaïe', in C.Hauret (ed.), *Aux grands carrefours de la révélation et de l'exégèse de l'Ancien Testament*, Louvain 1967, 107-28; P.E.Dion, 'L'universalisme religieux dans les différentes couches rédactionelles d'Isaïe 40-55', *Bibl* 51, 1970, 161-83; J.Blenkinsopp, 'Second-Isaiah – Prophet of Universalism', *JSOT* 41, 1988, 83-103; H.Wildberger, 'Der Monotheismus Deuterojesajas', in *FS W.Zimmerli*, 506-30; for Deutero-Isaiah and the idols cf. J.L.Koole, 'De beeldenstorm van Deuterojesaja', in *Loven en geloven, Feestbundel N.H.Ridderbos*, Amsterdam 1975, 77-93. For the use of feminine imagery see M.I.Gruber, 'The Motherhood of God in Second Isaiah', *RB* 90, 1983, 351-9; for the oneness of God, H.Klein, 'Der Beweis der Einzigkeit Jahwes bei Deuterojesaja', *VT* 35, 1985, 267-73.

5. A.Bentzen, *King and Messiah*, ET Oxford 1955; C.Stuhlmueller, *Creative Redemption in Deutero-Isaiah*, Rome 1970.

26

HAGGAI

1. The prophet and his age

We know little or nothing about the person of this prophet who has given his name to one of the shortest books of the Hebrew Bible. We only know that together with Zechariah he preached to the community which had returned from the Babylonian exile, exhorting them to rebuild the temple, since the coming of the Lord was near.

Our sources for the reconstruction of the events which underlie this preaching are the books of Ezra and Nehemiah (below, 43). As we shall see, these sources are not easy to use because they have been revised extensively; however, it emerges from them that after the fall of Babylon in 539 Cyrus, king of Persia, allowed all the exiles, including those from Judah, to return to their native lands and to rebuild the sanctuaries which had been destroyed (Ezra 6.3-5; 1.2-4; cf. II Chron. 36.2f.). Acts like these were an integral part of Persian religious policy, tending not only to avoid any unnecessary friction with the peoples incorporated into the empire but also to present the new monarchy as the liberator from Babylonian oppression. Among other things, this policy provided for the granting of religious liberty to individual peoples: Cyrus presented himself to his subjects as the great restorer of the religions trampled down by Babylon; in the so-called 'Cyrus cylinder' he puts special emphasis on this aspect of the restoration of cults which had been suppressed. In this fashion he won not only the sympathy of the peoples of the empire but also the support of the priesthood, now the only ruling element which offered some degree of institutional continuity. The last king of Babylon, Nabu-na'id (Nabonidus), incurred the enmity of the priesthood with his attempts to install archaic cults, and this tendency made no small contribution to his fall (cf. my *History*, XII).

It would thus be reasonable enough to imagine a return of the exiles to Judah *en masse*. However, nothing of the kind happened. Most of them had followed the advice given them by Jeremiah (cf.

chs.28; 29) and had established a strong economic position in Babylon; to give up overnight this new position which they had secured with so much effort would have seemed absurd. Meanwhile they contributed generously to the needs of the few who did return. On the other hand, the situation of those who returned very soon proved to be a far cry from the epic descriptions formulated by Deutero-Isaiah. Here was no second exodus! The way was long and difficult, the country had been devastated and had gone to seed after having been abandoned for more than half a century. The land lay desolate or, if it were particularly good, had passed into other hands (Nebuchadnezzar had distributed the land belonging to the deportees to the lowest classes in the country and in the cities, II Kings 25.12; Jer.52.16). This had created a complex situation in both legal and human terms: someone who had been given land more than half a century before would not readily be inclined to hand over the fruit of his labour to a family which had once owned it, or had some kind of claim to it. Some bad harvests followed, and the company of the returned exiles soon found themselves in a position of hopelessness and economic restrictions, ultimately depending almost entirely on money which might reach them from Babylon. No one had imagined that coming home would be like this; indeed those who returned had been promised the opposite.

About eighteen years elapsed between the return home and the beginning of the work of rebuilding the temple: Ezra 4.1-5.24 refers to a first attempt in this direction. It was, however, interrupted by the hostility of the neighbouring peoples, who denounced the returned exiles as nationalists who were about to re-fortify the city so as to be able to rebel. Doubts about them were easy to stir up; the temple walls, which today form the south-east corner of the city, were at that time the fortification towards the north-east, and their rebuilding could very well be interpreted as an attempt to reconstruct the defences of the city. Furthermore, the material difficulties which had meanwhile arisen meant that it was too much for the small community to be able to hope and dare to embark on an enterprise of this kind. Judah, incorporated into the Persian empire and therefore deprived of all political autonomy, was a tiny fraction of the old kingdom; the normal calculation is that in a day's march a man could easily walk across from one extreme boundary to another.

As I have said, the legal situation was complicated; the drought, the locusts and the resultant famine did the rest (Haggai 1.5-11; 2.15-19; Ezra 5.1ff.). In the north was the community from which the Samaritans were later to emerge, composed of a mixed population which practised a syncretistic cult, if we accept what II Kings 17.1ff. says. If we make a comparison with the Samaritan traditions themselves, this judgment is probably unfair in both historical and religious terms; if nothing else, it at least shows the relationship between the community of those who had returned from exile and the people on their immediate northern borders, a relationship which Ezra 4.1-5 reveals to have been very tense from the beginning. It also seems that there was a lively debate about who was to be considered the 'true Israel', those who had remained after the catastrophe of 587 or those who had returned; it seems that each group regarded itself as the 'remnant' announced by the prophets. There was not only the economic and political factor, but also a breach at the religious level, and all these elements counselled prudence: it was better to face the immediate problems than to embark on more large-scale projects like the rebuilding of the temple. At any rate, the cult continued to exist, albeit in a much reduced form; it was never interrupted even during the worst moments of the exile: Jer.41.4ff. speaks of pilgrims who came from the north to the ruins of the temple, while according to Ezra 3.3 an altar was erected where the temple of Solomon first stood. Things therefore did not seem to be too urgent.

The favourable moment seems to have arrived unexpectedly. On the death of Cambyses, son of Cyrus, the Persian empire was shaken by a series of grave disorders which threatened to cause its dissolution: this would not have been the first time that an empire of enormous dimensions dissolved into nothing in the course of a few years. Assyria and Babylon are the most impressive examples. Would this not be the warning of the imminent end, of the coming of the 'day of the Lord' already announced in Amos 5.18? In the person of the prophet Haggai this eschatological hope found its first interpreter. His own preaching began in August 521/520, as he called on the people to begin the rebuilding of the temple immediately, since the end was near. The Lord was about to come and ought to find his sanctuary ready to receive him. Ezekiel 43.1f. had already spoken in these terms (cf. Ezra 4.24-5.1; 6.14ff.): according to Ezekiel, YHWH himself would come and take up his abode in the midst of his people. Like the prophets of the past, Haggai too interpreted the events of the present and the imminent future as showing that the present ills of the people were the consequence of their sin and their lack of faith; they had allowed themseles to be diverted from their mission, letting themselves be caught up in immediate needs. These needs were pressing, but not so much as to justify their laziness in the face of the coming kingdom (1.9b-10). For this reason, God was now punishing them through certain reverses which in their turn were harbingers of even more severe judgment. Now the moment had arrived: the rebuilding of the temple was the most urgent matter and had to proceed apace, regardless of the economic, political or religious situation. The messianic kingdom was about to be inaugurated; its sovereign was to be the last scion of the house of David, Zerubbabel, grandson of Jehoiachin (note, incidentally, his Babylonian name, an all too evident sign of the degree to which the exiles had been assimilated in their new country). At that time he was the governor appointed by the Persian administration (for Zerubbabel and his functions see my *History*, XII, 5c). He was designated 'the elect of YHWH', his 'seal', his 'servant' (1.14; 2.23); we considered the third of these titles in connection with Deutero-Isaiah; for the second cf. Gen.41.42.

2. Analysis and text

Unlike the earlier prophetic books, Haggai has virtually no passages in poetry. Moreover, its messages are dated in a way which has no precedents in the Hebrew Bible and which is followed only in Zechariah. They run from 1.VI to 24.IX of the second year of Darius I Hystaspes (i.e. from August/September to November/December of 521-20). The third person, which is used right through the text, seems to presuppose the existence of a redactor, and the same thing could be indicated by the note about the effects of Haggai's preaching, the beginning of the work (1.12-15). But we cannot exclude the possibility that the prophet wrote in the third person to give the impression of greater objectivity. The book could also have been drawn up a little after the events which it describes, since Zerubbabel (who, as we shall see in connection with Zechariah, soon disappears mysteriously) is again presented as Messiah (2.23).

The text can be divided into four parts: (*a*) the summons to begin work (1.1-11), followed by the beginning of work (1.12-15); (*b*) an oracle about the building of the temple (2.1-9); (*c*) a series of questions about various matters (2.10-19); and finally (*d*) a messianic oracle about the person of Zerubbabel (2.20-23).

The text of the book is in good condition; only here and there do we find some irregularities in the arrangement of the material. For example, after 1.15 we would expect a date, as the text cannot be related to what has gone before, while in 2.10-19 we have two different themes: ritual purity and the conditions for being a member of the community – the second was understood until a short while ago as an adoption of positions in the face of the beginnings of the Samaritan schism. It has been suggested that the irregularity should be removed by transposing 2.1-19 after 1.15 and deleting the date in 2.18 as a spurious addition. This rearrangement makes the best sense of the text and only minimally affects the content, but there is no support for it in the ancient versions.

3. Thought

Anyone who wants to pass judgment on this book by making a comparison with the pre-exilic prophets in terms of content and aesthetics will certainly be misled; like the majority of the post-exilic prophets, Haggai is characterized by a clumsy and heavy style, and anyone accustomed to the themes discussed in the earlier books will find the problems with which he concerns himself often banal. Problems of political and social ethics, of faithfulness to one's calling, and so on, are now replaced by the observance of certain cultic rules and a more or less legalistic approach to life. It has been said of Haggai that he sought to incite his people 'with Utopian dreams of wealth and power as soon as the cornerstone of the Temple was laid' (R.H.Pfeiffer*, 603). Moreover, Pfeiffer continues, although the book is historically interesting for the information that it provides (otherwise we know little or nothing of the period), it has no importance from either a religious or a literary point of view. This is a harsh judgment, which in part is also shared by the Introductions* of Eissfeldt (426ff.) and Fohrer (458), who would prefer to translate *nābī'* in 1.1 as 'cultic prophet'.

We can leave aside any criticism which is based on exclusively modern aesthetic criteria: it now seems to be taken for granted that Haggai, like the majority of the post-exilic prophets, does not reach the level of his predecessors in this field. The problem seems more important, however, from a theological perspective; after all, art for art's sake was never the aim of any prophet, even those who composed works of notable artistic value. The theological problem of Haggai and then Zechariah arises directly out of the political situation: the Persian empire seemed to be in decline, and the prophet exhorted his people to look beyond their own difficulties, to go beyond their own confines and consider events on the world scene. To arrive at this position, however, the people needed a leading idea to guide them and courage to dare something apparently far beyond their own weak resources. The rebuilding of the temple in the hope of a messianic future was an act of faith in the unforeseeable strength of the divine promises, in the divine rule over the universe and in the kingdom which had been announced and was about to arrive. The rebuilding of the temple in the economic, political and religious situation of the 520s was a blow against present reality with a view to this future.

A faith of this kind is obviously open to a good deal of criticism: that it is removed from reality, that it interprets history almost mechanically, according to pre-established patterns, and that it is not a little reminiscent of the faith of certain Zealots and Sicarii from the time of Jesus and during the two rebellions which led to the destruction of the greater part of the Jewish community in Palestine: it is therefore easily written off. But we cannot deny that it was in effect the preaching first of Haggai and then of Zechariah which aroused the people from their torpor, revived their sense of vocation and enabled them to rise from the nadir which they had reached when the promises of Deutero-Isaiah had not been literally fulfilled. Thus the statement by W.Eichrodt that this position, while being inferior to that assumed by the other prophets, is still a notable testimony to the work of God in history, is a valid one. Instead of being overwhelmed and brutalized by the needs of everyday life, the believer praised the Lord whose coming he awaited and was concerned not to be found unprepared. This standpoint obviously leads to problems which go with any prophetic vocation, even if it is apparently less 'committed' than that of the great pre-exilic prophets.

BIBLIOGRAPHY

Commentaries

On the twelve minor prophets see above, 18; also A.Gelin, JB, [3]1960; T.Chary, *Aggée-Zacharie-Malachie*, SB, 1969; D.L.Petersen, *Haggai and Zechariah 1-8*, OTL 1984; C.and E.Meyers, AB, 1987.

1. F.S.North, 'Critical Analysis of the Book of Haggai', *ZAW* 68, 1956, 25-46; P.R.Ackroyd, 'Studies in the Book of Haggai', *JJS* 2, 1951, 163-76; 3, 1952, 1-13; id., 'The Book of Haggai and Zechariah I-VIII', *JJS* 3, 1952, 151-6; id., *Exile and Restoration*, London 1968, 153-70; W.A.M.Beuken, *Haggai-Sacharja 1-8*, Assen 1967; O.H.Steck, 'Zu Haggai 1, 2-11', *ZAW* 83, 1971, 355-79. For translations of the 'Cyrus Cylinder' cf. A.L.Oppenheim, in *ANET*[3], 215f.; T.Fish in *Documents from Old Testament Times*, 92-4. For the

general history of the period cf. P.R.Ackroyd, 'Two Old Testament Problems in the Early Persian Period', *JNES* 17, 1958, 13-27; K.Galling, 'Die Exilswende in der Sicht des Propheten Sacharja', in his *Studien zur Geschichte Israels im persischen Zeitalter*, Tübingen 1964, 109-26; R.A.Mason, 'The Purpose of the *Editorial Framework* in the Book of Haggai', *VT* 27, 1977, 413-21. For the messianic expectation in Haggai and Zechariah see K.Seybold, 'Die Konigserwärtung bei den Propheten Haggai und Sacharja', *Judaica* 28, 1972, 69-78; F.Sauer, *Die Tempeltheologie des Propheten Haggai*, Freiburg im Breisgau dissertation 1977; P.A.Verhoef, 'Notes on the Dates in the Book of Haggai', in *Text and Context... Studies for F.C.Fensham*, Sheffield 1988, 259-67.

3. Cf. W.Eichrodt, *Theology of the Old Testament* II, London 1967, 61f.

27

ZECHARIAH

1. The prophet and his age

As the dates given in the book clearly indicate, Zechariah is contemporaneous with Haggai; thus he too preached to the restored community at the beginning of the rebuilding of the temple. However, only the first eight chapters refer to the ministry of this prophet; chs.9-14, which are generally called Deutero-Zechariah, relate to a later period and will therefore be examined separately (cf. below, 31).

The ministry of Zechariah differs from that of Haggai in lasting over a number of years, from one month before the last prophecy of Haggai, at the end of 521-20, to about two years later, 519-18; here too the principal problem is that of rebuilding the temple.

We know very little about the person of Zechariah: Ezra 5.1 and 6.14 mention him with Haggai, whereas Neh.12.16 speaks of a Zechariah who may or may not have been the son or the grandson of a certain Iddo. According to Nehemiah, Zechariah belonged to priestly stock, which would be a good explanation of some tendencies which appear here and there in his book.

The ministry of Zechariah also began during the political upheavals which followed the death of Cambyses. Zechariah, too, and his audience, seem to have believed that these revolutions would be followed by the end of time and therefore be the inauguration of the kingdom of God. However, matters turned out differently. Darius I Hystaspes succeeded in bringing the various centres of rebellion under control one by one, since they were not co-ordinated, and overcame the rebels; he soon had the reins of power in his hands. His achievements have been immortalized in the trilingual inscriptions and immense bas-relief carved on the rock of Behistun in Persia, on the modern road from Baghdad to Tehran. Apart from its importance in the historical sphere, the inscription was a help towards the initial decipherment of Akkadian. Such a rapid conclusion to the events

which the people had interpreted, on the basis of the preaching of
their prophets, in an eschatological key, was another cause for
discouragement and distrust in the community. This appears clearly
from Zechariah's cry to the angel (1.12b).

Zechariah's preaching relates to the new situation which was
created following the victory of Darius and the collapse of the
messianic dreams of Judah. Its aim was to demonstrate that the
unexpected turn of events did not in the least compromise the
realization of the divine plans. Despite everything, the end-time was
near and the kingdom was at hand. So the work on the building of
the temple continued, through all kinds of difficulties, until one day
the Persian governor (satrap) of Syria came to Jerusalem for an
inspection. He believed, probably on the basis of tendentious information similar to that which had been received by the Persian
authorities some years before, that the messianic hopes of Israel and
the rebuilding of the temple posed a danger to the solidarity of the
empire (Ezra 5). Some scholars (cf. Pfeiffer*, 603 n.26) have thought
that hopes to this effect will have been cherished at least among some
groups and that 6.9-15 refers to them; moreover, the prophet will
have protested against such tendencies in 4.6-10. Be this as it may,
the inhabitants of Jerusalem succeeded in demonstrating their
innocence, producing as one of their arguments the fact that it had
been Cyrus himself who authorized the rebuilding of the temple. A
full authority to proceed was followed by an edict in which Darius I
confirmed the validity of Cyrus' decree, also ordaining that sacrifices
were to be offered in the temple for himself and his house (Ezra 5.3-
6.18). This is probably the origin of the practice attested in later
Judaism before the destruction of the temple of offering a periodic
sacrifice for the emperor. To be on the safe side, the Davidic
descendant Zerubbabel was removed from the governorship: he
disappears on the scene in mysterious circumstances and the last
visions of Zechariah no longer mention him. As we shall see later,
however, there is a passage which probably shows traces of a revision
which removed the mention of Zerubbabel from the text.

2. Analysis

The visionary style which had become a constitutive element of
prophecy with Ezekiel is considerably developed in Zechariah: after
an exhortation to conversion in general terms we find eight visions
in chs.1-6, some of them dated (those which are dated all bear the
date 24 XI of the second year of Darius, that is, 8 February 521-20).

Each time there is an explanation by an angel because the formulation of the visions is not intrinsically clear; this feature will later be typical of the apocalyptic genre. As we have seen, the purpose of the visions is to console the afflicted people who seemed cheated in their faith when their eschatological hopes failed to be realized. In Proto-Zechariah we rediscover the visionary element that we have already met in Ezekiel (cf. above, 24.21) but in a more advanced stage: the vision is now so complex, so rich in esoteric elements, that the prophet needs a heavenly figure, usually called an 'angelic surveyor', to explain to him what it is about. This, too, is a feature which we encounter again later in the sphere of apocalyptic literature.

(a) The first vision (1.7-17) describes a patrol of heavenly horsemen mounted on chargers of various colours. They bring the news that all the earth is now at rest, an alarming piece of information for those who are expecting the cataclysms which should have heralded its imminent end. The angel reassures the prophet: YHWH is still angry with the nations and will not fail to comfort Jerusalem very soon.

(b) The second vision (2.1-4: EVV, 1.18-21) shows four iron horns representing the nations of the four points of the compass; these are destroyed by four smiths. The action implies a judgment on the nations which are represented.

(c) The third vision (2.5-17: EVV, 2.1-13) presents a young man, 'a measuring angel', as J.A.Bewer has effectively described him; he proceeds to survey the ruins of Jerusalem with a view to the reconstruction of the city and its repopulation. The city will be inhabited by a multitude so great that it will not even be possible to build walls within whose perimeter everyone may return. However, there will be no need of walls, since YHWH himself will protect Jerusalem with a wall of fire.

(d) The fourth vision (ch.3) presents a dramatic scene: the high priest Joshua is accused before the heavenly tribunal presided over by an angel. He is clad in filthy garments, a visible sign of his sin and that of the people whom he represents; he is accused by a prosecutor who bears the title haśśātan = 'the Satan', a figure who appears in similar circumstances in the prologue and epilogue of the book of Job (see below, 37). In these two instances, the definite article indicates that what we have here is not a name but a function, and in addition this function is exercised within the heavenly court: evidently 'satan' is not yet a proper name, much less that of a devil. However, the president of the tribunal interrupts the accuser's speech: God now has pity on his people, a true 'brand plucked from the burning', as the phrase puts it; by a miracle it has escaped total destruction. And the angelic president announces the divine plan to give pardon instead of executing judgment. Then the priest is vested in clean garments, a sign of pardon.

(e) In the fifth vision (ch.4), we find a description of a lampstand. The passage is complicated by a series of technical questions about the nature, form and function of the artefact which have not yet been resolved. The lampstand is of gold and has seven lamps connected in some obscure manner with two olive trees from which it draws its fuel. The lamps represent the light of the eyes of God and the lampstand the community which mediates it to the world (again there is a clearly universalistic note); the two olive trees from which it draws its fuel are the two 'anointed' of YHWH: the high priest, Joshua, and the last member of the line of David, Zerubbabel.

(f) In the sixth vision (5.1-4) we see a scroll flying above the earth on which are written divine curses: this is the instrument by means of which YHWH will exterminate thieves and those who abuse his name by false oaths. There is often talk of the 'magic' character of the scroll, but it is probably better to speak in terms of 'symbolic actions', this time performed by God and not by the prophet. However, the two definitions are not exclusive: all of the ancient Near East believed in the objective value of blessings and curses, and the prophet is interested in what the divine word communicates, not the way in which this is brought about.

(g) The seventh vision (5.5 11) shows a woman, here a symbol of the people's sin, shut up in a measure of volume called an ephah (about nine gallons) and transported to Babylon by two female winged creatures. The significance of the action is that the sin is blotted out in Judah and transported to Babylon. This is probably the source of similar symbolism used in the New Testament (see Rev.14.8; 18.10,21).

(h) The eighth vision (6.1-8) shows God giving the heavenly patrol the command to carry out the orders which it has received. Four chariots (according to the restored text) leave for the four points of the compass: the one with black horses towards the north, i.e. Babylon, the seat of the Persian administration and, as we have seen, of sin, so as to execute judgment.

After the visions we have a prophetic act: Zechariah receives orders to make 'crowns' from the gold received from Babylon, both for the high priest (6.9-15). As I indicated above, at this point the text seems to be corrupt: the mention of crowns (in the plural) for one person, the use of a messianic term like 'shoot' which is a typical designation for the successor to the throne and the allusion to the throne and to kingship in vv.12ff., make it probable that the text originally also contained the name of Zerubbabel, which was eliminated a little later because it seemed inappropriate to introduce a person who was politically suspect and who was, in fact, eliminated from the scene, even if we are in ignorance about the circumstances. The alternative is to read either '*One* crown for Joshua' or '*Two* crowns, one for Zerubbabel and the other for Joshua'. The second is the *lectio difficilior*. In any case, the mention of two crowns for one person should be ruled out, since this is a feature which is only attested in Egypt and not in Israel. In Egypt, moreover, it has a special significance: the Pharaoh was the king of Upper Egypt and Lower Egypt, whereas in Israel the use of two crowns would have no significance. A third possibility put forward by Robinson and Horst and by Elliger in their commentaries has also been followed by Chary: we should read '*one* crown', but '*Zerubbabel*' instead of Joshua. In any case, an original connection with the now undesirable descendant of David seems probable. However, I prefer the second of the readings proposed because it reflects the dualism of the 'prince' (*nāśī*) and 'high priest' which is attested in Ezek.45-48.

These chapters end with a discussion of the problem of fasting (ch.7), presented in the terms of the pre-exilic prophets; this discussion took place about two years later and the reply to the question about the value of fasting is the same as that in Micah 6.8: 'Mercy is worth more than sacrifice.'

3. Thought

For Zechariah, as for Haggai, the kingdom of God is about to dawn and the sanctuary must therefore be finished. However, whereas the signs under which Haggai's preaching begins raise the hope of an imminent end or at least an imminent upheaval for the world, Zechariah's task is to announce that the people's hope is not vain, even if there are few outward signs to sustain it. God is not bound to signs. In addition, there is a fact which has yet to be mentioned: the book ends in ch.8 with a detailed description of the kingdom of God. It is one of those accounts which we might call 'naive' but also 'historical' and is similar to passages like Isa.9.1ff. [EVV 9.2ff.]; 11.1ff.; Ezek.34; 37. Israel's enemies are destroyed (2.4 [EVV 1.21]); Jerusalem can remain peacefully without walls because God is reckoned to be its protection and no surrounding wall is able to contain its population (2.8ff. [EVV 2.5ff.]); criminals wil be immediately deported (5.1ff.); the scattered remnants of Israel will return (8.7ff.), and many peoples will join them (2.15 [EVV 2.11], a theme which we met in Isa.2.2ff.//Micah 4.1ff. and examined in that context); old men and children will reappear in the squares of Jerusalem, the former sitting quietly and the latter intent on their games (8.4ff.); the fields will give copious crops (8.12), and the divine blessing will be visibly present everywhere (8.13). However, as has been said, this is not a 'bourgeois idyll' in an ancient Near Eastern key; it is the eschatological restoration of true humanity brought about by God, in communion with God and therefore with all humankind. In other words, it is the transposition of ancient messianic aspirations into everyday life.

As in the case of Haggai, the dates are precise, and we have seen how it is possible to date the work.

BIBLIOGRAPHY

Commentaries

On the twelve minor prophets cf. above 18. For Haggai and Zechariah cf. above, 26. Also A.Gelin, JB, ³1960; M.Bič, Berlin 1965; D.L.Petersen, OTL, 1984; C.L and E.M.Meyers, AB, 1987.

1. The division of Zechariah into a Proto- and a Deutero-Zechariah, the second possibly further sub-divided (cf. below, 31), has been recently subjected to a computer examination, cf. Y.T.Radday and D.Wickermann, 'The Unity of Zechariah in the Light of Statistical Linguistics', ZAW 87, 1975, 30-55. The result of this study is at first sight disconcerting: in linguistic terms there are not sufficient features to affirm the existence of breaks. However, it seems improbable that the work is a unity; it is usually divided along the lines previously suggested. Cf. W.A.M.Beuken, *Haggai-Sacharja 1-8*, Assen 1967; E.Lipiński, 'Recherches sur le livre de Zacharie', *VT* 20, 1970, 25-46; S.Amsler, 'Zacharie et l'origine de l'apocalyptique', *SVT* 22, 1972, 227-31. The Behištūn relief is reproduced in *ANEP*³, 249. For the text and its first decipherment see P.G.Couture, 'Sir Henry Creswicke Rawlinson: Pioneer Cuneiformist', *BA* 47, 1984, 143-5. For the figure of Zerubbabel cf. K.Galling, 'Serubbabel und der Wiederaufbau des Tempels in Jerusalem', in A.Kuschke (ed.), *Verbannung und Heimkehr. Beiträge W.Rudolph*, Tübingen 1961, 67-96; id., 'Serubbabel und der Hohepriester beim Wiederaufbau des Tempels', in his *Studien zur Geschichte Israels im persischen Zeitalter*, Tübingen 1964, 127-48; A.Petitjean, 'La mission de Zorobabel et la réconstruction du Temple', *ETL* 42, 1966, 40-71; G.Sauer,

'Serubbabel in der Sicht Haggais und Sacharjas', in F.Maass (ed.), *Das Ferne und Nahe Wort. FS L.Rost*, BZAW 105, 1967, 199-207. Galling argues that Zerubbabel is less likely to have been eliminated by the Persian authorities than rejected by the community in Jerusalem, in which theocratic ideals were increasingly gaining the upper hand, with the person of the monarch excluded. Sauer indirectly confirms this argument by showing how the importance of the person of Zerubbabel is markedly less in Zechariah than in Haggai. Political opportunism may also be involved in this. The textual problem of ch.6 is unaffected by this argument; Zerubbabel has disappeared from the present form of the text, in which the second crown is unexplained. For the relationship between Zechariah and apocalyptic cf. C.R.North, 'Prophecy to Apocalyptic via Zechariah', *SVT* 22, 1972, 47-71; S.Amsler, 'Zacharie et l'origine de l'apocalyptique', ibid., 227-31.

2. L.C.Rignell, *Die Nachtgesichte des Sacharja*, Lund 1950. For New Testament use of these texts cf. F.F.Bruce, The Book of Zechariah and the Passion Narrative', *BJRL* 43, 1960-1, 336-55. See also H.-M.Lutz, *Jahwe, Jerusalem und die Völker*, WMANT 27, 1968; A.Petitjean, *Les oracles du Proto-Zacharie*, Louvain 1969. On the horses in chs.1 and 6 cf. W.D.McHardy, 'The Horses in Zechariah', in *In memoriam Paul Kahle*, BZAW 103, 1968, 174-9; P.Fronzaroli, 'I cavalli del Proto-Zaccaria', *RANL* VIII. 26, 1971, 593-601; H.-F.Richter, 'Die Pferde in den Nachtgesichten des Sacharja', *ZAW* 98, 1986, 96-100. For ch.4 cf. C.R.North, 'Zechariah's Seven-Spout Lampstand', *Bibl* 51, 1970, 183-206. For ch.6 cf. G.Wallis, 'Erwägungen zu Sacharja VI 9-15', *SVT* 22, 1972, 232-37. Cf. also K.Seybold, 'Die Bildmotive in den Visionen des Propheten Sacharja', *SVT* 26, 1974, 92-10; id., *Bilder zum Tempelbau*, Stuttgart 1974; L.A.Sinclair, 'Redaktion of Zechariah 1-8', *BiblRes* 20, 1975, 36-47; C.Jeremias, *Die Nachtgesichte des Sacharja*, FRLANT 117, 1977; T.N.D.Mettinger, *The Dethronement of Sebaoth*, Lund 1981, 112f.; R.Mason, 'Some Echoes of the Preaching in the Second Temple? Traditional Elements in Zechariah 1-8', *ZAW* 96, 1984, 221-35; A.S.van der Woude, 'Zion as Primeval Stone in Zechariah 3 and 4', and S.Mittmann, 'Die Einheit von Sacharja 8, 1-8', both in *Text and Context... Studies for F.C.Fensham*, Sheffield 1988, 237-48, 269-82; J.Portnoy and D.L.Petersen, 'Texts and Statistical Analysis: Zechariah and Beyond', *JBL* 103, 1984, 11-21 (a polemical attack on the 1975 study by Radday and Wickermann).

28

TRITO-ISAIAH

1. The problem of the book

From 1892, the year in which B.Duhm suggested in his commentary that Isa.56-66 should be separated from Deutero-Isaiah, the independence of Trito-Isaiah from the texts which precede it has been generally accepted, outside conservative theological circles. The differences between ch.56-66 and the earlier chapters is too great for them to be considered as in any way a continuation. Throughout the greater part of Trito-Isaiah we continually find ourselves in the community of the restoration: there is mention of the temple and of rebuilding it, of sacrifices, of the observance of the sabbath and the regulations of the *tōrāh*, and the two last are considered to be essential qualifications for membership of the community. None of these arguments appears even once in Deutero-Isaiah, and since the setting of Deutero-Isaiah is Babylon, it is difficult to see how that would be possible. However, in a number of places there are notable analogies between Deutero-Isaiah and Trito-Isaiah: we have similar hopes for the imminence of the kingdom of God in 61.1-3 and 42.1-4 (the latter in a servant passage); and we have an almost identical concept of the work of the spirit of God in humankind. There are also notable affinities of style. The general setting for Trito-Isaiah is Jerusalem and the community described by Haggai and Zechariah, that is, about twenty years after the latest part of Deutero-Isaiah and perhaps even later; in 60.13 the temple has been built and it is only necessary to adorn it. However, the situation in the country has certainly not improved; it remains critical because of the high incidence of crime in some areas and of incompetence in others, the immediate result of which is that the righteous suffer (56.9ff.). For this reason God shows his judgment by continually postponing the fulfilment of his promises (cf.also chs.59-62), though he will not delay to intervene personally and to achieve justice for the elect. Another figure serves YHWH in place of Cyrus (63.1-6); foreign nations will not be the object of the divine judgment, which will fall instead on the people of God because of their unfaithfulness (65.11). However, the walls have still not been rebuilt (60.10), so that if Trito-Isaiah is a little after the time of Haggai and Zechariah, we have still not reached that of Ezra and Nehemiah (but cf. the theory put forward by Morgenstern, below, 48.3). Finally, according to Duhm, 66.1f. would refer to Samaritans who were building their own temple. However, this theory seems improbable, since quite apart from the fact that we know little or nothing about the final separation of the two communities, it is reasonably certain that the break did not come about before the fourth century BCE (cf. my *History*, XII.4); it seems better to think of criticisms directed against the hopes of Haggai and Zechariah, which were perhaps considered in some circles to be rather exaggerated. Duhm also tried to argue for the unity of chs.56-66, but hardly anyone has taken up his approach. Trito-Isaiah is a book of a composite kind if ever there was one. The majority of scholars in fact regard it as an anthology containing about twelve passages which are all different either in date or in purpose. Pfeiffer*, 480, seeks to explain the differences between Trito- and Deutero-Isaiah as the result of attempts to apply to the situation of the restoration the great promises formulated by Deutero-Isaiah, which had not been fulfilled. This theory is interesting, as it would explain both the analogies and also the obvious differences between the two works. It would remain to be seen whether the work were purely redactional or whether Deutero-Isaiah himself, whoever he may have been, continued his activity down to the last centuries of the sixth century BCE. Here, too, we have a solution proposed by the Scandinavian school: as in the case of Deutero-Isaiah, Trito- Isaiah will have been the product of the 'school of Isaiah' mentioned above, which will have continued its work over the centuries.

2. *Content*

Taking into account all these elements, let us attempt to classify the various units of which these chapters are composed, using as criteria either dating or connections with particular schools or tendencies.

(*a*) Two passages seem to be earlier than 521-20, when the rebuilding of the temple was put in hand, following the preaching of Haggai and later Zechariah. The first of them is 63.7-64.11 [EVV 12], which could even be dated to the last period of the exile. It contains a confession of sin followed by a prayer to YHWH not to sustain his anger for ever. The second is 66.1-2a, a brief poetic composition on the theme that God has no need of a temple because heaven is his throne and earth his footstool. It is impossible to date this passage, but it is probably an expression of polemic against the rebuilding of the temple, which was presented by Haggai and Zechariah as the most urgent task of the moment. Duhm's argument that this is a criticism of the building of the Samaritan temple certainly cannot be sustained. Be this as it may, the passage testifies to an interesting fact: even in the post-exilic period there was at least one line of thought which was extremely critical of the temple and the official cult, and which was a worthy continuation of pre-exilic prophecy. Others would see in the passage a form of consolation addressed to the exiles or perhaps even to those who had been first to return home and had no sanctuary. As can be seen, it is difficult to arrive at reasonably certain conclusions.

Next we have passages which come from the same time as the preaching of Haggai and Zechariah or a little afterwards.

(*b*) First of all, from the school of Deutero-Isaiah, we have 56.1-8, which is remarkable for its universalism in laying down conditions for admission to the community: 57.14-19; chs.60-62; 66.3-7 are similar passages. They could be attributed without difficulty to the hand of Deutero-Isaiah if, as was suggested above, it could be thought at all possible that he was also at work in Palestine among the exiles who returned. Pfeiffer* holds the strange view that 56.1-8 is quite simply an expedient to swell the somewhat reduced ranks of those who wanted to return to Jerusalem.

(*c*) Chapters 58; 59.1-15a recall Haggai and Zechariah because of their prosaic and moralizing tone.

(*d*) 56.9-57.13 and ch.65 recall Ezekiel by the way in which they present the internal situation of the community without any embellishment; in the view of Eissfeldt* (§ 45.2), 57.1-13 could be much older by virtue of its description of the sin of the many, the incompetence of the rulers and the tendency of many groups to paganism; the description would correspond quite well to the situation in the community before the reforms of Ezra and Nehemiah. In any case, the importance of these documents is considerable, especially for the historian: this is a situation about which otherwise we would know almost nothing. Among other things, we see an increasingly clear distinction between the 'righteous' and the 'sinners' which foreshadows the categories into which Judaism was to divide the members of the community some centuries later and which are reflected in the doctrines of Qumran and in those of the early church. Attempts have been made to see the Samaritans or their immediate precursors as the 'sinners', but the whole matter remains on a purely hypothetical level and is hardly probable. In any case, by means of these texts we are given information about the existence of syncretistic groups like those to be found before the exile, groups in quite a close relationship to the priesthood in Jerusalem. There were also contacts between Jerusalem and the syncretistic Jewish community of Elephantine in Egypt; the two parties were in constant correspondence at the end of the fifth century BCE. We shall be occupied with the question further in Appendix 2, 1-2.

(e) In 63.1-6 we have a minuscule apocalyptic fragment introduced by 59.15b-20; it is impossible to date either passage.

(f) Finally, 66.18-24 will be redactional. The passage is classified in this way for want of a better solution.

Such a complex composition is certainly difficult for a book as short as this one to deal with. The situation is complicated by the fact that for the most part we do not know the circumstances which accompanied or led to the composition of the passages in question.

3. Text

Some textual difficulties must be added to the problems I have already indicated. The most obvious is in 64.1, which reads, 'Who is this who comes from Edom, from Bozrah in crimsoned garments?' The conjecture generally proposed is to read 'Who is this who comes clothed in scarlet ('ādōm for 'ēdōm), with garments more crimson than those of a grape-harvester (mibbōṣer for mibboṣra)?' There is no support for the textual emendation from any ancient authority, nor is it absolutely necessary, but it does have the advantage of restoring the parallelism.

BIBLIOGRAPHY

Commentaries

See the bibliographies to Isaiah and Deutero-Isaiah.

1-2. W.Kessler, 'Zur Auslegung von Jes.56-66', *TLZ* 81, 1956, 335-8; id., 'Studien zur religiösen Situation im ersten nachexilischen Jahrhundert und Auslegung von Jes.56-66', *WissZ Univ. Halle* 6.1, 1956-7, 41-74; H.-J.Kraus, 'Die ausgebliebene Endtheophanie. Eine Studie zu Jes.56-66', *ZAW* 78,

1966, 317-32; K.Pauritsch, *Die neue Gemeinde: Gott sammelt Ausgestossene und Arme (Jesaja 56-66)*, Rome 1971; E.Sehmsdorf, 'Studien zur Redaktionsgeschichte von Jesaja 56-66', *ZAW* 84, 1972, 517-76. Doubts about the existence of Trito-Isaiah have been raised by F.Maass, 'Tritojesaja?', in F.Maass (ed.), *Das ferne und Nahe Wort. FS L.Rost*, BZAW 105, 1967, 153-63, and by A.Murtonen, 'Third Isaiah. Yes or No?', *AbrNah* 19, 1980-81, 80-2. J.J.Scullion, 'Some Difficult Texts in Isaiah 56-66 in the Light of Modern Scholarship', *UF* 4, 1972, 105-28, tries to explain a series of complex passages on the basis of Ugaritic parallels. In his review of the second edition of this book (*OA* 15, 1977, 357), H.Cazelles argued that the information at our disposal suggests, rather, that the temple had not yet been rebuilt (cf. 60.13; 64.10; 66.1f.). This last passage is better explained as polemic against the temple in general, before its rebuilding, rather than against the rebuilt temple. Note again in 66.5ff. the contrasting of old and new, this latter more in the eschatological future. Cf. further R.P.Carroll, *When Prophecy Failed*, London 1979, 151ff.; B.Wodecki, 'Der Heilsuniversalismus bei Trito-Jesaja', *VT* 52, 1982, 248-52; O.H.Steck, 'Der Grundtext in Jesaja 60 und sein Aufbau', *ZTK* 83, 1986, 261-96; id., 'Beobachtungen zu Jesaja 56-59', *BZ* 31, 1987, 228-46; id., 'Beobachtungen zur Anlage von Jes 65-66', *BN* 38/39, 1987, 103-16; T.D.Andersen, 'Renaming and Wedding Imagery in Is.62', *Bibl* 67, 1986, 75-80.

29

OBADIAH

The critics have written a great deal about this book, which is the shortest in the Hebrew Bible (only 21 verses long). The problem of dating it is particularly complex: many features almost certainly place it in the post-exilic period, but in the past there was no lack of scholars who would prefer to date at least the first part as early as the ninth century, thus making it the earliest of the prophetic books. Hardly anyone now holds this latter opinion: the events of which the first part of the book speaks cannot be connected with II Kings 8.20, as was earlier supposed.

The book falls into two parts: vv.1-14, an oracle against Edom, and vv.15-21, an oracle against the nations in connection with the 'day of the Lord'. Fohrer suggests a division into five oracles, but the main break is between vv.14 and 15.

As far as we can tell from the sparse sources at our disposal, relations between Edom on one side and Israel – Judah on the other never seem to have been particularly tense. The two peoples felt that they shared a common ethnic origin, as is shown by the stories of Jacob and Esau in Genesis and Deut.2.4-7; 23.7. However, it seems that after the destruction of Jerusalem in 587/6, refugees from Judah who sought safety in Edom did not receive the welcome that they had expected; it is also possible that the Edomites were allies (or had been forced to become allies) of Nebuchadnezzar, if it is permissible to draw conclusions from the list in II Kings 24.2. Anyway, even without pressing this possibility, which is at best doubtful, we can say that Edom seems to have been cheered by the fall of Jerusalem (Lam.4.21; Ps.137.7) and to have profited from it by occupying the southern territories (the Negeb) which were now virtually abandoned (Ezek.35.10-12; 36.5). Besides, in this case it was not so much a matter of territorial greed as the consequence of an invasion of Edom by Arab groups coming from the south. It seems that from then on Edomite domination of the Negeb steadily increased, to such an extent that from the beginning of the Christian era we find the south simply called Idumaea (see the New Testament and the work of Josephus). Be this as it may, Edom is reproached for having profited from the misfortune of its neighbour.

By contrast, the second part speaks of the 'day of YHWH', in an oracle against the nations.

The first part makes it quite clear that we are not in the ninth century but in the sixth, at a time later than 587. From vv.16-18 we know that hostility between north and south was very strong. This feature does not suggest the struggles between the two kingdoms of Israel and Judah so much as the constant disputes between the precursors of the Samaritans and the exiles who had returned to Judah after 539. In v.20 we have some rather obscure observations which scholars in the past have sought to connect with the wars of the Ptolemies in the third century or of the Maccabees in the second; however, a satisfactory solution does not seem possible, even in hypothetical terms. In a study written some years ago, M.Bič sought to interpret the work as an oracle pronounced on the occasion of the feast of the enthronement of YHWH in Jerusalem (a feast with which we shall be concerned below, 34.4). He argues that the oracle has been amplified on successive occasions, but his argument is not convincing.

An additional problem in the book is that of the relationship between vv.1-10 and Jer.49.7-22, which is also an oracle against Edom. The two passages are certainly parallel, and as usual raise the possibility of the dependence either of one on the other or of both on a common archetype. In any case, Jeremiah has the most ordered text, which might suggest that the text of Obadiah is of a secondary character; however, it is also possible, as we have seen in connection with this phenomenon elsewhere, that both quote an earlier passage, each in its own way.

If v.19 can really be connected with the migration of the Edomites into the Negeb under pressure from Arab groups coming from the south, it is without question an important note for the historian, since we know almost nothing about the situation in southern Arabia at this time. In v.20 the mention of *separād* (a term which much later was to include Spain), refers to Sardis, capital of the Persian satrapy of Sarda in Asia Minor.

Obadiah is of little theological interest, and its presence in the canon can easily be explained as a result of the anti-Idumaean polemic which was in full flood at the beginning of the common era.

The ancient sayings against a neighbouring people provided ready material for polemic against Herod and his house.

BIBLIOGRAPHY

Commentaries

On the twelve minor prophets cf. above, 18: also J.Trinquet, JB, [2]1959; J.D.W.Watts, Grand Rapids 1970; H.-W.Wolff, BK, 1977.

M.Bič, 'Ein verkanntes Thronbesteigungsorakel im Alten Testament', *ArchOr* 19, 1951, 568-78; id., 'Zur Problematik des Buches Obadia', *SVT* 1, 1953, 11-25; E.Olávarri, 'Cronología y estructura literaria del oráculo de Abdías', *EstBibl* 22, 1963, 303-13; G.Fohrer, 'Die Sprüche Obadjas', in *Studia Biblica et Semitica T.C.Vriezen dedicata*, Wageningen 1966, 81-93. Cf. further E.Lipiński, 'Obadiah 20', *VT* 23, 1973, 369f.; P.K.McCarter, 'Obadiah 7 and the Fall of Edom', *BASOR* 221, 1976, 87-91; G.I.Davies, 'A New Solution to a Crux in Obadiah 7', *VT* 27, 1977, 484-7; R.B.Robinson, 'Levels of Naturalization in Obadiah', *JSOT* 40, 1988, 83-97. H.-W.Wolff, 'Obadiah. Ein Kultprophet als Interpret', *EvTh* 37, 1977, 273-84, thinks that the prophet is interpreting ancient material. Cf. also G.S.Ogden, 'Prophetic Oracles against Foreign Nations and Psalms of Communal Lament: the Relationship of Psalm 137 to Jeremiah 49.7-22 and Obadiah', *JSOT* 24, 1982, 89-97.

30

MALACHI

1. Authorship and date

We know absolutely nothing about the author of this book, not even his name. The name given to the book is the result of a misunderstanding. *mal'ākī* means 'my messenger' and appears at the beginning of ch.3, which in fact talks of the arrival of a messenger at God's command. Owing to a confusion, the term then became the title of the book and was taken to be the name of the prophet. A reconstruction of the name as a theophoric name compounded with a Yahwistic element (*mal'ākī-yāhū**) is extremely dubious, quite apart from the fact that such a name is not attested in the Hebrew Bible. J.Pedersen and the Scandinavian school after him have very plausibly thought of an expected divine messenger, probably identical with the future messianic king or at least very closely connected with him.

Despite these problems, it is relatively easy to fix the date of the book: it comes from the Persian period. In 1.8 Judah is governed by a satrap (Hebrew *peḥāh*) and the temple is now rebuilt (1.10), so that we find ourselves at a time after 516-15; on the other hand, the abuses which the author bewails are those which appear at the time of Ezra and Nehemiah: marriages with foreign women (2.11f.); sacrifices offered with diseased animals (1.7f.). This would seem to bring us to a time before their reforms, probably at the end of the sixth century or the beginning of the fifth.

2. Analysis and content

In the EVV Malachi has four chapters, but in the Hebrew, LXX and Vulgate it only has three, which means that there is a difference over the numbering of the final verses, even though their content is identical. The text is usually divided into six oracles and an epilogue.

(a) 1.2-5 affirms that YHWH continues to love Israel despite everything.

(b) 1.6-2.9 reproves the faithful for offering sacrifices with blemished animals; for this fault they will be chastized by YHWH.

(c) 2.10-16, which is regarded by some scholars as an interpolation, accuses some men of Judah of having divorced their wives in order to marry foreign women who are pagans. The reasons for actions of this kind are now quite clear, although they are not mentioned here: marriage enabled the Jew to become part of one of the great families of the region, guaranteeing his protection and therefore a certain security on the economic and political level (as we have seen, his situation was very precarious in both areas). A similar procedure has been followed right down to the present day by some Christian Arabs living in the region of Syria; once allied to a powerful Moslem family, the Christian Arab enjoyed its protection and avoided a series of humiliations and sometimes persecutions. However, according to the prophet the end does not justify the means adopted, i.e. to divorce a legitimate wife and to marry a pagan woman. In Judaism even today, it is in fact the mother's religion which determines that of the children: her identity is always secure and she is responsible for the children's education (cf. below, 43.2).

(d) 2.17-3.5 deals with the 'day of YHWH', confirming the imminence and the proximity in time of the settling of accounts.

(e) 3.6-12 interprets the people's suffering (bad harvests, plagues like locusts, epidemics, etc.) as divine punishment for a failure to pay tithes.

(f) 3.13-21 [EVV 3.13-4.3] applies 2.17 to the final judgment.

(g) 3.22-24 [EVV 4.4-6] is the epilogue: the prophet Elijah, the precursor of the 'day of YHWH', is about to come, and the people are exhorted to observe the tōrāh. The figure of Elijah the forerunner is well-known in later Judaism; in the New Testament, Jesus himself was identified with him in some circles, cf.Matt.6.14, where one of the replies to his question 'Who do men say that I am?' is '... Elijah'; the theme is connected with the announcement in Deut.18.15.

3. Character, style and thought

The religious thought of Malachi is essentially centred on the cult, not to criticize it but to ensure that its execution is as correct as possible; as A.Lods*, 525, rightly observed, communion between YHWH and his people is in fact realized here. For some scholars this aspect of the prophet's thought is a negative feature, especially when it is compared with the position adopted by the pre-exilic prophets towards the cult. However, such an evaluation risks remaining on an abstract level, without taking into account the situation of the people involved; when this situation is considered, the prophet's message is quite coherent: the purity of the cult becomes a much more important problem in a Judaism which is now dispersed, and is surrounded by pagan or syncretistic elements. Even the intransigence of Ezra and Nehemiah on the problem of the cult and the question of foreign wives (cf. below, 43) does not fit the hypothesis of racism or nationalism but is governed by harsh necessity: the believer is moulded by the cult and by the family, so there can be no question of any compromise over the purity of these two elements. Jesus, too, will show similar intransigence over the question of divorce (though without the motive of preventing marriage with pagan women), allowing it in only one situation, the details of which are far from clear (Matt.19.1-12: Mark 10.2-12).

1.11f. is without parallel in the Hebrew Bible and presents special difficulties because of its ultimate implications. It has been interpreted in many different terms, ranging from a recognition of the monotheistic longing which extended through all the peoples under Persian rule, an imitation of the ruling power, to a recognition of the fundamental validity of all sincere religious expressions which are directed towards God, even if their intention is not clear. At any rate, the eschatological explanation attempted by some scholars must be excluded: they argue that the past is to be projected into the future. Now since the attitude of all biblical writers to other cults is without exception negative, this passage is remarkable, to say the least, and even more so in the context of a prophet like Malachi, who is completely preoccupied with the purity of the cult. It is not surprising, therefore, that it has been regarded as an interpolation. However, the method of removing difficult texts by declaring them to be interpolations is doubtful at the best of times. Eichrodt suggested another possibility: this is perhaps polemic against sacrifice understood as a meritorious work and therefore a demolition of the people's defence against the charges made by the prophet. In that case, following the lines of the pre-exilic prophets, Malachi too would be proclaiming that if the cult were only a matter of sacrifice, all religions would have it in abundance and Israel would have no reason to boast that the cult was its own prerogative.

The last passage in the book speaks of the coming of Elijah, the eschatological prophet who is to introduce the last times. As we have seen, the New Testament not only shows that some people attributed this characteristic to Jesus but in some passages identifies the mysterious person with John the Baptist (Matt.11.14; 17.12; John

1.21; 6.14; 7.40), while orthodox Judaism has continued to await the arrival of Elijah right down to the present day, even leaving an empty place for him at the passover meal. The book therefore rightly comes at the end of the proto-canonical Old Testament, even if it is clearly not its latest book.

The text does not present any difficulties; some scholars would prefer to put 3.6-12 after 1.5 so as not to leave it without a context.

BIBLIOGRAPHY

Commentaries

On the twelve minor prophets see on 18 above. Also A.Gelin, JB ²1960; T.Chary (above, 26); R.L.Smith, Word, 1985.

G.Wallis, 'Wesen und Struktur der Botschaft Maleachis', in F.Maass (ed.), *Das Ferne und Nahe Wort. FS L.Rost*, BZAW 105, 1967, 229-37. A.E.Hill, 'The Dating of the Book of Malachi: a Linguistic Re-examination', in *The Word of the Lord Shall Go Forth... Essays D.N.Freedman*, Winona Lake, Ind. 1983, 77-89, confirms this date by a linguistic study. On 1.11, cf. W.Eichrodt, *Theology of the Old Testament* I, London and Philadelphia 1971, 414; J.Swetnam, 'Malachi 1.11: an Interpretation', *CBQ* 31, 1969, 200-9; also the posthumous article by A.van Hoonacker, 'Le rapprochement entre le Deutéronome et Malachie', *ETL* 59, 1983, 86-9; B.Glazier-McDonald, 'Malachi 2:12', *JBL* 105, 1986, 295-8.

31

DEUTERO-ZECHARIAH

1. The problem of the book

It was the English scholar Joseph Mead (or Mede) of Cambridge who was the first to notice, about the end of the sixteenth century, that in the New Testament (in Matt.27.9) Zech.11.12f. is attributed to Jeremiah. This observation marks the beginning of studies of Deutero-Zechariah.

These soon made it quite clear that chs.9-14 have nothing at all to do with chs.1-8 of the book in question. There is no mention in them either of the rebuilding of the temple or of the political situation at the beginning of the reign of Darius I; neither the high priest Joshua nor Zerubbabel of the house of David appear. Stylistically the chapters lack the exact dating which we have seen to be a characteristic of both Haggai and Zechariah chs.1-8; this is replaced by the phrase 'oracle of YHWH'.

The book can naturally be divided into two units which are more or less independent of each other: chs.9-11 and chs.12-14. Finally, Lamarche's study has demonstrated the existence within Deutero-Zechariah of a degree of symmetry in construction, with pronouncements which either correspond exactly with each other schematically or form exact opposites.

2. The individual, his age and date

To give some idea of the complexity of the problems connected with the features which I have barely indicated, it is enough to note the various different opinions about the origin of the book.

(a) At the end of the last century and the beginning of this, the view that the book was composed in the pre-exilic period enjoyed considerable prestige. In its favour was the fact that, as we have seen, a tradition reported in the New Testament attributed the work to a pre-exilic prophet; chs.9-11 were assigned to the eighth century because in 10.10 Assyria and Egypt appear as enemies of Israel, while 11.14 was thought still to attest the existence of two states in Palestine, Israel and Judah. Again, 10.7ff. was supposed to speak of the destruction of the north and the exile of its people, but as a future event, which would put the chapters in question earlier than 722-21. In this case the episode of the 'three shepherds' who are destroyed (11.8) and the description of the precarious situation of the country would have to be connected with the facts narrated in II Kings 15.8ff., i.e. with the assassination of Zechariah and Shallum, who reigned briefly in Israel after the death of Jeroboam II. The mention of the *teraphim* in 10.2 would fit well in this context (these were a kind of domestic effigy sometimes compared with the *penates*: they are also mentioned in the patriarchal traditions, especially in Gen.31); so would that of the false prophets. According to some scholars of the last century, the Zechariah from whom the book derives would be Zechariah son of Jeberechiah mentioned in Isa.8.2, later confused by the redactor with the prophet of the same name from the end of the sixth century and added to his book. On this view, chs.12-14 would belong to a rather later date, the seventh century. In fact, only Judah is mentioned in them; the feast of booths is celebrated only in Jerusalem (14.16-19), an implicit indication that Josiah's reform has taken place (622-1: I Kings 22-23 // II Chron.34-35). The suppression of the false prophets seems to indicate that there are a large number of them about, while the mention of the earthquake in 14.5 could be connected directly with the end of the first half of the eighth century, given that this was the earthquake mentioned in Amos 1.1 (cf. above, 18). Of course the mention of these last two elements is not decisive; they could have been remembered some centuries later. Finally, the siege and plundering mentioned in ch.14 would have been those of 597 and 587/6.

(*b*) Later scholars are much more cautious in their evaluation of the data in question and have not accepted the importance that was previously attached to them. There are too many elements in Deutero-Zechariah which make him an apocalyptic prophet and put him at a relatively late date; some scholars have even gone so far as thinking in terms of Alexander the Great or the struggle between the Diadochi after his death, which would bring us to the end of the fourth century or the beginning of the third. Yet others would come down as far as the time of the Maccabees, in the first half of the second century (cf. below, 51-52), seeing in the three shepherds who are killed (11.8) the episode narrated in II Macc.4.5-13; they would also put the announcement of the 'good shepherd' (Zech.11.4ff.) in this context. Now without doubt the general style of the work favours a late date, as does the presence of obvious apocalyptic elements (those at the beginning, as we have seen, have connections with the work of Ezekiel and are developed in Proto-Zechariah). There seems to be no difficulty in construing a relationship of dependence of Deutero-Zechariah upon Ezekiel (cf.11.4 with Ezek.34; ch.14 with Ezek.38; 39, while 14.8 seems to develop the theme of Ezek.47.1-10). However, other passages seem to be based more on Deutero-Isaiah (12.2 on Isa.51.22; 12.10-13.1 on Isa.44.3; 53.5). Moreover, right through the book there is a particular insistence on the cult (cf. 9.7; 14.16, 21-28). Levi and the other priestly groups are mentioned on a level with the house of David (12.12f.), which is the sign of the existence of a theocratic régime; in 9.13 there is a mention of Greeks (Javan, i.e. the 'Ionians'). Finally, 9.1-8 is a passage which some scholars connect with Alexander the Great's conquest of Tyre in 332 by means of the dyke constructed between the mainland and the island on which the city was built. All these are elements which would put the book in the late post-exilic period. Given this 'dating, 'Assyria' would become the Syria of the Seleucids and 'Egypt' that of the Ptolemies, the two Western kingdoms which developed out of the division of the empire of Alexander the Great. The most that could be allowed would be that in some places the writer made use of earlier traditional material which can be recognized at certain points, following a procedure which is also attested among other authors, especially in apocalyptic (cf. below, on Daniel, 41).

(c) A third more recent position is that adopted by the Danish scholar B.Otzen, who would see chs.9-10 as a stratum dating more or less from the time of Josiah, deriving from the traditions of the 'am hā'āreṣ ('people of the land', cf. above, 9.5), but with an anti-monarchical tendency; in chs.12-13 he believes that we have a selection of texts from the exilic period which are hostile to Jerusalem, while in ch.14 we have a late passage of an apocalyptic kind. One of the most important arguments in Otzen's theory is that the mention of the Greeks does not necessarily indicate the time of Alexander the Great. Their presence is attested in Egypt before the sixth century, where they served as mercenaries, and in Judah they appear at the same period in the ostraca of Tell 'Arad (cf. below, appendix 1.10). In Deutero-Zechariah, though, they have more than an episodic, local character and assume the status of a people. This new interpretation of the work threatens to upset the two earlier approaches, of which the later one had the greater degree of plausibility.

(d) Another study by the Norwegian scholar M.Saebø is less

optimistic than its predecessors: he does not see any concrete possibilities of identifying the historical context of the work with any certainty. He is therefore content to study the literary and traditional settings, which prove to be extremely complex. A number of phases of redaction and interpretation follow one upon another, expanding the original texts by what he calls an 'additive procedure'; each unit then displays different characteristics, even if the divisions are usually essentially those of Otzen. Saebø proposes to examine the historical context of the work in a second volume.

In these circumstances it is no wonder that we know nothing about the person of the prophet.

3. Analysis and transmission of the text

As we have seen, the book can be divided into two parts:

(a) 9.1-11.3: the kingdom of God is about to arrive, the Israelite exiles are on the verge of being brought home and reunited in Palestine, while the powers of this world will fall. The 'peaceful king' will soon reach the capital.

(b) 1. Two important symbolic actions are described in rhythmic prose which is almost poetry (11.4-14, 15-17; 13.7-9). The details are not always clear.

2. The ultimate destiny of Judah and Jerusalem under the final attack and assembling of the hostile nations. They are saved by the miraculous destruction of their attackers (12.1-13.6; 14). Of course, this division presupposes the second interpretation of the work in sections (a) and (b) of the preceding paragraph and not that of sections (c) and (d).

The text is in a bad state, and is the most serious obstacle to a proper understanding. Because so much conjecture is needed and reconstructions are consequently open to extremely subjective elements, they tend to be of little help. One valuable aid towards objectivity in the examination of texts is the argument by Lamarche (put forward above) on the chiastic structure and therefore symmetrical character of the various units. Even here, however, it has been pointed out that Lamarche is perhaps rather too optimistic about the real condition of the traditional text, transferring the responsiblity for the variants which appear to the ancient translations.

4. Message

Eschatology in its apocalyptic forms now tends to hold the field. In the text we have at least two pericopes which were considered messianic, to some degree in later Judaism and always in the primitive church: 9.9ff.; 13.1ff. As we approach the common era, this eschatological messianic hope tends to become increasingly vivid, and finally constitutes the principal characteristic of the thought of Israel at this time.

BIBLIOGRAPHY

Commentaries

On the twelve minor prophets see above, 18, and on Zechariah, above, 27. Cf. also R.L.Smith, Word, 1985.

1. P.Lamarche, *Zacharie IX-XIV*, Paris 1961.

2b. K.Elliger, 'Ein Zeugnis aus der jüdischen Gemeinde im Alexanderjahr 332. v.Chr', *ZAW* 62, 1950, 63-115; M.Delcor, 'Les allusions à Alexandre le Grand dans Zach.ix,1-8', *VT* 1, 1951, 110-24. Cf. also I.Willi-Plein, *Prophetie am Ende. Untersuchungen zu Sacharja 9-14*, Cologne 1974; R.Tournay, 'Zacharie XII-XIV et l'histoire d'Israël', *RB* 81, 1974, 355-74 (interprets the book as an up-to-date commentary on the past history of Israel); R.A.Mason, 'The Relation of Zechariah 9-14 to Proto-Zechariah', *ZAW* 88, 1976, 227-39; A.S.van der Woude, 'Die Hirtenallegorie von Sacharja XI', *JNSWL* 12, 1984, 139-49.

2c-d. B.Otzen, *Studien über Deutero-Zacharia*, Copenhagen 1964; M.Saebø, *Sacharja 9-14*, WMANT 34, 1969. G.Wallis, '*Pastor bonus*', *Kairos* 12, 1970, 220-34, arrived quite independently at a variant of Otzen's position. He concluded that in content and language Zech.9-11 should really be called 'Trito-Zechariah'.

32

JOEL

1. Authorship and analysis

Nothing is known about the authorship of this brief but important prophetic book.

It can be divided into two parts: (*a*) the arrival of the locusts, followed by the 'day of YHWH' (chs.1-2 [EVV 1.1-2.27]); (*b*) the 'day of YHWH' (chs.3-4, [EVV] 2.28-3.21). Here we have two different works combined and co-ordinated at a later date. The book probably became a unity less on a redactional level than on a liturgical level. The studies by A.S.Kapelrud and M.Bič have brought to light some features of Canaanite origin; the work evidently arose in close conjunction with the fertility cults and their problems. This fact is now generally recognized and accepted by scholars, although the consequences to be drawn from it are not always clear. This uncertainty already appears in attempts to date the book. For Bič it is very old, perhaps the oldest of the prophetic books, because it reflects Elijah's struggles; it also has notable parallels to prophetic texts which he considers to be pre-exilic, like Isa.24.7; Jer.14.1-15,19. However, as we have seen above, the first of these passages is certainly late, while the text of Jeremiah is known for its Deuteronomistic revisions. There is a more widespread tendency to assign a post-exilic date to Joel, and H.-W.Wolff takes this position in his commentary, on the basis both of materials of an apocalyptic kind and of the historical allusions which are to be found in the book. A pre-exilic date (end of the seventh century BCE) has recently been proposed by C.A.Keller and W.Rudolph independently of one another, and was first argued for by Kapelrud. In any case, Joel is not to be dated as early as Bič's proposal. Here, too, it is possible that early material has been re-used in new contexts and new situations.

1.1-12 describes the arrival of the 'day of the Lord'; it is represented as an invasion of locusts which brings universal destruction. The prophet warns the people to repent and to show their repentance through prayer and fasting; the 'day' comes in 1.13-20 and is described in detail. In 2.1-11 we again have the scourge of locusts, but this time they have clear characteristics of apocalyptic creatures; from their mysterious and sinister character it is clear that they in fact represent a hostile army coming from the north, whose soldiers race like horses and penetrate everywhere like flames, even if in outward appearance they remain locusts. YHWH will allow the return of better times at the end of this scourge (2.18-27). Poetically this is one of the finest passages in the Hebrew Bible.

In ch.3 [EVV 2.28-32] the 'day of YHWH' arrives, preceded by the pouring forth of the spirit upon all the people of God ('all flesh'); this is a passage which reappears in the quotation in Acts 2.17-21 where the apostolic community proclaims that the prophecy has been fulfilled in the gift of the Spirit to its members. Finally, in ch.4 [EVV, ch.3] we have a description of judgment on the peoples in the valley of Jehoshaphat, followed by favourable times.

These are clearly post-exilic themes. The final attack of the nations on Jerusalem is a typical example; in 2.9 the walls seem to have been rebuilt, although the country has been reduced to Jerusalem and Judah only (4.1ff. [EVV 3.1ff.]). Because of this, most scholars think of a period a little before the conquest by Alexander the Great in 332. However, the theories of Keller and Rudolph are worth considering, and we should concede to them at least that earlier texts have been used again in a later context. At any rate, the literary genre is that of a collective lament over the catastrophe which has befallen the people, a portent of still worse things to come.

2. Style and thought

Joel is effective from a poetic point of view, and is very well written, but it does not succeed in concealing certain lexicographical elements which are thought to be late. However, this argument should not be pressed to its extreme conclusion: we now know in fact that many words which were at first considered Aramaisms and were therefore used as evidence for a late date for the text in which they appeared are sometimes western Semitic words and attested as such in non-biblical texts of undoubted antiquity, like those of Ugarit. Thus in 2.8 we have the term *selāh* = 'javelin', which is attested in Ugaritic and therefore cannot be considered late in itself, even if it only appears in the Bible in late texts. The fact remains that the language of Joel is classical, inspired by that of the eighth-century prophets, which is not surprising, seeing that the text must have been used from time immemorial in the liturgy. Only the eschatological adaptation, then, would seem to be late.

As things are, the prophet's thought seems totally directed towards the God who is coming, awaited at the same time with hope and fear. Only at his coming will the restoration of Israel take place, while the 'day of the Lord' (and here we notice a remarkable difference from the pre-exilic prophets) tends to become a day of judgment not so much for Israel as for the Gentiles. Before the exile, this type of religious feeling is connected more with popular religion on a nationalistic and syncretistic basis, against which all the prophets protested. Moreover, we must seriously consider the hypothesis that post-exilic eschatology had its roots at least partly in popular religious feeling and the prophets who gave it expression (prophets whom the Hebrew Bible does not hesitate on occasion to describe as 'false prophets'), rather than in the message of the 'great' prophets. As we have seen, such elements appear to a considerable degree in the book of Joel.

However, the presence of elements of this kind does not mean that Israel had renounced its traditions in this area. In 2.12-13 we see clearly that the people of God do not in the least exclude divine judgment on themselves, and by means of this element Joel too transcends the ethnic limitations of the faith of his time.

BIBLIOGRAPHY

Commentaries

On the twelve minor prophets see above, 18. Also M.Bič, Berlin 1960; H.-W.Wolff, ET, Hermeneia, 1977; C.A.Keller, CAT, 1965; W.Rudolph, KAT, 1971.

1. A.S.Kapelrud, *Joel Studies*, Uppsala 1948; W.S.Prinsloo, *The Theology of the Book of Joel*, Berlin 1985; cf. also W.Rudolph, 'Wann wirkte Joel?', in F.Maass (ed.), *Das Ferne und Nahe Wort. FS L.Rost*, BZAW 105, 1967, 193-8 (cf. also his commentary); H.-M.Lutz, *Jahwe, Jerusalem und die Völker*, Neukirchen-Vluyn 1968, 34ff., 51ff. For the origins of the work see G.Rinaldi, 'Gioele e il Salmo 65', *BeO* 10, 1968, 113-22, claiming that the text is a meditation on Ps.65 and therefore to be dated in the fourth century BCE. A rather earlier date is supported by G.W.Ahlström, *Joel and the Temple Cult of Jerusalem*, SVT 21, 1971. P.L.Redditt, 'The Book of Joel and Peripheral Prophecy', *CBQ* 48, 1986, 225-40, finds the origin of the book 'among a

particular group of people... which underwent a progressive move to the periphery of the Judahite religious consequence of Joel's criticism of the priestly hierarchy of the early post-exilic period' (239). Cf. also J.A.Thompson, 'The Use of Repetition in the Prophecy of Joel', in *On Language, Culture and Religion: In Honor of E.A.Nida*, The Hague 1974, 101-10; B.Kedar-Kopfstein, 'The Hebrew Text of Joel as Reflected in the Vulgate', *Textus* 9, 1981, 16-35; E.D.Mallon, 'A Stylistic Analysis of Joel 1.10-12', *CBQ* 45, 1983, 537-48; F.E.Deist, 'Parallels and Reinterpretation in the Book of Joel: A Theology of the Yom Yahweh?', in *Text and Context... Studies for F.C.Fensham*, Sheffield 1988, 63-79.

For the thought of Joel see J.Bourke, 'Le jour de Yahvé dans Joel', *RB* 66, 1959, 5-13, 191-212; W.S.Prinsloo, *The Theology of the Book of Joel*, BZAW 163, 1985.

33

JONAH

1. Analysis

Jonah contains not so much sayings and messages pronounced by the prophet as a narrative of his activities. It is a work which belongs to the literary genre of 'prophetic novel', as may be seen clearly from the fact that it has no historical connections (cf. below, § 3).

The content of the book enjoys more notoriety than it deserves because of the miraculous elements which make up a large part of it. YHWH orders the prophet Jonah to preach judgment on Nineveh, the capital of Assyria. However, the prophet is unwilling to assume a certainly burdensome and perhaps even dangerous task, and escapes in the opposite direction, taking a ship directly westwards, to Tarshish. During a severe storm the crew connect his presence on board ship with the danger to the voyage and finally, to placate the deity of the sea, Jonah is thrown into the waves. Devoured by a great fish, within which he remains for three days, he is then cast up by the monster on the eastern coast of the Mediterranean. This time Jonah prefers to obey and goes to Nineveh, where he preaches judgment, so that the inhabitants are converted. In these circumstances God decides to suspend judgment, and this irritates the prophet, who fears that he has cut a bad figure. He sits under a gourd which has miraculously sprung up as a shade from the sun, but God unexpectedly makes the tree shrivel. Still more annoyed, Jonah remonstrates with God, but is given the reply: 'You pity the plant... which came into being in a night, and perished in a night. And should not I pity Nineveh, that great city...?' With this thought the book ends.

2. The prophet

There is mention in II Kings 14.25, at the time of Jeroboam II, of a Jonah ben Amittai who is said to have announced forthcoming triumphs. This would make him an earlier contemporary of Amos, and would fit perfectly with the mention of Nineveh as the capital of Assyria. Thus there could in fact be an ancient tradition underlying the narrative, and this seems all the more likely since in the course of the reign of Adad-Nirari III, son of Semiramis, there seems to have been an attempt at religious reform in Assyria, with tendencies which might be considered monotheistic, in that they put the god Nabu in a place of prominence. However, this is only a question of appearances: even if we allow that the book used traditional material, it is obvious from the way in which it is presented that in fact we are dealing with a product of the later period, in the sense that, like Ruth, it has an 'open' attitude towards the pagan world (cf. below, 38.1). Moreover, the book is full of vague and even improbable remarks; there is no proof that the eighth-century Jonah was ever in Nineveh or that the protagonist of the book is to be identified with him.

3. The problem of the book

I have referred to one of the aims of the book, which is to proclaim openness towards the pagans: God does not want any human being to perish without having had at least the opportunity of being converted. The theme that salvation comes to those who hear and receive the word of God and not to an ethnic entity, however consecrated it may be, is directed against the tendency of groups in Palestinian Judaism to segregate themselves at all costs from their neighbours. However, this theme does not exhaust the content of the book, which also seeks to demonstrate to Israel that God is not necessarily bound to all his promises and his threats, and that in any case they are not fulfilled in a mechanical way; if the circumstances which produced the divine promise or threat change, its fulfilment can change or even be annulled.

If this is the ideological context of the book, there are also other features which indicate a relatively late date:

(a) Problems connected with its historicity:

1. Nineveh is not described as a city contemporaneous with the author, but seems to be set in remote times; the whole account is more reminiscent of the Hellenistic legend of Semiramis than of the testimony of a contemporary (cf.3.3; 4.11).

2. Miracle appears in the book as an obvious and customary event in the life of the believer, and occasions none of the surprise which would be the normal reaction of those who witnessed a happening

that in their opinion transcended the natural course of events. The story of the great fish, which is certainly the best known, is not unique in this context: the waters subside after the crew has thrown Jonah into the sea, the gourd grows and dies in the space of twenty-four hours, and thousands of inhabitants of the Assyrian capital are converted after preaching which we cannot even be sure was in Assyrian. Titles and descriptions are vague and sometimes even absurd: as Pfeiffer*, 588, remarks, to speak of the 'king of Nineveh' as in 3.6 is like calling the king of England the king of London.

(b) This brings us back to the problem of the character of the work. We have seen that it is not just a legend but a prophetic novel, though unlike the stories of Elisha, we are uncertain whether the protagonist is a historical figure. Some scholars have wanted to see the work as an allegory or a parable. The English scholar T.K.Cheyne saw it as an allegory: Jonah represents the elect people with a mission to convert the pagans. The people prefer to renounce their mission by leaving on a sea-going ship; the fish is the exile, which devours Israel like a monstrous dragon. This explanation is attractive, not least because it eliminates at a stroke the difficulties on a historical and scientific level. However, it should be remembered that when the Hebrew Bible makes use of literary genres of this type, e.g. in Judg.9.7ff.; Isa.5.1ff., it says so explicitly – and the fish helps Jonah instead of punishing him. By contrast, in 1907, H.Schmidt argued that Jerusalem was represented under the image of Nineveh, while the book sought to give an affirmative answer to the question whether God would suspend his judgment if it were converted, an argument which is also touched on in Ezek.33.11ff. Here too, however, quite apart from the objection already made against allegorical interpretations, the prophetic theme does not leave any room for doubt: in the message of the prophets, conversion is always a sufficient reason for divine forgiveness.

It therefore seems better to consider the book of Jonah as a parable elaborated with novellistic elements. The author, at any rate, means it to be historical, and his purpose was either to remind a people with introverted tendencies of his fulfilment of their mission according to the ancient phrase of Gen.12.3 (J), or to proclaim that God is not legally bound to his pronouncements, especially those of judgment, and that he remains free to modify them or cancel them at will, as new circumstances arise. As one can see, these positions are not mutually exclusive.

4. Chapter 2

Chapter 2 is immediately distinguishable from its context by being composed in poetry: moreover, it gives the only words which are said to have been pronounced by the prophet. On the other hand, it is not a prophetic discourse but a psalm of thanksgiving for escape from danger. Archaic elements abound. The suppliant is now dead and has gone to Sheol, the Hebrew Hades (v.3); in v.7 this concept is expressed by means of the word *'ereṣ*, which normally means 'earth' or 'region'. In Ugaritic, however, the meaning 'lower regions' is attested; cf. also the expression, 'the waters have gone over my neck', where the term *nepeš*, which normally means 'life principle', here has the archaic sense of 'neck', which is well attested in Akkadian and Ugaritic. It is from the nether regions that Jonah returns after his descent. Given the premises, we can easily understand how in the New Testament Jesus speaks of his own death and descent to hell as 'the sign of Jonah' (Matt.12.38ff. par.), evidence that even in the first century BCE the implications of the psalm were perfectly clear. The question of the fish also takes on quite new dimensions in this context: Jonah, thrown into the sea, has now become the prey of death and descends to Hades, which is symbolized by the sea monster; God rescues him from this desperate situation, for which the prophet gives thanks.

5. Date and text

It is impossible to assign a date to the text, even hypothetically. At most we might allow that ch.2 could be ancient; however, the problems dealt with in the book are clearly post-exilic. Some features of lexicography also point in this direction: in 1.7 the expression *bešellemī* = 'by means of whom' is clearly an Aramaism; in 3.2 *qeriāh* = 'announcement' is a late term, although it is not really an Aramaism, as was once supposed. Even here, however, we must be careful: there is evidence of the term, albeit in a slightly different form, in Ugaritic. Furthermore, the author seems to know Joel (cf.3.9a with Joel 2.14ff.; 4.2 with Joel 2.13b). Expressions and customs are connected with the Persian period: the expression 'God of heaven' in 1.9, the extension of mourning even to animals in 3.7f., a usage which is attested in Herodotus IX, 24. However, the book is already cited in Tobit 14.4-8 and Ecclus.49.10, so that it would be wise not to bring the date down beyond the end of the fifth or the beginning of the fourth century BCE.

The prose section, chs. 1 and 3, has some special features: there are different expressions to indicate the same people (the sailors) and the same object (the ship). We cannot, however, talk of sources here. For the rest, the style is lively and the argument sometimes subtle, and the language is correct.

BIBLIOGRAPHY

Commentaries

On the twelve minor prophets see above, 18; also A.Feuillet, JB ²1960; H.-W.Wolff, 1977.

1. For Tarsḧish, cf. G.Garbini, 'Tarsis e Gen.10.4', *BeO* 7, 1965, 12-19.
2. E.Bickermann, 'Les deux erreurs du prophète Jonas', *RHPR* 45, 1965, 232-64; H.-W.Wolff, *Studien zum Jonahbuch*, Neukirchen 1965; G.M.Landes, 'The Kerygma of the Book of Jonah', *Int* 21, 1967, 3-31; M.Burrows, 'The Literary Category of the Book of Jonah', in H.T.Frank and W.L.Reed (eds.), *Translating and Understanding the Old Testament. Essays in Honor of H.G.May*, New York and Nashville 1970, 80-107; E.G.Kraeling, 'The Evolution of the Book of Jonah', in *Hommages à A.Dupont-Sommer*, Paris 1971, 305-18; O.Kaiser, 'Wirklichkeit, Möglichkeit und Vorurteil. Ein Beitrag zum Verständnis des Buches Jona', *EvTh* 33, 1973, 91-103; A.Fáj, 'The Stoic Features in the Book of Jonah', *AION* 34, 1974, 309-45 (he finds numerous Stoic elements in the work); J.A.Miles, 'Laughing at the Bible: Jonah as Parody', *JQR* 65, 1974-75, 168-81 (he insists, as does H.-W.Wolff in his commentary, on the humorous character of the narrative); R.E.Clements, 'The Purpose of the Book of Jonah', *SVT* 28, 1975, 17-28; A.Fáj, 'La soluzione della "falsa" profezia di Giona', *BeO* 18, 1976, 141-9; G.I.Emmerson, 'Another Look at Jonah', *ExpT* 88, 1976-77, 86-9; J.C.Holbert, ' "Deliverance Belongs to Yahweh". Satire in the Book of Jonah', *JSOT* 21, 1981, 59-81; T.Nishumura, 'Le conflict des deux motifs dans le livre de Jonas', *AJBI* 9. 1983, 3-23; J.M.Sasson, 'On Jonah's Two Missions', *Hen* 6, 1984, 23-30; E.Levine, 'Jonas as a Philosophical Book', *ZAW* 96, 1984, 235-45; E.W.Hesse and I.M.Kikawada, 'Jonah and Genesis 1-11', *AJBI* 10, 1984, 3-19; A.J.Hauser, 'Jonah in Pursuit of the Dove', *JBL* 104, 1985, 21-37; D.L.Christensen, 'The Song of Jonah: A Metrical Analysis', ibid., 217-31. For Semiramis and the religious tendencies in Assyria see now G.Pettinato, *Semiramide*, Milan 1986.
3. Cf. recently L.Schmidt, *De Deo*, BZAW 143, Berlin 1976.
4. A.R.Johnson, 'Jonah II, 3-10: A Study in Cultic Phantasy', in H.H.Rowley (ed.), *Studies in Old Testament Prophecy presented to T.H.Robinson*,

Edinburgh 1950, 82-102; J.A.Soggin, 'Il "segno di Giona" nel libro del profeta Giona', *Lat* 48, 1982, 70-4.

5. For the Aramaisms cf. M.Wagner, *Die lexikalischen und grammatikalischen Aramaismen im alttestamentlichen Hebräisch*, BZAW 96, 1966, n.238.

Cf.E.J.Bickermann, *Four Strange Books of the Bible*, ET New York 1967.

PART FIVE

THE WRITINGS

34

THE PSALMS

1. Introduction

No book in the Hebrew Bible has been read more than the psalms, because, whether through Jewish or Christian liturgy or through personal piety, they seem to come closest to the hearts of believers. Many compositions contained in the psalter also have special importance on a linguistic and philological level.

In the Christian church we often find the psalms as an appendix to editions of the New Testament, in as much as they give a kind of compendium of the whole of the Hebrew Bible: some monastic orders rule that certain psalms are to be read every day. The study of the psalms is therefore complex, conditioned as it is by historical and ritual elements; that makes a critical examination all the more necessary.

The term 'psalm' and the title 'psalter' for the whole book both come from the Greek: *psalterion* is a stringed instrument and *psalmos* is a song accompanied by the instrument in question. The New Testament already speaks of the 'Book of Psalms' (Luke 20.42; Acts 1.20), and from here the expression has passed into the Christian church. In Hebrew the designation *t^ehillīm* = hymns is attested only at a relatively late period, but a study of literary genres immediately shows that hymns in the strict sense only make up part of the psalter. Psalm 72.20 speaks of the 'prayers of David...', which is evidently a designation for some parts of it. On the other hand, as we saw above (6.4,5), not all Hebrew poetry is to be found in the book of Psalms; some of this poetry consists of real psalms (e.g. Gen.49; Exod.15.1-18, 21; Deut.32; 33; Judg.5; I Sam.2.1-10; II Sam.1.19ff.; 3.33; 22.2ff.; 23.1-7; Isa.38.10-20; Jonah 2.3-10 and other lesser passages). We also have two real psalms in the New Testament, in Luke 1.46-55, 67-79, although they have of course been preserved only in Greek. There are also many compositions which should be classified as psalms in the deutero-canonical books and the pseudepigrapha and among the Qumran sect.

The canonical psalter contains 150 psalms. The numbering of these is complex. To simplify the situation somewhat: in some cases different compositions have been combined to form a whole, e.g. Pss.19; 24; 27; etc.; at other times a single composition has been subdivided into two parts, e.g. Pss.9 + 10; 42 + 43. In the case of Pss.9-10, LXX and the Vulgate have kept the original unity, dividing Ps.147 into two instead; this means that the two translations employ a different numbering from the Hebrew, though the content is identical. Some modern Roman Catholic Bibles still follow the numbering of the LXX and the Vulgate, but there is an increasing tendency to follow the Hebrew numbering, putting the other in parentheses. The Syriac translation (cf. above, 2.8b) has preserved a Ps.151, the Hebrew text of which was discovered in Cave 11 at Qumran together with other similar compositions in an incomplete manuscript which contains the psalter; these writings have never had canonical status, nor do we know to what degree they ever belonged to any collection of psalms before the problem of the canon arose.

Within the psalms themselves, too, numbering is complicated: in many cases the Hebrew text numbers the title, where there is one, as v.1, which means that its numbering is one ahead of many English versions; in Pss.51; 52; 54; 60 the Hebrew numbering is even two verses ahead.

The psalter is now divided into five books: I. Pss.1-41; II. Pss.42-72; III. Pss.73-89; IV. Pss.90-106; V. Pss.107-50. We know nothing of the criteria by which this division was made; however, it does not seem to have any historical or exegetical significance.

The psalter is thus a unique book in the Hebrew Bible, not least because it accompanied Israel throughout its history, from the monarchy probably down to the time of the Maccabees. The setting of the psalms makes the study of them particularly interesting, while the scarcity of clear and specific historical references at the same time makes them problematical. Because of the substantial differences in the material, it is impossible to give an overall explanation of the psalms; we must study the origin of each individual psalm, its setting, its literary genre and the possible transformations which it has undergone over the centuries. We can only look for general solutions where we have similar literary genres. In any case, the genres represented in the psalms are extremely old, quite apart from the date of any individual composition. Moreover, the late datings which were so frequently proposed a few decades ago (Pfeiffer*, 620, regarded the psalter as 'the great manifesto of the Pious' in the post-exilic period, while B.Duhm in his commentary wanted to date the majority of the psalms in the Maccabaean period, that is, towards the middle of the second century BCE, as does M.Treves today) can now be considered problematical; for example, how could we put a 'royal psalm' in the post-exilic period unless there had been a possible Maccabaean or messianic revision? However, the more obvious dating would be one prior to 587/86.

2. The use of the psalms

(a) Direct biblical testimony. Jeremiah 33.11 (cf. Pss.118; 136); II Chron.16.8ff. (cf.Ps.105.1-15; 96.1-13; 106.1, 47-49); Ezra 3.10ff. provide interesting information on the use of some parts of the psalter. The Chronicles passage is especially interesting, as it gives us first-hand information about the use of some of the compositions in temple worship. They were sung by choirs, and the community responded 'Amen', 'Hallelujah'. Earlier in this book we saw that the superscriptions at the beginning of the psalms are late, but they do give us information about the worship in which the psalms were used, at least at the time when the superscription in question came into being: that to Ps.30 speaks of the feast of the dedication of the temple (cf. below, 52.2); to Ps.100 of the sacrifice of thanksgiving; to Ps.92 of the sabbath; to Ps.24 (LXX) of Wednesday; to Ps.93 of Friday; to Ps.81 (Old Latin and Armenian) of Thursday. Thus it is evident that at some time (certainly before 70 CE, the date of the destruction of the temple), these psalms were connected with the morning sacrifice which was the beginning of each day's liturgy and which was called the *tāmīd*; moreover, this name appears in the superscriptions of some psalms. The Talmud knows the practice of singing some psalms (or parts of them) before prayer, and Pss.113-18 before the celebration of the passover; there is also independent evidence of this latter practice in Matt.26.30, and it has lasted down to today. There is therefore striking evidence of the use of the psalms in temple worship in Jerusalem in the post-exilic period, even if it is relatively late, though for the most part it is not possible to go back in time, still less to other sanctuaries than that of Jerusalem.

(b) In addition to the material already examined, the superscriptions offer other elements for determining the use of certain psalms. These are the psalms known as the 'Hallelujah' psalms (Pss.106; 111; 112; 113; 146-50), probably because the community replied with this formula at the end of each stanza; this feature, too, goes back to the cult. However, other expressions which recur in the superscriptions are not clear: we find *lamm^enāse^aḥ* = literally 'for the director (of the choir?)' 55 times; the term *selāh*, which is also attested in Hab.3, 78 times. It is sometimes understood as 'pause', but its meaning is uncertain and it should perhaps be translated 'for ever' (a kind of *per omnia saecula saeculorum*, Kraus). *mizmor* appears 57 times: it is translated *psalmos* by LXX, which means simply 'song', like the Akkadian *zamāru*; sometimes it is similar to *šīr* = song, though in a more specific form. Other terms like *miktām*, *maśkīl* and *šiggāyōn* are less clear: the second can be connected with the root *śkl* = 'understand', and perhaps mean 'instruction'; if we can connect the third with the Akkadian *šegū*, it perhaps means 'lament'. Other expressions are even less clear: Ps.22.1, 'the hind of the dawn' or 'a hind is the dawn'. Perhaps this is the title of the tune to which the composition was sung; we cannot rule out the possibility that the melody was of Canaanite origin, as there is explicit evidence of a deity *šḥr* = Aurora in Ugaritic. As we saw at the beginning of this book, the superscriptions often attempt to set the psalms to which they refer in the context of particular events in the history of Israel.

As a result, we see that there is decisive evidence of the use of the psalter at the time of the second temple. However, this does not mean that some of the compositions in it cannot be old. In other words, this is a *terminus ante quem*, not *a quo*.

3. The formation of the psalter

The few lines above are enough to show that when we study the origin of the psalter we are embarking on a particularly complex problem. There is a notable difference between the compositions which it contains in terms of chronology, aim and authorship. So it is not surprising that until a few decades ago there were scholars who thought that the psalter grew in size right down to the time of the Maccabees, i.e. to the second century BCE (and this view has still not been discarded). However, today the situation has changed: we have the Qumran psalms, the so-called *hōdāyōt*, and the manuscript of the psalter discovered in Cave 11a, even if it is incomplete. We can see from these writings not only that the psalter must have been complete by the second century BCE but also that the compositions outside the psalter which can be dated to this period are substantially different from those in the psalter itself. To this impossibility of a very late dating of the whole psalter we must add the fact, already noted, that many compositions (e.g. the royal psalms) presuppose a pre-exilic situation.

Another problem is the artificial character of some of the collections of psalms; this emerges clearly from the presence of obvious duplicates (cf. Pss.14 with 53: 40.14-18 with 70.1ff.; 57.8-12 and 60.7-14 with 108.1ff.). However, we should not rule out the possibility that in some cases this is the result of the same literary genre or analogous formulae. Moreover, in Pss.42-89 we find that the name YHWH has been replaced almost constantly with the title *ᵉlōhīm* = god, a substitution which seems to be entirely artificial. Consequently the term 'Elohist psalter' is regularly used; the designation does not, of course, have anything to do with the source in the Pentateuch. Perhaps we have here an example of the tendency of later Judaism to substitute one of the titles of God for the divine name, the pronunciation of which had been forbidden. On the other hand, this might be a special collection, since otherwise it would be impossible to explain why this work was not carried out consistently throughout the psalter.

On this basis we can now try to isolate some of the collections which are immediately recognizable:

(a) The 'Davidic psalter', which is so-called because the superscriptions connect the compositions in question in some obscure way with King David. It includes Pss.3-41 and chronologically is probably the earliest collection. The relationship with David is expressed by the formula *lᵉdāwīd* (= literally 'for David'); in ancient times it was believed that the *lᵉ* indicated authorship and so it was called a *lamed auctoris*; hence the attribution of a large part of the psalter to David. Like so many other attributions in the Hebrew Bible, however, this seems extremely problematical, as is the attribution of the Pentateuch to Moses. It arises from the account in I Chron.22.2-29.5, which describes how David reorganized worship in view of the imminent building of the temple of Jerusalem entrusted to his son Solomon; it finds its ultimate support in the tradition which makes David a skilful singer (cf.I Sam.16; II Sam.1.19ff.; 3.33), a tradition still related in Amos 6.5 (though that is a late tradition). The tradition which makes David the author of particular psalms appears explicitly only in the Babylonian Talmud (Pesaḥim 117a), where it is attributed to R.Meir, a disciple of R.Akiba (first half of the second century CE); it is therefore quite late, even if there are already evident traces of it in the New Testament. On the other hand, in the Davidic psalter also there are too many cases which presuppose not only the existence of the temple built by Solomon but also the exile and destruction of

Jerusalem, so that with the best will in the world it is impossible to connect these compositions with David. The formula *l·X* is also attested in Ugaritic, and sometimes in contexts which quite rule out the possibility that the person mentioned could be the author of the composition: *lkrt, l'qht, lb'l*. While the first two of these terms give the names of legendary kings and it would not be intrinsically impossible that the compositions should be attributed to them, the last is the name of a deity, Ba'al, who can hardly be envisaged as the author of a psalm. Thus the most logical explanation in the case of the mention of David remains that it means 'belonging in the Davidic collection', or something of this kind.

(*b*) The 'Elohistic psalter' (Pss.42-89), to which I have already referred above, is characterized by the fact that in 200 cases the name YHWH is replaced by the title *'elōhīm*; YHWH is left in only about 40 cases. In addition to a second edition of the compositions in question, in which this substitution was made, there are indications that this collection was added to the first. In it we can distinguish:

1. The psalms of the Korahites (42-49; 84; 85; 87; 88). The people in question appear in II Chron. 20.19, but we do not know the circumstances in which they came to undertake the role of temple singers. Similar to these are:

2. The psalms of Asaph (50; 73-83), probably a collection for another group of singers attested in Ezra 2.41; I Chron.15.19; II Chron 35.15, though we cannot establish the origins or the antiquity of the group.

3. We have a second 'Davidic Psalter' in Pss.51-65; 68-70; its conclusion has almost certainly been preserved in Ps.72.20. It is possible that before its revision it formed part of the collection mentioned in paragraph (*a*) above.

These are observations which relate particularly to the redaction and later use of the compositions in question; as we shall see, some of them could be significantly older.

(*c*) Psalms 90-150 do not have any features which allow us to place them in history or tradition. Psalms 120-134 are distinguished by a superscription which in a literal translation means 'songs of ascent'; it is possible that they were used as songs on a pilgrimage to Jerusalem, since the verb *'ālā*, 'go up', was used for this act. However, the remains of a great staircase discovered during excavations outside the modern city wall on the south side tend to suggest a processional ascent to the temple.

(*d*) Psalm 1 seems to have a special position. First of all it is a wisdom composition (we shall examine the significance of this statement shortly). Moreover there are traditions attested in the Talmud and the New Testament (Acts 13.33 in the 'Western text' of Codex D) in which it appears prefixed to Ps.2. There is no connection between the content of the two psalms, but Ps.2 sometimes appears as Ps.1. It is not easy to make a critical assessment of this discovery; however, it does not seem probable that the psalter once began with Ps.2 and that Ps.1 was added at some point as a kind of prologue.

4. The setting of the psalms

While the Hebrew and Christian tradition tended to attribute the greater part of the psalter to David, critical Introduction from the end of the last century and the first decades of this took the opposite course. In his commentary, B.Duhm argued that it was no longer a question of asking whether there were any psalms from the Maccabaean period, but rather of asking whether there were any earlier than this period, and the authority which his opinion enjoyed is amply demonstrated by the support given to it by R.H.Pfeiffer* (and now by M.Treves), and by the indecision of A.Lods*. However, we have already seen that it is impossible to put the question in these terms, not only because of the recent discoveries from Qumran but also because of the studies made in the 1920s by S.Mowinckel, H.Gunkel and H.Schmidt. The second in particular put forward a more moderate argument, pointing out the absence of any convincing proof for such a late date and showing at the same time that there could be no question of 'dating' pure and simple or of the 'origin' of a given psalm. The task was, rather, to establish in as exact a form as possible the literary genre of each composition, and within the field of the literary genre, the use which was made of it. As we saw above (6.3), this in fact is the only approach that really fits the material under consideration, which is largely anonymous and therefore difficult to date. A similar situation arises over other compositions which are virtually psalms: Gen.49; Exod.15; Deut.32; 33, Judg.5, etc. There was first a desire to attribute them to the two earliest sources of the Pentateuch, but we saw above (6.5) that they present problems of their own; they have obvious affinities with certain compositions in the psalter which today are generally recognized to be quite old (Pss.29; 68; 110). It must, however, be borne in mind that very often, and in all languages, poetry uses an archaizing style. One might recall the instances of the letter to

Dulcinea in Cervantes' *Don Quixote* or the preface to Manzoni's *The Betrothed*.

In any case, however late the dating of a particular psalm, there is no doubt that the psalms generally represent the development of a literary genre (or rather genres), the roots of which lie far back in the pre-Israelite past, though this does not rule out an independent development or a use substantially different from that of the literary genre from which they descended.

In this context we should take account of another feature which has also been mentioned above (6.2), that of oral tradition. This was the vehicle by means of which literary and liturgical material was transmitted throughout the ancient Near East. In this context the remembrance of the person of the author tends to become secondary, while features which would enable us to date the material cannot be established by comparing them with information known to us (the content is normally expressed in very general terms). The only guide is given by particular linguistic characteristics which enable us to establish a rough dating, with a great deal of room for manoeuvre. For example, the abundance or prevalence of Canaanite lexicographical features which tend later to disappear in Hebrew would obviously suggest an early date, but we must remember two factors. First, as indicated above, all poetry preserves a series of archaic elements much longer than everyday language; secondly, what we have may be artificial archaisms which are not really old. This feature is well attested in the ancient Near East, where a composition may display characteristics from centuries earlier. As we have seen, historical information is rarely to be found in the psalms, but it is obvious that the royal psalms must have arisen before the destruction of the monarchy, even if it is more than likely that they were used again in Maccabaean and messianic terms. Furthermore, the prayer for the speedy rebuilding of the walls of Jerusalem which comes at the end of Ps.51 at least presupposes their destruction in 587/86 and cannot be reconciled with the superscription which attributes the psalm to David. This observation, though, does not allow us to draw conclusions about the rest of the composition.

5. Literary genres represented in the psalms

(*a*) We have already discussed literary genres above (6.3). At this point we must examine them in rather more detail.

One of the most frequent genres in the psalter is the hymn or song of praise to YHWH; sometimes the praise can be given through a sanctuary, e.g. Zion (Pss.48; 74; 102, etc); at other times through a special form of hymn commonly called the 'enthronement psalm'. This designation was given to it by Mowinckel in the 1920s and continued through the British 'myth and ritual' school in the 1930s, 1940s and 1950s and the Uppsala school in Sweden in the 1940s and 1950s, because they postulate the existence of a festival during which, on New Year's Day, YHWH would have been solemmnly enthroned in his sanctuary after having been led in procession (perhaps by means of the ark). Psalms 24; 47; 93; 96-99 are hymns which fall into this category, and fragments are scattered here and there throughout the psalter. However, there is a certain amount of disagreement among scholars over the festival; some, like the Germans A.Weiser and H.-J.Kraus, instead tried to identify a 'feast of the covenant', though this too was problematical. In any case these are hymns which praise YHWH in particular forms. Psalms 2; 18; 20; 21; 45; 72; 89; 101; 110; 132; 144.1-11 etc. praise him through the person of the king, his anointed, and marked features of this genre are also scattered throughout the psalter.

The predominant themes of the hymn are: the history of the acts of YHWH, for which the community is exhorted to give thanks and praise; creation (and in this context, as among some of the prophets, interesting mythical elements appear which have now been partly eliminated from the Genesis narratives); the preservation of the world against the perils of chaos (Pss.8; 19a praise creation on this basis); and episodes in the history of Israel understood as the history of salvation. This feature, which we have seen to be predominant in the faith of Israel, also makes up a large part of the psalter; the hymn is certainly one of the forms of composition best represented not only in the psalter but also in the poetical compositions outside it, from earliest times to the New Testament. Sometimes (Pss.98; 150) we have indications of the musical instruments which accompanied the hymn, while at others we have an indication of the place where it was sung (Ps.100 at the temple gate). The main indications are of public use, but this clearly does not exclude private use also, in the worship of the individual and the family. Almost by definition, the hymn is characterized by its enthusiasm, expressed in a language which is full of adjectives and laudatory superlatives; there is a tendency to exaggeration and hyperbole. These are factors which those studying Israelite belief must take into account if they want to evaluate it properly.

The structure of the hymn is simple. It begins with an invitation or invocation to a cultic action: 'Sing...' or 'I will sing..', or even

'Praise/bless, my soul...' The invocation in the second person plural predominates. There follows the reason for the invitation or invocation: there are particular reasons which make it right and proper for the community and the believer to celebrate the praises of YHWH. In general these reasons are introduced by 'Because' and less frequently by a relative pronoun, 'Who has', or 'It is he who'; the latter is especially used if the preceding phrase ends with YHWH. These reasons are then followed by what we may call the 'body' of the hymn, which is composed of a selection of divine acts which are the reason for the exhortation to worship God. The genre recalls what we saw in the Pentateuch when studying the confessions of faith, though it is not possible to conjecture any kind of relationship between the two genres.

Of the royal psalms, Pss.2 and 110, the details of which are not always clear, probably refer to the coronation of the monarch (cf. Pss.21; 72; 101). Psalm 20 probably refers to the departure of the king for war, an occasion on which the divine blessing was called down upon him. Ps.144.1-11 seems to be similar, but it also has features which recall the lament. Psalm 18 seems to be a hymn of thanksgiving by the victorious king, while Ps.45 is probably an epithalamium on the occasion of his wedding. In v.5 the king is called by the title *'elōhīm*, 'god' (though this is not clear in some English versions [cf.v.6]). This is the only instance in the Hebrew Bible in which the divinity of the monarch seems to be supposed. In Pss.2.7-9; 20.7; 21.5; 110.1-5; 132.11f. we have a word of YHWH addressed to the monarch, probably in the form of an oracle from a priest or prophet; or it may be a stereotyped phrase, now fixed as a ritual formula.

(*b*) Another very frequent literary genre is the lament. First of all we may distinguish between public laments and private laments. In the former case, the people are assembled in the sanctuary on the occasion of some national or local disaster, an occasion which is foreseen with an abundance of detail in Solomon's prayer at the inauguration of the temple (I Kings 8.32-53, esp. vv.33-40); there is a special instance in Joel 1-2. In the psalter we have Pss.44; 67; 74; 79; 80, usually centred upon the theme of the injustices comitted by others against Israel, and on one occasion (Ps.44) accompanied by an impassioned prayer. There is frequent mention of the blessings which the people have experienced in the past, with which the present misery makes a sad contrast – again a connection, albeit remote, with the ancient confessions of faith; in Ps.79 the lament is probably accompanied by a vow. In Ps.60.8-10 we have a divine response, again communicated by means of an oracle from priest or prophet. The literary genre is already attested in Sumerian Babylon; the use made of this genre by the prophets from the eighth century onwards clearly demonstrates that the situation was similar in Israel (Amos 5.2ff.; Hos.6.1-6; 14.3-9; Jer.3.22b-4.2; 14.7-10, etc.). In some cases the genre is parodied, as with Amos.

The funeral lament has one of the few metres which we can identify with some certainty; it is a quintuple metre in two lines, one of three and the other of two beats, if it is permissible to use classical terms in this context. However, paradoxically this metre also appears in Isa.40.1ff. to announce liberation to the captives; is this perhaps a kind of proclamation which in form is *sub contraria specie?* Deuteronomy 32 is a public lament, and the book of Lamentations is composed exclusively of laments (for these two compositions see above 6.5 and below 38.2 respectively).

The individual lament can be distinguished by the use of the first person singular, a sign that it was recited by the individual at prayer. However, in Ps.129.1ff. the first person singular is identified explicitly with Israel, though there are no signs that a collective interpretation of the first person is known elsewhere in the psalter (it is also claimed as a possibility in the 'servant songs', cf. above 25.3c).

The argument of the individual lament is carried on through prayers and protests of innocence from the believer, who feels that he is unjustly the victim of the divine anger (with arguments which sometimes sound strange to modern ears, cf. Ps.6.6, a verse which until recently was interpreted as a kind of blackmailing of YHWH by the suppliant). The lament also normally has a 'body' in which the theme is expressed, followed at least by protests of innocence and a declaration which confirms the certainty of being heard; in this last case the certainty is the product either of the faith of the suppliant, an assurance that it is enough for him to turn to YHWH, who will surely hear the prayer, or of the declaration of an oracle, now inserted to a great or lesser degree into the liturgy, by means of which YHWH himself responded (Mowinckel and Gunkel). According to H.Schmidt, a special category of lament is one which he calls the 'prayer of the accused', brought before the court which is to try him (cf. I Kings 8.31ff.; Jer.26.1ff.). Psalms 7; 35; 57; 59 would fit this situation well. Once his case has been placed in the hands of YHWH, the accused can rest assured: his adversary will have dug his grave with his own hands.

(c) Psalms of trust, among which the well-known Ps.23 holds pride of place, are often regarded as identical to the 'certainty of being heard' which we have seen to have been added to many laments. In other words, the 'body' of the lament is thought to have disappeared, leaving only the certainty.

(d) Finally, there are not many instances of wisdom psalms in the psalter; they are all connected in the psalter with the exaltation of the *tōrāh* (Pss.1; 19b: 119 and some others).

6. Conclusion

The psalter, then, offers a cross-section of the cultic life of Israel from the monarchy to later periods. These 150 compositions thus make up a collection presenting the story of the faith of Israel. Studies of the question prove to be extremely complex, and we cannot exclude the possibility that at some time in the not too distant future, excavations at Ugarit will reveal the existence of similar compositions, of real parallels to the psalms, which would make their study very much easier. Thus the tendency of Christian faith to attach special importance to the psalms is fully justified, though some of the compositions which have been handed down to us are extremely difficult to interpret because of notorious textual difficulties. As we have seen, Qumran Cave 11 has produced a scroll containing some canonical psalms and others which lie outside the canon.

BIBLIOGRAPHY

Commentaries

B.Duhm, KHC, ²1922; H.Gunkel, HKAT ⁴1926; H.Schmidt, HAT, 1934; W.O.E.Oesterley, London 1939; E.J.Kissane, Dublin ²1964; G.R.Castellino, SacBib, 1955; H.-J.Kraus, BK ³1978; R.Tournay et al., JB, ³1964; A.Weiser, ET, OTL, 1962; A.González, Barcelona 1966; M.J.Dahood, AB, 1966-70; A.A.Anderson, NCB, 1972; L.Sabourin, New York ²1974; L.Jacquet, Gembloux, I, 1975; II, 1977; III, 1979; E.Beaucamp, Paris, I, 1976; II, 1977; G.Ravasi, I, 1981; II, 1983; III, 1984; L.Alonso Schökel, *Treinta Salmos*, Madrid 1980; C.Westermann, *Ausgewählte Psalmen*, Göttingen 1984.

General introductions and bibliographies: J.J.Stamm, 'Ein Vierteljahrhundert Psalmenforschung', *TR* 23, 1955, 1-68; K.Seybold, 'Beiträge zur Psalmenforschung', *TR* 46, 1981, 1-18; id., *Die Psalmen*, Stuttgart 1986; B.Feininger, 'A Decade of German Psalm Criticism', *JSOT* 20, 1981, 91-

103; R.de Langhe (ed.), *Le Psautier*, Louvain 1962; R.Martin-Achard, *Approche des Psaumes*, Neuchâtel 1969; E.Gerstenberger, 'Literatur zu den Psalmen', *VuF* 17, 1972, 82-99; id., 'Psalms', in J.H.Hayes (ed.), *Old Testament Form Criticism*, San Antonio, Texas 1974, 179-223. Cf. also J.-N.Aletti and J.Trublet, *Approche poétique et théologique des Psaumes*, Paris 1983. For the text cf. O.Loretz, 'Psalmenstudien I, II, III, IV, V', *UF* 3, 1971, 110-15; 5, 1973, 213-18; 6, 1974, 175-210, 211-40; 8, 1976, 117-21.

1. For historical themes in the Psalms cf. A.Lauha, *Die Geschichtsmotive in den alttestamentlichen Psalmen*, Helsinki 1945; F.H.Jasper, 'Early Israelite Traditions and the Psalter', *VT* 17, 1967, 50-9; J.Kühlewein, *Geschichte in den Psalmen*, Stuttgart 1973; for individual themes cf. L.Vosberg, *Studien zum Reden vom Schöpfer in den Psalmen*, Munich 1975. For style cf. N.H.Ridderbos, *Die Psalmen*, BZAW 117, 1972. For parallel psalms see W.Zimmerli, 'Zwillingspsalmen', in *Wort, Lied und Gottespruch. FS H.Ziegler*, Würzburg 1972, 105-13 (= his *Gesammelte Aufsätze* II, Munich 1974, 161-71). For the fourth book see M.D.Goulder, 'The Fourth Book of the Psalter', *JTS* 26, 1975, 269-89; A.H.W.Curtis, 'The "Subjugation of the Waters" Motif in the Psalms: Imagery or Polemics?', *JSS* 23, 1978, 245-56; J.Goldingay, 'The Dynamic Cycle of Praise and Prayer in the Psalms', *JSOT* 20, 1981, 85-90; M.D.Goulder, *The Psalms of the Sons of Korah*, Sheffield, 1982; H.Seidel, 'Untersuchungen zur Aufführungspraxis der Psalmen im altisraelitischen Gottesdienst', *VT* 33, 1983, 503-9; G.H.Wilson, 'Evidence of Traditional Divisions in the Psalms', *VT* 34, 1984, 337-52; E.Jenni, 'Zu den doxologischen Schlussformeln des Psalters', *TZ* 40, 1984, 114-20; S.Wagner, 'Das Reich des Messias. Zur Theologie der alttestamentlichen Königspsalmen', *TLZ* 109, 1984, 865-74; G.H.Wilson, 'The Use of "Untitled" Psalms in the Hebrew Psalter', *ZAW* 97, 1985, 404-13. Marco Treves, *The Dates of the Psalms. History and Poetry in Ancient Israel*, Pisa 1988, is a staunch defender of à late dating for the Psalter.

2. For the superscriptions cf. J.F.A.Sawyer, 'An Analysis of the Context and Incoming of the Psalm Headings', *TGUOS* 22, 1967-68, 26-98; B.S. Childs, 'Psalm-Titles and Midrashic Exegesis', *JSS* 16, 1971, 137-50; J.W.McKay, 'Psalms of Vigil', *ZAW* 91, 1979, 229-47; W.Brueggemann, 'Psalms and the Life of Faith', *JSOT* 17, 1980, 3-32. For the psalms without superscriptions see G.H.Wilson, 'The Use of "Untitled" Psalms in the Hebrew Psalter', *ZAW* 97, 1985, 404-13. For music see J.H.Eaton, 'Music's Place in Worship: A Contribution from the Psalms', *OTS* 23, 1984, 85-107; for prayer see A.Aejmalaeus, *The Traditional Prayer in the Psalms*, BZAW 176, 1986.

3c. C.C.Keet, *A Study of the Psalms of Ascent*, London 1969; B.Houlk, 'Syllables and Psalms: A Statistical Linguistic Analysis', *JSOT* 14, 1979, 55-62; K.Seybold, *Die Wallfahrtspsalmen*, Neukirchen 1978; id., 'Die Redaktion der Wallfahrtspsalmen', *ZAW* 91, 1979, 247-68; M.Mannati, 'Les Psaumes graduels constituent-ils un genre littéraire distinct à l'intérieur du psautier biblique?', *Sem* 29, 1979, 85-102.

4. S.Mowinckel, *Psalmenstudien*, 6 vols, Oslo 1921-4 (reprinted 1961); id., *The Psalms in Israel's Worship*, 2 vols, ET Oxford 1962; H.Gunkel and J.Begrich, *Einleitung in die Psalmen*, Göttingen 1932 (reprinted 1966); G.Fohrer*, 285-93, gives a useful synopsis of the dates assigned to individual psalms. For the problem of the relationship of some psalms to texts from Ugarit cf. J.H.Patton, *Canaanite Parallels to the Book of Psalms*, Baltimore 1944; J.Coppens, 'Les parallèles du Psautier avec les textes de Ras Shamra-Ougarit', *Muséon* 59, Louvain 1946, 113-42; R.T.O'Callaghan, 'Echoes of Canaanite Literature in the Psalms', *VT* 4, 1954, 164-76; H.Donner, 'Ugaritismen in der Psalmenforschung', *ZAW* 79, 1967, 322-50 and O.Loretz, 'Die Ugaristik in der Psalmeninterpretation', *UF* 44, 1972, 167-9, counsel caution. D.A.Robertson, *Linguistic Evidence in Dating Early Hebrew Poetry*, Cambridge, Mass. 1972, discusses the problem of the use of comparative linguistic material to date ancient Hebrew poetry, but he arrives at ambivalent results.

For the problems of the individual psalms see the monographs indicated by the various commentators and bibliographical studies.

For the enthronement psalms cf. E.Lipiński, *La royauté de Yahvé dans la poésie et le culte de l'ancien Israël*, Brussels 1965; J.Coppens, 'Les psaumes d'inthronisation de Yahvé', *ETL* 42, 1966, 192-7; O.Loretz, 'Strichometrische und theologische Probleme in den Thronbesteigungspsalmen', *UF* 6, 1974, 211-40; J.H.Eaton, *Kingship and the Psalms*, SBT II 32, 1976; J.H.Ulrichsen, '*YHWH mālak*. Einige sprächliche Betrachtungen', *VT* 27, 1977, 361-74. For a general survey see E.Lipiński et al., 'Psaumes', *SDB* IX, 1979, 1-125, and 'Königsherrschaft Jahwes und Thronbesteigung', *VT* 32, 1982, 297-310 (warns against the attribution to Israel of Babylonian festivals about which in the meantime scholars have substantially revised their views). For the problem of the relationship between the language of the psalms and that of the extra-biblical inscriptions cf. P.D.Miller Jr, 'Psalms and Inscriptions', *SVT* 32, 1981, 311-32. See also T.N.D.Mettinger, *The Dethronement of Sebaoth*, Lund 1983, passim.

5. Cf. H.Gunkel and J.Begrich, *Einleitung*; O.Eissfeldt*, G.Fohrer*, s.v., and C.Westermann, *Praise and Lament in the Psalms*, ET Atlanta 1981 and Edinburgh 1982.

5a. For the 'Uppsala School' cf. I.Engnell, *Studies in Divine Kingship in the Ancient Near East*, Oxford ²1967; A.Bentzen, *King and Messiah*, ET, London 1955. The possibility of a 'covenant festival' on Zion during the autumn festival has been examined by H.-J.Kraus, *Die Königsherrschaft Gottes im Alten Testament*, Tübingen 1951; cf. also his commentary, 197ff., and that of Weiser, 27ff., where the emphasis is different. From a critical point of view the two festivals seem phantoms. Cf. also P.D.Miller, Jr, ' "Enthroned on the Praises of Israel" ', *Int* 39, 1985, 5-19; J.Jeremias, *Das Königtum Gottes in den Psalmen*, Göttingen 1987.

5b. G.R.Castellino, *Le lamentazioni individuali e gli inni in Babilonia e in Israele*, Turin 1939; C.Westermann, 'Struktur und Geschichte der Klage im

Alten Testament', *ZAW* 66, 1954, 44-80; J.W.Wevers, 'A Study in the Form-Criticism of Individual Complaint Psalms', *VT* 6, 1956, 8-96; G.W.Anderson, ' *"Sicut cervus"*: Evidence in the Psalter for Private Devotions in Ancient Israel', *VT* 30, 1980, 388-97; G.Gerleman, 'Der "Einzelne" der Klage und Dankpsalmen', *VT* 32, 1982, 33-49. For the enemies and malefactors cf. H.Schmidt, *Das Gebet des Angeklagten im Alten Testament*, BZAW 49, 1928; H.Birkeland, *Die Feinde des Individuums in der israelitischen Psalmenliteratur*, Oslo 1933; id., *The Evildoers in the Book of Psalms*, Oslo 1955, G.W.Anderson, 'Enemies and Evildoers in the Book of Psalms', *BJRL* 48, 1965-6, 18-29; G.Sauer, 'I nemici nei Salmi', *Prot* 13, 1958, 201-7; E.Gerstenberger, 'Enemies and Evildoers in the Psalms', *HorBTh* 5, 1983, 61-77; E.Cortese, 'Poveri e umili nei Salmi', *RiBib* 35, 1987, 299-306. For the Psalms as literature and doctrine cf. N.Airoldi, 'L'antico mondo poetico dei Salmi', *BeO* 14, 1972, 97-105; G.Rinaldi, 'L'universo dei Salmi', *BeO* 15, 1973, 229-37; id., 'Il mondo per l'uomo nei Salmi', *BeO* 16, 1974, 163-76; id., 'Popoli e paesi nei Salmi', *BeO* 17, 1975, 97-111. For thanksgiving cf. W.Beyerlin, 'Kontinuität bei "berichtenden" Lobpreis des Einzelnen', *Wort und Geschichte. FS K.Elliger*, AOAT 18, 1973, 17-24. For wisdom in the Psalter see A.Hurvitz, 'Wisdom Vocabulary in the Hebrew Psalter: A Contribution to the Study of Wisdom Psalms', *VT* 38, 1988, 41-51. The possibilities of a structuralist approach are examined by T.Collins, 'Decoding the Psalms. A Structural Approach to the Psalter', *JSOT* 37, 1987, 41-60. For parallels with other literature cf. recently G.R.Castellino, 'Mesopotamian Parallels to Some Passages of the Psalms', *Beiträge zur alttestamentlichen Theologie. FS W.Zimmerli*, Göttingen 1977, 60-8. For the message of the Psalms see W.Brueggemann, *The Message of the Psalms*, Minneapolis 1984.

35

INTRODUCTION TO WISDOM

1. The wisdom books in Israel

The wisdom books make up an important part of the thought of the Hebrew Bible, not only because of their number but because we continually find their influence in other books. For all the differences in detail, they have a fundamental element in common, which is their principal characteristic and is not to be found in the other books: faith in a divine cosmic wisdom which rules and governs the universe with rational and immutable norms. The wise man is the one who adapts himself to these norms and discovers the way in which they work, perhaps even their essence; the fool or even the wicked man is the one who fails to do this and does not care. Each person receives his deserts in accordance with his wisdom or his foolishness: the wise man is given wisdom and through it a serene and fruitful life, while the fool and the wicked man have a life full of troubles.

This divine cosmic wisdom for which all human beings must search with every means at their disposal is called *ḥokmah* in Hebrew, but the concept can also be expressed by means of derivatives of the root *ṣdq*: *ṣᵉdāqāh* = 'justice'.

Now a glance at the thought of the ancient Near East will immediately show that the worlds of Mesopotamia and Egypt were also aware of a cosmic wisdom, Egyptian *ma'at*, which governed the world justly and to which the wise man therefore had to try to adapt himself. We have to do here, then, with the insertion into Yahwistic belief (or the survival) of a typically non-Hebraic, unhistorical element, so it is no surprise to find throughout the wisdom books a contrast with the essentially historical approach which is character-istic of the other books of the Hebrew Bible. There is no religious, social and political criticism here such as we find in the prophets; here we only have wise men and fools: the former intent on living in accordance with a cosmic principle, guaranteed by YHWH, the latter without this concern and therefore, at least in theory, destined to perish.

The wisdom books of the Old Testament are Proverbs, Job, Ecclesiastes in the Palestinian canon and the Wisdom of Solomon and Ecclesiasticus in the Alexandrian collection; we may also note strong influence from wisdom in some prophets and psalmists, in the Song of Songs, the book of Tobit and perhaps even in Deuteronomy and Dtr. It is beyond the scope of a work like this *Introduction* to deal with the complex problem of relationships between Israelite wisdom and that of the Near East; anyone who wishes to pursue matters further should consult the books listed in the bibliography. However, I shall try here to give some basic information for a critical reading of the wisdom literature, so that it is possible to understand the range of problems involved, and the means and ends of wisdom.

We have considered the feature which is common not only to the wisdom literature of the Hebrew Bible but also to that of the ancient Near East. It has two more obvious and to some degree disconcerting consequences, if we remember the strong polemical note which pervades the whole of the Hebrew Bible where it touches on the problems of Yahwistic belief and its relationship with the religions of the pagan world. In the first place, while we may note the due differences between the cosmic wisdom of YHWH and the theologically neutral wisdom of Egypt and Mesopotamia (neutral only up to a certain point, since it tends to assume characteristics which come increasingly close to those of a fate or destiny), we also discover a fundamental affinity at the level of content and effect. Moreover, affinities of form have been noted for some decades, and in at least one case it is easy to see the existence of a real dependence of a major Hebrew text on an Egyptian text. These affinities even extend to the crisis in wisdom which developed at a relatively late and more critical phase of thought, a phase in which the naive idea of reward and punishment outlined above proved untenable when put to the test. In the second place, the more typical themes which characterize the faith of Israel, like the proclamation of the acts of God in historically verifiable events, the election of Israel, promises about the people and the land, and so on, are almost completely absent in the wisdom literature. The scholar cannot avoid the impression that this is a matter more of a lack of interest than of ignorance: the wise man is preoccupied with the cosmic order; the rest seems irrelevant. It is not, therefore, surprising that the biblical theology movement sometimes passed a harsh judgment on the wisdom literature, regarding its thought as an element alien to the faith of Israel, an erratic block of material, a theologically false vein; and this valuation seemed to be supported by the obvious parallels with Near Eastern wisdom. Only in the last few years have these characteristic elements of wisdom been examined in a coherent fashion, even if the problem of their insertion into the message of the Bible sometimes seems to have been obscured, if not deliberately avoided.

Today the situation may be said to be very different. From the middle of the 1960s onwards Israelite wisdom has been the object of many studies primarily focussed on the phenomenon; apart from discovering the presence of wisdom features in other sections of the Hebrew Bible, these studies are concerned to examine the position and the limits of wisdom within the message of the Bible generally.

2. Proverbial wisdom and wisdom literature

A first distinction which the student of wisdom, whether Israelite or Near Eastern, is led to make is a formal one, though closer consideration shows that it is also valid in terms of content. This is a distinction between proverbial wisdom and wisdom tractates. The former is expressed in brief sentences which are either of universal validity or conditioned by particular situations; it provides brief affirmations or negations, and gives practical advice. It makes use of maxims which are usually composed of a single verse in two lines, sometimes of rather larger units, and is essentially to be found in the books of Proverbs and Ecclesiasticus, and (in part) in Ecclesiastes and the Wisdom of Solomon. Its aim is principally to offer the hearer or reader observations on day-to-day life, and therefore practical rules for behaviour in particular circumstances. If he follows these instructions, a man will fit in with the social order, which is a reflection of the cosmic order. He will behave wisely, and live a social life which is harmonious, integrated and free from conflict. This form of wisdom is not concerned with the ultimate realities of existence, and does not conceal its pragmatic character or the complete lack of criticism of the society within which it is developed: that society is seen, rather, as a fact which the wise man must not seek to change. He must attempt to fit in with it by discovering the rules of the game. As can be seen, this is an attitude which differs profoundly and in essentials from that assumed by the prophets towards society. On the other hand, it is not an attitude which is completely lacking in faith: Prov.1.7 solemnly affirms that 'the fear of YHWH is the beginning of all knowledge'. However, the attentive reader who is versed in the history of religion will not miss the fact that the mention of the God of Israel is made more in the form of a concession to the dominant faith than as a personal confession: we could easily substitute the more general phrase 'fear of God' or even 'of the deity' for the expression 'fear of YHWH', without facing the problem of the identity of the deity to whom reference was made. The expression could very well be considered equivalent to the popular modern saying that a bit of religion never did anyone any harm. It is only with the wisdom psalms and then with Ecclus.24.23ff. that the identification of wisdom with the *tōrāh* is made, thus bringing Israelite wisdom so to speak into the bosom of orthodoxy.

The content of the wisdom tractates is different. Sometimes, as in Job, they take the form of a dialogue and sometimes, as with Ecclesiastes, they are a confession in the form of a monologue. They rarely speak of minor questions and instead tackle the fundamental problems of human existence. The two best-known examples are certainly those of Job and Ecclesiastes, and the solution which they put forward is submission to the divine plan. This is typically Israelite, although it does not have the historical approach which we find outside the wisdom literature.

3. The setting of wisdom

In Israel, as throughout the surrounding nations, wisdom was taught and practised in wisdom schools. Jesus ben Sirach, the author of Ecclesiasticus, was the head of one of these schools, as we shall see shortly (below, 48.2). These schools cannot, however, be compared with the philosophical schools of Greece and the Hellenistic world; in Israel and the surrounding countries their aim seems to have been eminently practical: to educate state officials, especially among the ruling classes. The existence of such officials in Israel is explicitly attested among the time of David onwards. It is also a quite indisputable fact, supported as it is by irrefutable evidence, especially from nomenclature, that the ancient Israelite bureaucracy (if it is permissible to use the term for this period) not only was organized along Egyptian lines but also made use of Egyptian officials, whose names appear in the Hebrew Bible, sometimes in a distorted form (II Sam.20.25; I Kings 4.3; I Chron.18.16). This is sufficient explanation for the conservative sociological orientation of the proverbs. The way to behave at court, the good name which the wise man must guard jealously, and other elements of this kind were either outside the horizons of the common man or were evaluated by him in a substantially different way. They were, however, extremely important subjects for anyone who found himself in an elevated social position. We can also see the explanation of the favourable attitude towards society as it was, if we accept that proverbial wisdom was essentially addressed to high officials. It is therefore substantially correct to see the ethics of Proverbs as a 'group ethic' or even a 'class ethic', as W.Richter has put it. It is the ethic of the class of leading officials, educated for the posts which they will be occupying. But since, leaving aside differences in structures, the needs of a state tend to be essentially the same in the same historical and social situations, it is not surprising that this type of wisdom has an essentially international form: behaviour at the Babylonian court will not have been all that different from that required at the court of Judah or even at the court of Egypt. Material thus circulated from one nation to another with the greatest of ease, despite the relatively closed character of the society of the time. One example which we might consider typical is that of the romance of Ahikar: it was written in Assyria at some point after the eighth century and circulated throughout the ancient Near East; we even find one copy in the archives of the Jewish colony at Elephantine (cf. Appendix 2) in southern Egypt at the end of the fifth century BCE.

Of course the more speculative aspects of wisdom go beyond this approach, which is at the same time didactic and pragmatic, aimed at an adequate professional training. This does not, however, mean that the officials did not continue to be occupied with wisdom during the years when they were at work. Thus in the ancient Near East (and indeed in the modern Near East until a few decades ago) the figure of the wise man has never been a rarity, not to mention the figure of the wise monarch, of which there are many examples, from Solomon to Saladin.

This explanation of proverbial wisdom has now been accepted for some decades; over against it, however, there now stands another, which offers another, incompatible theory. In an article based on years of study, F.W.Golka begins from completely different presuppositions. In non-Islamic Africa down to the present day we have so-called 'segmentary' societies, agricultural societies without a central government, ruled by the elders of particular villages with a minimum of structure and organization. I have mentioned these in my *History* (57, 171ff.), to which I would refer for an application of the concept to Israelite prehistory. Golka notes the presence of proverbs of a biblical kind in these societies, proverbs which have more or less the same themes, and all of which provide very pragmatic solutions. He goes on to argue that proverbial biblical wisdom must also have arisen in analogous circumtances, as the popular response to power, an element which is regarded as being both necessary and oppressive. The norms of proverbial wisdom would therefore have arisen out of the need to use power and at the same time to neutralize it, in the latter case when it assumed prerogatives and rights which had a negative effect on everyday life.

BIBLIOGRAPHY

J.Fichtner, *Die altorientalische Weisheit in ihrer israelitisch-jüdischen Ausprägung*, BZAW 62, 1933 (a pioncer work); J.C.Rylaarsdam, *Revelation in Jewish Wisdom Literature*, Chicago 1946; id., *Les sagesses du Proche-Orient ancien (Colloque de Strasbourg, 17-19 May 1962)* [by various authors], Paris 1963; W.Zimmerli, 'The Place and Limit of the Wisdom in the Framework of the Old Testament Theology', *SJT* 17, 1964, 146-58; H.H.Schmid, *Wesen und Geschichte der Weisheit*, BZAW 101, 1966; W.Richter, *Recht und Ethos*, Munich 1966; J.L.McKenzie, 'Reflections on Wisdom', *JBL* 86, 1967, 1-9; F.Festorazzi, 'La sapienza e la storia della salvezza', *RiBib* 15, 1967, 151-62; R.E.Murphy, 'Assumptions and Problems in Old Testament Wisdom Research', *CBQ* 29, 1967, 407-18; A.M.Dubarle, 'Où en est l'étude de la littérature sapientielle', *ETL* 44, 1968, 407-19 (with valuable bibliography); H.-J.Hermisson, *Studien zur israelitischen Spruchweisheit*, WMANT 28, 1968; H.H.Schmid, *Gerechtigkeit als Weltordnung*, Tübingen 1968; J.L.Crenshaw, 'Method in Determining Wisdom Influence upon "Historical" Literature', *JBL* 88, 1969, 128-42; R.E.Murphy, 'The Interpretation of Old Testament Wisdom Literature', *Int* 25, 1969, 289-301; A.Barucq, 'Israele e Umanismo', *BeO* 11, 1969, 97-107; G.von Rad, *Wisdom in Israel*, ET, London and Nashville 1972 (a basic introduction to the material and its understanding, which should be read in conjunction with the review of the original German edition by W.Zimmerli, *EvTh* 31, 1971, 680-95); W.Brueggemann, 'Scripture and Ecumenical Life-Style. Study of Wisdom Literature', *Int* 24, 1970, 3-19; R.B.Y.Scott, 'The Study of Wisdom Literature', ibid., 20-45; B.L.Mack, 'Wisdom, Myth and Mythology', ibid., 46-60; F.C.Fensham, 'The Change of Situation of a Person in the Ancient Near East and Biblical Literature', *AION* 31, 1971, 155-62; H.-J.Hermisson, 'Weisheit und Geschichte', in H.-W.Wolff (ed.), *Probleme biblischer Theologie. G.von Rad zum 70.Geburtstag*, Munich 1971, 136-54; O.Plöger, 'Zur Auslegung der Sentenzensammlung des Proverbienbuches', ibid., 402-16; J.Harvey, 'Wisdom Literature and Biblical Theology', *BTB* 1, 1971, 308-19 (with an

444   THE WRITINGS

exhaustive analysis of the problem); G. von Rad, 'Christliche Weisheit?', *EvTh* 31, 1971, 150-5; R.B.Y.Scott, *The Way of Wisdom*, New York and London 1971; J.L.Crenshaw, 'Wisdom', in J.H.Hayes (ed.), *Old Testament Form Criticism*, San Antonio, Texas 1974, 225-64; R.N.Whybray, *The Intellectual Tradition in the Old Testament*, BZAW 135, 1974; W.Gispen, 'What is Wisdom in the Old Testament?', in *Travels in the World of the Old Testament. Studies presented to M.A.Beek*, Assen 1974, 75-9; G.E.Bryce, 'Omen-Wisdom in Ancient Israel', *JBL* 94, 1975, 19-37; J.P.J.Olivier, 'Schools and Wisdom Literature', *JNWSL* 4, 1975, 49-70; P.Sacchi, 'La protesta della sapienza', *RiBib* 24, 1976, 137-63; J.L.Crenshaw, *Studies in Ancient Israelite Wisdom*, New York 1976; A.de Pury, 'Sagesse et révélation dans l'ancien Testament', *RTP* 110, 1977, 1-50. For wisdom and history cf. R.Rendtorff, 'Weisheit und Geschichte', *Evangelische Kommentare* 9, 1976, 216-18; id., 'Geschichtliches und weisheitliches Denken', in *Beiträge zur alttestamentlichen Theologie. FS W.Zimmerli*, Göttingen 1977, 344-55; A.Jenks, 'Theological Presuppositions of Israel's Wisdom Literature', *HorBTh* 7, 1, 1985, 43-75; H.-D.Preuss, *Einführung in die alttestamentliche Weisheitsliteratur*, Stuttgart 1987.

For wisdom in late Judaism cf. B.Otzen, 'Old Testament Wisdom Literature and Dualistic Thinking in Late Judaism', *SVT* 28, 1975, 146-57; J.Halbe, 'Altorientalisches Weltordnungsdenken und alttestamentliche Theologie', *ZTK* 76, 1979, 318-418 (against Schmid's theory, but is not really relevant); M.Küchler, *Frühjüdische Weisheitstraditionen*, Fribourg CH 1979; E.T.Sheppard, *Wisdom as a Hermeneutical Construct*, BZAW 151, 1980; the whole issue of *Semeia*, 17, 1980; M.Barre, ' "Fear of God" and the World View of Wisdom', *BTB* 11, 1981, 41-5 (rightly stresses the similarity between the concept of the fear of God and similar concepts in the ancient Near East); E.Kutsch, 'Weisheitsspruch und Prophetenwort', *BZ* 25, 1981, 161-79; J.L.Crenshaw, 'Wisdom and Authority: Sapiential Rhetoric and its Warrant', *SVT* 32, 1981, 10-29; P.Nel, 'Authority in the Wisdom Admonition', *ZAW* 93, 1981, 418-26. For the studies of Mesopotamian and Egyptian wisdom cf. G.Buccellati, 'Wisdom and Not: The Case of Mesopotamia', *JAOS* 101, 1981, 35-47; R.J.Williams, 'The Sages of Ancient Egypt in the Light of Recent Scholarship', ibid., 1-35. Cf.also R.E.Murphy, *Wisdom Literature*, Grand Rapids, Mich. 1981; E.Lipiński, 'Ancient Types of Wisdom Literature in Biblical Narrative', in *I.L.Seeligmann Volume III*, Jerusalem 1985, 35-55.

3. For Israelite officials and their training cf. T.N.D.Mettinger, *Solomonic State Officials*, Lund 1971, which has an extensive bibliography and an analysis, on 25ff., of the Egyptian names of the officials discussed. The alternative theory on the origins of proverbial wisdom can be found in F.W.Golka, 'Die Königs- und Hofsprüche der israelitischen Weisheit', *VT* 36, 1983, 13-36.

36

PROVERBS

1. Author and title

At the beginning of the book we find a superscription which makes King Solomon, famed for his wisdom, the author of the work. True, it could also be translated, 'The proverbs of Solomon serve to make known wisdom...' and so on, but with this approach the problem is only shelved, and has to be dealt with later on another level. What would be the proverbs mentioned here? Thus it seems evident that the redactors wanted to attribute the work to King Solomon. However, not only can that not be proved, but as in the cases of Moses and the Pentateuch and David and the Psalms it seems impossible, even if it is true that the origins of wisdom in Israel are traditionally connected with the king in question. The passages which speak of the wisdom of Solomon are I Kings 5.9-14 [EVV 4.29ff.] and 10.1ff. The former is particularly important because it lists the areas with which Solomon was concerned: the king is credited with 'three thousand proverbs, and his songs were a thousand and five. He spoke of trees, from the cedar that is in Lebanon to the hyssop that grows out of the wall; he spoke also of beasts, and of birds, and of reptiles, and of fish' (5.12f. [EVV 4.32f.]). However, this precise description cannot be applied in any way to Proverbs: themes like those described do appear in other passages of the Old Testament like Judg.9.7ff.; II Kings 14.9, but they are not to be found in Proverbs!

The book as we have it is made up of seven collections, beginning at: 1.1; 10.1; 22.17; 24.23; 25.1; 30.1 and 31.1. We find the same material in LXX, but it is arranged differently, which is evidently proof of redactional work. As a further check we can detect numerous duplicates and variants. The Israeli scholar Y.M.Grintz suggests some means of checking what has just been said:

1. Each collection has its own typical vocabulary;

2. The first, third and fourth collections have enough elements in common to suggest the same academic basis;

3. The first and second collections have many elements of vocabulary in common, despite the difference in the themes;

4. There are, however, notable differences between the first and fifth collections.

Grintz therefore concludes that the first collection had access to the second collection but not to the fifth; the third and fifth collections had a common 'heredity'; finally, 1.1-6 embodies the characteristics of the first collection perfectly. Chapters 30 and 31 are considered separately.

2. Date

The date of the composition of Proverbs is as difficult to determine as that of the Psalms and poetry in Israel generally. The first collection (chs. 1-9) seems to be the latest part of the book, and this impression is confirmed both by the fact that wisdom is personified here (1.20; 9.1ff.), and by the presence in 7.16 of the term *'ēṭūn* = flax, equivalent to the Greek *othōne*, which would put the passage in the Hellenistic period. However, both these are words of Egyptian origin. Another feature which points to a late date is the dimensions of a number of passages, which are too long for classical Hebrew style. However, these arguments are not definitive.

On the other hand, the second section (10.1-22.16) seems to be older: 16.12ff.; 21.1; 22.11 presuppose the existence of the monarchy, and while it would not be impossible in theory for this to be a mention of a king in general terms, it seems more natural to think of the kings of Judah and Israel. This last possibility would be logical if it could be proved or at least be shown to be probable that the passage in question came from the north. The customs described also go back to the eighth century BCE rather than to another period, and we cannot rule out the possibility that in this case we have material which, if it does not come from the time of Solomon or even earlier (taken over from Canaan?), is at least of considerable antiquity. Another section of great interest is the third (22.17-23.12). In the 1920s, it was discovered to be dependent on a text by the Egyptian sage Amenemope (in Greek Amenophis) who lived during the second half of the second millennium BCE (we cannot determine the date exactly). A.Lods*, 657, gives an interesting synopsis of the two texts, but Richter's comparison has demonstrated the composite character of the two entities, the Egyptian text and the Hebrew text. He argues that the latter goes down to 24.22 and will have given a translation, sometimes literal, of material from Amenophis. Be this as it may, it seems that in this case, too, the Hebrew text has to be dated in the pre-exilic period.

In the fifth section (25.1ff.) we have words of Solomon which according to the superscription were collected by men of King Hezekiah's time (second half of the eighth century). We should therefore reckon with a long oral tradition down to the redaction in writing (that is, if the superscription is to be trusted). A large part of ch.25, specifically vv.2-27, has recently been connected with the work of the Egyptian Seḥetepibrē of the Twelfth Dynasty in the second half of the nineteenth century BCE, but studies of this complex subject are still in process.

In 30.1 (emended text) and 31.3 we have a mention of the North Arabian tribe of *maśśā'*, of which there is also evidence in Gen.25.14; I Chron.1.30. The wise man who spoke the words in question would have been its king. It is difficult to find any kind of indication of date here except for ch.30, where there are obvious lexicographical affinities with Ugaritic literature. Unless we want to argue for artificial archaisms, this would suggest an early date for the text in question.

BIBLIOGRAPHY

Commentaries

H.Duesberg and P.Auvray, JB, ³1961; B.Gemser, HAT, ²1963; A.Barucq, SB, 1964; R.B.Y.Scott, AB, 1965; W.McKane, OTL, 1970. For the text cf. W.A.van der Weiden, *Le livre des Proverbes*, Rome 1970; L.Alonso Schökel and L.Vílchez Lindez, 1984.

For bibliographical material cf. F.Vattioni, 'Studi sul libro dei Proverbi', *Aug* 12, 1972, 121-68.

1. C.(Bauer-)Kayatz, *Studien zu Proverbien 1-9*, WMANT 22, 1966; Y.M.Grintz, 'The "Proverbs" of Solomon', *Lešonēnū* 33, 1968-69, 243-69 (Hebrew; English summary); O.Plöger, 'Zur Auslegung der Sentenzen-sammlung des Proverbienbuches', in *FS G.von Rad*, Munich 1971, 402-16; D.Michel, 'Weisheit als Urform von Humanität', in H.D.Foerster (ed.), *Humanität heute*, Berlin 1970, 11-21; W.McKane, 'Textual and Philological Notes on the Book of Proverbs', *TGUOS* 24, 1971-72, 76-90.

2. M.V.Fox, 'Aspects of the Religion of the Book of Proverbs', *HUCA* 39,

1968, 55-69. For Proverbs 1-9 cf. A.Meinhold, 'Vierfaches: Struktur, Prinzip und Haüfigkeitsfragen in Prov 1-9', *BN* 33, 1986, 53-79; for 10-31 cf. W.Bühlmann, *Vom rechten Reden und Schweigen*, Fribourg and Göttingen 1975. The text of the Wisdom of Amenemope is in *ANET³*, 421ff.; for the problem cf. P.Humbert, *Recherches sur les sources égyptiennes de la litterature sapientale d'Israël*, Neuchâtel 1929; W.Baumgartner, *Israelitische und altorientalische Weisheit*, Tübingen 1933; A.Alt, 'Zur literarischen Analyse der Weisheit des Amenemope', *SVT* 3, 1955, 16-25; S.Morenz, *Ägyptologische Beiträge zur Erforschung der Weisheitsliteratur Israels*, Berlin 1963; W.Richter, *Recht und Ethos*, Munich 1966. For the dating and the character of Amenemope cf. I.Grumach, *Untersuchungen zur Lebenslehre des Amenemope*, Munich 1972. This study arrives at some interesting conclusions which in the present state of research seem conclusive: both the writings depend on what the author calls 'an ancient Egyptian doctrine', the order of which is reproduced more or less faithfully by the text of Proverbs; Amenemope then revised its text towards the twelfth century, while Proverbs uses its texts in an independent way.

Part of the text of Seḥetepibrē is in *ANET³*, 431; for the problem cf. G.E.Bryce, 'Another Wisdom "Book" in Proverbs', *JBL* 91, 1972, 145-57.

For the Instruction of 'Onchsheshonqy with numerous parallels to Proverbs cf. B.Gemser, 'The Instructions of 'Onchsheshonqy and Biblical Wisdom Literature', *SVT* 7, 1960, 102-8; see also his commentary, above, and M.C.Betrio, 'Considerazioni in margine ad un testo: Anchscescionqi ed il suo mondo', *Egitto e Vicino Oriente* 5, 1982, 25-33. See also J.L.Crenshaw, op.cit. (in the previous chapter), 66ff., 57ff.; G.Garbini, 'Proverbi per un anno. Il libro dei Proverbi e il calendario', *Hen* 6, 1984, 139-46; D.Daube, 'A Quartet of Beasties in the book of Proverbs', *JTS* 36, 1985, 380-6. For Prov.30 cf. G.Sauer, *Die Sprüche Agurs*, Stuttgart 1968. For Wisdom and its relations with Canaan cf. W.F.Albright, 'Canaanite and Phoenician sources of Hebrew Wisdom', *SVT* 3, 1955, 1-15; M.J.Dahood, *Proverbs and Northwest Semitic Philology*, Rome 1963; R.N.Whybray, *Wisdom in Proverbs*, SBT 45, 1965. The basic work on the relationship between Israelite and Egyptian wisdom is H.Brunner, 'Zentralbegriffe ägyptischer und israelitischer Weisheiten', *Saeculum* 33, 1984, 185-99. Cf. also B.Lang, *Wisdom and the Book of Proverbs*, London and New York 1986; N.Shupak, 'The "Sitz im Leben" of Proverbs in the Light of a Comparison of Biblical and Egyptian Wisdom Literature', *RB* 94, 1987, 98-119; T.P.McCreesh, 'Wisdom as a Wife: Proverbs 31:10-31', *RB* 93, 1985, 25-46; E.L.Lyon, 'A Note on Proverbs 31.10-31', in *The Listening Heart... Essays R.E.Murphy*, Sheffield 1986, 237-43.

37

JOB

1. Character, division and content

(*a*) The Hebrew name of the book is *'Iyyōb*, whence the Greek and Latin name *Iob* and the English Job. The book is a wisdom tractate which discusses the problem of theodicy and the suffering of the righteous that is intimately conected with it. However, other problems are discussed in the work: how the righteous sufferer must behave when faced with obviously undeserved sufferings, or how it is possible to continue to be a believer in an evil world. In this last question what is considered is not so much belief in the God of Israel as the validity of the wisdom axiom that the world is governed in a rational manner by the divine wisdom. And as always happens in these cases where the faith of Israel is being discussed, the final reply may seem inadequate from a philosophical point of view, in that none of the tormented questions put by the protagonist is given a logical and systematic reply; rather, they are resolved in the sphere of faith, that is, in a sphere where ultimate reality transcends the possibility of a rational and intellectual analysis. Thus the only thing to come out the worse for wear is Hebrew wisdom, the principles of which are challenged by the reality of the facts. The problem as such appears among all the people of the ancient Near East, and there are some Mesopotamian writings which are rightly compared with Job; however, the solution put forward here is acceptable only to those who, like Job, abandon the idea of an ordered and harmonious universe of wisdom and enter into the sometimes hard and irrational world of faith, accepting its paradoxical categories of thought.

(*b*) The book is easy to divide up. First of all we have a prose prologue (chs.1-2), which describes the felicity and patriarchal life of the righteous Job, an upright and pious man. However, this idyllic picture is disturbed by a meeting of the celestial court. Here the satan (as in Zech.3 the figure denotes a function, not a name, and is therefore the title of an official, not the name of a 'devil'), who, as the prosecutor, is always in search of culprits with whom to pursue his office, enters into discussion with God about the virtue of the righteous Job: is his virtue authentic or is his much-vaunted righteousness simply part of an astute calculation aimed at winning the divine favour? The result of the discussion is that YHWH subjects him to a series of tests, designed to bring out his righteousness even more. A series of catastrophes deprives Job successively of his family (apart from his hypercritical wife), his goods, and finally his health, so that though at first he is honoured and respected by all, at the end of the trials he finds himself sitting on a heap of rubbish, with only his life to call his own. This too is threatened, since he has been smitten with a foul disease. The second part (3.1-42.6) makes up the main body of the book. First of all, three of Job's friends – Eliphaz, Bildad and Zophar – arrive. In chs.3-14 we have a first series of disputes between Job and his friends, in chs.15-21 a second series and in chs.22-27 a third series, from which only Zophar is missing. Job replies to each series of discourses. The argument of Job's friends can be reduced to the following point: if Job is being punished in this way, something must have happened, or else he would be blaspheming, accusing God of injustice and denying his just and wise ordering of the world. But Job replies that he does not know what fault he can have committed, and that if God is dissatisfied with him, it is enough for him to indicate what is wrong and the reason for it. There is an interpolation in ch.28, a short poem about the inscrutable character of the divine wisdom, which has nothing to do with the context in which it appears. Chapters 29-31 contain Job's self-defence and a challenge to God to explain the reasons for his attitude. This reply by Job has led the Swedish scholar J.Lindblom to compare him with the figure of Prometheus, but the fundamental difference between the two narratives lies in the fact that in the case of Prometheus it is Zeus who has unjustly punished the man out of envy, while in this case, even if Job is finally won over, God has simply put him to the test and recognizes his righteousness. A fourth person, Elihu, enters the scene in chs.32-37. He is a friend who was not mentioned to begin with and does not appear later; he, too, delivers some speeches, which have a different content from the rest. In chs.38-39 we have the first speech by YHWH, to which Job replies in 40.1-5 (or 39.33ff. according to another numbering); in this reply he submits to the majesty and the will of God, which he is incapable of understanding. In 40.6-41.26 we have YHWH's second speech, to which Job replies in 42.1-6, in words which show his complete submission. Finally, to conclude the book we have an epilogue edited in the same style as the prologue, but which continues the body of the book. God judges the first three friends severely (42.7-9), while in 42.10-17 we have a final scene in which Job is completely restored to the social and economic position which he enjoyed to begin with.

The construction of the book is quite complex, but has its own internal logic; it justifies the assertion by Westermann that, as well as being a piece of wisdom literature, the book of Job is a dramatic representation of the literary genre of the individual lament in a dramatic form. We have already come across this genre in our discussion of the Psalms (above, 34.5b). This also explains the affinity of many passages with the Psalter.

(c) One difference between the various parts of the work which immediately strikes the eye is that between the prologue and the epilogue on the one hand and the body of the book on the other, although, as we have seen, there is a connection betwen them. The difference is first of all one of form: the prologue and the epilogue are presented in prose in a clear narrative style, while the body of the book is in poetry. However, there are notable differences in content, too. In the prologue Job is resigned; he is ready to receive evil from the Lord just as hitherto he has received good (cf. 1.21b; 2.10). In the body of the book, on the other hand, he struggles to defend his righteousness either towards his friends or – and this is much more important – towards God, whose wisdom must be the guarantee of the cosmic order, even if it seems to be absent in the moment of trial. In 16.11 the concept of suffering is markedly different from that contained in the prologue, and in the body of the book we have a whole series of wisdom features which are completely lacking in both prologue and epilogue. Despite the obvious fact that the three parts of the book are for the most part interdependent, in other ways than being connected with the same protagonist, we can discover at least two different traditions, without counting independent parts like ch.28, even if they have now been skilfully joined so as to show a consistent pattern of thought. For this reason it is customary to call the prologue and the epilogue the 'framework' of the book. This framework relates the legend of a just man called Job, a wise man and a patriarch who, although afflicted by God in many ways, still bears the suffering imposed on him with courage, in the certain belief that God himself will sooner or later secure justice for him – and this is in fact what happens. This legend could be placed towards the end of the pre-exilic period.

Moreover, there is evidence of a person with this name in two Old Testament texts (Ezek.14.14,20). He is mentioned along with Noah and a certain Daniel, obviously not the protagonist of the book of this name, since he could not be put alongside Noah (he has been identified as being probably connected with the legendary Ugaritic king known under the name *dn'il*; in Ezekiel, too, the name is written in a defective form without a *yod* after the second consonant). This is an indication that we can connect Job with the heroes of prehistory (the Ugaritic text comes from the fourteenth century, but it obviously refers to an earlier figure). The problem of the historicity of the person of Job as it has been handed down in the framework of the book thus arises almost automatically, and a negative response is already given in the Talmud (Baba Bathra 15a) and by rabbinic exegesis (Bereshit Rabba 57), despite their tendency to attribute a historical character to the most improbable episodes. We shall return to this question later.

(d) As we have seen, some passages in the book do not seem to fit well into their present context. I have already mentioned ch.28 (the theme of which would nullify the words of YHWH in chs.38; 39). To this should be added the speeches of Elihu (chs.32-37), which interrupt the context in which they are set. Job challenges God to show himself, but what happens is the arrival of Elihu. The divine response which ought to follow the challenge appears only in ch.38, after Elihu's speeches. Elihu's argument, that suffering serves to purify human beings, and therefore has an eminently pedagogical function, is substantially different both from that of the three friends and from that of YHWH (chs.38ff.). These are features which have been known for some time. Gregory the Great already expressed grave doubts about the legitimacy of the present position of such passages in the book, at least in the case of Elihu's speeches, which discuss an analogous theme. The descriptions of exotic animals in 40.15ff., 25ff. [EVV 41.1ff.] and of the various animals throughout chs.38-41 are also an independent element: the first animal bears the name *bᵉhēmōt*, usually translated 'hippopotamus', by analogy with a hypothetical Egytian term which is not attested, *p-ehe-mau* = 'water-ox'; others render it 'crocodile'. In the second instance the animal is called *lewyātān*, a name which appears in Ugaritic as *ltn* and which there (as in other passages in the Hebrew Bible) is a mythical monster; it is usually translated 'crocodile'. It is possible that these were originally mythological monsters which have now been reduced to the hippopotamus and the crocodile. Effective as the mention of them is from an aesthetic point of view, along with the other animals, it disrupts the development of the theme here, in the context of the acceptance by Job of his fate.

The situation of the book thus seems to be complex in every respect, and its complexity is increased by the fact that almost all the literary genres of the Hebrew Bible are represented in the book.

2. Date, place and problems of composition

As can easily be seen, the information at our disposal is very uncertain. There is no direct or indirect mention of any events which can be identified in a historical context, and the geography of the book is a mystery. There is no mention of the book of Job in other books of the Hebrew Bible except at a late date (only in Tobit 2.12, from the third to second century BCE, see below, 44). The dating of the 'framework' has been put in the late pre-exilic period; a post-exilic dating seems advisable for the body of the book. The problems are seen in an individualistic key, and we know that this approach is sometimes to be found during the exile (cf. Deut.24.16; Jer.31.29ff.; Ezek.18.1ff.). The basic issue discussed in the book is that of the legalistic application of the understanding of the cosmic order put forward by wisdom, an understanding which also underlies the idea of reward and punishment proclaimed by Deuteronomy and Dtr.

The problem of the language of the book has yet to be resolved; in this respect it is one of the most complex in the Hebrew Bible, In fact it contains the largest number of *hapax legomena*, and there is an abundance of Aramaisms - to such a degree that N.H.Tur-Sinai has been able to suggest a Hebrew translation of an Aramaic original. Other scholars have thought to discover a large number of Arabisms in the book (Guillaume counted 41 of them), but Fohrer in his commentary is sceptical about their existence. On the other hand the extraordinary richness of the vocabulary of Job should not surprise us excessively; once we accept its character as a wisdom tractate and the complexity of the theme with which it is concerned the problem is much more one of our inadequate linguistic knowledge. At all events, it will not do to speak of a particularly corrupt text, as was the custom until a few years ago. Of course, the ancient translations also found themselves up against similar problems, and they provide little help in solving them. The publication of the Targum on Job discovered in Qumran Cave 11 is not much help in resolving problems, since its text belongs in the same tradition as the Massoretic text.

At the end of the book, in 42.17b, the LXX identified the person of Job with that of Jobab, a king of Edom in Gen.36.33. This identification is linguistically possible, but there is no concrete evidence to support it.

Job is said to have lived in the East, in a country called Uz which Lam.4.21 connects with Edom: the very frequent use of *ĕlōᵃh* instead of *ᵉlōhīm* for God (a title which the ancient psalm in Hab.3 connects with Teman, a region probably situated either in north-western Arabia) also points in this direction; in the first case we would have another pointer towards Edom. However, many features of the book do not fit in with this locality: the mention of reeds in 8.11, of papyrus in 9.26 and of the animals in 40.15,26 [EVV 41.1]) suggests swamps or the broad deltas of rivers, and certainly not the desert of north-western Arabia. But in all these cases we could have interpolations, or notes that could have been made by any cultured person (and we have seen that the language of Job is of such a kind that we may suppose elements of high culture in the redaction of the book). For the rest, the problem of suffering is resolved in typically Israelite categories, even if the problem itself occurs throughout the ancient Near East. The very character of the work as a wisdom book makes it difficult to put it in any geographical and historical setting, given the international and cosmopolitan character of wisdom, even in Israel.

Thus for the prologue and the epilogue we come near to the time of the exile: Satan is still a title and not a proper name; the character of the Chaldaeans mentioned in 1.17, however, seems to be old; it would take us back to the end of the second millennium or the beginning of the first millennium BCE; in fact in the Hebrew Bible 'Chaldaeans' always denotes the neo-Babylonian empire (from the seventh century BCE on).

3. The problem and thought of Job

The ancient traditional narrative of the suffering of the righteous and pious Job, whose loved ones and possessions are later restored, thus seems to have been used as a starting point for the redaction of the body of the book and as a vehicle for discussing problems like theodicy and the behaviour of the righteous in a world which concrete reality has shown to be very different from that presupposed by wisdom. The problems dealt with in the book, then, are typically those of wisdom, but with the difference that, as among neighbouring peoples, Israelite wisdom also disputed the fundamental thesis of wisdom elsewhere, displaying a remarkable degree of scepticism over the existence of a universe governed by cosmic wisdom. But whereas among other peoples a practical solution could not be found, in Israel it was discovered in submission to the divine will, many aspects of which could not be understood by human beings, however hard they tried (contrary to the argument of wisdom). Nor could they always adapt themselves to this will (as wisdom argued). In other words, the approach made by wisdom to the problem of the government of the world proved to be too simplistic. However, whereas among other peoples this discovery led men to cynicism or despair, the Hebrew Bible made it an occasion for proclaiming its faith. According to the solution which God himself proposes to Job, it is not for human beings to ask God to give an account of his works, seeing that they have neither the competence nor the right to do so; God has sovereign freedom, and this freedom cannot be comprehended in any categories of thought, whether theological or philosophical. God reveals to a Job who has not asked for material or spiritual goods, but simply for what is his due, that his plans are not human plans and his wisdom is not human wisdom. This declaration satisfies Job. God has taken him seriously, and at the same time has recognized that the way in which the problem has been posed by Job's friends is not a serious one – though this approach is in fact that of wisdom. Precisely in his acceptance of the irrationality of YHWH, Job rediscovers his peace and escape from the vicious circle into which he had been led by a presentation of the problem according to the categories of wisdom. There is a New Testament parallel in Paul's discussion of the divine wisdom as opposed to human wisdom (I Cor.1.17-25), as there probably is also in the total reversal of values concerned in the Sermon on the Mount.

BIBLIOGRAPHY

Commentaries

G.Ricciotti, Turin 1924; E.Dhorme, ET, London 1966; C.Larcher, JB, ^{2}1957; G.Hölscher, HAT, ^{2}1952; A.Weiser, ATD, ^{5}1968: N.H.Tur-Sinai, Jerusalem 1957; N.H.Snaith, 1958; G.Fohrer, KAT, 1963; M.H.Pope, AB, ^{3}1974; F.Horst, BK, 1968; P.Pedrizzi, 1972; H.H.Rowley, ^{2}1976 (posthumous): D.Gualandi, 1976; G.Ravasi, 1978; L.Alonso Schökel and J.L.Sicre-Diaz, 1983; N.C.Habel, OTL, 1985.

Monographs

H.Richter, *Studien zu Hiob*, Berlin 1959; R.Gordis, *The Book of God and Man. A Study of Job*, Chicago 1965; N.H.Snaith, *The Book of Job*, SBT II 11, 1968: J.Lévèque, *Job et son Dieu*, Paris 1970; J.Vermeylen, *Job, ses amis et son Dieu*, Leiden 1986. See also H.-P.Müller, 'Altes und Neues zum Buch Hiob', *EvTh* 37, 1977, 284-304; id., *Das Hiobproblem*, Darmstadt 1978. The whole of the annual review *Semeia* 7, Missoula, Mont. 1977, is devoted to the book of Job, as is *Concilium* 169, 1983.

1. J.Lindblom, 'Job and Prometheus, a Comparative Study', in *Dragma, M.P.Nilsson dicatum*, Lund 1939, 280-7; W.A.Irwin, 'Job and Prometheus', *Journal of Religion* 30, 1950, 90-108; C.Westermann, *Der Aufbau des Buches Hiob*, Tübingen 1956; H.H.Rowley, 'The Book of Job and its Meaning', *BJRL* 41, 1958, 167-207 (= his *From Moses to Qumran*, London 1963, 141-83); D.N.Freedman, 'The Elihu Speeches in the Book of Job', *HTR* 61, 1968, 51-9; J.J.M.Roberts, 'Job and the Israelite Religious Tradition', *ZAW* 89, 1977, 107-14, argues that it is useless to look for historical features in the work; this goes against the literary genre which it represents. D.Michel, 'Hiob – oder der inhumane Gott', in H.Foerster (ed.), *Humanität heute*, Berlin 1970, 37-50; J.Barr, 'The Book of Job and its Modern Interpreters', *BJRL* 54, 1971-2, 28-46; H.McKeating, 'The Central Issues in the Book of Job', *ExpT* 82, 1971-72, 249-52; E.Laurin, 'The Theological Structure of Job', *ZAW* 84, 1972, 86-9, argues that ch.28 is now also an integral part of the work. For the 'framework' of the book cf. R.Polzin, 'The Framework of the Book of Job', *Int* 28, 1975, 182-200; A.Hurvitz, 'The Date of the Prose Tale of Job Linguistically Reconsidered', *HTR* 67, 1974, 17-34. The former brings out the artificial character of the framework; the latter its relatively late (post-exilic) character, contrary to what is so often asserted. Cf. also F.Scapella, 'A Reading of Job', *JSOT* 14, 1979, 63-7; A.Lacocque, 'Job and the Symbolism of Evil', *BiblRes* 24/25, 1979-80, 7-19; M.Görg, 'Ijob aus dem Lande 'Uṣ', *BN* 12, 1980, 7-12 (stresses the 'theological' geography of the book); Y.Hoffman, 'The Relation between the Prologue and the Speech-Cycles in Job', *VT* 31, 1981, 169-70; J.Lévèque, 'La datation du livre de Job', *SVT* 32, 1981, 206-19; A.de Wilde, *Das Buch Hiob*, Leiden 1981: H.Gese, 'Die Frage nach dem Lebenssinn: Hiob und die Folgen', *ZTK* 79, 1982, 161-79; N.C.Habel, 'The Narrative Art of Job: Applying the Principles of Robert Alter', *JSOT* 27, 1983, 101-11: R.G.Albertson, 'Job and Ancient Near Eastern Wisdom Literature', in W.W.Hallo et al. (eds.), *Scripture in Context* II, Winona Lake, Ind. 1983, 219-30; W.E.Aufrecht, *Studies in the Book of Job*, Waterloo, Ont. 1985; C.Schmitt, 'Die Heimat Hiobs', *ZDPV* 101, 1985, 56-63. For particular topics cf. also H.-P.Müller, 'Keilschriftliche Parallele zum biblischen Hiobbuch: Möglichkeit und Grenzen des Vergleiches', *Or* 47, 1977, 362-75; J.Kahn and R.Solomon, *Job's Illness*, Oxford and New York 1980; J.L.Crenshaw, op.cit., 16ff., 100ff. Cf.also P.Zerafa, *The Wisdom of God in the Book of Job*, Rome 1978; S.Prabakhara Rao and M.Prakasa Reddy, 'Job and his Satan. Parallels in Indian Scripture', *ZAW*

91, 1979, 416-22; M Perani, 'Crisi della Sapienza e ricerca di Dio nel libro di Giobbe', *RiBib* 28, 1980, 157-84; W.Vogels, 'The Spiritual Growth of Job', *BTB* 11, 1981, 77-80; I.Diez Merino, 'Manuscritos del Targum de Job', *Hen* 4, 1982, 41-64; R.D.Moore, 'The Integrity of Job', *CBQ* 45, 1983, 17-31; M.Perani, 'Sulla terminologia temporale del libro di Giobbe', *Hen* 5, 1983, 1-20; E.C Webster, 'Strophic Patterns of Job 3-27', *JSOT* 26, 1983, 33-60; E.Kutsch, 'Die Textgliederung in hebräischen Iobbuch, sowie in 4QTgJob und in 11QTgJob', *BZ* 27, 1983, 221-8; T.J.Gorringe, 'Job and the Pharisees', *Int* 40, 1986, 17-48; also J. van Oorschot, *Gott als Grenze. Eine literar- und redaktionsgeschichtliche Studie zu den Gottesreden des Hiobbuches*, BZAW 170, 1987; A.A.DiLella, 'An Existential Interpretation of Job', *BTB* 15, 1985, 49-55; J.H.Eaton, *Job*, Sheffield 1985; D.W.Jamieson-Drake, 'Literary Structure, Genre and Interpretation in Job 38', in *The Listening Heart. Essays... R.E.Murphy*, Sheffield 1986, 217-25; W.Morrow, 'Consolation, Rejection and Repentance in Job 42:6', *JBL* 105, 1986, 211-25. On the Elihu speeches see N.C.Habel, 'The Role of Elihu in the Design of the Book of Job', in *In the Shelter of Elyon - Essays... G.W.Ahlström*, Sheffield 1984, 81-98. On the LXX see J.G.Gammie, 'The Septuagint of Job', *CBQ* 49, 1987, 14-31; P.van der Lugd, 'Stanza Structure and Word Repetition in Job 4-14', *JSOT* 40, 1988, 3-18.

2. M.J.Dahood, 'North-West Semitic Philology and Job', in *A.Gruenther Memorial Volume*, New York 1962, 33-74; A.Guillaume, 'The Arabic Background of the Book of Job', in F.F.Bruce (ed.), *Promise and Fulfilment. Essays for S.H.Hooke*, Edinburgh 1963, 106-27; A.C.M.Blommerde, *Northwest Semitic Grammar and Job*, Rome 1969; A.Guillaume, *Studies in the Book of Job*, Leiden 1968. For Babylonian and other ancient Near Eastern parallels cf. J.J.Stamm, *Das Leiden des Unschuldigen in Babylon und Israel*, Zurich 1946; A.Kuschke, 'Altbabylonische Texte zum Thema "Der leidende Gerechte" ', *TLZ* 81, 1956, 69-75; J.Lévèque, op.cit., 13ff ; H.D.Preuss, 'Jahwes Antwort an Hiob und die sogenannte Hiobliteratur des alten Vorderen Orients', *Beiträge zur alttestamentlichen Theologie. FS W.Zimmerli*, Göttingen 1977, 329-43; M.Weinfeld, 'Job and its Mesopotamian Parallels - A Typological Analysis', in *Text and Context... Studies for F.C.Fensham*, Sheffield 1988, 217-26. For the Job Targum from Qumran cf. J.P.M.van der Ploeg and A.S.van der Woude, *Le Targum de Job de la Grotte XI de Qumrân*, Leiden 1971; N.Sokoloff, *The Targum to Job from Qumran Cave XI*, Ramet Gan 1974. For the text cf. I.G.Rignell, 'Notes on the Peshitta of the Book of Job', *ASTI* 9, 1972, 98-106; J.Gray, 'The Massoretic Text of the Book of Job, the Targum and the Septuagint Version in the Light of the Qumran Targum', *ZAW* 86, 1974, 351-6.

3. M.Müller, 'Die Gerechtigkeit Gottes des Schöpfers in der Erfahrung seines Knechtes Hiob', *Theologische Versuche* 6, Berlin 1975, 25-36; E.Ruprecht, 'Leiden und Gerechtigkeit bei Hiob', *ZTK* 73, 1976, 424-5; N.Habel, 'Only the Jackal is My Friend', *Int* 31, 1977, 227-36.

38

RUTH – LAMENTATIONS

1. Ruth

This superb short story deals with events supposed to have taken place in the time of the Judges (and therefore LXX and the Vulgate, followed by modern translations, insert it after that book; in the Hebrew Bible, however, it appears in the third part of the canon).

The content is simple: its purpose is to establish the genealogy of King David by showing that he is descended from, among others, a Moabite woman who, after losing her husband, a man of Judah who migrated to Moab and settled there, follows her mother-in-law back to her homeland. In this way Ruth renounces her own people and joins that of her husband, accepting their faith. In Judah she meets Boaz, a close relation of her dead husband, to whom she is married by means of a somewhat obscure combination of levirate marriage and the law of redemption.

As a literary genre, the narrative belongs to the class of popular legends, with features of the novella. It should probably be dated after the exile, but this does not exclude the use of earlier material. The names are symbolic: Ruth means 'companion'; Orpah, Ruth's Moabite sister-in-law who is in the same position but chooses to remain in Moab, means 'disloyal'; Naomi, the mother of the two dead men of Judah, is 'peaceful'; 'Boaz' means strength, and so on. The practice prescribed in Deut.25.9 is quoted in 4.7 as a feature of past times; the attitude of the book to non-Israelite people is positive and is reminiscent of that of Jonah. Here, too, there seems to be a polemical note against the tendency of post-exilic Judaism to be shut in on itself, while the book maintains the thesis, later to be taken up by the Pharisees in particular, that no one should be excluded from joining the people of God if they so wish. Maybe there is also a polemical note against the injunctions of Ezra and Nehemiah that foreign wives are to be expelled (Ezra 9; Neh.13). Here, however, we are already on less solid ground. Be this as it may, the book maintains the thesis that nationality is a secondary element: what really counts is the choice of faith.

The language of the book contains a series of Aramaisms, and despite the simplicity of the argument, it is not always easy. Nor is the text in the best of condition: indeed Ruth is a book which has one of the largest number of Massoretic notes. In any case, it is not possible to date it before the fifth or fourth centuries BCE. That does not mean that it has not preserved the memory of much earlier customs: for example, the village tribunal meets at the gate, and I was able to use the book, following L.Köhler's study, in the reconstruction of trials in Israelite law (see above, 11.7). The book does not show any signs of disruption, and there are no omissions or additions of any substance. It may be that the genealogy, which is the feature which gave the book its place in the canon, is an addition. It is interesting that the work sustains its argument by making David the descendant of a converted foreigner.

The atmosphere which the reader finds is that of a trusting abandonment to divine providence.

2. Lamentations

While LXX and the Vulgate, followed by modern translations, put this book after Jeremiah, in the Hebrew Bible it belongs to the third part of the canon. The Hebrew title, i.e. the first word of the text, is *'ēkāh* = 'Alas, how...', which introduces a lament (Hebrew *qīnāh*). The superscription in LXX[B] connects the work with Jeremiah, and that is perhaps why it occupies its present position in the LXX: its origin should probably be sought in II Chron.35.25, which speaks of a funeral lament by Jeremiah on the death of Josiah. However, four-fifths of the book speaks of the destruction of Jerusalem, and cannot have anything to do with this lamentation.

The work is made up of five laments, one for each chapter. However, they are not all composed in the same way. Chapters 1-4 are acrostics, but in terms of content chs.2; 4; 5 describe the situation of Jerusalem after the destruction of 587/6, while ch.3 belongs to a different literary genre. It is an individual lament, and has nothing to do with the exile. The despair expressed in 1-2; 4-5 could be a sign that the work is not far removed in time from the events which it narrates, so that, historically speaking, an attribution to Jeremiah would not be impossible. The author was not in fact deported, but is one of the survivors left behind by Nebuchadnezzar in the ruins of the capital: the details of the description in chs.2; 4 indicate this. It would also be impossible to understand 2.9 on the lips of the exiles among whom Ezekiel worked. However, we should recall that the liturgy could retain this kind of ritual for centuries.

With the exception of ch.3, Lamentations seems to have been recited very soon on the occasion of the commemoration of the fall of the capital, an observation which is already attested in Zech.7.1-5; 8.18f. for the first groups of those who returned from exile.

The historical interest of the book lies in the fact that it is the only document which originated among those who were left behind in Judah after the catastrophe of 587. Among them we find seriousness, composure, feelings of penitence and readiness to accept the lesson which they had been given. All this differs markedly from what we know to have been the dominant attitude only a few years earlier.

BIBLIOGRAPHY

Commentaries

H.Ringgren and A.Weiser, ATD, 1958; G.Gerleman, BK, 1965.

On Ruth only: P.Joüon, Rome ²1953; A.Vincent, JB, ²1958 (with Judges); E.Würthwein, HAT, 1969; J.Gray, NCB, ²1987 (with Joshua and Judges); J.M.Sasson, 1979. There is a monograph on the whole book: C.Lepre, *Il libro di Ruth*, Naples 1981.

On Lamentations only: H.-J.Kraus, BK ²1960; O.Plöger, HAT, 1969; D.R.Hillers, AB, 1972. Cf. also above, on Jeremiah.

1. D.R.Ap-Thomas, 'The Book of Ruth', *ExpT* 79, 1967-8, 369-74; J.L.Vesco, 'La date du livre de Ruth', *RB* 74, 1967, 235-47: O.Eissfeldt, *Stammessage und Menschheiterzählung in der Genesis. Wahrheit und Dichtung in der Ruth-Erzählung*, Berlin 1965; A.Baumgartner, 'A Note on the Book of Ruth', *JANESCU* 5, 1973, 11-15; D.R.Beattie, 'The Book of Ruth as Evidence for Israelite Legal Practice', *VT* 24, 1974, 251-67; O.Loretz, 'Poetische Abschnitte im Ruth-Buch', *UF* 7, 1975, 580-2; H.H.Witzenrath, *Ruth*, Munich 1975; É.Lipiński, 'Le mariage de Ruth', *VT* 26, 1965, 124-7; G.H.Cohn, 'The Names in the Book of Ruth', *Amsterdamse Cahiers* 1, 1980, 62-5; B.Green, 'The Plot of the Biblical Story of Ruth', *JSOT* 23, 1982, 55-68; H.Fish, 'Ruth and the Structure of Covenant History', *VT* 22, 1982, 425-37; A.Brenner, 'Naomi and Ruth', *VT* 33, 1983, 385-97; J.C.de Moor, 'The Poetry of the Book of Ruth', *Or* 53, 1984, 262-83; K.Nielsen, 'Le choix contre le droit dans le livre de Ruth', *VT* 35, 1985, 201-12; I.J.Petermann, 'Travestie oder Exegese?', *DBAT* 2, 1985 [1986], 74-117 (criticizes the

studies and their 'patriarchalization' of an originally feminist text);
G.R.H.Wright, 'The Mother Maid at Bethlehem', *ZAW* 98, 1986, 56-72;
L.Hongisto, 'Literary Structure and Theology in the Book of Ruth', *AUSS*
23, 1985, 19-28; A.Phillips, 'The Book of Ruth - Reception and Shame', *JJS*
37, 1986, 1-17; D.N.Fewell and D.M.Gunn, ' "A Son is Born to Naomi".
Literary Allusions and Interpretation in the Book of Ruth', *JSOT* 40, 1988,
99-108.

2. T.F.McDaniel, 'Philological Studies in Lamentations', *Bibl* 49, 1968,
27-53, 199-220. G.Brunet, *Les Lamentations contre Jérémie*, Paris 1968, has
argued that the first four laments are directed *against* Jeremiah, but the
theory has found little support.

Cf. also W.C.Gwaltney, Jr, 'The Biblical Book of Lamentations in the
Context of Near Eastern Lamentation Literature', in W.W.Hallo et al.
(eds.), *Scripture in Context* II, Winona Lake, Ind. 1983, 191-211; M.S.Moore,
'Human Suffering in Lamentations', *RB* 90, 1983, 534-55; Bo Johnson,
'Form and Message in Lamentations', *ZAW* 97, 1985, 58-73.

39

ECCLESIASTES – SONG OF SONGS

1. Ecclesiastes

The very name of this book, in Hebrew *qōhelet* (hence its name Koheleth in some modern translations), presents a problem: in 1.1,12 the person who is given this name is called 'son of David, king in Jerusalem', a designation which could only be applied to Solomon. But the gender of the noun is feminine, which would suggest rather a title or a description of function; this explains why in many languages it is sometimes translated 'preacher', from the etymology of the word, which seems to be connected with the term *qāhāl* = 'cultic assembly'. Be this as it may, the note which seeks to make Solomon the author of the book is similar to the one which attributes the book of Proverbs to him or the one which makes David the author of various psalms, and will not stand critical examination.

Ecclesiastes has a distinctive content, which is unique in the Hebrew Bible: for good reason the work has always perplexed scholars. It takes the form of reflection, confessions, maxims and meditations of various kinds, almost always put in autobiographical form; in them the author seeks to attract the attention of his readers to the scope of human existence, a problem which is characteristic of wisdom. He knows that human existence inevitably leads to death (and in this sense, after the Second World War he was seen as a precursor of existentialism). For him, everything, however noble and lofty, is 'nothing but vanity', the famous *vanitas vanitatum* of the Vulgate. Even the wisdom of which the wise men are so proud, believing that they can acquire adequate knowledge of the mechanism which rules the universe, so that they can adapt themselves to it, seems to the author to be a vain and futile thing, and he looks at the values human beings cherish in the same way. Thus Ecclesiastes is a sceptic and comes to conclusions which we can see to be disastrous for wisdom; this characteristic of his is in contrast to the attitude of the Hebrew Bible: both traditional theology and wisdom there are usually optimistic. However, this pessimism is to be explained not so much from the context of a crisis of faith as from a crisis of wisdom, of which the book of Job is another expression, as we have seen. And in any case, for a biblical author to come to the conclusion that 'a living dog is better than a dead lion' is quite sensational (9.4b).

The author is particularly hard on women, whom he considers 'more bitter than death', so that 'he who pleases God escapes her' (7.27-29). This is an anti-feminist attitude which is by no means isolated in Hebrew wisdom (cf. below, 48.3d).

The fact that only one problem is discussed, and the characteristic language, make the book a unified composition, although there have been some scholars who have seen it as a collection of different fragments. However, even if this latter theory were correct, it would be necessary to recognize that the fragments have been reconstructed as an organic unity with a marked artistic and logical sense, so that in practice it is impossible to identify such a unity or sometimes even to see what its argument is about.

The language of the book is a particular problem. Pfeiffer*, 729, gives a substantial list of Aramaisms and expressions taken from the Greek, and on the basis of this he assigns a late date to the work; this is the most commonly held opinion and is also supported by the content of the work. However, the theory has been put forward that the forms supposed to be Aramaisms are in fact features of western Semitic which are well attested from Ugaritic onwards; this might be an indication of the 'northern' origin of the work. It is not easy to see what value these observations have for a dating of Ecclesiastes, though for some scholars they are the sign of an earlier dating than that usually assigned to the book. On the other hand, in 9.7-10 we have parallels to Mesopotamian and Egyptian texts, and in 8.1f. to the romance of Ahikar which, as we shall see (44.2), was also well known by the deutero-canonical book of Tobit. Despite everything, the problems with which the book is concerned seem to be those of a late date; above all it reflects the crisis of wisdom which was attested throughout the ancient Near East and which in Israel was aggravated by contacts with Hellenistic philosophy from the end of the fourth century onwards. There came into Israelite belief elements like resignation, which is otherwise unknown in the Hebrew Bible; one unique element is a valuation of time as a cyclical entity, whereas the rest of the Hebrew Bible sees it only in linear and historical terms. As J.S.M.Mulder has it, 'Nobody can understand God!' In the other wisdom books, regardless of their thought, the problem is carefully avoided; there is still no hope for the future. Nevertheless, the author never goes so far as practical or theoretical atheism; he continually insists on the power of God and the weakness of humankind, although some writers have seen these affirmations as indications of insecurity, of a lack of personal communion, of a more rationalistic faith from which encounter and dialogue are absent. On the other hand, considering the general tone of the book, the conclusion is extremely positive: 'The sayings of the wise are like goads, and like nails firmly fixed are the collected sayings...' (in other words, the author does not deny the validity of wisdom, but assigns it a determinate position beyond which it should not enquire): 'Fear God and keep his commandments, for this is the whole duty of man' (12.13). If wisdom fails as a human attempt to dominate existence, faith remains, and we return to the more particularly Israelite element of thought. From the point of view of wisdom, Israel might have been inferior not only to the Greeks, as will be obvious, but also to its neighbours, yet in the realm of faith its insecurity vanishes to leave room for unconditional faith. What I said at the end of the discussion of Job therefore also applies here, and the reader is referred again to the passage.

In other words, Ecclesiastes concludes the work of limiting wisdom which Job had begun; he deprives man of the vain hope of being able to recognize the supposed order of the universe. He knows only one thing, that we must all die and that here the wise man and the fool are on the same level. Ecclesiastes thus puts all human sentiments in a new perspective, however noble they may be, by showing the vanity even of what seems unshakable, indicating that this is not the way for Israel. Only in this way can it truly prepare Israel for the new difficulties and the new tasks which lie ahead.

2. The Song of Songs

The traditional translation of the title of this book is equivocal: it can be translated either 'The best song' or 'The song *par excellence*', an alternative which is well known to anyone familiar with Hebrew grammar (cf. the *vanitas vanitatum* in 1). This work, too, is traditionally attributed to Solomon, who was a great singer as well as the possessor of a harem of notable dimensions. However, Solomon is mentioned only in general terms (3.7, 9, 11; 8.11f.) and there is not the slightest indication that he might in any way be the author. Scholars have always been divided over the character of the book, whether it is fragmentary or a unity. Origen was already in favour of the former alternative. Here, too, the linguistic question complicates matters considerably: Aramaisms abound (which could also be understood as western Semitisms), but so do terms of Persian and Greek origin.

The most probable explanation of the book seems to be that it is a collection of various songs on similar themes, if not the same theme; this would also explain the linguistic variations which can be found in the work. Firm ground has been discovered since J.G.Wetzstein, Prussian consul in Damascus, made an investigation into the practices and customs of Arab peasants in the area which he completed in 1873. Among other things, he established that during the long marriage festivals the married couple bore the title of king and queen of the festival; they sat at a special table which was called the 'throne' for the occasion, while the gathering sang hymns for the occasion in honour of the wife. Meanwhile available material has been increased considerably, to such a degree that we have now virtually reached certainty. The identity of the king and the Shulamite of the book has thus unexpectedly become clear: they were the bride and bridegroom during the feast in their honour.

In Scandinavia, however, an attempt has been made to go back to an earlier phase of the composition. It is argued that before the Song of Songs was democratized and applied to a wedding feast, it was a series of liturgical songs in the sphere of the cult which celebrated the sacred marriage of Ishtar and Tammuz and was transplanted to Judah, perhaps at the time of Manasseh, during the first half of the seventh century BCE. This was a time when the surviving Israelite state was a vassal of Assyria, and it may well have accepted, among other things, elements of the victor's cult. Research here was carried out before the work of O.Loretz, which confirms these two phases in the use of the composition.

As had already been noted by Ugo Grozio and has recently been pointed out by G.Garbini, the Song has some remarkable parallels with Hellenistic poetry, especially with Theocritus (first half of the third century BCE), the founder of bucolic poetry. This observation too brings forward the period of writing quite considerably.

The book did not become part of the canon without discussion. The collection was still controversial in the first century CE, and we have an echo of the discussion in the Mishnah (Yad. 3.5; cf. Ta'an.4.8). As an image of the marriage between YHWH and his people (a concept which is already present in Hosea) and then as an image of the marriage between Christ and his church, the book enjoyed canonical status only thanks to an allegorical interpretation which falsified the content, besides making it useless; both Israel and the church have always accepted marriage with all its implications, and it is quite consistent with this acceptance that marriage songs like those in the Song of Songs should have found a place in scripture alongside the history of religion and ethnology.

BIBLIOGRAPHY

Commentaries on Ecclesiastes

K.Galling, HAT, [2]1969; R.Pautrel, JB, 1948; H.W.Hertzberg, KAT, 1963; L.di Fonzo, SacBib, 1967; P.Ellermeier, Herzberg 1967-8; R.B.Y.Scott, AB, 1965; A.Lauha, 1978; J.Crenshaw, OTL, 1987. Cf. now also D.Michel, *Qohelet*, Darmstadt 1988.

Commentaries on the Song of Songs

G.Ricciotti, 1928; A.Robert, JB [2]1960; H.Ringgren, ATD, [5]1962; W.Rudolph, KAT, [2]1962; G.Gerleman, BK, 1965; R.Gordis, New York [3]1968; E.Würthwein, HAT, 1969; O.Loretz, *Das althebräische Liebeslied. Studien zur althebräischen Poesie* I, Neukirchen 1971; M.H.Pope, AB, 1977; G.Ravasi, 1985; O.Keel, ZBK, 1986.

1. J.Pedersen, 'Scepticisme Israélite', *RHPR* 10, 1930, 317-70; H.Ginsberg, *Studies in Koheleth*, New York 1950; M.J.Dahood, 'Canaanite-Phoenician Influence in Qohelet', *Bibl* 23, 1952, 191-221; R.Gordis, *Koheleth, The Man and His World*, New York 1955; A.G.Wright, 'The Riddle of the Sphinx: the Structure of the Book of Qohelet', *CBQ* 30, 1968, 313-34; P.Magnanini, 'Sull'origine letteraria dell'Ecclesiaste', *AION* 28, 1968, 363-84; D.Michel, 'Humanität angesichts des Absurden', in *Humanität heute*, ed. H.Foerster, Berlin 1970, 22-36; E.Horton, 'Koheleth's Concept of Opposites', *Numen* 19, 1972, 1-21 (on the relationship with Greek philosophy and the thought of the ancient Near and Far East); for a Christian evaluation, W.Vischer, 'L'Ecclesiaste testimonio di Cristo', *Prot* 9, 1954, 1-19; M.A.Klopfenstein, 'Die Skepsis des Qohelet', *TZ* 28, 1972, 97-109; D.Michel, 'Vom Gott, der im Himmel ist', *Theologia Viatorum* 12, Berlin 1973-4, 87-100; R.K.Johnson, ' "Confessions of a Workaholic". A Re-Appraisal of Qohelet', *CBQ* 38, 1976, 14-28; B.Pennacchini, 'Qohelet, ovvero il libro degli asurdi', *Euntes Docete* 30, 1977, 494-510. For the interpretation of the book cf. S.Brenton, 'Qoheleth Studies', *BTB* 3, 1973, 22-50; S.Holm-Nielsen, 'The Book of Ecclesiastes and the Interpretation of it in Jewish and Christian Theology', *ASTI* 10, 1975-76, 38-95; for the conclusion cf. G.T.Sheppard, 'The Epilogue to Qohelet as Theological

Commentary', *CBQ* 39, 1977, 182-9; H.-P.Müller, 'Der unheimliche Gast. Zum Denken Qohelets', *ZTK* 84, 1987, 440-64. Cf. also D.Lys, *L'Ecclésiaste ou que vaut la vie*, Paris 1977; J.Chopineau, 'L'image de Qohelet dans l'exégèse contemporaine', *RHPR* 59, 1979, 595-603; C.F.Whitley, 'Koheleth and Ugaritic Parallels', *UF* 11, 1979, 811-24; id., *Koheleth*, BZAW 148, 1979; J.A.Loader, *Polar Structures in the Book of Qoheleth*, Berlin 1979; T.Nishimura, 'Quelques réflections sé miologiques à propos de la "crainte de Dieu" de Qohelet', *AJBI* 5, 1979, 67-87; D.J.Lane, 'The Peshitta Text of Qoheleth', *VT* 29, 1979, 481-90; G.S.Ogden, 'Qohelet's Use of the "Nothing is Better" Form', *JBL* 98, 1979, 339-50; J.S.M.Mulder, 'Qoheleth's Division and also his Main Point', *Von Kanaan bis Kerala. FS J.P.M.van der Ploeg*, Kevelaer and Neukirchen-Vluyn 1982, 149-59; W.C.Delsman, 'Zur Sprache des Koheleth', ibid., 341-65; A.G.Wright, 'The Riddle of the Sphinx Revisited: Numeral Patterns in the Book of Qoheleth', *CBQ* 42, 1986, 38-51; O.Loretz, 'Altorientalische und kanaanäische Topoi im Buche Koheleth', *UF* 12, 1980, 267-78; A.G.Wright, 'Additional Numerical Patterns in Qoheleth', *CBQ* 45, 1983, 32-43; R.N.Whybray, 'Qoheleth: Preacher of Joy', *JSOT* 23, 1982, 87-98; L.Rosso Ubigli, 'Qohelet di fronte all'apocallittica', *Hen* 5, 1983, 209-34; E.Schoors, 'Koheleth', *ETL* 61, 1985, 295-300. E.J.Bickerman, *Four Strange Books of the Bible*, New York 1967, has an introduction and commentary. Cf. also H.-P.Müller, 'Theonome Skepsis und Lebensfreude', *BZ* 30, 1986, 1-19; I.von Loewenclau, 'Kohelet und Sokrates – Versuch eines Verglcichs', *ZAW* 98, 1986, 327-38. For dependence, albeit indirect, of Ecclesiastes on Theognis, cf. H.Ranston, *Ecclesiastes and the Early Greek Wisdom Literature*, London 1925; R.H.Pfeiffer*, 729f.

2. R.Gordis, *The Song of Songs*, New York 1954; H.Schmökel, *Heilige Hochzeit und Hohelied*, Wiesbaden 1956; A.Robert, R.Tournay and A.Feuillet, *Le Cantique des Cantiques*, Études Bibliques, Paris 1963; A.M.Dubarle, 'Le Cantique des Cantiques dans l'exégèse récente', *RechBibl* 9, 1967, 139-52; E.Würthwein, 'Zum Verständnis des Hohenliedes', *TR* 32, 1967, 177-212; D.Lys, *Le plus beau chant de la création*, Paris 1968; J.Angénieux, 'Le Cantique des Cantiques en huits chants à refrains alternants', *EphThLov* 44, 1968, 87-140 (= *De Mari à Qumrân, Hommage à J.Coppens*, ed. H.Cazelles, Gembloux 1969, 192-245); C.Carniti, 'L'unità letteraria del Cantico dei Cantici', *BeO* 13, 1971, 97-106. For a study of allegorizing and spiritualizing exegesis of the work cf. S.Grill, *Die Symbolsprache des Hohenliedes*, Heiligenkreuz ²1970; for the figure of Wetzstein cf. H.-J.Zobel, 'J.G.Wetzsteins Schrifttum', *ZDPV* 82, 1966, 233-8; for the thought of the Song and its origins cf. S.N.Kramer, 'Sumerian Sacred Marriage Songs and the Biblical "Song of Songs" ', *MIO* 15, 1969, 262-74; O.Loretz, op.cit.; J.C.Exum, 'Literary and Structural Analysis of the Song of Songs', *ZAW* 85, 1973, 47-9; R.E.Murphy, 'Form-Critical Studies of the Song of Songs', *Int* 27, 1973, 413-22; W.E.Phipps, 'The Plight of the Song of Songs', *JAAR* 42, 1974, 82-100; H.-P.Müller, 'Die lyrische Reproduktion des Mythischen im Hohelied', *ZTK*

72, 1976, 23-41; R.E.Murphy, 'Interpreting the Song of Songs', *BTB* 9, 1979, 99-105; id., 'The Unity of the Song of Songs', *VT* 29, 1979, 436-43; J.M.Sasson, 'On M.H.Pope's Song of Songs (AB 7c)', *Maarav* 1.2, 1979, 177-96; G.Garbini, 'La datazione del "Cantico dei Cantici" ', *RSO* 66, 1982 (1985), 39-46; id, 'Calche lessicali greci nel "Cantico dei Cantici" ', *RANL* VIII, 39, 1984, 149-64; H.U.Walter, 'Das Hohelied', *DBAT* 22, 1985 [1986], 140-79; E.C.Webster, 'Pattern in the Song of Songs', *JSOT* 22, 1982, 73-93; R.Tournay, *Quand Dieu parle aux hommes le langage de l'amour*, Paris 1982; M.V.Fox, 'Scholia to Canticles', *VT* 33, 1983, 199-206; M.D.Goulder, *The Song of Fourteen Songs*, Sheffield 1986; H.-P.Müller, *Vergleich und Metapher im Hohelied*, Freiburg 1984; M.V.Fox, *The Song of Songs and Ancient Egyptian Love Songs*, Madison, Wis. 1986.

40

ESTHER

The story of Esther is well known and has been the subject of numerous studies. She is said to have been queen of Persia after the deposition of Vashti, the queen who had refused to appear at the banquet of King Ahasuerus (Xerxes I), and to have thwarted a plot hatched by some Persian nobles against the Jewish community in the country (probably the first indication of an anti-Jewish persecution that we have, leaving aside the Pharaoh of the exodus). The book is now presented as the aetiological legend of the feast of Purim, which Jews still celebrate today as a kind of carnival; the word is interpreted in the text as the plural of *pūr* = 'lot', from the method by which the date of the massacre was fixed. The book is quite familiar with the customs of the Persian court of the fifth century BCE, but it also contains some puzzling information. In 2.5ff. Mordecai is described as one of the people deported under Jehoiachin, i.e. in 597, whereas the term *pūr*, the etymology and origin of which were unknown until recently, is Akkadian rather than Persian or Hebrew, and seems to be unknown to the readers of the text, for whom it has to be translated (3.7; 9.24). Furthermore the relationship between the word and the narrative is obscure, and it could be removed altogether without the narrative being any the worse. The idea that the word is given an artificial explanation by means of a tradition which describes the difficulties encountered by the Jewish community in Persia at the time of Xerxes (and the same goes for the feast) is therefore very probable. Others have noted that the names of the characters belong to Mesopotamia rather than to Persia: Esther is a phonetic variant of Ishtar, Mordecai of Marduk, both important Babylonian gods; indeed the latter was the patron deity of the city. Thus the question arises almost of its own accord whether we are not dealing with fragments of an ancient myth which has now been secularized and connected with the feast in question, in which two of the supreme deities of Babylonia are contrasted with other gods. On the other hand there is no reason to exclude a more prosaic explanation, namely that these are simply theophoric names of Babylonian origin given to Jews living in Babylon or Persia: Zerubbabel is a similar case.

There is mention in the book of the 'Chronicles of the kings of the Medes and Persians', but we do not know whether this is an official document, a chronicle of the life of the Jews resident in the region, or a literary fiction; no form of literature of this kind to be found on the Persian side, which favours the third possibility most.

Some scholars have sought to see in the story echoes of an event which in fact took place and is described by Herodotus (III, 68-79): on the death of Cambyses a magus made himself out to be the dead man's brother, the legitimate heir to the throne, though Cambyses had earlier had this man killed. He was, however, unmasked by a certain Othanes with the help of his daughter, who was a member of the royal harem. The people then killed all those who had taken part in the plot, an event which was commemorated in a 'feast of the killing of the magi'. The attempt, but not the feast, is also attested in Persian sources; it seems to have been connected with the New Year festival. If there is any relationship between this narrative and that of Esther, the historical basis of the book would be even more complex than it already seems to be. However, a close examination of the dates and the names reveals a still more prosaic reality: as Kaiser*, 207, indicates, what we have is not details of events which actually took place but a historical romance. Xerxes never had a first wife by the name of Vashti nor a second by the name of Esther: in Greek the name of his wife was Atossa. In the seventh year of his reign (2.16) he had other things to think about: the battle of Salamis in fact took place in 480. Finally, by that time Mordecai, deported by Nebuchadnezzar along with Jehoiakim in 597, will have been about 120, and his niece is hardly likely to have been very beautiful!

The book has marked nationalistic accents, a characteristic that can easily be explained from the frustration of a people constantly under foreign domination, which was often felt to contrast greatly with the mission they felt they had received from God. It is characteristic that the name of YHWH does not appear once in the book; this negative element was recognized later in the deutero-canonical additions to it, which among other things try to make up for this lack (cf. below, 46.1). Judaism at the beginning of the common era took account of this anomalous situation, as is shown by the discussions which preceded the admission of Esther to the canon. In the end, the book only found a place because it explains the institution of an annual feast which was very popular among Jews, and not because of its intrinsic content.

However, a study by B.W.Jones offers an alternative explanation: he thinks that the book is a Rabelaisian and humorous narrative, so that it caused scandal and indeed can still do so today because people seek to read it as theological literature and in a literal historical way. According to this argument, the work is meant to be hyperbole, a deiberately absurd story.

Historically the book is also interesting because it is evidence of the voice of nationalism, which is rarely heard in the Hebrew Bible. However, this theme should not be exaggerated: the very connection betwen the book and a carnival tends to show the absurd, ridiculous and humorous side of events rather than their cruelty. On the other hand, the history of the people of Israel shows that often the distance between tragedy and humour is not great.

BIBLIOGRAPHY

Commentaries

A.Barucq, JB, ²1959; H.Ringgren, ATD, ²1962; H.Bardtke, KAT, 1963; E.Würthwein, HAT, 1969; C.A.Moore, AB, 1971; G.Gerleman, BK, 1973; D.J.A.Clines, NCB, 1984. Cf. also W.Dommershausen, *Die Esterrolle*, Stuttgart 1968. E.J.Bickerman, *Four Strange Books of the Bible*, New York 1967, has an introduction and commentary.

There is a bibliography of recent works in H.Bardtke, 'Neuere Arbeiten zum Estherbuch', *Ex oriente Lux* VI, 19, 1965-6, 519-49; id, 'Der Mardochäus-tag', *Tradition und Glaube. FS K.G.Kuhn*, Tübingen 1971, 91-116; W.L.Humphreys, 'A Life-Style for Diaspora: A Study on the Tales of Esther and Daniel', *JBL* 92, 1973, 211-23; R.J.Littmann, 'The Religious Policy of Xerxes and the Book of Esther', *JQR* 65, 1974-5, 15-55; C.A.Moore, 'Archaeology and the Book of Esther', *BA* 38, 1975, 62-79; R.Gordis, 'Studies in the Esther Narrative', *JBL* 95, 1976, 42-58; A.Meinhold, 'Die Gattung der Josephsgeschichte und des Estherbuches: Diasporanovelle II', *ZAW* 88, 1976, 72-93; W.H.Shea, 'Esther and History', *AUSS* 14, 1976, 227-46; B.W.Jones, 'Two Misconceptions about the Book of Esther', *CBQ* 39, 1977, 171-81; A.R.Millard, 'The Persian Names in Esther and the Reliability of the Hebrew Text', *JBL* 96, 1977, 481-8; J.A.Loader, 'Esther as a Novel with Different Levels of Meaning', *ZAW* 92, 1980, 145-8; R.Gordis, 'Religion, Wisdom and History in the Book of Esther', *JBL* 100,

1981, 359-88; J.Craghan, 'Esther, Judith and Ruth', *BTB* 12, 1982, 11-19; E.Tov, 'The Lucianic Text of the Canonical and the Apocryphal Sections of Esther', *Textus* 10, 1982, 1-25; A.Meinhold, 'Zu Aufbau und Mitte des Estherbuches', *VT* 33, 1983, 435-45; D.J.A.Clines, *Ezra, Nehemiah, Esther*, London and Grand Rapids, Mich.1984; id., *The Esther Scroll*, Sheffield 1984. R.Zadok, 'On the Historical Background of the Book of Esther', *BN* 24, 1984, 18-23; id., 'Notes on Esther', *ZAW* 98, 1986, 105-10, attempts to recover a historical dimension and basis for the work. Cf. also C.A.Moore, *Studies in the Book of Esther*, 1982, which includes some of the articles listed here.

41

DANIEL

1. Character and content

We have already seen that in the Hebrew Bible Daniel is put among the Writings; the LXX puts it after Ezekiel, thus making it one of the prophets. In fact Daniel is an apocalyptic work, but this classification could easily have been used at a time when apocalyptic was tending increasingly to take the place of prophecy.

The book can clearly be divided into two parts: chs.1-6, in the third person, which tell the story of Daniel and his three companions at the court of Babylon; and chs.7-12, which contain our visions, narrated in the first person and explained by an angel. The situation here is similar to the one that we found in the case of proto-Zechariah.

In ch.1 we have a description of the hero of the book: he was deported to Babylon in the third year of Jehoiakim, i.e. in 607 BCE, together with his three friends, and educated at the court of Nebuchadnezzar II, where he kept the dietary laws of the *tōrāh* with exemplary zeal, even though this meant being restricted to an exclusively vegetarian diet. However, this had no adverse physical effects on the four, who in fact prospered. In ch.2 Daniel interprets to Nebuchadnezzar a dream which had baffled the wise man of Babylon and receives a rich reward from the king. In ch.3 the three friends have to undergo a harsh test: after refusing to pay divine homage to a statue which has been erected by the king, they are thrown into a fiery furnace: the heat is such that none of their escorts can survive in the vicinity, but the heroes are miraculously saved, to the king's understandable astonishment. In ch.4 we have another of Nebuchadnezzar's dreams, the content of which is very soon realized in the person of the king; he remains mad for seven years until he is finally cured by Daniel and praises YHWH. In ch.5 we have the famous account of Belshazzar's feast with the mysterious writing on the wall, which is interpreted by Daniel and soon fulfilled. In ch.6 Daniel is accused of having violated a law of Darius the Mede through his mode of prayer and is thrown into a den of lions; however, he miraculously escapes from it unharmed, thus achieving recognition of the cult of YHWH from the king by means of an edict.

In the second half of the book, first of all, in ch.7, we have four beasts which nowadays are unanimously interpreted as symbols for Babylon, Media, Persia and Macedon: ten horns grow out of the last beast, one of which is particularly virulent in language and action and is generally understood as a symbol for Antiochus IV Epiphanes (the horns represent the 'Diadochi' who succeeded Alexander the Great). In ch.8 we have a struggle between two more symbolic beasts, a ram and a he-goat, which symbolize the kingdoms of Persia and Macedonia respectively (8.20); in ch.9 the angel Gabriel reveals to Daniel the meaning of the prophecy in Jer.25.11, cf. 29.10, where the duration of the Babylonian exile is reckoned at seventy years, a round figure to indicate two or three generations: this is probably from the destruction of the temple, 587/6, to its rebuilding in 517/16. This is said really to be seventy weeks of years, 490 years in all. This calculation evidently brings us down to the time of the Maccabees and the period immediately following, the end of the second and beginning of the first century BCE. However, to say that does not yet overcome all the difficulties. G.R.Driver has made what I believe to be a definitive analysis of the problem, arriving at the following results. (By way of preliminaries it should be said that the figures are not to be taken precisely, as though they were the results of exact calculations.)

We should note how the weeks are divided:

(a) Seven weeks of years, i.e. 49 years (v.25);

(b) 62 weeks, i.e. 434 years (v.25b);

(c) One week of years, i.e. seven years (v.27a).

The first series, calculated from 587-6, brings us down to the year 538-7, i.e. that of the 'anointed prince' Cyrus in Isa.45.1, who at that time promulgated the edict for the liberation of those who had been deported. 434 years, calculated from the same date, give a wrong result: if it is in fact true that the text refers to the suppression of the high priest Onias III in 171, the accounts do not square. There are two possibilities. We can begin the calculation from the year of the accession of Nebuchadnezzar II, given in the oracle Jer.25.1,11, i.e. from 605, in which case we reach 171 exactly (cf. the commentaries by Plöger and Lacocque), but it seems strange that the calculations in question have two different starting points. Alternatively, we can follow Driver in postulating an error (a deliberate one?) in order to maintain the multiples of seven: 434 is written instead of 367 years.

For Driver the explanation of the error is simple: the author would have had inexact or incomplete chronological information (as, moreover, is the case for us in this period) and would therefore have chosen a multiple of seven without being bothered whether it was exact. Finally, the seven last years run from 171 to 164, the year in which the temple and its altar were reconsecrated. The period is in turn subdivided into:

1. 3½ years (171-168), i.e. from the assassination of Onias III to the desecration of the temple (v.26b);

2. 3 years, from 168-165, the year of the insurrection and the reconsecration;

3. Half a year, from 165 to 164, to the end of the 'author of desolation', i.e. the death of Antiochus IV (v.27b).

At all events, Driver warns, these are round figures, giving no more than an approximate guide.

The peace will be followed by the inauguration of the kingdom of God. In these chapters the sea often appears as an element of chaos, which is a widespread theme in the Hebrew Bible, just as the horns and the beasts described are symbols of force. In ch.11 an angel reveals to Daniel the course of history from Cyrus to Antiochus IV, while in 11.40-12.3 we have details of the events which will follow the death of the oppressor. The nations will fall, the kingdom of God will dawn, the dead will rise: the pagans to eternal death and the just to eternal life (12.2; cf. Isa.26.19). In 12.5-13, by way of conclusion, there is mention of a date by which these things will have happened: between 1290 and 1335 days respectively (12.11f.).

2. Authorship and origin

The text is silent about the authorship and origin of the book. The tradition of the synagogue and the church takes the author to be Daniel, the protagonist of the work, but he is a person who is otherwise unknown: in fact we saw when considering Job that the Daniel of Ezck.14.14,20 cannot be identical with the exilic Daniel. The question of authorship cannot therefore be resolved.

The first difficulties in the historical classification of the book begin with the deportation of Daniel and his companions. We do not in fact know anything of a deportation which took place in the third year of Jehoiakim, i.e. in 607 BCE. If we allow its basic historicity, the event might be connected with the conquest of Syria and Palestine by Nebuchadnezzar II a little later, after the battle of Carchemish in 605-4 and the victory over Egypt; it was on this occasion that

Jehoiakim moved out of the sphere of Egyptian influence and into that of Babylon (cf. II Chron.36.5). Complex problems of foreign policy followed, to which I alluded in the discussion of Jeremiah. Until recently the note in Chronicles was considered spurious, since there was no point of comparison, but discoveries during the 1950s of other fragments of the Babylonian Chronicle unexpectedly made sense of both this passage and II Kings 24.1ff. But even if we were to admit the substantial historicity of the events narrated, there remains the problem of chronology, which is evidently some years out. Other elements are no less perplexing; in 5.11 Belshazzar is implicitly called the son of Nebuchadnezzar and in 7.1 he appears as king of Babylon. However, he was neither one nor the other, but the son of Nabonidus, one of Nebuchadnezzar's successors who came to the throne as the result of a conspiracy. (The only other possibility is that 'son of...' is intended in a generic sense, as 'descendant of..', a usage which is attested in Hebrew and in Akkadian.) On the other hand, the statement that Belshazzar was king may simply be imprecise wording: towards 553 he was resident in Babylon as a king or vice-gerent for the king during his numerous absences and could therefore have been called king, at least by the people. Again, in 5.31, as we have seen, a certain Darius the Mede appears, who is considered to be king of Persia after the fall of Babylon. In 9.1 he appears as son of Xerxes, whereas in 6.29 Cyrus succeeds a Darius. If we are to be precise, the question arises what Daniel is doing at the court of the Medes before the Babylonian empire has fallen, always assuming that we take the term 'Mede' seriously. This question has never been answered. We must therefore accept that Media is in reality Persia. But the order of the kings of Persia is well known: Cyrus, Cambyses, Darius I Hystaspes, Xerxes. If the Darius mentioned here was Darius I from the last quarter of the sixth century, how old would Daniel be? These are features which were already pointed out by the anti-Christian polemicists Celsus and Porphyry at the end of the second century CE.

Although the chronology of the work thus seems confused, at least in the first part elements of considerable historical value also appear: Herodotus (I,191) and Xenophon, *Cyropaedia* (VII, v,15), report that Babylon was in fact conquered during a feast and that its inhabitants had no idea of what was happening. Eusebius of Caesarea, *Praeparatio Evangelica* IX, 41, confirms the note about Nebuchadnezzar's madness through a tradition which is independent of that of the Bible. It is thus evident that here we have traditions which, quite independently of their intrinsic value, are certainly not the product of the imagination of the person who wrote the book.

The language of Daniel is certainly post-exilic, and terms of Greek and Persian origin abound. Whole passages are written im imperial Aramaic, whereas logically we would expect early Aramaic. Some of the concepts expressed in the book are also late: the development of the dietary laws in a legalistic sense, prayer with the body turned towards Jerusalem, angelology, the doctrine of the resurrection (12.2), which we know still to have been the subject of lively debate at the time of Jesus (Matt.22.23ff.) and which was never defined in Judaism. In the first part of the book we thus find ourselves at some remove from the exile and certainly not at its beginning. The second part, however, is an apocalyptic writing pure and simple, and is to be assigned a late date.

On the other hand, in recent times there has been a tendency not to date the book too late: it is true that Daniel is not mentioned in Ecclesiasticus, but many fragments of it have been found among the writings of the Qumran sect, so that the book had already acquired some importance in the second century BCE. This position is confirmed by an analysis of the historical information given in the second part of the work: it becomes increasingly exact the closer it gets to the time of Antiochus IV and the Maccabees, i.e. the first half of the second century, while the earlier account of the Babylonian and Persian period is rather inaccurate. The book is quite familiar with Antiochus IV's two campaigns aginst Egypt (cf. my *History*, XIII.6ff.), in 170 and 169 BCE, and with the repression of Jewish worship down to the introduction of the 'abomination of desolation' into the temple in 167 (cf. 7.1ff.; 11.21-39). In 8.14 we probably have an indication of the purification of the temple by Judas Maccabaeus which took place in 163. The question becomes more complex when we get to 11.40, which announces the death of the oppressor in the course of an attack on Jerusalem. This is clearly a variant of the theme of the onslaught of the peoples in the last times (above, 24.4b); in reality Antiochus died on an expedition to the East in 163. Thus it is clear that Daniel is quite familiar with events connected with the life of Antiochus IV, but does not know of his death, which is presented only as an event in the future. We shall not go far wrong in dating the book betwen 168 and 164; this theory was already put forward by the neo-Platonist Porphyry in his anti-Christian polemic.

The book is not a unity in either content or language: from 2.4b to 7.28 it is composed in Aramaic – as we have seen, in imperial Aramaic. The change of language from Hebrew to Aramaic has still not been explained adequately, but Rowley is probably right in affirming that the author seems to be using Aramaic material of the Maccabaean period for chs.2-6; ch.7, also in the same language, was added a little later. The latest commentary on Daniel by J.-C.Lebram (1984) suggests the following explanation for this disconcerting phenomenon: as during the second century BCE Hebrew was the official language of Judaism and there is no apparent reason why the book should suddenly use Aramaic, the only possible explanation is that the Aramaic section was written by a different person; and that the text was not eventually translated into Hebrew can only be because it was a more ancient, authoritative text.

On the other hand, the author himself wrote in Hebrew the visions of chs.8-12, which are addressed not so much to lowly people as to the educated. In content we have a clear break between narrative passages (chs.1-6) and apocalyptic passages (chs.7-12). In the first part, feelings towards the Gentiles are only moderately hostile, while in the second part the hostility is obvious; we might conclude that the first part is made up of elements which circulated in the eastern Jewish diaspora, whereas the second part refers to events of the time of the Maccabees and was intended to strengthen the Jewish population in the homeland for the struggle.

The LXX gives a text of Daniel with some additions which, as in the case of Esther, we shall study below (46.2). In any case, the text is in extremely bad condition, so much so that Theodotion's version was soon used instead; the original was forgotten until it was rediscovered in modern times among the Chester Beatty papyri; according to a recent theory, what is thought to be Theodotion's text is really that of Symmachus. Be this as it may, the important fact is that here we have a unique example of one of the minor Greek translations of the Hebrew Bible being preserved at some length.

3. Purpose and message

From time immemorial the book of Daniel has been the favourite text among sects, who use the dates in it to calculate the end of the world, to condemn certain political régimes often rightly considered to be demoniacal, and for other speculative exercises. It is therefore perhaps even more necessary than with the other books of the Bible to be particularly careful in reading it and to avoid making the text say things which it cannot say. The four kingdoms symbolized by the four beasts represent those which we have seen, and cannot in any way be applied to persons and institutions from our own time.

The horn is Antiochus IV Epiphanes and not, say, Hitler, Stalin or any other baneful figure of our day. Even if attempts of this kind often arouse strong feelings, they are to be rejected by anyone, believer or unbeliever, who means to read the Bible seriously.

Once it has been established that the work is addressed to Palestinian Jews in the time of distress during the first half of the second century BCE we must surmount a second barrier: we must overcome the obstacle presented to modern people by the pseudonymity which is so markedly represented in the apocalypitc books. Its sole aim seems to have been to lend greater authority to the books, and the idea that this might be a fraudulent proceeding never entered the heads of the writers. On the other hand, according to the criteria governing admission to the canon, the book only found a place because it was attributed to the Daniel of the exile. In other words, without the phenomenon of pseudonymity, Daniel would never have entered the canon.

Thus the book of Daniel is an authoritative representative of the thought of Palestinian Judaism in the first half of the second century. It could be that it took up pious legends which were in circulation about the faith of individuals and groups of deportees during the sixth century; it is certain that it was addressed to contemporaries using these traditions as a comparison. If it was possible then to resist the guile and threats of the enemy, how much more was it possible now, when the people were united in their own country and the enemy was much less powerful. If he wished, a pious Jew could continue to observe the ritual prescriptions by which he made public confession of his faith to the pagan world. The first part of the book also seeks to show that relationships with Gentiles need not necessarily be as bad as they were at the time; and if they were, this was due to the intolerance of the pagans and not to any fault of Israel in this sphere. Moreover, with the help of God Israel could survive all the tests: consider Daniel and his friends, first in the furnace and then in the lions' den.

On the other hand, the second part of the work reacts to a paganism which had unexpectedly become intolerant and irrationally aggressive, contrary to its principles of rationality and tolerance. Here there could only be war, whether on an ideological level or, where restrictions had taken forms which were physically or morally intolerable, even on the level of armed struggle. Otherwise that would have been the end of Israel, which like all the people of the ancient Near East would have been absorbed into the Hellenistic world. By taking up this intransigent position Israel, by contrast, succeeded in resisting guile and threats, persecution and war, and emerged victor from the conflict.

The apocalyptic compositions in the second part have a variety of features. On the one hand we have a genuinely prophetic interest in the future development of history, and on the other a purely speculative approach (one has only to think of the 'exegesis' of the seventy years in Jeremiah), and an expectation of divine intervention with strong mythical elements which leave human beings completely outside their perspective. These concepts in fact seem to be a form of escapism, a flight from the historical reality in which the prophets lived intensely, into metaphysics and myth. This refusal to face history and to live in it was a mark of regression in Israel, an adaptation to the ruling mentality in the Hellenistic world, and in the last analysis was one of the causes of the catastrophes of 70 and 134/5 CE.

BIBLIOGRAPHY

Commentaries

J.A.Montgomery, ICC [2]1949; G.Rinaldi, SacBib, 1947; A.Bentzen, HAT, [2]1952; J.de Menasche, JB, [2]1958; N.W.Porteous, OTL, 1965; O.Plöger, KAT, 1965; M.Delcor, 1972; A.Lacocque, 1976; C.F.Hartman and A.A.Di Lella, AB, 1978; J.J.Collins, 1984; J.-C.Lebram, ZBK, 1984.

1. W.Baumgartner, *Das Buch Daniel*, Giessen 1926; H.H.Rowley, *Darius the Mede and the Four World Empires in the Book of Daniel*, Cardiff [2]1959. For the history of the period see H.Jagersma, *A History of Israel from Alexander the Great to Bar Kochba*, ET London and Philadelphia 1985, 44ff.

2. E.Gross, 'Weltreich und Gottesvolk', *EvTh* 16, 1956, 241-51; O.Eissfeldt, 'Daniels und seiner drei Gefährten Laufbahn im babylonischen, medischen und persischen Dienst', *ZAW* 72, 1960, 134-48 (= his *Kleine Schriften* III, Tübingen 1966, 513-25). For II Chron.36.5 cf. D.J.Wiseman, *Chronicles of Chaldaean Kings*, London 1956, 26f., 46f.; E.Vogt, 'Die neubabylonische Chronik über die Schlacht von Karkemisch und die Einnahme von Jerusalem', *SVT* 4, 1957, 67-96; A.Lenglet, 'La structure littéraire de Daniel 2-7', *Bibl* 53, 1972, 169-90; W.L.Humphreys, 'A Life Style for the Diaspora: A Study of the Tales of Esther and Daniel', *JBL* 92, 1973, 211-23; J.C.H.Lebram, 'König Antiochus im Buch Daniel', *VT* 25, 1975, 734-72; P.Grelot, 'La Septante de Daniel IV et son substrat sémitique', *RB* 81, 1974, 5-23; H.Burgmann, 'Die vier Endzeittermine im Danielbuch', *ZAW*

86, 1974, 543-50; J.C.H.Lebram, 'Perspektiven der gegenwärtigen Daniel-forschung', *JSJ* 5, 1974, 1-33; J.G.Gammie, 'The Classification, Stages of Growth and Changing Intentions in the Book of Daniel', *JBL* 95, 1976, 191-204. For the 'seventy weeks of years' cf. G.R.Driver, 'Sacred Numbers and Round Figures', in *Promise and Fulfilment. Essays Presented to S.H.Hooke*, Edinburgh 1963, 62-90. For Belshazzar see K.Galling, 'Politische Wandlungen in der Zeit zwischen Nabonid und Darius', in his *Studien zur Geschichte Israels im persischen Zeitalter*, Tübingen 1964, 1-60, esp.12ff. For Dan.7 cf. E.Dhanis, 'De Filio hominis in Vetere Testamento et in Judaismo', *Greg* 45, Rome 1964, 5-59; J.Coppens and L.Dequeker, *Le Fils de l'Homme et les Saints du Très-Haut en Daniel VII*, Louvain 1961; M.Delcor, 'Les Sources du chapitre VII de Daniel', *VT* 18, 1968, 290-312; L.Dequeker, 'The "Saints of the Most High" in Qumran and in Daniel', *OTS* 18, 1973, 108-87; J.J.Collins, 'The Son of Man and the Saints of the Most High in the Book of Daniel', *JBL* 93, 1974, 50-66; G.F.Hasel, 'The Identity of "The Saints of the Most High" in Daniel 7', *Bibl* 56, 1975, 173-92; V.S.Poythress, 'The Holy Ones of the Most High, Daniel VII', *VT* 26, 1976, 208-13; J.Coppens, 'La vision du Très Haut en Dan.VII et Hén. ethiop.XIV', *ETL* 53, 1977, 187-91. For the language of the book cf. H.H.Rowley, *The Aramaic of the Old Testament*, London 1929; id., 'The Bilingual Problem of Daniel', *ZAW* 50, 1932, 256-68; id., 'The Meaning of Daniel for Today', *Int* 16, 1961, 387-97; E.M.Cook, *Word Order in the Aramaic of Daniel*, Afro-Asiatic Linguistics, Undena, Malibu, Cal. 1986; J.Wesselius, 'Language and Style in Biblical Aramaic: Observations on the Unity of Daniel II-VI', *VT* 38, 1988, 194-209. For the Greek text cf. P.Grelot, 'Les versions grecques de Daniel', *Bibl* 47, 1966, 381-402; A.Schmitt, *Stammt der sogenannte Θ Text bei Daniel wirklich aus Theodotion?*, Göttingen 1966. He thinks that Symmachus is a more likely source. Also F.F.Bruce, 'The Oldest Greek Version of Daniel', *OTS* 20, 1977, 22-40; P.-M.Bogaert, 'Relecture et refonte historicisantes du livre de Daniel attestés par la première version grecque', in R.Kuntzmann and J.Schlosser (eds.), *Études sur le Judaïsme hellénistique*, Paris 1984, 197-224. For relations with the Qumran texts cf. A.Mertensen, *Das Buch Daniel im Lichte der Texte vom Toten Meer*, Stuttgart and Würzburg 1971; G.Bampfylde, 'The Prince of the Host in the Book of Daniel and the Dead Sea Scrolls', *JSJ* 14, 1983, 129-34; M.Casey, *Son of Man*, London 1979; I.Willi-Plein, 'Ursprung und Motivation der Apokalyptik im Danielbuch', *TZ* 35, 1979, 265-74; E.J.Bickerman, *Four Strange Books of the Bible*, New York 1967; G.L.Archer, 'The Hebrew Daniel Compared with the Qumran Sectarian Documents', in *The Law and the Prophets. FS O.T.Allis*, no place of publication, 1980, 470-81 (tries to demonstrate that the Hebrew of Daniel is ancient); P.R.Davies, 'Eschatology in the Book of Daniel', *JSOT* 17, 1980, 33-53; J.Day, 'The Daniel of Ugarit and Ezekiel and the Hero of the Book of Daniel', *VT* 30, 1980, 425-37; J.C.H.Lebram, 'Zwei Danielprobleme', *BO* 39, 1982, 510-17; W.Shea, 'Daniel the Mede; an Update', *AUSS* 20, 1982, 229-47 (an attempt to explain the chronology); H.Gese, 'Die Bedeutung der

Krise unter Antiochus IV Epiphanes für die Apokalyptik des Danielbuches', *ZTK* 80, 1983, 373-88; W.Shea, 'Nabonidus, Belshazzar and the Book of Daniel – A Rejoinder', *AUSS* 20, 1982, 133-49. *Int* 39.2, 1985, is devoted to Daniel. J.C.Trever, 'The Book of Daniel and the Origin of the Qumran Community', *BA* 48, 1985, 89-102; P.W.Coxon, 'The "List" Genre and Narrative Style in the Court Texts of Daniel', *JSOT* 35, 1986, 95-121; J.Goldingay, 'The Stories of Daniel: A Narrative Politics', *JSOT* 37, 1987, 99-116; T.Seidl, 'Volk Gottes und seine Zukunft nach den Aussagen des Bishes Daniel', in J.Schreiber (ed.), *Unterwegs zur Kirche*, Freiburg im Breisgau 1987, 168-200; A.Bonora, 'La storiografia del libro di Daniele', in *Atti della XXVIII settimana biblica*, Bologna 1986, 77-91.

3. On apocalyptic, a topic which we cannot discuss here in detail, cf. D.S.Russell, *The Method and Message of Jewish Apocalyptic*, London and Philadelphia 1964 (a basic work); cf. also K.Koch, *The Relevance of Apocalyptic*, ET SBT II 22, 1972; cf. above, 17.10 and also R.Martin-Achard, 'L'apocalyptique d'après trois travaux récents', *RTP* 103, 1970, 310-18; P.D.Hanson, 'Old Testament Apocalyptic Re-examined', *Int* 25, 1971, 454-79; B.Corsani, 'L'apocalittica fra Antico e Nuovo Testmaento', *Prot* 27, 1972, 15-22; James Barr, 'Jewish Apocalyptic in Recent Scholarly Study', *BJRL* 58, 1975-76, 9-35 with bibliography; J.M.Schmidt, *Die jüdische Apokalyptik*, Tübingen 1969; W.Schmithals, *The Apocalyptic Movement*, Nashville 1975; *Apocalypse et théologie de l'espérance: Congrès de Toulouse* (various authors), Paris 1977. See also, *inter alia*, J.A.Soggin, 'Profezia ed apocalittica nel Giduaesimo postesilico', *RiBib* 30, 1982, 161-73; P.Sacchi, 'Riflessioni sull'essenza dell'apocalittica', *Hen* 5, 1983, 31-61. A recent study by G.Boccaccini, 'È Daniel un apocalittico? Una (ri)definizione del pensiero del libro di Daniele in rapporto al Libro dei Sogni e all'Apocalittica', *Hen.* 9, 1987, 267-302, has argued on the basis of a comparison with other apocalyptic texts that Daniel cannot be considered as belonging to this genre.

The interpretation of the book of Daniel in terms of individuals and events contemporary with the interpreter is ancient; it goes back to the second-century apologists, cf. Dodenmann, *Naissance d'une exégèse*, Tübingen 1986.

42

CHRONICLES

1. Character, analysis and date

'Chronicles' is a translation of the Hebrew title *dibrē hayyāmīm* = lit. 'facts of the days'; the Greek, followed by the Vulgate, has *paraleipomena*, as though Chronicles were a kind of complement to the books of Samuel and Kings. In reality, the majority of scholars believe that, along with Ezra and Nehemiah, it is a large independent historical work, although it sometimes draws on the same sources as the 'former prophets' and thus appears so to speak in a parallel form to them. It was Jerome who proposed the title *Chronicon totius divinae historiae*, a title which corresponds well with the intentions of the compiler.

The content can easily be divided into four parts: I Chron. 1-9, the genealogies from Adam to David, with interesting variants and new information in comparison with the books of the Pentateuch and the 'former prophets' (however, in 3.17ff. the genealogies have six generations after Zerubbabel [cf. above, 26.2, 27.1], which gives an important *terminus a quo* for the dating if the boo':); I Chron. 10-29, the life of David; II Chron 1-9, the life of Solomon; II Chron. 10-36, from the schism to the exile. From the death of Saul onwards we have an obvious parallel narrative to Samuel and Kings, though this parallel does not detract from the originality of Chronicles in both choice of sources and ultimate intention. In the earlier part, however, the parallel appears only on the level of nomenclature, since (as we have seen) Chronicles here gives only genealogies and lists of places.

For Chronicles, the centre of the history of Israel is to be found in the temple and its worship, its priesthood and even in less elevated personnel. History before David, the history of the kingdom of Israel after the separation of the two kingdoms, and all forms of worship earlier than and then parallel to that of the temple, are thought to be devoid of interest and can therefore be ignored. David appears essentially as the spiritual father of the temple; although he was not allowed to build it, he organized all its worship and prepared the material for its construction (I Chron.22; compare with this I Kings 5). On his death he hands over to Solomon to continue the work thus begun and to bring it to a conclusion. David is also seen to have reorganized the cult, and especially its music; this is still within the context of the tradition which makes him a singer and a psalmist. His spiritual successors are Solomon, Jehoshaphat (the pious king who was zealous for the law), and of course Hezekiah and Josiah. These people appear as the embodiment of a synthesis of national saints and heroes, thus taking to an absurd degree a tendency which is already present in Dtr. Almost every feature which does not fit in with the hagiographical character of the biographies of these kings disappears: the story of David's family, certain aspects of the life of Solomon and so on. The direct intervention of YHWH is often the decisive element in the victorious solution of a conflict; we have a particularly clear instance of this approach in II Chron.20.1-30. Thus Chronicles is deliberately sacred history, perfecting historiographical tendencies which were earlier represented by Dtr and the prophets. Chronicles accepts the approach to certain historical problems in terms of reward and punishment which is well attested in earlier history writing, but it now takes this to excess. For example, the authors raise the problem how a king like Manasseh, who was considered the embodiment of the wicked ruler, could have reigned for so long a time; the explanation of the fact, which contradicts their theory, is sought along the following lines: the king, who was deported to Assyria, was converted there (II Chron.33.10f.). This explains the divine favour towards him. In reality, Manasseh, a vassal of Assyria, arrived in Asshurbanipal's capital along with other vassals, around 650, to pay tribute and supply military contingents (cf. the Assyrian Chronicle inscribed on the so-called C cylinder I, lines 24ff., *ANET*[3], 294). There can therefore be no question of a spiritual crisis, much less of a conversion.

As well as being particularly interested in worship, the priesthood and the levites, Chronicles is very familiar with the Pentateuch, especially the Deuteronomic legislation, the application of which is presupposed even in cases where the parallel passages of Samuel and Kings know nothing of it.

2. Sources

We saw above that the Chronicler knew the Pentateuch and cites people and places from it. He probably also knew Dtr, or at least its sources, since he agrees with it in many passages. He also cites the 'Book of the Kings of Judah' (I Chron.9.1; II Chron.20.34) and knows the 'Chronicles of the Kings of Israel' (II Chron.33.18). It is difficult to know whether these are the works cited in Kings (cf. above, 16.2b-c), different works, or literary fictions to give the work greater credibility. A *midrash* (= commentary) on the book of Kings is mentioned in II Chron.24.27, but we know nothing about it.

The work of the Chronicler has always been held in low esteem by bibical scholars: its crude interpretations in terms of reward and punishment, the episodes in Israelite history interpreted in a mythical and miraculous fashion, and other elements of this kind, give the critical reader too many reasons for discrediting the work. So it is all the more surprising that it has been recognized that in Chronicles we have a series of pieces of information from a reliable source which are not recorded in the books of Samuel and Kings. We have seen above (9.1), for example, that the chronological details about Josiah's reform in II Chron.34.3-7 is perhaps better than that contained in II Kings 22-23; according to them the 'reform' will in fact have begun about ten years before the discovery of the 'book of the law' during the restoration of the temple, while II Kings 22; 23 makes the two events coincide, as though it had been the discovery of the book which prompted Josiah to the reform. Here Chronicles offers the following view: Josiah begins the reform in the eighth year of his reign, probably in the context of a progressive disengagement from the Assyrian empire, which was now in decline, whereas the 'book of the law' was found in the eighteenth year, a date on which Kings and Chronicles agree. It is also II Chron.35.20ff. which gives detailed information (even if it is by no means clear) about the death of Josiah in the battle of Megiddo against Necho II of Egypt, an element which is absent from Kings. In II Chron.32.30 we have a note that Hezekiah developed the aqueduct and the water system of the capital with a view to a long siege: this aqueduct was rediscovered and explored in the second half of the last century. The lists of fortresses in II Chron.11.5-10; 16.1-6 and various notes about conspiracies and rebellions contained throughout the work are also authentic and early. There are a number of cases where Chronicles gives the exact names of particular people which in Dtr have been distorted for polemical reasons: Ishbaal in I Chron.8.33; 10.39 for Ishbosheth; Meribaal in I Chron.8.34 for Mephiboshet; and so on. It is also Chronicles which gives the correct interpretation of the delegation from the king of Babylon to Hezekiah in terms of 'negotations', according to the probable translation suggested by H.Cazelles for II

Chron. 32.31. This detail does not emerge from the parallel passages
in II Kings 20.12f.//Isa.39.1f. We must therefore be very cautious
over this information in Chronicles which does not reflect the theology
of the book in any particular way, and remember that in cases of this
kind the burden of proof is always with the prosecution, and not with
the defence.

At other times, however, the theology of Chronicles is actively at
work in the revision of information that we can verify through other
sources available to us. We have examined the cases of I Chron.14.2
and II Chron.33.10ff.; another similar case can be found in I
Chron.21.1ff.: the parallel passage II Sam.24.1 relates, 'The anger
of YHWH was kindled against...', whereas I Chron. reads 'Satan
stood up against Israel...' (incidentally, this is the only case in the
Hebrew Bible in which Satan appears as the proper name of a person
and as a demon). It is clear what has happened between the two
versions: in II Sam. God himself acts to punish David; in I Chron.
hagiography already has the king in its grip and therefore no
punishment took place; instead, the king is 'tempted' by Satan, who
has now taken over the role assigned to the Tempter, a role which
he will have in later Judaism, the New Testament and Islam.

3. Thought

In Dtr the theological interpretation served as an interpretative key
for explaining the events which were reported; they were considered,
if we may put it that way, as 'proof texts' for certain theories, for a
particular theology of history. The texts did not emerge substantially
transformed, but were simply cited outside their original context.
Paradoxically, in Chronicles we may say that the theological theory
existed first and that the facts came second and were often forcibly
made to fit it: the case of Manasseh's conversion may be considered
typical. That does not mean that the Chronicler was deceiving the
reader or the hearer: terms like 'pious fraud' have often been applied
to him in the past, but they do not get to the heart of the phenomenon.
In any case we cannot disregard the good faith of the author: in fact
the Chronicler saw events from the creation of the world to the time
of Ezra and Nehemiah and beyond – as the genealogies show – as
having taken place in the way in which he describes them. However,
it is difficult to call this process historiography. The modern reader
continually has the impression that, given the theory and the
premises, the results can only be what the Chronicler wants them to
be, and the impression which this situation makes is not a favourable

one: without insisting on an impossible degree of objectivity in the history, we ask at least that we shall not be asked to know *a priori* the result to which the investigations are taking us.

In other words, instead of selecting examples for his preaching from history, like Dtr, the Chronicler adapts history to his preaching, taking to absurd lengths doctrines like that of reward and punishment, well-known to the prophets and the Deuteronomistic writers, not to mention wisdom.

As Noth has rightly recognized, there are probably other reasons for the implicit protest against the attitude of the northern kingdom of Israel made by the omission of all favourable mentions of it (we may note a fundamental difference from Dtr, which condemns the 'sin of Jeroboam' but does not conceal the reasons which led to the separation). Here we have incipient anti-Samaritan polemic, and the Samaritans considered themselves, not unjustly, as the legitimate heirs of the kingdom of Israel. In other words, the Chronicler takes up an ancient condemnation to renew the present condemnation of a movement which was considered schismatic or even heretical, whose members were involved in the guilt of their fathers. The reduction of the Pentateuch to genealogies and lists of places could also be explained as a desire not to give the hated neighbours material which they might use in self-defence. Still, as J.Hausmann's recent work has shown, the political hopes of Chronicles are for a reunification of the north with the south in some way or other.

The danger inherent in the approach made by Chronicles to theological and ethical problems, not to mention the obvious tendentiousness in its account of the greater part of the past history of Israel, should be evident: the legalistic application of the doctrine of rewards and punishments; the distortion or the invention of facts to fit the theory; belief in the correctness of the cult, which is even enough to win battles – all these indicate that the theology of the Chronicler is something of a regression from that of his predecessors. However, we must be particularly careful here, and in any case we should avoid crude and dogmatic judgments; we know too little of the time at which Chronicles was written, nor do we know the need in response to which it was written. Just as the tendentiousness in Dtr can be explained from the need to give a theological interpretation to the catastrophe of the exile, so some of the elements which we rightly criticize in Chronicles may perhaps be explained when we know the need to which they are a response. This might also resolve much of our obvious perplexity.

In any case, we can see one thing from Chronicles. The preaching of the prophets and Dtr have had a salutary effect on post-exilic piety; the various forms of syncretism or idolatry have either disppeared or have been absorbed in such a way as no longer to be recognizable. The rule of Israel is theocratic and the great social injustices seem to have been overcome within the community, the centre of which is now the cult at Jerusalem. To some the price paid for this will seem to be high: orthodoxy and spiritual tranquillity have been attained through the introduction of certain forms of legalism which were developing while Israel was becoming a diaspora. Here too, however, a healthy balance betwen the two things is easier to look for than to obtain.

BIBLIOGRAPHY

Commentaries

W.Rothstein and J.Hänel, KAT, 1927 (I Chron. only); W.Rudolph, HKAT, 1955; K.Galling, ATD, 1958; H.Cazelles, JB, ³1961; J.M.Myers, AB, 1965; L.Randellini, SacBib, 1966; F.Michaeli, CAT, 1967; P.R.Ackroyd, TBC, 1973; R.J.Coggins, Cambridge 1976; H.G.M.Williamson, NCB, 1982.

Monographs and synopses

M.Noth, *The Chronicler's History*, Sheffield 1987, ET of pp.1-110 of his *Überlieferungsgeschichtliche Studien* I, Halle ²1957 (still a basic work). Cf. P.Vannutelli, *Libri Synoptici Veteris Testamenti*, Rome 1931-34, and recently J.Kegler and M.Augustin, *Synopse zum Chronistischen Geschichtswerk*, Frankfurt 1984 (for a comparison with Samuel and Kings, with LXX and Vulgate); T.Willi, *Die Chronik als Auslegung*, Göttingen 1972 (a study of the hermeneutical principles underlying the parallels with Samuel and Kings). There is a bibliographical study by E.Jenni, 'Aus der Literatur zur chronistischen Geschichtsschreibung', *TR* 45, 1980, 97-108.

1. S.Japhet, 'The Supposed Common Authorship of Chronicles and Ezra-Nehemiah Investigated Anew', *VT* 18, 1968, 330-71, produced significant arguments that Chronicles, Ezra and Nehemiah could not have been written by the same author; this theory was then endorsed by H.G.M.Williamson in his commentary and elsewhere (see below). Cf. W.G.E.Watson, 'Archaic Elements in the Language of Chronicles', *Bibl* 53, 1972, 191-207; R.Mosis, *Die Theologie des chronistischen Geschichtswerkes*, Freiburg im Breisgau 1973; J.Goldingay, 'The Chronicler as a Theologian', *BTB* 5, 1975, 99-126; J.D.Newsome Jr, 'Towards a New Understanding of the Chronicler and

his Purpose', *JBL* 94, 1975, 201-17; R.North, 'Does Archaeology prove Chronicles' Sources?', in *A Light unto my Path. Studies in honor of J.M.Myers*, Philadelphia 1975, 375-401; P.R.Ackroyd, 'The Chronicler as Exegete', *JSOT* 2, 1977, 2-32; R.L.Braun, 'A Reconsideration of the Chronicler's Attitude towards the North', *JBL* 96, 1977, 59-62; H.G.M.Williamson, *Israel in the Books of Chronicles*, Cambridge 1977; id., 'Sources and Redaction in the Chronicler's Genealogy of Judah', *JBL* 78, 1979, 351-9; S.Japhet, 'Conquest and Settlement in Chronicles', *JBL* 98, 1979, 205-218; R.L.Brown, 'Chronicles, Ezra and Nehemiah; Theology and Literary History', *SVT* 39, 1979, 52-64; M.Saebø, 'Messianism in Chronicles', *HorBTh* 2, 1980, 85-109; J.P.Weinberg, 'Die Natur im Weltbild des Chronisten', *VT* 31, 1981, 324-45; id., 'Die sozialen Gruppen im Weltbild des Chronisten', *ZAW* 98, 1986, 72-95; D.J.McCarthy, 'Covenant and Law in Chronicles', *CBQ* 44, 1982, 25-44; M.P.Graham, 'A Connection proposed betwen II Chr.24, 26 and Ezra 9-10', *ZAW* 97, 1985, 256-8; S.L.McKenzie, *The Chronicler's Use of the Deuteronomistic History*, Atlanta 1985. The 1979 article by S.Japhet is important; it follows from this that the Chronicler did not know of an Israelite 'conquest' of Canaan but seems to presuppose a residence there from time immemorial. Cf. also S.Japhet, 'Historical Reliability of Chronicles', *JSOT* 33, 1985, 83-107; W.Johnstone, 'Guilt and Atonement: the Theme of 1 and 2 Chronicles', in *A Word in Season. Essays... William McKane*, Sheffield 1986, 113-38; J.P.Weinberg, 'Die soziale Gruppe im Weltbild des Chronisten', *ZAW* 98, 1986, 72-96; J.Hausmann, *Israels Rest*, Stuttgart 1987, 5-23, shows that politically speaking the Chronicler wants an 'all Israel' which would also include the north; L.C.Allen, 'Kerygmatic Units in I and II Chronicles', *JSOT* 41, 1988, 21-36; U.Kellermann, 'Anmerkungen zum Verständnis der Tora in den chronistischen Schriften', *BN* 42, 1988, 49-82, shows that Chronicles' understanding of the Torah is a continuation of that of Deuteronomy and Dtr. On a linguistic plane there seems to be no possibility of distinguishing between the author of Chronicles and the author of Ezra-Nehemiah, cf. M.A.Thorveit, 'Linguistic Analysis and the Question of Authorship in Chronicles, Ezra and Nehemiah', *VT* 32, 1982, 201-16; D.Talshir, 'A Reinvestigation of the Linguistic Relationship between Chronicles and Ezra-Nehemiah', *VT* 38, 1988, 165-93.

43

EZRA AND NEHEMIAH

1. Character and content

The conclusion of II Chron.36 is identical with the beginning of Ezra; this fact is usualy interpreted as a sign of the continuity between the two works, despite the fact that Ezra and Nehemiah precede Chronicles in the Hebrew Bible. In the LXX, which has two more books of Ezra, the deutero-canonical III Ezra becomes I Esdras, while the canonical Ezra-Nehemiah is caled II Esdras.

The division is simple, as in Chronicles. In Ezra 1-6 we have the account of the restoration down to the rebuilding of the temple, events to which Haggai and Zechariah also refer, as we have seen. In Ezra 7 – Neh.13 we have an account of the two persons in question from their arrival from Persia: the reforms they introduced, the difficulties they encountered, the religious and moral situation prevailing in Judah, and so on. In language, content and theology the two works are usually thought to belong to the tradition of the Chronicler, though they have also drawn on sources contemporaneous with the events, which we shall be examining in due course. This theory has been challenged by Sara Japhet and H.G.M.Williamson (for whose writings see the bibliography to the previous chapter; we shall be discussing their view in due course). Ezra and Nehemiah share with Chronicles an interest in the cult, the priesthood, genealogy, the levitical families and so on.

2. Sources

What material formed the basis for the composition of the present text of the two biblical books? This is a complex question. At the very beginning, in Ezra 1.1-4.5, it is impossible to establish whether we have a creation of the redactors. This possibility arises particularly in connection with the numbers, which are inflated and therefore out of touch with reality. It does not in fact appear possible that in 538 and in the years immediately following, a little after the edict of liberation promulgated by Cyrus concerning the deported populations, such a vast population movement could have taken place before there had been time to reorganize the civil administration, at least in Palestine, if not throughout the empire. On the other hand, the list of the sacred vessels of the temple restored by Cyrus could well have been compiled at the moment of liberation and delivered to the rightful owners, on the basis of the inventory existing in the Babylonian administration, without this in the least implying that they were transported to Palestine. One solution to the first problem might be that the list of those returning does not refer to 539-38, but to 520, when another group moved from Babylon to Judah, as Zech.6.9 informs us, and began the rebuilding of the temple.

4.6-6.18 are written in Aramaic; as in the case of Daniel this is imperial Aramaic. For a long time the text has been thought to be a memorandum sent by the Jews in their defence to Artaxerxes I Longimanus, to reaffirm their loyalty to their new imperial lord and to defend themselvs against the opportunist calumnies which were being circulated by the neighbouring peoples on their account. This would have been produced on the basis of material dating from the time of Cyrus onwards. However, this theory finds no support in the facts; there are contradictions in the supposed 'defence' (e.g. 4.24 with 5.16). Noth thought that there were two original documents here, which were fused together at a later stage: one from the time of Artaxerxes, mentioned above, concerned with the rebuilding of Jerusalem, and the other from the time of Darius I Hystaspes, concerned with the rebuilding of the temple. The redactors would then have combined them and confused them, because of the affinity of the material and because three kings of Persia each bore the names of Darius and Artaxerxes. Be this as it may, even now scholars are divided on the essential authenticity of this documentation (some of those who consider it authentic would not, however, rule out redactional intervention). Whereas E.J.Bickerman in his classic 1946 study, F.M.Cross and S.Talmon are in favour; A.H.J.Gunneweg already offers such a complex explanation of the authenticity as to render it doubtful: O.Kaiser*, 180, firmly disputes the authenticity, and he has collected together the views of other scholars on the subject.

In chs.7-10 of Ezra and Neh.8 we have what have been called the 'memoirs of Ezra'. On these, scholars are divided. M.Noth, the latest of a number of scholars, thinks that they are the work of the Chronicler, either drawing on contemporary Aramaic sources or his own free creation. Other scholars, however, down to W.Rudolph, have thought that these are real memoirs or, probably better, a memorandum composed by Ezra in his capacity as local commissioner for Jewish religious affairs (but cf. below, § 4). The alternation of the first and third persons has been considered an indication of the validity of this theory: first person in Ezra 7.27-9.15, third person in 7.1-26; 10.1-44; Neh.8.1-8. However, as S.Mowinckel has demonstrated, this is a common stylistic element which also appears in other writings from the ancient Near East, so it cannot be considered a deciding factor.

In Neh.1-7,10; 12.17-43; 13 we have a collection which has been called the 'memoirs of Nehemiah'; he too was an official at the Persian court (but cf. below, § 4). However, here we have a desire more for self-glorification than to inform the court. In favour of this is the list of works completed under his leadership: the rebuilding of the walls of Jerusalem and other lesser acts. Be this as it may, the texts suggest two missions of Nehemiah, the first lasting twelve years and the second a little less, quite apart from the explicit chronological details. It is possible that these 'memoirs' have preserved the lists to which I have aleady referred (and that would explain the duplicate Ezra 2/Neh.7), while Neh.3 also gives a list of names of the workers used in the rebuilding of the walls of Jerusalem. These 'memoirs' too, however, have gone through many redactions, not excluding their embellishment with 'novellistic ornaments' (Kaiser*), so that it is no longer possible to recover the original text even in part.

Finally, in Ezra 9 and Neh.13 we have the problem of foreign wives and their expulsion, with which we were concerned above (30.2c).

3. Chronology

The problem of the chronology of the protagonists of the two books is also complex, this time historically. No satisfactory solution has yet been found, and here we are moving only in the realm of hypothesis.

According to the two books, Ezra arrived at Jerusalem before Nehemiah in the seventh year of Artaxerxes I, that is in 458, whereas Nehemiah will have arrived in the twentieth year of the same king, i.e. 445 (cf. Ezra 7.7; Neh.2.1). This theory has traditionally been maintained down the centuries and apparently presents no difficulties; it was put in doubt for the first time with arguments of considerable weight by the Belgian scholar A.van Hoonacker in 1890 and in the years up to the end of the last century. That starting point is the fact mentioned in Ezra 10.6 that Ezra is accompanied by a certain Jehohanan ben Eliashib; but Eliashib, whether father or grandfather of Ezra's contemporary, is clearly connected with Nehemiah and his ministry, which would suggest that Nehemiah, and not Ezra, was the first to come to Jerusalem, and did so half a century earlier. In other words, in fact the two will always have worked separately and not together as in the traditional scheme: they were only made contemporaries by the redactors; they were not really so.

This theory immediately enjoyed considerable success among scholars, though from the moment it was presented it inevitably caused a great dispute. There were also other elements in its favour which I list briefly:

(a) Nehemiah never mentions Ezra's work: a strange omission, even if this is an argument from silence.

(b) When Nehemiah arrives, the city seems to be sparsely populated and the walls have not yet been rebuilt, details which conflict with the account in Ezra.7-10.

(c) In Neh.5.15 Nehemiah's predecessors are blamed for the disorder reigning in the city; this is somewhat strange, to say the least, if we put Ezra among these predecessors and if the critical situation is the result of a full thirteen years of his rule.

(d) In Ezra 9.9 it is asserted that God allows the people to rebuild the ruined temple and then he gives the people a wall: but we know that the walls of Jerusalem (and this is what must be meant here) were rebuilt under Nehemiah. A spiritual interpretation of 'the wall' is not convincing since it has an artificial character and does not conform to the Hebrew spirit, nor can we invoke Zech.2.9, since this passage announces the situation in Jerusalem in an eschatological age.

(e) Under Nehemiah, the country is dominated by some local noblemen, a feature which does not appear in the texts dealing with Ezra.

(f) Neh.12.22 mentions a series of high priests, and it is here that the problem of Jehohanan ben Eliashib arises, which was mentioned above. In 10.6 he was a contemporary of Ezra, while according to the Elephantine papyri (cf. Appendix 2 below) he would be dated towards 410 BCE!

Of course, taken individually, none of these arguments is particularly strong, and those who would maintain the tradition can obviously call attention to the following points: (a) and (e) are arguments from silence and do not prove anything; (b) does not prove anything, because even so sparsely populated a city could succeed in bringing together an assembly of a considerable size if the population was disposed to collaborate; (c) can be explained by saying Ezra simply did not succeed in eliminating all the abuses, while (d) has recently been explained by J.Morgenstern with the hypothesis of a second destruction of the city following a second rebellion. Such a situation would seem to underlie the conversation reported in Neh.1.3; 2.3 where there is a reference to the precarious situation of Jerusalem, which is in ruins with its gates consumed by fire. Now if this were a description of the city as it had remained from the time of the rebuilding of the temple, there would be nothing sensational about the news, but it is the case if we suppose a new destruction. Finally, (f) proves little or nothing, since there could have been different priests of the same name: the incidence of papponomy seems to have been frequent (Cross).

For this reason scholars are still divided: G.Ricciotti, J.Pedersen, H.H.Rowley, N.H.Snaith, M.Noth, W.Rudolph, P.Sacchi and G.Widengren put the arrival of Ezra after Nehemiah (and the seventh year of Artaxerxes would then refer not to Artaxerxes I but to Artaxerxes II, which would bring us down to the beginning of the fourth century); a few – Y.Aharoni, D.Kellermann and F.M.Cross – are in favour of the traditional sequence, finding the alternative date assigned to Ezra too low.

A third solution has been proposed but does not seem to have found much of a following. The celebrations mentioned in Neh.1-7 seem to be an integral part of a sabbatical year and its liturgy. We know the dates of at least two of these, 164/3 (cf. I Macc.6.49) and 38/7 (cf. Josephus, *Antiquities* 12, 378; 15,7). It is thus relatively easy, by calculating backwards, to arrive at a sabbatical year celebrated in the time of Artaxerxes I Longimanus; this date falls in 430-29, that is, in the thirty-seventh year of the monarch's reign. It is then necessary to suppose an error in the dating: instead of reading 'In the seventh year of Artaxerxes' we should read 'In the thirty-seventh year of Artaxerxes'. In this case Ezra would indeed have come after Nehemiah, but not so late as a connection with Artaxerxes II might suggest. The greatest defect of this theory is obviously the fact that it not only requires a textual emendation at a vital point but is also based on the celebration of the sabbatical year, a festival the origins and celebrations of which are still shrouded in mystery. In fact we have no proof that it was ever celebrated before the time of the Maccabees.

A fourth quite radical way of solving the chronological problem and that of the relation between Ezra and Nehemiah would be to assume that Ezra never existed, but is the creation of later speculation. This theory was first proposed at the end of the last century and at the beginning of this, and has recently been revived by G.Garbini. According to him the book of Ezra is a creation of the first half of the second century BCE. The argument is well worth exploring, especially as it runs against today's consensus. It leaves open one question: what about Nehemiah?

4. The legal status of Ezra and Nehemiah in the Persian administration

Another disputed problem which is far from being solved is that of the legal status of the two protagonists of the book in the Persian administration, with which they obviously had contact. There is a degree of unanimity among scholars that they were officials at the Persian court (cf. above, § 2). However, without going into details which are of little value in understanding the book, I would cite the conclusions reached by R.North, which seem to take the discussion a good deal further forward:

(*a*) Nehemiah was never governor, since the text of Neh.5.14, on which the theory is based, is corrupt. The term *peḥah* = 'satrap' is not to be found in the Massoretic text, and has been reconstructed only on the basis of LXX[B-A] and the Vulgate; it is also completely isolated in the two books.

(*b*) Nor was his adversary Sanballat governor, although he was an important official.

(*c*) Nehemiah was only a page at the Persian court, and in Judah he exercised the functions of a master-builder.

(*d*) Ezra was only a priest and a scribe, with functions which were exclusively religious and never political.

(*e*) Neither Ezra nor those involved in rebuilding the temple had unlimited financial resources at their disposal.

(*f*) Ezra was never given any form of authority; he was an ordinary subject who enjoyed special favours from his sovereign.

BIBLIOGRAPHY

Commentaries

W.Rudolph, HAT, 1949; A.Gelin, JB [2]1960; B.M.Pelaia, SacBib, 1957; K.Galling, ATD, 1954; J.M.Myers, AB, 1965; F.Michaeli, CAT, 1967;

L.H.Brockington, NCB, 1969; P.R.Ackroyd, TBC, 1973; R.J.Coggins, Cambridge, 1976; F.C.Fensham, NICOT, 1982; A.H.J.Gunneweg, Ezra 1985, Nehemiah 1987. A bibliographical study has been made by R.W.Klein, 'Ezra and Nehemiah in Recent Studies', in *Magnalia Dei, Essays in Memory of G.E.Wright*, Garden City, New York 1976, 361-76.

1-2. A.Van Hoonacker, 'Néhémie et Esdras: une nouvelle hypothèse sur la chronologie de l'époque de la restauration', *Muséon* 9, 1980, 151-84, 317-51, 389-401 (published the same year as an extract); M.Noth, *The Chronicler's History*, ET Sheffield 1987 (see bibliography on previous section); A.S.Kapelrud, *The Question of Authorship in the Ezra Narrative*, Oslo 1944; H.Cazelles, 'La mission d'Esdras', *VT* 4, 1954, 113-40. For Nehemiah see U.Kellermann, *Nehemia: Quellen, Überlieferung und Geschichte*, BZAW 102, 1967. Cf. also S.Talmon, 'Ezra and Nehemiah (Books and Men)', *IDB-SV* 1976, 317-28; A.H.J.Gunneweg, 'Zur Interpretation der Bücher Esra-Nehemia', *SVT* 32, 1981, 146-61; id., 'Die aramäische und hebräische Erzählung über die nachexilische Restauration. Ein Vergleich', *ZAW* 92, 1982, 299-302; S.Japhet, 'Sheshbazzar and Zerubbabel. Against the Background of the Historical and Religious Tendencies', ibid., 66-98, 218-29; R.Zadok, 'Remarks on Ezra-Nehemiah', ibid., 296-8; W.Schottroff, 'Zur Sozialgeschichte Israel in der Perserzeit', *VuF* 27.1, 1981, 46-68; H.G.M.Williamson, 'The Composition of Ezra I-IV', *JTS* 33, 1983, 1-30; E.Cortese, 'I problemi di Esdra-Nehemia (e Cron.)', *BeO* 25, 1983, 11-19: M.E.Stone, 'The Metamorphosis of Ezra', *JTS* 33, 1982, 1-18. For relations with the Pentateuch cf. C.Houtman, 'Ezra and the Law: Observations on the Supposed Relation between Ezra and the Pentateuch', *OTS* 21, 1982, 91-115; R.Rendtorff, 'Esdra und das Gesetz', *ZAW* 96, 1984, 165-84; for the marriage legislation cf. D.Mossmann, 'Ezra's Marriage Reform: Israel Redefined', *BTB* 9, 1979, 32-8; for relations with the prophets cf. J.G.McConville, 'Ezra-Nehemiah and the Fulfilment of Prophecy', *VT* 36, 1986, 205-24. For the thought of the two books cf. F.C.Fensham, 'Some Theological and Religious Aspects in Ezra-Nehemiah', *JNWSL* 11, 1983, 59-68; D.J.A.Clines, *Ezra, Nehemiah, Esther*, London and Grand Rapids 1984; P.Sacchi, 'Testi palestinesi anteriori al 200 a.C.', *RiBib* 34, 1986, 183-204; H.G.M.Williamson, *Ezra and Nehemiah*, Sheffield 1987; D.L.Emery, 'Ezra 4. Is Josephus Right After All?', *JNWSL* 13, 1987, 33-44; C.T.Begg, 'Ben Sirach's Non-Mention of Ezra', *BN* 42, 1988, 14-18; T.Krüger, 'Esra 1-6: Struktur und Konzept', *BN* 41, 1988, 65-75.

3. J.Morgenstern, 'Jerusalem – 485 BC', *HUCA* 27, 1956, 101-79; 28, 1957, 15-47; 31, 1960, 1-29; id., 'Further Light from the Book of Isaiah upon the Catastrophe of 485 BC', *HUCA* 37, 1966, 1-28. For the third suggestion on the dating see A.Pavlovský, 'Die Chronologie der Tätigkeit Esdras. Versuch einer neuen Lösung', *Bibl* 38, 1957, 273-305, 428-56. Y.Aharoni, *The Land of the Bible*, London 1957, 358, and U.Kellermann, 'Erwägungen zum Problem der Esradatierung', *ZAW* 80, 1968, 55-87, support the traditional chronology with solid arguments. Cf. also K.Galling, *Studien zur*

Geschichte Israels im persischen Zeitalter, Tübingen 1964, chs.2, 3, 4, 6, 7; W.T.In der Smitten, 'Nehemias Parteigänger', *BiOr* 29, 1972, 155-7; C.G.Tuland, 'Ezra-Nehemiah or Nehemiah-Ezra?', *AUSS* 12, 1974, 47-62; F.M.Cross, 'A Reconstruction of the Judean Restoration', *JBL* 94, 1975, 4-18 (the two last-mentioned support the traditional order, for different reasons, but cf. against this G.Widengren in J.H.Hayes and J.M.Miller, *Israelite and Judaean History*, London and Philadelphia 1977, 503ff.). For the theory that Ezra never existed cf. G.Garbini, *History and Ideology in Ancient Israel*, ET London and New York 1988, ch.13 (which also has an exhaustive bibliography).

For the 'memoirs' cf. S.Mowinckel, 'Erwägungen zum chronistichen Geschichtswerk', *TLZ* 85, 1960, 1-8; id., *Studien zu dem Buche Ezra-Nehemia*, Oslo, Vol.I, 1964; II-III, 1965. For the whole problem cf. finally H.Jagersma, *A History of Israel in the Old Testament Period*, London and Philadelphia 1982, 201ff.

4. C.R.North, 'Civil Authority in Ezra', in *Studi in onore di E.Volterra*, Milan 1971, 377-404.

PART SIX

THE DEUTERO-CANONICAL BOOKS

GENERAL BIBLIOGRAPHY ON THE
DEUTERO-CANONICAL BOOKS

1. R.H.Charles (ed.), *Apocrypha and Pseudepigrapha of the Old Testament*, 2 vols., Oxford 1913 (text and commentary on all the relevant works)
2. R.H.Pfeiffer, *History of New Testament Times*, New York 1949
3. L.H.Brockington, *A Critical Introduction to the Apocrypha*, London 1961
4. L.Rost, *Einleitung in die alttestamentlichen Apokryphen und Pseudepigraphen*, Heidelberg 1971
4. The Roman Catholic *Introductions* listed in the general bibliography and those of Eissfeldt*, F.Michelini-Tocci*, G.Fohrer* and G.Stemberger*
5. H.Jagersma, *A History of Israel from Alexander the Great to Bar Kochba*, London and Philadelphia 1985

44

TOBIT

1. Characteristics and content

Apart from a few fragments discovered at Qumran, the book has
been transmitted only in Greek. It bears the title 'Book of the Words
of Tobit', which is an exact translation of the Hebrew *sēper dibrē tōbīt*;
the phrase could also be rendered 'Acts of Tobit', which would be
an apt title, considering that the work is largely narrative. The
Vulgate has simply *Liber Tobiae*. The book contains a series of
narratives centred on the persons of Tobit and his son Tobias. The
Vulgate uses the same name for father and son, and is followed by
many modern translations; both figures are said to have been
deported from the northern kingdom in 734.

We have three recensions of the text.

(*a*) That attested by codex א or Sinaiticus) of the LXX, compiled
in the fourth or fifth century CE, is probably the best; it has been
confirmed by the surviving fragments of the Old Latin. It served as
a basis for the Vulgate translation and for retrotranslations into
Hebrew and Aramaic;

(*b*) That attested by codex B (or Vaticanus) and A (or Alexandrinus) of the LXX existing before the discovery of Sinaiticus. The
Syriac, Coptic, Ethiopian and Armenian translations are dependent
on this, as is another retrotranslation into Hebrew. There are some
scholars who continue to regard it as better than Sinaiticus;

(*c*) A third recension is attested by some fragments of a Syriac
translation and some papyri from Oxyrhyncus; it is certainly later
than the two preceding texts, from which it seems to have been
compiled. We cannot go into the complex problem of the variants
here, for which I refer the reader to the critical edition.

Tobit is naturally divided into four parts (or into seven if we divide
the second part into two and the third part into three):

1. The prologue (1.3-3.17) tells of the vicissitudes of Tobit and his
family during the exile, where he remains faithful to the law, the

faith and the customs of his people; leaving aside life at the court, this is a theme which is reminiscent of that of Daniel and his three companions. Even before deportation to Assyria, however, the group had been opposed to the laxity of their compatriots in the religious and ethical spheres, and were thinking of the possibility of moving to Judah, where the spiritual situation seemed better. However, the deportation (cf. my *History*, X.4.1ff.) made these plans fruitless.

One night Tobit, having buried the body of one of his compatriots who had been assassinated in the street, had to remain outside because of the ritual impurity which he had contracted. While he was sleeping in the open, the droppings of some birds fell into his eyes, making him completely blind. The doctors did not know how to cure the illness and Tobit was soon reduced from prosperity to complete destitution.

Without warning, the scene of the narrative shifts to Ecbatana in Media, where a pious Hebrew woman by the name of Sarah was living. She had been married seven times, but each time had been made a widow before the marriage could be consummated, because of a demon caled Asmodeus who regularly broke in and killed her husbands on the first night. Public opinion made the woman responsible for this situation. Tobit on the one hand and Sarah on the other turned to God in prayer and he sent the angel Raphael to them, to cure Tobit and to free Sarah, who in due course became Tobias's wife.

2. Chapters 4-9 show Tobias' journey to Media, whither he had been sent by his father to recover a sum of money which had been deposited there. In ch.4 Tobit gives Tobias some advice and in ch.5 he entrusts him with the documents relating to the deposit. Tobias leaves, and on the way meets the angel Raphael in Hebrew dress. The young man takes him into service and the two go on their way. While Tobias is washing in the Tigris a fish tries to devour him (LXX[B-A] and Vulgate, whole; LXX only a leg), but the young man succeeds in catching it; on the advice of the young man he keeps the heart, liver and gall of the creature, which might be useful as medicine. When they arrive at Ecbatana they spend the night in Sarah's father's house and Raphael begins negotiations with a view to a marriage between the pair (ch.6). They are married, chase the demon away by means of the smell of the liver and heart of the fish, which they burn, and finally Sarah's marriage is consummated without incident. Meanwhile Raphael recovers the sum of money to save time (ch.9).

3. Chapters 10-13 describe the return of the young couple to

Nineveh. Tobias applies the gall from the fish (a medicine which is also known elsewhere in antiquity), to his father's eyes and cures him, and after that Raphael takes his leave without revealing his true identity and ascends to heaven, In ch.13 Tobit intones a psalm and praises God for his great works.

4. An epilogue (ch.14) shows Tobit dying at the ripe age of 99 or 127 years (depending on the recension), having given instructions to his son Tobias.

2. History and literature

To speak of the historicity or even of the legendary character of what is evidently a pious novella seems out of place; Raphael himself in 12.19 reveals to Tobit that his own presence is only a vision. On the other hand, the author of the book is concerned to establish some historical synchronisms which are an attempt to add verisimilitude to the narrative in 1.1. We have a reference to the deportation of Naphthali during 734 (II Kings 15.29), but this in fact took place under Tiglath-pileser III and not under Shalmaneser V, as the author supposes. Here we have a confusion of dates: 734, if we accept that the deportation happened under the former of the two kings; 722-21, if we suppose that it happened under the second. The last note contained in the work is about the fall of Nineveh at the hands of Cyaxares, king of Media, in 612 (two variants have Nabopolassar and Ahasuerus, i.e. Xerxes I) (14.15). Thus despite the preoccupations of the author or redactor, the chronology is far from precise and presupposes, among other things, a much longer life for Tobit than that indicated in 14.1. The supernatural and visionary element is another factor of historical uncertainty, but to rob the book of it would be to deprive it of its point, namely faith in divine providence which intervenes directly whenever it is needed and which brings everything to a good end, despite difficulties of every kind.

The author is familiar with the scriptures, which he calls 'the law and the prophets', an expression which is also well attested in the New Testament; it thus seems that he presupposes the existence of something like a canon, which puts him at a relatively late date, even if it is earlier than that of the Maccabees. The Pentateuch appears as the 'law of Moses' (7.13) or the 'book of Moses' (7.12), designations which, as we saw at the beginning of Part Two (above, 7.2a), are attested from Chronicles onwards. The 'golden rule', which is found in the New Testament (Matt.7.12), is presented in its negative form in 4.15. Throughout the work we find features classified as 'the tradition of the elders', sometimes Jewish traditions which were first taught orally and then codified in the Mishnah in the second century BCE; however, there is no lack of heterodox customs or even customs prohibited in scripture: in 4.17 we have an offering on a grave, a practice expressly forbidden in Deut.26.14 (cf. Hos.9.4; Isa.8.19; Jer.16.3) and later in Ecclus.30.18. Of course this kind of practice continued for many years in popular piety, but it is surprising to see it praised here rather than condemned. In 5.16 Tobias and Raphael are accompanied by a dog which then follows them in 11.4. However, in Deut.23.18 and Ecclus.13.18,22 the animal is considered unclean, as it still is today by Moslems in the Near East, where the word is a serious insult, so it is not surprising to find the mention of the animal omitted in the Aramaic version. On the other hand the author draws on the moral precepts of the Pentateuch and the prophets: in 2.6 he cites Amos 8.10 with remarkable exactitude; in 14.4 he cites Nahum 3.7 and Zeph.2.13f. with reference to the imminent fall of Nineveh (LXX[B-A] wrongly has Jonah instead). Moreover, throughout the book the author shows himself to be quite familiar with the content of the prophetic books. Again, in 1.21f.; 2.10; 11.18 and 14.10 there is mention of the oriental sage Ahikar, to whom I have already referred (above, 35.1). This is an oriental wisdom novella centred on the court of Sennacherib; the *terminus post quem* of the work is thus the end of the eighth and beginning of the seventh century, and a complete copy of it has been found in Elephantine, as we shall see in Appendix 2 below. Finally, the narrative of Tobit is interwoven with features from folklore and from fairy tales. It is therefore easy to come to the conclusion that the work is dependent on the Pentateuch and the prophets for its theological formation, while the rest of the material belongs to the world of wisdom, of folklore and popular piety. It would therefore be more precise to call the book a historical romance, in the sense that its characters may very well have existed in reality; however, the narrative seeks not so much to recount their fortunes as to edify the reader by their example. It may be said that this aim is fully achieved, since the narrative abounds in original touches, which are very attractive, and is a unique instance of its kind, even if the traditional themes of Jewish faith tend to become secondary and to be replaced by the observance of the law and the prophets (not too strict in the case of the popular piety which we have examined).

3. Problems of language and origin

(a) Origen did not know of the existence of a Hebrew text of Tobit, and affirmed that the book was not used among the Jews (*Epist. ad Africanum*, Migne, PG 11, 80); in his prologue to the work, Jerome knew of an Aramaic version from which he translated (perhaps belonging to the same tradition as the Qumran fragments), but his information cannot now be verified and we cannot exclude the possibility of a retrotranslation from the Greek. However, scholars agree that Tobit had a Semitic archetype, in either Hebrew or Aramaic; in fact we have a series of semitisms, the presence of which would be impossible if the work had been originally composed in Greek. In 1.11 we have the expression 'my soul' for 'I'; in 3.7 'someone... not' for 'no one'; in 3.10 'I am the only one of my father...' for 'I am his only daughter'; in 3.6 (LXX*) 'the face of the earth' for 'the (surface of the) earth'; in 13.13 the 'sons of the just' to indicate individuals belonging in this category; in 12.15 (LXX*) 'stand in the presence of' for 'serve', and so on. Of course one might think of a diaspora Jew writing in Semitic-type Greek or deliberately adopting a style of this kind to confer greater authority on his words; however, the theory that we have a more or less literal translation into Greek of a Hebrew or Aramaic text seems more probable. Scholars are in general inclined to accept the latter possibility.

(b) When we seek the place of origin and date of the book, an examination shows that we must immediately rule out the two countries mentioned in it, Assyria and Persia. Information about them is either vague or inaccurate; the Assyrian people and dates mentioned in 1.1 and 14.15 present problems in the different variants which are attested, and the corrections which we find in some cases seem to have been made with the aim of remedying these difficulties. They are therefore of no value for the historian since they contradict the critical principle of the *lectio difficilior* (cf. above, 3.3). The geography of the book also presents problems; the journey from Assyria to Media and Persia evidently reflects situations more appropriate to the Persian period and perhaps even to the Macedonian era: they certainly do not come from the eighth and seventh centuries BCE. The date of the book cannot therefore be earlier than the fourth century and probably should be brought down to the end of the third century or even to the second. It is debatable whether the origin of the book is to be sought in oriental Judaism of the diaspora in Babylon and adjoining countries (and the geographical information, for all its problems, points in this direction) or in western

Palestinian Judaism, as is suggested by the insistence on the temple and the elements connected with the canon. However, no definitive statement can be made to resolve this argument.

4. Thought

Pfeiffer has defined the message of Tobit in succinct terms: 'By example and by precept the Book of Tobit inculcates the noble religious and moral principles of Judaism in the first third of the second century BC' (*History of New Testament Times*, 278). The variants attested throughout the work do not detract in any way from this definition. At the centre of Tobit's religious thought stands the temple (1.4; cf. 13.10f.; 14.5 etc.). The problem of the observance of the food laws which has already occupied us in the book of Daniel is typical of the Judaism of the Hellenistic period, which was in contact with a paganism that was somewhat intolerant in this sphere; this was particularly the case with diaspora Judaism. The book is also distinguished by a firm personal piety (4.5) and a universalistic vision (13.13; 14.6); the law has marked ethical dimensions (2.11-14, etc.). There are a large number of prayers, contrary to what we find in the other books of the Hebrew Bible (3.1-6, 16; 12.25, etc.).

BIBLIOGRAPHY

Commentaries

G.Priero, SacBib, 1953; R.Pautrel, JB, ²1957; J.C.Dancy, Cambridge, 1972.
Bibliographies and critical studies: J.Gamberoni, *Die Auslegung des Buches Tobias*, Munich 1969; F.Vattioni, 'Studi e note sul libro di Tobia', *Aug* 10, 1970, 241-84.
2. W.von Soden, 'Fischgalle als Heilsmittel für Augen', *AfO* 21, 1966, 81f. (= his *Bibel und alter Orient*, BZAW 162, 1985, 76ff.); A.A.DiLella, 'The Deuteronomic Background of the Farewell Discourse in Tob.14.2-11', *CBQ* 41, 1979, 380-9; P.Deselaers, *Das Buch Tobit*, Fribourg CH 1982. For the Greek text see J.D.Thomas, 'The Greek Text of Tobit', *JBL* 91, 1972, 463-71; for the book generally cf. H.C.Brichto, 'Kin, Cult, Land and Afterlife. A Biblical Complex', *HUCA* 44, 1973, 1-54, esp. 28f. (for Tob.4.17; Deut.26.14). For Ahikar in Tobit cf. L.Ruppert, 'Zur Funktion der Achikar Notizen im Buch Tobias', *BZ* 20, 1976, 232-7, and the critical edition by

J.M.Lindenberger, *The Aramaic Proverbs of Ahiqar*, Baltimore and London 1983.
3b. J.T.Milik, 'La patrie de Tobie', *RB* 73, 1966, 522-30.

45

JUDITH

1. Characteristics and content

Judith is the name of the heroine of this book; by means of a violent act, which proves to be the only way out, she succeeds in saving her city from capture. Given such a theme, it is not surprising that the work has nationalistic tendencies of the kind that we have met in the book of Esther.

The book can be sub-divided into three parts: (*a*) chs. 1-7; (*b*) 8.1-16,20; (*c*) 16.21-25.

(*a*) To begin with, we have a confused historical reference: Nebuchadnezzar, king of Assyria (sic) and Arphaxad, king of Media (1.1), are at war (1.5). Nebuchadnezzar occupies Media and then turns westwards, conquering a series of places which are for the most part unknown to us, and only Israel resists him (chs.4-7), having recently returned from Babylon (4.3; 5.19). Holofernes, commander of the Assyrian troops, then attacks Israel with the aid of Edom and Moab and lays siege to Bethulia (a place unknown to us), succeeding in cutting off its water supply.

(*b*) Judith, a descendant of Jacob (!), chides her fellow-citizens for their lack of faith and their use of venal means to save themselves from the imminent danger (8.11-24). She had been left a widow some years earlier, and is beautiful, pious and rich. The young widow makes a plan to seduce Holofernes and goes into the camp of the besiegers accompanied by a servant girl who carries a basket containing ritually pure food, so as to avoid all contact with pagan fare. The general (ch.12) is bewitched by the woman and holds a banquet for her; at the end, when they are left alone, Judith succeeds in cutting his head off. She gives it to the servant girl, who carries it to Bethulia in the basket. The inhabitants then hang the head on the walls and attack the Assyrians, who are disconcerted by the disappearance of their commander and are defeated. Judith sings a hymn of thanksgiving.

(*c*) In the last part of the book Judith lives the life of a pious widow faithful to the memory of her dead husband.

2. Text, date and historicity

Contemporary Roman Catholic scholars have no hesitation in admitting the obvious historical and geographical difficulties presented by the work, usually limiting themselves to giving more or less probable reasons for this disconcerting phenomenon. Some suggest textual corruption. On the other hand, we have other parallels in the Hebrew Bible, even if they are not so obvious, in Esther, Daniel and Tobit (though, as we have seen, this last work makes no claim to historicity), which bear witness to an equally approximate or sometimes inaccurate knowledge of the events of a remote past. Jerome already supposed that this was a similar instance. The author evidently wants to describe events which he puts between the eighth and the sixth century in terms of his own time, presenting the whole affair as an allegory of the triumph of Israel, with God's help, over the assaults of the pagans.

The most obvious inaccuracies and inconsistencies in the historical sphere seem to be as follows (I indicate them following the basic study made by A.M.Dubarle). First of all, there is the question of Nebuchadnezzar of Assyria and Arphaxad of Media in 1.1, then the presentation of the Babylonian exile as a past event in 4.3 and 5.19. The claims to divine honours made by these monarchs in 3.8; 6.2 bring down the date of the work quite considerably, so that it cannot be before the time of the Diadochi (end of the fourth century). One explanation has been sought in a little-known episode of Babylonian history: towards 521, during the disorders which followed the death of Cambyses, a certain Arakha seized the throne of Babylon and on occupying it took the name of Nebuchadnezzar; for a short time he sought to reconquer the territories which belonged to the Babylonian empire, but was then swept away, along with many others, by Darius I Hystaspes. However, to associate the book with these somewhat obscure facts is a feeble basis for affirming its historicity. The Israeli scholar Y.M.Grintz has pointed out the parallels between the theme of the book and an episode which took place during the siege of Lindus, on the island of Rhodes, but here again the comparison is very weak. A more probable theory is that according to which the generals Holofernes and Bagoas are to be identified with the two generals sent against Phoenicia, Palestine and Egypt by Artaxerxes III around 350. However, there are many difficulties, unless we accept that Judith is a fictional account of one of the episodes in this campaign. Holofernes' itinerary in ch.2 also seems impossible: he covers almost 300 miles in three days, passing through places which are either unknown or absurd when they are known. No account is taken of the fact that an average of 100 miles a day is beyond an army consisting of infantry as well as cavalry, and in a mountain area. As we have seen, the identity of Bethulia is also unknown.

Until recently we had only a Greek LXX text known through B,A, ℵ, a codex connected with the Old Latin and the Syriac, and another independent codex. However, Jerome asserts that he translated from an Aramaic text, and this is not surprising, since the Greek text shows evident syntactical and stylistic characteristics of Hebrew and Aramaic, even if the biblical quotations are taken from the LXX. But more or less extensive fragments of the Hebrew text of the work are in existence, and lesser fragments contained in quotations, commentaries, etc., which remained partially unknown until Dubarle's study. In his work he collected them together systematically, succeeding in reconstructing the greater part of the Hebrew text. From this he demonstrated that the Hebrew was original in comparison with the translations. This was an important step forward in textual criticism, even if it was of no consequence for the historical and geographical problems presented by the book.

3. Thought

It is impossible to reduce the message of Judith to purely nationalistic categories, even if this feature is recognized to play a dominant part. For example, important elements of a religious and ethical character make an appearance, and they are by no means limited to the sphere of food regulations. God is presented in the book as omnipotent and omniscient, to such a degree that he knows of events before they take place (9.5f., where the Greek text, but not the others, uses the term *prognosis*). He is just (5.15), but also full of compassion (7.20; 9.14). On the other hand, his help to Israel is not unconditional: in 8.25-27 he does not hesitate to present precise conditions to his people; the way in which he exercises judgment on his people is the traditional one of making their enemies triumph (5.18-20; 11.10-15).

Although the book is interesting for the spiritual practices and problems of Israel at the time of the Maccabees, its historical and geographical inaccuracies and its novelistic character fully justify the perplexity over its status. It was never admitted to the Hebrew canon, and in the Catholic Church the discussion over its place in the Christian canon lasted in effect down to the Council of Trent.

BIBLIOGRAPHY

Commentaries

A.Barucq, JB, ²1959; C.A.Moore, AB, 1985; J.C.Dancy, Cambridge, 1985.
1. Y.M.Grintz, *The Book of Judith. A Reconstruction of the Original Hebrew Text*, Jerusalem 1957 (Hebrew, English summary); A.M.Dubarle, *Judith*, Rome 1966 (with bibliography); id., 'L'authenticité des textes hébreux de Judith', *Bibl* 50, 1969, 187-221; H.Y.Priebatsch, 'Das Buch Judith und seine hellenistischen Quellen', *ZDPV* 90, 1974, 50-60; A.M.Dubarle, 'Les textes hébreux de Judith: un nouveau signe d'originalité', *Bibl* 56, 1975, 503-11; M.Heltzer, 'Eine neue Quelle zur Bestimmung der Abfassungszeit des Judithbuches', *ZAW* 92, 1980, 437; J.Craghan, 'Judith Revisited', *BTB* 12, 1982, 50-3; P.M.Bogaert, 'Le calendrier du livre de Judith et la fête de Hanukka', *RTL* 15, 1984, 67-72.

46

ADDITIONS TO PROTO-CANONICAL BOOKS

1. Additions to Esther

The Alexandrian collection provides additions to the books of Esther and Daniel. We shall begin with the former.

(a) Character and content. In this case also the textual situation is complicated by the presence of several recensions. The LXX in its various uncial and minuscule codices, the fragments of Origen's Hexapla, the versions of Hesychius and Lucian, and the text of Josephus, *Antt.*9,184ff., between them offer at least five different recensions, all of which, however, agree in presenting a total of about 107 verses more than the Hebrew text. In the Greek text they appear in their logical context: before 1.1; after 3.13; 4.17; 8.12; 10.3 and at the end of the book. However, Jerome put them all in an appendix to the book because he considered them controversial in terms of the canon; modern Roman Catholic Bibles tend to follow the LXX order and the numbering of the Massoretic text.

We have the following passages:

(i) Mordecai's dream (11.2-12.6), through which he discovers a plot against the king of Persia by the eunuchs. He denounces the culprits and receives a reward, but incurs the enmity of high Persian officials.

(ii) The edict of Artaxerxes (13.1-7) for the extermination of Jews accused of disturbing the peace of the realm.

(iii) Mordecai's (13.8-18) and Esther's prayer (14.1-9);

(iv) Esther appears before the king (15.1-16 [Vg vv.4-19]);

(v) Decree for the rehabilitation of Israel (ch.16);

(vi) Mordecai recognizes that his aim has been achieved (10.4-13), followed by a colophon which ends the work (11.1).

(b) Literary problems. Without going into the problem posed by the variants of the Greek text, there is that of the relationship between the Greek and the Hebrew text: it is evident that we have two substantially different narratives about the same event. The purpose of the additions seems clear. In a context in which Esther ran the risk of not being accepted in the canon because of its nationalistic standpoint and its lack of theological elements, the additions seek to remedy the situation by supplying what is absent from the work: prayers, a theological approach to particular problems, and so on. Furthermore, they set out to demonstrate the historicity of the narrative by attaching documents to the text which are meant to enhance the positive impression caused by the addition of theological elements.

The scholar is faced with three principal problems:

1. Were the additions originally composed in a Semitic language, Hebrew or Aramaic, and if so, to what extent?

2. Are they contemporary with or later than the proto-canonical text?

3. Finally, do they have any relationship, other than that described, with the original text, or are they completely independent of it?

Until about a century ago, the most widespread view among Protestant scholars was that the additions were originally composed in Greek and were therefore later than the Hebrew text. However, according to the studies by Wellhausen, Nöldeke, Cheyne and Torrey, the sections referred to above as (i), (iii), (iv) and (vi) are certainly translations of a Hebrew or Aramaic original, while (ii) and (v), that is, the edicts, were originally composed in Greek, the official language of the time. Scholars are then divided over the antiquity of the additions: among Catholic scholars it is commonly argued that the additions are more or less contemporaneous with the proto-canonical text, whereas Torrey sees the Massoretic text as no more than the summary of what was originally a much more extensive original Greek text, some of which has been preserved in the deutero-canonical additions; this Greek text would in turn have been the translation of a Semitic original which has also been lost. The position over the additions, then, is quite complicated, and is difficult to resolve in the present state of research. In any case, the most widespread opinion continues to be that the additions are later than the proto-canonical text.

(c) The aim of the additions is also their message. As we have seen, the proto-canonical book does not mention the name of God once, nor is it very concerned with Jewish belief; these elements appear continually in the additions. It is therefore easy for those who defend the need to read Esther with the additions to show that without them the book would be theologically void and its presence within the canon incongruous, to say the least. But despite the presence of these theological elements, the additions, like the Hebrew text, have a strongly nationalistic attitude which is also projected on to almost a cosmic plane, in this way far transcending the original dispute between Mordecai and Haman. They thus become a kind of anti-Gentile manifesto, taking forward a discourse which we have seen to be extremely problematical in itself. This is probably the reason why they were not admitted into the Jewish canon, despite the theological element, which admirably completes what is lacking in the proto-canonical Esther.

2. Additions to Daniel

(a) *Introduction.* Like Esther, in the Alexandrian collection Daniel has some additions which have been transmitted in the LXX and the translation of Theodotion (or Symmachus, according to the theory mentioned above) which supplanted the LXX. There are three additions, but they give five different compositions, depending on which Greek text we use; unlike the additions to Esther, they have no theological value of their own. They are:

(i) The Prayer of Azariah (3.24-45 [EVV vv.1-22]);

(ii) The Song of the Three Young Men in the Furnace (3.52-90 [EVV vv.29-68]);

(iii) The stories of Susanna and Bel and the Dragon (chs.13; 14).

In Theodotion (or Symmachus) Susanna precedes the text, and the variants between the two Greek versions are remarkable.

(b) *Content.* (i) The Prayer of Azariah is preceded by an introduction which shows how the three young men are placed in the furnace and then how Azariah, one of the three, sings a hymn in which he praises God for his justice, confesses his sin and that of his people, and ends by expressing trust in the Lord.

(ii) The Song of the Three Young Men, which appears in the same context, is also preceded by an introduction, which describes how the king's servants continually fed the flames; in their midst, however, the young men sang a song which later entered Christian liturgy as the Benedicite, a liturgical invitation to all creation to praise and bless God.

(iii) The story of Susanna has different connotations depending on the recension of the text. In Theodotion we have Joakim, a rich Jew living in Babylon, married to the pious and chaste Susanna. During a feast two young Jews come to her husband's house and, after seeing her walking in the garden, become infatuated with her. One day while she is bathing in the pool in the garden, they surprise her and try to seduce her under the threat that if she refuses she will be charged with adultery. The woman prefers to be accused of adultery, and the court, in view of the social position of her accusers, believes them and not her. However, Daniel intervenes under divine inspiration, cross-examines the accusers and succeeds in confounding them. According to the law recorded in Deut. 19.18ff., in the rigorist interpretation of the first century BCE, the two are condemned to death, while the family praises God who has made justice triumph through Daniel. Daniel comes out of the affair with his prestige markedly enhanced by the position he has adopted. As I have indicated, the variants in the LXX text are remarkable: the two elders had been elected judges and regularly frequented Joakim's house, where they became infatuated with his wife. One night they sought to rape her, but she resisted them, preferring to accept the consequences of their threats rather than dishonour. Brought before the assembly of the synagogue she was humiliated and would certainly have been condemned had not Daniel intervened; from this point on, the narrative continues more or less as in Theodotion.

(iv) In the story of Bel and the Dragon in Theodotion we in fact find two narratives: in one, Daniel is asked by Cyrus, Astyages' successor (cf. Herodotus I, 130, but there is a good deal of uncertainty here), to prostrate himself before the god Bel. Naturally, Daniel refuses, since, as he explains to the king, it is an image of clay. When the king objects that the deity eats and that therefore Daniel's explanation cannot be true, Daniel lays a trap in the temple where the statue is, and by this means is able to prove to the king that the offerings are being consumed by the priests, not by the deity. The sanctuary is destroyed and the priests are put to death. In the second story the Babylonians worship a dragon, but Daniel refuses to join them. He kills it, but as a penalty for his misdeed he is thrown into a lions' den where the lions have been deliberately starved for seven days. However, God sends a certain Habakkuk (presumably not the prophet) to bring them food. The lions do not touch Daniel, and the king praises God for the miracle. In the LXX the content is the same, but in the first episode Daniel is a priest and is accompanied by the king of Babylon.

(c) Text, problems and date. In his preface to Daniel, Jerome (Migne, PL 28, 1291) asserts that the LXX departed considerably from the 'Hebrew truth', praising the church for having preferred Theodotion's version. We are also made aware of this preference of the early church by the fact that Theodotion seems to be used at the end of the first century CE by Clement of Rome.

The Song of the Three Young Men belongs in the same literary genres as those represented in the Psalter, and the general opinion is that it is a translation of a Hebrew or Aramaic original. The story of Susanna, which R.H.Pfeiffer* somewhat irreverently but aptly compared with a detective story, in all probability echoes the content of a popular tale, adapted by Israel to its beliefs and used to celebrate divine omniscience and conjugal virtues. Julius Africanus (Migne, PL 11, 44f.) in a letter to Origen already expressed his doubts about the Hebrew origin of the story, since it is full of word-plays which are only possible in Greek. However, the question cannot be said to be resolved. Of course it is futile to discuss its historicity, given the novelistic character of the narratives and the liturgical character of the poetical compositions, or to consider its relationship with the proto-canonical book of Daniel.

The story of Bel and the dragon tends to ridicule paganism, showing that pagan worship primarily served particular well-determined interests. However, we have no evidence of any cult of this kind, while the narrative fits in well with the novelistic theme of the brave young man who kills a monster and which is already atttested in Sumeria (one variant has a damsel who is threatened by the monster, cf. the story of St George).

Jerome (PL 25, 492f.) describes these narratives as *fabula*.

BIBLIOGRAPHY

Commentaries

See the Roman Catholic commentaries on Esther and Daniel, and C.A.Moore, AB, 1977.

1. C.A.Moore, 'On the Origin of the LXX Additions to the Book of Esther', *JBL* 92, 1973, 382-93; R.A.Martin, 'Syntax Criticism of the LXX Additions to the Book of Esther', *JBL* 94, 1975, 65-72.

2. J.Schüpphaus, 'Das Verhältnis von LXX- und Theodotion-Text in den apokryphen Zusätzen zum Danielbuch', *ZAW* 83, 1971, 49-73; M.Heltzer, 'The Story of Susanna and the Self-Government of the Jewish Community in Achaemenid Babylonia', *AION* 41, 1981, 35-39; H.Engel, *Die Susanna Erzählung*, OBO 61, 1985.

47

THE WISDOM OF SOLOMON

1. Character and content

The book which bears this title (in Latin simply *Sapientia*) belongs to Hebrew wisdom literature, as the title itself indicates, although no Semitic original has come down to us. The principal argument of the book is that there is no wisdom without justice, which only comes from God. Therefore the work is presented as an exhortation addressed by Solomon to pagans, first of all to seek wisdom, and to seek it where it is to be found. They will receive great benefits from it because (*a*) it brings salvation to pious Jews (chs.1-5); (*b*) it is divine in essence, so that kings cannot do better than to follow it (chs.6-9). Finally, (*c*) the history of Israel shows sufficiently that wisdom has brought blessings to Israel and calamities to the Gentiles (chs.10-19). The attribution of the work to Solomon indicates that it is a pseudepigraphical book.

2. Principal problems

The principal problems presented by the book are: (*a*) the original language in which it was written; (*b*) its authorship, or at least the circle from which it comes; (*c*) the place and date of composition; (*d*) its aim and therefore its ideological content. We shall examine each of these in turn.

(*a*) At least in the view of those who attributed the work to Solomon (who certainly did not write in Greek), the original language of Wisdom would seem to have been the Hebrew of the classical period. On the other hand, traditions handed down by the Muratorian canon and by Origen, Jerome and Augustine among the church fathers contrast with the theory of an original Hebrew text. Jerome in particular insisted on the Hellenistic character of the work, especially as regards the book's oratory. In passing, one might point out that this is probably the first case of the application to a biblical book of the method of the history of literary genres. Practically all scholars, even in conservative circles, agree that the book should not be attributed to Solomon, while a linguistic examination of the work also rules out with a reasonable margin of certainty that its original language might have been Hebrew or Aramaic. There are too many technical terms and expressions typical of the world of Hellenistic philosophy for one to be able to conjecture that Wisdom was originally written in a Semitic language. It might be conceded that in ch. 1 we still have the relics of a translation of some kind, but the treatment has been so free that the final result is very far removed fom the archetype.

(b) Authorship and division of the book. The division indicated at the beginning of this chapter is the most logical one, although it is also possible to put forward others. However, the book presents a literary and ideological coherence which indicates a single author or redactor. This theory is confirmed by a remarkable uniformity of style. It is perhaps possible to reconstruct Palestinian characteristics in chs.1-5, and more Alexandrian characteristics in chs.6-19, with nationalistic elements in the first half and universalistic elements in the second, but if this statement can be substantiated, it could be explained by the fact that the first part is addressed to Israelites and the second to Gentiles. Such a unitary character is certainly rare in Hebrew wisdom, and it recalls, rather, a Western philosophical tractate. We therefore have here yet another feature which indicates that Wisdom may derive from the Hellenistic Jewish diaspora. Of course the author may have been a Jew who was assimilated to his environment but familiar with the Jewish wisdom tradition and the mentality and the customs of the surrounding peoples, and also driven by a strong desire to convert this non-Jewish audience to Judaism.

(c) The place and date of composition thus follow almost automatically. If the original language is Greek, it is improbable, though not impossible, that the work was composed in Palestine. (The LXX fragments discovered at Qumran and part of the correspondence of Bar Kochba from the first half of the second century CE bear witness to the use of Greek in the Holy Land, even in quite nationalistic groups, but the content, style and thought of the work do not suggest Palestinian Jewish circles.) Rather, everything indicates that the place of origin of Wisdom is Alexandrian Judaism, which was so well assimilated in language and ideas to its setting (the most famous example is Philo of Alexandria, who lived in the first half of the first century CE; Wisdom does not show knowledge of his work). We may thus date the book about the first half of the first century BCE.

(*d*) Ideology. I have drawn attention to the fact that the author makes use of terms and expressions which recur in Hellenistic philosophy at the end of the first millennium BCE. We find them in 7.22, 24; 11.17; 14.3; 16.21; 17.2; 19.2 and in other passages where they are less obvious. The orientation of the book reveals strong Platonic, neo-Platonic and Stoic influences. On the other hand, an examination of it shows that although the author took over philosophical concepts typical of his time, he was not a philosopher and did not have a creative mind; rather, he seems to have been a brilliant popularizer of philosophical concepts, which are expressed in affirmations taken from the proto-canonical Hebrew Bible. This is another feature which is typical of the educated diaspora Jew, especially in this case, where the aim of the book is the conversion of Gentiles. In 7.22-30 we have a description of wisdom in terms which, we might feel, reflect a form of primitive gnosticism; in 8.7, on the other hand, we have a presentation of the four cardinal virtues.

When the author discusses scientific or philosophical themes, he seem to opt for poetic forms rather than for a precise terminology, and here we find a limit to what was said above about the use of technical terms: these are also used in an often uncritical and indiscriminate way. This is another feature which indicates that the author is not a philosopher. Sometimes we find omissions, as in 7.16 when he speaks only of the human body; at other times he takes over neo-Platonic concepts in an uncritical way: in 8.19f. that of the pre-existence of the soul, in 9.15 the idea that the body 'weighs down' the soul. In 2.23 we have an interpretation of Gen.1.26 which does not accord completely with the original; in LXX^{BAx}, we have here an 'image of his own nature' (*idiotētos*); elsewhere 'of his own eternity' (*aidiotētos*), which comes very close to Philo's doctrine in *De opificio mundi* 13. Hebrew Sheol has now simply become Hades, and exists only to punish the wicked (2.1ff.).

The points described in § 1 above in fact serve three aims: (i) to confirm Jewish believers in their faith and make it more profound; (ii) to restore to these Jews what they have lost; (iii) finally, to convert the Gentiles by showing them the absurdity of their religion.

To begin with the first aim: it seems that the author is addressing Jews whose hopes have been shattered. They have lived much of their lives in an oppressive and difficult environment, sometimes leading to open persecution; they have often been saddened and sometimes dismayed by the prosperity in which the Gentiles or the wicked have been living, a prosperity which has cast doubt on the reality of divine justice. The author deals with these problems on either an individual or an ethnic and collective level, by examining the past and the present, to develop a theory which he takes up in 11.13-16, based essentially on the argument that God, whose sovereignty over the world is beyond question, is also just and merciful (11.23; 12.15-18). This is a line of argument with which we are also familiar from the proto-canonical Hebrew Bible. The author does not seem to take account of the hypothesis of a conflict between divine omnipotence and divine justice, at this point proving himself to have a less developed sensibility than that of Job. In this context suffering can appear as a trial (3.4-6), with the aim of purification and spiritual progress, a kind of divine education of the believer (12.2; 16.5-13). Basically (the author's argument runs), Israel has been punished relatively little compared e.g. with Egypt (11.6ff.; 12.20-22), and moreover (as is shown by a series of examples from Adam to Moses), goodness and right conduct in this life unfailingly receive their reward, while wickedness is punished (ch.10). Here, too, the range of problems considered by the author is less developed than that in the book of Job: almost as if the book of Job had never existed, he returns to the wisdom concept of a just and right order of the universe, without taking into account either the possibility that this concept may not prove capable of validation from the facts, or the irrational element which lies at the root of relationships between God and man. Moreover, what are material goods like riches, a long life, children, and so on, compared with virtue and wisdom (4.1-9)? The author also does not seem to be aware of the problems considered in Ecclesiastes.

Finally, one typical feature of Israelite wisdom is its lack of interest in the hope of Israel and the great themes of its past history. It is striking enough that these themes are absent when the wisdom is addressed essentially to Israel; that is even more the case here, where it is addressed to Gentiles!

As for retribution, this befalls the individual rather than the community, as in Joel (cf. 4.20-5.1); no direct statement is made about the resurrection, but 4.18ff. seem to exclude it for the wicked.

The second aim of the work is to restore the faith of the apostate or indifferent Israelites. The author begins by posing the question: 'What must I do to obtain eternal life?' There seems to be an answer to the question in 15.3: a man can gain immortality only if he knows God and does his will. Here, too, the argument adopted is of a philosophical kind; it has an ontological character in 13.1ff., cf. Plato,

Timaeus 27d, where we find the theme of the builder who, being immortal, is also the source of immortality (12.1; cf.6.19 and again Plato, *Timaeus*, 29e-30b). Of course, it is not possible to claim that Wisdom is dependent on the *Timaeus*, but in any case it seems to know its content well, including its cosmogony. On the other hand, the author of Wisdom differs from Plato (and comes close to Philo's position) when he admits as a good Israelite that miracle can change the natural order of things, even if, again, like Philo, he knows the concept of the harmony of creation (19.18). Wisdom, too, poses the problem of evil and its origin, but it not only fails to provide a solution, but even arrives at a contradictory position: on the one hand it accepts the Platonic concept of the evil of matter (9.15), and on the other a variant of the traditional Hebrew view (Gen.3) that 'evil came into the world through the envy of the devil' (2.24). This is one of the earliest attempts known to us to explain the origin of the serpent in demonic terms, a theory which is soon afterwards taken up by the New Testament.

Finally, the author seeks to convert the pagans. Deutero-Isaiah (40.17-20; 41.6f.; 44.9-20) had directed all his irony towards the cult of idols, interpreting the effigies in a crudely materialistic way as identical with the person of the deity worshipped. Few pagans would have recognized themselves in this form of worship, which in any case is so easy to demolish; all the more so, since many ancient thinkers showed all their scorn for what they considered to be the product of superstitious popular piety. Wisdom discusses the problem in chs.13-15, beginning with the general question of worship of this kind and ending in 13.11-19 with the grosser forms of idolatry (following Isa.44). I have already commented on this kind of argument (above, 25.4a). The corrupt character of the pagans is attributed to their idolatries and in 14.21ff. we have a catalogue of distinctive pagan vices, a catalogue on which Paul draws fully in Rom.1.18-32. Wisdom 14.15ff. attributes this idolatrous worship to a twofold love, that of a father towards his dead son and that of the people for a distant king. This theory is reminiscent of the view put forward by Euhemerus of Messene (a place in the Peloponnese, or Messina in Sicily) in his *Hiera anagraphe*: Euhemerus in fact argued that the origin of the worship of the gods was to be sought in the veneration of rulers or deceased wise men. The argument, which despite its rationalistic and psychologizing features is obviously simplistic, was also used in the early Christian church by the apostolic fathers of the second century in their polemic against the pagans, probably on the basis of Wisdom. However, it has no foundation in the history of religion, The worst taunts are directed against theriomorphic Egyptian polytheism in 15.14-19, but here again many educated pagans would have taken the side of the author, among them Plutarch, Cicero and Horace.

However, the comparison with Deutero-Isaiah is only formal. The author is not interested in the *berīt* (covenant) on which Israel still based its relationship with YHWH in the post-exilic period; he is more interested in wisdom, which is defined in 7.22f. by a list of twenty-one characteristics in a form which is as prolix as it is systematically inadequate.

BIBLIOGRAPHY

Commentaries

J.Fichtner, HAT, 1938; E.Osty, JB, ²1957; D.Winston, AB, 1979. For the complexity of the work cf.C.Larcher, *Études sur le livre de la Sagesse*, Paris 1969; id., *Le livre de la Sagesse ou la Sagesse de Salomon*, Paris I, 1983; II, 1984; III, 1985; P.Bizzeti, *Il libro della Sapienza*, Brescia 1984.

2a. J.Reider, *The Book of Wisdom*, New York 1959; C.Romaniuk, 'Le traducteur du livre de Jesus ben Sira n'est-il pas l'auteur du livre de la Sagesse?', *RiBib* 25, 1967, 163-70; cf. G.Scarpat, 'Ancora sull'autore del Libro della Sapienza', *RiBib* 15, 1967, 171-89: C.Romaniuk, 'More about the Author of the Book of Wisdom – an Answer to G.Scarpat', *RiBib* 15, 1967, 543-54.

2d. For relations with Greek and Hellenistic philosophy see S.Lange, 'The Wisdom of Solomon and Plato', *JBL* 55, 1936, 293-302; J.M.Reese, *Hellenistic Influences upon the Book of Wisdom and its Consequences*, Rome 1970. For faith as understood in the book cf. C.A.Keller, 'Glaube in der "Weisheit Salomos" ', in H.-J.Stoebe et al. (ed.), *Wort – Gebot – Glaube. W.Eichrodt zum 80. Geburtstag*, Zurich 1970, 11-20; M.Conti, 'L'umanesimo ateo nel libro della Sapienza', *Ant* 49, 1974, 423-47; for the anti-idolatrous polemic cf. M.Gilbert, *La critique des dieux dans la livre de la Sagesse*, Rome 1973; id., 'Les raisons de la modération divine (Sagesse 11,21-12,2)', in *Mélanges bibliques et orientaux en l'honneur de M.Henri Cazelles*, Kevelaer and Neukirchen-Vluyn 1982, 149-62; id., 'La figure de Salomon en Sg 7-9', in R.Kuntzmann and J.Schlosser (eds.), *Études sur le Judaïsme hellénistique*, Paris 1984, 115-49; cf. also A.Pelletier, 'Ce n'est pas la sagesse mais le Dieu sauveur qui aime l'humanité', *RB* 87, 1980, 397-405; A.Sisti, 'Vita e morte nel libro della Sapienza', *BeO* 25, 1983, 49-61.

48

ECCLESIASTICUS OR THE WISDOM OF JESUS BEN SIRACH

1. Character and content

(*a*) Ecclesiasticus is the only book among those that we are considering whose author we know, even if his name has not been handed down clearly. There are variant forms: Simeon, son of Jesus called *ben Sīrā*; or Simeon, son of Jesus, son of Eleazar *ben Sīrā*; or also, in the Talmud, the Book or Instruction of *Ben Sīrā'*. Another feature of the work is that we have a good deal of it in the original Hebrew: fragments were found principally in 1896, then in 1931, in 1955 at Qumran and in 1964 at Masada, the fortified palace of Herod on the western side of the Dead Sea; a fragment from the first century CE has also been found in Qumran in Cave 2. This solves the problem of the original language of the work: it is a late form of Hebrew, of particular philological interest.

The book presents a series of sayings composed in the style of the proto-canonical Proverbs, with which indeed it often shows a marked relationship; unlike the Wisdom of Solomon, it thus has a fragmentary character and its content is difficult to classify. It gives its date as the beginning of the second century BCE, and the preface dates its translation into Greek about fifty years later. This dating of the work, which follows from the prologue of the Greek translation, has, however, been put in doubt: the prologue is said to be inauthentic, and the whole work to date from between 170 and 132 BCE. This confirms what H.P.Rüger has pointed out in a work of textual criticism. He has argued for the existence of a first Hebrew recension written in late Hebrew and very close in content to the Greek translation of the work, made in Alexandria towards 130 BCE, and of a second Hebrew recension written in a language close to that of the Mishnah, connected with the Syriac translation and forming the basis of a number of later Greek variants attested for the first time in Clement of Alexandria. The Syriac translation would have been made later on the basis of these two texts. It is interesting to note that the text resulting from this last operation in some cases resembles that of the Targum. The present text is thus the product of a complex literary process and is certainly removed from the original intentions of the author.

We find many quotations from, or allusions to, Ecclesiasticus in the New Testament, especially in the Epistle of James.

(b) The work can be divided into two parts. In the first (chs.1-23) we find initially a celebration of wisdom, which in all cases is given by God (1.11; cf. 1.16). In 2.1-4.10 there is praise of the virtues connected with it: patience, humility, mercy, trust in God and obedience to his commandments, filial piety, solidarity with the poor and so on; in 4.11-6.17 we have a series of instructions from a wise man or from wisdom itself, the promise of reward after trials have been undergone, and various pieces of practical advice. 6.18-8.7 describes the best way of finding wisdom, by avoiding wickedness and following some advice on the company to keep (advice which is also given from a social point of view). 9.17-11.19 is addressed to the rich and powerful, exhorting them to use justly the power which they derive from their social position, and to make good use of their money. 14.20-15.20 delivers a eulogy on wisdom, while 16.1-18.14 presents the doctrine of God the Creator with some examples drawn from biblical history. In 18.15-20.26 we have a series of counsels on love, foresight and self-control. 20.27-23.28 contrasts the wise man and the fool, the righteous and the sinner.

(c) The second part (chs.24-50) begins with wisdom's own account of herself (24.1ff.); she identifies herself with the 'tōrāh of Moses' (24.23, cf. below, 49.3). Chapters 25-26 deal with the theme of marriage, and in 26.29-29.28 we have an exhortation to honesty and prudence in word and deed. 30.1-32.13 discusses the education of children, health and manners, especially at banquets; 32.14-33.18 gives advice about how to find wisdom. 33.19-36.17 instructs heads of families about various themes: the administration of a patrimony, true piety (cf.34.18-25, etc.). 36.18-38.23 deals with some difficulties in which a man might find himself; in such cases, however, he is aided by wife, children, friends, the counsellor, the wise man, the doctor and so on. 38.1-15 discusses the interesting theological problem of the relationship between the doctor's cure and faith in God: which of the two is it better to trust? The reply is similar to that given by James 5.14 in the New Testament: the divine wisdom enlightens the doctor and gives him his gifts; therefore the two positions are complementary. 38.24-39.35 praises the scribe, whose profession is the most noble of all, while 40.1-41.13 considers suffering and death. In 41.14-42.14 we have considerations on shame, whether or not it is justified or not; the text ends in 42.15ff. with a song of praise to God for the virtue of which the fathers have given proof. We have a list of the fathers in chs.44-49, followed by a mention of the last legitimate high priest, Simeon II son of Jonathan (50.1). The book ends with praise to God (ch.51).

2. Authorship

Jesus, son or grandson of Sīrā' (also written Sīraḥ), lived in Jerusalem at the beginning of the second century BCE and will have composed his book towards 180 BCE. We can infer this from the praise of Simeon II mentioned above. Simeon seems to have died before the work was finished, though in LXX 50.1ff. he still seems to be alive. Flavius Josephus (Antt. 12,43, cf. 12,157) mentions a Simeon I, 'the Just', who lived about 300 BCE, while in Antt. 12,227 and 238 he mentions a Simeon II whose son, Onias III, was deposed by Antiochus IV Epiphanes at the beginning of the anti-Jewish persecution which led to the Maccabaean revolt (cf. II Macc.3; 4). Simeon II lived some time after 200 BCE and also bore the title 'the Just' (cf. Mishnah, Aboth 1, 2; Eusebius of Caesarea, Dem.ev. VIII, 2.71; Jerome, Comm. in Dan. 9 (Migne, PL 25, 545). For the identification of Simeon with Simeon II the information given by the Greek translator of the work, the grandson of the author, is decisive. He is writing towards 132 BCE (the thirty-eighth year 'of king Euergetes', who is almost certainly Ptolemy VII Euergetes), which obviously rules out a date earlier than the end of the third or the beginning of the second century BCE, and obliges us to take the Simeon whom it mentions as the second of that name. Antiochus IV and his persecutions are not yet mentioned in the work, so that its composition can certainly be put in the time before his ascent of the throne. For the authenticity of this prologue see above, § 1.

Ben Sirach also gives some information about his identity and work. In 51.23 he makes propaganda for his school, inviting the ignorant to enrol in it. It is in fact possible to acquire wisdom 'without money' (51.25); on the other hand the charges of the school seem to have been quite high, if according to 51.28 the author can say, 'Get instruction with a large sum of silver, and you will gain by it much gold'. In other words, the price is high, but it's worth it! In 51.29 we have an interesting variation between the Greek and Hebrew texts: whereas the former read: 'and your spirit will delight in his [viz.

God's] help', the Hebrew has, 'And I will rejoice *byšybty*', a term which can be rendered 'in my *yešībāh*', and from then on has been used to denote the seminary-school of pious Jews. Given the nature of the terms, it is not rash to suppose that the members of the school belonged to the ruling class in Jerusalem, the only ones who would be able to pay. This confirms what we have already seen in connection wih wisdom in general (above, 35.3).

The definition of wisdom which the author gives throughout the work is interesting: in the words of R.Smend Sr, the first editor of the Hebrew fragments, 'subjectively wisdom is the fear of God, and objectively the law of Moses'.

In 51.13ff. we have a somewhat confused account of the author's past life of study. Ben Sirach's ideal is expressed in 38.24-39.11: to be a scribe and to have enough to be able to devote oneself full-time to that work without being preoccupied and without having to work elsewhere. The traditional rabbinic ideal is rather different: every wise man has to work, to carry on a trade or profession as well as being occupied with wisdom. This is still attested in Paul's remarks in I Cor.4.12 and in the early church (cf. Didache 12.3, with its maxim: 'Those who do not work do not eat'). At heart the ideal put forward by Ben Sirach is Hellenistic rather than Jewish (and this explains the difficulties encountered by Paul when living in a Hellenistic community). In Jewish belief, manual labour and work of other kinds has always been held in high esteem, in contrast to the views of the surrounding world.

Be that as it may, Ben Sirach succeeds in remaining faithful to his ideal. Moreover, he shows a good knowledge of traditional wisdom, both Hebrew and Near Eastern, and perhaps also of the Greek language. This is so much the case that some scholars have thought to detect echoes of quotations of Euripides and Theognis in the text; if they are there, their value is not so much cultural as proverbial, in that they constitute material known by all.

In 1.22-24 we have what is perhaps a polemical phrase addressed to the Hellenizers in Jerusalem, whose attitude was probably one of the reasons why Antiochus IV believed that he could import Hellenism into Israel (cf. my *History*, XIII, 7-8). In 30.18f. the author attacks idolatry, and in 34.1-8 prophecy and the interpretation of dreams. Here too, then, he is completely within the milieu of the orthodox Judaism of his time. However, this traditional view of Ben Sirach has been found wanting by G.Boccaccini, who argues that the author of the book is a much more complex figure; his attempts at a synthesis already belong completely to late Judaism.

3. Thought

(a) Faith. Jesus ben Sirach knows of salvation on both the individual and the collective level, and follows the terminology introduced by Deuteronomy and Deutero-Isaiah; moreover, this will be the basis of Jewish resistance to Hellenistic attempts at spiritual and cultural assimilation. 17.17 attests both his patriotism and his universalism, which he bases on Deut.32.8; however, he docs not quote this according to the Massoretic text, but according to the important LXX variant which is also attested in a Qumran text. This has 'sons of God' instead of 'sons of Israel'; the latter reading does not make any sense. The Gentiles are often condemned (50.25), especially when they oppress Israel (36.1-10; cf. 35.18-20); the author's love of Jerusalem and of the land of his ancestors also appears throughout the work (24.1off.; 36.14).

Whether or not Ben Sirach knew of the synagogue is a disputed question: it is perhaps mentioned in 39.6, while the term in Greek in 24.23 probably refers to the assembly generally.

There is strong interest in the temple and its worship, and here the author is notably different from his predecessors (cf. 24.10-15; 36.12-17). In the description of Simeon the Just, there is probably a mention of the Day of Atonement (cf. 50.11); the priests are called 'sons of Aaron' in ch.51. Despite these references, it seems that worship and ritual are a secondary element for the author, who sees their importance as being in the realm of tradition. Sacrifice offered by the wicked is openly condemned (34.18-26; 35.11-20); observance of the law and the demands of mercy, moreover, are as good as sacrifice (35.1-3, cf. 17.11-27). Prayer appears as the expression of the author's mind (23.1-6; 36.1ff., etc.). The fulfilment of the law occupies a central place in Ben Sirach's piety. He seems to know a concept of resurrection, but often speaks of Sheol (14.16; 17.27; 28.21). The doctrine of divine rewards and punishments, which he knows well, is nicely orientated on the life to come, according to the best in Hebrew tradition, whether on an individual or a collective level (11.14; 16.6; cf. 1.11-13, etc.).

Monotheism is now accepted as a given fact in Israel, but at the same time it is proclaimed with vigour, perhaps in polemic against the Hellenistic world. Israel is the elect people of YHWH (45.19ff.; chs.48; 49, where the concept is expressed in the praise of the fathers of old); the power and majesty of God are proclaimed in 16.26-18.14.

(b) The tōrāh. I have already made several references to the importance of the tōrāh (traditionally translated 'law') in Ben Sirach's message. He does not yet know it in the rabbinic sense of the term as a written and oral revelation of God's teaching and will, though it often has a sense which goes beyond the bounds of the Pentateuch. In 39.1ff. he mentions the law, the prophets and wisdom, cited in parallel form, but as a technical term he speaks of 'the Law which Moses commanded us' (24.23; cf. 45.5). As in Chronicles, there is no definite proof that in these instances the author meant to refer to the Pentateuch, but this does seem probable. Ben Sirach is also a witness to the tendency to set alongside scripture the oral tradition which was later to be codified in the Mishnah; this is one of the elements which appear in the polemic of Jesus against the Pharisees. This tendency has only just begun to appear with him, and for want of a systematic study of the theme it is enough to cite an example. One of the earliest traditional prohibitions was against pronouncing the divine name of YHWH; the only exception to this was the high priest during the blessing in the temple on the Day of Atonement (cf. Mishnah, Yoma 6.2; Sotah 7.6). There is also provision for other instances in which the divine name can be pronounced, but there is no definition of blasphemy here or elsewhere. Now in 50.22 we have a blessing which is very clear in Hebrew: *'attā bārᵉkūnā 'ēt Y...*, 'and now, bless the Lord' (cf. the abbreviation of the name), whereas in the Greek text we simply have *ton theon*, a translation of the name by a title. In 23.9 the author criticizes the misuse of the name, especially in oaths, a tendency which returns in the New Testament.

Thus in the application and the fulfilment of the law the accent is more on the ethical element than on the ritual element, cf. 17.17ff., a passage in which we have a kind of summary of the law like those which will later be given by Jesus and some masters of late Judaism like Hillel and Akiba.

(c) As in the rest of Hebrew wisdom literature, wisdom is essentially directed towards everyday life, with the qualification discussed above, that *tōrāh* and wisdom coincide (24.23f.). Such a convergence did not come about in other wisdom literature, and we have had occasion to note how, in these works, Jewish wisdom moved more in the milieu of international wisdom than in a specifically Israelite context. We may therefore attribute to Ben Sirach an attempt at synthesis, intended to bring Jewish wisdom into the sphere of orthodoxy instead of leaving it on the periphery of Israelite faith.

The author askes all his pupils and hearers not to seek to investigate too far; despite this, he shows remarkable openness towards the problems of the universe (3.23ff.). His anthropology is expressed in a strange tension between optimism and pessimism as regards human nature, a tension which is never resolved: man is 'dust' (33.10), his life is 'flesh and blood' (i.e. humanity, without any participation in the divine nature, 17.31), and death makes him 'dust and ashes' (10.8-17). His life goes quickly and is soon over (18.7; 17.2), that is, apart from some privileged figures like Enoch and Elijah. Survival in Sheol is terrible, according to the best traditions not only of Judaism but of the ancient Near East (14.17; 17.27ff.), even if it has its good side for the infirm and the afflicted. An optimistic note appears in the affirmation that God has created man in his own image, giving him power and lordship over creation (17.1ff.) and a free judgment (15.11ff.); on the other hand, the world is fundamentally good (39.16ff.). Throughout the work we hear an exhortation to man to be content with what he has.

This is the starting point for the practical advice about order, the family, honesty, mercy, a sense of responsiblity, which appear throughout the work. As throughout the ancient Near East and also in Israel, the perspective is typically masculine (cf. Prov.31.1ff.): the view is that of a man understood as the patriarchal master of his family. The utilitarian theme which we have seen to be so important in the author's thought underlies his social ethics (cf. 16.1-6; 30.1-6; 11.29). There are a number of egotistic themes in the discussion of the problem of money; as well as knowing its value the author throughout the work gives advice about how to become rich, but at the same time exhorts his readers not to take too much account of riches. Health, for example, is better than riches (30.14ff.), while the wise man can attain a good social position even without being rich himself (10.30-11.1); the love of money can also cause ruin (11.10-13; 31.5ff.). On the other hand, an unregulated life can soon destroy a considerable inheritance (9.6; 18.32-19.1). These are questions which do not have a particular theological or ethical value, but are simply a matter of common sense.

(d) For Ben Sirach ethical norms derive from the divine will, a principle by which he puts himself in the tradition of prophetic preaching (2.15-17; 15.11-13; 32.14; 35.3-5). This will is revealed to man by means of the tōrāh (2.16); thus to love and honour God is the same as to observe the commandments (cf.10.19; 17.14).

We have seen that Ben Sirach accepts man's free will (15.15-17) and stresses his reponsibility. On the other hand, as we have seen, man is also dust and ashes (17.27). All men are sinners and therefore guilty (8.5); they are 'flesh and blood', (17.26), but they are also free. As in many biblical writers, the tension between free will and determinism is not resolved here. Similarly, there is no solution to the problems of theodicy and human nature. Sin appears as deliberate transgression; involuntary sin is deemed irrelevant to the author's ethical scheme. He too knows the doctrine of reward and punishment, as we have already seen (35.12ff.).

4. Text and style

In § 1 above we examined the character of the Hebrew text and saw what an advantage it was to us to have a considerable part of it. The complexity of its transmission is an indication that the work was not considered canonical in Israel, a reason why when studying the text it is necessary to keep an eye on the Hebrew, the Greek and the Syriac. The theme of the work is within the sphere of the thought of the proto-canonical books but is very original; new elements are the negative evaluation of work, which (as we have seen) is a feature of Hellenistic origin, and of woman. Had it not been for the chronological limits imposed on the Palestinian canon, it is probable that Sirach would have found a place there, given its extremely high theological and ethical level.

BIBLIOGRAPHY

On the Hebrew text

R.Smend, *Die Weisheit des Jesus Sirach*, Berlin 1906; M.Z.Segal, *Sēfer ben-Sirā' haššalēm*, Jerusalem ²1959; F.Vattioni, *Ecclesiastico*, Naples 1968 (synopsis of the Hebrew text together with Greek, Latin and Syriac versions).

Commentaries

H.Duesberg and P.Auvray, JB ²1958; H.Duesberg and I.Fransen, SacBib, 1966; J.G.Smith, Cambridge, 1974.

1. The basic studies for textual criticism are A.A.DiLella, *The Hebrew Text of Sirach: A Text-Critical and Historical Study*, The Hague, 1966, and H.P.Rüger, *Text und Textform im hebräischen Sirach*, Berlin 1970. The same author is producing a critical edition of the Hebrew text as fascicle 16 of *BHS*.

2. The identification with Simeon II the Just of 'Abot 1.2 is not universally accepted, cf. K.Marti and G.Beer, *'Abot*, Die Mischna IV.9, Giessen 1927, ad loc. The importance of the problem is lessened by the availability of other factors for dating.

3. G.von Rad, 'Die Weisheit des Jesus Sirach', *EvTh* 29, 1969, 113-33; J.Marbock, *Weisheit in Israel. Untersuchungen zur Weisheits-Theologie bei Ben Sira*, Rome 1971; W.Dommershausen, 'Zum Vergeltungsdenken des Ben Sira', in *Wort und Geschichte. FS K.Elliger*, AOAT 18, 1973, 37-43; J.L.Crenshaw, 'The Problem of Theodicy in Sirach: on Human Bondage', *JBL* 94, 1975, 47-64; P.Höffken, 'Warum schwieg Jesus Sirach über Esra?', *ZAW* 87, 1975, 184-201; T.Middendorp, *Die Stellung des Jesus ben Sira zwischen Judentum und Hellenismus*, Leiden 1973; J.Marbock, 'Gesetz und Weisheit. Zum Verständnis des Gesetzes bei Jesus Sirach', *BZ* 20, 1976, 1-21; J.T.Sanders, 'Ben Sira's Ethics of Caution', *HUCA* 50, 1979, 73-106; P.S.Bentjes, *Jesus Sirach en Tenach*, Nieuwegein, Netherlands 1981; id., 'Some Misplaced Words in the Hebrew Manuscript *C* of the Book of Ben Sira', *Bibl* 67, 1986, 397-401; A.A.Di Lella, 'The Poetry of Ben Sira', *EI* 16, 1982, 23*-33*; id., 'Sirach 10:19 – 11:6 – Textual Criticism, Poetic Analysis and Exegesis', in *The Word of the Lord Shall Go Forth – Essays... D.N.Freedman*, Winona Lake, Ind. 1983, 157-64; id., 'Sirach 51: 1-12: Poetic Structure and Analysis of Ben Sirach's Psalm', *CBQ* 48, 1986, 395-407; F.Saracino, 'Risurrezione in Ben Sira?', *Hen* 4, 1982, 185-203; B.J.Diebner, ' "Mein Grossvater Jesus" ', *DBAT* 16, 1982, 1-37 (for the lack of authenticity in the prologue and th⟨ ⟩ing between 170 and 132) and J.D.Martin, 'Ben Sira's Hymn to the Fathers. Messianic Perspective', *OTS* 24, 1986, 107-23; id., 'Ben Sira – A Child of his Time', in *A Word in Season. Essays... William McKane*, Sheffield 1986, 141-61; G.Boccaccini, 'Origine del male, libertà dell'uomo e retribuzione nella sapienza di Ben Sira', *Hen* 8, 1986, 1-37; T.R.Lee, *Studies in the Book of Sirach 44-50*, Atlanta, Ga 1986. For relations with ancient Hebrew poetry and Western Semitic generally cf. T.Penar, *North-Western Semitic Philology and the Hebrew Fragments of Ben Sira*, Rome 1975. For the 'praise of the fathers' (chs.44-50) see now B.L.Mack, *Wisdom and the Hebrew Epic*, Chicago 1985.

49

BARUCH AND THE EPISTLE OF JEREMIAH

1. Introduction to Baruch and its content

As we saw when studying Jeremiah (above, 23.1b), Baruch the son of Neriah is preseted as the prophet's amanuensis who, around 606 BCE, is said to have written two editions of prophecies at Jeremiah's dictation, the first of which was destroyed by King Jehoiakim after he had read it (Jer.36). The work with which we are concerned is presented as a writing of similar origin, read after the destruction of Jerusalem. 1.1-3.8 is in prose; 3.9-5.9 in poetry. In the first part we find a confession of faith composed in the fifth year of the exile and read to the exiles and to King Jehoiachin in prison; in some respects the style recalls that of Jeremiah (cf.2.23 with Jer.7.34), but it is even more like that of Daniel (cf. Dan.9.4-19). The second part contains first of all a writing in honour of wisdom, which is considered the source of all good things (3.9-4.4); in 4.1ff., as in Ecclesiasticus, wisdom is identified with the law of Moses. 4.5-5.9 announces the consolation of Jerusalem, while in ch.6 we have the 'text' of the letter which Jeremiah sent to the exiles (Jer.29).

2. Authorship and date

The mention of Jehoiachin and the fact that temple worship appears to be functioning (2.26) has suggested to some scholars that the exile mentioned is that of 597, so that the fifth year would be 593, and therefore a little while after the events narrated in Jer.27; 28. Difficulties begin when we try to see whether Baruch was in Babylon, and if so when; there is nothing to support this, and the information that we have tells against this theory. In Jer.43.5f. Baruch still áppears at his master's side, even after the fall of Jerusalem in 587, and it seems more probable that he was deported with Jeremiah to Egypt. A rabbinic tradition, reported in *Sēder 'ōlām rabbā'* 26, relates that after conquering Egypt, Nebuchadnezzar freed Jeremiah and Baruch and brought them back to their native land, but this is legendary and therefore has no bearing on our narrative. Another strange feature is the note contained in 1.6-11, that some of the sacred vessels were handed back in Babylon and were sent to Jerusalem; this happened to the bulk of the material brought back in the second half of the sixth century, but that was a result of the edict of Cyrus and the liberation of Judah. In 1.1 Belshazzar again appears as son of Nebuchadnezzar, an error which we already find in Dan.5.2 (unless we understand the word in the widest sense possible, as 'successor'). There are also other elements than the two indicated which show links with Daniel (cf. 1.15-20; 2.1-3, 7-14, 16-19; Dan.9.7-11.18). Now since Baruch is clearly fragmentary, whereas Daniel is relatively a unity apart from the dichotomy between 1-6 and 7-12 and the difference in language, it is logical to suppose that the former is dependent on the latter and that at least the first part of Baruch is to be connected with Daniel rather than with Jeremiah and his Baruch.

It is difficult to date the book and to identify the author; but it is certain that they both belong to a late period. The original language in which the writing was composed was almost certainly Hebrew; this is indicated by the marked Semitisms, which are difficult for anyone to understand who does not have a certain acquaintance with Hebrew. This also goes for the first part.

On the other hand, the second part is made up of two unrelated writings which do not have any connection even with the fictitious framework of the book. They, too, are late and were originally composed in Hebrew, even if this is not so obvious as in the first part; however, the text often uses strange expressions which can only be explained if we admit errors in orthography or reading which are possible only in Hebrew. 4.5-5.9 is radically different from the preceding sections and seems to be inspired by Deutero-Isaiah. Liberation from exile is expected in the immediate future, and the destruction of Babylon is imminent (4.22); there will be a return to Zion in miraculous circumstances (5.5-9). The alternative is therefore clear: either what we have here is ancient material which was used again at a later date, as may have happened in the case of Daniel (which is improbable), or we have yet another example of pseudonymity. We do not know when this section of the book was composed.

3. Thought

There is nothing original about the message of Baruch. It assumes forms borrowed from Daniel and Deutero-Isaiah, but it lacks precision and its affirmations are generic and without force. The God of Israel is the creator (4.35), and wisdom is identical with the *tōrāh* as in Ben Sirach (above 48,1c); 4.37 seems to refer to the election of Israel. God is merciful to his people, but they respond to his attitude with sin.

4. The Epistle of Jeremiah

Chapter 6 sets out to give the text of the writing sent by Jeremiah to the exiles (Jer.29). Israel must remain in exile for seven generations, which brings us down to the middle of the fourth century BCE, counting forty years for each generation; however, this is much earlier if we reduce a generation to thirty years. At the end of this time God will be pleased to free his people, but in the meantime they will do well not to allow themselves to be led astray by idolatry, which seems very easy in their present surroundings; to this end they are strengthened with useful advice.

The book is not a letter, nor can it be attributed to Jeremiah. In the preface to his commentary on Jeremiah (Migne, PL 24, 706), Jerome already called the work 'pseudepigraphical'. It is impossible to establish the date and the circumstances of composition exactly, but the calculation of generations brings us down to the fourth century, while other elements in the text suggest an even later date. The problem to which the question about the generations seeks to give an answer is the same as in Daniel: how is it that the divine curse continues for so long after the exile? Here, too, no reply is given.

Compared with other late writings, whether proto- or deutero-canonical, the present book raises one marked difficulty: it gives evidence not only of a good writer, but also of one who is well informed about the situation of the people in Babylon. Verses 1f. are typical of the style of Jeremiah, but the rest of the work lacks any features which might connect it with the prophet: for example, there is no trace of his tenderness, his despair and his hope, or the profound evangelical character of his message. Marduk is called by his late name of Bel, a corruption of Ba'al, as he is in the additions to Daniel (vv.40f.); the writing's admiration of the stars contrasts strangely with the polemic against astral worship in Deutero-Isaiah and in P. In general the work is directed against paganism; at a time of persecution it can be a good tactic for the oppressed to go over to the attack, and the author adopts this course. We probably have here a Jew of the Babylonian diaspora, well informed about the situation and history of that part of the world.

BIBLIOGRAPHY

Commentaries

See the Roman Catholic commentaries on Jeremiah; C.A.Moore, AB, 1977.
    2. B.N.Wambacq, 'Les prières de Baruc (1,15-2,19) et de Daniel (9.5-19)', *Bibl* 40, 1959, 463-75; C.A.Moore, 'Towards a Dating of the Book of Baruch', *CBQ* 36, 1974, 312-20 (puts the dating between the fourth and second centuries BCE); J.R.Busto Saiz, 'Baruc 3,9-4,4: estructura y contenido', in *Palabra y Vida, Homenaje a José Alonso Diaz*, Madrid 1984, 121-9. For problems of detail cf. E.Tov, *The Septuagint Translation of Jeremiah and Baruch. A Discussion of an Early Revision of Jeremiah 29-52 and Baruch, 1,1-3,8*, Missoula, Mont. 1973; id., *The Book of Baruch also called I Baruch*, Missoula, Mont. 1975.

50

THE PRAYER OF MANASSEH

As we saw earlier, in II Chron.33.11-13 we read that the wicked King Manasseh was deported to Assyria and there converted. We examined the historical value of this note, and therefore the occasion on which the prayer given here is thought to have been pronounced. It came to form part of the LXX, but did not find a way into the Catholic canon and can be found only in some Catholic Bibles. We do not know how it came to be part of the Alexandrian canon; at all events, there is no mention of it by Origen or Jerome.

The text seems to be studded with Hebraic and Hellenistic expressions, so it is difficult to establish which was the original language; here too we probably have a translation from a Hebrew original. The prayer has no theological relevance, but from a literary point of view it is an interesting example of a lament.

BIBLIOGRAPHY

Commentary

J.C.Danby, Cambridge, 1972.

H.Volz, 'Zur Überlieferung des Gebetes Manasses', *Zeitschrift für Kirchengeschichte* 70, 1959, 293-307.

51

I MACCABEES

1. Introduction

'Maccabee' is the nickname borne by Judas, son of Mattathias, the priest who began the revolt against the Syrians of Antiochus IV Epiphanes in 167 BCE. As the years went by, the nickname gathered such associations that it turned into a kind of surname for the whole family. Etymologically it is connected with the Aramaic *maqqābā'* = 'hammer', and thus means 'the hammerer'. However, the term does not refer to a weapon used in war but to a tool; for this reason other etymologies have been proposed, or none at all (for the period see my *History*, XIII.8ff.). The first two books of Maccabees are recognized as deutero-canonical in the Roman Catholic Church; the other two are not.

I and II Maccabees are particularly important for the historian. I Maccabees begins with the year 175, the date of the coronation of Antiochus IV Epiphanes, and goes down to the death of Simon Maccabaeus in 134; II Maccabees extends from 176 to 161. Consequently I Macc.1-7 is more or less parallel to II Macc.4-15. III and IV Maccabees, with which we shall be concerned in due course, are not in the Alexandrian collection and have nothing to do with the Maccabees: III Maccabees reports events which took place at the end of the third century under Ptolemy IV Philopator; IV Maccabees is a sermon with Stoic tendencies on reason as the mistress of the emotions. There is even a V Maccabees in Syriac, which in fact is a version of the six books of Josephus' *Jewish War*. The reasons against the canonicity of III-V Maccabees are obvious even to those who accept the Alexandrian collection.

2. Content

The content can be divided into the following sections: an introduction (1.1-9) which refers to Alexander the Great and the struggles among the Diadochi after his death. The first part (1.10-2.70) describes the origins of the revolt: first of all the manifest hostility of the Syrians (who in 198 succeeded the Ptolemies of Egypt as rulers of Palestine) against Israel and its cult (1.10-64), then the rebellion of Mattathias (ch.2). The second part (3.1-9.22) celebrates the work of Judas Maccabaeus in his struggles against the Syrians (3.1-4.61) and in his conflicts with other peoples, including the Idumaeans and Ammonites (chs.5-6); also in his battle against Demetrius I Soter, successor to the more reasonable Antiochus V Eupator, who was ready to drop the matter (7.1-9, 22). In the third part, Jonathan Maccabaeus first fights against Bacchides (9.23-73); there follows his alliance with Alexander Balas who, as alleged son of Antiochus IV, laid claim to the throne (10.1-11.19); finally, there is the relationship between Jonathan and Demetrius II (11.20-12.53). Simon Maccabaeus appears in the fourth part, which describes his relations with Trypho and Demetrius II (13.1-14.3); his rule (14.4-49); his relations with Antiochus VII Sidetes (chs.15; 16); and his death.

The book thus presents the following sequence of Maccabaean commanders, all brothers: Judas, died 160; Jonathan, died 142; Simon, died 134.

3. The relationship between I and II Maccabees

A comparison between the two books which, as we have seen, for part of the time cover the same period, reveals common features, features which appear in I Maccabees and not in II Maccabees, and vice versa. This suggests that the two books are independent of each other. It could be that I Maccabees made use of the work of a certain Jason of Cyrene who is mentioned in II Macc.2.23 and whom we shall meet in the next chapter. This theory was put forward by Eissfeldt*, but there is no evidence for it, and in fact he abandoned the argument in the last edition of his *Introduction*. Be this as it may, the period treated by both works extends for about fourteen years.

From a historical point of view I Maccabees seems to be the more trustworthy source, even if it does not succeed in making all the chronology agree. (For this problem see Hanhart's study.) The same problem arises in an examination of the statistics given, the number of troops involved, and so on. It might be possible to solve the problem of chronology by accepting two different systems of calculation, but here too we cannot go beyond the realm of hypothesis.

The content of the two works also differs. As we shall see, I Maccabees has a patriotic and nationalistic approach, while II

Maccabees puts more stress on divine power and retribution in the world to come. Furthermore, as we shall also see, I Maccabees is of Palestinian origin while II Maccabees is Hellenistic.

4. Literary problems

(a) The first problem to arise is that of the original Hebrew text. The LXX version which has come down to us is obviously the translation of a Semitic original which was still known to Origen and Jerome, though Jewish tradition is unaware of it. Flavius Josephus already quoted the Greek text when he used I Macc.1-13, including some points which are clearly erroneous; he seems to be unaware of the existence of a Hebrew original. Thus we can be sure that I Maccabees is the translation of a Hebrew or Aramaic text, though we cannot establish what the text was or what it looked like. Despite his evident Hebraisms, the author is obviously an effective writer even in the Greek translation. His model seems to have been the historical work of the Chronicler; like him he reports official documents (cf. especially Ezra and Nehemiah), genealogies and dates. Rather than being a reflection of reality, the speeches and prayers are recollections constructed in a polished rhetorical form, following a custom which is well-attested elsewhere. It is interesting to note that in the epic narratives the accent is more on human bravery than on divine intervention. Military pride and trust in God are strangely combined within the book, and there are a number of comparisons with figures from antiquity: the judges and the first kings (cf. I Macc.9.73).

I Maccabees abounds in copies of contemporary documents, accounts of missions accomplished or the results of conversations with the important people of the time. In this sense it almost seems as if the author meant to continue the work of the Chronicler by bringing it down to the second century. However, it is not clear whether the copies are authentic, and if so up to what point, or whether they are revisions of authentic material, or simply apocryphal. One thing is certain: the material is an integral part of the text, and the remarkable degree of historicity shown by the text is also an element in favour of the historicity of the material included.

(b) The author of the work is not mentioned once. Whoever he was, he must have composed his text in the last years of John Hyrcanus, and in any case before the occupation of Jerusalem by Pompey, that is, about the end of the second or the beginning of the first century BCE. He was a Palestinian Jew who knew Hebrew and Aramaic well; we do not know whether he also knew Greek. He was an ardent patriot, for whom religion and nation were identical. The celebration of the action of the Maccabees stands out here against the modest way in which it is described in the last chapters of proto-canonical Daniel. The author does not seem to have had any close contact with the sect of the Pharisees, since he never speaks of resurrection or of the messianic hope; it is possible that he wanted to write a kind of unofficial history of his time, glorifying the Maccabees. However, he does not conceal some of the misdeeds of Simon, the founder of the dynasty: 14.4-8; 15.15-24 are the only texts which give him unqualified praise. In reality the author admires those who have made a substantial contribution towards liberating his country from Syrian oppression, but he also tries to show that they were subordinate to an institution which is historically obscure but mentioned on a number of occasions, and which he calls 'the Great Synagogue' (3.44; 14.26-28): in the last analysis this decides policy and confirms Simon in his position.

Like the Chronicler, the author of I Maccabees sees the people as a religious community, a feature which is absent from II Maccabees; however, those who do not observe the law are excluded from this group (2.67 and other passages). Like Daniel, the author is well aware of the danger presented by militant paganism to those who observe the law.

(c) The LXX Greek text is all that is left after the loss of the original Hebrew. We have it in codices א and A, but it is lacking in B. Sometimes it seems as if the translator knew Greek well and was less familiar with Hebrew: in 1.28 he says 'Against its inhabitants' in Greek, instead of 'For its'. In 2.34 we have an obscure text which can, however, be reconstructed by someone who knows Hebrew as 'We do not wish to violate the sabbath'; 4.24 has the translation 'heaven' for 'God' or 'YHWH'; according to some, this is a way of not mentioning the divine name, but more probably it is an erroneous quotation of Pss.118 and 136 with a confusion between šēm = 'name' and šāmāyīm = 'heaven'; in the same passage the phrase 'For good and everlasting is his mercy' should obviously read 'For he is good and his mercy is everlasting' (Semitic languages do not use the verb 'to be' as a copula); in 6.1 (cf. Tobit 2.10) the Hebrew must certainly have been something like 'the province of Elam', but the translator, who did not know the double meaning of the Hebrew medīnā, invented a non-existent Elymais! In cod.A the quotations from the LXX are recognizable and the Greek is better.

For bibliography see below on 52.

52

II MACCABEES

1. Content

The introduction presents the reader with two letters written to the Jews of Alexandria; the first speaks of the restoration of the temple and the second of events a little earlier, with a legend about how the sacred fire was kept alive during the exile in Persia (sic!) and a reference to archives of Nehemiah in which were deposited books about the kings and the prophets, works of David, royal letters and so on. It ends by saying that the author, a certain Jason of Cyrene, wrote the deeds of the Maccabees in a work made up of five books, which have been condensed into one. There follow three parts and an epilogue. The first begins with the prelude to the rebellion (chs.3-7), the intrigues between the Israelite high priests and the Syrian kings (chs.3-4), and the persecution by Antiochus IV (chs.5-7, with the famous episode of the martyrdom of the mother and her seven sons in ch.7). The second part (8.1-10.9) describes the rebellion, the first victories (ch.8), the death of the tyrant (ch.9) and the purification and dedication of the temple (10.1-9; cf. I Macc.4.36-61). The third part (10.10-15.36) describes the campaigns of Judas Maccabaeus. The work ends with an epilogue (15.37-39).

2. Authorship

(a) Although we do not know much about the person who wrote the book, there can be no serious doubt as to who he was. The two introductory letters seem to have been added at a later stage and prefixed to the work, as was the preface which says that the five original books have been compressed into one (2.19-32); the epilogue also seems to fall into this category (15.37-39). However, the original text certainly goes back to Jason of Cyrene, mentioned above, and there is no reason to doubt that the summary was in fact made on the basis of his work. Still, we know nothing at all about this Jason;

we do not even know whether his work continued after the events of the year 161.

(b) The drama of this book revolves around the temple in Jerusalem. It is threatened, profaned, liberated and dedicated at what is to become an annual feast in Israel: the feast of dedication, Hebrew ḥᵃnukkāh, which is still observed today and which normally falls round about Christmas. Indeed, in the course of time it has even taken on popular elements and folklore from Christmas.

The book abounds in explanations of the law, either for the use of the pagans or for Israel (cf.6.5 and 5.17-20; 6.12-17 respectively). In fact II Maccabees has a much greater interest in theology than I Maccabees, although this theology is expressed in a somewhat rough form of reward and punishment. The pagans are defined as 'blasphemous and barbarous nations' in 10.4, but there are also severe censures of apostate Jews, of whom there must therefore have been considerable numbers. We find a series of theological features in II Maccabees which were absent from I Maccabees: for example, the resurrection of the body in 7.11; 14.46, a feature which is quite a contrast first to wisdom and then to Philo, both of whom, following Neo-Platonic lines, tend rather to teach the immortality of the soul. In 7.28 there appears for the first time in Hebrew thought the doctrine which will later be called *creatio ex nihilo*, though not in the absolute form in which it has sometimes been presented: the Greek is *ouk ex onton epoiesen auta ho theos*, that is, 'God made the world not from things which were', which is not identical with 'nothing' in the philosophical sense of the term. In 7.9, 14 (cf.14.46; 12.43) we have concepts of eternal life and death, and in 12.43 the intercession of the living for the dead, an element on which the Catholic Church sought to found the doctrine of purgatory. There is also a well-developed angelology (3.24-28; 5.2-4; 10.29ff.; 11.8, etc.). As Pfeiffer* has well observed, the fact is that II Maccabees is more a work of edification than of history. The author, Jason of Cyrene (in Cyrenaica), seems to have been a diaspora Jew who lived at Alexandria about 100 BCE.

(c) From a literary point of view the book does not seem to have known I Maccabees in either its Hebrew or its Greek form; it seems, rather, to have used a history of the Seleucids in Greek, i.e. a history of the dynasty of Antiochus IV, which seems also to have been known by Josephus, though he in turn does not know II Maccabees. The use of this non-Hebraic source probably explains the references to the cult of Dionysius in 6.7; 14.33 and some copying errors in 11.5; 12.17. Hence the author of II Maccabees can give an opposite version of the facts to that in I Maccabees; cf. I Macc.5 with II Macc.10.15, etc.

Following a method which is well-attested in this period, the author confines himself to summarizing the work of Jason of Cyrene, leaving him with the responsibility for his statements; the summary is justified by the excessive length of the original (2.24).

Finally, the book also seems to take some liberties both with chronology, often disagreeing with that of I Maccabees, and with doctrine, which is stressed or not depending on the view of the epitomizer. To this extent the original thought of Jason has been distorted, and it cannot of course be established, since we do not have even fragments of the text.

BIBLIOGRAPHY

Commentaries

F.-M.Abel, EB, [2]1949; A.Penna, SacBib, 1953; F.-M.Abel and J.Starcky, JB, [3]1961; J.A.Goldstein, AB, 1976 and 1983; J.J.Collins, 1981.

2c. K.Toki, 'The Dates of the First and Second Books of Maccabees', *AJBI* 3, 1977, 69-83, has argued that II Macc. was written to discredit I Macc.; the latter book was written before 124 BCE and after 134. This study opens up some interesting perspectives, especially after what I have said about the text in 2c. above. Cf. also R.Doran, *Temple Propaganda. The Purpose and Character of II Maccabees*, Washington, DC 1981.

4. A.Jepsen and R.Hanhart, *Untersuchungen zur israelitisch-jüdischen Chronologie*, Berlin 1964; H.Sahlin, 'Antiochus IV Epiphanes und Judas Mackabäus' (sic), *StTh* 23, 1969, 41-68; W.Wirgin, 'Judah Maccabee's Embassy to Rome and the Jewish-Roman Treaty', *PEQ* 101, 1969, 15-20; G.O.Neuham, *Studien zu den poetischen Stücken im 1.Makkabäerbuch*, Würzburg 1974.

For the two books see recently E.Nodet, 'La Dédicace, les Maccabés et le Messie', *RB* 93, 1986, 321-75. For the Maccabaeans-Hasmonaeans see 'Die Herrschaft der Hasmonäer. Idee und Wirklichkeit', *TV* 11, 1979, 45-65. For prayer in I and II Maccabees see now 'A.Enermalm-Ogawa, *Un langage de prière juif en grec. Le témoinage des deux premiers livres des Maccabées*, Lund 1987.

53

III MACCABEES, IV MACCABEES, I ESDRAS

1. III Maccabees

The book appears in the Alexandrian collection but it was not accepted into the Catholic canon; as we saw above, it has nothing to do with the Maccabees. It tells how after his victory at Raphia over Antiochus III at the end of the third century, Ptolemy IV Philopator of Egypt sought unsuccessfully to enter the temple at Jerusalem. He then tried to outwit the Jews of Alexandria, but did not succeed in his attempt. In the face of such determined opposition, a violent persecution broke out against the Jews, but three times they were miraculously saved. The king was converted and granted them letters of protection which at the same time authorized them to exterminate the apostates. The affair ends with a feast of thanksgiving and thus seems to be a kind of Alexandrian parallel to the feast of Purim.

Historical features in the narrative are: Ptolemy's victory, the celebration of the feast, and the anti-Jewish sentiments prevailing in certain circles in Alexandria. The rest, however, seems to be a romance centred on these features. Finally, the account is insignificant from an ideological standpoint.

There are no elements here which allow us to suppose the existence of a Semitic original; the original language is almost certainly Greek, and the work has been handed down in that language.

2. IV Maccabees

Like III Maccabees, IV Maccabees has nothing to do with the Hebrew liberation movement of the second century BCE; however, whereas III Maccabees has narrative elements which belong to the antecedents of the revolt and appears in the Alexandrian collection, the present book has such events only as illustrations and is not in the canon, so that it does not deserve its title. In fact it is a philosophical-type tractate dealing with the theme that reason has power over passions. The argument is presented on the basis of examples taken from the Hebrew Bible: Joseph, Moses, Jacob, David. However, the really telling examples are drawn from the Maccabean revolt, which is why the book has been given its present name: these are martyrs whose fates have already been recorded in II Maccabees. Thus the book has what Eissfeldt*, 614, has called 'Greek form and Jewish content'.

The work is also important because the author, who was certainly a Jew, tries to demonstrate the eternal value of Jewish culture to the pagan world, making use of features from Hellenistic rhetoric. Furthermore, his knowledge of Jewish culture and indeed of Hellenism does not seem to be very profound. Since the work presupposes the existence of II Maccabees, it cannot have been written before the first century BCE and was perhaps written even later.

3. I Esdras

This book is called III Ezra in the Vulgate, in which, as we have seen, Ezra and Nehemiah are called I and II Ezra respectively; it is more often called I Esdras (sometimes also the Greek Ezra), following the LXX, in which Ezra and Nehemiah together make up II Esdras. In the Vulgate it appears after the New Testament and is not canonical in the Roman Catholic Church. It sets out to give the history of Israel from the passover celebrated under Josiah in 622-21 to the proclamation of the law under Ezra, and in fact runs parallel to Chronicles, Ezra and Nehemiah, with some differences of order and of detail. Ezra 4.7-24 precedes 2.1; Ezra 4.6 and Neh.1.1-7.5; 8.1-13.31 are missing; instead, it has the story of the three young men at the court of Darius. A contest is won by Zerubbabel who, as a reward, receives permission to rebuild the temple (I Esdras 3.1-5.6, cf. Josephus, *Antt.* 11, 33ff.). The Greek of the texts which are parallel to the work of the Chronicler has remarkable style, whether as a translation or as an original. It always keeps its independence from the LXX and is much closer to the Hebrew text; sometimes the translation is very free, but at other times it offers readings which are superior to the Massoretic text. In other words, it is an extremely useful work for textual criticism.

There are, however, also chronological differences which Pfeiffer lists in a table (*History*, 242). In any case it would not be strange if what we had here was revision of the work of the Chronicler which, for reasons that we cannot explain, remained outside the present canon. As I have indicated, it is interesting that Josephus followed the text of I Esdras rather than Chronicles.

One section without parallels is the account of the adventures of the three young men at the court of Darius. Some scholars have seriously considered the possibility that it is a lost chapter of Chronicles, but in that case we would have to read 'Cyrus' instead of 'Darius'. However, there are considerable difficulties here; e.g. in Ezra and in I Esdras it is Sheshbazzar who, under Cyrus, brings back the temple vessels which had been carried away by the Babylonians, whereas II Ezra puts Zerubbabel under Darius without any possibility of a confusion. That is, unless, as Eissfeldt* has suggested, the name of Zerubbabel was simply added at a late stage.

Although the text is written in the best Greek, it equally seems to presuppose a Semitic type, perhaps in Aramaic. Its relationship with Jewish and international wisdom is also clear; as in the case of the book of Tobit, the latter is essentially represented by the story of Ahikar. However, we also find Persian features in the narrative: the exaltation of the truth at the expense of lies as the supreme virtue, as can be seen in 4.34-40, a hymn of praise to truth in which some scholars have found the echo of an ancient Persian hymn with a similar content. However, since it does not appear in the Avesta, ultimate certainty is impossible. Another feature characteristic of wisdom is the subtlety of the work on a psychological as well as a literary level. It is impossible to assign a date to it or to indicate the circumstances in which it was composed.

BIBLIOGRAPHY

1. M.Hadas, 'III Maccabees and Greek Romance', *Review of Religion* 13, 1949, 155-62; I. Levi, 'Ptolémée Lathyre et les Juifs', *HUCA* 23, 1950-51, 127-36; M.Hadas, *The Third and Fourth Books of Maccabees*, New York 1953; F.Jesi, 'Notes sur l'édit Dionysiaque de Ptolémée IV Philopator', *JNES* 15, 1956, 236-40.

2. A Dupont-Sommer, *Le quatrième livre des Machabées* (sic), Paris 1939; E.J.Bickermann, 'The Date of Fourth Maccabees', in *Louis Ginzberg Jubilee Volume* I, New York 1945, 106-240.

3. Critical text: *Esdrae liber I*, ed R.Hanhart, Göttingen 1974. Commentaries: W.Rudolph, 1949; J M.Myers, 1974. Cf. also A.L.Allrik, 'I Esdras according to Codex B and Codex A as Appearing in Zerubbabel's List in I

Esdra 5,8-23', *ZAW* 66, 1959, 272-92; A.Shalit, 'Koile-Syria from Mid-Fourth Century to the Beginning of the Third Century BC', *Scripta Hierosolymitana* I, Jerusalem 1954, 64-77; K.F.Pohlmann, *Studien zum dritten Ezra*, FRLANT 14, 1970; W.T.In der Smitten, 'Zur Pagenerzählung in 3 Ezra (3 Ezra III 1 – IV 6)', *VT* 22, 1972, 492-5; A.E.Gardner, 'The Purpose and Date of I Esdras', *JJS* 37, 1986, 18-27. For the historical and textual-critical value of the work see now G.Garbini, *History and Ideology in Ancient Israel*, London and New York 1988, 158-62.

APPENDICES

APPENDICES

I

PALESTINIAN INSCRIPTIONS FROM THE FIRST HALF OF THE FIRST MILLENNIUM

1. Introduction

Once we leave aside the discoveries at Ugarit relating to the second half of the second millennium BCE and those at Qumran in the period immediately preceding the end of the first millennium, the region of Syria and Palestine is notoriously poor in finds of inscriptions and manuscripts. Thus the few texts that have been found over the last century are all the more interesting to us, even if they may not seem very relevant from an aesthetic and literary point of view. They are important not only historically, but also linguistically, in that they allow us to reconstruct ancient phases of the Hebrew language. Moreover they can almost all be dated and have not been revised subsequently, an evident advantage that they have over the text of the Hebrew Bible. Of course we shall be examining only those which belong to Israel or to peoples of particular interest for biblical history.

Among the most important texts are: the so-called agricultural 'calendar' of Gezer; the stele of Mesha, king of Moab; the Samaria ostraca; the inscription on the Siloam aqueduct; the epitaph of a high royal official; a funeral inscription found near Lachish; the ostracon of Yabneh-Yam; the ostracon of Ophel; the Lachish ostraca; and finally the ostraca of Tell 'Arad and the Deir 'Alla inscription. Of these we cannot examine the Ophel ostracon because it is too badly damaged and therefore illegible; we must also refrain from examining the large amount of important material preserved on seals or as stamps on jars. This material is very important evidence for names, but is composed only of a few words: usually the name, patronym and sometimes the functions exercised by the owner, so we never have a proper literary text. The ancient Aramaic material will also be left out of account: it is easily accessible in a number of collections of texts.

2. The agricultural 'calendar' of Gezer

The small tablet which was soon given this name was discovered at Gezer in 1908 during excavations carried out there. The archaic form of the writing and the archaeological stratum in which the tablet was discovered allow a date in the second half of the tenth century BCE, probably towards 925; some scholars would prefer to put this dating some decades further back, but others want to bring it down at least a century. Be this as it may, this is the earliest Hebrew text that we have outside the Bible; some scholars date it before the Israelite occupation of the area and others immediately afterwards (I Kings 9.15-17). The text has some marked peculiarities of grammar, syntax and orthography in comparison with classical Hebrew; as in Ugaritic and ancient Phoenician, there is no article and it has final endings in -w, the exact significance of which has yet to be explained. Some scholars would understand it as an archaic ending for the dual (W.F.Albright), which then fell into disuse and was kept only for proper names. The translation of this ending as a dual would give a working cycle of twelve months, hence the title agricultural 'calendar'. The text would be as follows:

> There are two months of ingathering, two months of sowing, ²two months of late sowing, ³one month of pulling flax, ⁴one month of barley harvest, ⁵one month of harvesting (grain) and counting (?), ⁶two months of vine-tending, ⁷one month of summer fruit.

However, another translation made by Garbini and recently adopted by Gibson, which does not consider the endings in -w as duals, runs:

> Months of vintage and olive harvest; months of sowing; ²months of spring pasture; ³month of flax pulling; ⁴month of barley harvest. ⁵month of wheat harvest and measuring (?), ⁶months of pruning; ⁷month of summer fruit.

In the margin we also read 'by..., which Albright has understood, probably rightly, as 'byhw = 'Abiyahu, i.e. the name of the writer. The theophoric name ending with YHWH would of course be a feature in favour of dating the writing later than the occupation of the place by Solomon.

The writing is generally understood today to be a school exercise by a pupil whose name is indicated in a mutilated form in the margin; this would explain the rather clumsy look of the writing. Others would see it as a tablet deposited in the local sanctuary, with the aim of seeking a favourable harvest throughout the year. The two possibilities are not mutually exclusive.

3. The stele of Mesha, king of Moab

On the stele of King Mesha we have the longest text of the series, amounting to 34 lines. It is particularly important as an essentially historical text, because it gives the Moabite version of the facts narrated in II Kings 1.1ff.; 3.4ff., 24ff. It was discovered at the end of the last century in Transjordan in adventurous circumstances. While the person who discovered it was away looking for means of transportation the inhabitants of the area broke it up, thinking that it had valuables hidden within it. Fortunately a mould had been taken of the stone, so that most of it could be recovered, together with the fragments. The text agrees with that of the Hebrew Bible in saying that Israel had to abandon Moab. For the Moabites this was an understandable triumph. We then learn how the king had to reorganize his territory after he had won it back. The language of the text is very similar to biblical Hebrew, though it has some important grammatical peculiarites: for example, verbal forms with an inserted *t* which in Hebrew are limited to verbs beginning with a sibilant; we also have the pronominal suffix of the third person singular masculine in *h*, the plural in *-n* instead of *-m*. These elements, however, seem more a matter of dialect in comparison with biblical Hebrew and may reflect northern Israelite dialect; it has therefore been supposed that the author of the inscriptions was a Hebrew. In lines 11f. we have an interesting parallel to the institution of the ban, well-known in the context of the holy war in Israel; the vanquished are massacred in honour of the national god Chemosh, to whom they have consecrated. The stele can be dated not later than the second half of the ninth century BCE. The text reads:

[1]I am Meša', son of Kᵉmōš-yat, king of Moab, the [2]Dibonite. My father was king of Moab for thirty years, and I became king [3]after my father. I built this 'high place' for Kᵉmōš in *Qrḥh*, a high place [4]of salvation, for he saved me from every attack and let me see my desire on all my enemies. Omri, [5]king of Israel, had oppressed Moab for many years, since Kᵉmōš was angry with his country. [6]His son succeeded him on the throne and he too said: 'I will oppress Moab.' He said this in my days. [7]But I enforced my will on him and his house, and Israel perished totally and for ever. Omri had taken possession of the region of [8]Medeba, and he dwelt

in it during his days and the days of his son, forty years, but [9]K*mōš dwelt in it in my days. I rebuilt Ba'al Ma'ōn, and made a reservoir there; I also rebuilt [10]Kiryatayim. Furthermore, the men of Gad had settled in the region of 'Atārōt from time immemorial; [11]the king of Israel had fortified 'Atārōt for himself. [12]But I fought against the city, conquered it and put its inhabitants to the sword: [13]a spectacle for K*mōš and Moab. I brought from there ...[an unclear expression, which refers to David]... and I dragged him [or it] before the face of K*mos at Keriyot; and I settled there men of *šrn* and men [14]of *mḥrt*. Then K*mōš said to me, 'Go take Nebo from the hands of Israel.' Therefore I [15]went by night and fought against them from dawn until midday. I [16]took it and put every one to the sword; residents and foriegners, seven thousand men, women [17]and slaves; I had consecrated it to K*mōš. And I took from there the vessels belonging to YHWH [18]and dragged them before K*mōš. And the king of Israel had fortified [19]*yḥṣ* and had occupied it during the war against me; but K*mos drove him out before me. [20]I took two hundred men from Moab, all its troops; I led them against *yḥṣ* and conquered it, to annex it to Dibon...'

There follow lists of works done in various places and to various buildings.

4. The Samaria ostraca

The Samaria ostraca offer material of another kind: they are delivery notes for jars of wine and precious oil sent to the royal palace of Samaria. Almost all of them were discovered during the course of excavations in 1910; a last one was discovered in the excavations of 1932. They give us not only important information about nomenclature and topography, but also valuable details about the administrative situation in the kingdom of Israel under Jeroboam II (first half of the eighth century), the time of Amos and the beginning of Hosea's ministry. The system initiated by Solomon to get supplies for his palace, which was one of the reasons why the north separated from the south (I Kings 12), remained in force throughout the eighth century. The dates which appear in the ostraca point to the years between about 778 and 770 or a few decades later.

According to G.Garbini, the language of the ostraca is not a northern ('Israelite') variant of Hebrew but actually Phoenician. However, one might ask whether this is not rather evidence of the substantial identity of the two languages, northern Hebrew and

Phoenician. That would not be surprising, seeing that we know the constant and almost always cordial relations between Israel and the Phoenician city states.

5. The Siloam inscription

During the reign of Hezekiah, in the second half of the eighth century, the water system of the capital was extended and in part renewed by order of the king (II Chron.32.30; Ecclus. 48.17); it brought water from the spring of Gihon, in the bottom of the valley, to within the city, and was still partially working until a few years ago. An inscription describes the last phases of the work; it is on the lower part of a surface which was dressed for the purpose; no inscription has been put on the upper part.

Some of the text has been damaged, but the rest is quite legible:

... the piercing through. And this is the way (in which) the piercing through (was done): ²While (the stone-cutters were swinging their) axes, each towards his fellow, and while there were still three cubits to be pierced through, (there was heard) the voice of a man ³calling to his fellow, for there was a *zdh* (?) in the rock to the right (and to the left). When the ⁴piercing through was complete, the stone-cutters struck through each to meet his fellow, axe against axe. ⁵And the water ran from the spring to the pool for 1200 cubits, and 100 cubits was the height of the rock ⁶above the head of the stone-cutters...

The inscription was discovered in 1880 and is generally dated towards the end of the eighth century, a little before the arrival of Sennacherib in 701; it is also probable that the improvement of the aqueduct was made with a view to a siege. There is an incomprehensible term in line 3, perhaps 'perforation'.

6. The epitaph of a high royal official

Discovered in 1870 in present-day Silwan, on the east slope of the Kidron valley, this contains an important text, though slightly damaged, from the end of the eighth century BCE. Restored, it reads:

This is [the sepulchre of...] *yhw* who is over the palace. There is no silver and no gold here, ²but [his bones] and the bones of his concubine with him. Cursed be the man ³who opens this.

The style is that customary for this literary genre.

Overseers of the palace appear often in the Hebrew Bible, and are also to be found on many of the seals which have been discovered. However, we do not know of anyone whose name ends in -yāhū and who was buried in Jerusalem. Y.Yadin has suggested that this is Shebna, object of the invective in Isa.22.15, written in its full form as *Sᵉban-yāhū, abbreviated in Isaiah to Shebna, since it is said that he had a tomb constructed in Jerusalem (22.16).

7. The inscriptions in the burial cave near Lachish

These were discovered in 1961 in a cave used for burial from ancient times, at Khirbet bet-Leyy, about five miles from Lachish. The inscriptions are graffiti, not engraved, and part of their importance lies in the fact that they are the surviving texts with a religious subject. Their date can be fixed at the end of the eighth or the beginning of the seventh century BCE on the basis of palaeographical and historical features. Among the lesser ones we have the inscription at the entrance to the mortuary room, the reconstruction of which reads 'Cursed be he who robs this room'; among the major ones, the reconstructed texts read: 'YHWH is God of the whole earth [cf.Gen.24.3; Isa.54.5]; the mountains of Judah belong to him, to the God of Jerusalem'; another is 'The Mount of Moriah thou hast favoured, the dwelling of Yah, YHWH', cf. II Chron.3.1. This would then be the earliest identification of Moriah, a name which we find in Gen.22.2 for a country, with the temple mount. A last inscription reads: 'YHWH, deliver us.'

8. The ostracon of Yabneh-yam or Meṣad Ḥašabyāhū

The text in question was discovered along with two other obscure ones during the excavations carried out in 1960 on the perimeter of the ancient fortress in the area, in the neighbourhood of the gate. On the basis of palaeographical features, the text has been dated in the last decades of the seventh century.

(a) As now understood, the text reads:

¹Let my lord the governor hear ²the word of his servant. Your servant ³was reaping, your servant, in the heat ⁴of the day. Your servant had reaped, ⁵had measured and had piled up as on any day, before stopping, ⁶after your serv[ant had finished] the harvest and had pil⁷ed up as on any day. But Hōšiyāhū (or Hāšabyāhū) son of Sobai came ⁸and took your servant's cloak, after I had

finished ⁹this my reaping (as on) any day; he took the cloak of your servant. ¹⁰And all my companions who had reaped with me in the heat [of the day...] will bear witness ¹¹for me. If I am free from ¹²[guilt, return] my cloak. And if I was not, (it is possible) for the governor to return to me ¹³[the cloak of your servant and to show] kind[ness...¹⁴...]your servant and not reject him...¹⁵

(b) Another suggestion has been made for lines 5-6:

I reaped, ⁵gathered in and wanted to put it in store while it was still the middle of the day before the sabbath. ⁶After your servant had gathered his share and wanted to put it in store while it was still the middle of the day, there came...

And in line 9:

When I had gathered my share, while it was still the day which...

On the basis of this interpretation an attempt has been made to see the writing as the text of a petition sent to the governor by someone who had violated (or who was thought to have violated) the sabbath. However, he denies his guilt and puts the blame on the one who made the distraint, certainly a levite to judge from the name; we also know from Neh.13.22, though this is some centuries later, that the levites were responsible for supervising sabbath observance. The term 'put in store' used in the alternative translation is certainly wrong, since when the harvest was gathered it was not put in store, but left to dry before threshing.

(c) A third interpretation has been proposed:

³Your servant stood reaping ⁴in the area of the shares of the grain; he had reaped ⁵and measured, and the quota of the grain accorded with the daily quota before the day of rest. ⁶After your servant had measured the harvest and the daily ⁷quota of grain was in accordance with the daily quota, H. son of S. came ⁸and took the cloak of your servant after he had measured ⁹my harvest, exactly the daily quota.

The three possibilities considered show clearly that we are still far from an accepted reading of the text, though despite the complexity it is intelligible. It speaks of a band of harvesters, each of whom is paid for what he reaps; a harvester is accused of not having done his quota and is fined; to guarantee that he will pay he has to leave his cloak; he appeals to the governor for the restitution of the garment, a case which is expressly provided for in Exod.22.25-27; Deut 24.10-13; cf. also Amos 2.8; Prov.20.16

and 27.13; in the case of a pledge of this kind the law provides that it shall be handed back before dusk. This injunction does not seem to have been respected by those who took the pledge, hence the appeal. From Amos' invective we can conclude that cases of this kind must have been quite frequent. The theory of a failure to observe the sabbath (cf.Jer.17.19-27) seems improbable here. As can be seen even in the translation, the language is very poor and full of repetitions; perhaps the petition was dictated to a scribe, to whom the introductory formula is attributed.

9. The Lachish ostraca

The ostraca from Lachish (coord.135-108) are another set of documents the importance of which cannot be put too highly. The first eighteen were discovered during the excavations of 1934-35, and nos.19-21 during those of 1938. The letters belong to the last years preceding the fall of Jerusalem, probably the period betwen 590 and 587: in Jer.34.7 we read that only Lachish and Azekah were still resisting Babylonian pressure; the enemy tactics were to isolate Jerusalem progressively from all the surrounding strong-points, so as to be able to lay siege to it on all sides; this tactic had already been used by Sennacherib in 701 and was repeated much later, in 67-70 CE, by Titus. In letter IV, line 12, we read: 'We no longer see (the signals of) Azekah', while those of Lachish are still visible from other strong-points (for the system of signals see Jer.6.1b). In XI, line 4 the son of a certain Jeremiah appears; however, this Jeremiah is not the prophet, because we know that he was not married (Jer.16.2). III, line 20 talks of an anonymous 'prophet' and VI, line 4, of a defeatist (cf. Jer.38.4), but it does not seem possible to identify this figure with the prophet Jeremiah.

10. The ostraca of Tell-'Arad

The ostraca of Tell-'Arad (coord.162-076), which number about ten, were found during the excavations carried out in the area in 1962 and 1963. They can be dated in 598-7 and thus fall shortly before the first siege of Jerusalem; they are largely administrative texts: they speak of rations given to mercenaries and similar matters. Among the mercenaries we have the *kittīm*, a term to which I drew attention in the discussion of Deutero-Zechariah. This name was to be used at the time of Qumran for the Romans or for Westerners in general.

Here it probably refers to mercenaries originating from Greece and the islands: we cannot identify them more precisely.

11. The fragments of Tel Deir-'Alla

In the spring of 1967 a Dutch expedition under the leadership of H.J.Franken discovered a series of fragments belonging to different texts in the course of excavations on Tell Deir-'Alla (in Transjordan, coord.208-178, a few miles north of the mouth of the Jabbok, the present-day Wadi Zerqā, a tributary on the left bank of the Jordan). The writing has been done on plaster, which probably comes from a cultic object, perhaps a stele, rather than from a wall. It fell and was thrown outside the building in the course of an earthquake. This feature, along with the condition of the material, which was very fragile to begin with, makes the work of deciphering the texts extremely difficult. So far it seems possible to divide the fragments into twelve combinations, two of which are particularly important. These are two texts written in a language between Hebrew and Aramaic, which can be dated to about 700 BCE. The words still appear without *matres lectionis*, as we would expect, except at the end of a word, where a rudimentary system seems to have been in use for the personal pronominal suffixes.

The first combination contains a prophecy of Balaam son of Beor, apparently the same figure as the one who appears in Num.22-24; Deut 23.5f. and in other texts, where he is a Moabite prophet. Here too he has nothing to do with the faith and the worship of Israel; he is a 'divinely inspired clairvoyant' who announces destruction to his hearers according to orders received from a goddess. It is possible that the text, the end of which is badly damaged, calls for repentance, In the second combination we have a series of curses of the kind that we find attested in the Hebrew Bible and the Ancient Near East, probably from the mouth of the same person. A different combination of the fragments has recently been suggested by G.Garbini.

BIBLIOGRAPHY

1. Texts: D.Diringer, *Le iscrizioni antico-ebraiche palestinesi*, Florence 1934; S.Moscati, *L'epigrafia ebraica antica 1935-50*, Rome 1951; T.C.Vriezen and

J.Hospers, *Palestine Inscriptions*, Leiden 1951; H.Donner and W.Röllig, *Kanaanäische und aramäische Inschriften* (3 vols), Wiesbaden ³1971-6; J.C.L.Gibson, *Textbook of Syrian Semitic Inscriptions*, Oxford, I, 1971; II, 1975; III, 1981; a good presentation with a reproduction of a large number of the originals and accompanied by an accurate commentary is to be found in *Inscriptions Reveal*, Catalogue 100, 1973, of the Israel Museum in Jerusalem.

Translations: D.W.Thomas (ed.), *Documents from Old Testament Times*, London 1958 (reprinted New York 1961), 195ff.; K.Galling (ed.), *Textbuch zur Geschichte Israels*, Tübingen ²1968, 51ff.; *ANET*, ³1969, 320ff.; cf. also A.Lemaire, *Inscriptions hébraïques*, Paris, I, 1977 (II in preparation). The texts from Jerusalem and surroundings have been examined by F.Israel, 'Le iscrizioni ebraico-antiche da Gerusalemme', in *Gerusalemme. Atti della XXVI Settimmana biblica*, Brescia 1982, 163-80.

For a general introduction cf H.Michaud, *Sur la pierre et l'argile*, Neuchâtel 1958; there is a philological and linguistic study in F.M.Cross Jr and D.N.Freedman, *Early Hebrew Orthography*, New Haven 1952.

2. W.F.Albright, 'The Gezer Calendar', *BASOR* 92, 1943, 16-26; J.Février, 'Remarques sur le calendrier de Gézer', *Sem* 1, 1948, 33-41; A.M.Honeyman, 'The Syntax of the Gezer Calendar', *Journal of the Royal Asiatic Society*, 1953, 53-8; G.Garbini, 'Note sul "calendrio" di Gezer', *AION* 16, 1956, 123-30; W.Wirgin, 'The Calendar Tablet from Gezer', *EI* 6, 1960, 9*-12*; J.B.Segal, ' "Yrh" in the Gezer Seasonal Cycle of Ancient Canaan', *JAOS* 83, 1963, 212-21; S.Talmon, 'The Gezer Calendar and the Seasonal Cycle', *JAOS* 83, 1963, 177-87. Garbini, followed by Gibson, suggests 'put in store' at the end of line 5 instead of the improbable 'count'. He argues that the language of the calendar is a dialect more or less related to Hebrew and with archaic elements: the final *w* is not dual but a nominative plural construct to be read as *u*. So this is not a 'calendar' but simply a list of agricultural tasks to be carried out, some of which take one month and some two. Cf. also R.Rach and B.Brandl, 'Gezer under the Assyrian Rule', *PEQ* 117, 1985, 41-54, who favour a later dating.

3. S.Segert, 'Die Sprache der moabitischen Königsinschrift', *ArOr* 29, 1961, 197-267; for the problem of the syntax see F.I.Andersen, 'Moabite Syntax', *Or* 35, 1961, 197-267. The historical problems have been discussed by J.Liver, 'The Wars of Mesha, King of Moab', *PEQ* 99, 1967, 14-31, with a bibliography of earlier studies. A second very fragmentary inscription discovered in 1963 now allows Mesha's patronymic to be established; cf. W.L.Reed and F.V.Winnett, 'A Fragment of an Early Moabite Inscription from Kerak', *BASOR* 172, 1963, 1-9; D.N.Freedman, 'A Second Mesha Inscription', *BASOR* 175, 1964, 50f.; I.Schiffmann, 'Eine neue moabitische Inschrift aus Karcha', *ZAW* 77, 1965, 324f.; cf. also the archaeological surveys by M.Weippert, *ZDPV* 80, 1964, 169f.; 82, 1966, 328f. For the chronology of the events described cf.G.Wallis, 'Die vierzig Jahre der achten Zeile der Mesa-Inschrift,', *ZDPV* 81, 1965, 180-6; B.Bonder, 'Mesha's Rebellion against Israel', *JANESCU* 3, 1970-71, 82-8 (taking forty years as

equivalent to a generation); cf. also E.Lipiński, 'Etymological and Exegetical Notes on the Mesa' Inscription', *Or* 40, 1971, 325-40; J.M.Miller, 'The Moabite Stone as a Memorial Stela', *PEQ* 106, 1974, 9-18; P.Auffret, 'Essai sur la structure littéraire de la stèle de Mésha', *UF* 12, 1980, 109-24; J.Blau, 'A Short Philological Note on the Inscription of Mesa'', *Maarav* 2.2, 1980, 143-57; S.H.Horn, 'The Discovery of the Moabite Stone', in *The Word of the Lord Shall Go Forth, Essays... D.N.Freedman*, Philadelphia 1983, 297-505; A.Lemaire, 'Notes d'épigraphie nord-ouest sémitique: 19. La stèle de Mésha: épigraphie et histoire', *Syr* 64, 1987, 205-14.

4. B.Maisler (Mazar), 'The Historical Background of the Samaria Ostraka', *JPOS* 21, 1948, 117-23; Y.Yadin, 'Ancient Judean Weights and the Date of the Samaria Ostraca', *Scripta Hierosolymitana* 8, 1960, 9-25; A.F.Rainey, 'Administration in Ugarit and the Samaria Ostraka', *IEJ* 12, 1962, 62f.; id., 'The Samaria Ostraka in the Light of Fresh Evidence', *PEQ* 99, 1967, 32-41; A.Lemaire, 'L'ostracon C 1101 de Samarie – nouvel essai', *RB* 79, 1972, 565-70; W.A.Shea, 'The Date and Significance of the Samaria Ostraca', *IEJ* 27, 1977, 16-27; cf. also the review by G.Garbini, *AION* 37, 1977, 241-3; id, *I Fenici*, Naples 1980, 9 (on the language of the texts); W.H.Shea, 'Israelite Chronology and the Samaria Ostraca', *ZDPV* 101, 1985, 9-20.

5. H.-J.Stoebe, 'Überlegungen zur Siloainschrift', *ZDPV* 71, 1955, 124-40, with bibliography; G.Levi della Vida, 'The Siloah Inscription Reconsidered', in *In Memoriam Paul Kahle*, BZAW 103, 1968, 162-6, where he takes up and develops themes expressed in *RSO* 33, 1964, 311f.; he is followed by G.Garbini, 'L'iscrizione di Siloe e gli "Annali dei re di Giuda" ', *AION* 29, 1969, 261-3: the fact that the inscription does not have any stylistic parallels in other contemporaneous analogous inscriptions is explained by the suggestion that it will be an extract from the annals of the court of Judah (cf. above 16.2). Cf. also E.Puech, 'L'inscription du tunnel de Siloé', *RB* 81, 1974, 196-214. Cf. also M.Görg, 'Ein Problem-Wort der Siloah Inschrift', *BN* 11, 1980, 21-22 (the term *zrh*, which I have read, following the majority, as *zdh*, derives from the Egyptian and means 'perforation'); V.Sasson, 'The Silwan Tunnel Inscription', *PEQ* 114, 1982, 111-17; J.R.Abercrombie, 'A Short Note on a Silwan Tomb Imscription', *BASOR* 254, 1984, 61f.

6. A.Reifenberg, 'A Newly Discovered Hebrew Inscription of the Preexilic Period', *JPOS* 21, 1948, 134-7; N.Avigad, 'The Epitaph of a Royal Steward', *IEJ* 3, 1933, 137-52.

7. J.Naveh, 'Old Hebrew Inscriptions in a Burial Cave', *IEJ* 13, 1963, 74-92; F.M.Cross Jr, 'The Cave Inscriptions from Khirbet Beit Lei', in J.A.Sanders (ed.), *Near Eastern Archaeology in the Twentieth Century*, New York 1970, 299-306 (reading the first inscription differently and proposing 587 as a date). Cf. also A.Lemaire, 'Prières en temps de crise: les inscriptions de Khirbet Beit Lei', *RB* 83, 1976, 558-68.

8a. J.Naveh, 'A Hebrew Letter from the Seventh Century BC', *IEJ* 10, 1960, 129-39; S.Yeivin, 'The Judicial Petition of Mezad Hashavyahu', *BeO*

19, 1962, 3-10; S.Talmon, 'The New Hebrew Letter from the Seventh Century BC in Historical Perspective', *BASOR* 176, 1964, 29-38; J.D.Amusin and M.L.Heltzer, 'The Inscription from Meṣad Ḥasjavyahu: complaint of a Reaper of the Seventh Century BC', *IEJ* 14, 1964, 148-57.

8b. L.Delekat, 'Ein Bittschriftentwurf eines Sabbatsschänders', *Bibl* 51, 1970, 453-71; A.Lemaire, 'L'ostracon de Mesad Ḥasavyahu replacé dans son contexte', *Sem* 21, 1971, 57-79; D.Pardee, 'The Judicial Plea from Meṣad Ḥashavyahu', *Maarav* 1.1, 1978, 33-66; id., 'A Brief Note on Meṣad Hashavyahu Ostraka', *BASOR* 239, 1980, 47f.; Y.Suzuki, 'A Hebrew Ostracon from Mesah Hashavyahu', *AJBI* 8, 1982, 3-49.

8c. G.Garbini, 'L'ostrakon ebraico di Yavne Yam', *AION* 32, 1972, 98-102.

9. Cf. *Lachish* I, Oxford 1938 (nos.1-18); O.Tufnell, *Lachish* III, Oxford 1953; W.F.Albright, 'The Lachish Letters after Five Years', *BASOR* 82, 1942, 18-24; H.Michaud, 'Les ostraca de Lakiš conservés à Londres', *Syria* 54, 1957, 39-60; W.Richter, 'Lakīš 3 – Vorschlag zur Konstitution eines Textes', *BN* 37, 1987, 73-103; A.F.Rainey, 'Watching out for the Signal Fires of Lachish', *PEQ* 119, 1987, 149-51.

10. Critical edition: Y.Aharoni, *Arad Inscriptions*, Jerusalem 1975 (Hebrew, ET 1981). Cf. id., 'Hebrew Ostraka from Tel Arad,', *IEJ* 66, 1966, 1-7; id., 'Arad, Its Inscriptions and Temple', *BA* 31, 1968, 2-32; id., 'Three Hebrew Ostraka from Arad', *EI* 9, 1969, 10-21 (= *BASOR* 197, 1970; 16-41); A.F.Rainey, 'A Hebrew "Receipt" from Arad', *BASOR* 202, 1971, 23-9: M.Weippert, 'Zum Präskript der hebräischen Briefe von Arad', *VT* 25, 1975, 202-12; Y.Aharoni, 'The "Nehemiah" Ostrakon from Tell Arad', *EI* 12, 1975, 72-6 (in Hebrew, with an English summary); Y.Yadin, 'The Historical Significance of Inscriptions from Arad', *IEJ* 26, 1976, 9-14; cf. also D.Pardee, 'Letters from Tell Arad', *UF* 10, 1978, 289-336; V.Sasson, 'The Meaning of *whbst* in the Arad Inscriptions', *ZAW* 94, 1982, 105-11.

11. The main edition is J.Hoftijzer and G. van der Kooij, *Aramaic Texts from Deir 'Alla*, Leiden 1976. Cf.also J.Hoftijzer, 'The Prophet Balaam in a 6th Century Aramaic Inscription', *BA* 39, 1976, 11-17. Meanwhile various combinations of texts have been proposed: A.Caquot and A.Lemaire, 'Les textes araméens de Deir 'Alla', *Syria* 54, 1977, 189-208; G.Garbini. 'L'iscrizione di Balaam bar Peor', *Hen* 1, 1979, 166-88; M.Delcor, 'Le texte de Deir 'Alla et les oracles bibliques de Bala'am', *SVT* 32, 1981, 52-73; P.K.McCarter, 'The Balaam Texts from Deir 'Alla: The First Combination', *BASOR* 239, 1980, 49-60; H.-P.Müller, 'Die aramäische Inschrift von Deir 'Alla und die altesten Bileamsprüche', *ZAW* 94, 1982, 214-44 (supports the division made by Hoftijzer and van der Kooij); H. and M.Weippert, 'Die "Bileam" Inschrift von Tell Deir 'Alla', *ZDPV* 98, 1982, 77-103; J.A.Hackett, 'The Dialect of the Plaster Text from Tell Deir 'Alla', *Or* 53, 1984, 57-65 (independent confirmation of Garbini's suggestions); H.Ringgren, 'Balaam and the Deir-'Alla Inscriptions', in *I.L.Seeligmann Volume* III, Jerusalem 1985, 93-8; V.Sasson, 'The Book of Oracular Visions

of Balaam from Deir 'Alla', *UF* 17, 1986, 283-209; A.Lemaire, 'Les inscriptions de Deir 'Alla et la littérature araméenne ancienne', *CRAIBL* 1985.2, 270-85; J.A.Hackett, 'Some Observations on the Balaam Tradition at Deir 'Alla', *BA* 49, 1986, 216-22; E.Puech, 'Le texte "Ammonite" de Deir 'Alla: les admonitions de Balaam (première partie)', in *La Vie de la Parole... Études... offerts à Pierre Grelot*, Paris 1987, 13-30; V.Sasson, 'The Language of Rebellion in Psalm 2 and in the Plaster Texts from Deir 'Alla', *AUSS* 25, 1986, 147-54.

NB. A particularly full bibliography has been provided for this appendix, since the material is not usually examined in *Introductions* to the Hebrew Bible.

2

MANUSCRIPT DISCOVERIES FROM THE FIRST CENTURIES AFTER THE EXILE

1. The Elephantine papyri

The island of Elephantine is on the border between Egypt and Nubia at the level of the first cataract, where the Aswan dam has now been built; at the end of the fifth century BCE it housed a Jewish military colony in the service of the Persian occupation. Traces of it disappear with the end of Persian domination, at the beginning of the fourth century BCE. The colony is already attested in the pre-Persian period, before 525, the year in which Cambyses occupied Egypt. It is therefore probable that it was stationed in the region at the end of the seventh and the beginning of the sixth century BCE, under Pharaoh Psammetichus I or Amasis.

Some of the archives of this Jewish military colony were discovered towards the end of the last century, probably about 1890. They contain papyri composed in so-called imperial Aramaic, very close to that of Ezra and Nehemiah; they refer to people and events at the end of the fifth century BCE.

The archive is composed for the most part of contracts, transactions of various kinds and other documents in the realm of private law which shed important light on the practices and customs to be found in a setting and during a period about which we know almost nothing. The correspondence between the authorities of the colony and the religious authorities in Jerusalem is particularly interesting for anyone studying the Hebrew Bible: from it we learn that at Elephantine there was a temple built by members of the colony in honour of Yahu (an abbreviated form of YHWH) which had been destroyed about 410, so it seems, at the instigation of the priests of the local Egyptian god Khnum. Either they were afraid of the competition, or they were scandalized by the sacrifice of sheep and goats, which was sacrilegious to them: in fact the Egyptian god was represented with the head of a he-goat. The destruction took place with the connivance of the local authorities. Among other things, the correspondence deals with the reconstruction of the ruined temple and is addressed to the local governor and to the religious authorities in Jerusalem. Names appear in it which are also attested in the books of Ezra and Nehemiah, as we have seen; since the letters themselves are dated, the dates of these figures can be established objectively.

When the colonists received no reply to their initial protests, towards 408 they renewed their requests, and this time it seems that their efforts were crowned with success; it proved possible for the temple to be rebuilt very soon.

2. The religion of the Jews of Elephantine

The religion of the Jews of the colony is a problem of notorious complexity. First of all we have the question of the temple. How was it possible for the construction of another sanctuary to be authorized after Josiah's reform, not only outside Jerusalem but even outside the Holy Land, in Egpyt, without giving rise to endless polemic? At this point we are shortly before the period when the schism between Jews and Samaritans finally came to a head, and one of the reasons for the disagreement was the construction of a sanctuary by the Samaritans on Mount Gerizim, near Shechem. Furthermore, two other deities appear alongside the figure of YHWH, Anath-bethel and Asham-bethel. It is beyond question that these were gods worshipped alongside YHWII; their names are mentioned on lists of offerings and tithes together with that of YHWH, and these are lists which refer only to the Jewish inhabitants of the region. A temple outside Jerusalem and a cult which was at best syncretistic: these are two facts the origin and implications of which are still a matter of controversy.

First of all, it seems obvious that the reforms of Ezra and Nehemiah did not reach as far as Elephantine. Many scholars would prefer to go further back: the group, they claim, was formed even before Josiah's reform and maintained practices and religious traditions earlier than the last quarter of the seventh century BCE. The relationship of the two deities with Bethel seems to indicate a northern origin for this cult, but the term might also be a divine designation, which is also attested. For Kraeling (83ff.), it would simply be a matter of compromise: the colonists worshipped their God, YHWH, but to be on the safe side they did not overlook the other deities of their homeland, who were considered his vassals or subordinates. However, there is no proof for this theory. In any case, it seems strange that dealings with the religious authorities of Jerusalem, who were otherwise so jealous in their defence of orthodoxy, were frequent and normally cordial, without there being any trace of a conflict. The problem is for the moment destined to remain unsolved.

The so-called 'passover papyrus' (AP 21) is of particular interest to the reader of the Bible. It was studied fully by Grelot, and I follow his reconstruction here.

> [To] my [brethren [2]Ye]doniah and his colleagues [the J]ewish gar[rison], your brother Hanan[iah], [3]Now this year, the fifth year of King Darius, an order was sent from the king to Arsames (a third of a line is missing) [4](a third of a line is missing). Now therefore do you count four[teen days from the first day of Nisan] [5]... (Another lacuna) and keep [the passover]. And from the fifteenth day until the twenty-first day of Ni[san] will be a feast of unleavened bread: [6]for seven days eat unleavened bread. Be ritually clean and take heed, (do not do any) work (on the fifteenth and the twenty-first day) [7]... (another lacuna)... For the rest do not drink [beer] and do not eat anything [in] which the[re] is leaven... (another lacuna)... [8](Eat unleavened bread after the fourteenth day of Nisan at) the setting of the sun, until the twenty-first day of Nisa(n at the setting of the sun. For seven days, [9]let not leaven be found among you and do not intro)duce it into your houses, and keep it far from you during [those] days (a third of a line missing)...[10]... (a third of a line missing). (address); '[To] my brothers Yedoniah and his colleagues, the Jewish garrison, your brother Hanan[iah].'

It should be obvious, even to the reader who is unfamiliar with this material, that the papyrus is badly damaged and therefore mutilated in the key passages, so that it is far from clear to read and understand, despite Grelot's brilliant reconstruction. For example, Kraeling rejects the introduction of the term 'passover' into the lacuna in lines 4f., and this objection was already raised by Cowley and Vincent. But if this conjecture were correct, we would also have here the distinction between the passover and the feast of unleavened bread attested in P in the Pentateuch (Exod.12; Lev.11-5, against Deut.16.8, which tries to make the two feasts into one). Line 7 has been restored on the basis of the practice attested in the Mishnah (Pesahim 3.1) of not drinking any kind of drink fermented on a cereal base (in this case beer made from barley) during the week of the passover. It is interesting that the passage is dated in the fifth year of Darius II, i.e. 419; it also bears witness to a direct intervention by the king in internal matters of worship.

3. The Samaria papyri

About twenty fragments of papyri were found during 1962 and 1963 in a cave near the *wādī dāliye* in the Jordan valley, at about the thirty-second parallel, none of which has so far been fully reconstructed; they are documents of a legal and administrative character. The latest date attested in the papyri is 18 March 335 BCE; the earliest papyrus comes between the thirtieth and fortieth year of Artaxerxes II, i.e. between 375 and 365, though the figure is not exact because of a lacuna which has destroyed part of the number.

We await a thorough study and the definitive publication of the documents; meanwhile we can expect that they will be of considerable interest to the historian, either because they give information about the Persian administration and features of public and private laws connected with it, or because they give a complete list of five governors of Samaria, thus filling a gap left by Flavius Josephus, *Antt.*11, 302f.

BIBLIOGRAPHY

Texts

A.E.Cowley, *Aramaic Papyri of the Fifth Century BC*, Oxford 1923 (= 1967); E.G.Kraeling, *The Brooklyn Museum Aramaic Papyri*, New York 1953; G.R.Driver, *Aramaic Documents from the Fifth Century BC*, Oxford 1957; B.Porten, *Archives from Elephantine*, Berkeley and Los Angeles 1972.
There is a translation in *ANET*[3], 222f., 491f.
The legal questions are studied by A.Verger, *Ricerche giuridiche sui papiri aramaici d'Elefantina*, Rome 1965 (with a bibliography of 324 entries); cf. also Y.Muffs, *Studies in the Aramaic Legal Papyri from Elephantine*, Leiden 1969.
The northern origin of the colony has been argued for by K.Galling, 'Der Gott Karmel und die Ächtung fremder Götter', in *Geschichte und Altes Testament. FS A.Alt*, Tübingen 1953; there is also a thorough treatment of the question by E Volterra, ' "Yhwdy" e "'rmy" nei papiri aramici del V secolo provenienti dall'Egitto', *RANL* VIII.18, 1963, 131-73. For the date of the rebuilding of the temple cf. P.Grelot, 'La réconstruction du temple juïf d'Éléphantine', *Or* 36, 1967, 173-7; id., *Documents araméens d'Égypte*, Paris

1972; B.Porten, 'Aramaic Papyri and Parchments', *BA* 42, 1979, 74-104; I.Gottlieb, 'Succession in Elephantine and Jewish Law', *JSS* 26, 1981, 193-203; M.H.Silberman, 'Biblical Name-Texts and the Elephantine Onomasticon: A Comparison', *Or* 50, 1981, 265-331; B.Porten, 'An Aramaic Oath Contract', *RB* 90, 1983, 563-75; M.Görg, 'Noch einmal die Namenlisten von Elephantine', *BN* 22, 1983, 12-15; K.van den Toorn, 'Herem-Bethel and Elephantine Oath Procedure', *ZAW* 98, 1986, 282-5 (puts forward the curious proposal that Herem does not denote a deity but the treasure or some other element no longer available, by which he swears). Cf. also recently R.Contini, 'I documenti aramaici dell'Egitto persiano e tolemaico', *RiBib* 34, 1986, 71-109.

2. A. Vincent, *La religion des judéo-araméens d'Éléphantine*, Paris 1937, is a classic study. For the 'passover papyrus' cf. P.Grelot, 'Études sur le "papyrus pascal" d'Éléphantine', *VT* 4, 1954, 349-84; id., 'Le papyrus pascal d'Éléphantine et le probleme du Pentateuque', *VT* 5, 1955, 250-65; id., 'Le papyrus pascal d'Éléphantine: nouvel essai', *VT* 17, 1967, 114-17; id., 'Le papyrus pascal d'Éléphantine', *VT* 17, 1967, 201-7 (on which the text reproduced here is based); id., 'Le papyrus pascal d'Éléphantine et les lettres d'Hermopolis', *VT* 17, 1967, 481-3. Cf.also D.Golomb, 'The Date of a New Papyrus from Elephantine', *BASOR* 217, 1975, 49-53; K.van der Toorn, 'Herem-Bethel and Elephantine Oath Procedure', *ZAW*, 1986, 282-5 (disputes that worship was offered to Herem-Bethel); and an article in *JNES* 47, 1988, 99ff.

In *The Prophet Amos*, ET London 1987, 140ff., I argued that the term *'ašmat* in Amos 8.14 (and *ʾªsīmāh* in II Kings 17.30) could be attestations of one of these deities already in the Hebrew Bible; that is, provided that we do not have *šem*, 'the name', with a prosthetic *aleph*.

3. F.M.Cross, Jr, 'The Discovery of the Samaria Papyri', *BA* 26, 1963, 110-21; K.Galling, 'Die Liste der Statthälter von Samaria im 5/4.Jahrhundert', in his *Studien zur Geschichte Israels im persischen Zeitalter*, Tübingen 1964, 209f.; F.M.Cross, 'Papyri of the Fourth Century BC from Daliyeh', in *New Directions in Biblical Archaeology*, ed. D.N.Freedman and J.C.Greenfield, Garden City, New York 1969, 45-69 (with bibliography). A first papyrus, no.1, has recently been published by F.M.Cross, 'Samaria Papyrus 1', *EI* 1985, 7*-17* and fig.II; F.M.Cross, 'A Report on the Samaria Papyri', *SVT* 40, 1988, 17-26.

CHRONOLOGICAL TABLE

CHRONOLOGICAL TABLE

(C = century; *c.* = approximately)

Century BCE	Israel (Judah)		Egypt	Phoenicia and Transjordan
13	Beginning C13 BCE: Exodus from Egypt (?)		*c.* 1290–1224: Ramses II	
12	End C13-end C12 BCE: 'Conquest' of Palestine?		*c.* 1223–1211 (1224–1204): Merneptah	
11	*c.* 1020–1000 (1012–1004): Saul *c.* 1000–961 (1004–965): David			
10	*c.* 961–922 (965–926): Solomon *c.* 922 (926): Division of the empire		*c.* 964–956 (978–959): Siamun *c.* 935–914 (945–924): Shishak I	*c.* 976–930 (973–942): Hiram of Tyre

Century BCE	Kingdom of Israel	Kingdom of Judah	Egypt	Phoenicia and Transjordan
	c. 922–901 (926–907): Jeroboam I	*c.* 922–915 (926–910): Rehoboam		
	c. 901–900 (907–6): Nadab	*c.* 915–913 (910–908): Abijah		
9	*c.* 900–877 (906–889): Baasha	*c.* 913–873 (908–868): Asa		*c.* 891–859 (873–842): Ittobaal of Tyre
	c. 877–6 (883–2): Elah			
	c. 876 (882): Zimri			
	c. 876–3 (882–878): Tibni			
	c. 873–869 (878–871): Omri	*c.* 873–849 (868–847): Jehoshaphat		
	c. 869–850 (871–852): Ahab			
	c. 850–849 (852–1): Ahaziah			*c.* 850: Mesha of Moab
	c. 849–42 (851–845): Jehoram	*c.* 849–842: Joram		
	c. 842–815 (845–818): Jehu	*c.* 842 (845): Ahaziah		*c.* 814/3: Foundation of Carthage

Syria	Mesopotamia (Assyria)	Greece	Events
		C12: Trojan War	So-called 'Israel' stele
			c. 1050: battle of Song of Deborah, Judg.5(?) *c.* 1050–1000: struggle with the Philistines
c. 900–875 (885–870): Bar Hadad I			
c. 875–843 (870–842): Bar Hadad II (= Hadadezer)			
			C9: Aramaean wars
	c. 858–824: Shalmaneser III		853: battle of Qarqar
c. 845–842: Bar Hadad III? *c.* 843–806(?) (841–806): Hazael			841: Jehu pays tribute

Century BCE	Israel	Judah	Egypt	Syria
8	c. 815–801 (818–802): Jehoahaz c. 801–786 (802–787): Joash c. 786–746 (787–747): Jeroboam II c. 746–5 (747): Zechariah c. 745 (747): Shallum c. 745–738 (747–738): Menahem c. 738–7 (737–6): Pekahiah c. 737–732 (735–732): Pekah c. 732–724: Hoshea c. 723–2: Fall of Samaria c. 720: End of resistance after 720: Assyrian province	c. 842–837 (845–840): Athaliah c. 837–800 (840–801): Jehoash c. 800–783 (801–787): Amaziah c. 783–742 (787–736) Uzziah/ Azariah 750–742 (756–736): Jotham regent c. 735–715 (736–729/ 726): Ahaz c. 715–686 (728–700): Hezekiah		c. 806–775: Bar Hadad IV (III) = Mari' c.?: Rezin of Damascus 732: fall of Damascus
			c. 710/09–696/5: Sabako	
7		c. 687–642: Manasseh c. 642–640 Amon	c. 690–664: Tirhaka	
	End C7: Josiah reconquers part of Palestine	c. 640 (639)–609: Josiah 609: Jehoahaz 609–598: Jehoiakim	c. 663–609: Psammetichus I 655: independent again 609–594: Necho II	

Mesopotamia (Assyria and Babylon)	Media	Greece	Rome	Events
c. 810–783: Adad-nirari III				
c. 782–773: Shalmaneser IV		c. 776: First Olympiad		796: Joash pays tribute c. 760: Earthquake (Amos 1.1)
		754–3: year 3, VI Olympiad	753: foundation of Rome 753–509: the seven kings	
c.744–727: Tiglath-pileser III				
		C8: Hesiod		738: Menahem pays tribute to Tiglath-pileser III 734: Syro-Ephraimite war 734: Ahaz pays tribute to Tiglath-pileser III
726–722: Shalmaneser V 721–705: Sargon II				733–2: Tiglath-Pileser III conquers Galilee and Transjordan 732: Death of Pekah 731: Hoshea pays tribute to Tiglath-pileser III 724: Siege of Samaria begins 722: Samaria falls to Shalmaneser IV 721: deportation by Sargon II 713–12: campaign by Sargon II in south 701: siege of Jerusalem
704–681: Sennacherib c. 703: Merodach-Baladan of Babylonia 680–69: Esarhaddon 668–27: Asshur-banipal 625: First fall of Nineveh 612: Second fall of Nineveh 607–5: Nabopolassar of Babylon	625–585: Cyaxares of Media	c.640: Solon end C7: Thales		609: Battle of Megiddo and death of Josiah 605: Battle of Carchemish

Century BCE	Israel (Judah)	Egypt	Syria
6	597: Jehoiachin 597–587/86: Zedekiah 587/86–539: Babylonian exile	589–570: Hophrah 568–526: Amamis	
5	c. 539/8: Edict of Cyrus 538–521: Zerubbabel 'governor' 521–c. 330: Seven civil governors known (?) c. 485–385: Five Sanballatids known for Samaria	525: occupation by Cambyses	
4	332: Alexander conquers the region c. 300: Simon I high priest 323–198: Under the Ptolemies of Egypt	After 323: Ptolemy Lagids	After 312: Seleucids
3	c. 200: Simon VII high priest	285–246: Ptolemy II Philadelphus	223–187: Antiochus III
2	after 198: Under the Seleucids of Syria ?–175: Onias III high priest 174–171: Jason high priest 171–162: Alkimus high priest 165–160: Judas Maccabaeus 160–142: Jonathan Maccabaeus 142–134: Simon Maccabaeus		187–175: Seleucus IV 174–164: Antiochus IV 169: Invasion of Egypt 168: Invasion of Egypt 164–161: Antiochus V 161–150: Demetrius I 153–145: Alexander Balas

Mesopotamia (Assyria)	Media and Persia	Greece	Rome	Events
605–561: Nebuchadnezzar II		C6: Anaximander, Anaximenes, Xenophon		597: First fall of Jerusalem, deportation summer 587 or 586; second fall of Jerusalem, destruction and deportation
555–539: Nabonidus	559–530: Cyrus II			
	530–522: Cambyses 522–486: Darius I		509: Republic	561: Liberation of Jerusalem
		492–490: First and Second Persian wars 431–04: Peloponnesian war		
	335–332: Darius II			333: Battle of Issus 312–198: Conflict between Diadochi
			281–272: Pyrrhich wars 264–241: First Punic War	LXX translated
			218–201: Second Punic War	
			200–197 Second Macedonian War	
			192–187: War against Antiochus III	167: Desecration of temple
			171–168: Third Macedonian War	165: Maccabaean revolt 164: Reconsecration of temple c. 125: Qumran monastery founded
			149–146 Third Punic War	

Century BCE	Israel (Judah)
I	134–104: John Hyrcanus 104–103: Aristobulus 103–76: Alexander Jannaeus 76–67: Alexandra Salome 67–63: Aristobulus II 63: Pompey intervenes 37–4: Herod

Century CE	Israel (Judah)
I	6: Palestine a Roman province. Beginning of Zealot movement. Census 26: Pilate procurator c. 27–30: Ministry of Jesus 41–44: Agrippa king 52: Felix procurator 59?: Festus procurator 64: Gessius Florus procurator 66: Beginning of first Jewish revolt 67: Roman expedition under Vespasian; reconquest of Galilee 69: Vespasian temporizes 69: Titus commands the troops 70: Conquest and destruction of Jerusalem 74: Massada falls 115–117: Jewish revolt in various provinces 132: Second Jewish revolt begins 135: Revolt finally tamed; *Judaea* now becomes *Palaestina*

	Rome
	91–88: Social wars 60–53: First triumvirate 49–45: First Civil War 44–30: Second Civil War 43–36: Second triumvirate
	14: Augustus dies 14–37: Tiberius emperor 37–41: Caligula emperor 41–54: Claudius emperor 54: Nero emperor 68: Death of Nero 68–69: Galba, Otho and Vitellius emperors 69–79: Vespasian emperor 79–81: Titus emperor 87–117: Trajan emperor 117–138: Hadrian emperor

INDEXES

1. SUBJECT INDEX

Ancient authors are cited here only where they do not form the subject of a chapter or section.

3. INDEX OF MODERN AUTHORS